THE KREMLIN'S SCHOLAR

DMITRII SHEPILOV

EDITED BY STEPHEN V. BITTNER

TRANSLATED BY ANTHONY AUSTIN

The Kremlin's Scholar

A MEMOIR OF SOVIET POLITICS UNDER

STALIN AND KHRUSHCHEV

YALE UNIVERSITY PRESS   NEW HAVEN & LONDON

Set in Scala and Scala Sans by Duke & Company, Devon, Pennsylvania.
Printed in the United States of America.

Library of Congress Cataloging-in-Publication Data

Shepilov, D. T.
The Kremlin's scholar : a memoir of Soviet politics under Stalin and Khrushchev / Dmitrii
Shepilov ; edited by Stephen V. Bittner ; translated by Anthony Austin.
p.   cm.
Includes bibliographical references and index.
ISBN 978-0-300-09206-6 (alk. paper)

1. Soviet Union—Politics and government—1953–1985. 2. Shepilov, D. T. I. Bittner, Stephen V.,
1970– II. Austin, Anthony. III. Title.
DK274.S395 2007
947.085′2—dc22

2006035330

A catalogue record for this book is available from the British Library.

The paper in this book meets the guidelines for permanence and durability of the Committee
on Production Guidelines for Book Longevity of the Council on Library Resources.

10 9 8 7 6 5 4 3 2 1

CONTENTS

AFTER DMITRII SHEPILOV DIED in 1995, Dmitrii Kosyrev, Shepilov's grandson, and Mikhail Makovkin, Shepilov's son-in-law, located a copy of a memoir written in Shepilov's hand. Kosyrev prepared it for publication by deleting unnecessary quotations from published sources, reordering some passages to maintain thematic continuity, dividing two long chapters on Andrei Zhdanov and the trip to China into shorter ones, adding titles to the new chapters, and typing the manuscript. Slightly abridged versions of the memoir were published first in serial form (*Voprosy istorii,* nos. 3–11 [1998]) and then as the book *Neprimknuvshii* (Unjoined [Moscow: Vagrius, 2001]). The book before you is the fullest version of Shepilov's memoir published in any language, and is based on the manuscript that Kosyrev compiled. The photographs included here are likewise reproduced courtesy of Kosyrev.

Anthony Austin's translation maintains the chapter titles and divisions that Kosyrev added. As much as possible, it also maintains Shepilov's unique and sometimes frustrating style: his penchant for describing past events with the present tense, switching verb tenses without reason, and sometimes avoiding verbs entirely. I have edited the memoir for clarity and have abridged the epilogue (Kosyrev's interview with Shepilov) to avoid redundancy. In instances where Shepilov used ellipses to indicate dramatic pauses or continuation, I have substituted more conventional punctuation. All remaining ellipses in this book are also present in the original typescript; they indicate stammered or elided speech or thought, or material that Shepilov himself removed when quoting other works, rather than editorial abridgement on my part. To improve the accessibility of the memoir, I have attached explanatory notes to identify persons, places, and events that may be unfamiliar to the reader the first time they are mentioned in the text. Because Shepilov's interests were so broad, these include references to Russian, European, and Asian history, politics, and culture. I have corrected some of Shepilov's factual mistakes and inconsistencies in notes as well. In the final chapters on Khrushchev's trip to China, Shepilov's descriptions of Chinese history and culture reflect his own understandings as an outsider, and should not be taken as authoritative. Brackets designate text that Anthony Austin and I added to the memoir for clarity. I have also included a biographical appendix of persons who appear repeatedly. Shepilov's skills as a scholarly writer were considerable, and he often digressed from the narrative of his own life to provide background information about the people he encountered and the places he visited. In these instances I did not clutter the text with unnecessary notes. I transliterated Russian words according to Library of Congress guidelines unless they are conventionally rendered otherwise (Fyodor Dostoevsky instead of Fedor Dostoevskii). Likewise, I transliterated Chinese words into Pinyin unless they are conventionally rendered otherwise (Sun Yat-sen instead of Sun Zhongshan).

I want to thank Anthony Austin for promptly responding to the many questions I had while editing his translation and for patiently adapting his own schedule to the demands of my own. In addition, I am deeply indebted to Ethan Pollock for sharing his considerable knowledge of Stalinist politics and science with me and for rifling through his own files for materials about Shepilov. Thanks also go to Ethan, Willard Sunderland, and Steve Harris for reading the introduction with a critical eye, to Richard Hellie and Eleonory Gilburd for helping translate obscure words, to my colleague Randy Dodgen for helping transliterate Chinese words into Pinyin, and to the Office of the Dean of Social Sciences at Sonoma State University and to Matt Etzler for helping compile the index. Finally, I am grateful to my wife, Christel Querijero, who diligently proofread the entire memoir and who single-handedly put our kids to bed when I was too busy with Shepilov to help. As any parent of one- and three-year-olds knows, that's no easy task.

Stephen V. Bittner

THE RISE AND FALL OF DMITRII SHEPILOV
Stephen V. Bittner

DMITRII TROFIMOVICH SHEPILOV had two very different professional lives. The first was as an upwardly mobile lawyer, economist, and official in the Soviet Communist Party. Joseph Stalin reputedly deemed him too talented to go to "waste" when the secret police took an interest in him. The second was as a disgraced and forgotten politician who spent twenty-five years working in obscurity, first in Central Asia and then in Moscow. The turning point in Shepilov's career came in June 1957, when he was implicated in an unsuccessful coup to remove Nikita Khrushchev from power. In official parlance, Khrushchev vanquished the "antiparty group of Molotov, Malenkov, and Kaganovich [Stalin's former colleagues], and joining them was Shepilov" (*i primknuvshii k nim Shepilov*).[1] The phrasing of Shepilov's indictment was supposed to tar him as deeply unprincipled. Like a general who defects to the enemy after being outflanked, Shepilov allegedly "counted the votes" in the party's ruling Presidium and decided at the last minute to side with the majority, which wanted to oust Khrushchev, his friend and confidant, from power. This memoir is, in part, Shepilov's attempt to rebut Khrushchev's charge and restore his reputation. It is also much more than that: a personal account of high politics under Stalin and Khrushchev.

Dmitrii Shepilov was born in 1905 in the Central Asian city of Ashkhabad (Ashgabat). His father, Trofim Mikhailovich (1870–1951), was a peasant from Kursk province, a fertile agricultural region south of Moscow. In 1892, a year after he married Dmitrii's mother, Praskov'ia Fedorovna (1873–1949), the elder Shepilov was conscripted into the army and stationed with a railroad regiment near the city of Kizyl-Arvat, in Turkestan (Turkmenistan), near the Russian Empire's southern frontier. When his military service ended in 1898, Shepilov found work on the railroad line that connected Ashkhabad and Krasnovodsk on the Caspian Sea. He soon joined the Russian Social Democratic Workers' Party, the precursor to the Bolsheviks, and moved to Ashkhabad so he could enroll his children in a proper school. By 1907 the Shepilovs had six boys and a girl; Dmitrii was the second youngest. A few years later, the Shepilovs moved to Tashkent, their refuge during the Civil War.[2] Although the family was not wealthy, Dmitrii Shepilov gave no indication that his time in Central Asia was uncomfortable or unhappy, a common trope in Soviet coming-of-age narratives set in the tsarist period.[3] Instead, Shepilov recalled a childhood filled with adventure. He spent hot summer nights with his siblings on the roof of his family's adobe house. He delighted in the strange sights and diversions of the desert. And he sang songs and played music—his life's passion—with friends, some of whom remained close for decades.

As the son of a peasant turned worker and Bolshevik, Dmitrii Shepilov benefited from Soviet affirmative-action policies that targeted persons with favorable class identities and political ties. He matriculated at Moscow State University at a time when workers were the preferred students. In 1926 he graduated from the law faculty, joined the communist party, and dutifully accepted a job as a prosecutor in Iakutsk, a city in remote eastern Siberia. Two years later he transferred to a similar position in Smolensk, near the Soviet Union's western border. In the early 1930s, in the midst of collectivization, Shepilov gave up the practice of law to enroll in a program in agricultural economics at the Institute of Red Professors in Moscow. Shepilov did not specify the reasons for his career change, nor did he indicate any misgivings about being a prosecutor during a period of growing repression. While still a student at the Institute of Red Professors, Shepilov worked as a scientific editor at the *Great Soviet Encyclopedia,* the first of many editing jobs. In 1933 he graduated from the institute and became the head of a political department at a sovkhoz (state farm) in western Siberia. It was his second trip to the hinterlands at the party's behest.

In the late 1930s, Shepilov was back in Moscow, first as a staff member in the Central Committee's Science Department and then as an economist at the Academy of Sciences. Shepilov also moonlighted as a lecturer at the Institute of Red Professors, the Higher Party School, and the Soviet Trade Institute. It was during this time that the People's Commissariat of Internal Affairs (NKVD) took notice of him. In 1938, during the Great Purges, Shepilov was summoned to Lubianka, the headquarters of the NKVD, and asked to become an informant. Shepilov claims that he refused as a matter of principle, even though he fully understood what the repercussions might be for himself and his family. For several weeks he lived with the fear of imminent arrest. Bound by an oath to keep silent about his visit to Lubianka, Shepilov confided only in his friend Boris Ponomarev, a former classmate and future Central Committee member, perhaps so Ponomarev could inform his family should he suddenly disappear. After Shepilov's fall from power in 1957, he decided that the "writ" of the NKVD had expired. He told his family how "at the most difficult moment" of his life he did not "succumb to cowardice and dishonor." Implicit was a juxtaposition with his nemesis, Nikita Khrushchev, who "did not flinch from any obstacles or sacrifices" to please Stalin in his ascent to power.

When the war began in June 1941, Shepilov enlisted in the 21st Division of the People's Home Guard. He served on the outskirts of Moscow during the grim days in late 1941 when the city hung in the balance. As the chief political officer of the 24th Army and then a member of the Military Soviet of the 4th Guards Army, he fought at Stalingrad in 1942–43 and in the battles of liberation across Ukraine, Romania, Hungary, Yugoslavia, and Austria. When the war ended, Shepilov remained with the Soviet occupation forces in Vienna. He was promoted to major general and helped supervise reconstruction aid and relations with the Austrian government. In his free time he compiled an authoritative history of the 4th Guards Army with his friend Il'ia Arginskii and explored the Austrian countryside, a rare treat for a Soviet citizen.

Shepilov returned to civilian life in February 1946. He was forty years old. He found work as chief of the propaganda department at the newspaper *Pravda* and then as deputy director of the Central Committee's Bureau of Propaganda and Agitation (Agitprop). Shepilov found a party apparatus that was riven by competing loyalties and still adapting to the postwar context. He wrote that the leading figures in cultural politics during the war were the "Aleksandrov boys," Petr Fedoseev, Leonid Il'ichev, Vladimir Kruzhkov, and Pavel Satiukov, who owed their professional advancement to Georgii Aleksandrov, a philosopher by training who was in charge of Agitprop from 1940–47. Shepilov described Aleksandrov as a "classroom communist" who lacked practical experience. His protégés had similarly limited horizons: they were recruited directly from university, they had never been abroad, and, most important in Shepilov's mind, many had managed to avoid military service during the war. They were the antithesis of what Shepilov called the "Komsomol of 1920," the generation (in which he counted himself) that was willing to sacrifice all personal comfort and safety for the good of the party.

Opposed to the Aleksandrov boys were Andrei Zhdanov, the Politburo member who oversaw ideological matters, and Mikhail Suslov, the Central Committee secretary who was Shepilov's boss at Agitprop. Shepilov admired Zhdanov, who was responsible for his promotion to the Central Committee. Zhdanov "was a master of applying the laws and analyses of Marxist dialectics to explain, dissect, and analyze the most diverse intellectual concepts." Of course, many of these diverse intellectual concepts were victims of the *zhdanovshchina*—the campaign against Western culture that Zhdanov orchestrated at Stalin's behest after the war. On this topic Shepilov was far more ambivalent. On one hand, he claimed that modern, Western music had "a painful, sacrilegious effect" on him. Consequently, he supported the intent of the Central Committee's decree in February 1948 that chastised Vano Muradeli and several other Soviet composers for formalism. On the other hand, he was pained by the public self-criticism that Dmitrii Shostakovich, Sergei Prokofiev, and others were forced to perform. Shepilov was deeply saddened when Andrei Zhdanov, his friend and patron, died of heart disease in 1948. He also recognized that Zhdanov was responsible for a "whole series of undemocratic measures and declarations in the fields of literature, theater, cinema, music, and other ideological spheres."

Shepilov's work at Agitprop was not without peril. In the postwar years came not only the zhdanovshchina but a mounting wave of official anti-Semitism and the so-called Leningrad affair, trumped-up charges that a group of party and state leaders had conspired to use an international trade fair to remove Leningrad from the Soviet Union. Shepilov writes that he skirted disaster on two occasions. The first was in the spring of

1948, when Stalin summoned him to a Politburo meeting in the Kremlin with Suslov and Iurii Zhdanov, Andrei Zhdanov's son and the head of the Central Committee's Science Department. Stalin was upset about a speech that the younger Zhdanov had delivered to a meeting of party propagandists on April 10. Zhdanov had criticized the work of Trofim Lysenko, a biologist who achieved official favor by arguing, contrary to the findings of modern genetics, that acquired characteristics were inheritable. When Stalin demanded to know who had authorized the speech, Shepilov shouldered the blame, or so he claims. He then launched into an impassioned defense of genetics and asked Stalin to authorize an investigation of Lysenko's work.[4] "As a rule, no one ever made speeches in Stalin's office," he recalls. "The most complex questions were dealt with by terse comments of 'Yes,' 'No,' 'That's right,' 'Approve,' 'Look into.' No one spoke loudly, either. . . . My statement came out as a cry from the heart." Stalin instead promised Shepilov an investigation that would "debunk our homegrown Morganists," a reference to the American geneticist T. H. Morgan. The next day, Andrei Zhdanov, visibly disturbed by the episode and suffering from worsening heart disease, told Shepilov that he had "behaved very carelessly": "It could have ended tragically for you, and not only you."

Shepilov's second misstep was more serious. On March 5, 1949, Nikolai Voznesenskii, a rising star within the Politburo and the chairman of Gosplan, the agency that oversaw the economy, was fired from his posts. He was arrested later in the year and was executed in 1950 for complicity in the Leningrad affair. Shepilov's ties with Voznesenskii were tenuous: on two occasions, Voznesenskii tried unsuccessfully to lure him to Gosplan. Yet Shepilov proved vulnerable on the issue of Voznesenskii's book, *War Economy of the USSR in the Great Patriotic War*. The book won the Stalin Prize, the Soviet Union's highest award for cultural and scientific achievement, after it was published in 1947. It was widely praised in the press. Shepilov even heard (unsubstantiated) rumors that Stalin had himself edited it. A better imprimatur was hard to imagine. One of the journals that praised the book was *Bolshevik,* a Central Committee publication that was under Shepilov's purview at Agitprop. After Voznesenskii fell out of favor, the Central Committee reprimanded Shepilov for failing to provide adequate supervision at *Bolshevik* and for recommending *War Economy* to regional party secretaries. Shepilov was soon fired and had every reason to fear arrest. When he approached Georgii Malenkov to plead his case, Malenkov icily confirmed that his days were numbered.

But Shepilov was not arrested. He spent several anxious months doing copyediting work for a friend at *Bolshevik* and then, on January 31, 1950, reputedly on Stalin's orders, was appointed a Central Committee inspector. It was a decidedly less glamorous position than deputy director of Agitprop, but hardly the catastrophe that Shepilov feared. In fact, Shepilov's career soon took a positive turn. In the spring of 1950, Stalin summoned Shepilov to his dacha on the outskirts of Moscow to discuss a long-delayed textbook on political economy.[5] Stalin told Shepilov that writing the textbook was a "historic task" that was essential for the success of communism. Without the textbook, "our people will degenerate, and we'll perish. We need this textbook like we need air to breathe."

For the next two and a half years Shepilov helped draft and revise the textbook. Stalin provided the authors with a comfortable dacha outside Moscow so they could devote themselves to their task without interruption. Shepilov occasionally met with Stalin and spoke with him on the telephone about problems the authors encountered. He was impressed by Stalin's theoretical acumen and his ability to present complex topics in a concise manner—virtues he later discovered were entirely lacking in Nikita Khrushchev. Each contact with Stalin left him "in a state of intellectual ferment and eager to get to work," even though he admitted that Stalin's "seemingly faultless and brilliant generalizations regarding contemporary reality" turned out to be false. It appears that Stalin, too, was impressed with Shepilov. At the Nineteenth Party Congress in October 1952, Shepilov was elected to the Central Committee. In December, as work on the textbook was winding down, Stalin appointed him chief editor of *Pravda,* despite Shepilov's protests that he was not well suited for the job.

Shepilov's opinion about Stalin was conflicted. While at Agitprop he was proud of his proximity to the Soviet leader. He marveled at Stalin's generosity in dispensing Stalin Prizes and his stated reluctance to honor artists who distinguished themselves mainly by glorifying Stalin. But Shepilov also noticed that these were the very artists typically nominated for prizes. At the Central Committee plenum in October 1952, the first that he attended as a member, Shepilov felt a "slab of ice" on his heart when Stalin contemptuously accused Viacheslav Molotov and Anastas Mikoian of being too conciliatory to the United States. Both were subsequently excluded from the new ruling bureau within the expanded Presidium (formerly the Politburo). Shepilov was especially sympathetic to Molotov. In the late 1940s, Molotov's wife, Polina Zhemchuzhina, was arrested on charges of Zionist conspiracy. Nonetheless, "Molotov's devotion to Stalin did not seem to lessen." (Shepilov did not know, apparently, that Molotov and Zhemchuzhina divorced on Stalin's orders in 1948. Nor was he aware that Molotov abstained from a vote in the Politburo about whether to expel Zhemchuzhina from the party, a reluctance for which he later apologized to Stalin.)[6] Shepilov and other Central Committee members listened "with heavy hearts" to Stalin's report on the Doctors' Plot, far-fetched charges that a group of mostly Jewish doctors had conspired to assassinate Kremlin leaders with misdiagnoses and poor treatment. And Shepilov wrote of nagging doubts about Stalin's "egomania" and "persecution mania" and of the deep shame of official anti-Semitism.

It may be the case that Shepilov's ambivalence about Stalin reflected moral judgments he made after Stalin's death. On this topic, too, Shepilov was contradictory. He wrote about "frightful thoughts" that "rose from the depths of consciousness" during the last years of Stalin's life. But he also described his confidence that "the mighty and perfectly fashioned Soviet governmental system worked flawlessly" under Stalin.

Shepilov remained editor of *Pravda* until 1956. He led *Pravda* through the uncertain days of March 1953, when Stalin's inner circle wrestled with the issue of the succession. He was at Stalin's dacha late in the evening on March 5, only hours after the leader's death, to consult about the official announcement that would come at daybreak. He was in Stalin's Kremlin office on March 7 to discuss funeral arrangements. He helped smear Lavrentii Beria, the powerful chief of the secret police, after Khrushchev engineered his arrest in June 1953. And he traveled with Khrushchev to China in September and October 1954 to mark the five-year anniversary of the People's Republic, and to Yugoslavia in March 1955 to restore relations with the Tito government.

Shepilov rapidly ascended the political ranks during these years. In October 1953 he became a corresponding member of the Academy of Sciences, and in July 1955 a Central Committee secretary. In February 1956 he was chosen to be a candidate member of the Central Committee Presidium, the leading body in Soviet politics. From June 1956 to February 1957 he served as minister of foreign affairs. Shepilov visited Syria,

Egypt, Lebanon, and Greece in this capacity. In August and September 1956 he represented the Soviet Union at the London conference on the Suez crisis. Later in the fall he led the Soviet delegation to the eleventh session of the General Assembly of the United Nations.

After Stalin's death Shepilov formed a close relationship with Khrushchev, who tops Beria and Malenkov for the role of chief villain in his memoir. Shepilov first saw Khrushchev at a party meeting in the fall of 1937, when Khrushchev was secretary of the Moscow Party Committee. He was impressed by Khrushchev's modest background and folksy disposition. Khrushchev's promotion to the leading ranks of the party seemed to be proof of the Soviet Union's commitment to egalitarianism. They finally met in 1943, after the Battle of Stalingrad, when Khrushchev visited the headquarters of the 4th Guards Army. Again Shepilov was impressed. Khrushchev showed genuine concern for the welfare of rank-and-file soldiers and later sent Shepilov, whom he magnanimously called the liberator of Ukraine, a care package on behalf of the Ukrainian people. After the war Shepilov ran into Khrushchev, then secretary of the Ukrainian Communist Party, at the Central Committee compound on Old Square in Moscow. They shared stories from the front, and Khrushchev invited Shepilov to visit him in Kiev. Thereafter, Shepilov worked closely with Khrushchev on a number of occasions. During walks in the countryside, Khrushchev told Shepilov "things that only he knew": how Nikolai Bulganin punched Voznesenskii on the side of the head when he visited him in jail, and how Mikoian hedged when Khrushchev tried to gauge his opinion of Beria. Their relationship was close enough that in 1956 Khrushchev enlisted Shepilov's help in writing the secret speech denouncing Stalin. Shepilov drafted the sections that described Stalin's bungling war effort and foreign policy. Even though the speech was thoroughly revised and reshuffled before Khrushchev took the podium at the Twentieth Party Congress, Shepilov recognized "bits and pieces" of what Khrushchev said.

In a biography of Khrushchev, William Taubman suggests that the Soviet leader saw a potential heir in Shepilov, "the first veritable intellectual" whom he took "under his wing."[7] Yet Shepilov was less and less a compliant protégé. As early as 1951, Shepilov recalled being skeptical about Khrushchev's short-lived proposal to construct "agrocities" in the countryside. He later argued that Khrushchev's Virgin Lands campaign—

the cultivation of untilled steppe in Kazakhstan, the southern Urals, and Siberia—diverted scarce resources from the country's breadbasket and set a bad precedent by promoting extensive rather than intensive development. Shepilov viewed Khrushchev's enthusiastic embrace of corn as nothing short of ridiculous. He feared that Khrushchev soured relations with China by trying to be too charitable. And he was opposed to Khrushchev's plan to transfer the Crimea from Russia—where it had been for nearly two centuries—to Ukraine.

In Shepilov's mind, Khrushchev's schemes were not simply naive; they were examples of *manilovshchina,* the pathetic foolishness that the character Manilov embodied in Nikolai Gogol's *Dead Souls.* Khrushchev made important political decisions "on the basis of intuition" and then became irate if anyone questioned their correctness. He meddled in affairs he knew little about. He caused international crises with careless pronouncements. He did not hesitate to lecture the erudite leader of the Italian Communist Party, Palmiro Togliattii. He crudely told the Chinese not to carry on about communism until they had "pants to put on." And when the discussion turned to agriculture, supposedly his forte, Khrushchev tapped his forehead to indicate that he, not Stalin or anyone else, was the expert.

Shepilov thought that Khrushchev's chief fault was a lack of education. His favorite epithet for his former benefactor was "utter ignoramus." Khrushchev had "no taste for the painful grind of book learning to come to the wisdom of Pythagoras, the secrets of the Marxist law of surplus value," or—referring to the protagonist in Fyodor Dostoevsky's *Crime and Punishment*—"the psychological agonies of Raskolnikov." Shepilov contrasted Khrushchev with other communist leaders whose intellects he admired. Mao Zedong was an accomplished theoretician. Zhdanov immersed himself in nineteenth-century art criticism before drafting the seminal decrees of the zhdanovshchina. Voznesenskii wrote an 822-page book, *The Political Economy of Communism,* his "credo as a scholar and a communist," while awaiting arrest. Stalin told Shepilov that he regularly read three hundred pages a day. When Shepilov visited his dacha to discuss the political economy textbook in the spring of 1950, he was astonished at how quickly Stalin found the appropriate quotations from Marx and Lenin to illustrate his ideas. Shepilov had similar kind words for Iakov Sverdlov, Feliks Dzerzhinskii, Anatolii Lunacharskii, and other old Bolsheviks. He claimed that Khrushchev, in contrast, could barely sign his name. Khrushchev made spelling errors in his directives to the Presidium and the Central Committee. He mispronounced words and mangled foreign names. And in his interaction with foreign leaders, he was "Rassian" (*raseiskii*), a mocking word that suggests an unintelligent and chauvinistic lack of concern for the feelings of others.

At the core of Shepilov's critique of Khrushchev was an idealized view of the party. Shepilov envisioned the party as an intellectual meritocracy that traced its philosophical roots to Thomas More and Tommaso Campanella. The party was open to all true believers, but only the most talented rose to the top. The Central Committee was "the brain, the soul, and the heart of the party"; it was "the country's supreme forum of wise men." At its head was the philosopher-king—first Lenin and then Stalin—who divined truth in the canonical works of Marx and Engels. Yet Khrushchev climbed to the top by sycophancy and betrayal. Khrushchev gained Stalin's favor by "toadying, maneuvering, and fawning." To prove his devotion, he sent "thousands upon thousands of completely innocent people . . . into the abyss of unimaginable suffering." In 1953, Khrushchev skillfully orchestrated the arrest of Beria and then took advantage of the trusting natures of Molotov and Malenkov to reestablish "one-man rule." Once he was ensconced in power, he enlisted the help of political figures who were as morally compromised as he. And he set about covering up his own unscrupulous behavior with the myth of the simple miner who became the Soviet leader. Stalin was dead, but the "well-oiled machinery" that assured his "one-man rule was still running perfectly." Khrushchev, a political engineer par excellence, "pulled one lever after another."

By 1957 differences between Shepilov and Khrushchev were no longer confined to Shepilov's private musings. In February, Andrei Gromyko succeeded Shepilov as minister of foreign affairs, reputedly because Shepilov did not give a speech denouncing imperialism that Khrushchev had ordered.[8] Shepilov recalled discussions with Mikoian, Ekaterina Furtseva, and Kliment Voroshilov, all full or candidate members of the Presidium, about where Khrushchev's policies were leading the Soviet Union. It appears that Khrushchev, too, was aware of his growing rift with Shepilov. Shepilov was absent from the wedding of Khrushchev's son, Sergei, two days before the coup began. He told Voroshilov that he, Shepilov, had not been invited. Nonetheless, Khrushchev appeared to be genuinely hurt by

Shepilov's involvement in the coup and by the depth of his vitriol. "You dealt me the cruelest blow of all," he told Shepilov after the coup failed. During the Presidium meeting on June 18, when the plotters still had the upper hand, Shepilov read excerpts from his journal about Khrushchev, perhaps to counter suspicions that he had opportunistically joined the plotters at the last moment. Khrushchev later said that Shepilov described him scratching his armpits during a meeting with the president of Finland as if "they had been invaded by an army of fleas."[9]

As the coup dragged on and the Presidium opened its doors to the full Central Committee, the advantage shifted to Khrushchev. The ensuing discussion focused less on Khrushchev's shortcomings and more on the roles of Molotov, Malenkov, and Lazar Kaganovich in the repressions of the Stalin era. By the time Shepilov took the podium on June 24, he had to defend himself against charges that he had abetted a group of inveterate Stalinists. He was eventually cut off when someone said he was "rambling" and "wasting time for no reason, not saying anything." Punishment was swift. Molotov, Malenkov, and Kaganovich were expelled from the Central Committee and the Presidium on June 29 and assigned to unattractive posts in the hinterlands. Shepilov, then fifty-one years old, also lost his party posts and was sent to Frunze (Bishkek), where he became director of the Kyrgyz Institute of Economics. When Kyrgyz party leaders warmly received Shepilov, Khrushchev reminded them that Shepilov was a political exile and should be treated accordingly.[10]

There were additional indignities in the years to come. In 1960, Shepilov's corresponding membership in the Academy of Sciences was revoked, allegedly on the orders of Leonid Il'ichev, a former Aleksandrov boy who served as head of Agitprop from 1958–65. After Khrushchev denounced the antiparty group at the Twenty-second Congress in 1961, Shepilov, then working in Moscow, was excluded from the party. Shepilov even broke with his old friend Boris Ponomarev, allegedly because Ponomarev refused to support him during the coup, despite pledging otherwise. When Shepilov faced the possibility of arrest in 1949, he asked Malenkov to let him go "in peace" and resume his scholarly work. Shepilov could not have anticipated that Khrushchev would one day grant his request. From his return to Moscow in 1960 to his retirement in 1982, Khrushchev's former protégé edited collections of historical documents for publication at the archive of the Council of Ministers. His name, he claimed, never even appeared in the books he produced. It was fitting punishment for a man whom Khrushchev considered a pompous snob.

Shepilov wrote the bulk of his memoir in 1965–66, after Khrushchev was removed from power and when he himself was no longer under constant surveillance. He initially titled it *khrushchevshchina,* a pejorative word for the era of Khrushchev. Shepilov likely envisioned the memoir as a way to call attention to his own anti-Khrushchev credentials in a political climate that had suddenly become hostile to the miner from Ukraine. He wrote the final three chapters on Khrushchev's 1954 trip to China at a later date, probably in the early 1970s.[11] By that point, Shepilov likely realized that he would not be able to resume his previous career, and did not hesitate to criticize the Soviet invasion of Czechoslovakia in 1968 and border hostilities with China in 1969. As his manuscript became less a polemic against Khrushchev and more an account of his own life, Shepilov changed the title to *Tak slozhilas' zhizn'* (How It Was).

Shepilov's memoir is an unfinished work. He does not write about his time in Siberia and Smolensk as a prosecutor, nor his years at Moscow State University and the Institute of Red Professors. He refers only in passing to his stint as minister of foreign affairs. He does not relate what role he played at the Twentieth Party Congress, how he became involved with the antiparty group, nor what happened at the Central Committee plenum in June 1957. (Shepilov discussed the latter subjects in a brief 1991 interview, attached as an epilogue to this book.) According to his grandson, Dmitrii Kosyrev, Shepilov frequently told his friends that he was continuing to revise his memoir. But whether for reasons of age or for reasons of inclination, he never got around to it.[12] Perhaps he decided that the political climate, even under Mikhail Gorbachev, was not favorable for publication. His depiction of rampant cynicism and personal animosities in lofty party institutions undermined the idealistic myths that surrounded them. And his dim view of Khrushchev challenged the credentials and morality of a man whom Gorbachev and other reformers championed.[13] Shortly before his death in 1995, Shepilov distributed copies of his memoir to close friends to guarantee its survival, an act more akin to a dissident's than to a party leader's. It was safer, he thought, to keep the memoir hidden away.

Because the purpose of Shepilov's memoir changed during the years he wrote, it is an amalgam of different styles. Shepilov was often critical of Agitprop hacks who could write only by stringing together quotations and statistics. Their prose, he thought, betrayed a lack of independence. Yet passages in Shepilov's memoir are exactly like that: they were obviously written in consultation with a statistical almanac or clippings from *Pravda*. Shepilov proudly spouted Soviet economic and cultural achievements under Stalin. He cited statistics to prove the superiority of socialism over capitalism. He emphasized Soviet benevolence in world affairs and the evil intentions of imperialist adversaries. Shepilov also used his Agitprop voice for more subversive ends. He reproduced letters sent to *Pravda* in response to Stalin's death to underscore the pervasiveness of the cult of personality, not to celebrate Stalin. He tallied Khrushchev's encomiums for Stalin at the Eighteenth Party Congress in 1939 to prove Khrushchev's complicity in the cult. He systematically savaged a biography of Khrushchev, *Tale of an Honorary Miner,* with spleen normally reserved for oppositionists. He related rumors that Khrushchev was the son of a "kulak-exploiter" who fled to the Donbass, a coal-mining region in southern Russia and eastern Ukraine, to mask his true class identity. He made fun of the assertion in the biography that Khrushchev, "the main star in the firmament of the great days of October," had single-handedly established Soviet power in the Donbass and was a hero of the Civil War. He claimed that Khrushchev's only credential as a worker was a brief stint as a machinist. He questioned when and where Khrushchev had joined the party. He alleged that Khrushchev was an "active Trotskyite" in the 1920s. And he mocked Khrushchev with the sort of exhortation typically found at the end of an Agitprop pamphlet: "Forward, Nikita Khrushchev! Forward, with no fear or doubt!"

Shepilov's Agitprop voice reflected his own entanglement with Stalinist values. Shepilov used criteria from the 1930s to denigrate Khrushchev: Khrushchev had a dubious class background; he did not distinguish himself in the Civil War; he did not take advantage of the party's offer of education; he abetted the left opposition. Shepilov's criticism of Khrushchev's provincialism was similar. Khrushchev was not only an unrefined bumpkin, he lacked the essential *kul'turnost'* (level of culture) that was a hallmark of Soviet civilization.

Shepilov also wrote long passages of his memoir in an overtly literary style. He had an eye for detail. Sverdlov Hall in the Kremlin, the countryside surrounding Moscow, the Danube Valley, Lamaism, and the cities of Hangzhou, Beijing, and Shanghai were cause for digression. His descriptive sentences are staccato and often without verbs. He describes the journey to Nagornoe, the party's resort on the outskirts of Moscow where he revised the political economy textbook, as if he is looking out the window of a speeding car, taking occasional snapshots: "Leningrad Highway. The gargantuan Moscow-Volga Canal. Khimki Reservoir. Not far off the highway, the small village of Kurkino. Log cabins. Lilac bushes in front of a garden pinched by the cold. Ancient linden trees and white willows weighed down with rooks' nests and laden with snow." Shepilov moves back and forth in time to create dramatic tension. He begins the first chapter with Suslov's phone call announcing Stalin's death (a scene repeated later in the memoir). He then describes the events of Stalin's final days and the background of each of the potential successors who stood watch at Stalin's deathbed. Soon he is in a car racing toward the Kremlin, reflecting on its pre-Petrine history. Then he remembers a visit to Stalin's dacha in 1950 to discuss the political economy textbook. It is sometimes hard to tell where Shepilov's reminiscences end and hearsay begins, but some passages are clearly fictional. Shepilov imagines Beria's mindset, for instance, when Beria was in solitary confinement awaiting trial in 1953. Beria raged against Khrushchev "like a wild animal" and distracted himself by masturbating to memories of past sexual escapades. At these moments, Shepilov's writing resembles not a memoir but Anatolii Rybakov's fictional account of Stalin's inner circle in *Children of the Arbat* (1987).

Through most of his memoir, Shepilov casts himself as a loyal communist and scholar who is proud to be close to the apex of power but shocked by what he discovers there. In 1950, after his near arrest, Shepilov was nominated to be a delegate to the Supreme Soviet. He took the honor seriously and even traveled to Sverdlovsk oblast in the southern Urals to campaign in factories and collective farms. After his election, he marveled at the talents of the "best of the best," his fellow delegates in the Supreme Soviet, and was pleased to see that Igor Kurchatov, an atomic physicist, and Georgii Zhukov, a war hero, represented nearby districts. But the realization that the Supreme Soviet was utterly impotent soon supplanted Shepilov's pride. Its delegates came to Moscow not for meaningful debates (there were none), nor crucial votes (they were all unanimous), but to be wined, dined, and treated to consumer goods in short supply. He and Zhukov even joked about the annual "puppet show" they were forced to endure.

The personal transformation at the heart of Shepilov's memoir thus recalls the archetypical narrative of Soviet conversion "from darkness to light," albeit with different points of origin and destination.[14] Shepilov went from being a naive outsider who unquestioningly believed in the unanimous goodwill of party leaders to being an experienced insider (and after 1957, an experienced outsider) who was much more ambivalent about what he witnessed. After describing an awkward encounter with Stalin in 1949, Shepilov remarked that he was still "innocent . . . of the Kremlin's secrets and unversed in the conventions and niceties of the Stalin court." But Shepilov's learning curve was steep, and he soon realized that political life at the top of the party had its own unexpected rituals of obeisance. At his first Central Committee plenum in October 1952, Shepilov noticed that Stalin got upset when the "novices" in the hall, those with even less experience than Shepilov, gave Stalin a standing ovation: "Stalin at once gestured at them in displeasure, muttering something like, 'Never do that here.'"

Shepilov was also disappointed to find that the party leadership was not the unselfish brotherhood he had imagined, but was riven with cynicism and ambition. For Khrushchev, Malenkov, and Beria, policies seemed to be merely a means to power and had no value otherwise. Beria proposed an amnesty in 1953 not to reduce the suffering of innocents but to strengthen his reputation among the public. Malenkov gleefully manipulated Iurii Zhdanov's denunciation of Lysenko in 1948 to discredit Andrei Zhdanov. Beria and Malenkov used the Leningrad affair to destroy Voznesenskii. Khrushchev trumpeted the merits of collective leadership to disguise his own efforts to consolidate his power. Shepilov was more gracious toward Zhdanov, Voznesenskii, and Molotov. But like himself, the latter two were casualties of Stalin and Khrushchev. In Soviet politics, it seemed, nice guys finished last.

In this climate, survival was contingent on connections. There is ample evidence in Shepilov's memoir of the centrality of personal networks in the upper ranks of the party. After Aleksandrov and Malenkov fell into disfavor, the Aleksandrov boys hitched their fates to Khrushchev. Beria was held in solitary confinement in a military facility to prevent him from contacting any of his allies in the secret police. Promotions and demotions within the party leadership resulted in personnel shake-ups at lower levels, as "every high official" wanted to be "surrounded by a coterie of 'his own men.'" After Stalin's death, Shepilov watched how Khrushchev expanded his own coterie of devoted followers during a visit to Leningrad. Khrushchev encountered a near insurrection among the city's party members, who could not fathom why Frol Kozlov, one of the instigators of the purge following the Leningrad affair, was still secretary of the oblast committee. Contrary to Shepilov's advice, Khrushchev did not sack Kozlov; instead, Khrushchev made Kozlov beholden by emphasizing the precariousness of his position. Khrushchev's new protégé quickly realized "that his welfare, titles, posts, and entire comfortable life depended totally on his benefactor." Khrushchev reportedly took Ivan Serov, the head of the KGB in the mid-1950s, under his wing in a similar fashion.

A corollary of strong personal networks was weak institutional loyalties.[15] Shepilov admitted that Khrushchev's plot to arrest Beria in 1953 was "undemocratic and unconstitutional," but he doubted that the arrest could have been engineered any other way. If the effort to remove Beria had occurred through legal channels, Beria would have rallied his allies in the secret police to arrest his opponents. Their loyalty was to their patron, not his office.

Shepilov had at least two patrons during his tenure at the top: Zhdanov and Khrushchev. His brush with arrest in late 1949 and early 1950 came after Zhdanov's death and before he knew Khrushchev well. It may be the case that Stalin, who pulled Shepilov out of copyediting purgatory and assigned him to the political economy textbook, also considered himself Shepilov's patron. Shepilov later heard from Il'ia Arginskii, his friend from the war, that the secret police had tried to fabricate a case against him in 1951. Already in prison camp, Arginskii was sent back to Moscow in 1951 so that he could be questioned about his ties to Shepilov. His daughter Iren, then in the tenth grade, was also arrested and questioned about Shepilov. Although Shepilov found out about the episode only after Arginskii was released and rehabilitated, he attributed it to the threat that Beria and Malenkov perceived in his new relationship with Stalin. In the strange logic of Kremlin politics, Stalin was the most powerful patron, but a relationship with Stalin could produce dangerous envy among others.

It is not clear whether Shepilov served as a patron for individuals further down in the political ranks. He presented himself as a friend of

high culture and wrote at length about his lifelong love of opera and ballet. Wherever he traveled—New York, Vienna, Beijing—he visited opera
houses and historical sites. At the Second All-Union Congress of Composers, Shepilov told a sympathetic audience that American rock-and-
roll and jazz induced "wild orgies of cavemen" at the same time that he
emphasized the party's newfound flexibility in music.[16] After his party
membership was restored in 1976, there were even rumors that Shepilov
might become director of the Bolshoi Theater. Dmitrii Kosyrev writes that
there was a certain "legend" surrounding Shepilov: of all the party leaders,
he "knew the difference between an opera and an operetta" and could be
counted on to be a defender of the intelligentsia.[17] Judging from the memoir, there was some basis for this belief. In the late 1930s, while Shepilov
was a staff member at the Central Committee's Science Department, he
was sent to Astrakhan to investigate charges that former aristocrats and
White Army officers were sabotaging research at a wildlife preserve and
fish reservation. After meeting with the suspects and discussing their
scientific work, Shepilov determined that the charges were spurious and
managed to have them dismissed. Beyond that, however, it is difficult to
pinpoint instances in the memoir where Shepilov intervened on behalf of
cultural figures. He did not try to soften the blow of the zhdanovshchina
on composers who were friends. Nor did he strongly advocate or oppose
any candidacies during the annual discussions with Stalin on the awarding of Stalin Prizes. After his own disgrace in 1957, Shepilov may have
wanted to avoid implicating others as allies. Or maybe he realized early
on that patronage had its own risks. After telling Stalin what economists
he liked during the meeting at his dacha in 1950, Shepilov grew defensive
when Stalin joked, "Aha! You're revealing what faction you belong to!"
Given Shepilov's low regard for Khrushchev's legendary political skills,
perhaps he thought patronage was unseemly and thus kept silent about
his own coterie.

Shepilov's criticism of Khrushchev was not unique. Other critics also
questioned Khrushchev's sincerity as a reformer, his moral culpability for
Stalinism, and his intellect. After Khrushchev began to meddle in literary
affairs, the writer Boris Pasternak told the young poet Andrei Voznesenskii that Khrushchev was a "fool and a pig."[18] The sentiment was widely
shared among the intelligentsia. It is also true that Shepilov's criticism
of Khrushchev was sometimes so hostile that his credibility suffered.

He argued, for instance, that Khrushchev's "dictatorship . . . turned out to be infinitely worse and more offensive than Stalin's." Hundreds of thousands of persons who were released from the gulag after Stalin's death would have disagreed. Yet in equating Stalinism with the so-called khrushchevshchina, Shepilov denied that the latter was entirely contrary in spirit to the former.[19] In Shepilov's political world, there were many shades of gray. Shepilov complimented Khrushchev for ending terror, emptying the camps, and trying to patch relations with Yugoslavia. But he also thought that Khrushchev betrayed equally significant reforms by trampling efforts to create a truly collective leadership after Stalin's death. In the desire for one-man rule, Stalin and Khrushchev had much in common.

Shepilov used his memoir to distinguish himself from Khrushchev, who he thought was deeply flawed as a political leader and morally compromised as an individual. In opposing Khrushchev, Shepilov allied himself with people who were later labeled Stalinists. It was not merely a marriage of convenience. Like them, Shepilov admired Stalin and was proud to have worked with him. He defended Stalin's economic and agricultural policies. He even found much that was constructive in the zhdanovshchina, the epitome of Stalinist obscurantism and xenophobia. Unlike the Stalinists, however, Shepilov was critical about the past. He thought that Stalin's crimes had to be made public. And despite his personal animosity for Khrushchev, he admitted that the Soviet Union changed in positive ways under Khrushchev's watch. To borrow a word from the decree that removed Shepilov from power, Shepilov's mind was not fully "joined" to either faction at the Presidium meeting on June 18, 1957.

In the Manichaean politics of the party, there was little room for such subtleties. In language reminiscent of the show trials of the 1930s, Khrushchev linked Shepilov to an "antiparty group" of unrepentant Stalinists. To the end of his life, Shepilov was convinced that the phrase "and joining them was Shepilov" was meant to deny the sincerity of his own beliefs. Regardless, it was tacit recognition that Shepilov did not have the same clouded past as his co-conspirators and that his reasons for participating in the coup were not theirs. Shepilov wrote this memoir because he wanted people to know his reasons.

THE KREMLIN'S SCHOLAR

CHAPTER ONE

Stalin Is Dead

I WAS SITTING IN MY OFFICE at *Pravda*. We were putting out the paper for March 6, 1953. At about 10 P.M. there was a ring on the special Kremlin phone on my desk.

"Comrade Shepilov? Suslov[1] speaking. Stalin has just died. We're all at the 'nearby dacha.' Come right away. Phone Chernukha and get here as soon as you can."

Vladimir Chernukha was Stalin's second-ranking aide, after Aleksandr Poskrebyshev.

Stalin dead.

I did not say anything at the office. I told them to go on putting out the next edition. I ordered a car and left word that I was going to the Kremlin to see Poskrebyshev.

Stalin dead.

The news was so incredible that I could not fully grasp it. It seemed unreal. All the great achievements of the Soviet Union, all its greatness and glory, were linked with Stalin's name. And now Stalin was gone.

To be sure, for several days Moscow had been rife with ominous rumors that Stalin was gravely ill. Some said Stalin had a heart attack, others that he had been paralyzed by a stroke, still others that he'd been poisoned.

From people in the Kremlin I had heard that on March 1, Stalin had spent a normal working day at his "nearby dacha," as we all called it. It was no secret that for the past twenty years, after his wife, Nadezhda Alliluyeva, committed suicide, Stalin had not spent a single night at his apartment in the Kremlin. He lived and worked at the nearby dacha, on a turnoff from the Mozhaisk Highway just before Kuntsevo, on the Setun River.

A massive forest: mighty oaks, pines, fir trees, maples, birches. The whole area encircled by a solid wooden wall four to five meters high, painted green. At the foot of Poklonnaia Hill, not far from the historic hut of Marshal Kutuzov,[2] a striped barrier. From this point a paved road led to the dacha. Driving along, you caught an occasional glimpse of security guards among the trees.

A large green gate with a small square window. At your approach the window opened and you were inspected by a pair of eyes. Two guards came out through a small doorway. After checking your credentials and searching the vehicle they let the car through. A narrow driveway through the woods—and there was Stalin's dacha.

The two-storied house still wore its wartime camouflage. At the entrance you were met by a guard and escorted to the waiting room. No other security trappings visible. A coat rack, and to the right a small room used apparently as a library: many bookshelves filled with books.

In this room, summoned one night by Stalin, I had a long conversation with him about a projected textbook on political economy. Now in this room he had suffered a stroke.

Another door from the waiting room opened onto a large room used as both a dining room and a living room; the walls, as elsewhere in the dacha, paneled in pale wood. A big table, heavy chairs. On the walls, several color reproductions, in simple frames, of some of the most popular paintings by Russian artists, printed in *Pravda*'s new pressroom.

Here at this table members of the Politburo and the Central Committee Presidium often gathered for late supper after their official meetings. Here, too, Stalin had a few select government and party leaders and top foreign dignitaries over for supper.

An almost indistinguishable door in the wall separated the dining room from Stalin's bedroom: a bed; two small armoires for underwear, coats, and jackets; a sink.

To the left of the waiting room, a third door led to Stalin's spacious private office. A large writing desk, with a second desk placed against it to form a T, were both piled high with books, manuscripts, and papers, as were all the little tables around the room—indications that Stalin preferred to work mostly in the small room to the right and not in his formal office.

For some years Stalin had shown certain symptoms of hypertension and arteriosclerosis. We commented to each other about how well he looked, how fresh and pink-cheeked he was, not realizing that this high coloring was a sign of hypertension and that Stalin, as those around him reported later, did not believe in doctors. It appeared that for years on end he did not go in for medical checkups. Only on vacation at the seaside did he sometimes permit a visit from one of his dentists. After the fabrication of the monstrously pathological Doctors' Plot,[3] Stalin saw every doctor as a secret enemy and terrorist. That was why no one really knew the true state of his health.

He seemed quite fit. His suppers with guests after meetings of the Presidium sometimes went on for hours. He helped himself to heavy, highly spiced, and well-seasoned dishes. He mixed different kinds of cognac, wine, and fruit soda in a glass, following a recipe known only to himself. That was another reason everyone thought he was well.

Of course, those closest to Stalin could not help but notice in him the growth in recent years of psychopathic tendencies. For example, in the middle of a lively supper with fellow members of the Central Committee Presidium, Stalin would suddenly get up from the table and step briskly into the hall. Closing the door behind him, he would stand tensely, poised for a long time, listening: What were they saying in his absence? Of course, everyone knew that Stalin was eavesdropping behind the door, but they all pretended not to notice.

On other occasions Stalin cast a suspicious glance at someone who seemed pensive or sad. Why was he lost in thought? What was going through his mind? What was behind this? Without saying so, Stalin made it clear that he wanted everyone in his presence to be cheerful, sing, even do a turn on the dance floor, but not sit there and think. This could be embarrassing, since none of the Presidium members except Anastas Mikoian knew how to dance, but to pander to the boss they would improvise some kind of jig.

With Stalin's growing suspiciousness, it was necessary to be extremely careful around him. I remember one incident. In 1949, at a meeting of the Central Committee Presidium chaired by Stalin, there was a discussion of awards for the year's Stalin Prizes.[4] The meeting was held in the historic hall where Lenin once presided at meetings of the Council of People's Commissars; where the chair he sat in still stands as a memento of those days.

As head of the Central Committee's Department of Propaganda and Agitation, I was present and spoke. When the meeting was over, I decided to ask Stalin where we stood in regard to that textbook on political economy, whose latest draft had long been in his hands for a critique. Many of the economists who worked on the book asked me about it.

Almost everyone had left, and Stalin was on his way out; a few people were still clustered at a side door when I walked hurriedly up to him. Giving me a piercing and frowning look, he stopped for a second, then turned sharply and made for the side door. Catching up with him, I put my question to him. The guarded and puzzled look in his eyes gave way to a glint of cordiality and good humor. As Andrei Zhdanov, Georgii Malenkov, and a few others came up to us, Stalin said: "Well, here's Shepilov asking us to let our economists put out this textbook on political economy on their own. But this is a serious business. Not only for us in the government, but internationally. So you cannot do it without us." Turning to me with a smile he added, "You're not against our taking part in it, are you?"

I answered that of course I wasn't. "But you're very busy, Comrade Stalin, and the textbook is desperately needed."

"What do you mean busy?" Stalin objected. "For something that important we'll find time."

Zhdanov told me later that I had not behaved with enough circumspection. Innocent at the time of the Kremlin's secrets and unversed in the conventions and niceties of the Stalin court, I didn't quite comprehend his warning. Many things became clear to me much later, the most important of them after Stalin's death.

With the passing years, Stalin's suspiciousness, apprehensions, and manic delusions became increasingly evident. Racked by fears, Stalin usually spent the whole night at his desk going over his papers, writing, and reading. He read copiously, both scientific works and literature, and everything he read he remembered and took to heart in his own way. As a rule he went to bed at dawn.

Before turning in, he would look attentively through the windows.

Any footprints in the earth or snow? Had someone stolen up to the house? Of late he had even given orders not to sweep the fresh snow under the windows so that footprints would be easier to detect.

In the grip of his fears he often went to bed without undressing, in his tunic and even his boots. As an added precaution he kept shifting from room to room, sleeping one night in the bedroom, another on the couch in the library, another in the office or dining room. Knowing this, his household made up his bed for him in several rooms at once. When it came time to be driven to the Kremlin and back, Stalin himself selected the route to be taken, and changed it repeatedly.

Aware of these increasingly pathological traits, Lavrentii Beria and his henchmen in the security services deliberately poured salt on his wounds, concocting and feeding him all kinds of wild inventions about assassination plots, treason, and so forth. As it was later revealed, the Ministry of State Security (MGB) cooked up some garish myth about "a plot to assassinate Stalin" and arrested persons who played parts in the planned scenario. Physical and psychological tortures were a ready weapon for extracting full "confessions" from those who were detained, and transcripts of the interrogations were sent to Stalin. The brief routine of indictment before a "special council" then followed.

For the investigators and their superiors within the secret police, all this promised promotions, awards, and material benefits. For those arrested: a bullet in the back of the head in the solitary-confinement dungeons of Lefortovo Prison or, at best, endless years in the mines of the convict colonies of Kolyma.[5] For Stalin, in the final period of his life, the exposure of "terrorists," "poisoners," and "conspirators" became as vital as vodka to a hardened alcoholic. Beria and his men gratified this craving with sadistic glee.

Only because of Stalin's serious pathological illness, because of the absence of any control over the security services and any accountability on their part, could such monstrous fabrications as the Leningrad affair[6] and the Doctors' Plot have been hatched. As members of the Central Committee, we heard Stalin say at our first plenary session after the Nineteenth Party Congress in 1952 that Kliment Voroshilov, Viacheslav Molotov, and Anastas Mikoian were politically untrustworthy. In his final years Stalin regarded Voroshilov as an out-and-out spy and would not meet with him; Molotov and Mikoian he put down as "capitulators" to American imperialism.

That is why, after the Nineteenth Congress, they were excluded from the bureau of the Central Committee Presidium, a decision that Stalin made to bar their way to power.[7]

But, I repeat, much of this became known only after Stalin's death. On the night of March 5, 1953, as I was driven to the Kremlin, what ran like a movie through my mind was a succession of events, facts, and scenes from Stalin's life.

On the evening of March 1 everything proceeded as usual. There was a meeting in the Kremlin. Then everyone went to the nearby dacha for supper. The customary rich and spicy Caucasian, Russian, and Ukrainian dishes—*kharcho, chakhokhbili,*[8] borsht, fried sausage, caviar, smoked fish. Cognac, vodka, wine, soda. As usual, there were no waiters; the guests served themselves. By the time they left, it was long after midnight.

No one knows exactly what happened after that. The next morning Stalin was found lying unconscious by the library couch. Apparently, after his guests were gone, he retreated to his library, puffing away at his pipe. There, during the night, he suffered a massive cerebral hemorrhage and fell to the floor, where he lay unconscious until morning, without medical treatment. In his demented fear he had forbidden his guards and house-hold servants to enter any room he was in.

On the morning of March 2, Stalin was placed on the library couch. He was still unconscious. The hemorrhage affected vital sections of his brain. His right arm and right leg were paralyzed; he lay on the couch, eyes closed, his chest rising and falling, his breathing uneven and spasmodic.

Gathering the same morning at the dacha, the members of the Central Committee Presidium arranged to take turns for a round-the-clock vigil at his bedside. The best doctors in the country were brought in. They took steps to try to regulate his breathing and circulation, but failed to bring about any improvement. His breathing remained irregular, and his blood pressure rose to 220 over 120. His brain function worsened and complete arrhythmia set in.

On Tuesday, March 3, the text of the government's announcement of the illness of the chairman of the Council of Ministers of the USSR and general secretary of the Central Committee of the Communist Party of the Soviet Union, Joseph Stalin, was sent to me at *Pravda;* it was made public the next day and was followed by periodic bulletins on his condition. The popular reaction was one of increasing anxiety. Stalin's villainies had decimated mainly or exclusively the top layers of the country's officialdom. Only those closest to him knew his pathological characteristics. By contrast, the people and party had been taught for thirty years that Stalin was responsible for everything good about Soviet society; he was the source of people's welfare and happiness. Stalin's authority within the party, among the people, and on the world stage—especially after the war—was unchallenged.

The constitution was Stalinist. The collective agriculture, Stalinist. The five-year plans, Stalinist. Stalin was the incarnation of the party's greatness, the banner of victory in the Second World War. To do without Stalin was inconceivable. The government's announcement that "Comrade Stalin's grave illness will necessitate a more or less protracted absence from his official duties" triggered the spread of anxious questions.

"What will we do now?"

"What's going to happen now?"

"How can we do without Stalin?"

Meanwhile, Stalin's condition kept worsening; he had increasingly severe attacks of cardiac failure, acute circulatory deterioration in the cardiac veins, and acute myocardial damage.

It was crowded and stuffy in the library, where the stroke occurred. The couch he was on was carried to the dining room. Members of the Central Committee Presidium kept up their vigil at his bedside around the clock.

At subsequent meetings of the Presidium, Khrushchev spoke at length about Stalin's last days and hours, as he did to me during our walks. So did some others. At that time, the significance of much of what I heard was lost on me. Later, everything fell into place.

The deathwatch at Stalin's bedside was part of a tense game. On the surface, the members of the Presidium were a closely bound fellowship enjoying frank and open personal relationships, in the tradition of the Bolshevik old guard. In reality, under the cover of total unity and comradely teamwork, two of the members were engaged in frenzied activity to have all organizational questions—and hence the succeeding order of events—settled in favor of their own advancement and their own careers. These two were Lavrentii Beria and Nikita Khrushchev.

All indications were that Stalin had never given serious thought to his death and the need to prepare the country and the party for succession. He carried on as though "his kingdom shall have no end." True, there were times when he pretended he was wearying of his duties and wanted to be released from them. For example, I remember the following episode.

In October 1952 we Central Committee members newly elected at the Nineteenth Party Congress met in Sverdlov Hall in the Kremlin for our first plenum. When it came time to select the party's leadership, Stalin rose and said it was hard for him to serve both as premier in the government and general secretary of the party.

"I'm not as young as I was; it's hard for me. I don't have the strength. What kind of premier can't even deliver an address?"

Saying this, Stalin peered inquisitively into our faces, as though watching our reaction. No one in the hall could even contemplate Stalin's stepping down. We all understood instinctively that Stalin did not want his words to be taken seriously. Malenkov stood up and said there was no need to prove that Stalin had to remain as premier and general secretary; "it would be impossible otherwise." And Stalin did not insist.

Yet the years were taking their toll. Delegated by Stalin, for whom the task was simply too much, Malenkov delivered the Central Committee's general report to the Nineteenth Party Congress. This, however, was by no means to be understood as an indication of Stalin's choice of successor.

Of course, who that successor would be was grist for constant guarded speculation within the party and among the people. Whatever the different shades of opinion, everyone agreed that there was only one man within the leadership adequately seasoned by years of revolution and intraparty struggle to take over the helm, and that man was Viacheslav Molotov.

A member of the Bolshevik party since 1906, disciple and brother-in-arms of Lenin and Stalin, Molotov was arrested several times for his revolutionary activities and received his "education" not only at secondary school in Kazan and the Saint Petersburg Polytechnic Institute but in various prisons and in exile in the Vologda region and Siberia. He was a delegate to most party congresses and was one of the founders of *Pravda,* serving for a time as its managing editor. After the February Revolution, Molotov was a member of the Military-Revolutionary Committee, which oversaw the October uprising in Petrograd, and was one of the leaders of the Petrograd Soviet of Workers' and Soldiers' Deputies.

After the establishment of Soviet power, Molotov served as chairman of the Economic Council for the Northern Region, political commissar with the Red Army, chairman of the Nizhnii Novgorod provincial executive committee, secretary of the Don provincial committee, and secretary of the Central Committee of the Ukrainian Communist Party. In 1921, on Lenin's recommendation, he was elected to the Politburo of the All-Union Central Committee and to its Secretariat. For the next thirty-five years, Molotov served variously in the Politburo, as a secretary of the Central Committee and the Moscow Party Committee, as chairman of the Council of People's Commissars and the Council on Labor and Defense, and as people's commissar for foreign affairs.

Everyone who met Molotov in any capacity was struck by certain of his traits—first and foremost his party training and self-discipline, which he carried to absolute and almost fetishlike lengths. Molotov took the decisions and orders of the Central Committee, or even a phone call from one of its executives, as holy writ. Everything he was given to do was done faultlessly, in time, and at any price.

This rule applied to his international activities. Given instructions by the Central Committee Presidium for the positions he was to take at the United Nations General Assembly or at some international conference, Molotov was inflexible and fanatical in sticking to his guns, summarily rejecting any overt or covert attempt by his opponents to draw the Soviet Union toward a compromise. In international diplomatic circles he became known as Mr. Nyet.

It was this unshakable faith in the infallibility of the Central Committee and its decisions and instructions that most likely lay at the heart of his dogmatism and explains why, with all his irreproachable honesty, he joined others in the Politburo as accomplices in Stalin's crimes, which history will never forgive.

Lenin was a collectivist who put a high value on the critical acumen of his colleagues, even when the criticism was directed against him. Stalin was different, both as an individual and as a statesman. He was very circumspect in every word he spoke. But he did not tolerate the slightest criticism; all his theoretical formulations, orders, and actions had to be accepted as immutable. And Molotov, with his dogmatic and zealous party discipline that he placed in total submission to orders from above, carried out Stalin's every wish with the obsession of a fanatic, convinced that it was all done in the interests of the party, the people, and communism. This certainty was paramount even when any reasonable human being would have asked himself, "Does this make sense?" and even when Stalin's actions were directed cruelly at Molotov himself.

For more than thirty years, Molotov was at Stalin's side, deferring to him with the utmost tact in everything. Despite that, Stalin, to discredit him politically and remove him from power, ordered the arrest of his wife, Polina Zhemchuzhina, a longtime communist and prominent government worker. For many days and nights she was held in horrifying isolation in an effort to turn her into an instrument for "exposing" her husband. Then, at a Central Committee plenum, Stalin expressed his distrust of Molotov, accusing him baselessly of "capitulation to American imperialism" and moving that he be dropped from the bureau of the Central Committee Presidium.

Molotov took all this without a word of protest. And when Khrushchev launched his frenzied abuse of Stalin, a campaign carried to unbelievable extremes without a thought for the interests of the government and the party, Molotov did not yield for a single moment to any sense of personal injury or any offense over the deeply unjust treatment he suffered at Stalin's hands. It seemed that not even superhuman willpower could have prevented someone under similar circumstances from indulging in the harshest criticism of Stalin. But Molotov was gifted with just such superhuman self-control. He objected strongly to any one-sided censure of Stalin that could hurt the communist party, the Soviet Union, or the international labor and communist movement. And he did not care to take advantage of this politically opportune moment to present himself in a better light. All manifestations of egocentrism and vanity were alien to his nature—traits that, say, in Andrei Vyshinskii bordered on pathological narcissism and in Khrushchev were inflated to such a degree that they gave rise to popular ridicule. Molotov was always calm, unflappable, laconic, and never tried to take center stage.

His industriousness was phenomenal. While occupying the highest posts in the party and government he did not shrink from the lowliest tasks. On several occasions I was entrusted by the Central Committee Presidium to collaborate with Molotov on some editorial in *Pravda* on international affairs. At the age of sixty-five and older, he could sit and work all day and night if necessary. He was scrupulous in everything. His prestige in the party and among the people, especially after our victory in the Second World War, was very high, and it seemed that of all those gathered around Stalin's deathbed he would take the most active role and would organize the party leadership around himself. But this was not to be.

While taking his turn at Stalin's bedside and carrying on as best as he could with his other duties, Molotov maintained the stoniest composure and gave no sign of being worried about what would ensue after the hour struck for Stalin. At the Nineteenth Party Congress, when Stalin chose Malenkov to give the keynote speech, it seemed that it was Malenkov who would now put forward his claims to the mantle of successor. But Malenkov was too experienced for anything so foolhardy. He knew as well as anyone how jealously Stalin guarded his monopoly on the role of supreme leader, and he was mortally afraid of giving Stalin the slightest reason to suspect him of wanting to infringe on that monopoly. It could cost him his head.

Toward the end, the most pressing affairs of state got stuck on Stalin's desk. For fear of arousing Stalin's suspicions no one dared propose a meeting of the Central Committee Presidium to resolve these issues. We relied instead on some opportune moment to remind him that these questions required his immediate attention. Malenkov clung unswervingly to that policy, finding ways to let him and everyone else know that the initiative for bringing up and deciding every pending issue belonged to Stalin alone.

There was nothing of the dictator about Malenkov; he seemed to me to be devoid of vanity and personal ambition. Mild-mannered and subject to every influence, he had a need to attach himself to some strong personality, and he attached himself to Stalin, Ezhov,[9] Beria, and subsequently Khrushchev. He was an ideal executor of someone else's plans, a brilliant organizer, hardworking to a fault, performing his chosen role with resourcefulness and zeal. His was not a flair for broad initiative or innovation, but once given an assignment by Stalin, he would surmount any problem, go to any lengths, and bear any sacrifice to accomplish his mission promptly and flawlessly and report back. The joke within the Central Committee was that Malenkov always wanted Stalin's instructions carried out "yesterday."

In his devotion to Stalin and his belief in the leader's infallibility, he never asked himself whether carrying out his orders benefited or harmed the country. In that sense he was even more orthodox than Molotov. Molotov, as Stalin's oldest and most influential brother-in-arms, could sometimes allow himself to cross Stalin with a half-question, brief response, suitable quip, or come to someone's defense, or bring up a whole new topic. Malenkov never did this; with him it was "ordered—done."

In those tense days of Stalin's final agony, Malenkov did everything that Khrushchev, Beria, Bulganin,[10] and Kaganovich[11] suggested, whether seeing that the leader received the best possible care or taking care of other urgent official business. At the same time, he did it in such a way that, should Stalin recover, his decisions could be interpreted as loyal in every respect. Indeed, his devotion to Stalin was sincere. To repeat, among the Presidium members gathered at the bedside in an air thick with alarm, confusion, and anxiety for the future, only Khrushchev and Beria knew what they wanted.

Naturally, within the party and country at large, there was no thought of either of the two as a possible successor to the post of chairman of the Council of Ministers or general secretary of the Central Committee; they themselves, however, had their own ideas on the subject. Each made every effort—through promises, flattery, intrigue, and threats—to advance his own cause. In all this, two-thirds of the Central Committee Presidium, expanded at Stalin's behest after the Nineteenth Congress to thirty-six members, took no part in the private discussions among the principals. The list of those who kept watch at the bedside included Georgii Malenkov, Lavrentii Beria, Viacheslav Molotov, Kliment Voroshilov, Nikita Khrushchev, Nikolai Bulganin, Lazar Kaganovich, Anastas Mikoian, Maksim Saburov,[12] Mikhail Pervukhin,[13] and Nikolai Shvernik,[14] and the last three only now and then.

These were the mild days of March. At the dacha the giant pines in their snowy armor stood like silent sentinels; over the garden and the icy lake lay a down blanket of pristine white. In the hothouse the citrus fruit basked in tender orange hues. In the trees the fluffy squirrels leaped frantically from branch to branch and scampered up the inside of their miniature wooden Ferris wheel. There was a time when Stalin stood before the contraption and chuckled, watching the little creatures do their somersaults. Sensing the coming of spring, the flirtatious tomtits in their black berets burst into song, the artful crossbills started their work on the fir cones. With their revolting cawing, the crows descended on the kitchen scraps. But now the deep silence and unbroken rhythm of life at the dacha were disturbed by the coming and going of people, supplies, and oxygen tanks and masks. Presidium members who were taking their turns at the dacha took walks alone or in pairs and groups in the garden, looked in on the billiard room, and pored over the latest government documents.

With his flair for the colorful, Khrushchev later reported on those watchful days. The principal question under discussion was how to reorganize the party leadership after Stalin died. Everyone was asked for his opinion, and Beria immediately proposed that the Ministry of State Security and the Ministry of Internal Affairs be merged into one, with him at the head.

"I knew right away what he was up to," Khrushchev often said. "A minister like that would be in control of the entire security guard for members of the government, of the whole police force, the MGB divisions, and the border troops. Of course, I didn't let on that I was on to him. On the contrary, I kept telling him, 'Sure, Lavrentii, that's what we'll do, that's the right way to go,' and to myself I was saying, 'Just you wait, buddy, everything's going to be different than you think.'"

As Khrushchev remembered it, Beria could hardly contain his gloating over Stalin's stroke. He kept quizzing and nagging the doctors about the slightest changes in the patient's condition and waited feverishly for the desired finale. At the same time, Beria could not free himself of a haunting fear: Who knew, maybe Stalin would survive the crisis, maybe he could pull through. And in fact, on the morning of March 4, the extraordinary measures that doctors took seemed to be having some slight effect. Stalin began breathing more evenly; he even half-opened one eye, in which those present thought they saw a stirring of consciousness. More than that, they imagined they saw Stalin give them a sly wink: Don't worry. We'll lick this yet.

Beria was at the bedside. Seeing these signs of returning life, he fell on his knees, seized Stalin's hand, and kissed it. However, the semblance of consciousness lingered for only a minute, and Beria had no further cause for worry. Khrushchev naturally did not tell us what thoughts spun around in his own mind during Stalin's final days and hours, but these very quickly began to make themselves evident.

Everyone close to the Central Committee knew that Khrushchev was Stalin's favorite. Stalin's growing pathological tendencies changed his relationships to his entourage. Beria he was now wary of and often avoided meeting. Molotov, Voroshilov, and Mikoian he now regarded as enemy spies. As one possessed, he constantly replaced and even executed members of the security services and his own staff. Yet at the very height of his suspiciousness, he moved Khrushchev to Moscow and made him a secretary of the Central Committee and chief of the Moscow Party Committee.

But Khrushchev was not content with being just one of the Central Committee secretaries. At the time, the second secretary, after Stalin, was Zhdanov; after Zhdanov's death the position fell to Malenkov. For Khrushchev, the importance of the top Secretariat post was that it enabled its occupant to appoint his own men throughout the governmental, economic, and social structure and to be in control of all republic and local party organizations, with all the levers of power in his hands. So his sights were set on the position of general secretary of the party. The ultimate ambitions he nurtured were the same as Beria's, but his labyrinthine road map was different.

At the outset of the preliminary discussions Khrushchev announced that he wanted to be freed of his duties as secretary of the Moscow Party Committee so that he could concentrate on his work within the Central Committee. Everyone agreed, failing to foresee where this was destined to lead. Molotov, as always, was silent, cold as granite, as though all these mounting passions were of no concern to him. The choice of the easygoing, pliable, and unpretentious Malenkov as chairman of the Council of Ministers seemed fully acceptable. For Beria and Khrushchev, with their long-range plans, it was acceptable for the time being.

The car that was sent for me at *Pravda* races down Gorky Street; a jumble of thoughts, recollections, questions, images, whirl through my mind. Outside the window, there is a multicolored glitter of streetlights, shop windows, and colorful signs, as though on New Year's Eve. Red Square, silent and majestic. The driver brakes abruptly before the Spasskii Gate. Security officers in their fur winter coats and hats recognize me and let us through.

Inside the Kremlin walls, there is a solemn and mysterious stillness. A handful of officials, passes in hand, trudge purposefully through a gate in an iron wall leading to the building of the Supreme Soviet or toward another checkpoint before the building of the Council of Ministers. The great Ivanov Square lies empty, its silence broken only by the measured stamp of sentries in a changing of the guard or by the rustle of some lone official car. Only on the occasion of party congresses, Central Committee plenums, or Supreme Court sessions does the Kremlin fill with lines of people confined to certain paths to certain destinations.

In this stony silence, visions of the Kremlin's tempestuous history come naturally to mind. Here, to the left of the Spasskii Gate, stood the Criminal Department, and there, to the right, on the present sites of the Supreme Court Presidium and the Kremlin Theater, the Voznesenskii and Chudov monasteries. Closer in are the Assumption and Archangel Cathedrals; the church and golden bell tower of Ivan the Terrible soar regally over Cathedral Square, with the great cracked tsar-bell at their feet.[15] There, before the dip toward the Moscow River, the Embassy Department had its entrance, and there the Military Personnel, Local Gentry, and Musketeer Departments teemed with activity. From early morning to late at night, an incessant clamor used to reign on Ivanov Square. Hundreds of people in motley clothing thronged the doors of the various departments. From their platforms the scriveners read out their full-throated proclamations of the decrees and edicts of the tsar. Clumps of idlers who were nibbling on sunflower seeds and munching on rolls and tripe drifted about the square and watched the spectacle of criminals tied to pillars and sawhorses being whipped with leather thongs or beaten with cudgels. An assortment of clowns, performing bears, and horn tooters put on their acts for the delighted crowds. A steady din filled the air. And now—what silence!

At the corner of Trinity Square, where once stood the court of the boyar Boris Godunov,[16] we turn right and go past the imposing Arsenal, past Stalin's Kremlin apartment, and turn again toward the Nikolskii Gate. Here, across from the Arsenal, on what was once the site of the court of the Trubetskoi princes, the great eighteenth-century Russian architect Matvei Kazakov designed an edifice for the assembly of the Russian nobility. The building was later turned over to the Senate, and in March 1918, after the seat of government was moved to Moscow, it became the official residence of Soviet leaders. Here Lenin had his office and his surprisingly modest four-room apartment, where he lived with his wife, Nadezhda Krupskaia, and his sister, Mariia Ulianova.

An ancient porch with an iron overhang—the entrance to Stalin's office. Because everything linked with his name was cloaked in secrecy, this spot was referred to as the corner; to be summoned here was to be "summoned to the corner." A small dark waiting room. As I take off my overcoat I hear the whisper of automobile tires, the slamming of car doors, and the sound of voices. It turns out that after Suslov's phone call instructing me to come to Stalin's dacha, the Presidium members who were gathered there decided to return to Moscow and discuss matters in Stalin's study, where the Politburo usually met.

We take the elevator to a small hallway and a broad corridor leading to a massive double door, which opens on Stalin's spacious anteroom. A big table usually piled high with the principal American, British, French, and other foreign newspapers and a supply of paper and pencils. Another door, leading to Poskrebyshev's office, where two or three colonels or generals of Stalin's personal guard were usually stationed during the Politburo's meetings or other official functions. But today no one lingers in the waiting room or in Poskrebyshev's office; everyone proceeds straight to Stalin's study. I, too, am invited in.

The room is large and familiar. To the right of the entranceway, there are tall windows with white pleated drapes looking out on Red Square. In the corner by one window is a big writing desk with an inkstand, books, papers, sharpened pencils, and model planes. On the left by the wall there is a long conference table covered in baize. On the wall hang portraits of Marx, Lenin, Suvorov,[17] Kutuzov. On the parquet floor there is a long runner. A half-open door to another room affords a glimpse of an enormous globe; here Stalin took breaks from work at his desk.

The atmosphere at that meeting of the Central Committee Presidium, the first since Stalin's death, is too complex to be described in a single phrase. But in the months and years to come, I often thought back to that nighttime meeting, held while the body of the departed dictator was still warm at the dacha. As the members seated themselves around the table, no one took the chairman's place at the head, an armchair occupied by Stalin for almost thirty years. On one side of the table the chair next to Stalin's was taken by Malenkov, the next by Khrushchev, the next by Molotov; on the other side, Beria, then Mikoian; the others sat on both sides in no particular order. What surprised me during that meeting was the shrill and casual tone taken by Beria and Khrushchev. Both were in an agitated state; scabrous expressions fell from their lips. Molotov's face was of a waxy pallor; a slight frown hinted at the turmoil within. Malenkov was clearly upset and crushed. Kaganovich was not as loud as usual. A combination of hidden anxiety, dejection, worry, and pensiveness hung in the air.

This was not the usual kind of meeting, with its preset speeches and predetermined votes. Disjointed questions, exclamations, and remarks vied with accounts of the last days and hours of the departed. There was no formal chairman, but in view of the agreement reached at the bedside on Malenkov's future role, everyone addressed himself to Malenkov, who summed up the questions that were ripe for decision.

And important decisions were reached—among them quick, unanimous agreement on holding an inquest and having the body embalmed and placed in the Red Square mausoleum next to Lenin's. As I recall, it was Suslov and Pospelov[18] who were assigned to draw up an immediate announcement by the Central Committee of the Communist Party of the USSR, the Council of Ministers of the USSR, and the Presidium of the Supreme Soviet informing all communist party members and all Soviet workers of Stalin's death. A commission to arrange for the funeral was put together, with Khrushchev at its head. Someone, I don't remember who, proposed the construction of a monumental pantheon to the memory of the great figures of Soviet history. The idea was to transfer Lenin and Stalin to the pantheon, as well as the remains of other leading figures buried in the Kremlin wall. I recall that Khrushchev suggested erecting the structure in the new southwest region of Moscow. But in the end it was decided to put the proposal aside and call a plenary meeting of the Central Committee for the following day to rule on the most urgent questions facing the party and country.

The Kremlin squares were deserted and silent, the streets of Moscow desolate for the night. At the entrances to buildings, janitors scraped the ice off the sidewalks. In front of the grocery stores, immense trucks unloaded their supplies. A few pedestrians hurried along, impelled by the cold. A military formation on its way somewhere pounded a rhythmic beat on the pavement. A light snow drifted down. Everything seemed normal in this ancient capital; nothing had changed. Nonetheless, sitting in the limousine on the way to putting out the funerary edition of *Pravda*, I felt that some central mechanism in the gigantic engine of government had cracked. The cogwheels, gears, and transmissions still functioned, but something had broken down, something big and serious, fraught with enormous consequences for our country—and not for ours alone.

"No, that can't be," I thrust the thought away. "What consequences? Why?"

The snowflakes swirled in the beams of our headlights. Through a gap in the car window came the mournful and ominous soughing of the wind.

Stalin's embalmed body lay in its coffin in the Hall of Columns in the House of Soviets, in a sea of banners and flowers. The solemn harmony of orchestra and choir suffused the room. In this hall, as a student and member of the Komsomol,[19] almost thirty years before, I said farewell to the greatly beloved Lenin. And now—to Stalin. This time it fell to me to be part of the honor guard on several shifts, to stand next to members of the *Pravda* staff, the Central Committee, and representatives of the armed forces. The coffin was lined in bright red silk; there was a red coverlet over Stalin's feet and a red pillow for his head. And around the coffin, white chrysanthemums, white hyacinths, white lilies, white roses. Against this virginal white, the red of the coffin had an indefinable but eerie air.

Stalin was dressed in his generalissimo's uniform with its rows of ribbons, a uniform he had devised himself while the professional designers put to work by the quartermaster corps were toiling away at their sketches, trying to create something extraordinary and unique. Stalin took a regular general's tunic, set it off with a couple of embroidered buttonholes, and donned it at a meeting, thereby putting an end to any further exertions on that score.

Stalin's face was unbelievably pale, with a trace of an expression that was new to him—a certain sorrow, as though in parting with his life he went through a moment of intense anguish. His hands, too, were pale, with brown spots. To me they seemed disproportionately big and very strong.

An endless line of mourners moved through the Hall of Columns from early morning and all night long. Around the country, huge crowds gathered in the streets and squares of cities and towns, in villages and workers' settlements. Fearfully and sorrowfully people asked each other aloud or with silent glances, "What will happen now?" At memorial ceremonies, speakers poured out their grief—not because they were ordered to do so, but from the heart.

Stalin's authority with the people had been immense. The historic victory in the Second World War, the rapid reconstruction and subsequent economic boom, the repeal of rationing, the annual reduction in prices, and the visible improvement in living standards—all this was embodied by Stalin. The restrained and judicious policies espoused by Stalin toward a whole range of complex international problems left in the wake of the Nazis' shattering defeat—his steady pursuit of peace among nations—won him the respect not only of workers and intellectuals throughout the world but of many political and social leaders. Streets, squares, and entire cities were named after him.

In light of this tremendous victory, even the crimes of 1937–39[20] seemed to fade and retreat to a distant past. Indeed, in the minds of many they were not directly associated with Stalin. It was thought that certain evil men perpetrated these villainies without Stalin's knowledge and that as soon as he became aware of them he meted out stern punishment on those who broke the law.

At *Pravda* we received a torrent of telegrams, letters, and articles about Stalin. They came from leading public figures, writers, scholars, workers and peasants, grown-ups and children, from all the republics of the Soviet Union, and from abroad. My telephone rang incessantly; the callers all wanted their articles and tributes published without fail. What was this—hypocrisy, humbug? No! With Stalin dead, there was no further need for pretense.

"We are children of the Stalin era," wrote the author Aleksandr Fadeev. "All the best in us and in our work took shape under the strong influence of Stalin's teaching, his organizational genius, his personality. . . . Stalin was the greatest humanitarian the world has ever known. . . . For many, many centuries his sacred name will shed its light, illuminating the road ahead for humankind!" (*Pravda,* March 12, 1953).

And here is a letter from the actress Alla Tarasova: "I can still see his face, his smile, his kindly eyes, still feel the warm clasp of his hand. . . . How much we all learned as creative artists from his wise, inspiring instructions and advice!"

The French writer Louis Aragon: "To whom but him are we indebted for becoming what we are? He was a great teacher whose mind, knowledge, and example nurtured our party, the party of Maurice Thorez,[21] thousands of whose sons died in the cause of liberty with the names of Stalin and France on their lips!" (*Pravda*, March 12, 1953).

The great leader of the Chinese people, Mao Zedong: "It was with infinite sorrow that the Chinese people, the Chinese government, and I personally learned of the death of the dearest friend of the Chinese people and their eminent teacher, Comrade Stalin. . . . The victory of the Chinese national revolution is indissolubly linked with the constant care, guidance, and support provided us by Comrade Stalin over the past thirty-some years. . . . The immortal light of Comrade Stalin will always shine along the road taken by the Chinese people."

Many of the letters were of an astonishing depth and sincerity. The words seemed soaked in drops of blood from hearts convulsed with unquenchable sorrow. Among the thousands who wrote with such feeling was the talented poet Olga Berggol'ts. I knew what inhuman suffering she endured during those terrible years of unbridled lawlessness. I knew what wretchedness was hers during the blockade of Leningrad.[22] And now, having endured all the agonies of the past, Olga Berggol'ts wrote:

> Our hearts are bathed in blood,
> Our own, our dearest.
> Cradling your head,
> The Motherland weeps for you.
>
> The Motherland weeps,
> Letting the tears run,
> Pledging herself to you,
> Her captain, her guide, her father.
>
> Our dear one, you are with us, with us,
> In every heart you live, you breathe,
> You, our shining banner,
> Our glory, our soul.

The Prime Minister of India, Jawaharlal Nehru: "Death has plucked from our times a figure of extraordinary talent and great achievements. The history of Russia and the whole world will always bear the imprints of his efforts and accomplishments!" (*Pravda*, March 7, 1953).

The poet Aleksandr Tvardovskii:

At this hour of utmost sorrow
I cannot find the words
To express to the full
Our national calamity.

Tractor team leader Pasha Angelina, a Heroine of Socialist Labor: "Stalin! This name, lapped in the nation's love and respect, I inscribe deep in my heart. The great Stalin taught me, a simple peasant woman, a farmhand's daughter, to live and work for the welfare of my country and my people!" (*Pravda*, March 8, 1953).

The writer Mikhail Sholokhov: "Orphaned is our party, the Soviet people, the workers of the world. . . . Father, farewell! Farewell, our own and, to our last breath, beloved father! How greatly are we in your debt! You will always be with us, and with those who come after us" (*Pravda*, March 8, 1953).

The cold March wind howled in the water pipes and slammed the front doors. With ferocious anger it swept up the remains of blackened leaves, old newspapers, and matchboxes on the sidewalks. Wholly occupied though I was by my editorial work, my mind in those funereal days kept going back to the times and places of my meetings with Stalin. Red Square, the Bolshoi Theater, Andreevskii Hall, the Kremlin, Stalin's office, the meeting room of the Politburo, Sverdlov Hall. Most often and most hauntingly I recalled the small library room at the nearby dacha and on the floor, by the couch, the prostrate body of Stalin.

This room was bound up with my vivid memory of a particular conversation with Stalin, one in which he exhibited his scholarly side.

It happened on a Sunday. My wife and I were at the theater, enjoying an operetta. The final act had just begun when someone whispered hurriedly in my ear, "Comrade Shepilov, come with me. You're being summoned by the Kremlin."

I was taken to the phone in the manager's office. "Comrade Shepilov? This is Chernukha. Comrade Stalin wants you to call him."

I replied, "Comrade Chernukha, I'm in a theater, a rather crowded one. There's no direct phone line to the Kremlin. With your permission I could go to the Moscow Soviet near here. I'll call from there."

"No need for that. I told Comrade Stalin where you are and asked if

I should disturb you. He said yes, and to have you call him. He's waiting; call him on a regular line. Here's his number."

I called. At once I heard the familiar, muted, toneless voice: "Stalin." I gave my name and said hello.

"I hear," he said, "you're in the theater. Anything interesting?"

"Oh, just a light musical comedy."

He said, "We need to talk. Could you come over now?"

"Of course."

"No problem leaving the theater?"

"No."

"Then come to the 'nearby.' Chernukha will arrange it."

In a few minutes I was in the Kremlin. Chernukha ordered a car, and I was soon being sped along the Mozhaisk Highway. Word had evidently been sent ahead, because the barrier at the foot of the Poklonnaia Hill was raised at our approach, and the dacha's green gates opened at once. At the door I was met by a colonel of the security guard, who escorted me into the waiting room and disappeared. For more than two and a half hours at the dacha I did not see a single other security officer.

I hung up my coat and, turning around, saw Stalin coming out of his office. He was wearing his gray tunic and gray trousers, his usual attire in the two decades prior to the war. The tunic, I could see, was carefully patched in several places. He was in his slippers instead of his usual boots, with his trousers tucked into his socks.

Greeting me, he said, "Let's go into that room. It'll be quieter there." This was the first room to the right that I spoke of earlier as the library, the room where Stalin would suffer a stroke. At his bidding I seated myself in an armchair, placing my notebook and pencil on the table beside me. Stalin gave these journalistic tools a disapproving glance, and I realized I was not to take notes. Stalin, I soon learned, did not like his words to be taken down. In the months ahead, at his meetings with those of us at work on the new textbook on political economy, he often said, "What are you scribbling for, with your nose in your papers? Listen and think!" And we would have to scrawl some kind of shorthand secretly under the table and try to decode it later. This time, however, there was no way of taking notes without being noticed.

Throughout our conversation Stalin paced up and down, slowly, as was his wont, shifting his weight from foot to foot. "All right," he began.

"You asked recently about speeding up work on this textbook on political economy. Well, it's time to come to grips with it. It's been in Leont'ev's[23] hands and he's bungled it.

"It's not working out," Stalin continued. "We've got to reorganize. And so we're thinking about including you among the authors. What do you say?"

I thanked him for the honor and the trust he was placing in me, and he asked, "And whom else would you recommend for membership?"

The question caught me unprepared, but after a moment's thought I named two of our most qualified economists.

Stalin chuckled. "Aha! You're revealing what faction you belong to."

I had no special liking for either of the two professors, no more than I had anything against them, but I felt that my prompt recommendation could be interpreted in the most unexpected ways. Whereupon I added that the choice of authors would need further careful consideration.

Stalin said, "Did you read the latest page proofs of the textbook? What do you think?"

I reported as briefly as possible on my reaction, knowing that what we needed to get things going was not my comments but as much of Stalin's own views and advice as I could extract from him. And indeed, from that point on, Stalin spoke almost uninterruptedly for two and a half hours. Much of what he shared with me he laid out later before the group writing the textbook. As time went on, I formed the impression that sometimes Stalin liked to think out loud as a way of testing his ideas and conclusions. This stemmed from his extraordinarily keen sense of responsibility for his every word.

In that respect, the contrast between Stalin and Khrushchev, when the latter came to power, was especially striking. Khrushchev suffered from a pathological case of logorrhea; he did not have the slightest sense of responsibility for his utterances. In a fit of impromptu bravado during a public speech, for instance, he would fling an ultimatum at the Western allies: "If a peace treaty with the German Democratic Republic is not signed within the next six months . . ." Then there were threats and reminders that the Soviet Union had enough atomic bombs to lay waste to the whole planet.

During the thirty years of Stalin's leadership, all foreign statesmen learned to give serious heed to the statements of the "Russians," the "Bolsheviks" who did not engage in loose talk. Hence, as was to be expected,

Khrushchev's ultimatums led to the commitment abroad of additional billions for arms production. The general staffs of the United States, Britain, France, and NATO panicked and prepared to defend West Berlin from a "Russian invasion." The world seemed to be on the brink of war. But when May, the final month of Khrushchev's ultimatum, came around, he repeated his ultimatum, setting the following May as the deadline. The international consequences were the same. The ones to profit most from this verbal incontinence were the arms-producing monopolies of the imperialist powers.

It was the same with other public statements. Like a gossipy cook who can't resist tattling to a crony about snooping on her employers, Khrushchev was absolutely incapable of keeping his mouth shut, even when it came to state secrets. He was bursting with a need to boast about what he had found out or seen. Here's an example: "Yesterday I dropped in on one of our missile plants. Know that we're churning out our ballistic missiles on an assembly-line basis. Our missiles come off the assembly line like sausages, one every minute."

Naturally, this bragging was put to expert analysis by the imperialist powers to see how much truth it contained. But the problem was that such statements by Khrushchev triggered new military spending by the American Congress and the European parliaments to catch up with the USSR, which already had "missiles coming off the assembly line."

When the American spy Gary Powers violated Soviet air space as far as the Urals in his special U-2 reconnaissance plane and was shot down by our antiaircraft defenses,[24] Khrushchev stated in public: "We now have automated antiaircraft and antimissile systems that can shoot down a fly in space!" That, of course, was another empty boast. But it led to additional large-scale appropriations for the United States Defense Department.

By contrast, Stalin, even one to one, spoke with great restraint, carefully and scrupulously formulating his thoughts. In the course of the conversation that night when I was summoned to his dacha, Stalin covered a wide range of theoretical problems. He reviewed such subjects as the manufacturing and mass-production phases of capitalist development, the role of wages under capitalism and socialism, the period of primitive capital accumulation, the pre-monopolistic and monopolistic forms of capitalism, the field of political economy, the great utopian socialists, the theory of surplus value, and many other complicated matters.

Even when discussing the most abstruse aspects of political economy, he spoke easily and simply. Clearly, he had long ago mastered the whole subject. When dealing with the purely theoretical, he often engaged in historical digressions regarding primitive societies and ancient Greece and Rome. In his mind, the most abstract concepts of the past were linked to the most pressing problems of our own day. One felt he spoke out of vast experience as a Marxist teacher and publicist.

He obviously was well versed in the classic works of Marx and Lenin. For example, speaking of the successive phases of capitalism, he went to his bookshelf and took out the first volume of Marx's *Das Kapital*. It had the frayed and soiled look of a book much in use. Flipping through the pages, Stalin readily found the quotations he searched for to underpin his own thoughts.

"But it's not just a question of Marx. Here's how Lenin put it." Not finding the book he wanted, he left the room, returning in a few minutes with a bulky volume, which also bore signs of wear and tear. It was Lenin's *Development of Capitalism in Russia*. Again, he had no trouble finding the quotation he was looking for. Next he criticized some of the assumptions of Friedrich Engels, and his objections seemed quite sound.

Pacing up and down, Stalin continually puffed on his pipe. He took a cigarette from a box on the table, broke off the cork tip, and packed his pipe with the tobacco. Toward the end of our conversation he took a fat cigar, lighted it, and stuffed it into his pipe; the room filled with the strong odor of nicotine. Waiting for an opening, I said, "Comrade Stalin, you are smoking a lot. Isn't that bad for you?"

He replied, "You're not very observant. I don't inhale. Just puff-puff. I used to inhale, but not anymore."

What astonished me as he went on was the importance he placed on the theoretical. He spoke something like this: "Now you and your colleagues are set to write a textbook on political economy. This is a historic task. Without a new textbook we can't make any further progress. Communism doesn't spring like Aphrodite from the sea foam. And no one is going to bring it to us on a platter. We must build it ourselves on a scientific foundation. The Marxist-Leninist idea of communism must be made real. How? On a scientific basis. To do that, our people have to have a thorough grasp of economic theory, economic laws. If they do, we'll solve all our problems. If they don't, we're finished. We'll never achieve communism.

"And do our people really know about economic theory? They don't know a damn thing. The older generation knows, the old Bolsheviks. We pored over *Das Kapital*, we learned Lenin by heart. We took notes, we wrote summaries. All those times in prison and exile, they helped, they were good teachers. And the young today? They don't know Marx and Lenin. All they know is how to crib and use quotations.

"Your textbook must not be a crib, a series of quotes. No! It must provide a thorough explanation of all the economic laws and concepts contained in *Das Kapital* and other works by Marx and Lenin. It must serve as an introduction to further study of those works. Then we'll have educated Marxists to manage the economy intelligently and on a scientific basis. Without that, our people will degenerate, and we'll perish. We need this textbook like we need air to breathe."

The issue, Stalin repeated several times in forceful language, was one of "either-or." Either our people would master the essence of Marxism and we would prevail in the great battle for a new life, or we would fail in this undertaking and then—death. Saying this, he took the pipe out of his mouth and made a slashing gesture as though slitting his own throat.

"This textbook," he continued, "will have to be flawlessly honed and polished, every word weighed. And what do we have today? I've just read what that Leont'ev crowd turned out. What a lot of blather! What twaddle! First they give it to the imperialists—you so-and-so's—then they come out with a lot of Komsomol tricks, cheap agitprop. This textbook must influence people's consciousness, help them understand the laws of society. And here you don't know what they're trying to influence—the stomach maybe? Take Marx's *Das Kapital* or Lenin's *Development of Capitalism*— they're your models. Remember, this is not going to be easy. We're going to carp at every word."

I took advantage of the pause to ask, "Can we count on you to edit our work?"

"We'll see how it goes. But that isn't going to make it any easier. Don't think I'm going to let you off lightly."

Unexpectedly he asked, "When you write your articles, do you use a stenographer?"

I said no.

"Why not?"

"I write slowly. I do a lot of revising. Make inserts, transpose sentences and paragraphs. In other words, I keep polishing as I write. I can't do that without having the text down in front of me."

Stalin responded, "I don't use a stenographer either. Can't do anything with her hanging around."

Chatting, pulling on his pipe, he escorted me to the waiting room. "You get around to the stores, the marketplaces?"

I said I seldom did.

"Why?"

"Can't seem to find the time."

"Too bad. An economist ought to see for himself. In the final analysis these places show us how well we're doing with the economy."

Offering me his hand, he exclaimed, "Hold on, I forgot to order you a car," and went to a telephone.

Outside the giant fir trees stood like sentinels. Out of nowhere a colonel of the security guard rose on the steps. In the heavy silence came the whisper of automobile tires.

And now, in the massive flood of letters to *Pravda*, Stalin was among the dead, part of what used to exist. Physically, Stalin was now just a lump of mummified flesh.

In the Hall of Columns, the mourners queued up with grief-stricken, tear-stained faces. And meanwhile, elsewhere, a new party and government leadership was being organized. Not for a single day must there be any slackening of controls.

On March 6 the Central Committee met in plenary session. The meeting took place, as always, in Sverdlov Hall, with its great dome from which the red flag of the Union of Soviet Socialist Republics billowed proudly over Red Square. The first time I was in this hall was in March 1943: here the titular leader of the Soviet Union, Mikhail Kalinin, decorated me with the Red Banner for my participation in the Battle of Stalingrad. I was often here in later years, and each time I'd be filled with admiration for this grand achievement of the architect Kazakov. Massive columns and pilasters crowned with marvelous carvings against the wall of the circular interior. A gallery above a magnificent cornice. Above the windows, within the rotunda, bas-reliefs: Hippocrates surrounded by mothers; an allegorical depiction of the Neva River; Minerva on her throne receiving her commanders; Neptune and the naiads; the naval Battle of Chesme[25] and the brilliant victory of the Russian fleet over the Turks; Russia, holding up a bough with its bountiful yield of fruit. What a display of pride, grandeur, and beauty!

But now, as the Central Committee met, the hall was sunk in a tense silence, as though the coffin of the departed were right there.

All the organizational questions were settled, as always, unanimously, without debate: Malenkov was named as chairman of the Council of Ministers; Beria, Molotov, Bulganin, and Kaganovich as deputy chairmen; Voroshilov as head of state, chairman of the Presidium of the Supreme Soviet; and all the above, as well as Mikoian, Saburov, and Pervukhin, as members of the Central Committee Presidium. Bureaucratically, it was a turn toward radical centralization—major sectors of government and the economy were combined in one center, headed by a member of the Presidium.

Thus, Beria's plan was implemented. He became head of the enormous Ministry of Internal Affairs, which now included the former Ministry of State Security. There were numerous indications that Beria, from then on, would be number two in the highest levels of the government and the party. In view of Malenkov's pliant nature, Beria's role promised to be decisive in both spheres.

Everyone agreed on the need to draw the proper lessons from the situation that prevailed under Stalin, when the general secretary of the Central Committee functioned, in effect, as the one-man ruler of party and government, wielding colossal power and not answerable to anyone, a state of affairs that spelled utter disaster for the country. To prevent a repetition of anything similar, it was decided to eliminate the post of general secretary. But in that case, who was to preside at meetings of the Central Committee Presidium, where the most important issues facing the country—political, international, economic, and ideological—were ultimately decided? The answer seemed obvious: return to the Leninist tradition of having the Politburo meetings chaired not by its general secretary but by the head of government—which in Lenin's time meant the chairman of the Council of People's Commissars, or Lenin himself. Today it meant the chairman of the Council of Ministers, or Malenkov.

As for the party Secretariat, which dealt with day-to-day business, chiefly with overseeing the party's appointments of official personnel, it was assumed that several Central Committee secretaries would take turns at its head.

As events were soon to prove, this arrangement did not really suit Khrushchev at all. Under no circumstances was he going to back Malenkov as the presumptive leader of the party and the nation; he was hatching other plans. But for the time being he did not object to the proposed reforms. He only asked to be released from his duties as first secretary of the Moscow Party Committee so he could devote himself to his work within the Central Committee itself. This was approved at the March 6 plenum.

Khrushchev's appointment as a secretary of the Central Committee fulfilled his fondest wishes. It also raised the curtain on the first act of a tragedy that soon began to unfold before the eyes of the whole world, with destructive consequences. The decision to abolish the post of general secretary, or first secretary, was purely formal in nature; in effect, Khrushchev from this day on became the de facto leader of the party. Very soon he demanded that this position be legalized.

But in those days, which seemed to revolve around the coffin of the departed chief, everyone with the exception of Beria and Khrushchev, who had their own cards to play, understood how necessary it was to guard against the return of one-man rule. This was understood—but, as time showed, we did not have the resolve to take those radical measures that would have restored, in deeds and not just words, the Leninist form of party and government leadership and public life. Was it possible to achieve those measures? Yes, it was—through the broadest possible democratization of the party, government, and society at large.

This, however, did not come about, and in time the party and the people fell again under the burden of one-man rule. The only difference was that the new dictatorship—Khrushchev's—turned out to be infinitely worse and more offensive than Stalin's.

Stalin, with all his flaws, had many of the qualities of an outstanding leader. He was a well-rounded Marxist; he was tempered in the legendary school of political struggle, exile, and prison; he was wise and patient in deciding complicated affairs of state; in all his thinking, viewed from an objective standpoint, he sought to serve his people, and he was fanatically devoted to the idea of communism—all this without a trace of desire for personal material gain.

Khrushchev, on the other hand, soon showed himself to be lacking in lofty communist ideals or moral principles. What we saw was an ignoramus, a master of intrigue, elbowing everyone aside in his hurry to clamber onto the world stage. His was the philosophy of Prince Galitskii in Alexander Borodin's opera *Prince Igor:*

> If I could just get that honor,
> Be Grand Prince of Putivl',
> I wouldn't shed tears.
> I'd know how to live.
> I'd lay waste the treasury.
> Life would be sweet.
> That's what power is for!

But to get back to the March plenum. As part of the centralization scheme, Mikoian was made head of a unified Ministry of Domestic and Foreign Trade, Saburov of a gigantic machine-tooling department combining four former machine-tooling ministries, and Pervukhin of an equally huge ministry for electric power stations and the electrical industry. (In practice, however, these monstrous economic empires soon proved hard to manage, and the ministries in question were broken up into smaller entities.)

With all outstanding questions quickly resolved, the members of the Central Committee Presidium left for the House of Soviets. There, in the Hall of Columns, the mourners from the city streets continued streaming around the clock into a third day. What genuine grief on their faces, what tears, what sobs! It was as though the country was bidding farewell to its father. People stood for up to twelve hours in the cold March wind to pay their last respects. And not just Soviet citizens. From around the world, government delegations and public figures converged on the mournful capital to bow their heads before the dais where Stalin lay in state.

I often took time off from my editorial work to meet with prominent people in our country and the international communist movement who were then gathered with grim and clouded faces in the Hall of Columns: there, by the coffin, the Chinese delegation headed by Premier Zhou Enlai; the Italian communist leader Palmiro Togliatti; representing the Polish people, the head of the Polish Workers' Party, Bolesław Bierut, and Marshal Konstantin Rokossovskii;[26] the president of Czechoslovakia, Klement Gottwald; the veteran member of the Comintern[27] and of the Hungarian Communist Party Mátyás Rákosi; the leaders of the German Democratic

Republic Walter Ulbricht and Otto Grotewohl; the chairman of the Council of Ministers of the Romanian Republic Gheorghe Gheorghiu-Dej; the general secretary of the Bulgarian Communist Party Vulko Chervenkov; Finnish Premier Urho Kekkonen; the chairman of the All-India Peace Council Saifuddin Kitchlew;[28] the legendary tribune of the Spanish Civil War, the fiery "La Passionaria," Dolores Ibárruri; the Italian Socialist leader Pietro Nenni—everyone, everyone was there.

In Paris and Beijing, in Prague and Bucharest, in thousands of cities around the world, hundreds of millions of people emptied into the streets for mass ceremonies for the departed.

The final day of the great farewell was marred by tragedy. The funeral commission headed by Khrushchev announced that access to the hall would be terminated at 2 A.M. Yet the flow of people was still increasing. The throng packed Bol'shaia Dmitrovka Street all the way to Trubnaia Square. In the square itself the mass of humanity kept growing. From high up on Sretenka Street the crowds kept pouring down. At the steepest descent to Trubnaia Square they encountered barricades, but these obstructions did little to contain the pressure of the human avalanche from Kirov Street and Dzerzhinskii and Kolkhoz Squares. From the closely packed multitude rose moans, cries for help, warnings of danger.

Too late. The barricades at the abrupt incline from Sretenka Street to Trubnaia Square toppled. In the surge forward, a great number of people were knocked down and trampled by those behind them. There were sounds of rib cages breaking underfoot. Wails from hundreds of mouths were distorted with terror. Children on their fathers' shoulders were screaming for help from their mothers, but were drowned out in the bloodcurdling bellow of grown men being crushed like walnuts in a nutcracker.

All night long, ambulances, police, and military vehicles plied the streets, transporting their loads of mutilated bodies to the morgues. The ominous words, "Khodynka . . . Khodynka"[29] spread through the city.

On the morning of March 9, the Central Committee headed by its Presidium, the Presidium of the Council of Ministers, and the leaders of foreign communist and other workers' parties met at Stalin's coffin. There stood Molotov, expressionless as ever; there Voroshilov, cast down and bewildered; there Malenkov, pale and weary but composed. Behind his thick pince-nez, Beria's face kept twitching spasmodically. Khrushchev stood near me, his eyes red and inflamed, tears coursing down his cheeks. Now and then he brushed them away with the palm of his hand.

In time we became inured to the most surprising changes of mood and volte-face on Khrushchev's part. At a mass meeting attended by foreign correspondents and the diplomatic corps he would blurt out that "En-zen-hauer"—President Eisenhower's name as it came out of his mouth—"is a regular guy," and a few days later, because of some trivial occurrence, throw anathema at him. Even abroad, people got used to Khrushchev's excesses and stopped taking them too seriously.

That day he sobbed at Stalin's coffin. Knowing him to have been Stalin's favorite, no one was surprised by his tears. There was even something touching in this expression of sorrow when all need for pretense was past.

To the strains of Chopin's funeral march, the ritual begins. Wreaths are ceremonially removed. The famed marshals of the Soviet Union, Georgii Zhukov, Semen Timoshenko, Ivan Konev, Vasilii Sokolovskii, Leonid Govorov, Semen Budennyi, and others carry out Stalin's decorations on red pillows. Malenkov, Beria, Molotov, Voroshilov, Khrushchev, Bulganin, Kaganovich, and Mikoian bear Stalin's coffin out the door. Behind the coffin goes Stalin's ill-favored and unruly son, Vasilii, his face puffy with tears, and Stalin's likable daughter, Svetlana, dignified and reserved. Then we members of the Central Committee and the heads of foreign delegations follow the coffin.

Slowly down Hunter's Row, across Manege Square, and up toward Red Square move the serried ranks of the military escort. The coffin is placed on a gun carriage drawn by black horses, and the cortege moves toward Lenin's mausoleum. Through the coffin's clear plastic top I catch a glimpse of Stalin's waxen face and ash-colored hair. Red Square is inundated with troops, delegations of workers, and representatives of all the national republics. Utter silence: not a voice, not a whisper. The coffin is transferred to a high pedestal draped in red and black. The Central Committee Presidium and the heads of the major international communist parties take the steps to the top of the mausoleum. From there, Malenkov, Beria, and Molotov deliver eulogies.

Molotov speaks with calmness and restraint, yet with strong emotion: "Stalin was the great successor to Lenin's work. . . . We may take pride in having lived and worked for the past thirty years under the leadership of Comrade Stalin. We were brought up by Lenin and Stalin. We are pupils of Lenin and Stalin. And we will always remember what Stalin taught us, down to his final days."

I marveled hearing him speak. I knew that in the confusion of the five days since Stalin's death there simply hadn't been time to raise the question of Molotov's wife, who was still in solitary confinement in prison, even though she was innocent of any wrongdoing, and was at a fairly advanced age. I recalled how toward the end of Stalin's life Molotov sat humbly in the anteroom of the Central Committee Presidium, along with lesser party officials, waiting to be called to the meeting inside in regard to some specific question—this because Stalin excluded him from the Presidium bureau. I remembered the brutal flow of accusations of political and moral "capitulation to American imperialism" leveled at him by Stalin after the Nineteenth Party Congress.

And here was Molotov at Stalin's funeral. What iron discipline, to speak only in the nation's interests, to the exclusion of anything personal that could do the nation harm! I recalled that speech when Khrushchev much later jeered at Stalin's memory with a kind of roughneck malice and abandon, caring nothing for the country's interests and pursuing only his own selfish ends. Down the length and width of Red Square Molotov's weighty words fell; radio carried them around the world: "All his life Stalin devoted himself unstintingly to the struggle for communism, to the selfless struggle for the happiness of the workers, the happiness of the people. . . . Our aim is to be faithful and worthy pupils and followers of Lenin, true and devoted pupils and followers of Stalin."

There is an artillery salute. Stalin's brothers-in-arms raise the coffin and carry it into the mausoleum. One feels the whole country caught breathless for a moment of solemn respect. At noon all trains, ships, cars, trucks, machines, stop for five minutes of silence. At industrial plants in France, Italy, India, China, Poland, Czechoslovakia, and elsewhere, all work comes to a stop. Long factory whistles announce to the world that the last journey of the leader of a great nation has been completed.

Above the entrance to the mausoleum, the rose marble bears two names:

LENIN

STALIN

Who would have thought that only a few years later his most loyal favorite would subject Stalin's remains to gross outrage and indignity!

CHAPTER TWO

Ezhovshchina

LIKE ALL OF STALIN'S HEIRS on the political stage, Khrushchev emerged from the era defined by the last half of the 1930s, a time of sweeping and disastrous changes in the ranks of the country's leadership. In October 1937 the Great Terror that Nikolai Ezhov ran raged throughout the land. Many of the most senior party workers, the most trusted of Lenin's colleagues, were charged with villainies that made the blood run cold: poisoning wells, causing train wrecks, blowing up factories.

All the accused confessed their guilt. The sentence was always death. In trial after trial, the chief prosecutor, Andrei Vyshinskii, had but one demand: blood, blood, and more blood.

In time the venomous wave that became known as *ezhovshchina*[1] reached my own relatives. It crashed down first on the family of my wife's sister, Galina Paushkina. She and her husband, Emmanuil Ratner, both worked at the USSR State Planning Commission (Gosplan). At two in the morning on November 10, 1937, a group of GPU[2] agents burst into their small room on Palikh Street, ransacked the premises, and told Emmanuil to get dressed. They took him away and we never saw him again.

Thirty years later, we still do not know what happened to him. A loyal communist who was devoted to his party and country with every fiber of his being fell victim to that wholesale formula "enemy of the people." Where and how did he meet his end? What torture did he undergo? It is all a blank. After more than twenty years, the prosecutor's office informed Galina that Emmanuil Ratner had been posthumously rehabilitated.[3]

In January 1938 the wave engulfed my wife's stepfather, Garal'd Krumin. A member of the All-Union Communist Party (Bolshevik) since 1909, and a superbly trained Marxist, Krumin had been editor in chief of the newspaper *Economic Life* and later of *Izvestiia*. His correspondence with Lenin was well known.[4] Shortly before being picked up, he was expelled from the party for associating with "enemies of the people," the same slanderous accusation that had been brought against the Politburo members Jan Rudzutak and Robert Eikhe, both executed by Stalin.

Next on the list for expulsion was my wife's mother, Anna Unskova, secretary of the Voskresenskii district party committee in the Moscow oblast. Born into nobility and trained as a doctor, she joined the communist party in 1918 and ever after worked as one possessed on behalf of the party, the people, the ideals of Marxism-Leninism, and the world socialist revolution. Yet she, too, was expelled from the party.

Both Unskova and Krumin were part of that marvelous generation of Bolsheviks, Lenin's disciples, who were at the head of the Great October Revolution. I was always awed by their uncompromising loyalty to the ideas of revolutionary Marxism and their selfless commitment to their work. Both were utterly indifferent to any mercenary considerations. Both were consumed by their work with a kind of romantic exaltation, fervor, and love of life. Leaving on Sunday for a day's outing at Serebriannyi Bor,[5] Krumin would stuff his bag with Marx's *Das Kapital*, Rudolf Hilferding's *Finance Capital*,[6] Lenin's works on the role of gold and cooperatives, and a handful of pamphlets by Soviet economists.

"Garal'd Ivanovich," I once chided him, "all these books. . . . What kind of relaxation is that?"

He replied, "Poring over books—there's nothing I enjoy more. Besides, I've got a couple of ideas going. I want to make use of my free time to do an article on socialist accumulation. Expose once again, on the basis of the latest evidence, the ideological bankruptcy of those Trotskyite upstarts."[7]

When she was well past fifty, Anna Unskova managed to gain admission to the Institute of Red Professors and toiled day and night over scholarly tomes on scientific socialism. During the years of revolutionary ferment in Germany,[8] her only thought was to go there to work for the world revolution. When civil war came to Spain, she promptly added Spanish to her knowledge of French and begged to be sent to the land of Miguel de Cervantes. She revered the courage and heroism of the Spanish Communist Party. Consumed with impatience, she nagged me constantly for the works of Mao Zedong while they were still in typescript or page proofs. And now both of them, Garal'd and Anna, were crucified.

On January 20, 1938, as the wife of an "enemy of the people," Galina, too, was arrested, and her time of torment began. A cell in the Lubianka Prison. Harrowing interrogations; demands for incriminating evidence against "enemies of the people." Butyrskaia Prison. Convicts packed into airless freight cars. A concentration camp in the woods ringed by barbed wire and secured by guards and police dogs. That was how we relatives of the "enemies of the people" lived.

During this excruciating time, I was at work in the party's Central Committee. In 1933, I graduated from the Institute of Red Professors and then spent two years serving as head of the political section of a major animal husbandry sovkhoz in western Siberia. This was during the height of the socialist restructuring of the village. At a subregional party conference, I was elected to a party committee whose first secretary was Robert Eikhe. A metal worker by profession, Eikhe joined the Bolshevik party in 1905 and was tempered in tsarist and Latvian exiles, prisons, and camps. After the October Revolution he devoted himself for many years to organizing agricultural production and to the noble mission of the socialist reorganization of Siberia.

With the integration of rural political sections into the regular party, I was named deputy director of the scientific branch of the Agricultural Department of the party's Central Committee. The talented Bolshevik organizer and publicist Iakov Iakovlev headed the department. He had been a party member since 1913; his political activity began in his student days at the Saint Petersburg Polytechnic Institute and continued among workers beyond the Nevskii Gate.[9] In 1917 the tsarist police picked him up, and after the February Revolution he was active in organizing a workers' militia and soldiers' committees. As chairman of an underground revolutionary committee in Kiev and Kharkov and as one of the leaders of the rebellion against Petliura,[10] he helped bring about the victory of the socialist revolution in Ukraine.

During the grim years of the Civil War, Iakovlev headed the army's political section. All told, he contributed immeasurably to the effectiveness of Bolshevik political propaganda and the socialist reorganization of the village. He was one of the directors of the Main Political Education Committee of the RSFSR People's Commissariat of Enlightenment, then served successively as head of the Central Committee's publication section, editor of the popular newspaper *The Poor* and *Peasant Gazette,* chairman of the All-Union Council of Kolkhozes, deputy people's commissar of the Workers' and Peasants' Inspectorate of the USSR, and people's commissar of agriculture.

In 1935, while working in the Agricultural Department of the Central Committee, I worked with the Second Congress of Kolkhoz Shock Workers, held in the Kremlin, which was devoted to the exemplary rules for collective farms. Iakovlev spoke on this fundamental issue. I had to deal with him every day. A brilliant speaker, the author of many works on the problem of agriculture, Iakovlev devoted all his talent, all the skill of a Bolshevik organizer, to the great cause of collectivization.

Soon afterward, the Agricultural Department in which I worked was made part of the Central Committee's Science Department, which was headed by another old Bolshevik, a party member since 1907, Karl Bauman. This was a man of enormous erudition, a real revolutionary romantic. The spirit of revolutionary romanticism, Bolshevik innovation, and untiring enthusiasm energized all his activities in the demanding posts of secretary of the Moscow Party Committee, secretary of the Central Committee, and head of the party's top-level Science Department.

When I recall my meetings, conversations, and business dealings with people like Krumin, Iakovlev, Eikhe, Bauman, and many, many others of the Bolshevik old guard, I am struck by the thought that no revolution, no era of progress in the history of mankind, produced as many talented professional revolutionaries, public speakers, and brilliant academics, diplomats, economists, military commanders, writers, engineers, and builders as the Russian Revolution. This creative force has been the most valuable resource of the nation and party, their priceless ideological capital. It was this vital force that strengthened the energy and willpower of countless millions, raised them from the class of the oppressed and the persecuted, and set them on the high road of history.

The great tragedy of the next phase of the revolution lies in the fact that most of this glorious old guard was wiped out in Ezhov and Beria's torture chambers. The years 1937 and 1938 crept over the land. Eikhe, then a member of the Central Committee's Politburo and people's commissar for agriculture, was vilified and executed. His tragic letter to Stalin just before his death, a testament to his crystalline purity of spirit, was made public at the Twentieth Party Congress.[11] The story went that Bauman died of heart failure when agents of the NKVD came to his home to place him under arrest. Iakovlev was shot in 1939.

All of us rank-and-file members of the Science Department were removed from the Central Committee and scattered elsewhere. As a staff member, I was appointed executive secretary of the Economic Institute of the USSR Academy of Sciences, replacing the future diplomat Andrei Gromyko. All the while, the devastating whirlwind of arrests tore through the highest government and party bureaus, research centers, military units, industrial enterprises, design and construction offices, and rural administrations.

During the time I was with the Science Department, I once had a talk with Ezhov in his Central Committee office. For a long time there has been no mention of this bloodthirsty degenerate in any encyclopedia or historical reference book. So it may be useful to comment briefly on my impression of the man and the meeting.

To go by the official data, Ezhov's record is not at all bad. It contrasts favorably with Khrushchev's, which has many blank periods. Only future historians and psychologists with access to all the archives will be able to explain how a former worker with broad revolutionary experience could have sunk to the level of political and moral degradation that came to be reflected in a single word: *ezhovshchina*.

Nikolai Ezhov was born in 1895 in Saint Petersburg. From the age of fourteen, he was a worker at various local factories. In March 1917 he joined the communist party and took an active part in the October Revolution. During the incendiary years of the Civil War, he proved his mettle as a military commissar in different army units. Ezhov's major political activities began in 1922. He served successively as secretary of the party committee of Semipalatinsk province and the Kazakhstan subregion and, in 1929 and 1930, as deputy people's commissar for agriculture. Transferred to the Central Committee in 1930, he became head of its Department of Staff Assignments and its Personnel Department. At the Seventeenth Party Congress he was elected a member of both the Central Committee and the party's Control Commission.

Ezhov's incredible meteoric ascent dates from that period. He was appointed director of the CC's Industrial Department. He was elected to the Russian and Soviet parliaments—the All-Union Central Executive Committees of the RSFSR and the USSR. In 1935 he rose to the concurrent positions of secretary of the Central Committee, member of the CC Organizational Bureau, chairman of the Party Control Commission, member of the Comintern Executive Committee, and, finally, people's commissar for internal affairs. As a result, enormous power was placed in the hands of one man—he controlled the assignment of official personnel throughout the party and country, he supervised the entire system of governmental and party control, he commanded the NKVD's military units, and he took responsibility for the defense of the country's borders and the maintenance of domestic security, including the safety of the government and the whole mechanism for political information.

This state of affairs gave Ezhov an effective monopoly on reporting the political situation in the country and party according to his own views and inventions and on proposing "adequate" measures of control and repression.

I spoke earlier of the brilliant array of leaders drawn from the working class by the Russian revolutions—men like Ivan Babushkin,[12] Mikhail Kalinin,[13] and many others. Ezhov was not among them. He had no education of any kind. Unlike Lenin's other colleagues of working-class background, he never went through the school of Marxist study and development in political emigration, prison, and exile. He was a boor, and on theoretical questions he was completely illiterate. At the same time, according to those who knew him well, Ezhov was an able organizer, ruling with an iron hand. He was totally devoted to Stalin, and to carry out the leader's schemes and assignments he was ready to smash every obstacle and impose every sacrifice. Stalin fully exploited these qualities. In the period when Stalin's benevolent attitude toward his favorite was in bloom, Ezhov's authority grew and grew until it became limitless. He was even awarded a place in Stalin's *Short Course on the History of the Communist Party*[14] and was obligingly included by compliant historians in the party's "Leninist core." Verses and songs were written about him. Leading artists painted Ezhov's portraits, depicting him crushing the enemies of the people with his hedgehog mittens with steel spikes.[15]

Dizzy with fame and glorying in the trust and favors that Stalin bestowed on him, Ezhov kept widening the scope of his gory operations, and ultimately he could not stop. A stone thrown down a snowy mountainside travels faster and faster, gathering more and more snow, until it becomes a huge snowball and enormous rocks along its path are drawn into its violent descent. At this point, Stalin stopped Ezhov's churning meat grinder, sacrificing his favorite and presenting himself as the savior of the party and country from Ezhov's unbridled lawlessness.

Ezhov was declared anathema. But secretly, without publicity. "The Moor has done his deed; the Moor may leave."[16] I don't know to what degree Ezhov himself believed that those he sent to their deaths were "enemies of the people." What is incontestable is that Ezhov personally took part in the horrifying killings that took place in the clandestine backyards of the official establishment. After Stalin's death, Khrushchev told us several times that one day, while in Ezhov's Central Committee office, he noticed some spots of dried blood on the pockets and cuffs of Ezhov's tunic. He asked how they got there. Ezhov replied, almost ecstatically: "These are spots to be proud of. This is the blood of enemies of the revolution."

The question naturally arises: How could this ezhovshchina—and later its permutations, *berievshchina* and *khrushchevshchina*—have come about within the Soviet framework, taking into account the Marxist-Leninist party with millions of members and the whole system of party and government control? As I remarked earlier, historians will some day answer this question with all the necessary material in hand. Here I would like to note just one reason, among the very many, for the origin of ezhovshchina.

Lenin taught that all monopolies lead to decay. Lenin's postulate applies not only to the economy but perhaps even more directly to politics. Today, with the advantage of hindsight, it is incontestably clear that the entire system of leadership that Stalin adopted was based on his own monopoly of power. Stalin was able to create and maintain this monopoly by the use of trusted favorites, whom he kept changing. Rewarded with high rank and enjoying the leader's complete trust, the current favorite became, for a limited time, a monopolist himself. In the period in question, Ezhov was one such monopolist.

I have pointed out that as a secretary of the Central Committee, people's commissar of internal affairs, etc., etc., Ezhov wielded tremendous power.

In effect, he was under no one's control other than Stalin's, since he himself was the chairman of the Central Committee's Party Control Commission. It was his monopolistic and uncontrolled power, combined with his theoretical backwardness and uncouthness that led to his corruption and his political degradation. The nation and party paid for this with rivers of blood, the blood of their best sons and daughters. Ezhov himself paid for it with his life. But at the time I speak of, he was at the pinnacle of his power and glory.

With all his official posts, Ezhov had several offices, but most of his time was spent in his office at the Central Committee on Old Square. It was situated on the fifth floor, and we lower-level CC officials spoke of the "fifth floor" in whispers and with shudders. This was the floor where the secretaries of the Central Committee had their offices and where the Organizational Bureau and the Secretariat held their meetings. To be sure, Stalin himself was almost never there—he worked in his Kremlin office. Nonetheless, we were convinced that here, as well as in the Kremlin, the fate of the country and the whole world was decided.

At that time, the fifth floor was under Ezhov's complete control.

One morning, Karl Bauman, then head of the Central Committee's Science Department, summoned my section head, Ivan Doroshev, and me to his office. I had known Doroshev for many years. We were students together at the Institute of Red Professors; subsequently, he was made editor in chief of the CC's magazine *Bolshevik* and then rector of its Academy of Social Sciences.

"Here," Bauman said to us, "read this letter to Comrade Stalin and his instructions."

The letter said that certain former princes and White Army officers had embedded themselves in the administrations of the Astrakhan fish reservation and the Caucasus wildlife preserve and were hiding there in the guise of scientific researchers. The letter listed the names and biographical data of some of these employees. At the bottom left-hand corner of the page were these words, written in black pencil: "To Comrade Ezhov: Clean out the garbage. J. Stalin."

In addition to my work in the CC Science Department, I was then an instructor on political economy in the Agrarian Institute of Red Professors and a scientific editor of the *Great Soviet Encyclopedia*. As a scholar, I could not relish the job of carrying out a purge. Cautiously, in the form of a question, I said to Bauman that perhaps there was someone better suited than I for this mission. Bauman, a tactful and likable man, replied, "You wouldn't have to do anything yourself. You arrive in Astrakhan, you tell the whole story to the oblast party committee, and the committee takes care of everything. Also, before leaving, you will get Comrade Ezhov's personal instructions."

And there we found ourselves, on the mysterious fifth floor. I had never been there before, as we lower-level officials did not take part in the meetings of the Secretariat and the Organizational Bureau. To gain entrance to the fifth floor, a staff member of the Central Committee had to have a special pass. We were led to Ezhov's waiting room. At the precise time of our appointment we were invited into his office. An enormous room. The walls covered with light-blue patterned wallpaper. Wide windows opening on Old Square. An oversized writing desk covered in green baize. On top of the desk and a side table, a cluster of multicolored telephones and several piles of paper. At the back, the door to a lounge. Ezhov greeted us and asked Bauman and the two of us to sit down.

Prior to this, I had seen Ezhov several times at a distance, during the various meetings and sessions of the Presidium, but I had never seen him up close. And here we were, in the presence of the dreaded and all-powerful Ezhov. Before us was a small, frail man best described by the word "runt." His face was puny, with unhealthy yellowish skin. The reddish-brown hair stuck out in an untidy crew cut that was shiny with pomade. On one cheek, a scar from a bullet wound or something else. Bad, yellowing teeth. His eyes, however, I remembered for a long time—gray-green eyes fastened on me, as knowing as a cobra's. He was dressed in a khaki tunic and trousers of military cut; around his waist was an army belt disproportionately wide for his figure. His plain scrubby boots were turning ginger from lack of polish.

"So, my learned friends," he began, drilling into each of us with his piercing and clever eyes, "you've read the letter to Comrade Stalin? All right. You've also read the decision? Well, what's there for me to explain? Garbage is garbage. You have to go there with the oblast committee people and clean it out. Nothing could be simpler. Clean out and report back."

In the course of our conversation he was racked by heavy, painful coughing. There were rumors that he suffered from consumption. He would cough and spit his thick gobs of phlegm right on the luxurious red runner. "Why," it raced through my mind, "is he spitting right on the floor? How unprepossessing he is! Where does his strength lie?"

Two days later I was in Astrakhan. Hunchbacked cobbled streets. Everywhere a thick layer of white dust. The rumble of two-wheeled carts. The odor of Caucasian carp. Scraps of watermelon rind.

At the regional party committee, our impending arrival caused a terrible commotion. What? Stalin and Ezhov told them of a flagrant outrage in their own reservation, and they hadn't known anything about it? What a disgrace!

The next day I went to the reservation. The letter to Stalin named two of its staff members as "class-enemy elements." One was a former White Army officer and the other a woman who had belonged to the upper nobility. I decided to talk to them first.

A small settlement on one of the tributaries in the Volga River delta. A small, listing house. Inside, a room with a rusty iron bedstead, a felt cover, a blanket and a pillow. A wooden table with a newspaper for a tablecloth, and a sooty Red Army mess tin with the remains of some porridge. Books and manuscripts on the table, on the window sill, on small tables against the walls, on an ancient bookshelf—books, books, hundreds of books everywhere.

Seated before me was a man in some kind of light-gray shirt faded to the utmost by the sun. Worn trousers. A gray weather-beaten face with hair to match. The man was either humpbacked or the victim of some spinal injury that caused him to hunch forward, and he reminded me of some old mossy tree stump sunk in a bog, providing shelter for a school of sheatfish.

I introduced myself and asked him how he was doing. He gave me a long and steady look. His eyes were so pure, so kind, so wise, they radiated such light, that his appearance seemed transformed.

"As for my life, there's hardly any need to talk about that. Why waste time? But since we have the good fortune of a visit by a representative of the Central Committee to a backwater like our reservation, then I humbly request that you hear me out and take measures to place our fisheries on a sound basis." At first he spoke hesitantly, stumbling over his words and fixing me with a prying look: Was I to think the questions he raised were trivial? But the more he went on, the more his exposition became forceful and ardent. He seemed to straighten up, and his eyes took on a feverish glint. Not even the most fanatical sons of Muhammad offered up their prayers with such frenzied inspiration as my ichthyologist-interlocutor did while declaiming on the subject of fish.

I was struck by his erudition and his firm belief in the enormous scientific and economic importance of the unquestionable truths he was laying out. As he spoke, the evolution of the boundless world of sea life seemed to pass before my eyes.

"Take the Silurian, the third period of the Paleozoic era, 350 million years ago. A species of ancient round-mouthed fish makes its first appearance in fresh waters. In the Devonian period we see the testaceous and crossopterygian fish developing profusely in the seas. Hundreds of millions of years go by, and it is only in the Cretaceous period of the Mesozoic era, as a result of countless global evolutionary and revolutionary processes, that most of the modern species of fish emerge. What immeasurable riches nature offers us, and how foolishly we treat them, how meagerly we use them! Yet with rational exploitation of Russia's marine resources, Russia alone could supply the world with an abundance of seafood, caviar, vitamins, and organic fertilizer."

He spoke on, and it seemed to me that I was listening to a great magus or wizard. Let him wave his magic wand and billions of shoals of fish would rise from the depths of the lakes and rivers, the seas and oceans, and would be delivered by gigantic electric conveyors to spacious and well-lighted processing plants. There, snow-white assembly lines would take a thousand varieties of fish through all the culinary preparations. And then, endless columns of enameled, refrigerated trucks would speed the boiled, marinated, fried, and jellied preparations of sturgeon, whitefish, salmon, codfish, and herring, set off with tasty garnishes, seasoning, and spices, to stores, cafeterias, and homes around the country.

I don't know how long it took him to tell his story—or was it a testament?—three, six, eight hours? Listening to him, I mused: The Roman patriot Mucius Scaevola,[17] to demonstrate his disdain for the tortures awaiting him, placed his hand, for the sake of his country, on the flaming altar. My ichthyologist, to realize his dream of conquering the great fish kingdom for his country's good, would unhesitatingly sacrifice his life.

"I see," I said, "you have a lot of books. Titles in English, French, Spanish, and other languages. Do you know these languages well? Where do you get this literature?"

He replied, "I was given a classical education early on. My father was a general, killed in the First World War somewhere in Galicia.[18] My grandfathers and great-grandfathers were also in the military. And they wanted to make me into a soldier. I did see a little action in the First World War. After the revolution I volunteered for the Red Army. I was badly wounded fighting Denikin[19]—a broken back. I've been bent over ever since."

He went on. "The military life held no attraction for me. From childhood, I was fascinated by ichthyology. And so I plunged into that for good. My parents gave me a good grounding in French, German, and English. In school I studied Latin and Greek, and when I devoted myself to ichthyology, I had to read the specialized literature published in Japan, Norway, and Iceland.

"Of course, here in the reservation we don't get any literature, but I spend my vacations in libraries in Moscow and Leningrad. I find a thing or two there. And I get something from institutes abroad—I sometimes write for their journals."

The woman from the "upper nobility" also turned out to be a zealot and enthusiast—in the field of ornithology.

I sat at twilight on the sandy banks of the Volga. The rustle of reeds, the smell of slime and fish. In the distance, from time to time, the cackling of geese. A lemon-colored moon desperately raced somewhere through the smoky clouds. Involuntarily, my thoughts returned time and again to my conversation with the ichthyologist.

Yes, I said to myself, what a wealth of splendid people we have! An inexhaustible storehouse of gems, of talent—dreamers, master craftsmen, innovators. Take this reservation. A staff of just four researchers. They face difficult living conditions. Get miserable salaries. And here's this ichthyologist—all fire, action, and dreams of the people's well-being. I'm sure that never in his life has the thought occurred to him that he's doing something extraordinary. And here some loathsome informer calls him a "White Army officer" and "class enemy" and demands that he be purged.

At the party committee of the Astrakhan oblast I reported that there was no basis for purging the staff members named in the letter to Stalin.

But what about Stalin and Ezhov's instructions to "clean out the garbage"? Apparently, some drunk, dishonest chief economist who unearthed some "unsuitable elements" in the Caucasus reservation raised the fuss. One way or another, the case was closed.

My next, and I believe my last, mission for the Central Committee's Science Department was much more pleasant and productive. I was sent to look into the work of the animal-husbandry Institute of Hybridization and Acclimatization in Askania-Nova.[20] Prior to that, Academician Aleksandr Serebrovskii[21] briefed us Science Department staffers on the fundamentals of classical genetics. Academicians Mikhail and Boris Zavadovskii[22] told us about their experiments. We studied the work of Mendel,[23] Morgan,[24] Vavilov, and Kol'tsov.[25] We learned the secrets of the chromosome. In Askania-Nova I familiarized myself with experiments in crossbreeding different species of bison. At the time, there were hopes of producing a hybrid, a kind of musk ox with the body and meat of a cow and the wool of a sheep. I also learned of the work of V. K. Milovanov on the artificial insemination of sheep, and the results of many years of work by M. F. Ivanov on creating a new thin-fleeced crossbreed of a sheep and an Askanian rambouillet.

All this led me to a clearer comprehension of the pseudoscientific and fallacious fabrications of Trofim Lysenko,[26] who was just coming into vogue and who later did immeasurable harm to Soviet science and agriculture.

But soon the ominous shadow of the bloody purges fell on me for the second time. I went through an experience that forever filled me with great pride. It happened during the golden days of early autumn, 1938. I had just returned from vacation. I could close my eyes and vividly recall the ultramarine coverlet of the Black Sea, the joyous sun, and the silken rustle of the gentle shoreline waves. At night a path of silver moonlight sparkled along the smoothness of the sea. How delightful it was to cavort in these warm, enchanting waters, what an aroma of oleanders, tea roses, and carnations.

I returned to Moscow full of enthusiasm, with high hopes and big plans. We were living then in an old building on the Kotel'nicheskaia Embankment, next to where a high-rise stands today. On the first day of September I gave my first lecture of the new academic year at the institute. I was in top form. My students gave me a big bouquet of asters. With flowers in my hand and elation in my heart, I took a long walk through the sun-drenched streets of Moscow. There was a scent of yellowing leaves and freshly poured asphalt. How wonderful was God's world! "Life is good, and it's good to be alive."

At home, I went through some books and manuscripts, preparing myself with pleasure for the busy days ahead. Evening arrived, clad in lilac, and through the open windows the noises of the great city entered the room. Along the Moscow River, squat little tugs pulled their caravans of barges, their horns tooting gaily at each other.

The phone rang.

"Comrade Shepilov? This is the Moscow Criminal Investigation Department. We need to talk to you. Could you come in for a little while?"

I replied, "I'm afraid there's been some misunderstanding. What do you want to talk to me about? How can I be of any use to the Criminal Investigation Department?"

"We do not care to speak about it on the phone. We won't keep you long. May we send a car for you?"

I had no choice but to agree.

Twenty minutes later there was a ring at the front door. A young man in a dark worn suit and a crumpled cap came into the hallway. His face was severely blemished by smallpox; especially repulsive were his disfigured nostrils.

A dilapidated Black Maria[27] waited outside. We proceeded along the Kotel'nicheskaia Embankment, turned onto Red Square, then onto Revolution Square, and from there to Lubianka. The enormous building of the GPU-NKVD loomed ahead. The van stopped at one of the entrances, and the pockmarked man ushered me in. Everything became clear to me; asking questions was useless.

We were met in the waiting room by two uniformed officers of the NKVD. My escort handed them some kind of paper. We took the elevator—to what floor I didn't know. A wide corridor with innumerable closed doors. No one was there. A right turn, through one of the doors. A small office with just one window. By the window, a writing desk and two armchairs. To the right, a small table and two chairs. A tall, spare man in an immaculate gray suit stood up behind the desk. Under his jacket he wore an embroidered linen shirt. A long, well-groomed face. A thin, aquiline nose. Gray, clever eyes. Seeing his face and cold eyes, I for some reason recalled that the famous Italian criminologist Cesare Lombroso thought that a man endowed with a longish face, an aquiline nose, and steely eyes was the anthropological archetype of a murderer.[28] Actually, the man who awaited us made, in general, a favorable impression at first sight.

"Excuse us, Comrade Shepilov, for this slight ruse on our part. You, of course, can guess where you are, and that this is not the Criminal Investigation Department."

"Yes, I can," I replied, "although I don't see why the ruse was necessary."

During those years of Ezhov's terror, the public image of the NKVD had changed. Dzerzhinskii's Cheka[29] had been swathed in legendary glory and popular respect. Ezhov's NKVD filled people with horror. But at that moment I was completely calm, as though I had gone numb. The man with the steely eyes began to question me in the friendliest tones about my life, my work, and so on. I replied tersely, not seeing what this was leading to.

"Well, Dmitrii Trofimovich, we have been interested in you for a long time. We understand you perfectly. You were with the Central Committee. You were dismissed. Naturally, you couldn't help being embittered. After your dismissal from the CC all your comrades turned away from you."

"You're quite mistaken," I put in. "I don't feel bitter at all, and there would be no reason for it. My calling is scholarship. The transfer from the CC to scholarly work in the Academy of Sciences has been very much to my liking. Furthermore, I lecture at the Higher Party School and at the Soviet Trade Institute. I am published regularly and am involved in extensive editorial and propaganda projects. I am perfectly content and work with great enthusiasm and pleasure. How could there be any bitterness or even resentment?"

"Well, we won't argue about it. That is not the point," said the man with the steely eyes. "I do not have to tell you how serious the situation is around the country today. The Trotskyites, the Bukharinists,[30] the enemies of the people are active everywhere. And we must root out these enemy nests. You remember Lenin's instructions, that every communist must be a Chekist. So let us carry out Lenin's orders."

I said, "In my party, scholarly, pedagogical, and literary work, I do all I can to promote and popularize the party's policy."

"Yes, but the question now is one of your direct assistance to the NKVD in the struggle against our enemies."

"What can I say?" I responded. "I'm a party member. From my

Komsomol days on, I have answered to the party. I went to work wherever the party sent me, and I gave it my best. I repeat, I am perfectly satisfied with my current work. But if the CC finds it necessary to transfer me to some other kind of work, of course I will accept it unconditionally."

"No one is about to transfer you from your present work. We need you there, and you will stay there. What we are talking about is secret collaboration with the NKVD in your current scholarly position."

I felt a hot nauseous wad form in my throat and a cold snake crawl between my shoulder blades. Only now did I realize the purpose of my summons to the NKVD and this whole conversation.

The dead silence, I think, lasted a long time.

"So what do you say, Comrade Shepilov?" asked the man with the steely eyes.

I replied firmly, "I cannot accept your proposal."

"Why? As a matter of principle?"

"Yes, as a matter of principle."

"I see. You do not wish to carry out Lenin's instructions? You do not wish to join in the struggle against our enemies?"

"Lenin has nothing to do with it. I have been struggling and will continue to struggle against our real enemies as befits a communist, a party writer, a scholar. But your proposal is one I cannot accept."

"I would be interested to know," he said, "what these questions of principle are. You don't want to soil your delicate hands—let others do the dirty work? What, are we worse than you clean people?"

"No, I'm not afraid of any kind of hard work. And the questions of principle are these. As children, we were raised in a spirit of respect and love for the legendary Cheka of Dzerzhinskii. Later, as party propagandists, we brought up others in the same spirit. But lately the activities of the NKVD have taken on features that cannot help but arouse intense fear within the party and among the people. I cannot really say anything more, since there is a lot I probably don't know. But I do know that among many of those arrested recently, there are people who are close to me. I know their utter devotion to the party and people. And they are labeled 'enemies of the people.' I am absolutely certain that the party will sort all this out and everything will be corrected. To collaborate with you would be to take on moral responsibility for everything that is now happening. That I cannot do."

My mouth was dry; I was dying for a cigarette or a drink. But I did not ask for either.

Again, a long silence. I knew by then that I would not be leaving this building. Fragments of thoughts spun about in my mind. "Idiot, why did you come dressed for summer?" I had on white trousers and a cream-colored silk shirt. "I'll freeze in those cells. Why didn't I tell Marianna where I was going? And where was I going? To the Criminal Investigation Department. How will they ever find me?"

From somewhere far away, the following words reached me, heavy and cold as billiard balls: "Well now, you have fully exposed your true self. By the way, we thought you would. We know all about your ties to the enemies of the people and your hostile activities. And so, Shepilov," he dropped the "comrade," "I will leave you for a little while. Sit at that table and do some real thinking. Either you cooperate with us or . . . You're an educated person, a former prosecutor. You know very well what awaits you."

I moved to the small table. The man with the steely eyes and the vigorous and graceful way of moving left the office, and the pockmarked man came in. He walked up to the window, turned his back on me, drew the blinds, and stood staring vacantly through the pane. I don't know how long I sat there; I lost all sense of time. I did not reflect on the dilemma presented me. That question was settled instantly, not with my mind but my entire being, the moment the man with the steely eyes put it to me. A hodgepodge of random and fragmented thoughts, scenes, and recollections whirled about in my head.

I heard someone coming. With brisk and agitated steps a man walked in and stopped abruptly in front of me. The one who had interrogated me followed him. The pockmarked fellow by the window left at once. I was confronted by a smallish man with a pale face and disheveled black hair. He was dressed in rough cloth trousers and a khaki tunic and boots. A wide army belt girded his tunic. Perhaps he was aping his superior: that was how Ezhov liked to dress. A long army greatcoat was slung over one shoulder, one hem dangling on the floor. His face kept twitching convulsively, as though he were winking with sly and evil intent. His small, black, beady eyes flickered nervously. His shoulders twitched now and again, as though from an electric shock. Something about him was strongly reminiscent of Stalin's former assistant and the later editor of *Pravda,* Lev Mekhlis. "Well, Shepilov, what did you decide?"

I said I had already given my answer.

"I see," he yelped, "I see. As was expected." Turning to the man with the steely eyes, he said, "And what did you hope to get out of him? He's an enemy, an inveterate enemy. Do you think he'd ever collaborate with us Chekists?" Then he spewed a cascade of slimy insinuations and barnyard abuse, punctuated by disgusting and terrible threats. He twirled about the room like a top and flared the hems of his greatcoat like a peacock, screeching and spluttering. I was aware of the sour smell of dirty socks and an unwashed body and felt the flecks of his spittle on my forehead and cheeks. This painful and revolting performance lasted a long time, a very long time. I don't know how long.

I remained silent.

After one of his spells of hysterical yelping, the twitching dervish stopped abruptly before me and said, "Bear in mind, Shepilov, your fate is being decided here and now, and the fate of your family as well—don't think we're going to kid around with them. Well?"

I repeated my previous answer.

"Well, what can I say. You have pronounced sentence on yourself."

I had a mental picture of my daughter, Vitiusia, asleep in her little bed, of my mother's face, wasted by grief and wrinkled like a baked apple, with eyes as kind as a calf's. I saw again the golden banks of the Moscow River at Serebriannyi Bor, the cherry trees loaded with fruit.

The dervish went to the telephone and dialed a number. "Lefortovo? Get a cell ready—solitary confinement. Yes, strict regime. Yes. In an hour."

Whether he really gave an order or not, I don't know. At any rate he knew that as a former prosecutor, I had no illusions as to what solitary confinement at Lefortovo Prison signified.

Going toward the door, he once again stopped abruptly before me and shrilled, "Well?"

I looked him in the face, turned to the window, and did not reply. He swished the tails of his greatcoat, and I was assailed again by the nauseous odor of sweat. Silently, the pockmarked man reappeared.

I was sure that everything was lost, that the heavy headstone of my grave had thudded down on me. Suddenly I felt so tired that I was ready to collapse on the floor and sleep the sleep of the dead.

Much more time went by.

"Sign this," I suddenly heard a commanding voice say. Standing before me was the man with the steely eyes, holding out a piece of paper.

"I am not signing anything," I said.

"Don't be afraid. It's not at all what you think. Read it. This is the usual pledge not to reveal what we have been talking about. As a former prosecutor, you and your investigators have often required such signatures of your witnesses and visitors."

I read the printed text, satisfied myself that it was really so, and affixed my signature.

"You may go," said the man in icy tones.

The pockmarked agent escorted me downstairs, and the front door slammed shut behind me.

It was morning. A velvety Moscow morning. Janitors with dark-brown brooms swept the sidewalks. With a mighty squeal a streetcar made a turn around the square. A street vendor with a sleepy face clutched a tray of fried piroshki to her stomach.

I walked home by way of Old Square. With a kind of manic persistence, one and the same phrase kept hammering away in my brain:

"You have conquered, Galilean!"

"You have conquered, Galilean!"

"You have conquered, Galilean!"

And another voice clamored, "What does the Galilean have to do with it? Where did you get that? Oh, yes, those were the words of Julian the Apostate to Christ. But what does that have to do with it? You mean you are the Galilean?"[31]

I felt my entire soul lacerated. But through the pain and confusion, I really sensed my great moral victory. The victory of my honor and conscience. Now, let come what may.

I was convinced that I had only a few hours left, or at best a few days. I had to put everything in proper order.

At home I passed off a fictional version of my nightlong absence, drank a cup of strong coffee, and set about taking stock of my books. My library had several thousand volumes. In that plague-ridden period of our life, the possession of even a trivial brochure by some economist or philosopher branded as an "enemy of the people" was regarded as a criminal offense. I never led a double life. I was totally devoted to the party. I never departed from its policies, which I defended fervently against all manner of deviationists in my books, articles, and lectures. In line with the very strict instructions of the time, we had long since cleared our private libraries of such books as Bukharin and Preobrazhenskii's *The ABCs of Communism,*[32] Trotsky's *Lessons of October,* and other such literature. But there was always a chance of something banned being discovered on one's shelves.

These preparations took all day. No one came to search our home. Night fell, and during the night no one rang at the front door.

I spent the next day working as usual at the Academy of Sciences, and in the evening I paid a call on my friend Boris Ponomarev, the future secretary of the Central Committee. We were classmates at Moscow University, we worked side by side in the Komsomol, and we studied together at the Institute of Red Professors, although he preceded me there by a short period. Boris knew my parents, my brothers, every step of my life. I told him in detail of the events of that September night, having obtained his word as a communist not to spread it around.

Why my refusal did not lead to my arrest it's hard to say. Perhaps they could not find enough pretexts for starting a case against me. Or perhaps the end of ezhovshchina had already begun.

For almost twenty years, only Boris knew about this. Then, in 1957, a new storm broke over my head—the onslaught of khrushchevshchina. The way was cleared for all sorts of despotism and violence. While a patient at the Botkin Hospital, I told my family about the incident in September 1938. I wanted those closest to me to know that at the most difficult moment of our life I did not succumb to cowardice and dishonor and did not stain myself by participating in the bloody evildoing of that period. Moreover, by 1957 I reckoned that the writ of Ezhov's NKVD had run out, and I was no longer bound, not by law or ethics, by the promise extracted from me to remain silent.

At that earlier time, we placed a fanatical trust in Stalin, the decisions of the highest party institutions, and the press. We believed that the struggle for socialism was accompanied by an unprecedented exacerbation of class differences, that the Trotskyites and rightists had adopted the methods of White Guard terror, that some party members had joined forces with our class enemies, and that we had to smash the opposition of all hostile forces in open battle and ensure the full-scale triumph of socialism.

That was what we were taught. That was what we subsequently taught others. It was in that spirit that we wrote our articles and pamphlets and delivered our lectures. We did this convinced that we were right. True, we never stopped being aware of certain painful questions. Why, on the road to the victory of socialism, were there so many "enemies of the people"? Why were the ranks of the "enemies of the people" suddenly filled by the oldest Bolsheviks-Leninists? Why did these "enemies of the people" so readily confess to their crimes and so colorfully describe their most monstrous villainies? Why was there none of this under Lenin, when the country was still saddled with entire exploitative classes and when a weakling Soviet Russia stood alone against the whole imperialist world?

But these questions were stifled by the stock answers:

"Such are the laws of the class struggle."

"Such is the dialectic of the creation of the socialist society."

And just at that most agonizing stage of our lives, the political skies over Moscow revealed a new rising star—Nikita Khrushchev.

CHAPTER THREE

My First Meetings with Khrushchev

WE HEARD THAT A MINER had arrived from the Donbass to study at the Industrial Academy. He did not attend classes, but instead got involved in party work. When it came to general education and political knowledge he wasn't much, but he was a plainspoken fellow and quick-witted.

In the broad campaign of repression, the heaviest blows fell on the intelligentsia. It was as though all the party intelligentsia were under suspicion, especially those old Bolsheviks who had spent time in emigration. The wave of arrests swept through the Moscow city and oblast party committees, as well as the district committees. Consequently, when Khrushchev was elected first secretary of both committees, the reaction of the Moscow party leadership was positive. Perhaps in this difficult time for the party, this ordinary worker Khrushchev would prove to be a sturdy party leader and would end this bloated suspiciousness that paraded under the name of vigilance.

True, the election of Nikita Khrushchev to the post of Moscow secretary brought something unexpected to light: during the course of his work in Ukraine, he had at one time belonged to the Trotskyite opposition and had been an active Trotskyite. This was reported to Stalin, along with a request for his instructions: What should be done? Despite his violent opposition to the Trotskyites, Stalin displayed what was for him an unusual degree of tolerance. "Well, what can we do?" he responded. "If he was at fault, he was at fault; there's no getting away from it. But if he has realized his error and is doing good work, we can trust him and drop this question. Inform the presidium of the Moscow party conference of this fact, but there's no need to air the case before the whole conference."

That's how it was done. In the years to come, the great majority of those Moscow party leaders who were in the conference presidium were arrested, and the rest died off or disappeared from the scene for one reason or another. As for those party leaders who knew of this fact—Stalin, Molotov, Kaganovich, Malenkov, and others—they held it in the strictest secrecy, and for the next two decades it never surfaced. With this act of "magnanimity" toward Khrushchev, Stalin acquired, to his dying day, his most devoted, obedient, and zealous supporter, a man who did not flinch from any obstacles or sacrifices to please him. But I have gotten ahead of myself.

My first glimpse of Khrushchev was in the autumn of 1937. A meeting of the party leadership was being held in the great hall of the Moscow Conservatory. I don't remember what was on the agenda—I think the decisions of the June 1937 plenum of the Central Committee.[1] Khrushchev bobbed up in the presidium of the meeting, together with Kaganovich, then the people's commissar of transportation and heavy industry and a figure who lorded over the Moscow party organization. Everyone thought Khrushchev was Kaganovich's protégé.

Khrushchev was dressed in a worn dark-gray suit, his trousers tucked into his boots. A dark silk Russian shirt open at the neck showed under his jacket. A big head, a wide forehead, light hair, a broad open smile—the very picture of simplicity and goodwill. Looking at him, I and the people sitting around me experienced a blend of pleasure and a kind of benevolent compassion. "Good lad. An ordinary miner, and look at him—secretary of the Moscow committee. Means he has a good head on his shoulders. And so unassuming."

The audience gave Kaganovich and Khrushchev a warm welcome. Khrushchev mounted the rostrum to general applause. He began to speak. At the time, he was not as adept at public speaking as he became later, in his years as premier. He stumbled over his words, with long pauses and repetitions. True, when he warmed up, his speech flowed more evenly, although there were still plenty of blunders. It was hard to tell what he talked about. Everything that came to his mind, it seemed. This remained true of his speeches in the years to come. I remember he spoke of the need to prepare the city's apartments for winter. We cannot have the corridors and toilets of communal apartments lit by miserable bulbs. ("What penny-pinching!") We must provide buildings with central heating and stock up on firewood. Wholesalers and housewives must store preserves. "When you're pickling cabbage, you must add some sliced carrots and cranberries. Then, in winter, the whole thing will melt in your mouth."

Everyone laughed. And everyone liked it. True, there were a lot of words he mispronounced. But his language was colorful. His speech was peppered with jocular sallies, and somehow you did not want to notice all his mistakes. "You can see, he's a practical type, knows what life is like, plenty of experience. As for the rest, no doubt he'll learn."

But now and then, a clutch of bewildered and disturbing questions came to mind. "What's going on here? In the past, the Moscow organization was always headed by old Bolsheviks, Lenin's colleagues, talented speakers, the tribunes of the revolution. Where have they gone? Surely not all of them have fallen under suspicion. Yes, there's a lot that's unclear, painfully unclear. Still, everything that is happening must be right and proper. After all, the Trotskyites and the rightists—they're not a myth, they really do oppose the party's policies."

These were my first impressions of Khrushchev, and my first muted and confusing questions that were prompted by his appearance in the Moscow political arena. I met him personally during the war at the front. It was the year 1943. Our 4th Guards Army, whose political section I headed, emerged victorious from the battles around Stalingrad. Field Marshal Paulus and his army had been taken prisoner. We withdrew to the Voronezh sector for reinforcements.

In August 1943 the German army command launched a powerful offensive on the Voronezh and Stepnyi fronts to revenge the loss of Kursk, Orel, and Belgorod and to hang on to Kharkov. The enemy's forces in the Akhtyrka and Kolontaev sectors included the 7th and 11th Tank Divisions; the 10th Motorized Division; the most savage of the SS divisions, Great Germany and Death's Head, and many other units. The mighty new Tiger tanks and the self-propelled Ferdinand artillery, on which the German high command placed high hopes, bolstered the enemy's arsenal. On August 15 the Germans began their advance from the Akhtyrka and Kolontaev regions. The two sides were locked in fierce bloody battles in which the enemy, through a flanking maneuver, pushed back the opposing Red Army units and forced them to retreat to the east. On orders from our supreme command, the 4th Guards Army, reinforced by troops and new technology, was force-marched to the region east of Akhtyrka at the junction of the Voronezh and Stepnyi fronts and took up positions on the Voronezh front. We had to do some heavy fighting against enemy tank formations that advanced with powerful air support.

The Nazis cut a swath of atrocities. They burned villages to the ground, shot peaceful residents by the hundreds, reduced fields of grain to ashes, and exterminated cattle. Our army staff headquarters was located in a small and almost entirely burnt-out village. There was the incessant sound of artillery. The air was filled with charred smoke. It was hot, and high above, in the turquoise sky, the larks sang their hearts out as though nothing were amiss.

One morning, the commanding officer on the Voronezh front, the army general Nikolai Vatutin, and a member of the Military Council, Nikita Khrushchev, visited our headquarters. Our army commander reported on the situation, the state of the army, and the plan of operations. Our own army's representative on the Military Council was absent. I had just returned to headquarters from making the rounds of several divisions during the night. The previous evening we composed a message to the troops from the Military Council. Then, during the night, we went around the divisions and regiments to prepare the troops politically for battle.

I reported to Vatutin and Khrushchev on the political and moral state of the rank and file and the preparations we had made for the forthcoming battle. Vatutin's instructions for the battle plan were terse. Khrushchev, on the other hand, expatiated at length and in detail to me and the commanding general on the most patent truisms: that soldiers must be well fed, with no exceptions allowed; that we must see to it that each unit receives its due quota of vodka and tobacco; that there must be baths and medical stations where the troops can bathe during lulls in the fighting; that laundry must be disinfected of lice; and so on. We knew all that and always kept it in mind. But we were pleased that a member of the frontline Military Council delved so meticulously into the "trifles" of our army life.

In bloody battles in Ukraine, on the left bank of the Dnieper River, the enemy was crushed. We succeeded in crossing the Dnieper. In Operation Korsun-Shevchenko, we trapped the Germans in another "Stalingrad boiler room"; we did a superb job with Operation Umansk-Khristinov, forced our way across the Southern Bug and Dniester Rivers, and reached the borders of the USSR. Then came the brilliant Operation Jassy-Kishinev. After that, our glorious 4th Guards Army, in which I was the top member of the Military Council, fought successfully for the liberation of Romania, Yugoslavia, Hungary, and Austria. We crowned all this with the capture of Vienna.

When we crossed the Soviet border, Khrushchev regaled the army command with presents. Somewhere on the road from Jassy,[2] I received a case of Ukrainian delicacies, an embroidered Ukrainian shirt, and a tea thermos with the inscription "To the liberator of Ukraine, Col. D. T. Shepilov, from the grateful Ukrainian people." The army commander, chief of staff, and other top officers received similar presents with rather flattering inscriptions. We were all touched by these generous tokens of attention.

Five years passed. The war was over. After the capture of Vienna I was promoted to major general. My uniform was decorated with a score of ribbons that told of the difficult road traversed during the war years: two Battle Orders of the Red Banner; the Kutuzov Military Leadership Order, first class; the Orders of Bogdan Khmel'nitskii,[3] first class; of Suvorov, second class; of the Fatherland War, first class; and of the Red Star; the battle medals "For the Defense of Moscow," "For the Defense of Stalingrad," and "For the Capture of Vienna"; American and Hungarian medals; and many other military decorations.

After the war I worked in the Main Political Directorate of the Armed Forces of the USSR, then as an editor for *Pravda,* in its propaganda department, and then as head of the Bureau of Propaganda and Agitation in the party's Central Committee.[4] I recall the sultry summer of 1948, the respectful silence in the office of the head of Agitprop, the air of calm and solemnity engendered by the stately bookshelves, the massive table covered in dark-green baize, the polished chairs, and the rich silk drapes. In came Nikita Khrushchev, dressed in a white suit and an embroidered Ukrainian shirt tied at the neck by a cord with tassels. He had left the front right after the liberation of Kiev and was serving as first secretary of the Central Committee of the Ukrainian Communist Party. He was glowing with health, suntanned, and in excellent spirits.

In my work with the Soviet Union's Central Committee, I retained an interest in agricultural matters from my days as an agrarian economist, and I kept up as best I could with Khrushchev's speeches: Ukraine was still the country's most important source of grain. Now and then I, too, wrote on these questions.

Khrushchev laid out for me certain questions and issues concerning the Ukrainian newspapers he had brought with him. Then our conversation turned to agriculture.

"Yes," he said, "our Ukrainian comrades told me that before the war you used to write articles and books on agriculture. I must confess I never read anything of yours. But I'm an old fan of agriculture. Come see us, if you're interested, and we'll show you a worthwhile thing or two in the villages."

I reminded him that I had met him and General Vatutin on the Dnieper.

"Yes, Vatutin, Vatutin. . . . Lost a great man there, and in his prime.[5] But you know, I brought you a present—we've begun making tape recorders under the trademark 'Dnieper.' Marvelous gadget. You know, if you develop this, a tape recorder can take the place of a speaker and many actors. For you in Agitprop this should be important. If the Central Committee takes an interest in it, we in Ukraine can mass-produce it. You know, I have a dacha on the Dnieper. This spring I taped a nightingale singing. Simply switched on the tape recorder on the terrace. I'll give you the tape. It's terrific. Just listen, what trilling. Can't tell the tape from a live bird."

I thanked him and thought once again, "What a fine fellow. A member of the Central Committee Politburo, and so informal. He came to the reception. At the front he sent everyone a box of presents. And now, a tape recorder."

Our work together began after Stalin's death. At various times and for various reasons, certain questions cropped up about Khrushchev's past. He took great pleasure in talking about himself, his childhood, and the people he had met. His memory was phenomenal. He would remember the date and day of the week of an event or conversation that had taken place thirty, forty, or even more years earlier. He remembered the names and life stories of people he had met long ago. He was a superb storyteller, describing everything graphically, colorfully, with flavor and a dash of humor and spice. I listened to his many stories about himself and the past at meetings of the Central Committee Presidium and on trips abroad, as well as during our fairly frequent strolls at his dacha or mine.

But with all his love of delving into the past and all my curiosity about him, there were several points about his early years that he carefully avoided. In answer to a direct question, he would say something vague and quickly change the subject. His published biographies deliberately skirt some of these questions and deal with others in a very foggy manner.

Among these is the question of Khrushchev's social background. The entry in the *Great Soviet Encyclopedia* says that Khrushchev "was born into the family of a worker-miner in the village of Kalinovka in Kursk province." In Khrushchev's biography (or autobiography), *The Tale of an Honorary Miner,*[6] which was published by the Donbass publishing house Stalino in 1961, and which contained many factual misrepresentations, his father Sergei is styled as a "descendant of a Kursk peasant." Actually, there may be no inconsistency here, since each year in Russia millions of impoverished peasants moved to the cities looking desperately for work. Some day, some impartial historian will establish the truth on the basis of reliable documents.

However, as early as the 1960s, at the height of the orgy of khrushchevshchina, there were persistent rumors among the public that Khrushchev came from a kulak-exploiter family[7]—that his father owned a mill in Kursk province and had hired hands working for him. According to this version, after the October Revolution and at the beginning of the expropriation of the expropriators, Khrushchev's father, like many other kulaks, entrepreneurs, shopkeepers, moneylenders, and wholesale dealers of agricultural products, fled from his village and disappeared in the Donbass minefields. Lenin noted that these often illiterate dregs and bloodsuckers were "the cruelest, crudest, and most savage of exploiters." Of course, this popular hearsay about Khrushchev might have been based not on social-political but psychological factors: the rumors might have been inspired by Khrushchev's boisterousness, crudeness, and insultingly patronizing attitude toward groups and individuals.

Hundreds of times, in his speeches in the USSR and abroad, Khrushchev declared:

"I am a worker and miner."

"I like the smell of coal; it reminds me of my life as a miner."

"I know what a miner's pick is, and I enjoy shaking a miner's calloused hand."

And more in the same vein.

Our newspapers and magazines often depicted Khrushchev in a miner's hard hat, with a miner's light and pick in hand. In country after country, he was repeatedly voted an honorary miner. It was absolutely clear that these were deliberate attempts to disseminate a blatant lie. Not for a single day of his life did Khrushchev ever work in a mine; not with a hard hat or a pick did he ever work underground.

After moving with his parents from Kalinovka to the Donbass, Khrushchev very briefly attended school, and then he put in a stint as a metalworker who repaired equipment. That was all. All the rest about his days as a miner was invented in later years. After the Civil War he never engaged in physical labor, yet over the next thirty-five or forty years in his superprivileged position, he never tired of repeating, "I am a worker," "I am a miner," "I know what work-calloused hands are like." From these investments in an imaginary past he derived the most profitable dividends.

No wonder so many nasty jokes about Khrushchev's mining circulated about the country. Here is one of them:

QUESTION: Where is the mine where Khrushchev worked?
ANSWER: "Near an unknown village, at an undefined depth."

Khrushchev avoided talking about his education and was irritated when that side of his life came up. In his public statements he was often contradictory about this. He told me that while living in Kalinovka he attended school on a regular basis for only one winter; the next winter he rarely attended class, and then he stopped going to school altogether. When he became premier of this immense country, he dragged his teacher out into the open and outdid himself recounting how she had knocked sense into him—a tale that contained a good deal of exaggeration. But his poor teacher had nothing to do with it. Over the course of a winter or two he somehow managed to learn the alphabet, but during that period he never learned how to write. Of course, it might seem that this was not his fault: unfortunately, he simply was not cut out for study. That would be true—sort of.

For one reason or another, Khrushchev did not attend primary school. However, after the Civil War, at age twenty-seven, he was sent to a workers' school[8] attached to the Don Technical Institute. Millions of working-class people in the land of the soviets received an education in such workers' schools; they went on to become leading engineers, scholars, and statesmen. But instead of studying when he was a student, Khrushchev got involved in party work. Several years later, then secretary of his party cell, Khrushchev was listed among the school's graduates, but this did not make him educated. Even in the workers' school he did not learn how to write; only with great difficulty could he scrawl individual words on paper.

In 1929 he was again sent off to study—this time to the Industrial Academy in Moscow, which provided Stakhanovite[9] workers, self-taught industrial managers, and captains of industry with a general education and technical knowledge. But here it was the same story: Khrushchev became secretary of a party cell, and a few months later he left for party work in the Bauman district party committee in Moscow, abandoning his education altogether.

Thus, the Soviet system could hardly be blamed for denying an education to a gifted and active worker. On the contrary, it sent him to a workers' school and the Industrial Academy, but he did not take advantage of these opportunities. Why not? What happened? The answer, I believe, lies in several of Khrushchev's traits.

Khrushchev was a driven man. It was hard for him to sit and work at something for any length of time. He was always itching to rush off somewhere by plane or ship, to speechify, to be at a noisy banquet, to listen to honeyed toasts, to tell anecdotes, to sparkle, to lecture, to move about, and to bubble over. He could no more do without that than a vainglorious actor can do without applause, or a drug addict without drugs. People marveled: How did Khrushchev find the time to race about all those countries, give sumptuous dinners and suppers almost daily, be at all the exhibitions, attend all the performances, go on seaside vacations four or five times a year—again with dinners, cruises, distractions—and go on talking, talking, talking?

"When does he find time to work?" The puzzled question was one I heard many times.

But the point is that he never worked in the accepted sense of the word. He never read any books or magazines and never felt any need to; aided by the cribbing of others, he often passed off a sally about some book he had allegedly perused. His aides passed the gist of a few articles in the papers on to him. No one ever saw him bent over an analysis of figures or facts or preparing a report or address. Staff experts did all of this for him.

He merely "floated ideas." He did it mostly by feel, without acquainting himself with the facts, instead improvising as it suited the circumstances. This was often the tactic of all types of careerists and scoundrels, and the country and the party paid for it with tens of billions of rubles, with their prestige and moral values. All these traits fully bloomed in Khrushchev after he reached the pinnacle of power, but they were intrinsic to his nature, they were in his bones.

In short, diligence and Khrushchev were incompatible. Education of any kind, whether in a village school, a workers' school, or an academy, demands diligence above all—detailed, daily, painstaking work over many months and years. This was not for Khrushchev—anything but. That is why, on entering a technical institute or an academy, he promptly revealed himself as an uncommonly apt, albeit rambunctious, grassroots organizer. And a worker to boot—a miner, a man of strong will eager for furious activity, with no taste for the painful grind of book learning to come to the wisdom of Pythagoras, the secrets of the Marxist law of surplus value ("Away with the hydra of world imperialism!"—that will do), or the psychological agonies of Raskolnikov ("So he bumped off some old biddy—big deal"). Instead, Khrushchev became secretary of some party cell. Orders, minutes, meetings, speeches. As for studying, that would have been incomparably more laborious.

So while remaining semiliterate, Khrushchev forced his way to the highest levels of the leadership. Somehow or other, he learned to read. True, during all the years up to his fall, he read haltingly, mangling many words, placing the accent on the wrong syllables—but he read. As noted above, he never learned to write. He signed his own name with difficulty, usually scrawling just the first two letters: "*Khr.*"[10] There his powers of penmanship stopped. His written decisions were communicated verbally to his assistants, who wrote them down in the relevant documents.

In my two years of working with Khrushchev in the Central Committee, I saw only one document with comments in Khrushchev's handwriting. This was shortly after I was elected to the post of CC secretary. We received a telegram from one of our ambassadors. Khrushchev ordered it shown to Suslov and me. He wrote his instructions on it in his own hand—that we familiarize ourselves with its contents. The word "familiarize" was misspelled. All the words were written in a very large, uneven script, as though by someone unused to using a pen or pencil.

Future historians looking up original sources for that period will be surprised not to find a single document in the archives of the party CC or the Council of Ministers written in Khrushchev's hand. The explanation is very simple. That is why when reports from abroad spoke of Khrushchev visiting some institution and adding his comments to the guest book, the reports were actually inaccurate. Khrushchev himself could not write down his comments. This was done for him by one of his aides or one of the members of the delegation he headed. Khrushchev himself affixed his "Khr" or, at most, his "Khrushch." He did the same when someone nagged him for an autograph.

Of course, the very fact that the head of a great socialist state should turn out to be semiliterate was a terrible tragedy. The founders of scientific communism were among the greatest thinkers in world history—Marx, Engels, Lenin. In their erudition they were far ahead of their contemporaries. With all his dictatorial traits, Stalin had an expert knowledge of Marxist theory and questions of history, political economy, philosophy, and literature. Lenin's colleagues—Sverdlov,[11] Dzerzhinskii, Lunacharskii,[12] Chicherin,[13] Semashko,[14] Litvinov,[15] Frunze,[16] Krzhizhanovskii,[17] Krupskaia,[18] Kuibyshev,[19] and many, many others—were highly educated Marxists, publicists, and writers. Out of the depths, the great Russian Revolution produced a brilliant array of worker-revolutionaries.

Take the carpenter Stepan Khalturin, executed by the tsarist autocracy.[20] Take the weaver Petr Alekseev.[21] At the trial of "The Fifty" he concluded his fiery speech with the words: "Up will rise the muscular arms of millions of workers, and the yoke of despotism that soldiers' bayonets protected will be shattered to smithereens." Lenin called these words a great prophecy. Take the metalworker Viktor Obnorskii, who went abroad to study the western European labor movement and founded the Northern Council of Russian Workers. Take the weaver Petr Moiseenko, one of the main organizers of the famous Morozovskii strike.[22] Take the outstanding proletarian leader, the metalworker Ivan Babushkin, a student and Lenin's colleague, an agent and correspondent of the newspaper *Iskra* (Spark),[23] and the veteran of many prisons and exiles. Lenin called him a "national hero" and "the party's pride." Take the lathe worker Mikhail Kalinin, who became president of the great Soviet state. And hundreds and thousands of other celebrated leaders of the working class. All of them were well-educated Marxists, cultivated people, far more intelligent than many members of the old intelligentsia, talented publicists, and passionate voices of the revolution.

Now, twenty years after the greatest of revolutions, which raised millions of people to the heights of cultural development, we were faced with a paradox. At the head of the Moscow party organization—the group that created Marxist science, the party of innovators, the champion of the most progressive culture—stood a man utterly devoid of any intellectual endowment. What happened? How can this be explained?

These questions, which much later became so critical, only flared up briefly and then fizzled out. Khrushchev's working-class origins, his "detachment" (or so it seemed) from any oppositionist trend, were taken as guarantees that he, for one, would never prove to be an "enemy of the people." Combined with his practical outlook and common touch, all this appeared to outweigh certain minuses in his record. Who would have thought then that Khrushchev would become a one-man leader of the party, the head of state, and would give full rein to traits that would have such harmful consequences for the party, the country, the socialist camp, and the world communist movement?

With one subterfuge after another, Khrushchev tried to prop up the myth of his education. In his endless speeches, he plucked incidents of his own invention out of his years in the village classroom, the workers' school, and the Industrial Academy and referred to books he had never read and never even seen. Only once did he lift the lid on all this mystification. This happened in June 1957, when the question of transferring Khrushchev from the leadership of the party and government to a modest role more in keeping with his abilities arose for the first time in all its urgency.

In fervent speeches before the CC Presidium, most of its members called attention to Khrushchev's lack of restraint and his boorishness, to his habit of making, all on his own, half-baked decisions for which the party and the country had to pay dearly, and so on. At the start, Khrushchev could not know how things would turn out. Rising to reply to his critics, he declared with a guilty mien: "Comrades, please bear in mind that I never got an education anywhere."

But this was his only—and fleeting—moment of truth. In subsequent months he resumed his accustomed role and quite unabashedly issued categorical directives on questions of primary and secondary schooling, higher education, science, literature, and art.

One more thing. With all his garrulity, Khrushchev never spoke of where, when, and under what circumstances he joined the communist party or what he did during the initial period of Soviet power. On that score, his biographies, written at his own behest, pile up so many cock-and-bull stories that one cannot read them without smiling.

In the aforementioned book, *The Tale of an Honorary Miner,* Khrushchev and his obliging biographers assert that when the fourteen-year-old Nikita arrived in the Donbass, he started by herding cows and sheep for a landowner named Kirsh but soon apprenticed himself to a metalworker and, at a secret meeting of young workers, arranged to confront the plant manager, a man named Vagner, with an ultimatum for a wage increase. Vagner allegedly capitulated. Then Nikita and his friends, playing the accordion and getting the village constable drunk with vodka, planted a red flag on the chimney of a mill, just like Manolis Glezos[24] and the Young Guards of Fadeev.[25] The constable sobered up and pleaded with the townspeople to tear down the "treasonous flag" for a five-ruble reward. When no one accepted his offer, he called in a squadron of Cossacks from Iuzovka, and they began to shoot the flag with their rifles. Sensing the grave danger to the throne that the young Nikita represented, the local bailiff, one Krasnozhenov, demanded that the youth leave not only the plant but the entire area of his jurisdiction.

This account can be found not in the tales of Baron Münchhausen,[26] nor the libretto of an operetta, but on pages 13 to 21 of the biography.

Now we have the shepherd Nikita "under surveillance," standing before the cage of a mineshaft, delivering fiery speeches: "The capitalists—German, Austro-Hungarian, English, French, Russian, and so on—did not share the wealth they stole from the people, and unleashed a war among themselves." The biographer adds that to this day many remember Nikita's passionate political speeches before the mine cage (page 22).

Incidentally, recalling that the Leninist *Iskra* and *Pravda* played a major role in the history of the party and the Russian revolutionary movement, the biographer had to drag Khrushchev into that as well. So Nikita—we are now several years back—was an "able organizer" of group readings of *Pravda* (page 23). Soon he becomes a strike organizer at Rutchenkovka. Eventually the police try to arrest him. But the workers step forward in his defense and drive the gendarmes out of the workshops (page 25). Readers of Gogol's *The Inspector General* will remember how Khlestakov, completely drunk and basking in the admiration of all who were present, began his fib by claiming that he was not just a simple clerk but was on friendly terms with the department head. Falling into a frenzy of lying, he then claimed that he had once been a chief commander; another time he said he had been promoted to department director and had so many people working under him that the messengers alone numbered thirty-five thousand men who careened about the streets. He concluded his Himalayan lies by warning that the very next day he would be promoted to field marshal. For Khrushchev's sycophantic biographers, this serves as a model. They begin by portraying him as an ordinary political worker in a nameless division and conclude by promoting him, as it were, to field marshal—that is, they describe him as one of the organizers of the Red Army and an architect of its historic victories.

Everyone who has been involved in politics knows that from the 1905 revolution on, and especially after the Lena massacre,[27] the revolutionary movement grew and spread in the Donbass, as in many other proletarian centers of Russia, and that its soul and driving force was the Bolshevik party. The Bolshevik organizations of Lugansk, Iuzovka, Mariupol, and other cities in the Donbass rallied the working class, marshaled its assault on the autocracy, and subsequently led it in the great battles of October. At the head of these party organizations were such well-known proletarian leaders as Sergo Ordzhonikidze,[28] Fedor (Artem) Sergeev,[29] Kliment Voroshilov, Grigorii Petrovskii,[30] and others.

But wait! From Khrushchev's biography we learn that up to now our watchful historians have failed to catch sight of the main star in the firmament of the great days of October—Nikita Khrushchev. It turns out that he played the accordion, raised the flag on a mill, and toppled the autocracy in Rutchenkovka, arresting officials and disbanding the police (page 30). It turns out that "the problem was that Rutchenkovka did not have its own party organization, while the Iuzovka soviet had a majority of Mensheviks and SRs" (page 34). So Nikita Khrushchev himself took over. On the same page 34 he already figures as an "experienced leader." Never mind that he was not a party member and barely literate. "At meetings and workers' assemblies, Nikita Sergeevich exposed the opportunistic policy of the Mensheviks and SRs, exposed their deceptive policy of collaboration with the Kerensky[31] government, and called on the workers to rally behind the Bolsheviks" (page 36).

The book goes on to recount how, after the February Revolution, there was a mass demonstration with flags and how Nikita Sergeevich raised his flag aloft and proclaimed: "Down with the rotten government of Kerensky! Long live the Bolsheviks!" (page 36). After the October Revolution he is in Iuzovka, where, we are told, he demands that the Mensheviks and SRs be expelled from the local soviet, though he himself is still not a party member. Furthermore, it is revealed that he was the "organizer and soul" of the Red Guards of Rutchenkovka (page 41). There follows a mind-boggling abracadabra of fabrications.

Khrushchev disappears for a long time. (According to him, he was somewhere in Kursk province.) When and where he joined the communist party is carefully passed over in silence—for what reason, it is hard to say. The *Great Soviet Encyclopedia* says Khrushchev was a party member in 1918, without giving the exact date or place where he joined. The biographical narrative picks up his trail by saying that Khrushchev, "recruited by the party, proceeds to the front under the command of the political department (?!) of one of the rifle divisions" (pages 45–46). Then it speaks vaguely of a "young twenty-five-year-old commissar" without revealing what he was commissar of or how, as befits a commissar, he traversed the thousand-kilometer course to the shores of the Black Sea. Only forty-odd years later, Marshal Semen Budennyi would miraculously recall that in 1919, in the 19th Rifle Division, 74th Regiment, the commissar of the 2nd Battalion was Nikita Khrushchev. Let this assertion rest on the marshal's conscience.

But even if it were so—and it is contradicted by many other facts and remains at the very least an exaggeration—this alone should have stayed the brisk pens of Khrushchev's biographers when they elevated him to the ranks of the creators of the Red Army and its great commanders. On this score the biography says nothing less than the following: "It was Khrushchev who was among those who led the Red Army in foiling the sinister plot of the American, British, and French imperialists, who with the aid of the Entente fleet, tried to rescue Denikin's army from total rout." Further down: "On the shores of the Black Sea, the embattled road of the Civil War came to an end for Commissar N. S. Khrushchev, one of the dynamic creators of the Red Army and one of the organizers of the victory of the young Soviet republic over foreign intervention and domestic counterrevolution" (page 51). That, it turns out, is the kind of historic role

Nikita Khrushchev played during the Civil War while modestly staying out of the spotlight in the guise of a battalion commissar.

I have no intention of taking on the task of providing Khrushchev's true biography. Future historians will do that when the necessary data for such work become available. I merely take note of certain facts, observations, and impressions imprinted in my memory as a result of personal dealings with Khrushchev and what I heard from third parties.

For nine years Khrushchev headed the Moscow party organization and for twelve years the huge party organization of Ukraine. At various times, many comrades who worked with Khrushchev in Moscow and Ukraine told me about his way of clambering up the ladder of power. A good deal later, one of the most venerable figures of the communist party, a member since 1897, a former chairman of the Bolshevik faction in the government's Fourth Duma, chairman of the Central Executive Committee of the USSR, and deputy chairman of the Supreme Soviet of the USSR, Grigorii Petrovskii, told me through a third party: "You don't know what Khrushchev is all about. But I know. I came to grief on that. In January 1938, Khrushchev came to us in Ukraine as first secretary of the CC. Debunked Lenin. Confirmed the cult of Stalin. I was declared an enemy of the people. So it began."

During the devastating purges of 1937–38, and later in Moscow and Ukraine, no individual cases were decided without Khrushchev's personal knowledge and approval. In this way, thousands upon thousands of completely innocent people were plunged into the abyss of unimaginable suffering and went to their martyrs' deaths falsely stigmatized as "enemies of the people." Perhaps the most glaring and revolting aspect of Khrushchev's activity was that many of the persons whom he sent to the gallows, he later, with a hypocrisy unsurpassed in history, mourned the demise of from the highest party and government rostrums. In these lamentations there was the added twist that the men held responsible for the deaths of our glorious communists were, of course, Stalin and his colleagues, but never Khrushchev himself.

Intrigues, denunciations, flattery, calumny—no means were too base for Khrushchev to employ to solidify his position step by step and resolutely move upward. The decisive factor here was his skill in retaining Stalin's continued trust and favor. Over the many years of Stalinist leadership, an essential component of any speech, article, or book was a tribute to Stalin. Everyone had to submit to this unwritten but iron law. We all did so. But Khrushchev seemed to raise the art of unctuous fustian to hitherto unknown heights. His every speech, his every address, was a cascade of Staliniana. Of the many hundreds of possible examples I will cite just one.

It is 1939. The party is holding its Eighteenth Congress. There on the rostrum is the first secretary of the Central Committee of the Ukrainian Communist Party, Nikita Khrushchev. In his brief speech he invokes Stalin's name twenty-six times—with Stalin seated right there at the Presidium table. He is clearly running out of superlatives. With fawning glances at the table, he brims over with the following epithets:

"Our genius of a leader."

"Our guide."

"Our great Stalin."

"The Stalinist Central Committee."

"Our beloved leader, the great Stalin."

"The party of Lenin-Stalin."

"The Stalinist five-year plans."

"Like a steel wall, the party of Lenin-Stalin surrounds the Stalinist Central Committee and its beloved leader, the great Stalin."

"At the first call of Comrade Stalin."

"The historical directives of our great Stalin."

"The teaching of Comrade Stalin."

"The profound new concepts introduced by Comrade Stalin in his report."

"With all their heart, tenderly, lovingly, and solemnly, the Ukrainian people proclaim: '*Khai zhivi ridnyi Stalin!*' [Long live our own Stalin!]."

"The unprecedented solidarity . . . around our guide and teacher, the friend of the Ukrainian people, Comrade Stalin."

"Long live the greatest genius of humankind, the teacher and guide who is leading us triumphantly to communism, our own Stalin!"

And so on, throughout the speech (see the stenographic record of the Eighteenth Congress).

But these many years of toadying, maneuvering, and fawning; the eternal fear of perishing because of a slipup; the years of intrigue, plotting, and eliminating all rivals—all that is now gone. Stalin is no more. Now, the top of the mountain is within reach. All that remains is to surmount the last obstacles and remove or destroy the last competitors.

Forward, Nikita Khrushchev!

Forward, with no fear or doubt!

CHAPTER FOUR

Zhdanov Summons Me

THE ROOTS OF WHAT HAPPENED with the "Stalinist inheritance"[1] go back to 1946–47. At that time, after the end of the Second World War, I was caught up in a whirlpool of events whose driving force was Beria and which were linked with the ever increasing power exercised within the Central Committee by Andrei Zhdanov and Nikolai Voznesenskii.

I met Zhdanov soon after returning from the front to Moscow and worked closely with him right up to his death. After the war, when Zhdanov was Central Committee secretary and was put in charge of the party's entire ideological operation, the leading role there was played by the "Aleksandrov boys," so Zhdanov began to look for new people. Georgii Aleksandrov, for many years the head of the Bureau of Propaganda and Agitation, was intelligent and well read, although I don't think he ever studied the original sources or truly mastered the theory of Marxism-Leninism. An experienced teacher and propagandist, Aleksandrov was a typical example of a "classroom communist"—that is, a lecturer on communism. He had never done any practical work in the city or village. He had not fought at the front. He graduated from secondary school and then from a philosophy institute, began teaching philosophy, and soon was made head of the Bureau of Propaganda and Agitation and a member of the Academy of Sciences. Those were his credentials. Class struggle, socialist construction, difficulties and obstacles, the war, the imperialist world—all these were abstract notions for him, and revolutionary Marxism was a compilation of axioms and quotations acquired from books.

Taking over at Agitprop after the eviscerating purges of 1937–38, Aleksandrov proceeded to seed the CC organization and all the sectors of the ideological front with his own "boys." All of them came to the job from their classroom desks, none had any practical experience—thus, it was reasoned, they did not have any dealings with "enemies of the people." They had never been abroad, either—thus, they were not spies recruited by foreign intelligence. Lacking all principles and beliefs, they readily exalted whomever they were told to exalt on one day and pronounced anathema against anyone they were told to imprecate the next.

Selection and placement of personnel according to these considerations meshed with Stalin's suspicion of the old Leninist ideological staff and his policy of replacing them with compliant people who were ready to concoct and propagate whatever version of party history, the Civil War, and socialist construction was required of them. Typical of this legion of minions who were promoted to positions of leadership in the nation's intellectual life were Aleksandrov's deputies: Petr Fedoseev; Vladimir Kruzhkov, then the executive editor of the newspaper *Izvestiia* and subsequently of *Pravda;* Leonid Il'ichev, Aleksandrov's deputy at the newspaper *Culture and Life;* Pavel Satiukov; and many others.

All of them, taking advantage of their positions in the CC organization and elsewhere, frantically plundered the party and the government of all material and other benefits they could lay their hands on. At a time when the country was still far from recovered from its postwar difficulties and poverty, they lived in luxurious apartments and dachas. They secured fantastic incomes that accrued from concurrent posts. They wasted no time acquiring the stocks, shares, and vouchers needed to guarantee them affluent lives for years to come, whatever the circumstances. All of them, at one time or another, either managed to become academicians (even Il'ichev, who never in his life wrote a brochure or newspaper article on his own—subordinates did that for him) or were awarded the title of doctor, professor, and so forth.

Take Fedoseev, for example. At thirty-odd years of age he was still pondering whether he and the communist party were traveling along the same road. When he did join the party, he was immediately made deputy director of Agitprop in the Central Committee, although he lacked experience even at the level of the party cell. He saw workers and Red Army soldiers only in parades on Red Square and peasants only in the Voronezh Chorus.[2] Given this ideological deficiency, Fedoseev, like other classroom communists, was mainly interested in money grubbing. He acquired apartments; by hook or by crook he became a corresponding member of the Academy of Sciences, then a full academician, and finally the academy's vice president. The difficult years of socialist construction, and the even more difficult years of the Second World War, accentuated the cleavage between, on one hand, the revolutionary part of the party and the nonparty intelligentsia, which included most young people, and, on the other, its mercenary, careerist elements, which included the Aleksandrov boys.

I belong to the generation of young revolutionaries who emerged from the bowels of the working class and were known in our literature as the "Komsomol of 1920." We lived, worked, and studied in the heroic atmosphere of the Civil War. From early childhood, we had to go to work to earn our daily bread. At the age of twelve I went to work in a cigarette factory. We'd go to school in the evening. But there were some among us, children of wealthy parents—former manufacturers, high tsarist officials, priests—who had broken with their families and went to the factory in order to be "brought to a boil in a worker's pot," as the saying went, and to earn their credentials as warriors of the revolution, as communists. In fact, many of them did become Bolsheviks of that type.

We joined the Komsomol at age fourteen or fifteen. While studying at Moscow State University, we earned our living by hard labor, by unloading firewood at railroad stations, by sorting out stinking, greasy, woolen animal skins at tanneries, and so on. But our lives overflowed with ideas. We believed fanatically in the imminent victory of the world revolution. We avidly studied the works of Marx, Engels, Lenin, Hegel, Plekhanov,[3] Lassalle,[4] Kautsky,[5] Hilferding, and Fourier.[6] We haunted the lectures of Aleksandr Bogdanov[7] on political economy, Nikolai Bukharin on historical materialism, Mikhail Pokrovskii[8] on Russian history, Mikhail Reisner[9] on government law. We listened to the heated debates between Anatolii Lunacharskii and the Living Church archpriest Vvedenskii.[10] We made our way into the Polytechnic Museum, the Plekhanov Institute, and the Hall of Columns for the poetry readings of Vladimir Mayakovsky, Sergei Esenin, and Vikentii Veresaev. Somehow or other we slipped into the topmost balcony of the Bolshoi and Zimin Theater to listen to Leonid Sobinov and Antonina Nezhdanova in *Lohengrin* [Richard Wagner] and Grigorii Pirogov in *Faust* [Charles Gounod], and into the Moscow Art Theater and its studios for performances by Vasilii Kachalov, Ivan Moskvin, Mikhail Chekhov, Konstantin Stanislavskii, and Nikolai Khmelev.

Sometimes we argued heatedly until dawn, sustained by carrot tea or crackers. We argued about the meaning of life, about the revolution in Germany, about the *smenovekhovtsy*,[11] about new works by Aleksei Tolstoy, about Freud, and of course, about love. While coping with severe privation, chronic malnutrition, hard physical labor, and intensive study, we were afire with revolutionary romanticism. We did not wear stylish clothes or even neckties, spurning them as contemptibly bourgeois. We did not even dance the popular Western dances, but we had a wonderful time. Relationships between girls and boys were mainly strict and pure, although sometimes they were marked by a superficial affected comradeship, and even a certain abrasiveness—to differentiate ourselves, to be sure, from the despised "aristocracy."

We fell in love and we sang. On vacation we covered hundreds of kilometers on foot in unknown places in the Crimea, the Caucasus, and Central Asia. We were immensely happy. After completing our higher education, we volunteered, without being pressured in any way, for practical work in the distant beyond: there it would be harder, more interesting; there we'd be needed most.

Urged on by these sentiments and armed with a diploma from Moscow University, I left for work in Iakutiia.[12] Just think! More than thirty days to get there, and part of the way on dog- and reindeer-drawn sledges. (Air travel had not yet arrived.) And imagine! This was the "snow-white crypt," where the Decembrists,[13] the members of People's Will,[14] and the Bolsheviks were exiled—how interesting! Forget the Volokolamsk region of Moscow province and Chuvashia,[15] the choice that the party CC offered me. Only Iakutiia! I left for the country's most remote republic to spend more than three years there as a prosecutor with the central court, after which, again at my own request, I transferred to the Western oblast as a prosecutor.

With the Institute of Red Professors behind us, and in the midst of the great socialist restructuring of the village, we again left Moscow with an intercession from the Central Committee. Married and a father, I left for deepest Siberia to join a rural political department. It was there that the main front of the class struggle for socialism was now located. So it was there that I had to be.

Then—war. The terrible, fateful question of life or death loomed over our beloved fatherland. We, the Komsomol of 1920, were now researchers and professors with academic degrees, experienced teachers, and authors of numerous experiments. But for us there was no question of what to do. From the first days of the war we tore up our draft-exemption certificates, abandoned our comfortable Moscow apartments and university positions, left our families, and went off to the front to defend the country. In my 21st Division of the People's Home Guard from Moscow's Kiev district alone, some 12,500 Muscovite volunteers marched down the old Smolensk road[16] one morning in July 1941 to meet the enemy head on. The whole country sent millions of its sons to the front.

> To the sound of the war's alarm,
> In the dusk of a July night
> On the old Smolensk road
> The Muscovite regiments march.
> Under their heavy knapsacks
> Their broad backs will not bend.
> There goes a professor from Volkhonka Street[17]
> And there a metalworker with a rifle.

That was the military march of the 21st, later the 173rd, and then the 77th Guards Division.

We felt the full force of the bloody battle for Moscow. Then we endured the full burden and glory of the Battle of Stalingrad, from the advance of the Nazi armored divisions to the shores of the Volga, to the capture of Field Marshal Paulus. In battles of liberation, we swept across Ukraine and engaged in heavy fighting for the deliverance of Romania, Yugoslavia, Hungary, and Austria.

West of Vienna, joining up with the Americans, we celebrated victory. We fought our way for many thousands of kilometers. From Moscow to Vienna, we laid millions of our brothers-in-arms in the cold earth. We left Moscow in July 1941, and we returned to our homes only in the spring of 1946—almost five years later. We who made it through the war returned with a score of military decorations and medals on our chests, but with graying heads: time and again we had looked death in the face.

I must add that quite a different course was taken by that fairly large stratum of the petite bourgeoisie within the intelligentsia to which I referred earlier. It goes without saying that all these Il'ichevs, Fedoseevs, Satiukovs, and their ilk did not join the party's political sections when the fate of socialism in the villages hung in the balance, and not one of them left for the front when the life and death of the land of the Soviets was at stake. Throughout the war and following it, Satiukov, Kruzhkov, and Il'ichev busied themselves buying up paintings and other valuables. They and others like them turned their apartments into miniature Louvres and became millionaires. Academician Pavel Iudin, formerly our ambassador to China, once told me that Il'ichev, showing him his paintings and other treasures, had said, "Keep in mind, Pavel Fedorovich, these paintings—whatever the circumstances—represent capital. Money may lose its value. Anyhow, who knows what could happen? But paintings do not depreciate." That was why this whole cabal turned to collecting paintings and other valuables, not out of any love of art, which they did not understand.

During the war they expanded and consolidated their control of all the sectors of the ideological front. They met those of us who returned from the front with ill-disguised hostility. Not because we were a reproach to their consciences—no, there were no excess pangs of conscience for them! We just made them look bad.

For years after the war, I received many letters and verbal complaints from former political department staffers and war veterans who could not find work consistent with their qualifications, or even reenter the fields of science, literature, art, and so on, that they had left when volunteering for the front. In truth, a monopoly on top posts and disdain and hostility toward returning front-liners and wounded veterans were characteristic of other parts of state and party organizations.

However, the nature of our people's government and the foundations of our communist party are such that, sooner or later, political looters, careerists, and money-grubbers of whatever variety are forced to reveal their true colors, and their machinations and slanderous intrigues come to light. That is logical: people who have not undergone class, political, and front-line struggle cannot endure the trials of real life, and unmask themselves.

That is what happened here. Philosophical debates in June 1947 showed that Aleksandrov's *History of Western European Philosophy* was written in the spirit of "professorial objectivism" and amounted to an eclectic hodgepodge that bore clear traces of various bourgeois and petit bourgeois influences; its ideological basis was far from meeting the standards of Bolshevik party ethos. The same spirit characterized the articles and pamphlets of many other Aleksandrov boys. Soon an event occurred that debunked the leaders of the "Aleksandrov school" on moral and political grounds.

A letter to the Central Committee from an outraged mother prompted an investigation that established that a certain figure in our literary and theatrical circles had turned his luxurious apartment into a glitterati house of prostitution.[18] To provide for his clients, he mustered a bevy of comely movie actresses, ballerinas, female college students, and even schoolgirls. Here Aleksandrov, his deputies Aleksandr Egolin and Vladimir Kruzhkov, and certain others were wont to disport themselves. Kruzhkov made use of this fancy den for the additional purpose of buying paintings. The Central Committee, in a confidential circular, characterized all this for what it was, and took some action in regard to the guilty parties. However, they all retained membership in the party and their positions in the Academy of Sciences.

In the forty-odd years of political life that have passed before my eyes, many of the country's leaders were accused of various kinds of ideological deviations, opposition activities, and even state crimes. Only future historians will be able to tell the world which of these accusations were valid. But the kind of moral disrepute that Aleksandrov and his boys brought on themselves was unprecedented in the party's entire history. What made it particularly offensive was that the people involved were supposed to be the party's intellectual mentors.

At about the same time, Fedoseev, with plenty of help from Il'ichev, was busy writing slanderous and vile denunciations of the academician and CC Politburo member Nikolai Voznesenskii and an entire group of Soviet economists. The pair did not do their work out of some misguided overzealousness—they knew that they were peddling barefaced calumnies. They knew that given Stalin's pathological suspiciousness, their denunciations could well cost the innocent scholars their lives. But this was required of them, since it was required for the realization of Beria's schemes. They were promised appropriate financial rewards. They were all eager to play their parts.

In subsequent years, Aleksandrov sank ever deeper into alcoholism;

he died of cirrhosis of the liver. Many of the Aleksandrov boys, on the other hand, proved to have a tenacity not uncommon among people of that kind. Adopting a new guise when it was to their advantage, they became Khrushchev's fervent supporters. This disreputable cabal evolved into a kind of brain trust for Khrushchev and began to take charge of all ideological activity, with devastating effect on the country's intellectual life.

But this came later. In 1947, after the Aleksandrov affair, the burning question was how to replenish the ranks of ideological workers within the party's Central Committee and its doctrinal departments. Andrei Zhdanov distinguished himself trying to solve this problem. At this point, in the mysterious ways of the Almighty, the gaze of the party leadership fell, inter alia, on me.

This is how it happened.

After the end of the war, my 4th Guards Army was billeted in Austria. At first the army headquarters was located in an aristocratic neighborhood of Vienna. Then it was moved to Saint Pölten in the province of Lower Austria, and then to the town of Eisenstadt in Burgenland province. Far from decreasing at the end of the war, the scope of my work as head of the army's Military Council grew. The troops were deployed in a number of Austrian provinces and Vienna. We had to work hard to help them adjust to their new roles and duties in a peacetime army of occupation.

Some of the men had to be demobilized and sent home with all due honors. We had to billet, equip, and make other arrangements for new reinforcements. We were feverishly active. Political indoctrination among the troops and civilians was undergoing a change in form and content. In addition to these routine army functions, we had to take on entirely new responsibilities—political, economic, diplomatic, and cultural. The sphere of my duties and concerns seemed endless: it started with my role in the formation of the governing bodies of the republic that were headed by the leader of the right socialists, President Karl Renner, and the chairman of the Austrian People's Party, Chancellor Leopold Figl, and encompassed problems of education, health care, and food supplies.

To begin with, we had to take care of everything, even provide food for the hungry animals in the Vienna zoo. This work involved constant contact with Marshal Fedor Tolbukhin; Aleksei Zheltov, a member of the Military Council of the 3rd Ukrainian Front; the representatives of the American and British commands; the central and local officials of the republic; the

Soviet military commandants; and the leaders of the Austrian communist and populist parties.

While traveling about the country, I took pleasure in the incomparable landscape of the Austrian Alps, covered with forests of beech, silver fir, maple, elm, and spruce. I delighted in the magnificent alpine meadows with their emerald blankets of grass and the aquarelle brilliance of flowers. A lavish sun gloated over the endless gardens and vineyards of the Danube Valley, whose colors varied from yellow and light blue to matte green.

When I had the time, I went to see the ruins of the famous Vienna Opera that was destroyed by the American Air Force, a senseless act that prompted us to supply the Austrian government with all the materials and resources required for the building's complete reconstruction. I took in the Cathedral of Saint Stephen, founded in the twelfth century, Schönbrunn Palace, medieval castles, and the monasteries and churches of Lower and Upper Austria, Burgenland, and Styria.

What bloodstained storms swept, one after another, over these cities, villages, castles, monasteries, and churches! The invasion of the Roman emperor Augustus. The incursions of the Germanic tribes of Bavarians and Slovenes.[19] The Frankish dominion.[20] The Bavarian Eastern March.[21] The beginning of Hapsburg rule.[22] The frenzied inquisitions.[23] The Black Death, that epidemic of plague that claimed millions of lives. The Peasants' War.[24] The Austro-Turkish war.[25] The Napoleonic invasion. All the blows suffered by the Austrian people in the nineteenth and twentieth centuries. And now, everywhere, a blessed silence, as though the era of the Gospels had come to pass: "Peace on earth, goodwill toward men."

A word or two about the Hapsburgs. After the end of the war my fourteen-year-old daughter, Viktoriia, visited me in Vienna. One beautiful lilac morning we set forth together by car along the Danube to Krems. This was the site of the castle of Franz Josef I, emperor of the Hapsburg dynasty. Now it was occupied by his grandnephew, Otto Hapsburg, who claimed to be the sole heir to the Austrian throne.

The imposing castle was ringed by a traditional moat with a metal drawbridge. Otto Hapsburg met us at the gate—a man of unprepossessing appearance with a creased and unshaven face. Dark, slightly protruding eyes and a ponderous, jutting jaw, a congenital feature of the Hapsburg clan. He was dressed in the traditional Austrian gray suit trimmed in dark green, a feather in his gray hat.

At our approach he raised his hat and gave a deep bow. I introduced myself and my daughter. The owner of the castle said he was glad to have this opportunity for making my acquaintance and expressing his gratitude: the Soviet troops quartered on the castle grounds were models of good conduct; he and his family could not feel safer, and all their property was intact.

He took us on a tour of the castle, narrating along the way. An extensive collection of rifles; a hoard of trophy animals bagged on the territory of the castle—stuffed heads of mountain goats, chamois, and deer tagged with plates naming their royal owners. Magnificent canvases by prominent artists; porcelain; crystal. Through the wide French doors of the upper floors, a view of indescribably beautiful landscapes. The majestic sweep of the Danube sparkling with millions of ripples. The luxuriant gardens and vineyards of the Danube Valley. And in the distance, an amphitheater of alpine meadows and forests decked in the garments of the enchantress Nature.

In the formal halls and rooms, a wealth of cupboards and bureaus displaying dynastic treasures—gold boxes inlaid with precious stones; gifts from various monarchs and nobles; a saddle with a bridle and stirrups in gold used by Franz Josef; rare vases; crystal; porcelain; and carpets.

I asked Otto Hapsburg if everything that was there upon the arrival of the Soviet army of liberation had been preserved.

"Oh, yes," he assured me eagerly. "Everything is intact, everything was saved. The Russian troops are very disciplined and show great care for the safety of the population and its property."

It was true that we—the army's Military Council—had given the strictest orders to our troops to mount guard over all art galleries, museums, palaces, and churches of historical, architectural, and artistic value and to hand them over to the care of the new local Austrian authorities. The Soviet army saved an incalculable quantity of cultural riches for the people of Austria, Germany, Hungary, Czechoslovakia, and other countries.

I asked Hapsburg about the whereabouts of his family, and he replied that they were with him. Excusing himself, he left, and returned a few minutes later with his wife, daughters, and son, whom he introduced to Viktoriia and me. Their faces bore signs of fear, which quickly dissipated, and a burning curiosity: What were these Russians like?

In answer to my question, the boy told me that he was studying at an agricultural school in Switzerland and was home on vacation. His father, the heir to the Austrian throne, added, "I am a grain farmer." He used those precise words. "I quit politics completely a long time ago and have been devoting myself wholly to agriculture. I'm not interested in this palace. And I want my son to be a grain farmer, too."

On our way back to Vienna, Viktoriia said, "Papa, what a nice boy, that young Hapsburg."

"Well," I replied, "you'll graduate from your institute and he from his agricultural college, and we'll pair you two off. It'll be quite a novelty. Grandson of the serf Mikhail Shepilov of Kursk, son of the lathe worker Trofim Shepilov, the Soviet professor and general Dmitrii Shepilov is now related to the Hapsburgs, the dynasty that for seven hundred years tyrannized the peoples of Europe." We laughed. In later years I read in the papers that the "grain farmer" Otto Hapsburg turned up in Germany and was more than once discovered to be at the center of conspiracies to restore the Austrian monarchy and place himself on the throne.

In December 1945, I was recalled to Moscow for talks. The ultramarine Austrian sky glittered with primordial purity. The yard of the building where I lived in Saint Pölten was abloom with roses. Two peacocks, seemingly squeezed into tuxedo jackets the colors of precious stones from the Urals, flapped about with piercing screeches. We caught a ride to Moscow on a bomber going our way. In the freezing cabin, our fellow travelers, army generals on rear-line duty, warmed themselves with bottles of vodka.

At the Central Committee I was offered the post of director of the Telegraph Agency of the Soviet Union (TASS). I declined. A few days later I was told to report to Aleksei Kosygin, then chairman of the Russian Soviet Federated Socialist Republic (RSFSR) Council of Ministers. Kosygin received me late at night and offered me the post of RSFSR people's commissar of technological agriculture. Commissariats of that kind were being organized at the time at the union and republic levels. Evidently the basis for the offer was that after graduating from Moscow University, I completed a course at the Agrarian Institute of Red Professors and wrote quite a number of articles, brochures, and the like on the agrarian question. I replied that I had long stopped working on agricultural problems and could hardly be of any use in such a post. At the Central Committee I said that if the time had come for me to leave the army, I would request that I be put back where I was before volunteering for the front—at the Academy of Sciences.

I flew out of Moscow in a blinding snowstorm, wrapped in a fur coat. I returned to Vienna on a bright sunny noon. Sparrows hopped about in the sparkling puddles. High in the sky, the skylarks circled with triumphant song. Yes, I thought, only eternally sunny blue-domed Vienna could have given birth to the "waltz king," Johann Strauss.

In February 1946, I was demobilized and recalled to Moscow. I left my beloved 4th Guards Army with mixed feelings. On one hand, ever since the end of the war I had longed to return to my home on Bol'shaia Kaluzhskaia Street, to my work, my books. Or even to go somewhere other than Kaluzhskaia, to torrid Tashkent or a village in Riazan—anywhere, so long as it was home, my own native land. On the other hand, how sad it was to part with my wartime friends, with whom I shared the whole ordeal from Moscow to Stalingrad to Vienna. Our farewells were difficult, touching to the point of tears.

In Moscow I was appointed deputy chief of the Bureau of Propaganda and Agitation at the Main Political Directorate of the Armed Forces of the USSR. On August 2, 1946, I was confirmed by the Central Committee as chief editor of the propaganda department of *Pravda*. There the indescribably difficult and demanding work of a newspaperman began for me. It occupied me for most of the day and nearly all night; in those days *Pravda* was printed late, from 6 A.M. to 9 A.M. We had no days off. Frequent lack of sleep brought on headaches and showed in our puffy faces.

In my capacity at *Pravda,* I wrote a number of major articles: "A New Era in the History of Mankind," "The Great Soviet People," which later went through three printings as a brochure, "The Secret War against Soviet Russia," "Soviet Patriotism," "Achieving Abundance in Food Supplies: The Most Important Goal of the Soviet State," and others. Perhaps these articles contributed to the change in my career. Or perhaps other circumstances and facts unknown to me came into play. At any rate, one day I received an important telephone call.

Usually, after working all night and getting little sleep during the day, I went to the "Kremlin cafeteria" on Vozdvizhenka Street, which served as a meeting place for the Moscow elite: people's commissars, high officials of the Central Committee and the Council of Ministers, old Bolsheviks, marshals, prominent diplomats. Here I often met with Maksim Litvinov. I listened to many of his statements at various party conferences and meetings, read his brilliant speeches at international conclaves, and was his fervent admirer. By this time Litvinov had been relieved of all official positions and responsibilities in the Ministry of Foreign Affairs, to the great dissatisfaction of many party leaders. He gave the impression of leading the lonely life of an outcast.

This probably was consistent with the general situation. In those days, anyone who fell into Stalin's disfavor and was then subjected to Khrushchev's abuse found himself in a kind of void. Litvinov appeared to have been abandoned by everyone except his oldest friend and colleague in revolutionary struggle and political emigration, the diplomat Aleksandra Kollontai.

I was fortunate enough to hear several of her speeches. A collection of her popular essays on the problems of love, family, and morals—*Revolution of Feelings and Revolution of Morals*—came out in 1923. She lectured on those subjects and international issues. To us, the Komsomol of 1920, she was a communist divinity. A beautiful woman with refined and gracious manners, tastefully dressed, and fluent in several foreign languages, she was the world's first female ambassador. She spoke eloquently and passionately on issues of love and morality. We revered her no less than fanatical Tibetans revere their Dalai Lama. After the war, and after a quarter-century as ambassador to Norway, Mexico, and Sweden, Aleksandra Kollontai, like Maksim Litvinov, was removed from all diplomatic activity and, like him, lived in solitude.

Who in his wildest dreams could have imagined that I was destined to succeed Litvinov and Georgii Chicherin as foreign minister of the Soviet Union!

One day in mid-September 1947, as I was dining in the Kremlin cafeteria before the evening's work at *Pravda,* I was called to the government telephone and told that Andrei Zhdanov wanted me to report to him at once at the Central Committee.

A building on Old Square. Fifth floor. An enormous office finished in light beige wallpaper. A baroque writing desk and a long conference table. Bookshelves. Piles of books, newspapers, and magazines on the table. Standing before me, a shortish man with a pronounced stoop. A pale, bloodless face. Thinning hair. Dark intelligent eyes with sparks of merriment in their depths. A small black mustache.

Andrei Zhdanov was in a military tunic with the epaulettes of a colonel general. I don't remember why—perhaps because I had business that day with my aides in the Military-Political Academy, where I was still lecturing—but I, too, was in a general's uniform. His outward appearance, stance, and way of speaking gave him a likable air. This, my first conversation with him, was very lengthy and made a strong impression on me.

Zhdanov provided a candid appraisal of the situation on the ideological front and laid out his own thoughts on how best to solve the most urgent problems. He spoke animatedly, wittily, interestingly, with burning ardor, pacing up and down the room and punctuating his words with eloquent gestures. Now and then he came up to me and gazed searchingly into my eyes, as though to see whether his arguments were having effect. From time to time he stopped to catch his breath; everyone knew he had heart trouble. The gist of what he told me was this:

"Things have not worked out well for us in CC Agitprop. The war ended. We were faced with gigantic economic problems. Comrade Stalin's plan is not only to restore our socialist industry to the full in the shortest possible time but to raise production by significant levels. The same for agriculture. But to attain these goals we must do an enormous amount of ideological work among the masses. Without that we cannot move forward one inch.

"The situation is quite serious and complicated. The plans of the imperialists to defeat us on the battlefield have failed. From now on, they will be engaged in an increasingly determined ideological offensive against us. We must keep our powder dry. And it is completely out of place for us to indulge in hypocritical complacency: 'We won, so now we can do anything.'

"Things are difficult, and more difficulties lie ahead. Serious difficulties. Our people showed self-sacrifice and heroism that defies description. Now they want to live well. Millions of them tasted life abroad, in many countries. They saw not only the bad but some things that made them wonder. And much of what they saw they interpreted incorrectly, one-sidedly. Anyhow, people want to reap the fruit of their victory, live well—have good apartments like the ones they saw in the West, eat well, dress well. And we are duty-bound to give them all that.

"The mood among a part of the intelligentsia, and not only the intelligentsia, is 'To hell with all politics. We just want to live well. Be well paid. Breathe freely. Enjoy ourselves. That's all.' What they don't understand is that the road to a good life is paved with the right policies.

"Comrade Stalin has been telling us lately that politics is the vital basis for the Soviet system. If the party follows the right policies, if the masses recognize these policies as vital to their own well-being, then we shall resolve everything and create an abundance of material and intellectual riches. If we do not follow the right policies, if the masses do not accept the party's policies as their very own, we will be lost. So these apolitical, nonideological sentiments are very dangerous for our country. They are leading us into a quagmire. And these sentiments have lately made themselves felt. In literature, plays, films, a kind of mold has formed.

"These moods are all the more dangerous when they are accompanied by kowtowing before the West. 'Ah, the West!' 'Ah, democracy!' 'There is literature for you!' 'Look at those polling stations!' What a disgrace, how demeaning to our national dignity! There's just one thing these gentlemen sighing for the 'Western way of life' cannot explain: Why was it we who defeated Hitler, and not those others with their pretty ballot boxes in the streets?

"Stalin and the Politburo have lately been putting forward one ideological question after another. And what has Agitprop been doing all this time—Aleksandrov and his group? I don't know. They come to me and are in ecstasy over the measures taken by the CC for the intellectual mobilization of our people. But they do nothing to help the CC.

"And no wonder. All these Aleksandrovs, Kruzhkovs, Fedoseevs, Il'ichevs, who dug in on the ideological front and concentrated everything in their hands—they're not revolutionaries or Marxists. They are petit bourgeois. Actually, they are very remote from the people and concerned above all with their own personal affairs.

"You are a military man and you know what a 'fallback position' is. One has the impression that with their apartments, dachas, money, academic degrees, and titles, they have prepared their first-line fallback positions, then their second-line, then their third-line, to provide for themselves for the rest of their lives. The CC has received several letters about these operators. It's as though they sense that they floated up to the top by chance, and they're apprehensive—they might be dismissed, so they must insure themselves. What kind of intellectual mentors are these? Ideology indeed!

"That is why the Politburo has reached the conclusion that we cannot make progress on the ideological front without purging and strengthening

CC Agitprop. There are proposals to bring you in on this business—to appoint you, for now, deputy director of the CC Bureau of Propaganda and Agitation. The director would be Mikhail Suslov, but he'd be busy with other matters, so you, in effect, would be running the whole show."

I told Zhdanov I was grateful for the trust placed in me, but I did not feel I could shoulder the responsibility, as I lacked the necessary knowledge and experience.

"Now, now, my dear fellow," he retorted, "allow me to disagree with you. You've got two degrees—from Moscow State University and the Institute of Red Professors. Your humble servant wasn't lucky enough to get that kind of education. As for experience, good Lord—work in the Komsomol, work in the party CC, a party political department stint in Siberia, five years at the front, division commissar, member of the army's Military Council. . . . No, my dear fellow, you don't have the slightest grounds for refusal.

"Clear the ideological front of all these petite bourgeoisie," he continued, "bring in new people from the oblast committees, from the army's political sections, and everything will be fine."

So on September 18, 1947, a new phase of my life began.

CHAPTER FIVE

Agitprop under Zhdanov

IN ITS MISSION, functions, and scale, CC Agitprop in those days was a gigantic empire covering every aspect of Soviet intellectual life. From the campaign against illiteracy to the most minute questions of religion, aesthetics, and philosophy, everything fell under its purview: the whole system of public education, from schools and literacy courses to institutes of higher learning; the entire press, from mass-circulation factory bulletins to *Pravda, Izvestiia,* and *Publishing House;* an enormous network of scientific organizations, from factory laboratories to the USSR Academy of Sciences; physical education and sports; museums and libraries; literature and writers' unions; music and composers' unions; painting, sculpture, and artists' unions; the entire field of art, from amateur clubs in factories and kolkhozes to the Bolshoi Theater, the All-Union Folk Dance Ensemble, the Piatnitskii Chorus, and the USSR State Orchestra; a gigantic party education network, from political study groups to the University of Marxism-Leninism, the Higher Party School, and the Central Committee's Academy of Social Sciences; and much, much more.

All these different sectors of the ideological front had to be kept under observation. We had to know the gist and substance of the intellectual life of every corner of society. We had to put our staff members in the right places to make sure that the party's policies on ideological questions were being followed. All this demanded extensive knowledge and good sources of information. We had to do a huge amount of reading, watching, and listening. The work was intellectually and physically demanding.

Established customs made work even more difficult. Agitprop had to adjust itself to the work habits of the CC Secretariat, and the Secretariat and Politburo to those of Stalin. Even though the war was over, Stalin kept to a work schedule from the war years. He got up at six or seven in the evening. Meetings and discussions began even later. Work continued until morning. The Council of Ministers and the staffs of the Central Committee, the ministries, and all central government offices had to adapt to this schedule.

But the country, the people, the plants, and the factories kept normal hours. That had to be kept in mind. As a result, the end of one working day (night) would often coincide with the start of another. Just as during the war, every high official kept a bed in his office so that he could catch a nap at some opportune moment. The work was grueling. Heart attacks, strokes, and deaths were commonplace. I was pushed to my absolute limit.

During this period Stalin was especially preoccupied with ideological questions and gave them top priority. Agitprop was handed one assignment after another. Stalin set these forth at meetings of the Politburo, the Secretariat, by telephone, and often in informal settings.

Stalin frequently invited his colleagues to the "nearby dacha" after meetings of the Politburo. They viewed a new movie or some old favorite and had supper. All night long they discussed a multitude of questions. When necessary, other people were invited. Sometimes the Politburo reached decisions right away; at other times it set a time for discussing a new issue.

Zhdanov often invited me from my office on the third floor to his on the fifth floor. His face would be very pale and incredibly weary, his eyes inflamed by lack of sleep. He would gasp for air with his mouth open. For Zhdanov, with his heart disease, those nightlong vigils at the "nearby dacha" were catastrophic. But neither he nor anyone else wanted to miss a single dinner, even when ill. It was there that everything of any importance was brought up, discussed, and sometimes conclusively decided.

After the customary greetings, Zhdanov would speak more or less as follows:

"Yesterday, Comrade Stalin noted that our new publications treat the work and sociological views of Fyodor Dostoevsky[1] in a very one-sided and often wrong way. Dostoevsky is portrayed only as an outstanding Russian writer, an unsurpassed psychologist, a master of language and verbal imagery. He was all that, indeed. But to say only that is to present him in a one-sided way that throws off the reader, especially the young.

"What about Dostoevsky's sociological and political side? After all, his work was not limited to *Notes from the House of the Dead* and *Poor Folk*. What about *The Double*? His notorious *The Possessed*? He wrote *The Possessed* to tar the revolution, to portray the revolutionaries maliciously and viciously as criminals, oppressors, and murderers, to paint them as psychotics, betrayers, and provocateurs.

"As Dostoevsky saw it, there is an element of the satanic and perverse in each of us. If a man is a materialist, if he does not believe in God, if he—oh, horrors!—is a socialist, the satanic element wins out, and he becomes a criminal. What an abject, vile philosophy!

"Dostoevsky's philosophy spawned the murderer Raskolnikov. Even liberals were repelled by the base slander of *The Possessed*. And the philosophy of *Crime and Punishment* is essentially no better. No wonder Gorky[2] called Dostoevsky the 'evil genius' of the Russian people.

"True, in his best work Dostoevsky described with stunning power the lot of the humiliated and injured, the savage behavior of those in power. But what for? To call upon the humiliated and injured to struggle against evil, oppression, and tyranny? Far from it. Dostoevsky called for the renunciation of struggle; he called for humility, resignation, Christian virtue. Only that, according to him, could save Russia from the catastrophe of socialism.

"Our literati view Dostoevsky through rose-colored glasses and portray him as a quasi-socialist who couldn't wait for the advent of the October Revolution. But this is outright falsification. Don't we know that Dostoevsky spent his life repenting for his 'youthful delusions,' like his membership in the Petrashevskii circle,[3] and atoning for them? How did he atone? Through calumnies about the revolution, a zealous defense of the monarchy and church, and all kinds of obscurantism.

"Of course, Comrade Stalin says that we're not about to disown Dostoevsky. We have published him widely and will continue to do so. But our writers and our critics must help our readers, especially the young ones, see Dostoevsky as he is."

On another occasion, taking his smudged notebook out of his pocket, Zhdanov reported:

"Yesterday, Comrade Stalin advised us not to neglect Kuprin.[4] The writer gave us *Moloch,* a vivid exposure of capitalist swinishness and bourgeois morality. He gave us *The Duel,* a faithful picture of the tsarist army, with its lawlessness, its browbeating discipline, and its other serious faults."

In the same way, Zhdanov passed on Stalin's orders on improving the satirical journal *Krokodil,* on the Bolshoi Theater's production of Mussorgsky's opera *Boris Godunov,* on the works of Gleb Uspenskii,[5] on radio broadcasting, on the great traditions of Vissarion Belinskii,[6] on Vano Muradeli's opera *Great Friendship,*[7] and on many other subjects. Each order triggered an immediate response on the part of *Pravda,* the Agitprop newspaper *Culture and Life,* critics, publishing houses, theaters, and all the appropriate levers of ideological indoctrination.

While implementing Stalin's orders, Zhdanov was very demanding and scrupulously thorough. But what sort of man was Zhdanov? What were his views? What was it like to work with him?

Andrei Aleksandrovich Zhdanov belonged to that marvelous generation of the Russian revolutionary intelligentsia who gave all their strength, every drop of their blood, all their ardor, to the great cause of socialist development and the triumph of Marxism-Leninism on a worldwide scale. Born in 1896 to the family of a public-school inspector in Mariupol,[8] he joined the revolutionary movement at age sixteen and the Bolshevik party in 1915. After the October Revolution, he worked in the Urals, then in Tver.[9] In the Gorky oblast[10] he served on the provincial party committee, then on the provincial executive committee, and then as secretary of the regional party committee. He was elected a secretary of the party's Central Committee at the Seventeenth Party Congress,[11] a candidate member of the Politburo in 1935, and a full member at the Eighteenth Party Congress.[12]

After Kirov's murder in 1934, Zhdanov was appointed secretary of the Leningrad party organization, and remained at its head for ten years. In 1944 he transferred to Moscow as a secretary of the Central Committee. As a party leader, he had to deal with a wide variety of questions: the repatriation of factories and the repeal of bread rationing, enlarging the intake of fisheries and expanding book publication, the production of cement and pay raises for scholars, planting flax and developing television. But there was one sphere of activity in which Zhdanov was transformed into one possessed by a fervent quest for answers to the agonizing questions that gave him no rest. This was the sphere of ideology—questions of Marxist-Leninist theory, literature, theater, painting, music, film, and so on.

Zhdanov was a well-rounded Marxist. As was true of the entire old Bolshevik intelligentsia, his Marxism was not the fruit of cribs and quotations from anthologies. He continually and substantively enriched his thinking with Marxist theory from original sources. In my relationship with him, I often saw that the laws, principles, and conclusions of Marxist-Leninist theory were not stored lifeless in his head, to be peddled as citations when needed, like postcards from a vending machine. Zhdanov was a master of applying the laws and analyses of Marxist dialectics to explain, dissect, and analyze the most diverse intellectual concepts.

I was always greatly impressed by the way Zhdanov dealt with complex ideological questions. He never asked Agitprop or his assistants to write his speeches for him or to supply him with drafts of solutions to problems under consideration. He himself studied the problem in all of its aspects, listened carefully to scholars, writers, and musicians versed in the relevant subjects, compared different points of view, tried to visualize the entire history of the issue under discussion, and applied to it the relevant pronouncements of the founders of Marxism. In that capacity Zhdanov himself raised questions for Agitprop to study and himself formulated the basic conclusions and recommendations.

He never used ready-made speeches, speeches composed of quotations, or articles written from the first to the last page by omnipresent aides and slick journalistic hacks. Under Khrushchev, this method became standard for a wide range of party and government officials. In Khrushchev's time, people forgot how to think, analyze, and generalize for themselves. They lost, or never bothered to acquire, the knack for talking to people in plain language. The living word gave way to the ubiquitous quotation.

Zhdanov liked interesting, creative people and did his best to find them and draw them into the work of the Central Committee and the country's cultural institutions. He could not abide mediocrities, those conventional *agitpropshchiki*[13] whose mentality was confined to a limited number of memorized quotations and Marxist-sounding formulas. Lively, creative, and talented, Zhdanov wanted all sectors of the ideological front to be staffed by keen, resourceful people, people with a "divine spark."

Zhdanov scrupulously wrote his own speeches, pouring his heart into them. I remember him laboring over a speech on music, ablaze with inspiration. He mined Marx and Engels for their nuggets on the subject and pored over them. He studied Plekhanov on aesthetics; he went through Lenin's speeches, letters, and notes. His desk was piled high with the works of Vladimir Stasov,[14] Aleksandr Serov,[15] and the letters of Pyotr Tchaikovsky, all with bookmarks, marginalia, and underlining. Finding some striking image or wording, he could not wait to pour out his thoughts and feelings. Often he phoned me in my third-floor office at the most unexpected hour—in the middle of the night or early in the morning.

"Could you come over now?"

I would come.

"Listen to this. 'Music must strike fire in people's hearts'—Beethoven, on his Fifth Symphony. Imagine, what a sublime mission for music—to strike fire in people's hearts!"

Or, "Have you read Serov's *Critical Essays* on music? Ah, my friend, what a store of treasures! Listen. 'The greatest delight, the greatest charm of the art of sound, lies in the melody; without it everything is pale, colorless, dead, however intricate the harmonies, however wondrous the counterpoint and orchestration.' Our modernists have sent the melody packing—in other words, they deaden the soul of music!"

I was always impressed by the wide range of Zhdanov's intellectual interests and by the passion he brought to the study of any current issue, as if at that moment there was nothing more important in the whole world. He was released from the spell of this or that idea only when he finished grappling with it in his mind and arrived at a final concept and the means of solving pressing problems. That was why his speeches and recommendations were so forceful. Today, with hindsight, his positions on a number of ideological questions may seem dubious, but there is no denying the power of his arguments, or his passionate sense of purpose: to ensure the triumph of communist ideology.

In 1947–48,[16] Zhdanov oversaw the drafting of a series of party Central Committee decrees on ideological questions, and his speeches on philosophy, literature, art, and international problems enjoyed wide currency. These included his commentary on Georgii Aleksandrov's book *The History of Western European Philosophy*, his talk "On the Journals *Star* and

Leningrad,"[17] and such speeches as "On Our Theatrical Repertoires and Measures for Their Improvement,"[18] "On the Film *A Great Life,*"[19] and "On the Opera *Great Friendship* by V. Muradeli." These speeches unquestionably contributed in large measure to the ideological awareness of our intelligentsia and to the intellectual cohesion of the Soviet people in resolving the major problems of building communism.

But these decisions were not free of extremism and the unfounded abuse of a large number of prominent cultural figures who, like the entire country, went through fire and water while building a new life and who faithfully served the people. Among them were the Soviet writers Mikhail Zoshchenko and Anna Akhmatova and the outstanding film directors Sergei Eisenstein, Vsevolod Pudovkin, Grigorii Kozintsev, and Leonid Trauberg. The greatest Soviet composers—Dmitrii Shostakovich, Sergei Prokofiev, Nikolai Miaskovskii, Aram Khachaturian, the pride and glory of Soviet and world musical culture—were stigmatized as representatives of an "antidemocratic trend in music."

Stalin's polemical style, which is not artistic but political, was clearly visible in this denigration of our celebrated Soviet cultural figures. When he wanted to level his criticisms against an individual, group, or social phenomenon, Stalin lashed out mercilessly, engaging in untrammeled hyperbole. Sometime in the 1920s, in the period of intense struggle against the opposition, Leon Trotsky said of Stalin, "This cook will prepare only spicy dishes." Subsequent events showed this characterization to have been largely correct.

While noting the growth of revisionism in the social-democratic parties, Stalin could brand the entire worldwide social-democratic movement as "social fascism."[20] This mixed everything up and made it impossible for communists to reach the hearts of millions upon millions of social-democratic workers. Detecting the beginnings of a retreat from proletarian internationalism in the speeches of the leaders of the Yugoslavian Communist Party,[21] Stalin immediately branded them as bloody executioners and Turkish Janissaries.[22] Spotting an element of objectivism in the philosophic works of Academician Deborin,[23] Stalin labeled him a proto-Menshevik idealist.

Khrushchev adopted this Stalinist style and took it to the most extreme amoral lengths. Stalin seized on something that really existed, at least in embryo, and then subjected it to the wildest hyperbole to nip it in the bud.

Khrushchev would concoct a lie on the spot, from scratch, and proceed to defend it with all the powers of the government at his command.

By nature, Zhdanov was an intelligent and sensitive man. But when Stalin, in their conversations, criticized some aspect of the country's intellectual life and attributed to it great political significance, Zhdanov promptly trumpeted these views in public. Of course, in doing so he was not alone.

Linked to my image of Zhdanov are the events involved in the staging of Muradeli's opera *Great Friendship*.

As I mentioned, I went to work at Agitprop in the second half of September 1947. On the gala day of November 7,[24] the opera premiered at the Bolshoi Theater. Right after the performance, Zhdanov told me that Stalin was dissatisfied with it. In Stalin's opinion this was not music but some kind of cacophony.[25] Furthermore, in his opinion, the libretto distorted historical truth. Zhdanov asked me to have Agitprop look into the state of Soviet music and forward its conclusions to the Central Committee.

We enlisted a large group of Moscow's leading musicologists to help us in our study and sent on our recommendations to the Central Committee for a draft decree on music. All this, it seemed to me, was done quite professionally and could serve as the basis for further advances in Soviet musical culture and its proper development.

Personally, I have always been an ardent devotee of classical music. My father had a pleasing voice and was always humming old Russian songs around the house, and sometimes liturgical music. My brothers all played musical instruments by ear—one the balalaika, another the mandolin, guitar, and violin. When I was eleven, I became friends with my classmate Iurii Ostroumov, who has now been my friend for more than fifty years. Iurii had a piano at home, and his mother, Tatiana, was a music lover. To her accompaniment we learned and sang the love songs and lyrical pieces of Pyotr Tchaikovsky, Sergei Rachmaninov, Anton Arenskii, Mikhail Glinka, and Aleksandr Dargomyzhskii, arias from operas, and the old romances and songs of the Russian composers Aleksandr Varlamov and Aleksandr Gurilev.

Our voices at that age were starting to crack, yet Iurii was already developing into a tenor and I into a baritone. We often sang duets: Glinka's "Do Not Tempt Me," Konstantin Villebois's "How Empty Is Our Sea," and others. Another classmate who developed a bass voice at an early age, Zhenia

Polenskii, soon joined our musical group. Now we could sing in trio, and we didn't do a bad job performing "The Cloud Stayed the Night," "In the Wild North," and other compositions. It was in those days that music captivated me, and it became my love and a source of delight, happiness, and passion for the rest of my life.

In 1918 in Tashkent,[26] where I was in school after moving from Ashkhabad,[27] we students founded a theatrical company. From the very beginning, several girls, Iurii, Zhenia, and I were its stars. We performed musicals in schools around town, in barracks, in outlying villages, in the Coliseum opera house, in the House of the People, in the city park, and in front of the Modern and Khiva movie theaters. We put on the old high-school play *Ivanov Pavel,* the children's operas *Puss in Boots; Cat, Goat, and Ram; Luli-Muzykanty;* and others. We performed scenes from classical operas, *Evgenii Onegin* (Tchaikovsky), and others, and held concerts featuring lyrical songs of classical Russian and Western composers. Soon the girls in our club formed the nucleus of a fine group of ballet dancers.

The more I was imbued with the soul of music, the greater became my need to immerse myself in it. During the Civil War, Tashkent was a flourishing city. It attracted a host of splendid singers, and the Tashkent opera was famous for the high quality of its productions. As young singers, we were allowed to take any empty seats for free, and we made frequent, almost daily, use of this privilege.

In the mornings I had to earn my living, at first making cigarette paper in a tobacco factory and then running errands for a block committee in charge of housing nationalized by the revolution. After lunch I attended class in what was then known as an upper-level school. This, of course, often left me exhausted, but when evening came I was drawn irresistibly to the opera. For the fifth, tenth, and twentieth time I would sit enthralled by those arias, duets, choral pieces, and overtures I knew so well.

My father was a metalworker in the Tashkent railroad complex, and after the revolution he attended a workers' night school. To him, my passion for the theater was "nonsense" and a "waste of time," and he frequently made a scene about it, but not too severely. My love of music was so overwhelming that I soon quit the block committee and found work as a makeup assistant at the opera.

It would have been hard to find anyone less equipped for the task. Not even under pain of death could I have drawn anything faintly resembling a chair or a chicken. Nonetheless, I plunged bravely into the makeup game. Before the curtain and during intermissions I fitted wigs and pasted beards and mustaches on chorus members and extras and daubed their faces with greasepaint as I fancied. I tried to make everyone look as colorful and terrifying as possible, whatever they were performing that day—warlike Polovtsi[28] in *Prince Igor* [Alexander Borodin], courtesans at the court of the Duke of Mantua in *Rigoletto* [Giuseppe Verdi], or Egyptian high priests in *Aïda* [Verdi]. God only knows why the opera put up with my artistic frenzy as long as it did.

As soon as the third bell rang I sped backstage or to a seat in the stalls and surrendered to the magical world of sound.

My passion for music merged with my need to earn a living, and my days were divided between school and the theater. The compositions I heard were imprinted so vividly on my impressionable young mind that two or three years later I could still give a faithful rendition of the arias, choral parts, and even the female and orchestral parts in a dozen operas— *Mermaid* [Dargomyzhskii], *The Demon* [Anton Rubinstein], *Evgenii Onegin* [Tchaikovsky], *Faust* [Charles Gounod], *Carmen* [Georges Bizet], *The Queen of Spades* [Tchaikovsky], *La Traviata* [Verdi], *Rigoletto* [Verdi], *Les Cloches de Corneville* [Robert Planquette], *Aïda, Boris Godunov, I Pagliacci* [Ruggero Leoncavallo], and *Prince Igor.* To this day, I remember all the words and notes I heard almost half a century ago.

My lifelong attachment to chamber music has been no less passionate. Here, my idols were—and are—Tchaikovsky and Rachmaninov. Out of the distant past, memories emerge. With what excitement, joy, impatience, hope, and happiness did I respond to the music of these geniuses!

Scenes of yesteryear flit before my mind. It is March, the fields of wild tulips are faded, the apple trees and apricot and cherry orchards are snow-white in their wedding gowns. We are in Iurii's spacious room. The intoxicating aroma of spring floats in from the garden. In his velvety tenor voice Iurii sings:

> I opened the window—
> It was unbearably stuffy—
> And sank on my knees in front of it.
> The spring night breathed on my face
> With the blessed breath of lilacs.

Somewhere in the garden a nightingale sang.
I listened to it with piercing sorrow.
Wistfully I recalled my homeland.
My native land I remembered.

At fifteen years of age, I had no concept of my native land as a whole. To me, it was something directly experienced. It was the old whitewashed house on Smolensk Street. It was my beloved mother, her dear, sun-blotched face as wrinkled from cares, sorrows, and grueling toil as a dried apple. It was the apricot and peach orchards. It was my closest friends—Iurii, Vania, Lialia, Zhenia. It was the Salar River,[29] my brothers, the grass, the theater, the blue sky—everything I saw, breathed, and lived by.

Under the magic spell of music, I sensed with every fiber of my being that behind the melodies and words of pining for one's distant land there was something huge, excruciating, and sweet. My very soul yearned for something huge and heroic. I did not know what it could be. But I knew that I was ready for some great feat, some act of self-sacrifice, that would release the seething lava of emotions in my breast.

Another snapshot of the past:

A blazing August morning. Iurii and I go for a swim in the Karasa River. Giant poplars. A peach orchard. Green vines bending under the weight of bunches of grapes. To dive from the shore into the silvery water, to chase after the oversized dragon flies, to bury myself in the warm sand—what ecstasy! On the other side of the river there is a large melon field. We gorge ourselves on the fragrant melons.

Back in Iurii's house, the pale lilac evening fills the rooms, terrace, and garden. The windows and doors are open wide. The well-watered earth gives off a slightly tart aroma. The poplars whisper to each other with their silvery leaves. Tatiana Fedorovna runs her fingers softly over the keyboard, and the magic of Tchaikovsky's *Night* begins.

Why do I love you, moonlit night,
Love you so much that it hurts to admire you?
Why do I love you, quiet night,
When to others, not to me, you send tranquillity?

Pure as crystal, the music pours through the open windows into the garden. It mingles with the phosphorescent moonlight and the scent of carnations and nasturtiums into a kind of bewitchment. The worldly wisdom of the poet Polonskii's[30] words does not touch me; I don't muse over the meaning of the lines. I sense with exquisite poignancy the indescribable beauty of the summer night and the sounds of this lyrical song. Everything within me throbs with happiness.

The music plays, three pellucid chords, and as though melting into the night, the air, and the scent of flowers, the harmony, takes on melodic form.

> Oh, night, why should I love your silvery light?
> Will it sweeten the sorrow of hidden tears?
> Will it give my hungry heart the answer it craves?
> Will it resolve my onerous doubts?

The final chord fades away. Silence. Silence in the room. Silence in the garden. Silence in the skies. And I exult. My heart is filled with rapture. I want to do something good. Something exalted. So that everyone can be as happy as I. How good life is . . . my God, how good! This exhilarating effect of music on the mind, on the soul, on all my being, has stayed with me all my life. All my life I have worshiped music—real music—as reverently as a true Christian worships God.

That is why the modernistic trends that began seeping into the Soviet Union from the West had not only a negative but a painful, sacrilegious effect on me. Of course, I appreciated the great significance of Alexander Scriabin's innovations in his *Holy Spring,* and Igor Stravinsky's in *Petrushka,* as well as the outstanding works of Dmitrii Shostakovich.[31] Basically, I approved of the original, the avant-garde. But at the same time I saw the need to protect Soviet music from those Western trends that led to the collapse of musical structure and music's pathological transformation.

In this spirit we wrote our Agitprop brochures on music. Zhdanov, however, did not make use of them. He called them "academic." He wrote everything himself, with the help of his closest aides and chosen consultants. This led to his well-known speech at the conference of Soviet music officials and to the party CC's decree on February 10, 1948, on the opera *Great Friendship.*

Held in the white-marble hall on the fifth floor of the Central Committee building, the conference brought together the cream of the Soviet music world—the composers Dmitrii Shostakovich, Sergei Prokofiev, Aram Khachaturian, Vissarion Shebalin, Dmitrii Kabalevskii, Iurii Shaporin, Nikolai Miaskovskii, Vasilii Solov'ev-Sedoi, and Ivan Dzerzhinskii, the veteran professors of music Aleksandr Gol'denveizer, Mikhail Gnesin, and Elena Katul'skaia, and a collection of music critics, conductors, singers, and others.

It was here that I met Shostakovich. In later years I frequently attended his concerts, and I conversed and corresponded with him even after I no longer occupied any official positions. But my first glimpse of him remained my most vivid memory of him.

Dmitrii Shostakovich gives the impression of being constantly in a state of creative obsession, wound up like a spring. Pale, with furrowed eyebrows, he stares at you through thick glasses with his thoughtful, sharp, inspired gray eyes. Every now and then his face twitches as though from an electric shock. You feel that his words, his movements, are only a facade, and that behind this protective barrier he is working at something with unbelievable intensity.

I was always amazed by his modesty, which bordered on a kind of childlike shyness. When the concert hall rocked with applause after the performance of, say, his Seventh or Thirteenth Symphony, it was very difficult to coax him onto the proscenium. When he could resist no longer, he stood behind the footlights with an agonized look, gave a few stiff bows with his arms glued to his sides, and hurriedly, as though staggering from fatigue, left the stage.

At the Central Committee conference, he seemed traumatized by the course of events, his soul in tatters. He made two speeches. In the concluding one, he said: "My work has suffered from many failures and serious shortcomings, although in all my composing I think of the people, my audience, the people that raised and nurtured me, and I always try to write music that people will understand."

It seemed to me in later years that the outcome of the CC conference, as well as the public criticism of Shostakovich that followed, had a significant and positive impact on all his subsequent work.

As for Sergei Prokofiev, I seem to remember meeting him after the conference, at his home at Nikolina Hill.[32] Maybe I was wrong, but he seemed to react differently to the criticism brought against him. In his response I detected two contradictory yet related elements. The first was astonishment: What are they talking about? Does it make sense? Is all this any use to the country and to music? And the second was the purely professional reaction of a man who spent his whole life in intense creativity and who was accustomed to weighing and responding to any troubling question about his music by going back to his scores: Well, maybe I'd better do *The Tale of the Stone Flower* a little differently. . . . Maybe I ought to think about revising *War and Peace*.

For Khachaturian, Kabalevskii, and Shebalin, the discussion seemed to be extremely painful.

Apart from critiquing the composers' work, the conference did some reshuffling, appointing the young musician Tikhon Khrennikov as head of the Composers' Union and the well-known choral conductor and musicologist Professor Aleksandr Sveshnikov as rector of the Moscow Conservatory.

Both Zhdanov's speech and the CC decree "On the Opera *Great Friendship* by V. Muradeli" centered on two clear themes. One of them was progressive in nature. The CC warned the composers against the danger of their work being corrupted by the aesthetic principles, forms, and techniques that were characteristic of modern bourgeois music of Europe and America—music that was ugly, false, atonal, dissonant, unharmonious, and built on a jangling mixture of sounds that represented a cacophony for the depraved tastes of individualistic aesthetes. As Zhdanov said, "We must recognize the danger to music posed by this formalistic trend as an attempt to wreck the temple of art that the geniuses of musical culture built." These statements undoubtedly helped many of our composers guard against an infection of pathological modernism.

The other theme that sounded in the CC's decree and in Zhdanov's speech was antidemocratic in substance. It leveled a series of major political accusations at a large group of the country's leading composers. They were blamed for losing contact with the people, adhering to bourgeois ideology, and promoting subjectivism, constructivism, extreme individualism, and stale, outdated conservatism. They were branded as representatives of an antidemocratic trend that ultimately led to the destruction of music. No creative debate on a democratic basis was permitted, and the composers were saddled with the kind of mandatory artistic and creative standards that should always be the outcome of free democratic debate. Organizational measures bolstered the decree.

The same kind of political accusations had characterized previous CC decrees on literature, the theater, and cinema.

At roughly the same time, Agitprop was working on the upcoming Stalin Prizes for achievements in the fields of science, technological innovation, literature, and art. Candidates for the prizes were nominated by state and private organizations, scholars, writers, and artists. The candidacies were then thrown open to public discussion. With due regard for these views, the Stalin Prize Committee voted in secret on each candidacy. After that, all the files were transferred to Agitprop, which drew its conclusions and prepared a draft announcement for the CC Politburo.

Agitprop then sent all the materials to Stalin—but not before every nomination was considered and discussed exhaustively with Zhdanov. We went over the literary work produced during the past year. We viewed several movies. The chairman of the Radio Committee, Puzin, played recordings in Zhdanov's office of the symphonies, concerts, and songs nominated for prizes. Zhdanov examined every work thoroughly, from every aspect, weighing all its plusses and minuses. It was a pleasure for me to observe the erudition and originality of his approach to complex and sophisticated questions of science, literature, and art.

The Politburo (Presidium)[33] discussion of the nominated works usually took place in Stalin's office. Apart from the Politburo members, the conferences were attended by the president of the Academy of Sciences, Aleksandr Nesmeianov; the general secretary of the Writers' Union, Aleksandr Fadeev, or his deputy, Konstantin Simonov; and the heads of the departments of art and cinematography, Sergei Kaftanov and Ivan Bol'shakov. When the agenda included Stalin Prizes for the year's inventions, the government ministers involved in those matters were invited as well.

These meetings were always very lively and interesting. In contrast to most Politburo meetings, the time devoted for deciding on Stalin Prizes was dispensed with a generous hand. I still have my notes from the Politburo's meeting in 1949 on the Stalin Prizes for 1948. The meeting in Stalin's office on the nominations for literature took place on March 19. It began at 10:00 P.M. and ended at 11:50 P.M. The nominations for scientific research were discussed three days later, on March 22, from 11:00 P.M. to 12:35 A.M. The conference on March 31 on scientific and technical inventions lasted more than four hours, from 10:00 P.M. to 2:05 A.M.

Stalin was probably better prepared for these meetings than anyone else. He was always a close reader of current literature and found time to go over everything of any artistic, social, or economic significance. As he demonstrated on many occasions, he remembered everything he read, and interpreted it in his own unique way. He managed to read in proof form the literary "thick journals" like *Novyi mir* (New World), *October, Banner,* and *Star,* as well as scholarly journals like *Philosophical Issues, Economic Issues,* and *Historical Issues.* Once, in the course of our conversations with Stalin on political economy, the academician Pavel Iudin marveled, "Comrade Stalin, when do you have time to read so much literature?" With a sly grin Stalin replied, "I have a set quota—about 300 pages of literary or other writing every day. I recommend a daily quota to you, too." As a result, Stalin was often able to show up not only Agitprop staffers but members of the CC Politburo and even the writers themselves.

At one of the Politburo meetings on Stalin Prizes for literature, Stalin turned to me and said, "There was a story in *Star* at the beginning of last year." He gave the title and the author's name. "A very good story, I thought. Why wasn't it nominated?" There was a general silence. "Have you read it?"

"No," I replied, "I haven't."

"Well, I can understand that. You don't have enough time. You're busy. But I've read it. Anyone else?"

General silence.

"Well, I read it," Stalin repeated. "I think we could give it a second prize." Surprises of this kind were not infrequent.

Stalin's views on art were exceedingly varied. Sometimes he set extremely high artistic standards and ridiculed attempts to push through a prize for some work simply because of its politically topical subject matter. But he often did the same himself. "This is a revolutionary work," he would say. "This is a useful theme." "This story is on a currently vital theme." And the work got a Stalin Prize despite its artistic weakness.

For example, he supported the nomination of Konstantin Fedin for a first prize for his novels *First Joys* and *An Unusual Summer* and yet remarked, "In places this novel reads more like a list of events than an artistic work." And this about Fedin, a master of language who aimed above all else at artistic form!

On Aleksandr Korneichuk's play *Makar Dubrava,* there were comments that the story was of great current interest and that Makar Dubrava was a genuine Soviet miner. Then Stalin spoke up. "The question is not whether Makar Dubrava is a miner, whether he is of proletarian origin. We're talking about the play's artistic merits—does it create an artistic image of a Soviet miner? That's the decisive factor."

At another discussion someone referred to the ballet *Raimonda,* with its score by Aleksandr Glazunov. The chairman of the Committee on the Arts, Polikarp Lebedev, maladroitly remarked that the ballet had a "medieval plot." Stalin scoffed rather maliciously at this. "And aren't *Boris Godunov* and many other great works based on 'old themes'? Why does the Committee on the Arts have such a primitive viewpoint?"

Stalin often scoffed at statements that a certain writer was "in search of themes" or had gone on a "creative trip" to find a subject for a novel or "collect material" for a story. In one of his conversations with a group of writers, Stalin asked, "What would you say to this: She's married, has a child, but falls in love with another man. Her lover does not understand her, and she commits suicide."

The writers replied in one voice that the plot was banal.

"And with this banal plot," Stalin retorted, "Tolstoy wrote *Anna Karenina.*"

When Stalin saw real talent in a beginning writer, he took a personal interest. I remember that when Mikhail Bubennov came out with his novel *The White Birch,* Stalin inquired about the writer's career. He supported the novel's nomination for a first prize. At a Politburo meeting on the subject, he asked about the author's health. Informed that Bubennov was ill, he told me to see to his medical treatment. "And not somewhere near Moscow, either. Send him south and have him well cared for."

It is interesting to recall the debates over the work of Vera Panova.

During discussions, Stalin always pressed us on whether we took everything into consideration. Did we read all the works for the year? Was anyone worthy of attention being left out? He quizzed Zhdanov, Fadeev, and me: "And how about (he would name another writer). And whom did you nominate from the Baltic republics? Why is there no one from Moldova? The Stalin Prize Committee grabs and offers us what's under its nose and doesn't see the rest." He referred to works by Latvian, Lithuanian, and other writers in other Soviet republics, and asked: "Would this do? How about that? Would this deserve a prize?"

At one such questioning at a Politburo meeting on March 31, 1948, Stalin asked, "Has Panova's *Kruzhilikha* been nominated?" Someone present replied that Panova's novel *Kruzhilikha* had a mixed reception in literary circles; some were for it and some were against.

Stalin asked, "Why were they against it?"

"The book depicts workers' lives in rather dismal tones."

"And how," Stalin objected, "are people's lives depicted in *The Town of Okurov*?[34] Yet what a fine thing that is. The question is whether they are depicted truthfully. So why can't we award a prize to *Kruzhilikha*?"

One of the writers present said, "But isn't it important to take into account the writer's attitude toward events and people—with whom he sympathizes?"

"And with whom did Gorky sympathize in *The Artamanov Affair*? Panova is being blamed for not finding a happy resolution to the clash between the personal and the public. That's ridiculous. What if that's how it happens in real life? Who among our writers has been able to resolve those clashes?"

There were no more comments. Vera Panova received a second prize.

Stalin continued to clarify, supplement, and correct. "Did you nominate Pervomaiskii? How about moving Kostylev to a second prize for *Ivan the Terrible*? I think Iakobson should get a first prize for his *Two Camps*." That was what he called August Iakobson's play *Battle without a Front Line*. "Gribachev could get a prize for *The Kolkhoz 'Bolshevik.'* Except that the image of the party organizer in this narrative poem is not sufficiently developed."

Fadeev nominated Nikolai Tikhonov for a second prize for his cycle of poems *A Georgian Spring*.

Stalin laughed. "Doing a friend a favor, eh? I propose giving Tikhonov a first prize."

For all his exacting artistic standards, Stalin sometimes displayed a surprising tolerance, a kind of benevolence, toward certain works and writers. A case in point is the writer Fedor Panferov.

I had known Panferov for many years. When I was working in Pushkino with Pavel Iudin and others on the textbook on political economy, he dropped in sometimes for a cup of tea. On occasion I visited him and his wife, Antonina Koptiaeva, at their dacha at Nikolina Hill. I regarded Panferov as a writer of mediocre accomplishments. Only one of his novels,

Bruski, a broad historical canvas of life in a Soviet village, had any artistic merit. Gorky criticized the work for its copious vulgarisms, but its positive features are indisputable. The author's subsequent work took a downward turn from both an artistic and a sociological standpoint. His play *When We Are Beautiful* and his novel *Volga, Mother-River* (1952–53) were labored and stilted.

Nonetheless, at our CC Politburo meeting on the Stalin Prizes in 1948, and again in 1949, Stalin inquired, "How about Panferov?"

Both times the question was greeted with vague mutterings, and both times Stalin said we had to give Panferov something. "All right, he got criticized. But we have to give him a prize." In 1948, Panferov was awarded a second prize for the novel *The Struggle for Peace,* and in 1949 a third prize for the novel *In the Land of the Defeated.* This caused a certain flurry in literary circles and among readers in general, since neither novel was of the slightest artistic importance. Only a small group of mediocrities grouped around the journal *Oktiabr'*—edited by the same Panferov—approved of the awards and continued to extol the laureate.

Similarly, Stalin was inexplicably partial to the works of Semen Babaevskii. Among writers and readers, Babaevskii's novel *The Cavalier of the Golden Star* was regarded as a classic example of "gilded literature." In place of the real life of a kolkhoz village with all its difficulties and problems, with its intense struggle between the promising future and the outdated traditions of the past, the novel substituted tinsel idylls. All the same, Stalin liked the novel and its sequel, *Light over the Earth,* and Babaevskii was awarded three Stalin Prizes.

Stalin prepared just as thoroughly for discussions on prizes for painting and sculpture. Among the members of the Politburo, only Zhdanov ever went to the Tretiakov Gallery or other museums to see the works nominated for Stalin Prizes. So before a Politburo meeting, Agitprop sometimes arranged for an exhibition of the nominated canvases and sculptures in Catherine Hall of the Great Kremlin Palace. Stalin and the whole Politburo would stop by to look. For Stalin, however, this was not enough. He would sometimes come to meetings with a copy of the journal *Ogonek* containing reproductions or with postcards of paintings and ask the most surprising questions.

"Here in *Ogonek* there's a portrait of Stanislavskii by the artist Ulianov. Could we give it a prize?"

I say "surprising" because you could never tell what Stalin would propose or what changes he would make to Agitprop's selections. For instance, the president of the Academy of Art, People's Artist Aleksandr Gerasimov, was known to be highly favored in government circles. After Zhdanov's death, the Politburo took up the Stalin Prize Committee's nomination of Gerasimov's painting *I. V. Stalin at the Coffin of A. A. Zhdanov* and his portrait of Molotov at its meeting on March 26, 1949.

"There's nothing special about these pictures," Stalin said. "Gerasimov is getting on as an artist. He's been given his share of praise. Does he need more? We ought to give this some thought and weigh it carefully—does he deserve another prize?"

Everyone was silent. Stalin turned to me. "And what do you think of Gerasimov?"

I told him honestly what I thought. After a long pause during which he stroked his chin, always a sign of intense concentration, he went on. "And anyhow, what is this?—Stalin here, Stalin there. For Gerasimov—Stalin. For Toidze[35]—Stalin. For Iar-Kravchenko[36]—Stalin." But that was playacting. For even after his feigned condemnation of "Hurrah for Stalin" productions, books, paintings, and movies glorifying Stalin were invariably selected for Stalin Prizes.

At the same meeting, during a discussion of an award to Aleksandr Kibal'nikov for his sculpture of Nikolai Chernyshevskii,[37] Stalin asked, "Why did the sculptor depict Chernyshevskii in his youth? Without an inscription, no one will know it's Chernyshevskii. Ninety-nine percent of our people will recognize only the mature Chernyshevskii, with glasses." In the end, however, he agreed to give Kibal'nikov a second prize.

I remember the stir that the construction of Moscow's first high-rises caused. At a Politburo meeting, without any preliminary discussion by the Stalin Prize Committee and without taking public opinion into account, the secretary of the Moscow Party Committee and chairman of the Moscow Soviet, Georgii Popov,[38] proposed awarding prizes to the architects and sculptors who worked on these buildings. The president of the Architecture Committee, A. G. Mordvinov, was opposed to this on the grounds that none of the buildings were finished, and construction on some had not even begun. Stalin said, "I think Popov is right. The prizes for these high-rises can be awarded now. For the drafts. This is our first attempt to move on from old architectural forms to new ones. And in the case of

Moscow University, that's not just a building, it's a whole complex. As an exception to the rule, we could award prizes for draft projects."

When Kliment Voroshilov tried to raise some objection, citing the Soviet Army Theater as an architectural model, Stalin said, "Why is the Soviet Army Theater any better because it's in the form of a five-pointed star? Who except people in a plane can see the five-pointed star?" There and then we decided to increase the number of Stalin Prizes for architecture.

But the art form for which Stalin had a real passion was the cinema. Here his tastes and artistic standards were unquestioning and definite. What he liked most of all were historical movies on revolutionary themes, epic in conception and rich in social significance; he was generous in his awards for films of this kind. He was a champion, too, of documentaries—about Lenin (*A Day in a Victorious Country*), about life in socialist countries and in Soviet republics (*Democratic Hungary, Soviet Ukraine*). He frowned on movies of a lyrical or psychological bent, and adaptations of fictional work that he did not regard as particularly artistic or socially significant. At a Politburo meeting about film on June 11, 1948, Stalin spoke more or less as follows (I am referring to my notes on that meeting):

"The film ministry is pursuing a wrong policy. It keeps straining to make more and more movies. We shouldn't be increasing the number of movies every year. It's very expensive. There's a lot of junk being made. They don't keep to the budget. Yet the movie industry could yield two billion rubles in net profit.

"They want to produce sixty films a year. There's no need for that. That's wrong. We ought to make four or five feature movies a year, but good ones, first-rate ones. And several documentaries and popular-science films. Instead, we're concentrating on volume, as in agriculture. We ought to make fewer movies, but good ones. Increase the distribution network, make more copies.

"When it comes to movies we mustn't take the United States as a model. The goals there are different. They make a lot of pictures and make a colossal profit. We have other goals.

"I look at this plan for new movies. What a lot of nonsense there." (Stalin often used the word "nonsense.") "Here's a title: *A Commander's Night*. Why? What for? It'll be some kind of nonsense. Or this: *Sputniki*. What for? Or *The Tale of Tsar Saltan*. Who needs that? The movie about Matrosov[39] turned out badly.

"We shouldn't be giving the republics free rein; they're spending a lot of money on movies. And what do they put out? I see they want to make *Raid in the Carpathians.* What for? Vershigora is going to falsify things. Or *Zaslonov.* What is that?—a paean to partisans. Or a film about the *nakhimovtsy.* What can one say about the nakhimovtsy? We've got enough military themes as it is. The movie *Great Strength*—this one we need. But I don't like the director. Better have Pyr'ev take it on.[40]

"The Kliuev and Roskin affair made it clear that some of our scientists are lacking in national pride, in patriotism." (The Soviet scientists Kliuev and Roskin were accused of passing on to the Americans a cure for cancer that they allegedly had discovered. Both were found guilty by a court of their peers.)[41] "There's a lot of idle talk these days about the 'internationalization of science.' You even find it in Kedrov's book." (The reference was to Bonifatii Kedrov's work *Engels and the Natural Sciences.*) "This idea of 'international science' was cooked up by spies. The Kliuevs and Roskins should be beaten. That's why we need films like *Great Strength,* a film about Soviet patriotism, the national pride of the Soviet people.

"Generally speaking, all our important films should be entrusted to experienced directors. Romm—he's good. Pyr'ev, Aleksandrov, Ermler, Chiaureli. Use them. They won't let you down. Have them make technicolor films as well. That's an expensive business. Kozintsev is good. Lukov should be drummed out. Pudovkin is good.[42]

"We've got Bol'shakov clamoring that we need new blood, that we ought to make use of the young." (At the time, Ivan Bol'shakov was the USSR Minister of Cinematography.) "Go ahead, but experiment at your own expense, not with state funds.

"About documentaries: We need a movie about Lenin. But give it to Romm. I see we have Beliaev down for director. I don't know Beliaev. Or give the Lenin film to Pyr'ev. A film on Belinskii—we need that.[43]

"Cinematography is doing badly in Armenia. We have to correct that. Have to help.

"This film about Georgia—*A Film on the Motherland of the Great Stalin*—can't we throw out the title? And if there were no Stalin, would you be making a film about Georgia? Or take this, *Stalinist Urals.* What are the Urals, my own property? Dump the word "Stalinist." A movie on the Volga—we need it. It should be presented as a travelogue.

"We must ask Agitprop and the movie ministry to submit to the CC a project for expanding the network of movie showings so that there'll be films shown in every major regional center, and also a proposal for making many more copies of good films. We'll provide transportation to get the films out to those places."

I have cited only one of my series of notes from Stalin's comments on cinema, but these are quite typical. He was totally in love with movies. He saw pictures he liked again and again. He invited Politburo members, Soviet diplomats home on business, heads of foreign communist parties, and, as a mark of special favor, visiting foreign political leaders and other important guests to screenings of his favorite films. Yet his odd views served to undermine the movie industry.

As noted earlier, Stalin wanted to release only cinematic masterpieces, though in a huge number of copies for endless showings. This led to an annual decline in the number of feature films such that they could be counted eventually on one hand. Great directors were left idle; their skills went to seed. Actors left the cinema for other art forms. As a result, the Soviet movie industry ran into serious trouble.

But the movies that did manage to make it to the screen were rewarded with Stalin's full support. At Politburo meetings he would say, "Well, any more nominations? Did we forget anyone? Come on, come on. For good work we won't skimp on prizes." And when someone argued against a prize for this or that film or actor, Stalin usually disagreed.

I remember that some in the movie industry were incensed by prominent directors who invariably used only their wives in leading roles, even when the women were wrong for the parts because of their age or other reasons. The critics argued, among other things, that this stood in the way of younger talent; many letters on the subject were written to the government and the Central Committee.

At one Politburo meeting someone argued insistently and persuasively against a prize for an actress who was well along in years. The case was clearly one of unsuitability for her role and excessive pressure on the part of her director-husband. "You see," Stalin remarked, "when an actress is young and beautiful, she lacks experience. By the time she has that experience she is no longer young and beautiful. So what can you do about that paradox? I propose we keep this heroine on the list of prizewinners." It was done.

When nominations in the realm of research, scholarship, and technological inventions came up for discussion, Stalin's knowledge of technical detail was amazing. How did he find time to acquaint himself with major works of philosophy, economics, history, law, and biology? Even in these fields, however, Stalin was guided by his own predilections and eccentricities. At a Politburo meeting on March 22, 1949, that was devoted to Stalin Prizes for scientific and scholarly achievement and at one on March 31 for technological inventions, Stalin delved deeply into every nomination, and his assessment of a historical event flew in the face of the accepted interpretation and caught everyone by surprise.

One of the nominations was a historical work. "I didn't have time to read this book," Stalin said to me. "Have you read it?"

I said I had.

"And what do you think?"

I replied that Agitprop was in favor of giving it a prize.

"Tell me, does it include something about the Baku Commissars?"[44]

"Yes," I replied, "it does."

"Well, are they shown in a favorable light?"

"Yes, absolutely."

"In that case," Stalin said, "we cannot give this book a prize. The Baku Commissars do not deserve approbation. There's no need to publicize their actions. They yielded power to the enemy without a fight. Boarded a ship and left. We're lenient toward them. We don't criticize them. Why? They suffered martyrs' deaths, shot by the British. We don't tarnish their memory. But they deserve to be judged severely. They turned out to be bad leaders. When you write history, you must tell the truth. It's one thing to honor their memory; we've been doing that. It's another to give a true assessment of a historical event."

We were all bewildered, but no one voiced any objection. The nomination was dead.

Stalin was very critical in his questioning of economic ministers about inventions and industrial design. Addressing Minister of Aviation Mikhail Khrunichev, he asked, "Is this type of fighter plane really Lavochkin's original design? It isn't just a copy of a foreign model?" Turning to Minister of Armaments Dmitrii Ustinov: "Simonov is a very capable weapons designer." (The reference was to the head designer of one of our arms plants, Sergei Simonov.) "But why so little about our artillery designers in the Urals? Our precision industry is falling behind: measuring instruments and so on. Progress here should be encouraged. The Swiss still have a monopoly here. How are we doing with our cotton gins?

"We heard some talk here about America—is it going ahead with locomotive production? Listening, you'd think we'd done a thorough study of America and know the country well. Of course, that's wrong."

When a nomination appeared unconvincing at one of the meetings, Stalin asked (I think the question was addressed to Minister Kaftanov), "Which do you think is more important—the Nobel Prize or the Stalin Prize?"

Kaftanov hastened to reply that it was the Stalin Prize, of course.

"In that case," Stalin said, "nominations for that prize must be well founded. We're not dispensing charity here. We are judging on the basis of merit."

On the whole, however, he was liberal with prizes. At one of the discussions he was asked what to do about People's Artist Aleksei Dikii, who had been nominated simultaneously for two prizes—for his roles in the Malyi Theater production of *A Hardy Muscovite* and in the movie *The Third Blow.* Stalin replied, "Well, what of it? He's earned both. So he deserves them."

It was at this meeting that the question arose about awarding a first prize to Academician Trofim Lysenko for his book *Agrobiology.* In this connection, the country's leadership and Politburo would soon be embroiled in stormy events that were of great significance for everyone, myself included.

CHAPTER SIX

Zhdanov's Death

AT THE MARCH MEETING of the Politburo, some of those present spoke up cautiously against Lysenko. But when the president of the USSR Academy of Sciences, Aleksandr Nesmeianov, ventured a remark in that vein, Stalin stopped him short with a sarcastic reply.[1] He then spoke at length about Lysenko's merits. After reading aloud—and in full—some report on Lysenko's work with branched wheat, he went on:

"Just think, an ear of regular wheat has 30 to 40 seeds, while the branched kind has 150 to 200. What an increase in our grain resources if we could put branched wheat into production! Lysenko is working on that not as a peasant but as a scientist. Branched wheat used to be grown in America and Canada, but it died out. If Lysenko manages to develop this new strain, it would be a great achievement. So far, in his experiments and those of the Georgian plant breeders, the wheat has gone bad. We must watch this project and protect it. At one of our agricultural exhibits, someone tried to steal an ear of branched wheat."

It may seem strange: What did biology have to do with the struggle for power within the Politburo? The events that were connected with this question took a strange and most dramatic turn—and ended with Zhdanov's death.

At all the CC meetings I attended, Zhdanov was always very reserved and cautious. That was fully understandable. Since 1944, when he began

his work with the CC, he had been responsible for innumerable initia-
tives on major ideological problems. His speeches, reports, and talks on
philosophy, literature, art, and international affairs enhanced his popularity within the party and among the people. During that time, Georgii
Malenkov, dismissed as a CC secretary,[2] was more or less inactive within
the USSR Council of Ministers, and Zhdanov was left to supervise all
aspects of the party's program through the CC Secretariat.

Stalin became very close to Zhdanov, and they spent a lot of time together. Stalin thought highly of Zhdanov and gave him one assignment after
another of the most varied kinds. This reduced Beria and Malenkov to a
state of silent irritation. Their hostility to Zhdanov kept growing. With Zhdanov on the rise, they feared the waning or loss of Stalin's trust in them.

The reader will forgive my unwitting mistakes and misconceptions if
I try to re-create Beria's state of mind in the postwar period: the fear, the
constant, nagging, haunting fear, of Stalin. What does Stalin think of him?
Would some unknown band of Stalin's new praetorian guard burst into
his apartment on Sadovo-Kudrinskaia Street on some pitch-black night?
Wasn't that what had happened to his predecessors—Iagoda,[3] Ezhov, and
Abakumov?[4]

Why does Stalin look at him so intently of late? Why, on several occasions, did he pass him over, not invite him to dinner? Because of some
machinations against him by Zhdanov or Voznesenskii? Or both? In recent
years, Voznesenskii has had an inordinately rapid rise. Stalin has given
him enormous power on economic problems. His prestige is unassailable.
Zhdanov has become Stalin's intimate. He is Stalin's principal counselor
on all ideological questions. Stalin spends all his free time with Zhdanov.

The two most influential members of the Politburo, as well as its most
educated Marxists—Molotov and Voznesenskii—held Zhdanov in high
esteem. Beria and Malenkov, therefore, were clearly bent on using any
and all means to undermine Stalin's trust in Zhdanov, discredit him in
some fashion, and put an end to his role as first secretary of the Central
Committee after Stalin. This required undermining or even destroying
Stalin's trust in Molotov and Voznesenskii. Both Beria and Malenkov kept
a close eye on the situation and did not miss a single opportunity to tip
the scales in their favor.

With Stalin's pathological suspiciousness and his jealous guarding
of his absolute monopoly on power, such opportunities were not hard

to find, all the more so since Zhdanov, Molotov, and Voznesenskii were, from a moral standpoint, the complete opposites of Beria, Malenkov, and Khrushchev. They were men of principle, absorbed in their work and free of any inclination toward factionalism and intrigue.

Zhdanov's brilliant speeches were published in huge editions and broadcast on the radio. Molotov's articles and speeches were collected in many volumes. In 1948, Voznesenskii's work *War Economy of the USSR in the Great Patriotic War* was awarded a Stalin Prize, first class. Molotov and Voznesenskii became academicians. This alone enabled Beria to pour salt on Stalin's sorest wound: Zhdanov wants to be popular; Zhdanov wants to replace you as the party's theoretician; Zhdanov is surrounding himself with "his" people, "Leningraders," and others as well.

I have no doubt that Beria used every opportunity to say the same about Voznesenskii and Molotov—not openly and directly but more subtly, slyly, and perniciously.

Zhdanov was aware of these intrigues and was often angered by them. He would arrive from a meeting "upstairs" extremely worried and distraught. This had an immediate effect on his heart. He would turn deathly pale; he would become agitated, short of breath, and gasp for air while recounting what had transpired upstairs. But with his innate tactfulness he never allowed himself to say anything derogatory about other members of the Politburo.

Then an opportunity arose to strike a blow at Zhdanov from the most unexpected quarter.

Zhdanov was involved with Lysenko and had been grooming his own son, Iurii, for a political career. I met Iurii in the summer of 1947 in Sochi.[5] He impressed me with his good manners and erudition, his feeling for music, and his lively and cheerful disposition. We joined a group of young people on a trip to Ritza, a lovely mountain lake. The seaside smelled of seaweed and oleander. After five years in the army, after the mud, blood, and agony of war, everything before my eyes was wondrously beautiful: the sea, the giant eucalyptus, the vast ravines, the limitless turquoise sky, the tea roses of the most tender hue. One day while I was with that group, we gave a little performance at one of the government dachas. I sang some old Russian songs by Tchaikovsky and Rachmaninov, and Iurii accompanied me on the piano, improvising without the score.

Back in Moscow, after returning from "upstairs," Andrei Zhdanov remarked, "Yesterday Comrade Stalin said to me, 'Why are you hiding your son from me? You really must bring him to me some time and introduce us.'" Soon afterward I saw an announcement of Iurii's appointment to the CC Science Department. Our collaboration progressed from the musical to the professional.

In April 1948 the CC convened a seminar of lecturers from across the union.[6] Several days before the opening of the seminar, Iurii told me he would like to read a paper at the session on the state of Soviet biology, with some criticism of Academician Trofim Lysenko. He asked for my advice—which of Lysenko's assertions to speak to—and showed me a draft of his paper.

I met Lysenko in 1936 while with the CC Science Department, at a time when he was taking his first steps in the field of biology, and the CC staff was helping him, as an innovator, get on with his work. Lysenko was given generous support and publicity as a "practical-minded" man of the people, as opposed to "deskbound scientists out of touch with reality" who busied themselves with "abstract problems." At first, I, too, was inclined to see him as a real phenomenon: what do you know—a simple agronomist, brought up on the plow yet raising fundamental biological problems in his own independent and novel manner!

Lysenko quickly began to attract supporters such as Isai Prezent, Ivan Glushchenko, and Nikolai Nuzhdin, enterprising scientists who sensed that he was gaining favor at the highest levels and that they could safely back him. Lysenko himself was a theoretical know-nothing, incapable of putting his innovative ideas into literate form, and his new cronies couched his ideas—or simply his ordinary agronomic procedures—in conventional, scientific language. They gradually promoted Lysenko's assumptions and conjectures in the mass-circulation papers as "new discoveries," "biological laws," "laws of life," and "Michurinist biology."[7] Lysenko was pronounced a classic in his own lifetime. Lysenko and his circle dismissed all preceding advances in genetics, including the monumental discoveries and theoretical precepts of Gregor Mendel and Thomas Morgan, as idealist notions and bourgeois inventions.

In the developed capitalist countries, classical geneticists were making one great discovery after another. By plumbing deeply into the secrets of the living cell and the laws of heredity, it is possible to develop new strains of agricultural products, increase agricultural yield, and make new

advances in medicine. The Lysenkoists insisted with maniacal dogged-
ness that genes and chromosomes were nonexistent as material particles
in the core of a living cell and as the substrata of heredity. In the most
vulgarized and distorted ways, they cited Lamarck's's[8] well-known theories
on the decisive role of the environment in the evolution of an organism
and on the inheritance of acquired characteristics as the ultimate truth of
biology. Certain agronomic techniques, like the vernalization[9] of seeds and
the pruning of cotton fiber, and Lysenko's highly controversial proposals,
like sowing over unplowed stubble and crossbreeding cattle that produce
milk high in fat with those that produce low-fat milk, were hailed as great
discoveries that would lead to the transformation of agriculture.

Lysenko's "theory" came to monopolize all treatment of the subject
in the press and higher educational institutions. Classical genetics was
anathematized root and branch. Portraits and busts of Lysenko appeared
next to those of Darwin and Timiriazev[10] in all agricultural institutions.
Schools were named after him. And there was more. Lysenko became an
academician, director of the Institute of Genetics of the USSR Academy
of Sciences and president of the Lenin All-Union Academy of Agricultural
Sciences. He was thrice a Stalin Prize laureate. For any and all reasons,
valid or not, he was decorated six—six!—times with the Order of Lenin
and was awarded the Order of Labor of the Red Banner and the Red Star
of a Hero of Socialist Labor. He was elected standing deputy to the USSR
Supreme Soviet. And there was more.

The more outraged a wide spectrum of Soviet biologists and other scientists were over the vulgarizations that Lysenko spouted, the more fren-
ziedly his hangers-on shouted the genius of the newly consecrated pope.
He did not find it necessary, as is accepted in every branch of science, to
back with evidence and data from experiments the ideas he proclaimed.
With a kind of pathological obsession, Lysenko cast suspicion on the whole
Soviet biological establishment. The first to be denounced as idealists,
anti-Darwinists, and bourgeois naturalists were Mendel, Morgan, and
all other classical geneticists. Then one prominent Soviet scientist after
another was included in their company. This went on for three decades.
As a result, Soviet genetics was restrained for a whole era, and socialist
agriculture suffered an incalculable setback.

How and why did this colossal sham, with its enormous cost to socialist society, come about?

The Bolshevik party sees the major source of productivity in the creative power of the masses and supports in every way innovation and initiative from below. Hence, Lenin could extol a mundane event—the decision of the Kazanka workers to contribute their labor without pay on a Saturday—as a "great initiative."[11] He saw in it the seeds of a new, communist attitude toward labor, and he held up the episode as a model and symbol for a whole historical period.

Stalin wanted to follow in Lenin's footsteps. Thus, the biggest modernization campaign to take place in the country—the adoption of a communist attitude to labor—was given the name of an ordinary miner, Aleksei Stakhanov. People like Pasha Angelina,[12] Mariia Demchenko,[13] and Evdokiia and Mariia Vinogradova[14] became prototypes, models of heroic labor in agriculture and the textile industry. This symbolic role was bestowed on Lysenko as well.

Trofim Lysenko began his work as an experimental agronomist in Ukraine, first at the Umanskii School of Horticulture, then at the Belotserkov Plant-Breeding Station and the Odessa Plant-Breeding and Genetics Institute. Khrushchev, who was considered an expert on Ukrainian agriculture, supported and promoted him, and it was Khrushchev's praise of him that apparently put him in Stalin's good graces.

However, there was a radical difference between Lenin's and Stalin's approaches to supporting and popularizing the work of economists, scientists, and innovators. Despite his powerful mind and encyclopedic knowledge, Lenin often emphasized that he was not a "specialist" on this or that question. Depending on the nature of the problem, he forwarded it to the chairman of Gosplan, or Gleb Krzhizhanovskii, Anatolii Lunacharskii, Nikolai Semashko, or some other people's commissar or specialist. Moreover, Lenin valued all positive criticism of his own views on any given subject.

As for Stalin, he was patient and cautious before making up his mind, but once he came to a conclusion, it was cast in granite. Of course, those around him ascribed infallibility to his every word, but still, Stalin did not allow for the slightest hint of any criticism of himself.

Khrushchev was an utter ignoramus. Without consulting anyone or reading anything, he answered the most complicated questions on the basis of intuition and was furious if anyone had the slightest doubt that his views were right. In such cases he was quite vengeful.

All the fakery surrounding Lysenko stemmed from Khrushchev's pretentiousness and was backed up—on the basis of Khrushchev's own reports—by Stalin's unshakable authority. This explains how a young agronomist knowing nearly nothing of the storehouse of knowledge that biology amassed, and having as yet made no contribution whatsoever to agriculture, could suddenly be crowned the pope of "Michurinist biology."

The tragedy was that the entire might of the government and the party supported Lysenko. As president of the Lenin All-Union Academy of Agricultural Sciences (VASKhNIL), Lysenko repeatedly declared that our agricultural establishment was rife with "Morganists-Mendelians" and that membership in the academy should not be decided by elections, as provided for by its charter. He asked the government to appoint members from above, and this was done time and again. Moreover, those appointed to the academy under the banner of "Michurinist science" were people without the necessary scientific credentials or knowledge and sometimes with no connection whatever to the science of agriculture. The newly coined words "anti-Lysenkoism" and "anti-Michurinism" were freely batted about; they became political accusations that led to organizational shakeups in academic institutions.

Before long, Lysenko and his supporters had succeeded in pillorying all Soviet geneticists—Academicians Kol'tsov, Serebrovskii, Mikhail and Boris Zavadovskii, Professor Nikolai Dubinin, Professor Zhebrak, and hundreds of their colleagues. Then the smear campaign was turned against a large group of prominent Soviet plant breeders—Academicians T. N. Konstantinova, P. I. Lisitsina, N. V. Rudnitskii, and many others. Millions of hectares of land were sown with new strains that they developed—wheat, rye, clover, flax, barley, potatoes, and other crops—but each of these breeders objected to this or that aspect of Lysenko's pseudoscientific vulgarizations or to his dictatorial ways. This was enough to stigmatize these outstanding scientists as "Weismannists,"[15] "Morganists," "Mendelians," and "anti-Michurinists," with all the usual consequences.

A number of scientists wrote and spoke to the CC, government, and Stalin about these anomalies and the enormous damage they were inflicting on Soviet science and agriculture, but their efforts were in vain. Any scientist who dared to disagree with any of Lysenko's theories in a lecture or the press immediately came under public censure and was expelled from any editorial position he was holding. And Lysenko's stature rose another rung.

In Lysenko's view, his main critic was the internationally acclaimed Soviet botanist and geneticist, the president of VASKhNIL, Nikolai Vavilov. I met Vavilov in 1935. A scientist of encyclopedic erudition, a brilliant researcher and organizer, Vavilov was the pride of Soviet natural sciences. At many sessions and conferences, I saw how patiently and tactfully he heard out Lysenko's unbelievably pretentious speeches, trying to ferret out something rational from his fantasies.

During the Ezhov terror, Vavilov was arrested and died in prison. A number of other Soviet geneticists and plant breeders also met their demise then. Many were prevented from continuing with their research and university lectures. The more noisily and persistently the campaign against "bourgeois Morganist-Mendelian genetics" went on behalf of Lysenko's "great discoveries," the more Soviet biology fell below world standards, and the greater was the cost to Soviet society.

We consigned the gene to perdition and paid for it with millions of rubles in gold for the purchase of hybrid corn in America that was developed with the aid of classical genetics. We banished Gregor Mendel and his followers from our studies and spent a fortune in hard currency buying thoroughbred cattle raised on Mendel's laws of hereditary characteristics. We disposed of the entire theory of heredity as a bourgeois fabrication, while beyond our borders the same theory laid the basis for increasing the number of chromosomes in a seed, thereby enlarging the yield of grain crops and expanding the raw-materials base for the manufacture of medicines. We paid a heavy price for our backwardness.

Both intuitively and intellectually, we lay workers of the Central Committee's Science Department sensed the absolutely abnormal situation in our biological sciences. It seemed incredible that 99 percent of Soviet scientists—communist and nonparty, young and old—rallied against one innovator. Could everyone be out of step except Lysenko? We applied ourselves to Darwin, Mendel, Morgan, and Michurin; we pored over Soviet tomes on genetics, plant growing, and zoology. We asked Academician Aleksandr Serebrovskii, a professor at Moscow University, to take us through a short course on genetics and laboratory experiments.

We are in a university lab. We count up fruit flies (*Drosophilae*), interbreed them, arrive at various combinations, and clearly see for ourselves that the phenomena of heredity, gene division, and the conditions for permitting or preventing the division of various elements conform to certain established laws. The deeper we delve into the relevant literature, the more we discuss matters with genuine scientists, the more distinctly we see where true science lies and where rank vulgarization is the rule. It is vulgarization clothed in lofty catchphrases: Humankind must actively transform nature instead of adapting passively to it; no more plodding away for a decade over a single variety of grain—we must do it in a single year; and so on.

Yet we were powerless to rein in the know-nothings and back the real rather than the fictitious forces for progress in our science. This continued until Khrushchev's fall. Only then, haltingly, painfully, against the opposition of hardened bureaucrats, did the true face of Lysenkoism begin to emerge and its devastating effects begin to be acknowledged.

I have dwelt on this in such detail because Lysenkoism was not the only pathological episode of the time. It was part and parcel of a whole social phenomenon. It demonstrated the incalculable harm that favoritism did in a planned socialist economy. In a capitalist society, in the final analysis, capital investment is made at the individual's own risk or whim. It results either in personal loss or in personal profit. In an organized society, on the other hand, favoritism has entirely different consequences. The effects of Lysenkoism were as follows: For thirty years, an entire branch of science that was vitally important to the country was placed under an embargo; generation after generation of students, agronomists, and zoologists were raised in disciplines that rested on a fallacious scientific foundation; and to the detriment of the country's livestock and agricultural production, the work of a huge army of breeders and kolkhoz farmers was predicated on agricultural and cattle-raising methods that contravened the scientific principles of agriculture.

Unfortunately, systematic favoritism was in flower not just in certain branches of science. I could name singers who were showered with titles and honors because they were "liked upstairs." I could mention a painter of far from superior talent who stood on the pinnacle of our artistic Parnassus because he had painted someone "upstairs." I could name certain mediocre movie actors who were anointed immortals in their own lifetime because "someone" regarded them as geniuses. In a situation where literature, art, and science are under the direction of a single center, favoritism of this kind becomes extremely damaging to the country's intellectual life.

After these tumultuous years have passed, perhaps some future chronicler will conclude that Khrushchev was the Rasputin[16] of politics and Lysenko the Rasputin of science. But this became clear to everybody only after several five-year plans. At the time I am writing about, Khrushchev was Stalin's all-powerful brother-in-arms, and Lysenko was protected from any and all criticism by virtue of his lofty titles and posts—including the post of deputy chairman of the Union Council of the USSR Supreme Soviet.

As a scholar and a communist, I hold dear the prestige of Soviet science and the dignity of the Soviet Union. With all my being, I longed for the collapse of Lysenkoism, which discredited both our science and my fatherland. That is why I did not hesitate for a minute to back Iurii Zhdanov's plan to come forward at the lecturers' seminar with a critique of Lysenko. I reported to Suslov, head of Agitprop, on the seminar's program.

Iurii Zhdanov spoke as scheduled. His words were a model of tactfulness. His criticisms of Lysenko were couched in strictly scientific terms. The report had a very favorable reception. The next day I got a call from Malenkov: "Please send me the text of Iurii Zhdanov's speech at the lecturers' seminar."

I told Malenkov that the stenographic record would, as usual, be available in a few days; it would have to be transcribed and then corrected by the speaker.

"I'm not phoning just on my own behalf," Malenkov said. "Please understand that the stenographic record must be sent immediately and without any corrections."

I went to Andrei Zhdanov's office and told him of the phone call. He was very upset. "Malenkov is a pretty seasoned fellow. He wouldn't have called you unless the Boss[17] told him to. Send the stenographic record. How could you have permitted such a speech without checking with me? I don't want to complain about Iurii. He is well mannered and very respectful at home, in his family life. But he is a terrible romantic—he gets carried away. He didn't say a thing to me about his speech. He let himself go. But you, an experienced political worker, didn't you see what a speech like that could lead to?"

"Andrei Aleksandrovich," I objected, "after all that has happened, it's time to put an end to this disgrace. All our scientists are up in arms. Our agriculture is suffering tremendous losses. With this Lysenkoist mumbo jumbo we are becoming the laughingstock of real scientists throughout the world, including those who are friendly toward us."

"Oh, you naive soul," said Zhdanov, "do you think you have to prove anything to me? I can see you haven't learned how to keep in touch with reality."

The next evening Zhdanov, Suslov, Iurii, and I were summoned to a meeting of the Politburo in Stalin's office.[18] The first item on the agenda was Iurii's speech. Stalin was morose. As I learned later, he was holding the transcript of the speech in his hands.

Stalin asked, "Has everyone read Zhdanov's report—young Zhdanov's?" We answered yes.

"This is unheard of. Without informing the CC, you scheduled young Zhdanov's report at the lecturers' meeting. Gave Lysenko a dressing down. On what basis? Who allowed it?"

Everyone was silent. It seemed to me that the reply should come from Suslov, as head of Agitprop, to whom I had sent a written account of the seminar's program. But he remained silent. The silence became unbearably oppressive. Then I stood up and said:

"I allowed it, Comrade Stalin."

The room was absolutely still. Stalin stopped abruptly in front of me. I met his severe, searching gaze.

"On what basis? Don't you know that our entire agriculture depends on Lysenko?"

In the long seconds that followed, scenes of scientists and veteran breeders complaining to me about being hounded by the Lysenkoist cabal passed through my mind. I remembered all those reports that exposed the inflated character of Lysenko's "great discoveries" and achievements.

"Comrade Stalin," I said, "you have been wrongly informed about Lysenko's work. I was only recently appointed to Agitprop. But in these few months I have spoken to our leading scientists and breeders. Millions of hectares of land have been sown with strains of wheat, rye, clover, and buckwheat developed by them. Yet all of them have been stigmatized by Lysenko and his followers with the bywords 'Weismannists,' 'Morganists,' and 'anti-Michurinists.'

"The scientists I talked to could not name a single new strain actually developed by Lysenko, not a single major scientific recommendation that is improving our agriculture. I am prepared for any punishment. But I earnestly beseech you to appoint a special commission to look into Lysenko's work. Without a high commission composed of members of the CC, no one will dare decide this question correctly."

I blurted this out in one breath, loudly and passionately.

As a rule, no one ever made speeches in Stalin's office. The most complex questions were dealt with by terse comments of "Yes," "No," "That's right," "Approve," "Look into." No one spoke loudly, either. Stalin himself spoke in a quiet, toneless voice, and others followed suit. My statement came out as a cry from the heart.

Everyone was silent.

Stalin went to his desk, picked up a cigarette, tore off the tip, and emptied the tobacco into his pipe. He did the same with a second cigarette. He sucked on his pipe and slowly walked the length of the conference table. He gave me another long look. Then he spoke very quietly, but I thought I detected a sinister nuance in his tone.

"No, we can't leave this as is. We must appoint a special commission of the CC to look into this business. Those guilty must be punished as an example. Not Iurii Zhdanov, he is still young and inexperienced. We must punish the 'fathers': Zhdanov—he pointed the stem of his pipe at Andrei Aleksandrovich—and Shepilov. We must draw up a comprehensive decision of the CC. We must assemble the scientists and explain everything to them. We must back up Lysenko and debunk our homegrown Morganists."

He went on. "We must forbid Agitprop to be so high-handed. Who gave it the right to decide such questions by itself? By the way, who is head of Agitprop?"

Suslov stood up. "I am, Comrade Stalin."

"Then why are you so quiet? Did you give permission for this speech?"

"No," Suslov replied, "I did not. I didn't deal with this question. I was busy with other matters."

"Come off it, we're all busy with many other things. But we fulfill our assignments and take responsibility for them."

Stalin then named the Politburo members and other officials who were to form a commission headed by Malenkov.

Andrei Zhdanov did not utter a word during the whole meeting. But from all indications the episode had a traumatic effect on him. I don't know what transpired on the night after the session. But at noon the next day he called me in. He was pallid and puffy-eyed and had to space out his words with long pauses: he was suffering from angina pectoris, and any undue stress aggravated his asthmatic spasms. I was stunned that he did not tax me with a single serious misdeed. He only said with great compassion and even sympathy, "You behaved very carelessly last night. It could have ended tragically for you, and not only you. Now you must start everything from scratch."

At the time, I did not know what that meant.

"As for me," he continued, "I may have to go somewhere for a rest cure. Looks like my heart is acting up."

I don't know which springs and cogs of the great machine known as the leadership were set in motion during the following weeks. There were rumors that Andrei Zhdanov would be transferred to "other work" and that Malenkov would again head the Secretariat. All well-informed persons were sure that Beria and Malenkov would take advantage of the "Lysenko affair" to try to remove Zhdanov from power. We all waited for the decision of the commission that was investigating and for something more as well—exactly what, we did not know.

But this time, to everyone's surprise, nothing terrible happened. The decision in the Lysenko affair did not provide for any administrative measures against Zhdanov or me. Whether Zhdanov had a heart-to-heart talk with Stalin and was able to persuade him of something or other, whether the fervor and conviction of my outburst at the meeting had some lasting effect, whether Stalin stayed his hand in view of Zhdanov's rapidly worsening condition, or whether Stalin had just then learned that Iurii Zhdanov was to be his son-in-law, the husband of his only daughter, Svetlana—none of this do I know. I only know that on July 10 Iurii sent Stalin a letter in which he said that he had "made a number of serious mistakes" in his speech at the lecturers' seminar. At the same time he repeated that he "disagreed with several of Academician Lysenko's theoretical positions." A month later this letter was published in *Pravda*. Subsequently, Iurii showed me a letter from Stalin summarily condemning him as a "Mendelian-Morganist."

In accordance with the decision of the Central Committee, a well-attended conference of VASKhNIL was convened on July 31, 1948. Lysenko read a paper "On the Situation in the Biological Sciences." All the discoveries of modern biology, the great advances in unlocking the mysteries of the living cell that had laid the basis for a revolution in agricultural science, all this Lysenko dismissed as "metaphysics" and "idealism." To challenge anything he said was useless and impossible. Lysenko was authorized to announce at the meeting that the party CC had read and endorsed his report. After that, who would have dared question anything he said?

The session set off yet another smear campaign against Academicians Nikolai Kol'tsov, Mikhail Zavadovskii, Ivan Shmal'gauzen, Petr Zhukovskii, and Aleksandr Serebrovskii, Professors Anton Zhebrak and Sos Alikhanian, and many other scientists. Lumped together with them, of course, was a whole army of plant breeders, growers, and stock breeders who were pressing on with their important work under the most difficult circumstances, developing new high-yield strains and new breeds of cattle, raising the productivity of agriculture and animal husbandry on the basis of those very laws of classical genetics that had just been crucified yet again on the VASKhNIL cross.

Once again Lysenko was anointed—this time by an entire scientific conclave—as a living classic. It took eight long years before Khrushchev could be persuaded, and then with great difficulty, to dismiss Lysenko as president of VASKhNIL on the pretext that he was a weak administrator and would do better to concentrate on his research.

Zhdanov's serious condition—hypertension, arteriosclerosis, angina pectoris, and congestive heart failure—kept worsening. The enormous load of work, the frequent and lengthy night sessions and dinners at Stalin's dacha, and the constant stress all had an aggravating effect. He gasped while speaking, and his face came out in red spots. He paused between sentences and inhaled deeply to suck in some air.

One sunny morning, he called me into his office and said, "I've been ordered to go on a rest cure. I won't be all that far from Moscow, in Valdai.[19] They tell me the air there is easier to breathe. Well, we'll see."

He went on. "You must report to me regularly on anything of consequence, what's going on in our ideological work. I don't plan to put everything aside, and I don't think I'll be gone for long. Phone me. My assistants will be visiting me on a regular basis, so you can send your information with them."

A couple of times Zhdanov phoned me from Valdai to ask "What's new?" "Remember," he said, "I haven't dropped into oblivion. Inform me in more detail about everything."

In July 1948 the administration of the CC was reorganized. The Bureau of Propaganda and Agitation was made into a department. Stalin said the word "bureau" was more appropriate for the economic field. Agitprop's functions and area of responsibility remained the same—that is, limitless. I was named director.

This work literally took up my days and nights. Two rooms in a dacha in Serebriannyi Bor were placed at my disposal, and here I lived with my family during the summer. The air smelled sweetly of pine resin and grasses. Somewhere in the bushes, a nightingale sang all night long in the spring. But for me there was no time to enjoy the indescribable charms of nature. I would arrive at the dacha at dawn, sometimes even later. After a few hours of heavy sleep, often with the aid of sleeping pills, I would wake up still tired and try to perk up by taking a swim in the Moscow River. But the work went on, wearing me out completely.

With Zhdanov ill, Malenkov was reappointed head of the CC Secretariat. His fondest wish was thus realized. In giving orders, especially those he received from Stalin, Malenkov would set the most impossible deadlines. No sooner did Stalin express some wish than the whole country and the entire party would be shaken up, and all the levers of the government and the party would be shifted to full speed ahead. At his next meeting with the Boss, Malenkov would announce, "Comrade Stalin, your orders have been carried out." Or the same declaration would appear in the press in the form of a report addressed to the leader that was written by those responsible for carrying out these orders. Reports of this kind were sent to all the newspapers.

Overcoming all obstacles, Malenkov demanded the immediate implementation of Stalin's instructions. Sometimes his haste was detrimental to the matter at hand. But Malenkov gained in power and stature as the preeminent executor of Stalin's will.

As for me, for four years I had fought in the war under difficult front-line conditions. Then came the all-consuming night job at *Pravda*. Now the superhuman demands of my work at Agitprop. The work was accompanied by a continuous cycle of frenzy, bewilderment, prodding, and warnings. I knew instinctively that given the spit-and-polish style that Malenkov favored, I was not the best choice to be head of Agitprop. Nonetheless, every reprimand I received had a traumatic effect.

Finally, I suppose, my soul rebelled. One day, returning to my office from Malenkov's on the fifth floor, I fainted in the corridor. What happened later I remember only dimly. I came to in the Kremlin hospital.

After that, wearisome days in the solemn stillness of the hospital room. The diagnosis: blockage of the blood supply to the brain caused by nervous exhaustion. My intellectual motor, however, continued with its feverish work. My mind seethed with thoughts of incomplete publication work, the study of foreign languages in schools, plans for a new series of posters, deficiencies in the courses on political economy in universities, falling behind in the international soccer competition, the need to increase the production of newsprint, the selection of new students for the Academy of Social Sciences, and a hundred other subjects.

In some cases, draft decrees had to be submitted to the CC; in others, memos had to be sent around; still others required assistance from the Council of Ministers. Everything was important; everything was urgent. And here I was, prone in bed. The doctors' orders: complete rest. What rest? I was dying to phone someone, call someone to my room, write someone a note. The doctors kept coming in and trying to sever my remaining links with the outside world. Zhdanov was unavailable, and with my stupid illness, I was letting everyone down.

The news about Zhdanov was alarming: serious attacks of angina pectoris and progressive asthma were causing spells of suffocation.

At the end of August, the Politburo decided to have Voznesenskii call on the patient in Valdai. On the morning of August 31, Zhdanov got up, shaved, read the newspapers, and went through his mail. "How good I feel today," he said to those around him. "I haven't felt like this for a long time." At 3:55 P.M., Zhdanov was no more. The medical commission concluded that death was caused by paralysis of the damaged heart and severe edema of the lungs. Voznesenskii arrived to see his brother-in-arms on his deathbed.

Still hospitalized, I was not allowed to accompany Zhdanov to his final resting place.

At a CC plenum after the Nineteenth Party Congress, Stalin declared emotionally and with great conviction that Zhdanov had been murdered by his doctors: they allegedly reached a deliberately false diagnosis and followed a purposely improper course of treatment. These, of course, were the ravings of a sick mind. Yet I would not be at all surprised if some day someone in Beria's diabolical crew revealed that it was Beria who saw to it that Zhdanov's life came to a premature end during his stay in Valdai.

A final word on Andrei Aleksandrovich Zhdanov:

I believe that history will give this talented Bolshevik-idealist his rightful due for his contributions to the cause of the great proletarian revolution. But it will not remove from the scales the fact that Zhdanov's name was linked with a whole series of undemocratic measures and declarations in the fields of literature, theater, cinema, music, and other ideological spheres.

Zhdanov did much to bolster both the principles of revolutionary Marxism and Leninist party spirit and populism in various areas of intellectual creativity. But he worked just as assiduously to bring into line aspects of creativity that should not and cannot be brought into line, whose standardization, in fact, violates the principles of Marxism-Leninism. True, the dictatorial orders of Joseph Stalin, whom Zhdanov and all of us unquestioningly obeyed, loomed over all the demands for uniformity. But that does not alter the substance of the measures taken, nor the question of historical responsibility.

CHAPTER SEVEN

The Tragic Fate of Nikolai Voznesenskii

ON JANUARY 21, 1949, the twenty-fifth anniversary of Lenin's death, the traditional solemn memorial meeting was held at the Bolshoi Theater. I was invited to be on the proscenium as a member of the ceremonial presidium, the first time I was ever asked to attend in such an exalted capacity. As usual, members of the CC Politburo gathered to the right of the stage, behind the government box, and the rest of us in the presidium—heads of the Moscow Party Committee and Marshals Budennyi, Vasilevskii, and Meretskov—gathered to the left of the stage, behind the management box.

At 6:50 P.M. the presidium comes on stage. The house erupts in applause for Stalin. He is in his generalissimo's uniform. Squinting in the glare of the klieg lights, Stalin joins in the applause—and is followed by those around him—in an apparent greeting to those in the hall. He starts to sit down, but the hall still rocks with applause, and he rises from his chair and continues to clap slowly. Then, folding his hands across his stomach, he shifts his weight ducklike from foot to foot, waiting for the storm to subside.

Finally, vigorously using the bell, the chairman, Nikolai Shvernik, manages to restore quiet. Stalin sits. The presidium and the audience follow suit. Petr Pospelov takes the floor.

Although Pospelov's speech is officially devoted to Lenin, Lenin is the subject of only a few generalizations. The substance of the address centers on the tenets that Pospelov solemnly proclaimed at the outset of his speech:

"The historic victories of socialism around the globe are victories we owe above all to the fact that the banner of Leninism was raised aloft by Lenin's great comrade-in-arms and successor to his work, the wise leader of the party and the people, Comrade Stalin!

"Stalin formulated a coherent and complete doctrine on the nature of the socialist state, and with this doctrine he empowered the party and the people. . . .

"Stalin provided the theoretical basis of socialist industrialization for our country, its means and methods. . . .

"Stalin provided the theory of the collectivization of agriculture. He was the founder and organizer of the kolkhoz system."

(For the text of Pospelov's speech, see *Pravda,* January 22, 1949.)

It was in this vein that we delivered all our speeches and wrote all our articles in those days. The Russian language lacked enough superlatives to do justice to Stalin's greatness and genius, and all our orators and writers outdid themselves coining new encomiums.

As a speaker, Pospelov had always been boring, tedious, and flat. All his articles and speeches were nothing more than a string of citations, sometimes with and sometimes without quotation marks, and it would never have occurred to him to try to put these canonical, cast-iron clichés into plain speech. As he droned on, an air of dejection, like a persistent, unabating autumn rain, settled on the hall. It seemed as though not only people in the audience but Pospelov himself, who was spouting phrase after phrase from a prepared text, were dozing off. However, Stalin and the rest of the presidium maintained the stoniest front.

Suddenly, for no apparent reason, as though starting from an unexpected jolt, Pospelov unbuttoned the shirt collar above his Adam's apple with one hand and began to bark loudly in a threatening tone. The bark rose to a full-throated crescendo.

"As the mastermind inspirer and organizer of the universal-historic victory over fascism," he bawled, "there appeared the wise leader and teacher of the party and people, the strategic genius of the proletariat, the greatest military commander of all time and all peoples, Comrade Stalin!"

The hall exploded with applause.

People in the know said that Pospelov always had his texts marked with special signs telling him when to go into his ecstatic bark. While remaining outwardly impassive Stalin at times would lean over to Molotov or Voroshilov to whisper, "You see? Pospelov's getting angry. That means he'll now start talking about the great Stalin."

When the strictly allotted time for some speaker began to run out but the conclusion seemed nowhere near, Stalin would take out his gold Longines pocket watch, glance at the time, then at the speaker, and put his watch back in his pocket. A tremor of alarm would run the length of the presidium table like an electric shock. Glowering looks would be cast at the speaker and cautious, guilty ones at Stalin. Every speaker would know what that meant.

This time, however, when the speech was over and the Politburo was sitting down for dinner and awaiting the performance to follow, Pospelov was invited over to the table, and Stalin graciously raised a toast to his health.

That is how I remember the beginning of 1949. The political situation was complex and contradictory. New popular democratic states were arising on the crest of the mighty antifascist, anti-imperialist national-liberation struggle. The capitalist encirclement of the Soviet Union had collapsed. Of the *cordon sanitaire*[1] around our country, not a trace was left. In the countries of eastern and southeastern Europe a mighty coalition of socialist nations was coming into existence. In ancient Asia, the home of more than half of humankind, the forces of socialism scored a momentous victory with the establishment of the People's Republic of China. By 1948 the Soviet Union had not only rebuilt the industrial enterprises destroyed in the war but raised the gross industrial output 18 percent above the prewar level.

Agricultural production had also come close to prewar figures. However, compared to industry, agriculture was moving forward very slowly and was clearly lagging behind the country's needs.

Monetary reform took place in December 1947. Rationing of food and goods was abolished. The government adopted a policy of annually lowering the prices on the most essential commodities, earning citizens' heartfelt gratitude. In March 1949 a scheduled decrease in prices gave the population a savings of forty-eight billion rubles over the period of a year.

In May the Presidium of the Supreme Soviet adopted the decree "On the Abolition of Capital Punishment."

These trends, however, did not last long. It was then that the revolting and often openly anti-Semitic campaign against "cosmopolitanism" was born. The campaign was presaged by an article that took up four full columns of the January 28, 1949, issue of *Pravda:* "On a Certain Unpatriotic Group of Theater Critics." To this day, I do not know how and why the idea of this disgraceful campaign originated. But there can be no doubt that it did our party and country enormous harm.

At this time, Stalin was pretty much a recluse. He never showed up at construction sites, factories, or kolkhozes. He seldom received anyone. But thanks to the extensive information-gathering system run by the CC and the government, he was well informed of the situation in the country and abroad. Calmly, unhurriedly, and carefully he weighed the pros and cons of outstanding questions, settled issues ripe for decision, and put forward new goals and ideas. The entire administration of the great state functioned steadily and smoothly. Behind his back, however, forces seeking to draw closer to the levers of power and preparing for his hour of death were secretly active. They needed to exclude the possibility of surprises, to push aside—or, even better, eliminate—those who stood in their way.

After Zhdanov's death, they saw their main obstacle in the person of Nikolai Voznesenskii. This was a talented young man, well grounded in Marxism and bursting with energy. He had been close to Zhdanov and Molotov. There were times when Stalin seemed to favor him above everyone else. That was enough reason to set the blades of Beria's infernal machine against him.

Nikolai Alekseevich Voznesenskii was born in 1903 in the village of Teploe in Tula province. His father, a forester, died when the boy was thirteen, so Nikolai had to start earning a living at an early age. He dropped out of school, apprenticed himself to a carpenter, then got a job in a printing shop. In 1917 he organized a communist circle in his village, and at age sixteen he joined the communist party. He received his early party education at the renowned Sverdlov Communist University, where he attended lectures by Joseph Stalin, Feliks Dzerzhinskii, Anatolii Lunacharskii, and Valerian Kuibyshev, among others. In 1931 he graduated from the Institute of Red Professors, and his work for the state, the party, and science began.

In 1935, Voznesenskii was appointed chairman of the Leningrad Planning Commission, from 1938 he was chairman of Gosplan, and from 1939 he took on the added post of deputy chairman of the Council of People's Commissars. In 1934, at the Seventeenth Party Congress, he was elected to the Soviet Control Commission, and at the Eighteenth Congress to the CC. On the eve of the war he was elected a candidate member of the CC Politburo, and in 1947 a full member of the Politburo.

Despite his enormous load of responsibilities in Gosplan, the Council of Ministers, and the State Defense Committee, Voznesenskii found time to pursue his scholarly work. A highly educated Marxist, he gave priority to the scientific and technical measures required for putting state planning into effect. He promoted the concept of a general plan of economic development timed over several five-year plans. He stood for a balanced planning method and worked resolutely to make sure that the economy developed on a rational basis. As far back as the early 1930s he came out with a series of articles in which he tried to determine the fundamental laws of Soviet economic development, and in later years he continued working on this problem. The economic laws that his research uncovered were applied to the practical aspects of his planning projects. In 1935 he was awarded a doctor of economic sciences degree, and in 1943 he was elected to the USSR Academy of Sciences.

Voznesenskii's book *War Economy of the USSR in the Great Patriotic War* came out in 1947, and it was reliably reported that Stalin went over the manuscript and penciled in certain inserts and corrections. The book was awarded a Stalin Prize, first class. Voznesenskii donated the two hundred thousand rubles that came with the prize for the maintenance of orphanages for the children of soldiers, partisans, and workers who were killed by the Nazis during the occupation.

This did not prevent Stalin from turning against the book a year later. Voznesenskii by now was in prison awaiting his final hours. The book was withdrawn from circulation as anti-Marxist and hostile to the Soviet system. A year after that, when the time came for the next round of Stalin Prizes, Stalin said, "We have a proposal here for a prize to Professor Liashchenko[2] for his *History of the National Economy*. I'm for it. His book is much more solid and interesting than that book by"—snapping his fingers—"what's his name?"

"Voznesenskii," came several promptings.

"Yes, yes, Voznesenskii."

Voznesenskii's book was favorably received by party propagandists, scholars, and teachers. Nonetheless, as I was told several years later, it was the publication of this book that gave Beria and his collaborators their chance to move against him. By this time Stalin's suspiciousness had reached an acutely pathological stage and was accompanied by a hypertrophic degree of conceit. Only he could make new proposals and put forward new ideas; others could and should only propagandize, popularize, and systematize these ideas.

Beria went to work on these weaknesses. He used every opportunity to pour salt on Stalin's wounds with a remark, a comment, a whisper: Voznesenskii was emerging as a leader; his book was being pushed as though it would take the place of Stalin's *Problems of Leninism;* Voznesenskii was getting big-headed enough to imagine himself as head of government; without Stalin or the Politburo's knowledge Voznesenskii had recently cut back on existing plans for economic development; Voznesenskii was placing himself at the center of a new group of Leningrad workers.

Soon enough, Beria and Kaganovich came up with "evidence" of Voznesenskii's alleged abuse of power as chairman of Gosplan. As usual, they found an informer, a false witness. This time the role fell to a Gosplan staffer, Boris Sukharevskii. At one time Sukharevskii was a researcher in the Economic Institute of the Academy of Sciences. At the outbreak of war in June 1941, every decent, committed, and patriotic member of the academy, both communist and nonparty, volunteered for the front. They included people getting on in years, with party service going back to prerevolutionary times, people maimed in the Civil War, people with advanced scientific degrees and in high positions, among them the prominent expert on international relations Modest Rubinshtein, the old Bolshevik writer Mikhail Mashkevich, the historian Nikolai Rubinshtein, and many others. Boris Sukharevskii, an athlete, a tennis player, and the youngest of the lot, announced that he could not go to the front—primarily for health reasons, but also because, as a specialist, he could join the army only as a "military planner."

Those were turbulent days for us. Before we left for the front, we did not have time to look into the behavior of this creature. Sukharevskii found a comfortable niche in Gosplan and was fully beholden to Voznesenskii for his rapid ascent up the ministerial ladder. But now, at a nod from

Beria, there was an opportunity for him to step forward as Voznesenskii's denouncer and claim his thirty pieces of silver. Sukharevskii carried out his Judas mission flawlessly. After that, brilliant schemer that he was, Beria was able to heap one accusation on top of another, each more fantastic than the last.

Some kind of examining commission came up with the allegation that several documents classified as secret were missing from Gosplan's voluminous files. This was considered a state crime, and Voznesenskii was charged with it. An industrial fair of the Russian Federation was organized in Leningrad, and this was portrayed to Stalin as a conspiracy against the party leadership and the Soviet Union. According to this version, Aleksei Kuznetsov, a secretary of the party CC; Mikhail Rodionov, chairman of the RSFSR Council of Ministers; and many others joined Voznesenskii, a former secretary of the Leningrad oblast and city Party Committees, in a plot to use the fair as a cover for prying Leningrad loose from the USSR.

On March 5, 1949, abruptly and without any review of the charges against him, Voznesenskii was relieved of all his posts. A few days later he was expelled from the Politburo and then from the CC. He wrote a letter to Stalin, swearing that he had always been loyal to the party and was not guilty of anything. There was no reply. He tried to talk to Stalin, if only on the phone, but Stalin proved unreachable. As a doctor of economic sciences and an academician, he asked to be allowed to work on research in academy institutions. The request was shelved.

Voznesenskii, however, did not give up. Right after being fired, he applied himself to research. His seven months of forced unemployment became seven months of intensive work on a major theoretical treatise, *The Political Economy of Communism,* which was 822 typewritten pages in length. "This work," he said, "is my credo as a scholar and a communist."

All the while, Beria and Abakumov were feverishly at work concocting the components of what later became known as the Leningrad affair. Not even a diseased mind could invent anything more ridiculous or fantastic. Here we had sabotage, espionage, betrayal of the country, and other ravings spun out of thin air. Nonetheless, it was on the basis of these fabrications that Voznesenskii was arrested.

It happened in the late autumn of 1949. Voznesenskii, after working hard all day, stretched out on the couch. There was a ring at the front door, unfamiliar voices in the hallway. Men in Ministry of State Security (MGB) uniforms entered the room and proceeded to search for incriminating evidence. The senior one sat down at the desk and began to rifle through the drawers. He went through personal letters, typescripts of the book, decorations and medals, and tossed them all on the floor.

Then the door slammed shut on Nikolai Voznesenskii for good.

Just the day before, he had said, "I believe in the fairness of the Central Committee." Yes, with every fiber of his being he was devoted to the party, the people, the country, and the noble ideals of communism.

Arrested along with Voznesenskii were Aleksei Kuznetsov and Mikhail Rodionov, Petr Popkov, who was secretary of the Leningrad oblast Party Committee, Voznesenskii's brother, Aleksandr, who was the RSFSR minister of enlightenment, and many other party and government officials. Leningrad found itself with new party leaders, Vasilii Andrianov and Frol Kozlov, and was the object of a devastating purge. The proud name "Leningrader" was transformed into political invective. All of the city's official personnel fell under suspicion. The Leningrad affair gave rise to tidal waves of human misery.

Beria and his cohort appeared to have fully achieved their objectives. Zhdanov was no more. Voznesenskii was in solitary confinement, isolated from the outside world. But that was only the outward picture. In fact, the tragedy was only in its first act. The scenario that the Beria people devised for this new "conspiracy" continued to develop and expand because they had two objectives in mind.

The first was to have Voznesenskii executed by inflating the affair to fantastic proportions. To achieve that, they had to convince Stalin that the MGB had uncovered a gigantic plot that involved virtually the entire Leningrad party organization and that was headed by top executives of the Politburo and Council of Ministers (Voznesenskii), the Central Committee (Kuznetsov), the government of the Russian Federation (Rodionov), the secretaries of the Leningrad oblast (Popkov) and city committees (Iakov Kapustin and G. Badaev), and many others. Beria, Abakumov, and their cohort could then present themselves to Stalin as the "country's saviors" and reap the appropriate honors and rewards.

The second objective was to discredit Zhdanov in his grave. They had to prove retroactively that the strands of the conspiracy led to Zhdanov, who as the former longtime head of the Leningrad party organization, had "trained" the city's plotters and "placed" them in key positions in Moscow and the Russian republic. The purpose here was to raise Beria's status in the Politburo as Stalin's most faithful servant.

So the Voznesenskii-Leningrad affair snowballed to incredible size. More and more innocent people who were branded as conspirators filled prisons in Leningrad and Moscow. Leningrad underwent a massive purge. Some years later, with Stalin dead, I was told that he had insisted at the time on harsher measures to force those arrested to "confess" and implicate others. It was then that the practice of keeping prisoners handcuffed was introduced; Kuznetsov's wife was kept handcuffed for months in prison to make her provide the necessary evidence. The stage managers of the Voznesenskii affair wanted to make it seem as though he had his "supporters" and "followers" everywhere, and this led to the "affair" of the journal *Bolshevik* and Agitprop itself.

I was favorably impressed by Voznesenskii's scholarly articles during the 1930s, although I never knew him well. At the beginning of 1941, he called in several senior members of the Economic Institute of the Academy of Sciences, myself included, and offered us positions in Gosplan. Whereas some of us accepted, I told Voznesenskii I was quite satisfied with my current position and felt that I would be more useful to the party pursuing my scholarly work. He did not insist. While working for *Pravda* after returning from the front, I published a number of theoretical and propaganda articles that seemed to go over well with the intelligentsia. In 1946, Voznesenskii asked me to meet with him at Gosplan. He praised my articles and offered to take me on as deputy chairman of Gosplan and head of its Central Statistical Bureau. "You'll have available to you all of the state's statistical records. You'll be free to write all the scholarly works you please. This new position will make it easier for you to do your research, and all your work will have a solid statistical basis." Once again I cited my reasons against a transfer to Gosplan. With the CC's support, I won out.

Finally, when Voznesenskii and his Gosplan staff got down to work on the basic problems of the general plan for the country's economic development for the next twenty years, he invited me as an economist and head of CC Agitprop to one of the conferences on the plan.

That sums up my contacts with Voznesenskii during all those years.

Nevertheless, the directors of the conspiracy extravaganza decided for some reason to include me among the scholars and economists whom they portrayed as Voznesenskii's supporters and followers. Soon enough, storm clouds began to gather around my head.

In Petr Fedoseev, then editor of *Bolshevik,* Beria and Malenkov found a tool for implementing their plans. The journal gave wide publicity to Voznesenskii's book *War Economy.* That, of course, was only natural. The work was indeed praiseworthy. As noted above, everyone knew that the book had received Stalin's stamp of approval and a Stalin Prize, first class. But now Voznesenskii had been proclaimed a state criminal, and any good word about his book became criminal in intent. Fedoseev, to save his own skin, took on the shameful role of slanderer and informer.

With help from Leonid Il'ichev, who in addition to being my deputy at Agitprop, was on the editorial staff of *Bolshevik,* Fedoseev began sending patently false denunciations to the CC alleging the existence of a "Voznesenskii school" among the economists on his journal's staff and within Agitprop. His slanderous accusations covered a large group of academicians, corresponding members of the academy, and professors—Konstantin Ostrovitianov, Lev Gatovskii, Gennadii Sorokin, Ivan Kuzminov, Filipp Koshelev, me, and others; all of us were apparently chosen simply because we were economists.

In his groveling zeal to ingratiate himself and please, Fedoseev declared at a lecturers' seminar convened by CC Agitprop that the classics of Marxism-Leninism were being treated as supplementary material and Voznesenskii's book as fundamental; that the seminar's entire tone was set by Academician Ostrovitianov, a "supporter" of Voznesenskii; that the chapters on economic planning in the books *Political Literacy* and *Our Native Land* "exaggerated the role of Gosplan" in a bow to Voznesenskii—even though both chapters were written by the renowned party writer Viacheslav Karpinskii, a member of the All-Union Communist Party (Bolshevik), or VKP(b), since 1898. Today all this might look like trivia and nonsense. But at that time, accusations of this kind were enough to send people to the block.

Did Fedoseev know that his denunciations were absolute lies from beginning to end? Not only did he know that he concocted these lies, but he was fully aware that the more embellished the lie, the larger his payment would be for his Judas-like service. Did Fedoseev know that his denunciations would cost many renowned Soviet economists their heads, people who were completely innocent? Yes, he knew. Yet he did so to save himself and get one of the juicier morsels from Beria's table.

Whether for the sake of his philosophy or at the suggestion of Beria's department, Khrushchev subsequently picked out this individual. Fedoseev was made a member of the party CC, vice president of the Academy of Sciences, and part of Khrushchev's brain trust. He began instructing personnel on philosophy, ethics, and the moral principles of communism. Was the immortal Nekrasov[3] anticipating this future academician when he wrote in a lullaby, "A high official you may seem to be, but a scoundrel you remain"? Given the conditions and customs of the time, any attempt to reveal the truth was bound to fail. Whatever the price, everything had to conform to the preset scenario.

When I learned of the case being prepared against me, I called on Malenkov, then head of the CC Secretariat, and said, "Georgii Maksimilianovich, you know my record. I am a scholar. I left the Academy of Sciences for the front. My fondest wish is to return to scholarly work. But I'm a party member and have no right to make that decision. I was assigned to *Pravda*. Then I was made head of CC Agitprop. I grant that I may have been the wrong man for the job—I won't go into the reasons why. So let me go in peace. Believe me, I'm not hanging on to my present position. I'd be happy to go back to scholarly work. But why trump up charges for things I never did?"

Malenkov gazed at me and said in a calm, even good-natured tone, "We've been after you for a long time. We never could make it stick. But now you won't get away." Clenching his fist, he depicted a fish wriggling on a hook. I felt as though I were really dangling on a line, the hook in my throat, and any effort on my part would only make the hook sink in deeper.

I was dismayed: this was rank injustice. But even more distressing was the realization that this particular episode was casting a new light on something great and important, something that had always been sacred to me. In those days, I conceived of everything associated with the party leadership, the Central Committee, and the CC organization in the most idealistic terms, in the best sense. In my eyes, every member of the Politburo personified the most honorable and exalted characteristics and moral and political principles. Every decision of the CC, every measure taken by the CC administration, I accepted as holy writ. No critical judgments were possible. Every step taken and every word spoken by the party and government leadership served the truth, the great truth of communism. No personal or unseemly—to say nothing of selfish—motives were ever involved.

Then why did Malenkov say to me, "We've been after you for a long time. . . . Now you won't get away"? How vile! After all, Malenkov knew full well that my conscience was clear. I had never done anything reprehensible. Why was this falsehood being tolerated? How could something like this be going on within the Central Committee?

Actually, the truth here was of no interest to anybody. Everything had been prearranged. Those in charge of this political intrigue had to annihilate Voznesenskii; this was accomplished. Now, as an auxiliary operation, they had to have me expelled from the CC; this was to be done under any and all circumstances and at whatever price. Any resistance on my part would only hasten my doom.

On July 13, 1949, the CC Politburo announced its decision "On the Journal *Bolshevik*." There were two charges against me.

The first read: "Note that Comrade Shepilov, as head of the Bureau of Propaganda and Agitation of the CC of the VKP(b), failed to exercise adequate control over the journal *Bolshevik*."

The second: "Point out to Comrade Shepilov that he committed a gross error in authorizing the Bureau of Propaganda and Agitation of the CC of the VKP(b) to recommend the works of N. Voznesenskii as textbooks for use by secretaries of regional party committees and by propagandists. Cancel these instructions as erroneous."

It was clear to everyone that my days within the CC organization were numbered. Sure enough, I was shortly dismissed from my Agitprop post. After that—days, weeks, months, of tense, agonizing waiting.

Those were harsh times. In the wake of the glorious wartime victory, the country was going through another enormous purge for no good reason. All night long the Black Marias prowled the streets and courtyards. People who had only recently been released from concentration camps, where they had survived for ten years after 1937, were arrested all over again, as were people who had at any time belonged to one or another opposition group but had somehow escaped arrest in 1937–38, and relatives of "enemies of the people" who had also for some reason remained at liberty. Others were arrested for no apparent cause.

Seven years later, I met one of my university classmates. Considerably older than I, he had joined the party in 1917 and had fought in the Civil War from start to finish, ending up with a shattered arm. At Moscow University he was prominent in party and academic activities.

"Well, Feliks," I said to him, "how are you getting on?"

"So-so," he replied. "Did you know I did time, five and some years?"

"When? What for?"

"They picked me up in 1949."

"What for? For whom were you spying—the Americans, the Japanese, the Portuguese?"

"No, they charged me with belonging to the Trotskyite-Bukharinist opposition in 1918."

"There was no such opposition in 1918."

"So what? They charged me anyway. I told them that. I asked them to show me a single textbook or article on the party's history that mentioned any such opposition in 1918."

"And?"

"And? Well, look."

He rolled up his sleeve and showed me a web of scars on his arm.

"And you 'confessed,' of course?"

"I 'confessed.' The special committee gave me ten years. I served five and a bit. In 1954, I was released and rehabilitated. Now I'm getting my pension."

At times like that, to be unemployed as I was—and to be branded a "Voznesenskii supporter" to boot—was like living with a noose around your neck. We strained to hear the sound of footsteps on the stairs. A ring at the door in the evening cleaved the mind like a flash of lightning: Who was there? Did they come for me? Autumn arrived with its long dreary evenings, the wind howling in the windows, the coughs and flu. Then winter. I was still jobless. Officials versed in court etiquette were careful to give me a wide berth. On meeting me in the street, they did not acknowledge me.

I occupied myself with research on the history of collective farms. I studied English. As I had during my years at the Institute of Red Professors, I took pleasure in reading Hegel's *The Science of Logic*. On those interminable stormy nights I lost myself in my volumes of Chekhov, Blok, Esenin. I remember how much I enjoyed Viacheslav Shishkov's novels *Ugrium River* and *Emelian Pugachev*.

It seemed utterly absurd to keep me unemployed. Here I was, able-bodied, with my wits about me, capable of contributing much to my party and my people—and idle for months on end. What good did it serve? I asked the CC to give me work of any kind, if only on a temporary basis. After my insistent requests, I was told I could "for the time being help with editing" at the same miserable journal, *Bolshevik*.

As luck would have it, the journal's executive editor then was my wartime comrade Sergei Abalin. A historian by profession, like me he had volunteered for the front in June 1941, and we saw action together in the battles for Moscow, Stalingrad, and other places. Handsome, with curly brown hair and an athletic build, he was soft-spoken, tactful, and kindly by nature, and very impressionable and sensitive. An entirely decent man, utterly devoted to the party. (Several years later, his impressionability and sensitivity brought him to a sorry end. Suspecting that his superiors did not trust him as editor, he put his feelings into a brief letter that his wife later showed me. Then he packed his family off to their dacha, took an armchair into the kitchen, sat down, and turned on the gas. His corpse was discovered only after a day and a half. Rest in peace, dear Serezha.)[4]

Abalin greeted me warmly at the *Bolshevik* office and sympathized sincerely with my position. Avid for work, though lacking any official status, I buried myself in editing difficult and tricky material and in copyediting. I went through a pile of writings by American publicists and wrote a long polemic, "The Warriors of American Imperialism." I critiqued and corrected articles submitted to the journal. Working nonstop, I tried to fend off gloomy thoughts and somber forebodings.

Then the time arrived for celebrating Stalin's seventieth birthday. On December 3, 1949, the press published the announcement of the Supreme Soviet Presidium on the formation of a committee headed by Nikolai Shvernik to arrange for the festivities. Articles devoted to Stalin—couched, of course, in superlatives—began to appear in *Pravda* and all other papers. In honor of the anniversary, a campaign of socialist competition for fulfilling production plans ahead of schedule was launched throughout the country. Articles about Stalin by virtually the entire Politburo—Malenkov, Molotov, Beria, Voroshilov, Mikoian, Kaganovich, Bulganin, Khrushchev, Kosygin, and Shvernik—filled the columns of *Pravda*.

Leaders of the world communist movement—Maurice Thorez, Bolesław Bierut, Klement Gottwald, Harry Pollit, Palmiro Togliatti, Gheorghe

Gheorghiu-Dej, Dolores Ibárruri, and others—paid fervent and eloquent tribute, as did Soviet official and public figures, scientists, military commanders, and writers. With his usual skill and emotion in dealing with the public, Ilya Ehrenburg[5] wrote:

"Stalin was not one of those remote military leaders whom history knows. Stalin encouraged everyone; he sensed the grief of refugees, the creak of their wagons, the tears of mothers, the wrath of the people. Stalin, when need be, put the defeated to shame and shook the hand of the brave; he was present not only at headquarters but in the heart of every soldier.

"He appears before us as an ordinary worker, toiling from morning to night, shirking no difficulty, the first to control the Soviet land. . . .

"Gifts are sent to him. A Frenchwoman whose daughter was shot by the fascists sends him all that remained of her child, a little hat. No one else gets such gifts, and there are no scales to weigh such love."

Ehrenburg concluded his article with the words:

"In stormy weather at sea, the captain stands at the wheel. While others work or rest, gaze at the stars or read a book, the captain stands facing the wind, peering into the dark night. Great is his responsibility, great his deeds. . . . And he stands at the wheel, no matter what."

With equal artistry and emotional power, Leonid Leonov[6] wrote: "From the time Stalin appeared among us, every secret wish of the Soviet people has come true. And it cannot help but come true now—the victory of communism, the immortal glory of the Leader!"

Mikhail Sholokhov:[7] "Father! Our glory, our honor, our hope and joy —may your days be long!"

On December 16, the leader of the Chinese people, Mao Zedong, arrived in Moscow for the festivities. This was his first visit to our country, his first trip abroad. Stalin was not at the Iaroslavl' railroad station to meet him; Mao was met by Molotov and Bulganin. But Stalin received him the same day, and they met and held talks repeatedly after that.

Now the big day was here—December 21, 1949. The morning papers carried a long letter to Stalin from the party CC and the Council of Ministers. By decree of the Supreme Soviet Presidium, Stalin was awarded the Order of Lenin. Regarding decorations for himself, Stalin was always very strict and restrained.

I was still without work and in a state of suspense. Of course, no one thought of inviting me to the celebrations. Without expecting anything to come of it, I called Malenkov's office the day before the anniversary and to my surprise received a ticket to the ceremony—and a good seat, too, in the second box of the mezzanine very near the stage.

Here I am in the Bolshoi Theater. On the stage, in a sea of flowers and scarlet banners, an enormous portrait of Stalin. On the proscenium, members of the Politburo and the leaders of many foreign communist parties. Stalin in his generalissimo's uniform. Next to him, Mao Zedong in a dark gray civilian tunic like the one usually worn by Stalin.

Shvernik declares the meeting open. At his first congratulatory words, the excited audience rises to its feet, and a storm of ovations rocks the theater. Waves of applause, cries and shouts of hurrah, roll one after another across the hall. Stalin applauds slowly, evidently in response.

Representatives of all the union republics, the nation's workers, scientists, performers, writers, and young people, including the youth organization Pioneers, make many speeches. Among the representatives of foreign communist parties, the floor goes first to Mao Zedong. The audience greets him with thunderous applause. Though tall and well built, Mao turns out to have a soft and high-pitched voice. He speaks slowly and impressively and makes an excellent impression. "Comrade Stalin is the teacher and friend of all the peoples of the world, the teacher and friend of the Chinese people."

In his bell-like, mellifluous Italian, the charming Palmiro Togliatti: "We succeeded in becoming a large, popular party thanks to the struggle to overthrow the fascist regime that communists waged with every available means. But our hopes of advancing and scoring successes would have been dashed if we had not had you as our genius leader, our inspiration and guide. . . . All glory to you, Comrade Stalin!"

Togliatti turns this way and that and sees that there is no interpreter from Italian, whereupon he repeats his speech in perfectly good Russian.

The stage belongs to Dolores Ibárruri. A strong face of classical beauty, like that of Alonso Cano's[8] Madonna. It is hard to describe her irresistible power as an orator. A clear musical voice with beguiling nuances. A proud bearing; bold and expressive gestures with her hands. She speaks emotionally, with inspiration, and holds the audience completely in her sway: "Neither terror, persecution, nor death itself can extinguish the sacred flame of love that the Spanish people feel for Stalin and the Soviet Union."

At the conclusion of the speeches, applause for Stalin from the proscenium and the entire audience reigns in the hall. Everyone expects him to take the stage and, as usual, deliver one of his carefully crafted anniversary speeches. Or at least say a few words of gratitude or just a simple thank-you for the affection that all these guests from around the world showered on him. But Stalin does not approach the dais. Gazing apathetically at the audience, he claps slowly. The ovations keep mounting. Stalin does not react. The audience goes wild, demanding that he speak. Stalin remains impassive.

This goes on for five, seven, I don't know how many minutes. Finally Shvernik declares the meeting ended. And for months afterward, *Pravda* carries extensive lists of congratulatory telegrams that were sent to Stalin on his seventieth birthday.

January 1950 arrived with its buffeting snowstorms. From the ninth floor of my building on Bol'shaia Kaluzhskaia Street I looked out on the frosty elms of Neskuchnyi Garden. In the distance the Spassky Tower of the Kremlin rose proudly against the leaden sky.

My daughter Viktoriia was admitted to the Architectural Institute. Her student friends would come over in the evenings. They would talk about the latest literature, new plays, art exhibitions. I studied their faces and listened. A new generation was taking over, different from mine. What were these young people like? What did they think about? What did they hope for? What were their ideals? Would they carry on with the traditions of my generation, the Komsomol of 1920, or would they revise them? In what way? I was strongly drawn to these new budding shoots of humanity. I wanted to comprehend their souls and feelings. "Hello, young strangers."

I was glad to see the arrival of a generation of men and women more mature and educated than we had been at their age. And it was enormously thought-provoking and alarming to note their increasingly critical attitude toward many aspects of Soviet life. We had grown up fanatical communists, obsessed and possessed. We were intolerant of any criticism or skepticism. Our unconditional orthodoxy cemented the nation for decades. The moral and political unity of the people was the fortress against which the turbid waves of internal counterrevolution and imperialist intervention broke and retreated.

But had this absolute orthodoxy, zealous discipline, and fanatical faith in the infallibility of the leadership grown into blind submissiveness? The kind of submissiveness that eventually led to the one-man dictatorship of Joseph Stalin and to the monstrous lawlessness of Ezhov, Beria, and their likes? Was the burgeoning criticism of our extraordinary young people being proffered as a potent life-giving elixir that would rescue our society from the hardening of its arteries? Then we would see restored all those Leninist standards of criticism and that atmosphere of genuine freedom and democracy that were engendered by the great revolution and that permeated the party and the country in Lenin's day. Not just restored, but greatly developed and expanded. After all, we witnessed several decades of Soviet power. We saw the creation of a multinational state with a solid economic foundation. Now the whole momentum of history enjoined us to advance to a system of authentic rather than nominal sovereignty of the people, to a profusion of material and spiritual benefits, and to the broadest democracy, with political freedoms that secured the inviolability, dignity, and rights of the individual to a degree unknown in the most arch-democratic bourgeois society.

With these agonizing questions, thoughts, and internal arguments I wandered on snowy nights, in the grip of insomnia, up Kaluzhskaia Street to the Lenin Hills. From here I could see all of Moscow, hectic during the day and composed now. I love you, O my city, with a son's boundless love! With every breath in my body I defended you in your hour of mortal danger. Why must I now roam your streets like a pariah? Why do these hands of mine bring nothing to your treasure house? How absurd this all is!

My body was on fire. A few pedestrians gave me curious glances: I was probably speaking out loud to myself. An icy wind burned my face. The frozen branches of ancient maple trees sighed mournfully, like metal wreaths at a cemetery. With a broken spirit and a fevered mind, I trudged home, before me an interminable night of ragged sleep.

When would it all end?

Then, suddenly and unexpectedly, the end came. At noon one day, a phone call. "Comrade Shepilov? Tomorrow at noon, be at the meeting of the CC Secretariat."

Twenty-four hours of slow, tormented speculation and musings. What could this mean—the worst? But in that case, they would simply have sent over a Black Maria. An explanation of some matter? But then they would have told me so I could prepare myself. Could it be, in spite of everything, the end of my period of unemployment? What could they offer me? Where could they send me? What did it matter where? Even to Chukotka.⁹ To some dark hole. It wouldn't be hard for me. So long as I could work, work, work.

True, Viktoriia had just started at her institute. Well, we could find her another school. After all, I arrived in Moscow and was admitted to the university without knowing a single soul in the capital. Of course, after Iakutiia, Siberia, and the front, it would be nice to stay in Moscow so Viktoriia could graduate from the institute. But if the party wanted to send me somewhere else, so be it.

At noon the next day, January 31, I presented myself at the CC, at the Organizational Bureau conference hall on the fifth floor. A meeting was in session, dealing with an extensive agenda, but I was ushered in at once. Well, I thought, I can't be that much of a criminal if I'm invited to be present at a discussion of questions with no bearing on my case; that was seldom permitted.

Malenkov, who was in his customary gray Stalinist military tunic, chaired the meeting. There were brief reports on one issue after another, followed by brief discussion, the chairman's summary, and the decision. When all the items on the agenda were dealt with, Malenkov said: "All that's left is to examine the case of Comrade Shepilov. Right now he's not doing anything. Yet he's educated and experienced. We've been a little late with his assignment."

And he gave me the most good-natured and affable smile imaginable, as though he had never said to me, "We've been after you for a long time. . . . Now you won't get away." What could it mean?

Malenkov continued. "I hear that Comrade Shepilov once said he'd like to be a CC inspector. If he hasn't changed his mind and the job is to his liking, let us appoint him to be a CC inspector, and after that we'll see. What do you say, Comrade Shepilov?"

I replied that I accepted. And the matter was settled.

How come? What had happened? Why such a radical change? Why hadn't they tried to do me in as part of the Voznesenskii affair?

I learned the inside story only several years later, when I was a secretary of the CC. At a routine meeting of the Politburo, Stalin, surprising everyone—as had frequently occurred on other occasions—inquired: "Where is Shepilov? What is he doing? What is he working on?"

Everyone was silent. Malenkov seemed somewhat upset, unable to determine from the tone of Stalin's voice whether he intended to cast me down or lift me up. So he said with an impartial intonation calculated to please the leader, "In fact, we all wanted to consult with you, to ask you, Comrade Stalin, what to do about Shepilov."

Stalin said, "We gave Shepilov a dressing-down. But he is an educated Marxist. We can't let people like that go to waste."

So my fate was decided.

Why this unexpected change of mind on Stalin's part—from dismissing me as head of CC Agitprop to acknowledging my erudition and usefulness? It's hard to say. Only Stalin knew why.

At that time, the investigation of the Leningrad affair was in full swing. It is possible that Beria had proposed that I, and perhaps a whole group of Moscow economists, be charged formally in connection with the case, and that Stalin wanted to use this to make Beria once again aware that he, Stalin, had his own independent views. Or perhaps he decided not to blow up the Leningrad affair to a cosmic scale. After all, the main thing had been accomplished: Voznesenskii was out of the way. Perhaps Stalin just then read some of my latest writings, which always featured his theoretical positions and gave his works pride of place in the strongest and most positive terms. Perhaps while reading he remembered me and after careful consideration decided that even with the wildest imagination it would be difficult—and maybe unadvisable—to link me to the Voznesenskii affair. Or perhaps Stalin began to look for someone who could replace Zhdanov on the ideological front.

In short, it is hard to say what Stalin might have been thinking as he tossed off a few words about me. But after that, everything worked like magic. The very next day I was appointed a CC inspector, a post that in those days usually went to former first secretaries of oblast and regional committees and members of the party CC. A few days later Stalin invited me to his dacha for a long tête-à-tête on putting out a textbook on political economy; work on that project began soon afterward.

With February came the start of the campaign for elections to the Supreme Soviet, and one fine day I received a red-striped telegram marked "Official."

"The workers, employees, and engineers of the Ural'skii aluminum plant in the Kamensk-Ural'skii electoral district[10] have nominated you as a candidate for deputy of the USSR Supreme Soviet."

"The workers of the Ural'skii Novotrubnyi plant." The same.

"The workers of the Kamensk-Ural'skii aviation plant."

And so on and so forth.

Then the Nineteenth Party Congress came in the autumn of 1952, and I was elected to the Central Committee. Yes, it is frightening to be in a situation where your work, your freedom, your very life, and the life or death of millions of people, depend on the likes or dislikes of one man.

Meanwhile, the Leningrad affair kept being inflated. By now, hundreds of people arrested in the case were languishing in prison under the harshest conditions, subjected to forcible methods of interrogation to make them confess to crimes they had never committed. The emaciated and tormented prisoners were pummeled with one new charge after another, each more fantastic than the last.

Nikolai Voznesenskii, first deputy chairman of the USSR Council of Ministers and chairman of Gosplan; Aleksei Kuznetsov, a secretary of the CC of the VKP(b); Mikhail Rodionov, chairman of the RSFSR Council of Ministers; Petr Popkov, secretary of the Leningrad oblast Party Committee; Iakov Kapustin and G. F. Badaev, secretaries of Leningrad city Party Committee; P. G. Lazutin, chairman of the Leningrad city soviet; and many other leaders of the Leningrad party organization were charged with "sabotage and subversion within the party."

The Leningrad wholesale trade fair that they organized early in 1949 "squandered state funds and caused economic damage to the state."

Like the Zinovievites[11] of an earlier time, the accused allegedly wanted to turn the Leningrad party organization into a bastion for struggle against the CC. They allegedly heaped opprobrium on the party CC, violated state plans, and sabotaged work within state offices.

Of course, the accused were supposed to "confess" to all this wild, pathological poppycock. Nonetheless, in his final statement at the trial, Voznesenskii declared: "I am not guilty of the crimes of which I have been accused. I request that this be conveyed to Stalin."

The Military Collegium of the USSR Supreme Court sentenced Voznesenskii, Kuznetsov, Rodionov, Popkov, Kapustin, and Lazutin to death. The sentences were carried out.

The executions, however, marked not the climax but the beginning of a terrorist campaign against Leningrad party personnel. That decision was followed by many others. The special conference of the MGB was hard at work. It meted out death or prolonged incarceration in prisons or camps to more than two hundred leading party and government officials in Leningrad. After that, the new secretaries of the Leningrad party organization, Vasilii Andrianov, Frol Kozlov, and Nikolai Ignatov, began to arrest innocent people for having "associated" with Voznesenskii and Kuznetsov. These charges were enough to have hundreds of others imprisoned, banished from Leningrad, or expelled from the party.

After Stalin's death, I, as editor in chief of *Pravda,* accompanied Khrushchev to a meeting of party activists in Leningrad. The first secretary of the Leningrad party organization at the time was Frol Kozlov. The meeting was held in the Tauride Palace, and the meeting's presidium, of which I was a member, received many notes demanding that Andrianov and Kozlov be brought to justice for violating revolutionary legality, smashing the Leningrad organization, and deliberately defaming its members.

During the breaks, many party activists asked me, "Why is Frol Kozlov still secretary? Why aren't Kozlov and Andrianov made to answer for what they did?"

Late at night we met with Khrushchev at the house where we were staying and where Zhdanov had once lived. After supper we went out for a walk. The giant city was still. The waters of the Neva lapped softly against the boats tied up along the shore. There was a creaking of wooden oarlocks. The stars glimmered faintly in a pallid sky.

I told Khrushchev about the notes and what had been said to me at the meeting. "It's my impression," I said, "that the communists here are unanimous about the need to dismiss Kozlov immediately as Leningrad secretary. I think Kozlov himself recognizes that he has no respect or support from among the activists."

Khrushchev was silent. I continued along the same line, citing more facts and arguments.

"All right, all right," Khrushchev said, "we'll see."

I felt a cold breeze from the river. There was an odor of fish and slime.

Speaking at the meeting the next day, Khrushchev made an astounding statement: "As for Comrade Kozlov, if you support him, the CC will too."

There was utter silence.

I soon learned that Khrushchev made frequent use of such tactics.

He chose some failed and discredited official, appointed him to a high post, rewarded him with various titles, and made him into his most loyal and obedient servant. This protégé understood that his welfare, titles, posts, and entire comfortable life depended totally on his benefactor. One word from the latter, and all was lost. So the protégé constantly exerted himself to be louder than anyone else in trumpeting fulsome praise of Khrushchev, in rendering him any service, and in taking the vilest actions against anyone in Khrushchev's bad books.

It was simply on the basis of personal loyalty that someone like Ivan Serov,[12] who was responsible for the deaths of thousands of people and should have been put on trial, became head of the organs of state security and Khrushchev's closest associate. And on the same basis Kozlov soon became a secretary of the CC, deputy chairman of the Council of Ministers, and a member of the CC Politburo.

Глава IX

Девятнадцатый съезд.

Для того, чтобы реализовать все разумные замечания и предложения, сделанные в ход[е] экономической дискуссии, а также указания Сталина по проекту учебника, — дать нам решением Президиума Полит-бюро ЦК [...] переработ-чен [...] еще один год [...].

И вот вооруженные девяноста умами мы, авторы учебника, снова появляемся в "издании". Теперь уже не в диалоге-вечные Годы!" Наш [...]

The first page of a chapter on the Nineteenth Party Congress written in Shepilov's hand. In the published memoir compiled by Shepilov's grandson, the first paragraph appears at the end of chapter 9 and the second paragraph at the beginning of chapter 11.

Major General Shepilov (third from left) and the commander of the 4th Guards Army, Lieutenant General Nikanor Zakhvataev (fourth from right), outside Berlin, 1945.

American General George Patton pinning a medal on Shepilov in Vienna, May 1945.

Delegation at the Soviet residence in Beijing, 1954. First row, from left to right: Anastas Mikoian, Ekaterina Furtseva, Nikita Khrushchev, Nikolai Bulganin, and Nikolai Shvernik. Second row, from left to right: Georgii Aleksandrov, Shepilov, unknown man, Iadgar Nasriddinova, and Pavel Iudin.

Soviet reception in Beijing, 1954. First row, from left to right: Zhou Enlai, Liu
Shaoqi, Nikita Khrushchev, Nikolai Bulganin, Georgii Aleksandrov, and Anastas
Mikoian. Shepilov is first from the left in the second row.

Shepilov (tall man in second row, middle) meeting with Chinese citizens in Beijing in 1954. To the left of Shepilov are Iadgar Nasriddinova and Ekaterina Furtseva.

Shepilov (at rostrum) speaking at the Twentieth Party Congress, February 15, 1956.

Shepilov with writers at the Twentieth Party Congress, February 1956. From left to right: Shepilov, Aleksandr Korneichuk, Mikhail Sholokhov, Aleksei Surkov, and Mustai Karim.

Shepilov in Egypt, seated on sofa with Gamal Abdel Nasser (right), 1956.

CHAPTER EIGHT

A Hard Road

THE GALE OF CONFERENCES, public demonstrations, articles, and speeches devoted to Stalin's seventieth birthday gradually subsided, although fervent glorification of the great leader remained obligatory in any public statement. Meanwhile, life took its course, and that old harlot History kept astounding humankind with her new tricks.

It was ever more apparent that the hope of establishing "peace on earth, goodwill among men" had been illusory after the bloody Second World War. The North Atlantic Treaty Organization (NATO) was signed into existence in Washington, D.C., in April 1949 outside the framework of the United Nations. The pact set up an aggressive military bloc comprising the United States, Britain, France, Belgium, the Netherlands, Luxembourg, Canada, Italy, Portugal, Norway, Denmark, and Iceland. Greece and Turkey joined the bloc in 1952, and the Federal Republic of Germany joined in 1955.

NATO's principal objectives were to prepare for an imperialist war against the socialist countries and suppress all national liberation movements. An important part of its organizers' plans was to restore the military might of West Germany—even to provide it with atomic weapons—in order to convert the FRG into a powerful base for aggression against the East.

With every passing year it became clearer that in NATO's corridors the United States was striving for supremacy in the Atlantic bloc. The well-known American commentator James Reston wrote in 1951 that while Washington was depicting NATO as an alliance of twelve equal partners for public consumption, it had quietly created an organization in which all real power was concentrated in the hands of a small military cabinet representing the United States, Britain, and France. The decisions of the three, he added, were usually determined outside the organization, often to the annoyance of the French. However, even between the United States and Britain there was a rivalry for undisputed supremacy. All this gave rise to growing disputes in the NATO camp. Seventeen years later, the head of the French Republic, General de Gaulle, would announce that France was withdrawing from NATO's military command.[1]

At the time, the loudest denunciations of NATO came from the USSR deputy minister of foreign affairs, Andrei Vyshinskii. I met Vyshinskii in the winter of 1923; he lectured and conducted a seminar on criminal trial procedure that I took at the law school at Moscow University. In later years I heard many of his public lectures and speeches, and as a researcher, I met with him for various reasons at the Academy of Sciences, to which he was admitted as a full member in 1939.

Vyshinskii had acquired a kind of garish international renown as chairman of the special commission of the USSR Supreme Court and subsequently as prosecutor in the show trials in the so-called Shakhty affair[2] and the cases of the Industrial Party,[3] the United Trotskyite-Zinovievite Terrorist Center (1936),[4] the Parallel Trotskyite Center (1937),[5] the United Anti-Soviet Rightist-Trotskyite Bloc (1938),[6] and many others. He was unquestionably accomplished, a skilled orator and able debater with a flair for quick and often stinging retorts to his opponent's arguments. But his oratory, although it impressed many at the start, was based on a singular moral and ethical outlook.

First, Vyshinskii was an unsurpassed, pathological narcissist. Speaking at a seminar of party activists or a meeting, he would posture, flirt with the audience, and glow with self-admiration: Look, how talented I am, how witty, how quick. He would intersperse his speech with phrases like, "Well, there, of course, I put Eden's nose out of joint,"[7] "I drove U.S. Secretary Byrnes into a corner,"[8] "I explained it to that naive innocent Léon Blum."[9]

Second, Vyshinskii embodied the most repellent features of Machiavelli. To further his career and achieve his aims he was ready to lower himself to any depths. In a time of sinister purges, it was he who invented the doctrine of "presumption of political guilt" in the course of the trial and who developed and enriched Stalin's theory of intensifying class struggle as the country moved closer to socialism. The assumption was, "You are accused of being an American spy (or a Trotskyite or a Bukharinist). Prove that you are not." The accusation could be as fantastic and nonsensical as imaginable, and the chances of disproving it while isolated in prison were nil.

Typical of Vyshinskii's character was his utter lack of principle. Zealously, with all the brilliance of an actor or a lawyer, he would defend a given position; but if Stalin, Molotov, or some other leader voiced the slightest comment, or expressed displeasure or doubt by a gesture, shake of the head, or arch of the eyebrows, Vyshinskii would make an immediate 180-degree turn and proceed to defend the opposite with equal brilliance and wit.

It was that moral and political attitude that made Vyshinskii a handy instrument of Stalin's punitive policies during the darkest years. Taking shelter behind the high-flown phrase "Under the conditions of proletarian dictatorship the welfare of the state constitutes the highest law," Vyshinskii in his lectures on criminal law propagated his own formula: "Better to find ten innocent people guilty than exonerate one guilty person."

In his capacity as USSR prosecutor general, Vyshinskii condoned and sanctioned the wide-scale practice of unjustified arrests. He played a key role in staging many trials in which all the accused "confessed," and the most unproven charges were deemed proven. On his conscience lay a legion of snuffed-out lives.

But all this was before the war. Now Vyshinskii glittered in the arena of the United Nations, hurling a daily Niagara of words down on the heads of the trembling imperialists. His eloquence knew no limits and recognized no restraints. During the course of various international meetings, our major newspapers would carry two or three columns of his speeches. He himself would brag, "For each speech I prepare one text, deliver another extemporaneously, and publish a third."

Many years later, during the 1956 London conference on the Suez Canal,[10] U.S. Secretary of State John Foster Dulles called on me at the Soviet Embassy in London and touched on Vyshinskii in the course of our talk.

He said he had asked to see me because in my rather laconic statement on arriving in London he had discovered one word—just one—that gave him hope that he and I could find common ground for a sensible approach to the Suez problem. He added that it would have been most difficult to do this with Mr. Vyshinskii. Of course, he said, Mr. Vyshinskii deserved great respect, but he could not imagine anyone fully understanding his scintillating speeches and pronouncements.

True enough, Vyshinskii was so intoxicated by his own eloquence that for a turn of a phrase or a biting comment he was ready to sacrifice the business at hand.

At the same time, people on every continent were being mobilized to campaign against another war. Hundreds of millions of people signed the Stockholm Peace Petition.[11] The party sought to consolidate all the democratic forces of the world to overcome any tendency toward narrow sectarianism. Stalin was deep in conversations with representatives from India, working out new policies and tactics for ending the isolation of the Indian Communist Party and placing it in the vanguard of the international struggle for peace, democracy, and socialism. Stalin also held talks with the leader of the Italian socialists, Pietro Nenni, who had allied his party with the Italian communists to work for peace and the democratic reform of Italian society. Nenni was awarded the Stalin Peace Prize.

But of course the peace campaign among the masses did not obviate the need for continued strengthening of the country's defenses. In October 1951 the first Soviet atomic bomb test took place in the arid steppes of Kazakhstan.[12] It signaled the start of the inevitable competition among the great powers—the United States, the USSR, Britain, then France, and later the People's Republic of China—for expanding and improving their atomic arsenals.

More powerful than any atomic or hydrogen bomb, however, was the growing consolidation of the forces of socialism. After the proclamation of the People's Republic of China on October 1, 1949, Mao Zedong, as related above, visited Moscow for Stalin's seventieth birthday celebrations; the visit strengthened the bonds of friendship between the two great countries. Mao inspected the Stalin Automobile Plant and the kolkhoz Luch (Ray) outside Moscow; he attended a performance of *Swan Lake* at the Bolshoi Theater and paid a visit to Leningrad. A four-volume edition of his writings was published in Moscow. The Soviet people welcomed their Chinese friends with ineffable joy and love. Everyone understood that the close friendship between the USSR and China was the cornerstone of the international socialist fortress, a mighty bulwark for liberation movements throughout the world, and a critically important factor in global foreign policy.

In February 1950 the Treaty of Friendship, Alliance, and Mutual Assistance between the USSR and the PRC was signed in the Kremlin. The Changchun railroad line was unconditionally handed over to China, and Soviet troops were withdrawn from Port Arthur.[13] The Soviet Union provided China with long-term credits amounting to three hundred million U.S. dollars.

Yet as the forces of communism consolidated and strengthened, word of worrisome developments in certain communist parties filtered through. For example, it was reported that in the French party, one of the most renowned and aggressive, Maurice Thorez was copying much of Stalin's leadership style, making his own decisions in too arbitrary a fashion, rejecting all comradely criticism, and removing some of the oldest and most distinguished party members from top posts. That was why Moscow received the decision of the December 1952 CC plenum of the French Communist Party—"On the Factional Activities of André Marty and Charles Tillon"—with great concern and reserve.

André Marty was very popular in Russia. The son of a French communard[14] of 1871 and a worker, Marty bravely bore the punishments, prisons, and penal colonies of French reactionary rule. In the winter of 1918–19 the French imperialists sent a naval squadron and interventionist forces to the Black Sea. Marty, then a marine and mechanic, led the sailors aboard the destroyer *Proteus* and the cruiser *Waldeck-Rousseau* in a rebellion that raised the red flag and refused to open fire on the Russian Revolution. Marty was also renowned for his courageous speeches against Marshal Foch,[15] who called for a crusade against the USSR, and for his outstanding contributions to the struggle of the Spanish people against fascism.

Now this member of the Politburo of the French party, this parliamentary deputy who represented the workers of Paris, this former secretary of the Executive Committee of the Comintern, was suddenly accused of a series of grave political wrongdoings: factional struggle against party policy; leftist adventurism in wartime; belittlement of the leadership of Maurice Thorez in the French party; a bourgeois-nationalist assessment of the role of the USSR in the liberation of France; and even "ties to police circles." Moreover, in imitation of Stalin's methods in such cases, it was decided not to publish Marty's letters and statements to the Politburo; thus, one could not make out the precise nature of his antiparty actions.

The decision in the case was extremely harsh: to dismiss Marty from all party posts, relieve him of all his responsibilities as a Politburo member, and consider expelling him from the party. The same decision was reached in regard to the CC Politburo member Charles Tillon.[16] Both were soon expelled from the party. But we, as in all such cases, tried to stifle our feelings of apprehension and doubt. In all likelihood, both of them were really guilty before their party. It would probably have been inadvisable to inform us of the substance of the affair. Stalin and the other leaders of the VKP(b) CC undoubtedly knew the whole story and had given their approval.

Similarly alarming developments occurred in some other foreign parties. But on the whole, the immediate postwar period was characterized by an enormous rise in the prestige and authority of the Soviet Union and its communist party and by the growing role and influence of communists in the world's liberation movements. This was attributable primarily to the Soviet Union's spectacular economic progress.

The initial round of postwar reconstruction was completed in an incredibly short time, and the rate of subsequent industrial development remained very high. Thus, in 1950 the gross industrial product rose by 23 percent in a single year. The Fourth Five-Year Plan—the first of the postwar period—was fulfilled nine months ahead of schedule. Compared to the prewar year of 1940, industrial production had risen by 73 percent by the end of 1950, and electric power output by 87 percent. Agricultural production, though lagging behind industrial production, was placed on a solid technical and scientific footing.

Now it was necessary to decide on the basic features of the Fifth Five-Year Plan, on its core industrial and agricultural components. This was done. In 1950, at Stalin's initiative and in accordance with his instructions, the CC and the government approved a number of gigantic construction projects in the Volga region and Central Asia: the Kuibyshev Hydroelectric Station on the Volga River, which had a capacity of nearly 2 million kilowatts, an annual volume of 6.1 billion kilowatt-hours for transmission to Moscow, and 1.5 billion kilowatt-hours for irrigating the lands of the Volga region; the Stalingrad Hydroelectric Station on the Volga River, which had a capacity of no less than 1.7 million kilowatts and an annual transmission volume of 2 billion kilowatt-hours for improving the climatic conditions of the Caspian Sea lowlands, for developing arid and semiarid regions for cattle raising and agriculture, for irrigation projects in the southern part of the trans-Volga region, the Sarpinskii lowlands, the black-earth regions, and the Nogaiskii steppe; the Kakhovskii Hydroelectric Station on the Dnieper River, the Southern Urals Canal, the Northern Crimean Canal, and irrigation projects for southern Ukraine and northern Crimea; the Main Turkmen Canal from the Amu Dar'ia River to Krasnovodsk on the Caspian Sea, irrigation projects for the southern regions of the Caspian plain in western Turkmenistan, the lower reaches of the Amu Dar'ia River, and the western parts of the Karakum Desert; the Volga-Don Navigation Canal, and irrigation projects for the Rostov and Stalingrad regions.

These projects constituted a gigantic plan for socialist economic development. Completion of this plan would expand the country's newest sources of electricity and energy, transform the face of many major economic regions, modernize the technology of a number of highly important agricultural zones, and greatly increase agricultural production. It would also improve and reduce the cost of the country's transportation system.

After Stalin's death, that ignoramus Khrushchev often scoffed at this truly scientific plan, which had been carefully studied from every economic angle. Only half hearing something and not bothering to sort it out, Khrushchev pronounced himself against the construction of hydroelectric stations: hydroelectric stations were supposedly too expensive; any that were being built were put on hold, and construction resources were switched to thermal power plants.

It is easy to imagine what a catastrophic energy crisis would have overtaken the economy as a whole if Khrushchev's ban on hydroelectric stations had remained in force. Of course, his half-baked improvisations had to give way to common sense, and soon the wondrous giants of electric power began to rise along the Volga and Dnieper Rivers and along the Angara, Enisei, Irtysh, Naryn, and Nurek Rivers,[17] pouring new vitality into all areas of the economy, culture, and daily life. Khrushchev also mocked the Turkmen canal, but here, too, common sense prevailed, and a few years later the shining waters of the Amu-Dar'ia began flowing through the desert to the capital of Turkmenistan, Ashkhabad, and beyond to Krasnovodsk on the Caspian Sea.

Living standards were also improving. The monetary reform of 1947 stabilized the ruble. The initial reduction of prices on food and consumer goods in 1947 saved the population 86 billion rubles for the year, the second in 1949 saved 71 billion, the third in 1950 saved 110 billion, the fourth in 1951 saved 34 billion, and the fifth saved 28 billion. Year by year the Soviet people in both urban and rural areas ate and dressed better, although we still had far to go to attain the desired level of prosperity.

Moscow was being rebuilt. In August 1952 a twenty-seven story building arose on Smolensk Square,[18] one of eight projected high-rises. At first we Muscovites were astonished by the unfamiliar statistics—170.5 meters in height, 2,000 service and engineering facilities, more than 400,000 square meters in area, a hall with a capacity of 500 people, its own library and reading room, an in-house phone system, 28 elevators, and so on. We gazed with pride at this new architectural knight in shining armor.

Construction was going on everywhere, in town and country. But there was a dire housing shortage and other reasons for popular discontent. Masses of poorly paid employees grumbled about the high taxes and various deductions from their pay. The monthly and essentially compulsory loan deductions were most unpopular. But despite the many difficulties and shortages, the general atmosphere was one of confidence, economic and political improvement, and complete certainty that life was getting better day by day. Even visitors from abroad sensed this atmosphere and the unshakable faith in the future. As early as the 1930s, the discerning Lion Feuchtwanger wrote in his book *Moscow 1937:* "I was at first surprised and dubious when I found that all the people with whom I came into contact in the Soviet Union, and this includes casual and obviously spontaneous conversations, were at one with the general scheme of things, even if they were sometimes critical of minor points. Indeed, everywhere in that great city of Moscow there was an atmosphere of harmony and contentment, even of happiness."

Feuchtwanger continued: "They know that their prosperity is no vague possibility which may never materialize, but the inevitable outcome of a rational planning. They have been taught that the foundations of a house must first be laid before the interior can be fitted up. The raw materials had first to be procured, the heavy industries built up, and the machines obtained, before work could be started on the production of consumer goods and manufactured articles. The Soviet citizens realized this and were ready to bear with the deficiencies in their private lives. By now it is clear that the planning was right, that the sowing was rational, and that a rich and happy harvest will be reaped; and the Soviet people are enjoying, with intense satisfaction, the first fruits of this harvest. They see that today, just as they had been promised, there are thousands of things to be had, things of which no more than two years ago they would hardly have dared to dream. And the citizen of Moscow enters his stores, just as a gardener who has sown much goes into his garden to see what else has come up today. Daily he sees something new—contentedly he sees caps, perhaps, then buckets, then cameras. . . . And the fact that the leaders have been as good as their word so far is the people's guarantee that the Plan will materialize increasingly and that things will improve from month to month."

Feuchtwanger concluded: "There can be no doubt that the difference in the advantages and security which the Soviet citizen enjoys as compared with the subjects of the Western states, seems to him so enormous that the inconveniences of his daily life dwindle into nothing."[19]

Feuchtwanger's description of the mood of the great majority of the Soviet people in the 1930s applied equally well to the 1940s, except that in the postwar period there was a further strengthening of the people's faith in the party, its policies, the government, and the future and of its confidence that a life of genuine material and intellectual abundance would soon be secured for everyone. We shall see later how the Khrushchev regime undermined this popular faith in a bright tomorrow with its innate recklessness.

In the 1950s, however, everything was on the up and up. Of course, the gigantic task of transforming the daily lives of millions of people had its anomalies and setbacks, one of which concerned Khrushchev himself.

On March 4, 1951, *Pravda* carried an article by Khrushchev that covered the bottom halves of two pages, and was entitled "On the Growth and Well-Being of the Kolkhozes." Its thrust was that our old villages and settlements were worthless; our kolkhozes had become so entrenched and prosperous that we could let our old villages be razed. In place of these useless old villages, we had to build new ones—find the right locations, move the villages, and construct multistory buildings with sidewalks, plumbing, bathrooms, and other amenities. The old words "village" and "settlement" would be discarded, and the new communities would be given the names of "agrocity" (*agrogorod*) or "kolkhoz settlement" (*kolkhoznyi poselok*). Khrushchev called for design work on the new kolkhoz settlements to start immediately and gave his instructions on where to locate the agrocities, how to build them, what materials to use, and so on. In his speeches, Khrushchev said all this could be done in one to three years.

The utter rashness of the plan was self-evident. At that time, villages had a total population of 108 million. To pull down the old villages and erect new agrocities in new locations would require an investment of enormous sums, running to hundreds of billions of rubles, colossal manpower, a thousand-fold expansion of all branches of the construction industry, and more. Meanwhile, the village had just barely recovered from the terrible destruction of the war, especially in the formerly occupied areas; gross agricultural production in 1951 reached only 93 percent of the prewar figure. The kolkhozes were mostly still poor. The development of the construction industry was still at an early stage. Under these circumstances, to propose dismantling an old village and replacing it, as though by magic, with a new village was sheer *manilovshchina*[20] and recklessness that threatened to make a shambles of all real work on the village level.

I don't know how Stalin reacted to this issue on March 4. But the next day *Pravda* ran the following headline and text:

"From the editors—Correction.

"Due to negligence on the part of the editors in publishing Comrade N. S. Khrushchev's article 'On the Growth and Well-Being of the Kolkhozes' in yesterday's edition of *Pravda*, an editor's note specifying that Comrade N. S. Khrushchev's speech was being published as a basis for discussion was dropped from the page. This mistake is hereby corrected."

Several days later Professor Ivan Laptev and I were summoned to the CC Agricultural Department—at that time we were regarded as authorities in the field of agrarian economics. The department head, Aleksei Kozlov, received us in his enormous office, with two of his deputies present. Kozlov was said to be close to Malenkov, but I do not know whether that had any bearing on the reaction to Khrushchev's article. Kozlov told us that Stalin regarded the article as a mistake and had instructed the CC Agricultural Department to prepare an article or a party circular—I don't remember which—criticizing it. Kozlov added that his department had already prepared a draft article, which he gave to us to edit.

We were surprised by the draft's sharp and politically harsh tone. Khrushchev's approach to the issue was called leftist, and there were some hints at Trotskyism. I, of course, did not know at the time that Khrushchev had once been a Trotskyite. Professor Laptev and I regarded Khrushchev's article as wrong, both for its unrealistic proposals and for its emphasis on daily consumption in kolkhozes and not on production, which it ignored in the process of rebuilding villages.

Naturally, I was wholly in favor of fundamentally restructuring our settlements and villages, which in their appearance and their peasant ways retained the features of the old wooden antediluvian Russia. But every reasonably educated Marxist could see that to attempt to resolve these problems by erecting even the best multistory buildings complete with bathrooms was absurd. The only right way was through the mechanization and electrification of agricultural production, an increase in the peasants' productivity, and expansion of kolkhoz and national wealth. Only that could open the way to a basic restructuring of settlements and villages and lead to an improvement in the lives of the *kolkhozniki*.

It was in this vein that we wrote a critical article on Khrushchev's speech. Kozlov was quite annoyed by the bent of our criticism and our practical proposals. He kept insisting that we hone the article politically, which we did not do, as that seemed to be outside the scope of our discussion. Whether or not our "unresponsiveness" played a role in the matter, or some other reasons arose, Kozlov called us in again shortly thereafter and said that "Comrade Khrushchev had a talk with Comrade Stalin": my assignment with Professor Laptev was canceled.

I do not know who continued to deal with this question or how they did so. But ten years later, at the Twenty-second Party Congress, that pair of Khrushchev toadies Satiukov and Il'ichev, who never suspected that history had already consigned their patron to the dustbin, sought from the dais to prove to their master with nauseating servility how brilliant his 1951 article on the kolkhozes was and how sorely Shepilov's malicious criticism had hurt him.

This was not the only example of Khrushchev's forays on the agricultural front.

But let us leave aside Khrushchev's idiosyncrasies and improvisations.

There were many more to come, and they exacted a heavy price from the people. In the period under discussion, Stalin held the reins of government firmly in his hands. The economy, as noted above, was growing at a fast clip. However, in regard to the superstructure—everything from government to philosophy and aesthetics—things were moving in a different direction.

To me—yesterday, today, and to the end of my days—the majestic ideas that Marx, Engels, and Lenin proclaimed in *The Communist Manifesto, The Principles of Communism,* and *State and Revolution* are incarnated in the Soviet system, whose superiority over the capitalist system is incontrovertible. If one were to put aside all historical accidents, uncertainties, deviations, and distortions and take just the features, principles, and goals that are intrinsic to the Soviet socialist system, then they are—or must be—the following:

1. The struggle for peace on earth
2. Material abundance for all working people resulting from the expansion of public property
3. Real power for the people
4. Broad democratic freedoms for all and guaranteed protection of the rights, honor, and dignity of the individual
5. Abundant cultural benefits

As the Soviet system progressively strengthens and develops its socialist technological foundation, it must become increasingly democratic; the worker must feel increasingly free; and the full authority of the state must protect the constitutional rights and socialist moral standards that are inherent in society.

In the postwar period, the contrast between the rapidly developing economic foundation and the political and legal superstructure grew increasingly obvious. After Lenin's death, over a period of many years we witnessed a systematic retreat from Leninist norms of party, state, and public life. We went from authentic collectivism to a one-man leadership in government; from a real democracy that throbbed with renewed vitality to a formalist democracy, mere window dressing; from honest, open, and principled grassroots criticism within the party (the sort that Lenin consistently encouraged) to a purely external, deadening, false unanimity; from revolutionary legality to lawlessness that arose from revolutionary expediency.

Officially, of course, no one admitted any of this, and everyone asserted the very opposite of what was going on. As for those un-Leninist and undemocratic measures and institutions whose existence could not simply be denied, they were rationalized by the laws of the class struggle ("the closer to socialism, the fiercer the class struggle"), by the resistance being put up by the exploiters, by the need to smash the Trotskyite-Bukharinist opposition, and so on.

Actually, after the victorious end of the war, these reasons were no longer valid. All hostile classes had long since been eliminated. Within the party, no oppositionist trends or groups survived. The entire society was united on moral and political grounds. The Great Patriotic War had confirmed and strengthened this unity. Yet there was not the slightest sign of any movement toward Leninist norms of party, political, and public life, no symptoms of any absorption of the changes that had taken place on all the tiers of the base, no consideration of what their ramifications were for the superstructure.

There was still more. In January 1950 the death sentence, repealed in 1947, was reinstated for certain crimes. In the icebound silence of Kolyma and other regions, hundreds of thousands of completely innocent people languished behind barbed wire, branded as "enemies of the people." Things had reached a point where not a single prisoner was able to escape from this veritable hell, and no reliable information seeped through. And all the while the sinister assembly lines of the Ezhov-Beria workshops kept hurling additional human victims into the gaping maw of the new Moloch.

Stalin said on several occasions that "we struggled against all kinds of nationalists—Russian, Ukrainian, Cossack, Jewish—but we never touched the Georgian nationalists." Stalin threatened, "I'll get them." And he did. In 1951, catering to his sentiments on the score, the minister of state security of the Georgian republic, Nikolai Rukhadze, and the deputy minister of state security of the USSR, Mikhail Riumin, concocted the Georgian affair.

The producers of this affair alleged that a "Mingrelian nationalist group"[21] tied to a Georgian emigration center in Paris headed by Noe Zhordania, Gegechkori,[22] and others had been organized in Georgia. The group supposedly engaged in espionage and other subversive work against the Soviet state. A wave of arrests of party and government personnel accused of belonging to the group rolled over the republic. Apart from the mass arrests and sentencing of Mingrelians, several thousand people not charged with anything specific were deported from Georgia to the Far North and other remote regions.

The same period saw the staging of the affair of the Jewish Anti-Fascist Committee, which cost the lives of leading members of the Soviet intelligentsia—political workers, writers, and artists.[23]

The unbridled lawlessness of the security services gave rise to grave alarm throughout the country. When that happened in the past, Stalin sometimes placed the blame for such crimes on certain officials of the MGB and finished them off, thereby reaping more glory as a guardian of revolutionary legality and a champion of justice. The halo around his head grew all the brighter.

That's how it happened this time. At one of the plenums of the party CC, I heard Stalin subject the MGB and several of its individual leaders to severe criticism. Afterward, in December 1952, the CC circulated a directive to all party organizations: "It is considered highly important and urgent for the party, the leading party organs, and all party organizations to establish control over the work of the Ministry of State Security. It is essential to put an end once and for all to the lack of supervision of the activities of the organs of the Ministry of State Security and to place their work in the capital and the provinces under the systematic and permanent control of the party, leading party organs, and party organizations." However, the inconsistency of these measures is illustrated by the fact that at the same time work began on the new and monstrous Doctors' Plot.

The shift from the living, active, transformative democracy of Lenin's time to a purely formal, spurious, and ornamental democracy was increasingly evident in the work of local and central soviets. In the 1920s and 1930s, I was often a guest at the All-Union and All-Russian Congresses of the Soviets, I worked in different branches of the Sokol'niki district[24] soviet, and I listened to heated debates among the deputies at the Moscow city soviet. All these meetings pulsed with the life and spontaneous revolutionary creativity of the people—the great revolution crowned entire classes as the real masters of their enormous land. But gradually, year after year, from one five-year plan to the next, the focus of discussion and decision on important current issues and less important organizational, administrative, and procedural matters moved from the congresses, conferences, sessions, and meetings of soviets—and later from their executive committees and collegiums—to narrowly based presidiums, bureaus, and individual directors and leaders. As time went on, these new centers of authority fell captive to the machinery of the all-powerful apparat, on which everything depended—a party-state apparat, unelected, unchanging, and unaccountable to any democratic assembly.

All reasonable and appropriate divisions between the legislative and executive branches, between the deliberative and decision-making bodies, and between those governing and those held accountable were gradually erased. All power was concentrated in the hands of narrowly based agencies or individual leaders. The prerogatives and functions of the entire system of Soviet institutions kept shrinking. The higher levels of party governance—the bureaus and first secretaries of the regional, oblast, and territorial committees, and the central committees of the union republics—atrophied from disuse. The party's general meetings and regional, oblast, and republic-level conferences, as well as all party and soviet congresses, gradually became ceremonial occasions whose only function was to approve and confirm by unanimous vote whatever was proposed by some small-scale agency or leader.

We shall see later what monstrous distortions resulted from this development during Khrushchev's time. The most ridiculous and ignorant of his projects—like splitting the party into industrial and agricultural components, providing each oblast with two party committees and two executive committees, abolishing the entire system of industrial planning with its economic ministries and its sector distinctions and substituting for it a system of regional economic soviets (*sovnarkhozy*)—were discussed and approved unanimously at all levels of government. After Khrushchev's fall, all these projects, whose implementation cost the country hundreds of billions of rubles, were just as unanimously ridiculed and repealed.

Thus, the evolution of the system of government, party, and soviet democracy was far from what Lenin had envisioned and bequeathed in his works, first in *State and Revolution* and then, toward the end of his life, in writings like "Better Less but Better," "How We Can Reorganize the Workers' and Peasants' Inspectorate," and "Our Revolution." The cornerstone of the Leninist form of state and party is the proposition that the working class is the real creator of all of humanity's wealth and must be the real director of all affairs in Soviet society. As he figuratively put it, "Every cook must learn how to run the state."

Lenin emphasized this principle to safeguard against the bureaucratic ossification of state and party organizations and their loss of contact with the people. Especially in his last works, he carefully sought, and succeeded in finding, practical means for actively involving the individual citizen and the masses in the running of the state at all levels of government, from the village soviet and factory committee to the Central Committee Politburo.

Prior to the war, Stalin sometimes followed these behests. There were regular plenary sessions of the party CC, where basic economic, theoretical, and international questions were submitted to earnest debate. The CC convened congresses of Stakhanovite workers, kolkhoz specialists, the military, and other groups, and Stalin listened carefully to the speeches, clarified various issues, and gave his own well-thought-out and highly useful instructions. This served as a working model for all republic and local offices. After the war, however, Stalin's contact with party personnel and workers diminished rapidly, and he soon became a virtual recluse. This set the pattern for other leaders, since any personal initiative could arouse Stalin's suspicions with all the usual consequences. And the reclusive work habits of leaders in Moscow influenced the style adopted by republic and local leaders.

Things came to such a pass that party and government leaders addressed the country with "speeches from the throne" only once every four years, during elections to the Supreme Soviet. After the Eighteenth Congress of the VKP(b),[25] no party congress was held for thirteen and a half years. Two or three years would sometimes pass without any CC plenum. All discourse between the party and government leaders, on one hand, and representatives of industry and the intelligentsia, on the other, came to an end. In the provinces the situation was a little better, but for the most part local officials took their cue from the capital.

Only later, after Stalin's death, did the full tragedy of the political changes under way become clear to me and, I imagine, to millions of other communists and members of the intelligentsia. And prior to that? Were we rank-and-file communists really never vulnerable to doubt and alarm? Did we not sense that something had gone wrong, that things were not the way Lenin had intended? Of course these doubts and agonizing thoughts arose in our minds. Then why were we silent, why didn't we object and protest? Out of cowardice, careerism, fear? No, the overwhelming majority of party members were fine, upstanding people. But to ask, doubt, or object, even during discussions, became absolutely impossible. The remark would instantly be labeled either as "wavering from carrying out the party's general policy" (official questionnaires even had a special item: Did you ever waver in conforming to the party's general policy?) or as "compromising" with Trotskyism or rightist opportunism, again with consequences that were foreseeable.

How, then, did we square all this with our consciences? How could we look at ourselves in the mirror? We told ourselves that things were not always this way within the party and would not stay this way. As long as the country was still under capitalist siege by the exploiting classes that were fading from the international arena, we explained to ourselves that the events of 1937–38 and later years and the party and government's retreat from Leninist norms were necessary for the survival of the Soviet state. This, we reasoned, required iron discipline and complete unanimity within the party in resolving all outstanding questions. It was this that made us view the many troubling events of the time through a certain prism, to take pride in our party cards, to defend unquestioningly whatever was termed part of the party's general policy, and to be ready to sacrifice everything, even our lives, for its triumph.

The drift toward undemocratic forms of leadership and rule made itself felt on all levels of the party and government, including the institution that would have seemed to be democratic by its very nature—the USSR Supreme Soviet. In advance of elections to this body on March 12, 1950, I was on the road night and day campaigning before workers, kolkhozniki, and members of the intelligentsia in the Kamensk-Ural'skii election district—the Ural'skii aluminum plant, the Sinarskii pipe manufacturing factory, aircraft plants, the Kamensk-Ural'skii electric power station, the Berezovskii gold mines, and suburban kolkhozes and sovkhozes. Everywhere I went I was amazed by the powerful and sophisticated technology of the gigantic factories and by the intense industriousness and enormous productivity of all of the builders of socialism. Everywhere I was touched by the warmth and sincerity with which the voters welcomed me, a mere mortal.

So there I was, for the first time in my life a deputy to the Soviet parliament. I was happy and proud. First, because I found myself in that group of one thousand citizens —"the best of the best," as the press called us—

whom the great nation of two hundred million had honored with its votes. Second, because the workers of the Urals, the industrial backbone of the socialist state, had elected me deputy.

The newly elected Supreme Soviet met on June 12 in the conference hall of the Great Kremlin Palace. I had been there in previous years, before it was restored, when it was called Andreevskii Hall. Now I sat in the section reserved for delegates from the Sverdlovsk oblast; seated next to me were other newly elected deputies from the same oblast—Marshal of the Soviet Union Georgii Zhukov, the celebrated atomic scientist Igor Kurchatov, the Urals writer and fabulist Pavel Bazhov, and others.

I met Marshal Zhukov at the front in 1941, during the most critical days of the battle for Moscow, when the capital was in mortal danger. Zhukov was in command of the western front. I had just been appointed head of the political section of the 173rd Rifle Division, formerly the 21st Home Guards Division of the Kiev district of Moscow, composed entirely of Muscovite volunteers. Though wretchedly armed with obsolete weapons of the First World War, the division was imbued with a staunch determination that was nothing short of miraculous.

Our division had its first taste of battle on the Desna River west of the city of Kirov.[26] All October and November it engaged in bloody battle with one of General Guderian's shock tank units whose mission was to capture Tula and Kashira and then fight its way into Moscow from the south. No words can do full justice to the courage, heroism, and self-sacrifice that troops of our division displayed while defending their beloved ancient city of Moscow. The division's battle hymn included these words:

> The enemy sought to broaden
> The headlong advance of his tanks,
> But our troops made a stand at Kashira,
> Defending the capital with their lives.

Like our other units, the division suffered enormous casualties, but the enemy's tanks did not break through to Moscow.

The cold that November was exceptionally fierce. The division commander, Colonel Aleksandr Bogdanov, took me along to the headquarters of the western front, located in Perkhushkovo, near Kashira, to ask for reinforcements. On the way, we saw how Moscow was surrounded by barrage balloons and how its approaches bristled with trenches, barriers, antitank ditches, antiaircraft batteries, barbed wire obstructions and obstacles, artillery installations, barricades. Moscow was ready to die but not surrender.

We reached Perkushkovo at 11:00 P.M. and stopped at the house assigned to Nikolai Bulganin, a member of the Military Council for the western front. By then, even though I was in boots and a military greatcoat, my feet and whole body were icy, my fingers and lips as numb as wood. After the confusion of artillery fire and smoke, bloodstained bandages, shell craters, and the frozen bodies of men and horses, I was amazed by the peace and comparative comfort that met us. The waiting room was neat and warm. By a drawn curtain a potbellied Tula samovar hummed its soothing air.

Bulganin heard out my brief report on the division's combat operations with evident interest, praised the division and the Muscovites, and issued orders for awards and medals to those who had distinguished themselves in action. He promised to send us reinforcements of men and weapons as soon as possible. Shortly before three in the morning, the division commander and I were ushered into the office of the commander of the western front.

From the very first moment, Georgii Zhukov made an indelible impression on me. An intelligent and noble face, a high, clear forehead, keen gray eyes, a sturdy frame, a firm step, lucid and precisely worded thoughts and orders—everything spoke of great inner strength, self-confidence, unbending will, and superbly primed discipline. The division commander and I reported briefly on the division's engagements, its present state, and our request for reinforcements. The marshal rapped out:

"The division has done well. Those who distinguished themselves will be decorated. The division's ranks will be reinforced. Weapons will be delivered. Don't lose a moment preparing for immediate battle. Be in constant operational readiness."

The division commander reported that in the very first battle against enemy tanks, a commander of an artillery unit, Colonel Glotov, had deserted the division. Zhukov pressed a button. A general entered. Zhukov said:

"The commander of the 173rd reports that in the heat of battle, artillery unit commander Colonel Glotov deserted the division. Colonel Glotov is to be found and shot." (Twenty-five years later, at an academic conference during celebrations marking the anniversary of the German rout at the gates of Moscow, Zhukov was asked, "Is it true that Stalin was very cruel?" Zhukov replied, "It's true. I myself was very cruel. The situation demanded it.")

After ordering the colonel's execution, Zhukov took a few brisk steps around the room and said, "For certain commanders the concept of honor apparently does not exist. A marshal dons peasant burlap and bast shoes and slips out of encirclement. What a disgrace! To let encirclement scare you out of your wits. Fight like that and we'll lose the country. Lose everything. These are my orders to the troops: Whatever it takes in the way of reinforcements, maintain the division at peak combat readiness."

Subsequently I was to have another frontline meeting with Zhukov, this time far from Moscow, in my new capacity as head of the political department of the 4th Guards Army. After the fierce but victorious Battle of Stalingrad, our army was refreshed, reequipped, and reinforced. We now had first-class rifles, powerful artillery, and massive tank and air support. The one drawback was that the new army commander was singularly unqualified for the post, an uncultured man with little military knowledge. Ironically enough, this was the marshal who had escaped from encirclement in peasant clothes, as Zhukov had recounted to us that freezing night in Perkhushkovo in 1941. His name was Grigorii Kulik. Demoted from marshal to lieutenant general, he dwelt for a while in the bowels of the war ministry and then persuaded Stalin to give him a chance to rehabilitate himself at the front.

And so our army, its staff, corps units, divisions, and regiments that were headed by educated, capable, and battle-seasoned officers and generals, found themselves under the command of an utter ignoramus. This was a cavalryman of the Civil War who had not progressed an inch in his development over an entire historical period. In outlook, cultural level, and moral character, he was one of those dictatorial sergeant majors of the old regime. He had absolutely no concept of the complex new techniques of military engagement or the art of mutual support among different kinds of forces. His style of command was limited to shouts, curses, and the eternal precept: "If he doesn't follow orders, a lash across his mug." Now this tyrant, installed in our celebrated and battle-proven army, began to act up.

The army was advancing under fire from the Akhtyrka-Kotel'va-Oposhnia line in order to reach the Dnieper. Strong mechanized and tank units, including murderous fascist divisions like Death's Head, Great Germany, and Hitler Youth, opposed us. At the height of an operation, when the commander had to direct the course of battle, General Kulik would abandon his command post, join the ranks, plunk himself down behind a machine gun, and open fire on the enemy: "Let it get to high command and Stalin how brave Kulik is." Or, all on his own, without orders from headquarters, he would turn the army's flank in an unauthorized direction to "take part" in the capture of a major city and add to his laurels. I was forced to report to the front's Military Council on Kulik's total unfitness for his job.

In the course of the operation of September 21, 1943, our command post received a visit from a representative of the high command, Marshal Zhukov. Several corps and division commanders were gathered at the observation point. After receiving their brief reports, Zhukov gave his own appraisal of the situation in a few words of utmost clarity. He ordered changes in the deployment of some units and in the plan of operation and condemned Kulik's conduct and methods of command. He also ordered Kulik to interfere no further in the direction of military operations and transferred those duties to the army's deputy commander. Fortunately, Kulik was soon removed from the post of army commander, and his presence among us was remembered only as a brief, melancholy interlude.

Marshal Zhukov was—and remains—a highly gifted and outstanding Soviet military leader. At the front, he lacked the mildness and tactfulness of Marshal Aleksandr Vasilevskii or the reserve and correctness of Marshal Konstantin Rokossovskii (under whose command I served during the battle for Stalingrad). He was severe, unbending, and sometimes abrasive. But every frontline operation—maybe several at once—that he directed profited enormously from his talented leadership. His legendary fame was deserved and accompanied him wherever he went. "Where there's Zhukov, there's victory" was the catchphrase that followed him on all fronts. I regarded him with great respect and admiration.

Zhukov returned from the war a thrice-decorated Hero of the Soviet Union and was enshrined in the national consciousness as the country's most popular and famous military commander. Whether for this reason—Stalin did not like to share fame with anyone else—or for some other, he was suddenly released from all his Moscow posts and sent to Sverdlovsk to command the troops of the Urals military district.

Now on June 12, 1950, he and I were sitting next to each other in the deputies' rows in the Great Kremlin Palace, exchanging reminiscences of the front.

Another neighboring chair was occupied, as I mentioned earlier, by the prominent atomic physicist and the director of our work on the chain reaction, the missile expert Igor Kurchatov. Joining in the conversation, Kurchatov spoke shyly and almost guiltily about himself. He was so bound by security regulations and classified materials and so occupied with his work that he was not even allowed to go to the Urals to meet with his constituents, something he greatly regretted. Indeed, Kurchatov was a figure wrapped in top secrecy.

Prior to August 1945, when bombs of monstrous destructive power exploded over Hiroshima and Nagasaki, we Soviet scholars with no direct connection to atomic matters knew little about the subject. Even in the Academy of Sciences, the prevalent view was that research in the field of nuclear physics held little promise, since achieving nuclear fission would require more energy than would be released in the process. In the United States, all work on atomic energy was conducted in the strictest secrecy. Only occasionally did some information filter through: how the brilliant physicist and thinker Albert Einstein, the Italian atomic physicist Enrico Fermi, and the Danish patriarch of nuclear physics, Niels Bohr, all fleeing fascism, laid the foundations for this research in the United States; how the immigrants Emilio Segré, Leó Szilard,[27] and others contributed their talent; how, on behalf of a group of physicists, Einstein persuaded President Franklin Roosevelt to launch a mammoth research project to explore the use of atomic physics for military purposes; how Nazi Germany was engaged in preliminary work for producing a chain reaction using its own uranium and heavy water from Norway, and how the American Air Force, acting on a tip from British intelligence, blew up a transport vessel with a shipment of Norwegian heavy water that had been collected over two years, thereby foiling Germany's plans for building an atomic reactor; how toward the end of 1942, Fermi succeeded in producing a chain reaction fueled by uranium and graphite; how remote Los Alamos in the state of New Mexico became the center of American research on splitting the atom for the manufacture of atomic weapons; and how the first American atomic bomb was produced and tested.

As for our own research in the field of atomic energy, no one breathed a word. Only among a few persons close to the government was the mysterious figure of Kurchatov spoken of as the top theoretician and director of such work and then in hushed tones. Only much later was it revealed that as early as the spring of 1939, Kurchatov had alerted the government to the possible military significance of achieving a sustained atomic chain reaction, in view of Nazi Germany's frantic attempts to produce atomic weapons. As Academician Anatolii Aleksandrov reported later, it was estimated even then that splitting one kilogram of uranium would release as much energy as an explosion of twenty thousand tons of TNT.

So surmounting enormous difficulties, a team of Soviet physicists, chemists, metallurgists, engineers, and workers headed by Kurchatov solved the mystery of producing a plutonium-fueled explosive charge. The first Soviet experimental atomic reactor fueled by uranium and graphite was put into operation on December 25, 1946. In 1949 the Soviet Union, confounding the skeptical prognosis of the Americans, carried out its first nuclear bomb test. This signaled the end of the American monopoly on atomic weapons, with all its implications for the world.

Now there I was sitting next to Igor Kurchatov, looking at him and thinking: What mysteries of matter has the mind of this man penetrated! By what immense forces of the universe were his hands constrained! In later years, I heard many of Kurchatov's reports at the highest levels of government.

Then, next to us, was the writer Pavel Bazhov, with the kind, gentle eyes of Grandfather Frost[28] at Christmas time, charming us with his stories of the wondrous beauty of the Urals.

As on all previous occasions, the Supreme Soviet proceeded in a "normal" fashion. At all its meetings, all motions on appointing the chairmen and deputy chairmen of the Council of the Union and the Council of Nationalities, on setting the agenda, and on selecting the members of the standing commissions for the study of legislative, budgetary, and foreign-policy proposals were approved unanimously and without question. Several other commissions were added in later years—on the economy, science, and culture. But everyone knew that these commissions had no effect on ultimate decisions and, more often than not, did not meet at all, although they could have played an important role in Soviet parliamentary democracy.

After the approval of these motions, the Supreme Soviet customarily hears reports on the state budget and the economic plan for the subsequent year, and several days are spent debating these reports in both chambers. But a good 90 percent of the debates have no connection with the substance of the reports. The deputies assigned to speak arrive at the session with prepared texts that inevitably consist of either a personal disquisition or a report on the state of affairs (or the fulfillment of some plan) in the industrial and kolkhoz sectors or on the cultural life of a given republic or oblast. These debates have no impact whatever on the projected budget or economic plan, although for form's sake, after the conclusion of debate, some kind of sum is allocated to one or another program mentioned in the speeches.

If and when an international question arises, the CC staff and the editorial offices of *Pravda* prepare several speeches for selected deputies to deliver—secretaries of oblast committees, academicians, military commanders, steel workers, milkmaids, and teachers. The chairman of the Council of Ministers and other government officials never dream of having to persuade the deputies of the advisability of a particular policy or action of government or having to obtain consent on the most important measures for the year ahead. They know that in reality none of them are accountable to the parliament.

Not a single leader at these sessions need fear being subjected to criticism. All the deputies are disciplined enough to know that one may criticize a leader only on orders from "upstairs," in which case everyone who speaks must join in the criticism and throw a stone. Otherwise one may be suspected of sympathizing with whomever has been set up for reprimand.

The way Soviet democracy operates, it would be impossible for the following scenario to take place:

At a session of the Supreme Soviet, the chairman of the Council of Ministers, Nikita Khrushchev, proposes reorganizing economic management by eliminating the economic ministries and adopting a system of regional economic soviets (sovnarkhozy). Some deputies support the idea; others oppose it. Still others accept its basic premise but suggest revisions and amendments. The debate brings out the facts of the matter, and the vote on the measure establishes the will of the majority. Having gone through the mill of the deputies' collective wisdom and experience, the draft with all its revisions, changes, and amendments becomes law. The minority submits to the majority.

A similar, seemingly normal procedure for a top-level assembly would be, I repeat, completely impossible for us. No questioning of a draft bill, no raising of doubts, is permitted. The discussion becomes an unconditional endorsement of the report and the bill itself, without a hint of real debate. A vote on the proposal produces one and only one result, unanimous approval, which is devoid of the very meaning and aim of voting.

During my eight years as deputy to the Supreme Soviet, I did not witness a single instance when a deputy voiced disapproval of a proposal, even as a basis for discussion, or voted against it or abstained. There was no such incident, either before or after my tenure. If such an incident had occurred, if some deputy spoke or voted against, or even abstained, on some proposal that Stalin, Khrushchev, or any other top leader submitted, he would have been stigmatized as antiparty or mentally ill.

That is why all questions brought before the Supreme Soviet are discussed and decided with complete and unswerving unanimity. Between meetings, the deputies are given lavish free meals. Usually there is an exhibition of consumer goods that coincides with a Supreme Soviet session, or the opening of a secluded store where the deputies may buy goods in short supply—woolen sweaters, shoes, fruit, vegetables, and so on. In the evenings, they are treated to theatrical performances. On the fifth or sixth day, all the decrees issued since the previous session of the Supreme Soviet are unanimously approved without any discussion, questions, or individual objections, and at the first sessions after the elections, a show of hands confirms the membership of the Supreme Soviet Presidium and the Council of Ministers. Loaded down with purchases, the deputies depart for their homes until the next year.

And that's how it went this time.

At another session of the Supreme Soviet five years later, I again found myself seated next to Zhukov. Only then he was defense minister and I a Central Committee secretary. Both of us were candidates for the CC Presidium. We were sitting not in the chamber but on the dais. The meeting moved ahead with the pace and smoothness of a precisely regulated mechanism. Now and then an aide brought us files that required our immediate attention.

Suddenly Zhukov turned to me with a question. "Listen, Dmitrii Trofimovich. You're a theoretician. Please tell me—why do we put on this puppet show every year?"

"What puppet show?" I asked.

"These sessions. After all, we're all pretty busy. Everyone is up to his ears in work. Then why do we drag thousands of busy people to these sessions, which don't really discuss or decide anything? Whom are we fooling?"

I put him off with a joke. "You say, Georgii Konstantinovich, that I'm a theoretician. This, however, is not a theoretical question but an organizational one. So put it to Khrushchev."

We laughed—a bitter laugh, of course.

Another decade goes by. I write this in December 1966. Once again the Supreme Soviet is in session. I have long since ceased being a deputy. Marshal Zhukov, the recipient of four awards as Hero of the Soviet Union, has also retired as deputy. The ashes of Igor Kurchatov repose in the Kremlin wall. Pavel Bazhov is in his grave.

A new generation is succeeding the old. The young have been raised on the teachings of Marx and Lenin. They know nothing of the old life or the ideology of private property. They are aware of the full grandeur of the victories of socialism. But they also know of the suffering that many in their fathers' generation endured during the Stalin era and of the trampling underfoot of freedom, human rights, personal dignity, and the honor of the state that took place under Khrushchev. They do not want to reconcile themselves to such customs. Half a century after the greatest revolution known to mankind, they want to live a truly free and democratic life, in accordance with Lenin's legacy.

Taking account of the experience of our revolution and the socialist construction of the peoples' democracies, I am convinced a thousand times more firmly than ever that Lenin and the October Revolution opened the way to a form of authentic people's sovereignty and genuine democracy that is incomparably superior to the most democratic bourgeois parliamentary democracy. As Lenin said at the First Congress of the Communist International, "The essence of Soviet power is that the one and only basis of state power and the entire state apparatus is the mass organization of those classes that were oppressed by capitalism. These masses, while granted equality under the law, were in reality, even in the most democratic bourgeois republics, kept from participating in political life and denied the enjoyment of democratic rights and freedoms through thousands of devices and tricks; they are now drawn into constant, vital, and decisive participation in the democratic governing of the state."

Elsewhere Lenin pointed out: "The republic of soviets (of workers', soldiers' and peasants' deputies) is not only a higher form of democracy compared to the usual bourgeois republic . . . but the only form capable of assuring a painless transition to socialism."

A half-century has gone by since those words were written. In the meantime, the bourgeoisie has learned a lot from history. So have we. We have learned our Marxism the hard way. Most important, we have laid down a mighty material and technological foundation for socialism. On this foundation we can live as Lenin taught. We *must* do so. All the more so since Leninism itself has been enriched prodigiously these past fifty years, absorbing and adapting to the diverse experiences of all countries and the global liberation movement.

Now we can and must reorganize the functioning of the superstructure—from state policy to philosophy and aesthetics—on the socialist basis that is characterized by the broadest possible popular democracy and genuine individual freedom. In the postwar period, this became a dire necessity, without which it was impossible to continue to make rapid progress in any area of our public life. Yet the fear of taking this path came to the surface; we felt it within the government and the party. We felt it in the ideological sector as well.

The hard line taken by Andrei Zhdanov on literature, social sciences, theater, music, and films continued to develop and intensify. Stalin's terse remark that someone was "trying to extinguish the flame of the great teachings of Pavlov"[29] launched a campaign to expose the anti-Pavlovites. The campaign was a useful one in many respects, but as was often the case, it was not lacking in excesses. The attacks on Ivan Pavlov's outstanding pupil, the prominent Soviet physiologist and Hero of Socialist Labor Leon Orbeli,[30] damaged Soviet science.

In May 1950, *Pravda* ran an article by Professor Chikobava[31] of Tbilisi University, "On Certain Questions Regarding Soviet Linguistics." It inspired a broad-based discussion that culminated in Stalin's famous article "On Marxism and Linguistics." Even here Stalin could not refrain from politicizing this scholarly problem and inserting criminal insinuations into his criticism. He accused the world-renowned linguist and archaeologist, Academician Nikolai Marr of despotism. Naturally, Stalin's article was immediately declared a holy of holies, a classic. The "new teaching"[32] on language that Marr propounded was anathematized, and all discussion of linguistic issues was cut off. Lamentably, Stalin's heavy hand often treated theoretical questions from an administrative rather than an intellectual point of view.

In the sphere of literature and drama, every effort was made to favor works of a pompous, gilded, slanted nature, even though they were clearly far from the historical truth and low in artistic quality. As a result, Stalin Prizes went to such novels as the above-mentioned Semen Babaevskii's *Light over the Earth,* Anatolii Surov's play *Dawn over Moscow,* films like Ivan Pyr'ev's *Kuban Cossacks* and Mikhail Chiaureli's *Fall of Berlin,* and art like the Ukrainian painter Mikhail Khmelko's enormous tinseled and sentimental canvas *Triumph of the Victorious Motherland.*

At the same time, Aleksandr Prokofiev's work, Valentin Kataev's new novel, *Power to the Soviets,* and many other works were accused of being apolitical and ideologically hollow. From time to time, Stalin involved himself in questions of history, philosophy, political economy, and other social sciences if he thought the subject warranted his intervention. At such times, the political aspect of the discussion came to a boiling point, and the entire engine of government was set in motion. Here is an example from before the war:

The editors of a scholarly journal on history decided it was time to examine certain issues regarding German social democracy prior to World War I and the attitude of left-wing Russian Bolsheviks toward it. They ran an article with an editorial note saying it was being published as a basis for discussion. Stalin wrote a letter to the editor calling the article "anti-party" and "quasi-Trotskyite" in nature. The journal's editors were accused of "rotten liberalism," and the author of the article was branded a "prevaricator," "slanderer," "crook," "quasi-Menshevik," "disguised Trotskyite," "vulgarian," "turncoat," "liar," "anti-Leninist smuggler," and "Trotskyite contrabandist." One hardly need add that everyone linked to the publication of the article was promptly arrested. And these arrests were only the harbingers of what was to follow.

Stalin's letter ended with a grievance against Emelian Iaroslavskii,[33] "whose books on the history of the VKP(b), despite their virtues, contain a number of mistakes on fundamental issues and questions of historical accuracy." This comment led to a new round of repressions.

One of the contributors to the exhaustive treatise *The History of the VKP(b),* produced under Iaroslavskii's supervision, was Nikolai El'vov.

As the journalist Eugenia Ginzburg, the mother of the writer Vassily Aksyonov, recounted in her memoirs, El'vov and many other writers and propagandists were deported from Moscow to Kazan after Stalin's letter.[34] There, as coauthor of Iaroslavskii's treatise, he was arrested in 1937 as an "enemy of the people." Then the arrests caught up with those who consorted with those who consorted with the principals. And so it went, like a chain reaction.

The practice of transforming artistic criticism into grave political accusations had especially serious consequences for works produced in the national republics. Such episodes had a marked effect on the political atmosphere among the republic's intelligentsia. Take, for example, the case of the well-known Ukrainian poet Volodymyr Sosiura, who published a poem entitled "Love Ukraine."

> Love Ukraine like the sun, like light,
> Like the wind, the grass, the waters. . . .
> Love Ukraine, its age-old sweep.
> Be proud of your Ukraine,
> Its beauty, new and everlasting,
> And its nightingale voices.

Stalin concluded that these lines were in praise of "Ukraine in general . . . outside time and space," of "perennial Ukraine." Hence, they constituted a "nationalistic approach." A similar so-called artistic work might have appealed to "any enemy of the Ukrainian people from the nationalist camp, such as Petliura, Bandera, and others."[35]

Stalin, as we have noted, did not hold back on "serving up spicy dishes." Thus, his criticism linked the author to Bandera and Petliura. In the end Sosiura was accused of nationalism. *Pravda* rehashed all the faults that Stalin detected in the poem and the poet in a long editorial. Now nothing could save the author from the onus of his crime.

Political accusations were leveled in passing at the poet Maksim Ryl'skii, who had not been without serious ideological error in the past, for his favorable review of Sosiura's poem; at the poet Aleksandr Prokofiev for "sovietizing" the poem by translating it into Russian; and at the editor Valerii Druzin for publishing the poem in his journal *Star.*

Just as severe was the criticism that Stalin handed down after seeing Konstantin Dankevich's opera *Bogdan Khmel'nitskii,* which was performed during "Ukrainian week" in Moscow. Of course, after Stalin's comments the festival went sour, for Stalin was not disposed to use phrases like "the authors failed to include" or "the composer failed to account for." In everything he criticized he saw an antigovernment motive, a subversive plot. So he was inclined to say, "Polish gentry do not appear on stage; for some reason they were concealed from the audience." Stalin's ineradicable suspiciousness sometimes had the most disastrous consequences, as every department of the party and the government copied and internalized it.

To everyone's surprise, Stalin even found the militant—and seemingly politically impeccable—novel of Aleksandr Fadeev *The Young Guard* to be ideologically flawed. This novel, published in 1945, won immediate and widespread popularity and recognition among the young and the entire nation. It received a Stalin Prize, first class. A play based on the book was performed in scores of theaters around the country. The novel was widely published abroad. Then Stalin, who was generally well disposed toward Fadeev's work, suddenly confronted the author with a list of charges. First, in his opinion, the novel failed to give a sufficiently well-developed picture of the older generation—the Bolsheviks, the underground workers, "the fathers." Second, it exaggerated the political maturity of the characters drawn from the younger generation—Oleg Koshevoi and the other "sons." Third, the scenes depicting the early war period—the evacuation of industry and population to the rear and the army's retreat—painted a false picture of the time; in reality, of course, from the outset of the war all this took place in a planned and well-organized fashion.

Though highly sensitive and easily hurt, Fadeev found the inner strength to rewrite his novel. A new edition of *The Young Guard* came out in 1951. I'm not at all sure whether the rewrite was justified. From the standpoint of historical truth and artistic quality, the new edition was not an improvement. Fadeev went through a painful spiritual trauma. Like a good soldier, he carried out orders. But I doubt that he was convinced of the need to redo his book. Nonetheless, Stalin and the entire party press approved of the new edition. In December, in honor of his fiftieth birthday, Fadeev was awarded the Order of Lenin.

That New Year's Eve, I had guests at my home on Kaluzhskaia Street. Among them were Fadeev and his wife, Angelina Stepanova, an actress with the Moscow Art Theater; the academicians Pavel Iudin, Konstantin Ostrovitianov, and Aleksandr Topchiev, and the composer Tikhon Khren-

nikov, all with their wives; and the young singer and future Bolshoi Theater soloist Larissa Avdeeva, my wife, Marianna, and her sister, Galina. The
pine tree glittered with ornaments, its needles giving off a spicy aroma.
Larissa rendered Tchaikovsky's love songs in her beautiful mezzo-soprano.
Khrennikov sang soulful songs and arias from his operas, accompanying
himself on the piano. Then all of us sang together. Everything was relaxed,
pleasant, and festive.

Leaving the dining room for my study, we talked of science, music,
and theater. Fadeev sparkled with wit. His high-pitched voice and staccato
laugh dominated the room. In the middle of some animated argument
among the academicians, he came up to me and whispered mysteriously,
"I have an urgent and important proposal. Could we go into the dining
room?" He whispered the same to Iudin.

When the three of us were in the dining room, he said, "Let's knock
off a hefty glass to Stalin." We drank.

Gradually the others joined us. Fadeev told stories, mimicked certain
writers and actors, sang, and laughed more than anyone, in high shrill
peals. We parted company in the morning.

Fadeev was fanatically devoted to the party. The party's word, Stalin's
word, and the directives of the CC staff he took as immutable. Perhaps
I'm mistaken—I was not all that close to him—but to Fadeev, as to many
other communists, Stalin incarnated the party's greatness, wisdom, and
moral strength. Even to himself he would not cast any doubt on any of
Stalin's actions. The party was always right. Stalin and the party were one.
So whatever was done was necessary. Fadeev was irreproachable as general
secretary of the Soviet Writers' Union, just as thousands of other communists were irreproachable; their absolute honesty was beyond question.

But after the Twentieth Party Congress the veils began falling, and
behind them loomed the terrible truth of what we had not fully grasped.
It is possible that that was one of the factors, if not the main factor, in
the tragic denouement of May 13, 1956 [when Fadeev committed suicide].
From our great and simultaneously woeful historical experience, we must
draw this conclusion among others: we have to put more trust in people,
including members of our own intelligentsia.

The Soviet intelligentsia emerged from the depths of the people.
Alongside the people, members of the intelligentsia bore all the privations
of the period when the Soviet state was being established and consolidated:

they starved, dressed poorly, and lived in primitive surroundings. But they toiled in a spirit of total self-sacrifice. Under the party's direction, older professors, teachers, educators, engineers, and doctors brought up a young and powerful technological intelligentsia, which provided leadership for the country's great industrial revolution. It produced a large force of administrators and directors for a massive socialist system of agriculture. It gave impetus to a mighty cultural revolution in our multinational land. It suffered the greatest devastations in the years of sinister lawlessness, yet it retained its everlasting devotion to the people, the fatherland, and the socialist ideals. It contributed commanders and military, political, and technical personnel to the front, and it supplied construction experts, engineers, directors, and production managers to the rear, thereby securing our victory in the Great Patriotic War. In the tremendous process of socialist development, the intelligentsia have been the driving force in the political, social, cultural, and ideological life of Soviet society.

History has given us exemplary lessons—how large a price we paid and what irreplaceable losses we suffered for our unwarranted distrust of various individuals and whole groups in the Soviet intelligentsia. The political leaders Nikolai Voznesenskii and Jan Rudzutak, the military commanders Mikhail Tukhachevskii and Vasilii Bluecher, the scientists Nikolai Vavilov and Mikhail Pokrovskii, the engineers and economists Valerii Mezhlauk and Garal'd Krumin, the writers Boris Pasternak and Isaac Babel, the artists Vsevolod Meyerhold and Solomon Mikhoels—these are only a few names in the legion of senselessly lost talent.

Let us place greater trust in our people's wonderful intelligentsia! The intelligentsia will repay that trust a hundredfold.

CHAPTER NINE

A Textbook on Political Economy

I AM AN INSPECTOR IN THE PARTY'S Central Committee. I have a small office on the third floor of the CC building with a view of Il'inka Street. I even have a tiny waiting room with a battery of telephones and a young female secretary, Galia Pavlova. Compared to the round-the-clock bustle at Agitprop, my workplace is an utter oasis of calm. I get various assignments. All my spare time I devote to working on the new draft of the textbook on political economy.

Long before the war, Stalin decided on the need for a good, sound textbook on the subject and entrusted its preparation to a corresponding member of the Academy of Sciences, Lev Leont'ev. Over the course of a decade, Leont'ev produced one version after another, but Stalin wasn't satisfied with any of them and kept insisting on further improvements.

Several years before the war, Leont'ev submitted the final results of his latest effort, and a special commission of the CC Politburo was formed on Stalin's instructions to look over the text. On January 29, 1941, Stalin expressed his opinion of the book to the commission and the author. The war interrupted work on the textbook, but in the transition to postwar reconstruction the project was revived. Leont'ev prepared yet another version, the fourteenth or fifteenth, but Stalin was once again dissatisfied. On his orders, a commission headed by CC secretary Georgii Malenkov was formed on February 22, 1950, to revise the text and submit it to the Politburo within a month.

One day I was summoned to Malenkov's fifth-floor office. I found the enormous room the scene of an unusual, for these premises, flurry of acquisition. The walls were lined with tall bookcases with glass doors, and Malenkov's assistant, D. N. Sukhanov, was filling their shelves with books. Several hundred tomes were already arranged decorously in rows. I recognized familiar titles by Adam Smith, David Ricardo, Henri Saint-Simon,[1] and others. I learned later that this collection was assembled from the libraries of the Higher Party School and the Central Committee's Academy of Social Sciences. Walking over to the bookcases, Malenkov said with a somewhat guilty mien:

"As you can see, Comrade Stalin has us digging into political economy. How long do you think it would take to master this discipline?"

I replied, only half jokingly, "Well, if you freed yourself from all other work, you could do it in thirty to fifty years."

In any case, the commission members carried out their instructions and submitted the revised text within a month. Since there were differences of opinion among them, the draft was submitted in two versions, reflecting two points of view, although the differences between them were essentially fairly minor. Both variants were sent around to a number of expert economists for their opinion. I was among those consulted, and I plunged into the text with enormous interest, eager to contribute my bit to this useful enterprise.

Stalin, it appeared, was displeased with the commission's work; its draft had angered him.[2] At that point, something happened that upset all my plans and changed, perhaps, the rest of my life.

One Sunday my wife and I went to see an operetta. The production moved along smoothly and vivaciously. We were into the final act when someone whispered hurriedly in my ear, "Comrade Shepilov, come with me. You're being summoned by the Kremlin."

In the theater manager's office I was handed a telephone.

"Comrade Shepilov? This is Chernukha. Comrade Stalin wants you to call him."

"Comrade Chernukha, I'm in a theater, a rather crowded one."

What followed—my drive to the "nearby dacha" and my long talk with Stalin about the textbook, as described in the first chapter—filled me with joy and pride. I went over Stalin's comments one by one. I meditated on the harsh life of this extraordinary man, placed by destiny at the head of a great country and the world liberation movement. An old tunic, patched-up socks, almost constant isolation. It was said that not even his son, Vasilii, or his daughter, Svetlana, could visit him at his dacha unannounced—they had to ask his permission. Yes, "heavy lies the crown of Monomakh."[3]

Returning from the "nearby dacha," I burst into my friend Boris Ponomarev's home on Bol'shoi Kislovskii Lane. Incoherently, as though in a trance, jumping from one point to another, I told him what had transpired. I did not tell anyone else about it for a long time afterward; in those days it would have been considered impermissible and even dangerous. We knew of such an incident, a story that was whispered among close friends.

On a visit to the Soviet Union, an eminent Asian communist leader was feted by Stalin at his dacha, entertained at dinner, and regaled with choice Georgian wines. While saying good-bye, Stalin gave him a beautifully packaged box of chocolates as a mark of special goodwill. Touched by such kindness, the visitor asked Stalin for a signed portrait as a memento. Stalin acceded. But just before the statesman left for home, the photo, on Stalin's orders, was surreptitiously removed from his suitcase in his room at the Moskva Hotel, and only the chocolates were left. The man raised hell, swore he was ready to leave behind everything else he had with him and go only with the portrait, and begged everyone to find the stolen gift. But no one could help him.

What secret convolutions of the brain could have prompted Stalin to see danger in letting a picture with his dedicatory autograph be taken off to the impenetrable jungles of a distant republic, to be revered there as a sacred image? Only a psychopathologist could tell. There was also word of the tragic fate of an ordinary citizen whom, due to some peculiar circumstances, Stalin had presented with a signed copy of one of his pamphlets.

But thoughts of that nature flitted only momentarily through my mind. I was simply happy—happy to know that what lay ahead of me was a piece of important creative work, needed, according to Stalin himself, by the party, the country, and the entire world communist movement.

Soon enough, Stalin invited Leont'ev, Ostrovitianov, Iudin, and me to the Kremlin for a talk. Ushered into his office at the "corner," we found him looking healthy, vigorous, and rested. We sat at the conference table while Stalin paced the room puffing on his pipe. Once again, he subjected the Malenkov commission's draft to substantial criticism. Some of his points he had already made in his conversation with me; others he raised for the first time or in expanded form. We all took furtive notes, which we later put together to arrive at a unified record of his comments.

A talk with Stalin on these questions left you feeling that you were dealing with someone who had mastered the subject better than you had. There were other reactions as well. Here is an example.

Quite a bit later, at the beginning of November 1952, issue number 20 of *Kommunist* (as the theoretical and political journal of the party CC, *Bolshevik* was renamed starting with that issue) carried my article: "I. V. Stalin on the Economic Laws of Socialism." On November 24, at ten in the evening, I got a call from Poskrebyshev asking me to call Stalin at home. I did so, and Stalin answered at the first ring.

"Do you have the last issue of *Bolshevik* before you? I've read your article. It's good. But there's one mistake. In the second paragraph on page 42, you write that Stalin discovered the objective economic law of the mandatory correlation between labor relations and the nature of the forces of production. That is incorrect. I did not make this discovery. Marx discovered the law of the mandatory correlation between the state of labor relations and the nature of the forces of production in his introduction to 'A Critique of Political Economy.'[4] He points out that during certain historical periods, forces of production correspond to the state of labor relations. At a given stage of development, production forces begin to run counter to existing labor relations. Then a revolution occurs. Of course, you remember this assertion by Marx?"

I replied, "Yes, I am familiar with Marx's well-known assertion. But Marx did not formulate this assertion as an economic law. As I understood it, Marx was the first to propose this, but he did not formulate it as a law. In your work, Marx's assertion was developed further and formulated as an objective economic law of the mandatory correlation between labor relations and the nature of the forces of production."

Stalin said, "It's true, of course, that Marx did not formulate this assertion as an economic law. A number of other very important theoretical axioms he discovered were also not defined as laws. But that does not change the substance of the issue. All I did was single out and underscore Marx's assertion because it has largely been forgotten.[5] I think it would be better if you revised that part of your article. You could say something like this: Stalin clarified the well-known assertion that Marx discovered and put forward. Or perhaps you don't want to make this correction? Maybe it would be hard for you to do it. Look, I'm doing this for you, for your reputation. Otherwise, people may think that Shepilov does not know his Marx. Reissue the article with the correction."

I said, "Reissuing the article in the journal would be difficult. Maybe we could publish it as a brochure and revise that portion as you suggest."

To which Stalin replied, "Well, all right, do it that way. Because it's a good article and this part spoils it. Good-bye."

Each contact with Stalin left us in a state of intellectual ferment and eager to get to work. We were naturally proud of being entrusted with scholarly work of such importance and of doing it under Stalin's direct supervision. We repeatedly saw how thoroughly versed he was in political economy, philosophy, and history, how knowledgeable he was in regard to facts, including facts from much earlier historical periods, and how astute he was in applying abstract principles of political economy to current conditions. Everything he said to us we took as incontestable truth; everything in his instructions we accepted as new, important, and absolutely correct.

Today, fifteen years after Stalin's death, we are gradually beginning to sort out the past and to see that not all of Stalin's theories and assumptions should be taken as irrefutable Marxist truth. Stalin was a highly experienced popularizer of Marxism-Leninism. He was a master of seizing on the most salient and important feature of a classic work and laying out its complex historical conclusions, truths, categories, and laws plainly, clearly, and tersely, making them accessible to the average person. An example of this was his work *Foundations of Leninism*. In a half-hour lecture, Stalin could provide a thorough analysis of world events, the liberation struggle, and the socialist construction of an entire epoch, and do it on a sound theoretical basis, making it plain, clear, terse, and accessible to all. He did this, as we know, for thirty tempestuous and difficult years. All this is true. But it is also true that in some respects his theoretical works are deeply flawed and deviate from Lenin's positions. On closer analysis, his seemingly faultless and brilliant generalizations regarding contemporary reality portray it in a false light.

But this realization came to us later—tortuously, discordantly, and sometimes painfully. In the period I am dealing with, we were untroubled by doubts about the impeccable nature of Stalin's theoretical works and his instructions to us. Stalin was held by all to be the coryphaeus of Marxism-Leninism, and we, the coauthors of the textbook on political economy, had no latitude for any critical views of Stalin.

And no such views existed. We dismissed out of hand the anti-Soviet fulminations heard abroad, and rightly so: they did not contribute anything edifying. After the rout of the Trotskyites and rightists, the unanimous view in the Marxist camp at home and abroad was that Stalin's works, his ideas, his teachings, and his words were the pinnacle of Marxist thought. Over the three decades of Stalin's supremacy, criticism within the party on sociological issues gradually waned, and when all was said and done, there remained only one creator of theory and source of criticism—Stalin.

Only he could, and did, fire critical broadsides—yesterday against the "contrabandists" on the subject of party history, today against the "Menshevik-like idealists" in philosophy, tomorrow on the "counterrevolutionary Kondrat'evites" in agrarian theory,[6] the day after tomorrow on the "rootless cosmopolitans" in literature and the theater. Everyone else had only one right: to praise the brilliance of Stalin's ideas and to propagandize and popularize them. An absolute monopoly on questions of Marxist-Leninist theory, a gradual eclipse of Bolshevik critical thought—our party, our people, and the world communist movement paid dearly for these evils.

After one of our conversations with Stalin, the CC Presidium appointed a group of Soviet economists to write a textbook on political economy. The group included two full members of the Academy of Sciences, Konstantin Ostrovitianov and Pavel Iudin; two corresponding members, Lev Leont'ev and me; a member of the Academy of Agricultural Sciences, Ivan Laptev, and a corresponding member, Anatolii Pashkov. On Stalin's instructions, we were all released from our current duties and obligations and placed "in strict isolation" at the outskirts of the city so that we would not be distracted by lesser concerns and would complete the textbook within a year. Stalin ordered the "best possible conditions" to ensure that "they are not lacking in anything and have no concerns other than work on the textbook."

This was done. We were given a splendid house that Savva Morozov[7] at one time built in Gorki outside Moscow. From July 1931 to June 1936 it was the home and workplace of Maxim Gorky.

Gorky returned to the Soviet Union for good in May 1931,[8] and took up residence at 6 Malaia Nikitskaia Street, now Kachalova Street. But soon afterward, on June 27, he wrote to Adam Bogdanovich[9] that he had begun to spit blood, and in July he moved to Gorki. As his tubercular condition worsened, he made two trips, to Italy and the Crimea, traveled around the country, and paid frequent visits to Moscow. But Gorki remained his home. Here he wrote his last works. Here he died.

And so on a fragrant May morning in 1950 we arrived in Gorki, at an attractively designed two-storied house with a tree-lined driveway on a high bank of the Moscow River. A neglected garden; beyond it a pine forest. Across the river with its clear bluish waters, meadows as far as the eye could see. At the front entrance, bronze deer with branching horns. A decorated marble foyer. A large first-floor dining room.

Gorky followed a rigid routine: a set time for work and a set time for relaxation, when he would come down to the dining room where some guests were usually waiting—everything was strictly scheduled. In his prodigious creative work, which he pursued to his last breath, Gorky kept up with a wide circle of acquaintances—writers, artists, scientists, kolkhozniki, inventors, and musicians. He was often host to Stalin, Voroshilov, Shcherbakov,[10] and other government leaders. He exchanged views with them about the draft of the Soviet constitution, the building of the Moscow metro, the construction of giant planes, the Civil War, folk music, and much else.

Here in this house Gorky received the chairman of the French radical socialist party, Édouard Herriot; here he chatted with the writer H. G. Wells. Romain Rolland[11] and his wife visited him for three weeks, and together they conversed with the artists of the village of Palekh,[12] as well as with a large group of pupils of the NKVD's Bolshevskii Labor Commune.[13] They also met with leading Soviet movie directors—Vsevolod Pudovkin, Aleksandr Dovzhenko, Mikhail Romm, Grigorii Roshal', Grigorii Aleksandrov—and viewed the films *The Battleship Potemkin* (Sergei Eisenstein), *Mother* (Pudovkin), *Pyshka* (Romm), and others. After leaving, Rolland wrote to Gorky on August 4, 1935: "It is good to belong, as you do, to a great people striding forward and leading mankind. I am happy to have met and made contact with that people."

Among the Soviet writers who visited or stayed with him were Aleksei Tolstoy, Konstantin Fedin, Mikhail Svetlov, Semen Kirsanov, Igor' Sel'vinskii,

Leonid Leonov, and many others. There wasn't a single aspect of human activity that didn't excite Gorky's liveliest interest. After a conversation with the academician Aleksei Speranskii,[14] he applied himself diligently and at length to the establishment of an institute of experimental medicine—the Institute for the Study of Man, which later evolved into the Academy of Medical Sciences. After receiving a group of musicians he put forward the idea of publishing a collection on the "lives of extraordinary people." In a conversation with the staff of the Moscow Art Theater, he discussed problems of staging. In a letter to Fedor Khitrovskii,[15] he advocated the production of children's toys of a new kind, for group games, and in another letter he delved into the subject of Mari[16] folklore. Chatting with the Kukryniksy,[17] he set out his thoughts on painting; meeting with groups of kolkhozniki from Tatarstan[18] and workers from Iaroslavl',[19] he questioned them in detail on problems of agriculture, industry, and the lives and cultural interests of workers and peasants in towns and villages.

Truly, it would take several lives to accomplish even part of the work done by this extraordinary man as he sat at his desk in his study to the left of the living room. Here he began, completed, or revised his last plays—*Egor Bulychev and Others, Dostigaev and Others, Somov and Others.* Here he wrote his great epic, *The Life of Klim Samgin.* Here he wrote a large number of brilliant articles on a wide range of subjects. And all this accounted for only a small part of his work during those years.

Even though he was past sixty and his lungs were impaired by a forty-year history of tuberculosis (lesions, enlarged bronchial tubes, emphysema, asthma, sclerosis), he supplemented his creative work with a prodigious amount of editing and correspondence. He initiated the production of the multivolume *History of the Civil War* and then edited it himself. He initiated and supervised the writing of a series of books, The History of Factories and Industrial Plants. He was the editor of the journals *Our Achievements* and *Literary Studies,* a member of the editorial staff of the journal *USSR in Construction*, and the editor of the *Almanac, Sixteenth Year.* He worked out plans for a book, *The History of Women,* and for a lengthy series of books, The History of the Village. He was the director of the journal *Kolkhoznik.*

As I stood by his writing desk thumbing through shelf after shelf of books with his marks, underlines, and comments, I reflected on his energy and his lofty concept of his duty as a writer and citizen. Sadly, I compared it with the omnipresent phenomenon of young Soviet writers who, having published one novella or part of a novel, squandered the next twenty or thirty years on a few short stories and newspaper articles and on speeches at interminable, and in most cases quite unnecessary, writers' meetings, seminars, and conferences. Regrettably, such "writers"—or, more precisely, literary bureaucrats—often become secretaries of writers' unions or directors of one sort or another. They are quite satisfied with their high rank and good pay. But what a glaring contrast with the great creators of world literature—Balzac, Leo Tolstoy, Goethe, Chekhov, Gorky, and a host of others!

With bated breath we enter Gorky's bedroom. Strikingly plain and simple furniture: a bed, a wardrobe. Above the bed, our gaze is drawn to Mikhail Nesterov's canvas *The Sick Girl*. The girl is rendered as pale, consumptive, her bloodless skin stretched tight over her cheeks, her shrunken lips baring her teeth, in her eyes inexpressible sorrow and exhaustion, her body withered and inert. Everything tells you that the small flame of life is flickering, the girl is dying. And the most terrible thing about the picture is the fresh crimson rose clutched in her cold waxen hand. Perhaps this beautiful and, one imagines, incredibly fragrant rose evokes more than anything else the tragedy of a waning life.

Nesterov encountered the sick girl, Zoia Gurkova, in the Crimea, and asked her to sit for him. She replied, "If I can enable a great painter to create a canvas, then my life is not pointless." Seeing the painting at an exhibition, Gorky entreated Nesterov to let him have it. Knowing that the picture had a somber emotional impact and that Gorky was suffering from tuberculosis, Nesterov did not want to accede to his request. Nevertheless, with the help of the artist Pavel Korin, Gorky acquired the painting and hung it over his bed. There, under Nesterov's canvas, at 11:10 on the morning of June 18, 1936, the life of the great writer came to an end.

He struggled against his illness to the last breath, and wrote down his last observations on little pieces of paper:

"Highly complex reactions. Two related processes—a sluggish sensation, as though my nerve cells are being extinguished and covered with ashes and my thoughts are graying, and at the same time a wild desire to talk, to the point of delirium. I know I'm rambling, although the individual phrases make sense. They think it's pneumonia; my guess is I probably won't survive it. I can't read or sleep."

He dictated the following observation: "The end of the novel—the end for the hero—the end for the author. The final blow."

I was given a room once occupied by the writer's son, Maksim Alekseevich.[20] Ostrovitianov had the room that belonged to Gorky's wife, Nadezhda Alekseevna (Timosha), and so on.[21] As for the rooms that had been made part of a museum, they were the holy of holies for us. But at times when I was deep in thought, I would go in softly, leaf through his books, contemplate his desk and *The Sick Girl,* and almost see his remarkably kind eyes and hear his quiet, halting voice with its regional Russian accent.

We spent a whole year in Gorki intensely working on a strict schedule. Drawing on our conversations with Stalin, we laid out a work plan and the textbook's table of contents. When our work revealed areas of disagreement, we asked for another meeting with Stalin.

Stalin was quick to respond. The meeting took place on May 30, 1950, in Stalin's Kremlin office. Stalin was dressed in his usual worn prewar gray tunic, trousers, and boots. He was freshly shaven and looked hale and hearty. We posed our questions and he answered them. At times he would ask questions himself. The conversation lasted an hour, from 7:00 to 8:00 P.M. Saying good-bye, Stalin said he would be glad to meet with us whenever we felt the need.

On returning to Gorki we compiled a collective record of our conversation. Stalin held us to a very demanding standard of authorship. He repeatedly stressed that every word had to be carefully weighed so as to eliminate any redundancies ("blabber," he called it). He insisted on flawless scholarship that was at once wedded to a popular style but avoided all vulgarization. He had no time for oversimplification or glibness, which he called "cheap."

After completing chapters on political economy and pre-capitalist means of production, we sent them to Stalin for editing. He was amazingly thorough; nothing was too small for his attention; he carped about everything. I am not able to convey here the extent of corrections that he made in our text, but I can give a few examples.

The title we chose was *Political Economy: A Short Course.* Stalin crossed out *Short Course* and substituted *A Textbook.* In the chapter heading "Pre-capitalist Formation," he changed "Formation" to "Means of Production."

In the first chapter we wrote, "The origin of man was one of the greatest leaps in the development of nature." For "leaps" he substituted "turns." To our sentence, "Man's ancestors lived in herds," he added "and hordes."

In our second chapter, "Production by Slave Labor," there were many corrections as well. In our sentence "At first slavery was patriarchal in character," he inserted "and domestic" after "patriarchal." We wrote, "The rich loaned out money, enslaving their debtors"; Stalin changed it to "The rich made loans in seeds and money, enslaving their debtors, making them into slaves and seizing their land."

In addition to his many substantive and stylistic corrections, Stalin sometimes supplied his own often-quite-significant inserts. For instance, to the book's introduction to political economy, he added the following:

"As we can see, the study of political economy deals not with some abstract, irrelevant issues but with the most concrete and current questions involving the vital interests of people, societies, and classes. Is the end of capitalism and the victory of the socialist economic system inevitable? Do the interests of capitalism stand in opposition to the interests of society and the progressive development of mankind? Is the working class the gravedigger of capitalism and the bearer of ideas for the liberation of society from capitalism? These and similar questions are resolved differently by different economists, depending on which class interests they represent. This explains why at present there is no single model of political economy for all classes of society, but several models—bourgeois political economy, proletarian political economy, and finally, the political economy of intermediate classes striving to adapt the political economy of the working class to the preferences of bourgeois political economy.

"This also reveals the utter fallacy of those economists who assert that political economy is a neutral, nonparty science that is independent of class struggle and free of any direct or indirect links to political parties.

"Can there be a political economy that is objective, impartial, and unafraid to look truth in the eyes? Of course there can be. But such an objective political economy can belong only to a class that is not interested in covering up the contradictions and vices of capitalism, nor in preserving the capitalist order of things—a class whose interests coincide with the liberation of society from capitalist slavery and are at one with the progressive development of mankind. Such a class is the working class. Hence, only a political economy based on the interests of the working class can be objective and selfless. Marxist-Leninist political economy is precisely that."

In the chapter on slavery and production Stalin inserted the following:

"As we can see, society under the slave-ownership system presented a fairly diverse picture of strata and classes. Society consisted of two principal strata, the free and the slaves. The first enjoyed all the civil, property, and political rights of citizenship (except for women, who were held in virtual slavery) and were separated from the slaves. The slaves were denied all these rights and were barred from consorting with the free. The free, in turn, were divided into two classes, the big landowners, who were also the major slaveholders, and the small producers (peasants and tradesmen), among whom the better-off also made use of slave labor and had slaves of their own. Finally, there were the priests, who played a major role in the slave era and belonged to the class of big landowners and slaveholders.

"Thus, apart from the inherent difficulties between the slaves and the slaveholders, there were inherent difficulties between the big landowners and the peasants. As the slaveholding system developed, and as slave labor, the cheapest form of labor, took over the major areas of production and formed its basis, the contradictions between the slaves and the slaveholders became the basic contradiction within society as a whole.

"True, the contradictions between the small producers and the major wellborn landowners gave rise to a democratic movement among the free aimed at eliminating enslavement through debt, redistributing land, doing away with the privileges of the landed aristocracy, and turning power over to the demos (i.e., the people). However, none of this brought any relief to the small producers; it only increased the influence and power of the newly rich slaveholders from the ranks of the 'commoners,' who had profited from war and the slave trade at the expense of the landed aristocracy.

"The fact was that this democratic movement, far from trying to liberate the slaves or even ease their lot did not even allow this question to be raised. Besides, as we know, any time the slaves tried to raise their heads and demand their freedom, all the other free strata, with the exception of the poorest peasants, whose condition did not differ fundamentally from that of the slaves, forgot their differences and formed a solid front against the slaves. The democracy of ancient Greece and Rome, so ballyhooed in bourgeois history textbooks, was essentially a democracy of slaveholders."

However, Stalin had time to edit only the introduction and the first three of the textbook's forty-two chapters. After that, he told us to turn in the finished draft as a whole. The work was finished within a year, and the proofs were submitted to the CC Politburo.

It was spring. The trees filled with sap like the milk-swollen breasts of a wet nurse. The nightingales, robins, and finches filled the air with their songs. The bird cherries burst into bloom. The cherry trees and apple trees acquired a fragrant coverlet of pale pink petals. The meadow across the Moscow River dressed up in green. Above it, the skylarks victoriously trilled their silvery hymns.

Regretfully we bade good-bye to hospitable Gorki. It had been sheer happiness to be engaged in creative work in such ideal surroundings—to pore over the great intellectual heritage of Marx, Engels, and Lenin and the works of historians, philosophers, and economists, the precursors of scientific socialism, searching for the key to the laws of our complex reality. Shortly before leaving, we were honored by a visit from Nadezhda Peshkova and Liudmila Tolstaia, the widow of Aleksei Tolstoy. We sat late into the night listening to their reminiscences and sharing our impressions of two giants of Russian literature.

On the eve of our departure, I browsed once more through the rooms of the Gorky museum. In the evening we took a long stroll along the Moscow River. The moon bathed the world in a magical light. The frogs filled the night with their croaking serenades. There was a pungent odor of grass and fish. That very night the lilacs bloomed.

While waiting for Stalin and the other Politburo members to go over our draft, we returned to our regular jobs.

Just ahead was a significant date for Soviet music—the 175th anniversary of the Bolshoi Theater. I was to take part in the preparations for this jubilee—to help decide on awards of orders and medals to the theater's artists and confer honorary titles. I took this on with pleasure.

From my student days, the Bolshoi Theater had been my temple of world music, my seat of musical learning, my source of inexpressible joy and pleasure. Since 1922, I don't think I missed a single, even slightly notable production of the Bolshoi Theater or the former Zimin Theater, later the Bolshoi's affiliate. Getting in wasn't always easy, but I was so determined to fight my way through or die trying, even without a ticket, that I overcame the difficulties. Can you imagine missing a day's performance of Wagner's *Lohengrin* if Leonid Sobinov is singing the principal role and Antonina Nezhdanova is playing Elsa? Years later, when I had access to the government box at the Bolshoi, the main (formerly the tsar's) loge, and the box for the theater management, I remembered what delight overcame me after sneaking in when I perched somewhere in the gallery, waiting with bated breath. Soon the lights would dim and the heavy curtains would part on the sorcery of *Swan Lake*. How I feared the intermissions! What if they asked for my ticket and threw me out? This, I confess, did happen sometimes. Yet at the Bolshoi's next gala production, there I'd be again, trying to make myself invisible.

In the course of those decades I saw a wealth of operas at the Bolshoi and its affiliate, including *The Demon* [Anton Rubinstein], *La Traviata* [Giuseppe Verdi], *Manon Lescaut* [Giacomo Puccini], *Carmen* [Georges Bizet], *Lohengrin* [Richard Wagner], *Werther* [Jules Massenet], *I Pagliacci* [Ruggero Leoncavallo], *La Bohème* [Puccini], *Faust* [Charles Gounod], *The Sorochinsky Fair* [Modest Mussorgsky], *Die Walküre* [Wagner], *May Night* [Nikolai Rimsky-Korsakov], *Die Meistersinger von Nürnberg* [Wagner], *Tosca* [Puccini], *The Tsar's Bride* [Rimsky-Korsakov], *The Mermaid* [Aleksandr Dargomyzhskii], *Le Coq d'Or* [Rimsky-Korsakov], *Pskovitianka* [Rimsky-Korsakov], *Evgenii Onegin* [Pyotr Tchaikovsky], *The Huguenots* [Jakob Meyerbeer], *The Barber of Seville* [Gioacchino Rossini], *Dubrovsky* [Eduard Napravnik], *Yolanta* [Tchaikovsky], and *Cherevichki* [Tchaikovsky].

At the end of the war there was a new flowering of opera at the Bolshoi, which restaged many Russian and world classics, some as new productions. Thanks to the brilliant work of the set designers Fedor Fedorovskii, Petr Vil'iams, Vladimir Dimitriev, Vadim Ryndin, and others, the staging of the Bolshoi's spectacles not only rivals that of many of the world's other renowned theaters but often exceeds it. The direction of masters of the operatic art like Vladimir Losskii, Nikolai Smolich, Leonid Baratov, Boris Pokrovskii, and others is superlative. During the postwar years, the Bolshoi restaged *Boris Godunov* [Mussorgsky], *Sadko* [Rimsky-Korsakov], *Aïda* [Verdi], *Prince Igor* [Alexander Borodin], *The Queen of Spades* [Tchaikovsky], *Ruslan and Ludmila* [Mikhail Glinka], *Mazeppa* [Tchaikovsky], *Khovanshchina* [Rimsky-Korsakov], *The Power of Evil* [Aleksandr Serov], *Romeo and Juliet* [Gounod], *Lakmé* [Léo Delibes], *Madame Butterfly* [Puccini],

The Marriage of Figaro [Wolfgang Amadeus Mozart], *Fidelio* [Ludwig van Beethoven], *A Life for the Tsar (Ivan Susanin)* [Glinka], and other operas.

In later years I was able to acquaint myself with the operatic virtuosity of Prague and Paris, Budapest and Milan, Belgrade and New York. From the standpoint of the production as a whole, the performances of the Bolshoi's repertory that are listed above were without question masterpieces of operatic artistry. However, the hard truth is that the decisive element in opera is the quality of the voice and the sound of the orchestra. If either is inferior, no amount of staging will save the day.

Soviet opera in the postrevolutionary years owed its rise to a brilliant array of operatic singers at the Bolshoi. I was lucky enough to have heard them all many times. They were Leonid Sobinov, Antonina Nezhdanova, V. R. Petrov, Grigorii Pirogov, Kseniia Derzhinskaia, Nadezhda Obukhova, Elena Katul'skaia, Valeriia Barsova, Elena Stepanova, Aleksandr Pirogov, Mark Reizen, Nikolai Ozerov, Georgii Nelepp, Leonid Savranskii, S. I. Migai, Mariia Maksakova, Vera Davydova, Ekaterina Shumskaia, and others.

The creators and moving spirits of the Bolshoi's outstanding productions were highly talented directors like Viacheslav Suk, Nikolai Golovanov, Arii Pazovskii, L. P. Shteinberg, Aleksandr Melik-Pashaev, Iurii Faier, and Kirill Kondrashin. Under their supervision, the orchestra and choir excelled in splendor and emotion. Yet along with the Bolshoi's steady progress in the quality of its productions as a whole, the undeniable decline in its postwar vocal resources made itself distinctly and alarmingly felt. A whole number of operas had to be given up because the leading parts were beyond the vocal powers of a new set of singers with mediocre natural gifts and improperly trained voices. (Even then, however, there were some remarkable talents, such as Galina Vishnevskaia and Irina Arkhipova.)

The Bolshoi's ballet company, on the other hand, retained all its brilliance, gaining worldwide repute. My appreciation of choreography developed somewhat later than my infatuation with singing. But such immortal Bolshoi productions as *Swan Lake* [Tchaikovsky], *Don Quixote* [Ludwig Minkus], *The Nutcracker* [Tchaikovsky], *Giselle* [Adolphe Adam], *Coppélia* [Delibes], *Raimonda* [Aleksandr Glazunov], *Romeo and Juliet* [Sergei Prokofiev], *Sleeping Beauty* [Tchaikovsky], and others captivated me for all time. The ballet became as much of a necessity for me as books, the theater, the opera, classical music, and good folk songs.

I was fortunate enough to have seen many performances by the famous stars of the Russian ballet—the queen of them all, Ekaterina Geltser, M. P. Kondratova, Viktorina Kriger, Viktor Smoltsov, Galina Ulanova, Olga Lepeshinskaia, Raissa Struchkova, Maia Plisetskaia, Marina Semenova, Aleksei Ermolaev, Mikhail Gabovich, and Asaf Messerer, to name just a few. In the capitals of Europe, Asia, Africa, and America, the Bolshoi Ballet was greeted with boundless acclaim and appreciation.

I know my pen is too weak and my words too pale to convey even a minute fraction of the imprint that the great masters of the Bolshoi Theater left on the soul and consciousness of their audience. Take Antonina Nezhdanova. I heard her as Violetta [Verdi's *La Traviata*], Ludmila [Glinka's *Ruslan and Ludmila*], Gilda [Verdi's *Rigoletto*], Antonida [Glinka's *A Life for the Tsar*], Marguerite [Gounod's *Faust*], Elsa [Wagner's *Lohengrin*], and in several other roles and in concert. On the stage, she did not make a striking effect in appearance or dramatic talent, as was the case, according to his contemporaries, with Fedor Chaliapin.[22] But on leaving the theater after one of her performances you never asked yourself about her acting: her enchantment was in her voice, as pure as mountain crystal, soft, and tender. She sang with a captivating warmth, expressiveness, and soulfulness. No score was too difficult for her. Her artistry lay in her wide vocal range and virtuosity, which she combined with the subtlest emotional sensitivity.

So I can't answer the question of how well she performed. In my opinion, she did not act at all, in terms of movement, gestures, and other outward expressions. But whatever the role, she always entranced her listeners and left an impression that lasted for the rest of their lives. As we know, Sergei Rachmaninov's celebrated *Vocalise* was written for—and dedicated to—Nezhdanova. When she deplored the fact that the score had no words to it, Rachmaninov said, "Why do we need words when you can express everything better and more fully with your voice and performance than anyone else can with words?" Such was the miraculous power of her voice and artistry. And when Nikolai Golovanov[23] introduced me to Nezhdanova, then a professor at the Moscow Conservatory and already in her seventies, I must have behaved like a besotted schoolboy who meets the object of his admiration.

On a sorrowful day of June 1950, at the conservatory's Great Hall, which was draped in black, I paid my last respects to this great Russian singer. From time to time I still stop at the Novodevich'ii cemetery before the gravestone with its carved marble garland and pristine rose. And then I seem to hear her voice, like a nightingale's trills on a moonlit Moscow night.

In November 1951 an all-Union discussion on the contents of the political-economy textbook, drafts of which were circulated beforehand for comment, was held in the club of the Central Committee. The cream of the social-science community took part. There was a heated discussion, revealing how involved all those present—economists and specialists in other fields—were in the publication of a sound textbook. The overwhelming majority approved our draft but suggested various revisions and offered advice on the book's structure and certain wordings. As always in open debate, however, some of the speeches were patently abusive, vulgar, and ill informed. On the basis of the discussion, we sent Stalin our proposals for improving the draft and correcting a number of mistakes and inaccuracies and a rundown of questions left unsettled.

On February 1, 1952, Stalin responded with a major theoretical treatise, "Comments on Economic Questions Related to the Discussion of November 1951." We, the authors of the textbook, naturally took pride in Stalin's laudatory remarks about our work; ordinarily he was stinting on praise. In his comments, Stalin wrote:

"Some comrades at the discussion were much too zealous in panning the textbook draft, disparaging the authors for mistakes and omissions, and asserting that the work was a failure. That was unfair. Of course, there are mistakes and omissions, as there almost invariably are in any large-scale undertaking. All the same, the great majority at the discussion agreed that the draft could serve as the basis for the final version, requiring only a few corrections and additions. Indeed, one need only compare this draft with textbooks on political economy now in circulation to see that it stands head and shoulders above any of them. In this, the authors of the draft have rendered a great service."

We were fully satisfied, as well, with Stalin's reaction to our "Proposals for Improving the Textbook Draft." While making a number of important new theoretical postulates, he added: "As for all remaining questions, I have no special comments to offer on the 'Proposals' made by Comrades Ostrovitianov, Leont'ev, Shepilov, Gatovskii, and others."

On February 15, 1952, there was a wide-ranging conference in the Kremlin that was attended by members of the CC Politburo, the authors of the textbook, and the country's most prominent economists. With Stalin's "Comments" serving as a basis, the meeting was called so that we could exchange views on a number of questions that had not yet been clarified in the text. Economists asked questions, and Stalin answered. Stalin was in high spirits and willingly shared his thoughts. In the end, the CC Politburo gave us another year so that we could deal with all the worthwhile comments and proposals made at the conference and with Stalin's own instructions.

CHAPTER TEN

Under the Sword of Damocles

FIXING ARGINSKII WITH A COLD AND INDIFFERENT STARE, Riumin[1] said, "Tell us what you know about Shepilov's hostile activity."

This incident took place *after* I was placed under suspicion and relieved of all my posts, *after* Stalin suddenly remembered my situation and observed that "we can't let people like Shepilov go to waste," *after* he received me at his dacha for a long conversation and asked me to take part in writing a new political economy textbook, and *after* I was elected to the Supreme Soviet and, later, to the party CC. Yet despite all these intervening events, Beria's sinister machine kept moving on its predetermined course, and the sword of Damocles still hung over my head.

To describe how the net was being spun around me, and how, two or three years after the Patriotic War, it was attached to the cogwheels, assembly belts, and transmission of the horrendous machine that was again operating at full speed, I must make a fairly lengthy digression. I must speak of one of my wartime comrades, of a real communist and Soviet patriot, of Il'ia Arginskii, the principal hero of the episodes into which I was newly cast.

When our 21st Moscow Home Guards Division was formed in June and July 1941, among the volunteers for the front was a group of educators and writers, the founders of our division newspaper, *Battle Flag*. They were the historian and longtime party member Professor Vladimir

Miroshevskii, the economist Iakov Kronrod, whose later career earned him a doctor of economic sciences, the philosopher Professor Aleksandr Makarovskii, and the experienced writer, journalist, and poet Il'ia Arginskii. There were others, many others, all honorable men, worthy sons of their party and their fatherland. They started a first-class frontline newspaper, and later an army newspaper, both of which they published on a regular schedule no matter what, often while under heavy fire, trudging the rugged roads of war to its victorious conclusion.

Il'ia Arginskii served mostly as a war correspondent. He could be found in the ranks, at artillery positions, in the trenches, at observation posts. Wherever the fighting was fiercest, wherever some unit was in difficulty, wherever an assault unit was trying to breakthrough, there you would always find Il'ia Arginskii. Calm, unruffled, seemingly absent-minded and indifferent to his surroundings, even when mines were exploding around him or the sector was under murderous machine-gun fire, Il'ia was a scrupulous gatherer of information. He also wrote his own pieces, as well as poetry, and spent time chatting with the troops and filling them in on what was going on in the world. He was possessed by his work. Always alert, with stubble for a beard and sharp, gray eyes behind glasses that were thick enough for the half-blind, Il'ia was a master at enlivening his writing with ideas, artistic portraits of heroes, and bits of verse.

In his perpetual creative fever he seemed oblivious to his own self. If his comrades did not feed him, he would go for twenty-four hours without a meal. In the bitterest cold he would climb out of his dugout, distractedly leave his fur hat behind, and proceed bareheaded to the front line. Working around the clock, Il'ia slogged ahead with our division and army—literally slogged—through mud, dust, snow, and frost, all the way from Moscow and Stalingrad to Vienna.

He was thin and haggard to look at, although there was no kindlier creature on earth. It would be hard to imagine a more unselfish, honest, and upstanding person than Il'ia. He was devoted to his wife, Antonina, and their only child, their little daughter Iren, both of whom he left behind in Moscow. But he was so impractical and helpless in day-to-day matters that even during periods of calm, in between the fighting, he could not tear himself away from his work to mail them a food package. He often went hungry, and so did they. I remember on one occasion, when I was called back to Moscow after the war, he took me up on my offer to take something home to his family. Going to the army commissary, what did he buy? A box of candied fruit. Not bread, butter, or lard, the kind of solid food our starving relatives in the rear were dying for, but a box of candied fruit. He thought it would be inappropriate to send anything more substantial.

The spring of 1945 was ending when I encountered Il'ia again on a road west of Vienna, somewhere around Amstetten. The beige waters of the Danube rolled majestically to the east. The castle of Emperor Franz Josef, now the home of the aforementioned Otto Hapsburg, cast its proud gaze over the gardens and vineyards of the boundless estate. From the alpine meadows came the sweet breath of mountain grass. Everything around me radiated light and happiness. Even the sight of gutted tanks and self-propelled artillery, the torn up shell craters, and the withered remains of horses could not detract from this spectacle of nature in glorious bloom.

Il'ia was in a pair of warm, oversized boots, his forage cap askew, revealing a head much grayer than I remembered, a row of battle medals jingling on his tunic. Sheaves of manuscripts stuck out from his trouser pockets, and the latest issue of the army newspaper was rolled up under his arm. He was unshaven, as usual, smoking one cigarette after another as his gray eyes behind their thick glasses beamed with affection and warmth.

"So, Il'ia," I greeted him. "We made it, you and I, didn't we?"

"We made it," he replied.

I sang, "To the sound of the war's alarm, / In the dusk of a July night." It was our division's marching hymn, written by Il'ia in collaboration with the writer S. Berezko.

He said, "Now that the calls to battle are over, maybe we'll be going home soon?"

"Yes, soon, I would think. Tell you what, Il'ia, let's do one last thing, let's put out a book on our army's road from Stalingrad to Vienna before we go back home."

Il'ia played a big part in our work on this book. He stayed on in the army for more than another year, seeing it through to publication. Thanks to him, the comprehensive history of the 4th Guards Army, *From Stalingrad to Vienna*, was splendidly produced by a Vienna printing plant. Only then, after shipping the entire edition to Moscow, did Il'ia go home. In 1946 he resumed his journalistic career, joining the newspaper *Water Transport*.

In the hurly-burly of Moscow life we lost sight of each other. Suddenly, in the summer of 1948, I heard a rumor that Il'ia Arginskii had been arrested. I could not believe it. Il'ia, the most selfless and loyal man alive, arrested? For what? No, it could not be. But it was.

Early that year, there had been tenacious rumors that the mass arrests of the past were back. People who were arrested in 1937 and 1938, and who were rehabilitated or released upon the completion of their terms, were allegedly being picked up all over again for unknown reasons. One did not want to believe these rumors. More arrests after such a glorious victory? Impossible. It was all lies. Most would sooner expect a sweeping amnesty than new arrests. But the sinister rumors grew and spread. Certain incontestable facts and names of apprehended individuals began to emerge.

Several years later, Il'ia gave me an account of what happened to him. This is what he said:

On April 2, 1948, around two in the afternoon, Il'ia came out of the GUM department store and was approached by a man in civilian dress. "Pardon me, are you Arginskii?"

"Yes, Arginskii."

"I'm with State Security. Here are my credentials. We need to clear up something with you. Please come with me."

A car drove up, a door opened, and Il'ia found himself in the back seat between two men. The one who had introduced himself as a security agent sat next to the driver. Il'ia was absolutely calm, believing they really wanted him to help them clear up some mix-up. The car went the length of Nikol'skaia Street, rounded Lubianka Square, turned onto Stretenka, and stopped before the iron gates of the huge complex of the Ministry of State Security (MGB). The agent rang, the gates swung open, and the car proceeded under an arch to the entrance of a large inner building invisible to the square. An elevator took them to the second or third floor, where they stopped before a door marked "Admission of Arrested Persons."

That should have made everything perfectly plain. Yet even while standing before the door Il'ia thought, "They say the arrests have begun all over again. They must have arrested someone I know, and they need me to clear up something so they can let him go."

The agent rang, the door opened, and Il'ia found himself in a tiny room with a table and bench. The agent left. The room was deathly quiet.

No sound from the outside could penetrate. Two hours went by. Il'ia thought, "Why are they taking so long to bring in whomever it is? That's no good, keeping me here all this time. I've got work to do."

Finally a man in military uniform came in and said in a sharp, cold, mechanical voice, "Undress. Put everything on the table."

Only then, with the freezing of his heart rather than his mind, did Il'ia realize what was happening. With lightning speed, incidents in his life, images of his wife and daughter, of his desk strewn with papers at his editorial office, passed before his eyes. "They've probably begun looking for me at work. What will Tonia think?"

Undressing down to his underwear, he asked, "And these, too?"

"Those too."

Il'ia stood naked. The man in uniform took his time going over all the seams in the pile of clothing, snipped off all the buttons and metal buckles, removed the leather belt, and placed his documents and wrist-watch to one side.

"May I get dressed?" Il'ia asked.

"No," was the answer.

Another officer in uniform came in. "After me."

Il'ia was taken to a bathroom where he had his head shaved. Then he was led naked from one room to another, where some specific routine was performed in each. Everything suggested the impeccable function-ing of a gigantic conveyor belt. In the progression from room to room, Il'ia had his height and chest measured, his fingerprints taken, and was photographed from the front and in profile. Then he was told to say a few words, first loudly and then in a whisper, and his voice was taped. After that he was examined by a doctor.

The doctor's manner was businesslike and civil, but that did not lessen the humiliation of the entire procedure. With callous thoroughness, the doctor inspected his mouth, dental crowns, nose, ears, and anus: Had he perhaps secreted a bit of graphite on his body to write a letter, or a vial of poison, or any other prohibited item? The unexpected nature of his arrest would seem to have made such suspicions outlandish.

But all these absurd and debasing actions had their purpose. From the moment the iron gates of the Lubianka grate shut behind you, everything is calculated to break you psychologically, to strip you of your dignity and sense of self. You must understand—and the sooner the better—that from now on you are not a human being, and they can do anything they want with you. No one escapes from here, and no sound of yours can reach the world beyond these walls.

In accordance with strict procedure, the prison warden and even a prosecutor will visit you in your cell. With the tone of an evenly functioning automaton, they will ask, "Do you have any complaints?" "Do you have any requests?" At first, before being taught by experience, you may naively tell them of being subjected to monstrous lawlessness and indignity, expecting that such incidents will not be repeated, and that those responsible will be punished. Your outraged accusations will be heard with icy politeness. And soon enough you will realize that neither visits from wardens nor the inquiries of prosecutors and judges are meant to assure that legality is observed. In fact, the investigators, prosecutors, and members of the special courts are the cogwheels and levers of the superbly designed and flawlessly polished Ezhov-Beria machine.

Then the psychology of bowing to the inevitable takes hold. "Obey, give in, there is nothing, absolutely nothing, you can do about it." It was only under the thick layer of this inanimate submissiveness that the embers of hope still smoldered for most of those penned up here. "No, this cannot go on. The whole problem is that Stalin, the CC, the party don't know what's going on here, how the enemies of the party and the Soviet state are carrying on. But sooner or later Stalin will find out about everything, and then these scoundrels will pay dearly for their crimes, and all the innocent will be released, and everything will be set right." This unshakable faith in Stalin, the CC, the party, this belief in the justice and purity of Soviet moral principles, enabled people to put up with the cruelest suffering and deprivation and—for the fortunate few—to survive until the blessed day of release and rehabilitation.

After undergoing a physical examination, Il'ia was taken back to the cell where he had been made to undress. Here he was left in total isolation for what seemed an eternity. Agonizing over his past, his activities, his encounters, his statements, he could find nothing reprehensible. Then what's the matter? What's going on? No, this must be a mistake, everything will soon be cleared up and they'll let me out. The hardest to bear, like a hot iron to the brain, were thoughts of Tonia and Iren. Had they already been told about what had happened? What was happening to them?

While Il'ia was wrestling with these tormenting questions, two men in military uniforms showed up at his one-room apartment in Moscow's Arbat neighborhood, and presented Antonina with a search warrant and documents identifying them as MGB. They conducted a lengthy, meticulous search. Il'ia later surmised that they were looking for weapons or gold: Had he brought back any gold valuables from Austria? Of course, I am absolutely certain that Il'ia, a man who survived the whole campaign across the Soviet Union, Romania, Yugoslavia, Hungary, and Austria, would never have brought back any valuables, nor even a piece of burlap for foot wrappings. The search came to nothing. But it marked the beginning of Tonia's own search for answers to her husband's fate.

At two in the morning, two guards came into Il'ia's cell and took him with them. They walked down long corridors, took an elevator down and another one up. After being immobile for so long, it was very hard for Il'ia to walk. Shorn of its buttons and belt, his trousers kept slipping and had to be held up. Without their laces, his shoes kept falling off. At last Il'ia was led into a large room on the seventh floor. A big window. Two men in MGB uniforms sat at two desks. The older-looking of the two motioned toward a small table and stool next to one of the desks.

"Sit down. I am the MGB investigator in charge of your case. My name is Rozov. My assistant in your case is Senior Lieutenant Kravchenko. You may address me as Citizen Investigator. Your arrest was not a happenstance. Here is the arrest order. Here are the instructions for your arrest by Navy Minister Afanasiev. Here is the order from the secretary of the Sverdlovsk regional Party Committee, Riabov. They have knowledge of your case, evidence of the crime, and have approved of your arrest."

Il'ia said, "I have not committed any crime, and am not aware of any guilt on my part."

"You all say that."

What followed was an evidently well-rehearsed and frequently performed routine that was designed to break the detainee's resistance at a stroke, and force all manner of admissions out of him. As though on cue, three MGB men burst noisily into the room and asked Rozov, "Whom have we here?" "Oh, so this is Arginskii? Well, well." "Caught at last, my fine fellow. We've been after you for quite some time. Now you'll tell us everything." A few minutes later another group entered. "What have you got here? Arginskii!" "Well, well. Got him in the end, eh?" "You're going to lay it on him?"

"You bet," Rozov replied. "I'm going to throw the book at him."

About three hours later, a man in a general's uniform came in. Rozov rapped out: "Stand up!" And threateningly to Il'ia: "You—up!"

"Well," the general said, "got you in here, eh? Remember, we know everything about you. Remember, you're not going to leave this place alive until you clear your chest of it. Remember . . . "

That's how it went. Rozov and Kravchenko relieved each other as the revolting farce wore on. After about twenty-four hours, Major Rozov handed Il'ia a piece of paper. "Sign this—that today at such and such an hour and so many minutes you were charged with crimes under Article 58, paragraphs 8, 10, and 11, of the Criminal Code."[2]

Il'ia objected, "I don't know what those paragraphs say."

"You'll know later. Right now just write that you were served with the charge, and sign."

Il'ia was then taken to a cell.

At one time this building had been the site of a large hotel, the Lubian-skii Passage; later it was converted into an internal MGB prison. The higher floors were dubbed the "generals' penthouse." They had been added in 1937, and their first inmates were the renowned Soviet military leaders Tukhachevskii, Iakir, Uborevich, and others.[3] Il'ia was placed in cell no. 113. There was a window with a covered transom high up under the ceiling, so the inmate could not see the sky or be diverted by the sight of a pigeon or sparrow on the windowsill. The cell's bunk and table were screwed to the floor. The door had a peephole. A toilet bucket stood by the door.

All the cells in the "generals' penthouse" were built for solitary confinement. But at that time, because of the new wave of mass arrests or for some other reason, they had added a second bunk. Il'ia already had a roommate when he arrived in his cell, a man who introduced himself as an old Bolshevik arrested on false charges. But even to an innocent like Il'ia, it soon became obvious that the man was a plant to whom the new prisoner, crushed and bewildered, was supposed to pour out his heart and disclose all his "crimes." After a few days of failing in his advances, the plant disappeared.

The agonizing days and nights of an MGB victim stretched on and on. The charges, as always in such cases, were formulated long before the arrest. The techniques used in such cases were quite simple. Another myth of another conspiracy was concocted in the depths of the MGB's investigative section. The surest and most common fabrications were attempts on the life of Stalin and other party leaders. Depending on the investigator's powers of imagination, the details of each planned "attempt" were meticulously elaborated, and the plotters assigned their roles. Il'ia Arginskii was confronted with the charge that while working at *Resort Gazette* in Sochi before the war, and in collusion with the paper's editor and other employees, he had plotted to assassinate Stalin, who spent his annual vacations in Sochi, as well as Chkalov, Baidukov, and Beliakov, aviators and Heroes of the Soviet Union.[4] Now Il'ia faced all the torments of getting a guilty confession and denunciations of accomplices wrenched out of him.

There isn't enough space here to give even a brief description of the array of methods that were employed to achieve these ends. To some extent, this has already been done in a number of accounts that have appeared since the Twentieth Party Congress. There will undoubtedly be many more writings on the same subject, so that all the implements and methods of the monstrous Ezhov-Beria system of mass murder may be anathematized, buried deep in the ground, and the earth above it sown over with salt.

After being subjected to fiendish tortures that could leave them irreversibly maimed, very few prisoners were able to hold fast in their determination not to falsely implicate themselves and others. Most broke down during the interrogation. Il'ia, however, did not admit to anything. The investigation dragged on. After three months, Il'ia was transferred to solitary confinement in Lefortovo Prison.

Even under the heartless conditions of the MGB's internal prison at Lubianka, the thought of Lefortovo could send chills up a prisoner's spine. A transfer there portended a tragic turn in a case. The move was made in a special prison vehicle known popularly as a Black Raven. These were big, sealed, windowless, armored buses that were divided into separate metal cages, so that none of those arrested could see or hear each other. The guards sat in the back. With the renewal of mass arrests, the flock of Black Ravens multiplied, which gave rise to alarming rumors among the people and led to an improved form of transport. Inside the vehicles stayed the same, but their outward appearance changed. White, yellow, and light-blue vehicles with signs in large letters that read "Bread" and

"Meat" replaced the black buses with iron bars at the back. Who would have guessed that these colorful conveyances secreted people who longed for at least a moment's glimpse of the outside world?

Solitary confinement in Lefortovo was a far cry from the old-fashioned cells at the Butyrki or Sokol'niki Prisons. Lefortovo was a fully equipped, fully modern, American-style, maximum-security house of detention. The five-storied building was designed in the shape of a cross so that all the cells were visible from the points of intersection, floor by floor, gallery by gallery. All the cells were for solitary confinement and had iron bars facing the galleries, which were enclosed by metal webbing to prevent the inmates from throwing themselves down to the ground floor. Each cell had a heavy door with a peephole, and a small opening for food. Guards, whose soft-soled shoes gave no warning of their approach, patrolled the galleries day and night.

The cells were proofed against all sound and were comparatively roomy—eight steps in length, four in width. Each had a window high enough to be out of reach, covered from the outside, and protected by metal webbing. The glass was shatterproof. Every morning a guard opened the window with a long stick so as to air out the cell, and did the same when it was necessary to expose the prisoner to the freezing cold. There was a bunk and table, both screwed to the floor, and a sink and a toilet bowl. There were no toilet buckets at Lefortovo.

Once here, the prisoner lost his name. He became a number. He saw no other prisoners. He was strictly forbidden from approaching the peephole. Unless subject to special restrictions, he was taken out once a day for a fifteen- or twenty-minute walk. For that he was taken down the stairs to the courtyard. Metal webbing protected the inner staircase. At ground level, high wooden walls partitioned the yard at ground level into individual walking enclosures about the size of a small room. From a number of lookouts atop the walls, the guards watched the prisoner's every move.

No visitors or newspapers were allowed. Books were permitted. At regular times on set days, a book cart rolled up to the cell door, and the prisoner selected or ordered a book through the small opening, but not any work by Marx, Engels, Lenin, Stalin, or any volume of party decisions. The despicable "enemies of the people" were not fit to touch these tomes. The prisoners were fed three times a day—in the morning a bowl of thin, murky, revolting slop that claimed the name of soup, plus a mug of tea and a ration of black bread and sugar for the rest of the day; for lunch more of the same soup and some wheat, oat, or other gruel; for dinner more of the gruel and a mug of tea. Officially, the prisoner could sign for the receipt of food packages from his family, but in practice the packages were stored away and brought to him only if he confessed to the charges against him, and supplied the evidence the investigator wanted to hear. If he refused to sign the testimony that the investigator prepared in advance, there was no chance of getting the food.

Pressure was applied in other ways as well. The privilege of buying provisions from the prison commissary was granted only to those who signed the testimony that was demanded of them. Il'ia refused to sign. All forms of pressure were tried on him with no result. So they switched investigators. The new investigator began with a "carrot."

"Il'ia Vladimirovich, do you make use of our commissary?"

"No," Il'ia replied.

"Why not? That's too bad. Do you like white bread? Order him three loaves," the investigator told his assistant. "Would you like some sausage? Order him a kilogram."

But no sooner did it become clear that Il'ia had no intention of reciprocating with his signature than the offer of bread and sausage was withdrawn.

Month followed month. Grueling interrogations. Staged confrontations. Punitive incarceration, and other refined forms of punishment. Bleeding gums and the loss of teeth. Tormenting thoughts of the nation, party, home, family, and friends. At the end of August, Il'ia was taken back to Lubianka for yet another interrogation. But no interrogation followed. Instead, the interrogator handed him two thick tomes. "Here is the indictment and the record of your case. Go through it and sign that you have read it."

From the indictment, Il'ia learned of the accusation against him— while a correspondent at the newspaper *Trud* (Labor), he, the paper's editor Nemchik, and three other journalists received a directive from Leon Trotsky through the American communist artist, Fred Ellis, who had worked for *Trud* in the nineteen-thirties; following these instructions, they moved to Sochi, where they went to work for the newspaper *Resort Gazette,* and organized a terrorist group to plot the assassination of Stalin, Chkalov, Baidukov, and Beliakov.

Il'ia responded by saying that everything contained in the indictment and the rest of the account was a pack of lies and utter nonsense. The investigator asked him to sign that he had read through the case. Il'ia was now sure that these absurd allegations would be dropped, and the real investigation begun. But there was no further investigation, and no judicial proceedings. After several days, Il'ia was brought before the prison warden and one other official. The warden said, "Here, read this."

It was an excerpt from a decree of the Special Board[5] stating that Il'ia Vladimirovich Arginskii, born in 1906, was charged under Article 58, paragraphs 8, 10, and 11 of the Criminal Code, and sentenced to ten years in the strict-regime labor camps. To question the sentence, object, be indignant, or ask for mercy was pointless. After that, there was transfer to camp, and life under the rules and conditions that Aleksandr Solzhenitsyn described.[6]

The years crept by. Backbreaking labor. Tuberculosis. The loss of almost all his teeth. Then, at the beginning of 1951, a sudden summons to the camp commander, and transport in a prison train to Vologda, and from there to Moscow.

Once again, the MGB's internal prison at Lubianka. Once again, strip searches and solitary confinement. Brief walks after dark on the rooftop. Lilac Moscow nights. Stars, distant and serene. And close by, so close by, right over there in the Arbat neighborhood, people dear to his heart. "They're asleep. Could they even dream that I am here, a few blocks away, close to them, so very close, and yet so inexpressibly far, in another world more distant than another planet? It will take years for me to return to their world. Will I last that long?"

A few days later, Il'ia was transferred to solitary confinement at Lefortovo. Another three months or so passed by. There was no review of his case, no further interrogations. Then why was he brought back to Moscow?

And then one day the cell door clanked open, and in stepped a youngish man with a shock of black hair and a haughty expression on his good-looking face. He wore a brand new suit that was impeccably cut, and had an air of nattiness, complacency, and incontrovertible superiority. As Il'ia was to learn, this was none other than Riumin, an MGB investigator assigned to particularly important cases.

For several years, Riumin had been a minor and little-known opera-tive in the MGB system. All at once he rose to dizzying heights as Beria's principal and most intimate henchman, and helped concoct the most horrible and abhorrent cases. Their falsifications sprang from a seedbed of anti-Semitism that was reminiscent of the Black Hundreds;[7] their most monstrous and refined concoction was the infamous Doctors' Plot.

Fixing Il'ia with a cold and indifferent stare, Riumin said, "Tell us what you know about Shepilov's hostile activity."

Stunned by the question, Il'ia replied that he had known Shepilov at the front as a battle-tested general, and that he also knew that since the war Shepilov had been engaged in work that demanded unquestioned political loyalty. He had never heard of any "hostile activity" on his part, and would discount it out of hand.

Riumin heard out the reply with an icy demeanor and a disdainful moue. He repeated the same question in different forms, and got the same answers. He met with Il'ia several more times, but was unable to drag anything out of him.

By this time, Andrei Zhdanov was dead and Nikolai Voznesenskii destroyed. But Beria and Malenkov persisted with the plan they hatched some years earlier. Much later, I learned that in furtherance of their planned attempt to fabricate a case "against Shepilov," they even tried to exploit Il'ia's daughter Iren, then still a minor.

In those days, Iren was in tenth grade. She had been raised exclusively on communist ideals and interests. She loved her parents tenderly, and was devoted to them, her school, the Pioneers,[8] the Komsomol, the Arbat, Moscow, her country, and Lenin and Stalin. Like her mama, she was proud of her father for driving the Germans away from Moscow, taking them prisoner at Stalingrad and Korsun-Shevchenko, and pursuing and beating them at the Dniester and Bug Rivers, in Romania, Hungary, and Austria. Worried about her papa, she marked that route on her map, cried when she pictured him lying wounded on some battlefield, and waited impatiently for him to come home.

Papa returned thin, sunburned, and with ribbons and medals. Iren's friends gazed in secret admiration at these awards sparkling with gold and enamel. Papa resumed writing his articles. Mama worked at the factory. Iren studied in school. She was very happy.

Suddenly papa disappeared. He was arrested.

"They arrested my papa. What for? Could my papa have done anything wrong? No, I will never believe it. They arrested Zhenia's papa as well, and Irma's aunt, and the relatives of some kids in the eighth and ninth grades. Why them? The kids say they're not guilty of anything."

No one could answer these tormenting questions. And more questions followed. "Why are our laws being broken? Why can't we talk openly about it? How was it under Lenin? Would Lenin have allowed anything like this to happen?"

All this gave rise to a passionate desire to find out how things were in Lenin's day, what Lenin had taught. Her school friends, Boria Slutskii, Zhenia Gurevich, Vladik Furman, and other boys and girls in the ninth and tenth grades, as well as friends in their first year at the university, began to get together in school or at someone's apartment to read and discuss what Lenin had written.

"One day," I was told later by Il'ia's wife, "they met in our room. They were sitting around the table and on the sofa. The kittens crawled about underfoot. They read Lenin out loud, asked questions of each other, and argued. Then they broke off and played with the kittens, then argued again. Looking at them, it would never occur to anyone that anything was wrong. I was glad to see them studying Lenin so seriously." The members of this reading circle, about twenty in number, began calling themselves Young Leninists.

On January 18, 1951, Iren and fifteen other boys and girls were arrested. At nine in the evening two men in military uniform entered Arginskii's small, humbly furnished studio apartment on Arbat Street and asked for Iren's whereabouts. Antonina replied that Iren was at her aunt's watching television. Obtaining the aunt's address and telephone number, the men soon brought Iren home and began searching the premises. Iren did not cry, but her lips were white and trembling. Antonina broke into tears when they took Iren away. The girl was in her school uniform.

They took her first to Little Lubianka, the MGB's Moscow branch, but the "case of the Young Leninists" was soon assigned to an investigation team under Riumin, and all the students were transferred to Lefortovo. Iren went through the same tortures as her father. In accordance with a prearranged scenario, each child was charged with plotting to carry out terrorist acts against Stalin, Molotov, Voroshilov, Mikoian, and others.

To Iren fell the role of would-be assassin of Georgii Malenkov. Everything was vividly described in the prepared script—how she first got the idea of assassinating Malenkov, how she planned to obtain the murder weapon, how she staked out her prey, and so on. All she and the other students had to do was sign their confessions.

Then, during one of the interrogations, she broke down into tears. "I don't want to kill Malinovskii. He's a good man. He's a Marshal. He fought next to papa. Papa told me about him, he said he was good. I don't want to say that I wanted to kill Malinovskii."

The interrogator lost his temper. "You mixed everything up! No one is asking you to admit that you wanted to assassinate Malinovskii. You wanted to assassinate Malenkov. Get it? Malenkov, not Malinovskii. Malenkov is a secretary of the party CC. He's short, in civilian dress. Malinovskii is a marshal. Don't mix them up." And he went on to differentiate in detail the two leaders' physical appearance, dress, and official positions.

Iren kept on sobbing, but when it became clear to her that she was not supposed to have wanted to kill Malinovskii, who had fought side by side with her papa, she calmed down and signed the testimony that was handed her.

I don't know the full circumstances of the affair. What I relate I heard from members of the Arginskii family. I do know that Riumin prepared this scenario with an eye to political expediency. With the widening breach between the USSR and Yugoslavia, all the students were charged with having been recruited for espionage by Yugoslavian intelligence, and with being adherents of Marshal Tito. Since the disgraceful campaign against the "cosmopolitans" was in full swing, some of the students were charged with being "Jewish nationalists." And more in the same vein.

As the story went, some "grown up" began to frequent the Young Leninists' evening reading sessions, and volunteered his opinions and offered advice that went far beyond anything the students had in mind. Only much later, piecing things together, did it become clear that the man was an MGB agent and provocateur. He did all he could to create the appearance that he had participated in meetings of an illegal group. Such groups could be saddled with all the terrorist plans and scenarios that the MGB developed. The prefabricated case featured the testimony of this "grown up" as the principal piece of incriminating evidence. Yet this mysterious figure did not officially appear during the investigation, nor did he show up in court.

The Military Collegium of the Supreme Court found all sixteen students guilty of counterrevolutionary activity. Slutskii, Gurevich, and Furman were shot. Iren and eleven others were sentenced to twenty-five years in labor camps. And the youngest, Nina, a ninth grader, was sentenced to ten. Iren served her time in strict-regime labor camps, first in the lead mines of Dzhezkazgan in Karaganda oblast, then in a mica factory in the Taishet region of Irkutsk oblast, and then in an agricultural camp in Novosibirsk oblast.[9]

I have told of the tortures and hardships that the Ezhov-Beria lawlessness inflicted on just one Soviet family, but it would take the thousands, tens of thousands, hundreds of thousands of stories of families victimized by this lawlessness to convey the oceanic scope of the resultant human suffering. Only then can one fully understand the significance of the measures taken by the party and the Soviet government after the Twentieth Party Congress to restore revolutionary legality in the country.

At about the same time he was interrogating Il'ia about me, Riumin was grilling Iren on the same subject. Not surprisingly, he was unable to get anything out of her. Thereupon, Iren was ushered into the enormous and imposing study of Minister of State Security, Abakumov. Seated before her was a tall, well-formed, broad-shouldered man in a general's uniform, with several rows of ribbons on his chest. He had a patrician face, with gray eyes half shut under thick black brows. Now and again he would raise his eyelids and direct at her the glare of a wild boar.

"What can you tell me about Shepilov's hostile actions?" asked Abakumov, clipping his words as though hacking them with an ax.

"I don't know anything," Iren replied.

"Nothing?"

"Nothing."

"But you know Shepilov?" he persisted.

"No, I don't."

"What, never even heard his name?"

"I heard it."

"From whom?"

"From mama."

"What did you hear?" Abakumov asked.

"That he is a general, papa's superior at the front."

"Did he come to your home?"

"Yes, once."

"What did he talk about with your father?"

"He didn't, papa was at the front."

"Then why did he come?"

"He brought mama and me a package from papa."

"What did he bring?"

"Candied fruit, sweets."

"Then whom did he talk to?"

"To mama. He stayed only a few minutes."

"And where were you at the time?"

"In school."

"Then you never saw him?"

"No, never."

The ridiculousness, tragicomedy, and futility of the interrogation were obvious. But because the sinister Riumin and the Minister of State Security had stooped to interrogate personally an ordinary Soviet journalist whose relations with me never went beyond the customary relations between two frontline, friendly political workers, and since they even deigned to interrogate the journalist's daughter, a sixteen-year-old student, clearly the case was of interest to someone at the very top.

Fortunately or unfortunately, I did not know any of this at the time. Much later, I learned that at the same time the party and people placed their greatest confidence in me by electing me to the Supreme Soviet and the party CC, and by giving me extremely important assignments, sinister accusations against me were being concocted in the secret labyrinths of the MGB. Abakumov, it turned out, fabricated a report that while attending the Institute of Red Professors in the nineteen-thirties, I had made critical statements about the party's Central Committee. Then this same Minister of State Security interrogated a schoolgirl, the daughter of my wartime colleague, trying to dredge up some material to smear me as a patriot and soldier.

I do not know what kind of "case" was hatched in the depths of the MGB, and what role in what crimes had been assigned to me. I also do not know why the plot was not completed. Perhaps after further reflection, Beria and Malenkov concluded that I presented no obstacle to their plans. A Soviet intellectual, a scholar, I had consistently sought only one thing after returning from the front, a resumption of my research at the Academy of Sciences. I had never shown any ambition for any posts, and

in fact, had resolutely rejected them when they were offered to me. Perhaps Zhdanov's death and Voznesenskii's demise rendered the falsified
"case" unfeasible and unnecessary. Perhaps the two leaders needed a fresh
scenario and new actors for the roles of "plotters."

What is most likely, however, is that Stalin's death wiped out Beria's
previous plans and goals. He now had to have an entirely new strategy
and plan of action, since Stalin's death radically altered the political con-
figuration of the country and party.

CHAPTER ELEVEN

The Nineteenth Party Congress

ON A FROSTY MORNING IN FEBRUARY 1952, we authors of the textbook were again on our way into "exile." However, not back to our benevolent Gorki. This time they put us up at Nagornoe, the party CC's resort in the Moscow suburbs. Leningrad Highway. The gargantuan Moscow-Volga Canal. Khimki Reservoir. Not far off the highway, the small village of Kurkino. Log cabins. Lilac bushes in front of a garden pinched by the cold. Ancient linden trees and white willows weighed down with rooks' nests and laden with snow. Close to the village, two buildings of the Nagornoe resort. Farther off, a newly planted fruit orchard, a dairy farm, and fields of wheat and oats. On Saturday evenings and Sundays, members of the CC staff came here with their families. The dining-room tables were loaded with appetizers, main courses, plenty of meat pies and rich dishes, and rows of decanters and bottles of vodka and wine.

But we had no connection with that life. After our arrival, Nagornoe became the realm of political economy six days a week, all but Sunday. Total silence. The help staff whispered portentously among themselves, "The scholars are at work." We followed our own strict timetable for getting up, meals, work, and walks. We ate sparingly and sensibly—nothing in excess. Alcohol was out. We had a year to carry out a gigantic task—to rework totally the draft of the textbook. We gave it all we had. Our working day ran to no less than ten hours. The entire group subjected each revised chapter to comment and criticism. This often lasted late into the night. At times, the discussion became quite heated.

On April 21, 1952, we received a copy of Stalin's letter to Aleksandr Notkin[1] and later two of his theoretical works, "On Comrade L. D. Iaroshenko's Mistakes" and "Reply to Comrades A. V. Sanina and V. G. Venzher."[2] These works, together with his "Comments," later formed the substance of his book *The Economic Problems of Socialism in the USSR*. It went without saying that we had to pay full respect to these new treatises by Stalin in our own book. In short, we worked our heads off.

In our free time we slogged through the snow on skis or took walks in the countryside. Even though we repeatedly swore to one another to think of something other than political economy during our hours of recreation, we weren't always able to keep the subject from cropping up during these outings. That February, Nagornoe was hit by snowstorms. The village was buried in white and the woods were snowbound. In the mornings, bluish smoke curled up from sooty chimneys; there was a pleasant aroma of baking bread. Chickens coated with hoarfrost huddled against the snowdrifts. Ruffled sparrows darted to and fro. A vast stillness enveloped the church, the houses, the park, the Skhodnia River, which were all trimmed in ice.

I contemplated the cabins, which looked like chocolate candy coated in snow, this whole way of village life, and gave myself over to dreams of how nice it would be to move permanently into one of the cabins. Bring my library, and write and write and write. I pictured myself sitting by a window that was lashed with slanting autumn rains. During winter, snowstorms would whip the fields. I would sit and work. After all, what did I really need? I could boil a potato in its skin and cook up some buckwheat groats. In return, what stillness! How freely I would breathe! How clearly I would think!

Our walks in the countryside were all the more pleasurable after the arrival of spring. The dirt roads swelled with water and glinted with puddles; the horizon turned a light blue; the birches became a glistening aquarelle of tender lilac. The waters of the Skhodnia churned about in imitation of the mighty Terek.[3] The alder buds were swollen. In a noonday blaze that was hard on the eyes, the rooks arrived, clean and black as though varnished. A construction project began to unfold. Sitting at my desk, I could see, through the glass doors of the balcony, how the rooks, in a frenzy of activity, tore off chips of wood from the shed and added them to their capacious nests.

The whole mystery of the springtime transfiguration opened up before our eyes. The walls of the ravines turned to shades of brown, the winter crops to fields of emerald. Up on high, the skylarks filled the heavens with their silver song. We saw the first snowdrops. And then, so fast it took your breath away, everything turned springlike—the sky, the gardens, the children, the ravines, the aspens, the chickens, the hazel, the Skhodnia. Everything smiled, everything sparkled.

It would take a powerful pen to describe this poetic region outside Moscow. It is a piece of ancient Russia. Every stone and oak is embedded in Russian history. They say that Ivan the Terrible came here for his falconry, which gave the ancient estate that once stood here the name of Sokolovo.[4] Later, for almost 150 years, the estate belonged to the Davidov family of landowners. During the summers of 1845–46, Alexander Herzen[5] rented one of the houses on the grounds, a roomy place with Greek columns and a mezzanine. The house stood by an old park with ancient oaks; it had a magnificent view of the distant hills and a boundless sea of cornfields. Nearby was an arbor named Bellevue for its beautiful view. Through a deep ravine the Skhodnia winds its wayward course. You can still see the remains of an ancient dam.

Captivated by these images of Russian nature and forced to spend a quarter-century abroad, Herzen wrote of his beloved countryside on the outskirts of Moscow: "The vistas that my house offered me were never surpassed in my memory, not by Sorrento, not by the Roman Campagna, not by the somber *Aleppy*,[6] not by the opulent English farmlands. . . . There is something about our languorous countryside that resonates in Russian song and deeply touches the Russian heart."

The house where Herzen stayed no longer stands. But his contemporaries left for us a record of the centrality of the Sokolovo house in some of the most vivid chapters in the history of Russian social thought. We walk up to the old lawn. There is a bitter scent of oak bark. This must have been the site of the annex that Timofei Granovskii[7] occupied in 1846. Herzen's friend Nikolai Ogarev[8] lived on the mezzanine floor.

Later on, we took the Northern Road to Pushkino, outside Moscow, to continue our work. We settled ourselves in the Partisan House on the grounds of a Central Committee sanatorium. The small dwelling acquired that name because it served as the main headquarters of Panteleimon Ponomarenko's partisan movement.[9] In late autumn the driving rains beat against our cottage from all sides. Then the winter snowstorms wrapped it in gleaming white. But in our isolation, the rhythm of the elements was beneficial to our labors.

On October 5, 1952, the Nineteenth Congress of the Communist Party of the Soviet Union (CPSU) convened in the Great Kremlin Palace. Along with some of the authors of the textbook, I was invited to be a guest. I sat in a box off to one side, high up in the balcony. For the entire session, I sat next to Artem Mikoian, the famous designer of the MIG fighter plane and the brother of Anastas Mikoian. Several ministers, prominent military leaders, and members of the CC staff sat in the same box.

The Nineteenth Congress was held at a time when industrial production in the USSR had increased by 223 percent since 1940, and the production of capital goods by 267 percent. By 1952, industrial production in the USSR was 12.6 times higher than in 1929. In the United States it doubled during the same period; in Great Britain it increased by 60 percent; in Italy by 34 percent; and in France by 4 percent. In spite of all the difficulties and problems, agricultural production was also growing. That year, the state stores and the kolkhoz markets were piled high with products. The firmly established policy of annual price reductions was tantamount, in real terms, to appreciable increases in wages.

There had been no party congress for thirteen years. Now at the new congress, the great victory of the horrendous war and the enormous successes of socialist construction created an atmosphere of joyous and solemn elation. Molotov declared the session open. Respects were paid to the memory of those who had died in the interim: Aleksandr Shcherbakov, Mikhail Kalinin, Andrei Zhdanov. The congress presidium was chosen by vote: Bagirov,[10] Beria, Bulganin, Voroshilov, Kaganovich, Kuusinen,[11] Malenkov, Molotov, Stalin, Khrushchev, and several secretaries of the major party organizations. A stormy ovation met each mention of Stalin. Time and again the congress rose to its feet to hail the leader; every speech was punctuated by his name. Molotov set the tone in his introductory remarks, which ended with the words, "Long live our dear, our great Stalin!" It was in that spirit that every speech began and ended.

Aleksei Kosygin: "Long live our genius leader and teacher, our dear and beloved Comrade Stalin!"

Mikhail Suslov: "The party will lead the Soviet people with a firm hand to the complete victory of communism only under the wise guidance of our great leader and teacher, the coryphaeus of science, our dear and beloved Comrade Stalin!"

Nikita Khrushchev: "Long live the wise leader of the party and people, the mastermind and organizer of all our victories, Comrade Stalin!"

Leonid Brezhnev: "It is the great fortune of our fatherland that at the head of the multinational struggle for the development of our nation and the triumph of communism stands the greatest man of our epoch, the wise leader and teacher Joseph Vissarionovich Stalin. Long live our leader and teacher, the great and beloved Comrade Stalin!"

Today, such unctuous encomiums strike us as somehow debasing. Today, the frenzied glorification of Mao Zedong in China seems to us to be some kind of fanatical hysteria. But in those years, similar speeches about Stalin were routine for everyone.

Gathered at the congress were the flower of the party and the international communist movement. Among the foreign guests were most of the world's communist leaders, among them Bolesław Bierut of Poland, Klement Gottwald of Czechoslovakia, Liu Shaoqi of China, Maurice Thorez of France, Luigi Longo of Italy, Mátyás Rákosi of Hungary, Gheorghe Gheorghiu-Dej of Romania, Vulko Chervenkov of Bulgaria, Enver Hoxha of Albania, Dolores Ibárruri of Spain, Harry Pollitt of Great Britain, and Wilhelm Pieck and Max Reimann of Germany.

For the first time in thirteen years, the summary report of the Central Committee did not come from Stalin. Pleading that his health would not permit him to take on such a responsibility, Stalin handed the task over to Malenkov with the assent of the CC Politburo. At the same time, Stalin took a whole range of deliberate actions to show who was boss within the party and at the congress. A few days prior to the opening of the congress, all his latest works, which formed part of his new book, *The Economic Problems of Socialism in the USSR,* were published in *Pravda.* He thereby let it be known that this work, not the political report to the Central Committee, would form the basis for discussion at the congress. That, in fact, is what happened.

Then, at the opening of the congress, seeing that Thorez, Gottwald, and Ibárruri were sitting in the Presidium loge rather than at the Presidium dais, Stalin got up and invited them to the dais, holding the chair for each one and causing a commotion among the congress organizers. After that, Stalin sat at the side of the dais closer to the rostrum, so there were two empty chairs between him and Kaganovich. Throughout Malenkov's speech, which took up several hours, he remained almost motionless, gazing stonily ahead.

Malenkov went unbelievably fast through his speech, giving Stalin an occasional sidelong glance, as a well-trained horse might glance at its rider. As Stalin's longtime favorite who was accustomed to his master's ways, Malenkov was trembling inside: What if Stalin made one of his familiar, impatient gestures or took out his gold Longines watch? That would signal displeasure, and Malenkov would have to cut short his speech and end it no matter where he was. After all, to arouse Stalin's displeasure, to say nothing of his anger, would be much worse than to make a fool of himself before an audience of a thousand. But all was well. Stalin listened to the speech to the end.

Both the summary report and the instructions for the Fifth Five-Year Plan for economic development (1951–55) that Maksim Saburov delivered provided an analysis of Soviet development so far and set a course for the period ahead. The congress adopted the party's new charter that Khrushchev introduced, and set up a commission for revising the party's program.

Everyone waited impatiently for Stalin to speak. No one could imagine that Stalin would leave the palace without some word for the delegates and foreign guests who had spoken so warmly of the Communist Party of the Soviet Union. Indeed, on October 14, the final day of the congress, Stalin gave a brief speech.

It would be hard to describe the effect on the audience when the chairman, Voroshilov, uttered the long-awaited words, "Comrade Stalin has the floor." The entire hall rose to its feet as though galvanized. Thunderous ovations shook the building. Standing on the rostrum, Stalin gazed with seeming indifference into the distance. The expression on his face revealed nothing of his feelings at the moment. Now and then he shifted from one foot to the other, smoothed his mustache with his index finger, or stroked his chin. Twice he raised his hand as though requesting the audience let him begin, only to cause the ovation to redouble. I don't know how long the storm of applause lasted. But finally the delegates sat down and Stalin was able to speak.

As always, he spoke very softly, without expression, as though quite unconcerned with the impression he was making on his listeners. In my time I heard many orators from the ranks of the Russian and international communist movement—Leon Trotsky, Anatolii Lunacharskii, Grigorii Zinoviev, Sergei Kirov, Lev Kamenev, Georgii Chicherin, Maksim Litvinov, Andrei Vyshinskii, Sergo Ordzhonikidze, Andrei Zhdanov, Georgii Dimitrov,[12] Klement Gottwald, Dolores Ibárruri, Palmiro Togliatti, and others. I heard government leaders and outstanding speakers like Egyptian President Gamal Abdel Nasser, Indonesian President Sukarno, Indian Prime Minister Jawaharlal Nehru, and Belgian Foreign Minister Paul-Henri Spaak. I heard speakers from various countries at the United Nations. They all spoke publicly with different temperaments, styles, and emotional appeals, but I would say that none of them ever exhibited the same indifference to outward form, or the same cold disinterest in captivating the minds and hearts of those sitting in the hall, as Stalin. In spite of that, everyone listened to him with bated breath. Why?

Stalin rarely spoke in public. Sometimes he spoke only once over a period of years. To be present at one of his appearances, to see and hear Stalin in the flesh, was deemed a rare and great opportunity. Anyone lucky enough to be there did not want to miss a single word. Moreover, for thirty years the entire press, radio, and cinema and all of the oral propaganda and arts had been inculcating the view that Stalin's every word was a lofty revelation, absolute Marxist truth, a gem of wisdom that contained knowledge of the present and a prediction of the future. That was why the hall listened to Stalin as though under a hypnotic spell. At the same time, Stalin was well aware of the significance that was attached not only to his every word but to his every nuance. He prepared carefully for each public address and weighed the effect of each of his statements.

Stalin expressed his thanks to all the fraternal parties and groups whose representatives had honored the congress with their presence or sent their greetings. Then he focused on a single theme: The bourgeoisie had become reactionary. Not a trace remained of its former liberalism. There was no longer any so-called freedom of the individual. The principle of equality among people and nations had been trampled into the ground. The banner of bourgeois-democratic freedoms had been cast overboard. Also cast overboard was the banner of national independence and sovereignty. This banner, Stalin said, will have to be raised by you, the representatives of communist and democratic parties. There is no one else to do it.

Stalin called on the revolutionary parties of the capitalist countries to learn from the mistakes and successes of the Soviet Union and the people's democracies. He concluded his speech with a tribute to the fraternal parties and their leaders:

"Long live peace among nations!"

"Down with the warmongers!"

This was Stalin's last public speech, his swan song. In a sense, it revealed a great deal about the man.

Bit by bit, Stalin had chipped away at inner-party democracy and Leninist fundamentals, principles, and standards. He rid the party of any and all sources of healthy criticism and dealt ruthlessly with anyone he saw as an actual or potential critic of his dictatorial style. Stalin did everything he could to destroy and shatter elements intrinsic to the Soviet system—individual freedom, revolutionary legitimacy, and the broadest democracy for the people, from top to bottom. With unfounded arrests and every kind of purge, he ensured that state and society were firmly placed on a foundation of arrangements and behaviors that were wildly contrary to Marxist-Leninist doctrine.

By the time of the Nineteenth Congress, the course of modern history and the development of the Soviet Union urgently required a broad democratization of party, state, and society. Without that, we could not move ahead. It is hard to know whether Stalin came to this conclusion by intellect or by the instinct of an old revolutionary that told him that the country could not go on in the old mode. One way or another, he returned in his swan song to the themes of democracy, individual freedom, national sovereignty, and independence. Moreover, the congress was immediately followed by the implementation of a whole range of measures that were designed to suggest that Stalin had decided on a new course, one of reinvigorating the leadership with the principles of collectivism, eliminating the impunity of the security services, and ensuring revolutionary legality.

But as we shall see, all this was rendered stillborn by virtually simultaneous actions that ran directly counter, actions that bolstered one-man dictatorship and arbitrary lawlessness within the leadership and society at large.

Late on the evening of October 14, we authors of the textbook were working at Partisan House in Pushkino. There was a ring on the special Kremlin line.

"The electoral commission at the congress has just finished counting votes. From the authors' group, Pavel Iudin and Dmitrii Shepilov were elected members of the CC of the CPSU, and Konstantin Ostrovitianov was elected a candidate member."

I went out on the porch. The ancient forest held the house in a tight grip. From the fading ash trees to the whitish clouds overhead, everything was drenched in silvery moonlight. What stillness! How beautiful was this age-old world!

My breast was bursting with happiness. I was a member of the Central Committee of the great communist party: the party that had taken unto itself all the wisdom of the nation's life, the thousand-year experience of the struggle for the freedom and happiness of mankind, all the tortuous seeking of the road to the harmonious society of the future, from Thomas More,[13] Campanella,[14] Saint-Simon, Fourier, Herzen, and Chernyshevskii to Marx and Lenin; the party that lifted up the bullet-torn banner of the Paris Communards and was the first to issue a daring challenge to the old world; the party that in the sacred fire of the proletarian revolution laid the cornerstone of a new order. Now this party stood at the head of a great power and was universally recognized as the mentor of the world's communist and liberation movements. Its ranks encompassed seven million people. The entire CC numbered only 125. The CC was the brain, the soul, and the heart of the party. It was the country's supreme forum of wise men, its vital core. Here I stood, the grandson of the serf Mikhail Shepilov, the son of the metal worker Trofim Shepilov, a member of the highest echelon of the party and the state, the Russian intellectual Dmitrii Shepilov. Out of an electorate of seven million, only 125! And I a rank-and-file Soviet scholar, a rank-and-file party propagandist, was among them. I was part of that critical nucleus of the party and the nation that had been graced in the past by leaders and voices of the revolution like Lenin, Sverdlov, Frunze, Lunacharskii, Kuibyshev, Dzerzhinskii, Chicherin, Kalinin, and Kirov. How would I vindicate the great trust placed in me? How would I repay my party and my people for this honor and for the hopes they placed on me? To do so I was ready for any sacrifice. For the sake of the happiness of my party and my country, I was ready to sacrifice all my strength to the last drop of my blood and, if need be, life itself.

Iudin and Ostrovitianov came out on the balcony. We were all terribly excited. We knew we could not sleep. So, overcome with joy, we decided to dash off to Moscow.

We took the old Iaroslavskii Highway at full speed. Moscow was ready for bed. The lights in the windows were out. We headed for my place on Kaluzhskaia. How many questions we raked over before dawn, how many world problems we resolved in theory! We drank toasts to the party, to Stalin, to the people, to science, to the army.

The first plenum of the newly elected CC was held on October 16. In accordance with what was by now a longstanding tradition, we met in the Sverdlov Hall in the Kremlin. Precisely on time the members of the outgoing Politburo ascended the stage, Stalin at the head. Seeing him, some CC members—novices, evidently—rose to their feet and began to applaud. Stalin at once gestured at them in displeasure, muttering something like, "Never do that here."

In fact, at all celebrations and meetings Stalin and his colleagues thought they deserved all manifestations of the personality cult, like standing ovations and cheering, but not at CC and Politburo plenums. Perhaps the legacy of Lenin, who was fiercely opposed to any deification of himself or any other highly placed leader, still survived in that one respect, and Stalin deemed it important to back the tradition in this single instance. (Soon enough, Khrushchev abandoned even this tradition.)

The basic task facing the CC was to form the CC's executive bodies, the Presidium and the Secretariat, and approve the appointment of the chairman of the party Control Commission. As I mentioned earlier, Stalin gave the appearance of wanting to avoid reelection.

"Why elect me secretary? It's hard on me—head of the Council of People's Commissars and secretary. . . . Getting on, you know. . . . What kind of secretary is it who doesn't have the strength to deliver a summary report?"

At that point, Malenkov got up and tersely said, "I don't think it is necessary to prove that this is how it must be. There is no other way. Everyone knows it."

Stalin made a hopeless gesture as though to say, "Do what you will." But everyone in the hall knew that there was no alternative and that Stalin himself had no thought of letting anyone else head the Politburo (Presidium) as secretary. All the same, the title of general secretary was abolished.[15] (In time, however, Khrushchev, as first secretary, demanded that it be reinstated, and at the Twenty-third Party Congress[16] the title was revived.)

The ensuing discussion on the formation of the new leadership took a completely unexpected turn, one that made a very unpleasant impression—at least on me.

Everything that went on at the top of the party was wrapped in the utmost secrecy. People were afraid to ask or talk about anything going on there. Given the all-pervasive system of surveillance, denunciations, and wiretapping, that could cost you your life.

Word filtered down from above that Molotov's wife, Polina Zhemchuzhina, who had long headed the perfume industry, had been arrested. Why? No one knew. But the feeling was that the arrest did not compromise Molotov himself. The same was true when Kalinin's wife was arrested, and Kuusinen's as well. Everyone knew how devoted Molotov was to the party, to whatever assignment he was given, and to Stalin personally. Everyone remembered Stalin's expressions of high regard for Molotov, his toast on Victory Day:[17] "To our Viacheslav!"—which for Stalin, given his aloofness from any sentimentality, was positively mushy.

At the same time, many remembered Stalin's warm words for Nikolai Bukharin: "Our Bukharchik[18]—we'll see to it that no harm comes to him." On Stalin's orders, this same "Bukharchik" was later sentenced to death. Years later I read the last letter that Bukharin wrote before his execution. The letter was imbued with such sincerity, such pleading, such affection for Stalin, that it would melt a stone.

"Koba, Koba!"[19] Bukharin called out from his death-row cell. "You know that I'm not guilty of anything. You know my boundless love for you. Don't take my life. Send me off to the far north, if you like, to labor there to the end of my days. I will make the rounds of the nomad camps of the Chukchi, the Lamuts, the Iukagirs,[20] and read to them from newspapers and pamphlets, discuss things with them. . . . What do you say?" One self-sacrificing idea after another flowed from his pen. Just "don't have me shot; don't kill me."

Of course, Stalin knew that Bukharin was not really guilty of anything warranting the death penalty. But he showed no mercy. Bukharin was shot.

Stalin was also well aware of Molotov's fanatical affection for him, his devotion, his impeccable implementation of party directives and all

Stalin's instructions. It is hard to believe that Molotov's devotion to Stalin did not seem to lessen after his wife's unjustified arrest. Yet standing on the rostrum, Stalin spoke contemptuously of him, saying that he had been intimidated by American imperialism and had sent panicky telegrams back from the United States, that a leader like him was untrustworthy and had no place in the party leadership. In the same vein, Stalin expressed his distrust of the political reliability of Mikoian and Voroshilov.

Still an inexperienced newcomer to this hall, I listened to Stalin with bated breath. I felt as though a slab of ice had been placed on my heart. My gaze shifted from Stalin to Molotov to Mikoian and back to Stalin. Molotov sat immobile at the Presidium table. He was silent. Not a muscle twitched on his face as he stared straight at the assembly through his pince-nez, occasionally moving three fingers of his right hand over the baize tabletop as though kneading a ball of bread. Mikoian showed every sign of agitation. The speech that he delivered was shallow and morally reprehensible. Defending himself against a slew of fantastic accusations, he did not hesitate to point a finger at Molotov, claiming that he had always been close to Voznesenskii—which by then was incriminating evidence.

Stalin, for his part, ended his speech with the following conclusions:

The plenum had to elect a new and unprecedentedly large CC Presidium comprising the twenty-five full members and eleven candidate members whose names he put forward. These included a number of unprofessional, unrefined, and undistinguished people like Leonid Mel'nikov,[21] Vasilii Andrianov,[22] Averkii Aristov,[23] Nikolai Mikhailov,[24] Nikolai Ignatov,[25] Ivan Kabanov,[26] and Aleksandr Puzanov.[27] Thus, departing from a decades-old tradition, the Presidium (Politburo) was diluted by mediocrities unknown to the party and the people.

Perhaps Stalin, with his growing persecution mania, did this because he wanted to avoid any contact with men whom he regarded either as outright spies, like Voroshilov, or as capitulators to American imperialism, like Molotov and Mikoian. Perhaps his aim was to rid himself of the last representatives of the old guard in the Politburo, Molotov, Voroshilov, and Mikoian, who enjoyed wide respect in the party and throughout the country. Whatever his motive, he unexpectedly proposed the creation of a new body that the party charter did not envision, a separate bureau within the CC Presidium that was entrusted with the functions of the former omnipotent Politburo. He proposed that Molotov, Voroshilov, and

Mikoian be excluded from this top party entity. As always, his proposals were approved unanimously by the CC.

Despite all his egomania, however, Stalin realized that he could not simply toss aside three eminent party leaders who were Lenin's brothers-in-arms. So a certain decorum was preserved. Officially, Molotov, Voroshilov, and Mikoian remained members of the party's top executive body, although in fact they were removed from all leadership roles; at the same time, the creation of the Presidium bureau and the decision to close its doors to the party's three oldest leaders was kept secret and not aired in the press. (Before long, Khrushchev would dispense with such conventions. In one blow he would make short work of seven Politburo members, unabashed by the fact that one of them, Voroshilov, was head of government, three, Molotov, Malenkov, and Bulganin, were former heads of government, and three, Kaganovich, Pervukhin, and Saburov, had been deputy chairmen of the USSR Council of Ministers.)

With my blood running cold as I listened to Stalin's accusations of "espionage" against Voroshilov and his charges of "capitulating to American imperialism" against Molotov and Mikoian, I thought for what must have been the first time, "Could all this be a product of Stalin's schizophrenic paranoia?" But despite everything, I rejected the thought. "We probably don't know everything there is to know. . . . Some things probably cannot be disclosed. . . . In time they'll gradually let us CC members know what has been going on." To question Stalin or try to object—these outlandish ideas did not occur to anyone. The pronouncements and views of the genius Stalin could only be reverently and rapturously acclaimed.

The same frightful thoughts about Stalin's mental health rose from the depths of consciousness when the mind-boggling spectacle of the Doctors' Plot began to unfold before our eyes. Once again a CC plenum was in session. Stalin lashed out at the security services. Abakumov and his associates were fired from their security posts. Egged on unremittingly by the Beria gang, Stalin saw intrigues, conspiracies, and terrorist plots on his life. Playing to the great Moloch's obsessions, the security services capped the Leningrad affair with the Doctors' Plot—a detailed scenario, act after act. Then on January 13, 1953, the substance of the plot was laid out in the newspapers in an official TASS announcement that was headlined "Arrest of a Group of Doctors-Saboteurs."

The report said that the state security services had uncovered a terrorist group of doctors who had murdered a number of the country's leaders with treatment that was deliberately mistaken. As covert enemies of the people, these doctors allegedly undermined their patients' health with harmful procedures, false diagnoses, deadly medications, and so on. Using these methods, they had caused the deaths of two CC secretaries, Zhdanov and Shcherbakov. And they were planning to do away with a number of military leaders, including Marshals Aleksandr Vasilevskii, Leonid Govorov, and Ivan Konev. Accused of these monstrous depredations were the country's leading doctors, the cream of Soviet medical science—Miron Vovsi, Vladimir Vinogradov, M. B. and B. B. Kogan, P. I. Egorov, A. I. Fel'dman, Ia. G. Etinger, A. M. Grinshtain, and the internist G. I. Maiorov.

"Trampling on the sacred banner of science and besmirching the honor of their fellow medical personnel," the report continued, "these doctors-murderers became fiends in human shape and the hired agents of foreign intelligence. Most of the members of the terrorist group . . . were linked to the international Jewish bourgeois-nationalist organization 'Joint,' created by American intelligence. . . . Other members of the terrorist group . . . turned out to be longtime agents of British intelligence." Even before the publication of the TASS report, the CC plenum heard an account of the Doctors' Plot. When Cheka agents said something, Stalin was speaking.

In the course of the protracted Iagoda-Ezhov-Beria-Vyshinskii reign in the judicial bodies and security services, the Soviet people had become inured to the most incredible court trials and accusations. But even the hardened Soviet people were shaken by the brutal and ridiculous nature of the Doctors' Plot and were assailed by a whole slew of bewildering questions and doubts about its validity. Why would the outstanding Soviet internist Academician Vladimir Vinogradov, an honest soul and mentor to thousands of medical students, suddenly become an agent for British intelligence and start poisoning his patients? It was monstrous and absurd. Why would the loyal Soviet patriot and eminent scientist Professor Miron Vovsi, who was the chief internist of the Red Army during the war and who devoted his life to the service of Soviet medicine, suddenly ally himself with a "Jewish bourgeois-nationalist organization" created by American intelligence? Again, monstrous and absurd. The same for Professor V. Kh. Vasilenko, Professor B. S. Preobrazhenskii, and the others.

As though sensing the force of these irrefutable questions, Stalin persisted in trying to prove to us CC members who were seated in Sverdlov Hall that the doctors were guilty beyond all doubt. I did not write down his speech, but it went something like this:

"They killed Zhdanov. They killed Shcherbakov. They wanted to do away with our marshals. Look at Andreev sitting there—they deliberately made him deaf, the poor man. They admitted everything. We are sifting through their testimony. Still, some people have their doubts! One of the Kremlin doctors, Lidiia Timoshuk, helped our Chekists uncover this affair; she revealed their murderous methods."

We listened to all this with heavy hearts. On one hand, the records and moral reputation of the accused, to say nothing of plain common sense, belied the credibility of the plot. On the other hand, Stalin himself assured us of the incontestable nature of the evidence: Witnesses exposed the deeds, the arrested men confessed, they wrote down their testimony. What else did we need?

Was it possible that the immutable laws of class struggle led to such actions? The case had another specific feature. Although some of the arrested doctors were Russians, most were Jews, a factor that was underscored by the allusion to the "Joint."[28] Moscow was rife with rumors that a smear campaign was under way and that Jewish doctors were being dismissed wholesale. And not only doctors. Travelers from Ukraine reported that Jews were being purged from all organizations in Kiev and other cities on Khrushchev's orders. It was obviously part of a deliberate plan to foment a wave of anti-Semitism.

Why was this being done? For what purpose? Nothing like this had ever taken place under Lenin. Stalin had expressed himself forcefully and categorically against anti-Semitism. His comments were in print. Why was everything moving in the opposite direction? How could this be reconciled with the international precepts of Marxism-Leninism? Let me add that in my own family we lived by a set of healthy moral principles, and anti-Semitism was completely alien to us.

Today it is hard to imagine what would have happened if Stalin had lived a few more years. What bloody fictions would have been concocted for his benefit by the state security services? How many lives would their new, cannibalistic scenarios devour? But in those days, in the wake of the Nineteenth Party Congress, such thoughts did not occur to us. It seemed

to us that the mighty and perfectly fashioned Soviet governmental system worked flawlessly. On the captain's bridge stood the great helmsman
Stalin, and so long as he held the wheel in his hands, we could rest easy
about the country's fate.

Life went on. On October 20, 1952, Stalin summoned Iudin and me,
although I no longer remember whether it was for a meeting of the CC
Presidium with a group of experts on ideology or for a closed conference
on ideological questions. The meeting, attended by the entire Presidium,
the secretaries of the Central Committee, and several department heads
and ideological experts, began at 10:05 P.M.

Apparently Stalin had been agonizing since the Nineteenth Party Congress about how best to organize the control exercised by the party over
the various branches of agriculture, foreign policy, the military sector, and
so on. But what concerned him most was the mentality and outlook of
society as a whole. His comments at the meeting mostly concerned the
party's ideological program. According to the notes that Iudin and I took,
he said something like this:

"Our propaganda is no good—it's a hodgepodge, not propaganda at
all. Everyone is dissatisfied with it. There isn't a single member of the
Politburo who is satisfied with the work of the Propaganda Department.
Our propaganda personnel, especially the young, lack a real knowledge of
Marxism. Our older generation had the advantage of a thorough knowledge of Marxism and political economy. Our propaganda is especially
weak in our newspapers, including *Pravda*. As editor of *Pravda,* Il'ichev
is ineffective. He is not up to the demands of a job like this. We ought
to appoint someone stronger as executive editor of *Pravda* and give him
time to study.

"*Pravda* is our most important newspaper. It ought to embody the
best of all the other papers. It ought to reprint or excerpt their best articles. *Pravda* should be the principal base for the work of the Propaganda
Department.

"So, whom shall we name as executive editor of *Pravda?* After all, we
can't postpone this for a hundred years."

We were all silent.

"Yes, I see," Stalin went on. "You don't know your own people. We
must also think about better leadership for our industry. We should have
a separate department for industry and transport and place it under some

major figure. We must exercise control over our personnel, follow their progress carefully, and promote the young to leadership positions without excessive delay. We have plenty of able young people, but we don't know enough about our younger cadres. If we put someone in charge of something, and he sits there for ten years without moving further up, he stops growing and we lose a good man. How many people have we ruined because we did not promote them fast enough!

"Our agriculture is badly run. Our party people are not familiar with the history of agriculture in Europe or animal husbandry in the United States. All they do is sign papers that only make things worse.

"Our younger cadres are weak on theory. We have to help them develop. Lectures are useful, of course, but the main emphasis in helping with the development of our personnel should be placed on the printed word.

"We ought to create a standing commission on ideological questions under the CC Presidium to oversee the party's entire ideological program. Find ten to twenty qualified people for the commission staff. People with a knowledge of languages—English, German, French (although use of French is less widespread these days), Spanish (Spanish is the language of some one hundred twenty million people). We must find someone fluent in Chinese—maybe Fedorenko?[29] They should all be well paid.

"The commission on ideological questions must raise the level of Marxist propaganda in our press. The base for this work must be the journal *Bolshevik*. The journal is badly run by penny-pinchers. It ought to be an example to other periodicals. We must think about reorganizing its editorial staff. Why Il'ichev? We could even have two executive editors there.

"*Bolshevik* ought to carry reviews and critical articles on the work of provincial journals, prod them, help them improve. The commission must take on the journals *Philosophical Issues, Economic Issues, Historical Issues,* and maybe a few others. It's time to put an end to the disgraceful practice of reprinting various party and government decrees in our theoretical journals—that's just evidence that we lag behind events.

"We must place our propaganda on the subject of political economy and philosophy on a sound basis. Stop harping on the unity of opposites —that's Hegelian terminology. The Americans reject Marxism; they slander us, seek to undo us. We must expose them for what they are. We must familiarize our people with the enemy's ideology, bring it under attack—this will stiffen our ranks.

"Today we're pursuing not only a national but a global policy. The Americans want to bring everything under their domination. But America does not enjoy respect in any of the world's capitals. *Pravda* and our party journals must broaden our people's vision, expand their horizons—we are a world power. Stop poking about in petty issues. Our people are afraid to write about foreign policy; they wait to be told when to write.

"We need popular pamphlets on various subjects. In the old days we had pamphlets such as 'Who Lives By What?' and 'What Every Worker Should Know.' A lot of workers began their political-economic education with such pamphlets. Today popular pamphlets must be more serious, more advanced in nature, but we need them.

"Our lectures don't have much meat to them—still, they do some good. We ought to go out sometimes to the provinces to give lectures for a week or two.

"This ideological commission ought to include Shepilov, Chesnokov,[30] Rumiantsev,[31] Iudin, and Suslov. Who else? We must set up the commission secretariat."

After that, at 11:00 P.M., the conference ended.

I was subsequently named chairman of the Standing Commission on Ideological Questions of the party CC. As chance would have it, I was assigned an office on the fifth floor of the CC building that had been reserved for Stalin after the building's renovation. But Stalin always worked in his Kremlin office and was never there. Now, apparently in view of the great significance he attached to the ideological commission, his empty office was placed at our disposal.

My life entered a new phase. I continued to stay at the Partisan House in Pushkino and work on the textbook on political economy. But now I had to make trips to Moscow to set up the commission staff and direct its work. I did that reluctantly. Scholarship is a jealous mistress; she lays claim to all your thoughts and feelings and does not want to share you with anyone else. But when duty calls . . . Now I had to devote part of my time to another highly important and beautiful lady, the ideological commission, even though my heart remained at Partisan House.

In mid-November 1952, Suslov told me that the subject of *Pravda* had been raised again at a meeting of the CC Presidium. He said, "Il'ichev is obviously not up to the job of executive editor, and they've decided to let him go. They plan to appoint you to the position." With all the force I could summon, I objected to this plan and asked that no such decision be made in my regard. But Suslov said he doubted very much that the matter could be reconsidered.

Taking advantage of an opportunity to speak to Stalin, I pleaded with him not to appoint me editor of *Pravda*. Adducing a number of what I thought would be persuasive general arguments, I added, "I was given the great honor of working on the textbook on political economy. You told me what enormous importance the party attaches to the creation of such a textbook. I am the author of many of its chapters. In addition, Comrade Ostrovitianov and I are compiling and editing the chapters written by the other authors. If I were to leave our group, it could interfere with the submission of the textbook on schedule."

Stalin replied, "No one is about to release you from your work on the textbook. Why do that? Work on the textbook and for *Pravda*."

"I'm afraid," I objected, "that would prove impossible. *Pravda* is a serious business. I would have to answer for every word."

"Of course it's a serious business," Stalin agreed, "but does being editor of *Pravda* mean hanging about the paper day and night? No need for that. The editor must see to it that the paper follows the right political policy. Takes the right direction. He should set the tone. Edit only the most important and crucial material himself. The rest should be left to your staff of editors. The staff are always at the newspaper offices. Put together an able staff of editors. You could have not just one managing editor but two—they could take turns. Your editors are the newspaper's soul. You will be its conductor."

I argued that there were a number of other comrades much better suited than I was for such an exalted position.

"For instance?"

"For instance, Comrade Pospelov. Apart from everything else he is an old newspaper hand—worked for *Pravda* for a long time."

"Who?" Stalin exclaimed. "Pospelov?" Folding his hands across his stomach, he tossed his head back and gave a long peal of hollow staccato laughter. "To propose Pospelov means that you do not understand *Pravda*. Don't you see, he's burnt out. He looks back and not ahead. How can we succeed in the day-to-day leadership of the ideological and political (and not only political) work of a party as large as ours? Only through the press. How do we guide the press itself? Only through *Pravda*. This is the paragon of all newspapers, a paper like no other. It must be that. Yet *Pravda* has been frittered away. In a number of instances we have seen that Il'ichev is not an educated Marxist. He's an ignoramus. He needs to go to party school. So you'll have to take on *Pravda*. So that it won't be too hard for you, get some capable assistants."

In an ironic tone, Stalin said, "You like Pospelov? All right, you're welcome to Pospelov as an assistant, a deputy. Whom else do you want? We could have two editors for *Pravda,* the chief editor and number two. Think about it. Give the CC your proposals on how *Pravda* can be improved."

And that was that.

I took on my new assignment in low spirits. I had no bent for newspaper work. I volunteered for the front from the academic world, which I felt to be my calling. I always longed to return to the bosom of the Academy of Sciences. I had several economic research projects in mind, and I had made a start on some of them. I wanted very badly to finish them off. But again, when duty calls . . .

As best as I could, I set about remedying matters at *Pravda*. Very soon I submitted to the Presidium a draft of a CC decree on *Pravda* dealing with organizational questions and problems, as well as new appointments. The proposal passed quickly and easily. Stalin looked well and for some reason was in a good mood—he joked, laughed, and was very "democratic."

"You know," he said, "Shepilov told me that *Pravda* is hard to run. Of course it's hard. I thought maybe we ought to name two editors?"

This was met with loud objections. "No, that would create divided authority." "Things would get out of hand." "No one would have the last word."

Stalin laughed, "Well, I can see I lack popular support. All right, where the people lead, I go." He took his pipe out of his mouth and pointed the stem right and left, as though to say that he would be ready to follow the people, whatever direction they chose.

Everyone laughed.

"All right," he continued, "let us agree to what is in the draft: one executive editor, two managing editors, the first to put out the current issue, and the second to work on the next one. You think this will lead to opportunism? No?"

The decree passed.

So my new and, I must say, difficult life began. One night, not too long afterward, I was sitting in my *Pravda* office supervising the next day's paper, the issue for March 6, 1953. At about 10:00 P.M., there was a ring on the special Kremlin phone.

"Comrade Shepilov? Suslov speaking. Stalin has just died. We're all at the 'nearby dacha.' Come right away. Phone Chernukha and get here as soon as you can."

CHAPTER TWELVE

In Mortal Combat

THE WAVE OF POPULAR UNREST, alarm, and sorrow touched off by Stalin's death gradually subsided. Life returned to normal. However, the new leadership of the party and the country confronted a mind-boggling sea of international, organizational, economic, and ideological problems, which were all the more difficult because for years on end people at the highest level were accustomed to waiting for Stalin's instructions on everything. Nikita Khrushchev spoke about this at meetings of the CC Presidium and CC plenums:

"We relied totally on Stalin. We left everything to Stalin. We knew that Stalin would make the right decision about everything. We had no worries. Now there is no one on whom to depend. We must decide everything for ourselves. The decisions are complicated: issues of international affairs, the economy, literature. . . . Late just last night I phoned Bulganin. I asked, 'Nikolai, what are you doing?' He said, 'I'm reading.' 'What are you reading?' 'The journal *Kommunist.*'

"You see how it is. When did we ever read *Kommunist* or other journals? Now we must."

Of course, Khrushchev was speaking for himself. He never read anything, neither books nor journals; he felt no need to read and judged others by himself.

The CC Presidium, the Council of Ministers, the Central Committee, and the Supreme Soviet counted among their members many superbly educated Marxists and brilliant engineers, designers, economists, military leaders, and writers. On the cultural level, the Soviet people as a whole had advanced to the front ranks of mankind. Yet it was undeniable that Stalin's death placed incommensurably greater demands on the country's leadership. What were the most urgent problems? They were not in the economic sphere. Here the gigantic machine was still running smoothly and on its own momentum. Socialist industry was on the rise. In Moscow, majestic architecture was soaring ever higher—Moscow University and buildings on the Kotel'nicheskaia Embankment, in Smolensk Square, in Vosstanie Square, and on Kalanchevskaia Street. In April 1953 a splendid new line was added to the metro system, with stops at Arbat and Smolensk Squares and Kiev Station.

On April 1, 1953, in what had become a tradition, the nation was rewarded with another reduction in retail prices. Stalin strongly championed the policy of regular reductions in prices. He frequently characterized it as integral to the socialist political economy. His reasoning went something like this:

"Our socialist industry enjoys an absolute monopoly since there is no private manufacturing. The country is shielded from the world market by a monopoly on foreign trade. Given the strict control of prices, there is virtually no domestic competition among our enterprises. There is a shortage of consumer goods. Under these conditions, systematically lowering prices is the most effective means of stimulating higher productivity and better quality. Lowering consumer prices prevents sloth and stagnation and is the best way to raise wages in real terms."

One of the grave economic consequences of the khrushchevshchina was the abandonment of the policy of price reductions, and the shift to the policy of overt and covert price increases for consumer goods. This caused serious harm to the entire economic and political situation in the country.

The price reduction of April 1, 1953, included almost all food products and mass consumer goods—bread, flour, cereal, grain, meat, fish, butter, sugar, vodka, fabric, clothing, shoes, soap, and household goods, as well as public catering. It was the sixth postwar price reduction. The preceding five price reductions meant that prices were half of what they had been in the fourth quarter of 1947, and the sixth reduction was the biggest, saving people fifty-three billion rubles over the period of a year. It represented a great economic victory, especially when compared to the steady increase in prices in the capitalist world.

The dynamic upturn in the arts also continued. I remained true to the habits that were formed during the thirty years I lived in Moscow. My boundless love of music and art drew me irresistibly to the Bolshoi Theater, the Moscow Art Theater, the symphony concerts at the Conservatory, the Malyi Theater, and the operetta. I was overjoyed by every theatrical success and filled with pride at the glowing triumphs of our touring companies throughout the world.

The Bolshoi Theater put on a brilliant production of Verdi's *Aïda*. The talented director Boris Pokrovskii, the outstanding operatic conductor Aleksandr Melik-Pashaev, and the young, unknown, but extraordinarily gifted set designer T. G. Starzhenetskaia collaborated on an inspired recreation of the Italian master's dramatic work. The principal singers were superb—Georgii Nelepp as Radamès, Vera Davydova as Amneris, Ivan Petrov as Ramfis, and Pavel Lisitsian as Amonasro. During the intermission I was able to express my appreciation to Melik-Pashaev and Nelepp, and a few days later at a chance meeting at the theater, to Davydova.

Soon afterward the Bolshoi restaged Georges Bizet's immortal opera, *Carmen*. But the production proved mediocre in every respect. At the end of May, the Bolshoi also presented a new production of Alexander Borodin's *Prince Igor*. Here Fedor Fedorovskii proved himself an extraordinarily talented set designer, while Aleksei Ivanov, Aleksandr Pirogov, and Ivan Petrov scored enormous successes in the roles of Prince Igor and Prince Galitskii. The choreographer Kas'ian Goleizovskii staged the Polovtsian dances with great flair.

The Bolshoi did more than offer new productions of the classics, those precious jewels in the crown of operatic art. In June it premiered Iurii Shaporin's long-awaited opera, *The Decembrists*. The composer had been laboring over this work for almost a quarter-century. During my time as head of CC Agitprop, Shaporin, the director Nikolai Golovanov, and the composer Tikhon Khrennikov approached me on several occasions with requests for advice. The main problem lay with the book. The opera needed a historically accurate plot[1] and, at the same time, a dramatic and heroic framework that conformed to the operatic genre. This required consultations with historians, composers, directors, and musicologists. I tried to help as much as I could.

At last the score was done. The production was placed in the hands of one of our leading directors, Nikolai Okhlopkov, known for his rich imagination and excellent taste. The same Starzhenetskaia teamed up with Anatolii Petritskii to fit out the opera with artistically compelling sets while Melik-Pashaev took charge of the musical interpretation.

The premiere showed that Shaporin had written a deeply moving opera with splendid symphonic development, dramatic arias, and masterly choral effects—in short, an opera destined to find a permanent place in the repertoires of our musical theater companies.

The Moscow Art Theater put on Gorky's *Dachniki* (Dacha People) with renowned actors and actresses like Alla Tarasova, Klavdiia Elanskaia, Olga Androvskaia, Mikhail Ianshin, Mark Prudkin, Anatolii Ktorov, and Vladimir Ershov.

In short, Moscow remained a theatrical mecca. However, the country confronted major problems that required immediate solutions—first and foremost, problems of foreign policy.

By the time of Stalin's death the international situation had become tense. It was crystal clear that the great powers, once joined by the bonds of the anti-Nazi coalition, were going their separate ways after the war. The Soviet Union consistently pursued its policy of peace, freedom, and independence for all states, large and small. The countries of the Anglo-American bloc had reverted to their old imperialist course.

American planes carried out ferocious bombings of Pyongyang and other cities and villages of the Democratic People's Republic of Korea. French imperialists continued to wage a bloody war against the peoples of Indochina, who rose up in a sacred struggle for independence. On the German question, the Western powers trampled underfoot the wartime agreement that called for a single, peaceful, democratic Germany. By implementing two separate zones and subsequently creating the Federal Republic of Germany, they embarked on a separatist policy to perpetuate the division of Germany, remilitarize West Germany, and turn it into a hotbed of militarism and aggressive revanchism. This revanchism found its standard-bearer in Konrad Adenauer, the federal chancellor, whom Churchill dubbed the wisest German political leader since Bismarck in a speech on May 11, 1953. The United States, Great Britain, and France stalled in their negotiations on a democratic successor to the Austrian treaty.[2]

The fact that the Soviet economy was developing at a steady rate and the country was moving full speed ahead gave rise to intense alarm within the reactionary camp. Its leaders deliberately whipped up a campaign of anti-Soviet militarist hysteria, triggering a new arms race.

Among the dismal manifestations of this hysteria was the "Rosenberg case" fabricated in the United States. American security services grabbed two American citizens, Ethel and Julius Rosenberg, a sweet and unassuming couple, the parents of two little children, and charged them with spying for the Soviet Union. The whole world knew they were innocent. The working people of New York, Beijing, Rome, London, Moscow, and Paris held mass protests demanding their release. Outstanding writers like Thomas Mann, François Mauriac, and Ilya Ehrenburg joined in the protests, as did student organizations throughout the world—and just about everyone, up to and including representatives from the Vatican. Nonetheless, Ethel and Julius Rosenberg were sent to the electric chair.[3]

So much for one side of the picture. On the reverse side, the incipient collapse of the entire imperialist colonial system in Asia and Africa drew one people after another into national liberation movements. The centuries-old British dominion in India rapidly fell apart. India was divided into two nations, India and Pakistan, and power fell into the hands of the ruling classes of those countries.[4] The British colonies of Ceylon and Burma also gained their independence, as did the Dutch colony of Indonesia.[5]

In Egypt the nationalist parties asked the British to leave the Suez Canal zone. All the signs were that the seventy-year British reign in Egypt was nearing its end. Just the previous year—in July 1952—a revolutionary coup overthrew the tyrannical regime of the corrupt and morally depraved puppet King Farouk. In the years that followed, this glutton and phenomenal lecher led a dissipated life in Europe. He died while seated at a table in some dive in Rome in the company of a prostitute.[6] A hundred-dollar bill, a Browning, dark glasses, and a cigarette lighter—that was all that was found in the pockets of this Arab Croesus, whose fabulously luxurious retreats in Cairo and Alexandria I soon saw.

An anti-imperialist, antifeudal revolution gripped Egypt. The presidency of General Naguib proved short-lived; the general was dismissed and confined to some hideout in the desert. In 1954 power passed into the hands of a group of young military men who belonged to the Free Officers Movement. Gamal Abdel Nasser, a lieutenant colonel in the Egyptian army and a former general secretary of the liberation organization, filled the post of head of government and acting president of the Egyptian Republic.[7] This marked the beginning of an era of radical reform and struggle for Egypt's political and economic independence.

The events in Egypt produced a chain reaction of national liberation movements in the Middle East and Africa. Reporting in *Pravda* on each phase of this struggle, I could not, of course, imagine that it would soon be my lot to sit in the luxurious palace of the dethroned Farouk, in the shadow of the great pyramid of Cheops, holding discussions with President Nasser and his colleagues about the fundamental problems of the country's economic and political development.

By 1953 the anti-imperialist national liberation struggle had spread to Tunisia, Morocco, Madagascar, the Gold Coast [Ghana], Kenya, Malaysia, the Philippines, and many other countries. This led to a change in the global situation and created new opportunities for us.

Immediate responsibility for the conduct of Soviet foreign policy in this complex situation still lay with Molotov; the policy he pursued was characterized by a number of traditional features that had evolved under Stalin. The most important were as follows:

1. A comprehensive evaluation of all the economic, political, class, and other factors responsible for a given feature of international life
2. Skillful application of the laws and categories of Marxist dialectics to the analysis of specific international situations
3. An understanding of the need to differentiate between interim and constant factors in analyses of international events
4. The ability to exploit the inevitable differences among the capitalist countries and their blocs and alliances in order to weaken the forces of war and reaction in the interests of democracy, peace, and socialism
5. The sensible use of Leninist principles of compromise as a diplomatic technique, with consideration for the conditions and opportunities for compromise, the limits of compromise, the time covered, the pluses and minuses of the whole approach, and so on
6. Wisdom and patience in deciding on foreign-policy démarches, with careful consideration of the means to be employed, possible reactions, and the practical results
7. The ability to make sure that short-run diplomatic actions correspond with and are subject to the basic political and strategic interests of the

Soviet government, which is duty-bound in its foreign policy to consider the basic interests of the international working class and the peoples of colonial and occupied countries struggling for liberation

These principles of Soviet foreign policy and diplomacy won us significant victories in the international sphere—universal recognition of the Soviet Union, mindfulness of every word in our foreign-policy documents, the continued growth of socialist forces around the world, a corresponding weakening of capitalist forces, the rout of the German and Japanese military machines in the Second World War, and the creation of a great socialist coalition of European and Asian states that embraced a third of mankind.

The previous history of Soviet foreign policy and diplomacy led to two wartime triumphs that will astound generations of future historians. First, the Soviet Union split apart the prewar united front of capitalist countries and took its place in the ranks of the great anti-Nazi coalition, along with the United States, Britain, France and many other states that acted in concert against the fascist Axis. And second, throughout the war against Germany, the Soviet Union neutralized imperial Japan, thus averting the dire peril of a two-front war. To a large extent these two diplomatic victories predetermined the outcome of the Second World War and subsequent world history.

Molotov's habitual circumspection and thoroughness in considering and preparing for any foreign-policy move grew even more pronounced after Stalin's death. He increasingly consulted with academics and journalists with backgrounds in international affairs. After Molotov decided on a substantive position on a question, people gathered in his office and at the Ministry of Foreign Affairs to consider the various forms of implementation—either an ambassadorial statement; an interview with the deputy minister or minister of foreign affairs; a statement by the ministry itself, the head of government, or the government as a whole; or an official note (in case of the last, what kind of note—an aide-mémoire, a *note verbale*, or some other kind).

As experienced politicians, diplomats, and journalists (both at one time had worked for *Pravda*), Stalin and Molotov always attached great importance to the press as an instrument of foreign policy. Both saw the press as a fully adequate and effective means of dealing with many international questions. In such cases, the editor of *Pravda* or *Izvestiia* was instructed to publish an article. Sometimes the order was direct: assign David Zaslavskii[8] to write the required article or column.

After discussion with the executive editor and finalization, the draft was sent "upstairs"—to the CC Presidium—for review. Sometimes the final version was drafted then and there, and the executive editor could not change a single comma without permission. At other times the CC members submitted their individual comments, and the executive editor was left to work out and publish the final text. Occasionally Stalin wrote the article himself.

As I mentioned earlier, Stalin did not like to work with a stenographer. If the article was composed within the Presidium, Stalin, as a rule, dictated slowly and deliberately. Molotov, Malenkov, Zhdanov, Poskrebyshev, who was Stalin's secretary, or the executive editor recorded his words. Sometimes this took hours. Molotov followed Stalin's example. There were times when work of this sort began during the day and lasted through the night.

After the article was polished, we asked what form it should take in print: Should it be something written by a correspondent of this particular newspaper or someone else (if the latter, should it be signed with a pseudonym or "Observer"); or should it be an article or a front-page editorial by TASS? How prominently the piece was featured was also a matter for specific instruction. On what page? In the bottom half? Under a three-column headline? Or in some different way?

The same careful thought was given to diplomatic receptions, depending on whether the foreign guests were in favor or not. The answer determined who was host, where the reception was held, which Soviet officials attended, and so on.

I dwell on these seemingly technical matters because they are part of that apparatus whose skillful use is a prerequisite for the conduct of foreign policy. Later, under Khrushchev's one-man rule, all these procedural conventions were tossed aside, and the whole storehouse of diplomatic discourse was turned upside down. Things reached a point where any statement on any question, large or small, was left almost exclusively to Khrushchev. He gave speeches almost daily, sometimes several times a day, wherever he was, under whatever circumstances, without regard for the significance of the issues involved or the possible reaction abroad. Before the Supreme Soviet, he spoke hot-temperedly about minor diplomatic questions, but in passing or during chance conversations with strangers he referred to major international problems that required substantive governmental comment. The same was true of diplomatic receptions. The halls that the Ministry of Foreign Affairs normally reserved were abandoned to cobwebs. The ministry's staffers began to neglect the forms of diplomatic etiquette. Khrushchev received all foreign guests, both the important and the not so important. The venue was always the Great Kremlin Palace, where the entire Politburo, the CC Secretariat, and a motley crew of CC members, ministers, deputies to the Supreme Soviet, artists, writers, generals, and marshals were in attendance. All diplomatic receptions turned into sumptuous feasts.

As for the press, Khrushchev kept a jealous eye on just one thing—that all his speeches were published in all the principal newspapers. Because of that, a single issue was sometimes packed with two or even three of his interminable speeches. Anything else that appeared in the press held little interest for him.

But all Khrushchev's innovations came later. During the period in question, the priority that Molotov gave to the role of the press in the conduct of foreign affairs proved to have a direct effect on my own life and work. I spoke earlier about the enormous domestic and international significance that Stalin attached to the Marxist textbook on political economy. Work on the textbook was approaching its conclusion, but my life was still divided between night work as executive editor of *Pravda* and time snatched during the day for work on the textbook. While Stalin was alive I somehow managed to scrape along. But soon after his death things got more difficult.

Spring in all its splendor came to the outskirts of Moscow, where our work on the textbook was nearing completion. The earth, trees, grass, and skylarks seemed intoxicated by the sun. Washed by the warm rains, the winter wheat gave off an emerald glow. All the vital juices of the earth burst through its newly warmed crust; as if they were in nature's magic bowl, they became snowdrops, bird cherries, dandelions, grain, birch leaves, flowering lindens, and lilacs. Next to my window, among the delicate cherry and apple trees, there was an old shed topped with shingles. As in the previous year, I watched the black-lacquered rooks pull furiously at the roof, tearing off bits of shingle and flitting up to the tops of the ancient poplars and oaks to build their nests. The joyous hubbub of the avian kingdom filled the air. How mighty is the force of life!

One late afternoon Molotov called on the special government phone. "Comrade Shepilov, where are you right now?"

"I'm on the outskirts of the city with the commission on the political economy textbook."

"That's what I want to talk to you about. We're ready to put through a whole range of very important foreign-policy measures. We cannot do it without *Pravda*. But the executive editor is distracted by the textbook."

I replied, "I already spend all my nights at *Pravda,* even my days off. Anyhow, we'll soon be done with the textbook."

"I'm not questioning the importance of your work on the textbook," Molotov countered, "but now we have things here that are more important. You must now be totally focused on your work at *Pravda*. I've already discussed the matter with the others in the Presidium, and they all agree. I am conveying the Presidium's instructions to you."

It was sad to say good-bye to my snug little cell with its desktop volumes of *Das Kapital* and Lenin, to the woodland stillness that separated us from the hurly-burly of city life, to the ineffable joy of creative work in the propagation of the great ideas of Marxism-Leninism. But the writing and editing of the textbook really was coming to an end. Like my colleagues, I made one final effort. In 1954 millions of blue-covered volumes with the title *Political Economy: A Textbook* began cascading through countless distribution channels into the homes of workers, students, teachers, engineers, doctors, artists, soldiers, and propagandists. Later the book was published in translation in hundreds of thousands of copies in Czechoslovakia, Bulgaria, Japan, East Germany, Poland, Britain, China, Denmark, France, Norway, and Italy—in short, throughout the world.

It was true, of course, that many pressing foreign-policy problems needed work and required decisions. On these questions, Molotov's views were authoritative, if not decisive. But now many of the questions that previously had been decided in consultation with Stalin were submitted for discussion by the CC Presidium. The members still met in the office that Stalin once occupied. They still stared fixedly at the portraits of Suvorov and Kutuzov that were bulging out of their frames. Only now the long conference table had been moved away from the wall and up against the windows.

At first Khrushchev did not join in the discussions on international issues. The inertia of the past mindset apparently still held. Toward the end of Stalin's life, I was present at several Presidium discussions about certain international problems. I remember on one occasion how various Presidium members took opposing positions on a complex diplomatic problem. Stalin slowly paced about the room with his ducklike gait, puffing on his pipe. He was evidently weighing the yeas against the nays and had not made up his own mind. Abruptly, he stopped before Khrushchev and, squinting at him, said, "Well, let our Mikita come up with something."[9]

Some of those present smirked; others tittered. Everyone thought it was outlandish and funny that Khrushchev should be asked for his opinion on an international question. Khrushchev mumbled something unintelligible, and Stalin, dropping his jest, sank back in thought. I saw something similar on another occasion. Who could have imagined that the time was close, very close, when Khrushchev would fancy himself a great international authority and, without consulting anyone on anything, would make categorical pronouncements on all diplomatic issues, and that anyone who expressed the slightest doubt about his wisdom was dismissed? O History, you are a woman of easy virtue!

But for now we were still in the period when all the speeches, editorials, and propaganda articles in our newspapers and journals focused on the need for collective leadership. As chairman at meetings of the CC Presidium and the Council of Ministers, Malenkov did his best to run things in a fully democratic fashion. With a good deal of tact and consideration, he tried to encourage all the different personalities at the top level of government to pool their efforts to resolve current problems. In his own demeanor there was not a trace of pretentiousness. He did not try to stand out; his whole manner seemed to say, "I have no edge over the rest of you. Let us reason together. Make your suggestions. I am here only to coordinate our efforts." He did so naturally and sincerely. I do not believe he had any thought of personal aggrandizement. He had always worked like a dog; after Stalin's death he worked ten times harder.

The CC Presidium and Secretariat were fully present at all conferences, meetings, festivities, diplomatic receptions, and so on. The Presidium and the Council of Ministers, freed from the restraints imposed on them by Stalin, worked hard and in an orderly fashion. To preserve a semblance of unity, the members tried not to engage in polemics, or at least to smooth over points of disagreement. At the sessions immediately following Stalin's death, critical remarks often gave way to questions like, "But don't you think that the proposed solution would only complicate matters?"

Yet all this amounted to only an outward show of collectivism.

In his writings and speeches Stalin often spoke of the great importance of collective leadership. As a model of collectivism, he held up the party Central Committee, comprising as it did "our best industrial leaders, our best cooperative directors, our best supply agents, our best soldiers, our best propagandists, our best public workers, our best kolkhoz experts, our best experts on private farming, our best specialists on the nationalities of the Soviet Union and nationalities policy. Concentrated in this forum of sages is the wisdom of our party. Anyone can correct anyone else's personal opinion or proposal. Everyone is able to contribute experience." (See *Pravda,* March 16, 1953.)

He said this in 1931. Until the advent of the Khrushchev regime, it is true that the Central Committee comprised the best, the ablest, and the most educated elements of the party. But the more time that elapsed after Lenin's death, the weaker the principles of collective leadership became, especially within the party's critical institutions. Over the three decades of Stalin's leadership, the entire system of governmental and party administration gradually lost its collective character and adapted itself to one-man rule, which eventually reached its apogee. This led inevitably to the trampling underfoot of Leninist standards of conduct within the party and the country as a whole. Bureaucratic rust gradually covered the machinery of government. The cogwheels, transmissions, and driving belts that kept open channels of communication between the party leadership, party organizations, and individual members, as well as between the party and nonparty masses, functioned less and less well. A transition to authentic collectivism and broad democracy would have required major reforms aimed at the restoration and further development of Leninist standards. But that was out of the question.

Like a penniless gambler who is obsessed by thoughts of fortune, who peers at other card players to study their tactics and devise ways to knock the second-rate players out of the game, and who stakes everything to deliver the mortal blow to his most dangerous opponent, the uneducated vandal from Kalinovka, Nikita Khrushchev, patiently plotted his moves. Having been Stalin's favorite, Molotov's devotee, Kaganovich's protégé, Bulganin's colleague, and Malenkov's and Beria's friend, Khrushchev carefully and suspiciously studied the scene with his small, puffy, porcine eyes. What had transpired since Stalin's death? How was power distributed among his heirs? Who was allied with whom? Who was dangerous? Who was not? Future historians and psychologists will ask themselves in amazement: How did a semi-educated person like Khrushchev, an utter provincial hick in manner and mentality, manage to summon up such a wealth of skill, duplicity, cunning, treachery, hypocrisy, and immorality in the pursuit of his aims?

As I mentioned earlier, the consensus within the party and among the people was that Stalin's only rightful successor was Molotov. But Molotov did not show the slightest inclination to take the helm. With matchless discipline and decorum, he waited for the collective wisdom of the CC Presidium to determine his future role. That made things easier for Khrushchev. Even while he stood at Stalin's deathbed, he obtained the assent of Bulganin, Malenkov, and Beria to relegate Molotov to second-rank status within the leadership.

To all appearances, it was Malenkov who took the helm. I previously described how he delivered the summary report at the Nineteenth Party Congress on Stalin's instructions. At the March 1953 session of the Supreme Soviet, he was elected chairman of the USSR Council of Ministers.

Malenkov undertook the basic reconstruction of Stalin's Kremlin arrangements. He was only now beginning to assume his role as head of government in relation to the diplomatic corps. But Khrushchev had already made it pretty clear to him how illusory his position as Stalin's young successor was and how submissive he had to be to hold on to his post. A large wolfhound condescendingly pats with a heavy paw the head of an affectionate poodle and nuzzles the poodle's belly with its nose. Then it bares its fangs and growls menacingly: "Hey . . . easy there." The sweet and gentle poodle finds that prudence demands that it lick its protector on the nose and try to coax him into a benevolent mood.

Sniffing about him, Khrushchev realized from the outset that the complacent Malenkov was not his main obstacle in his climb to the top. Malenkov treated Khrushchev with astonishing tact and goodwill. He forgave the frequent jibes Khrushchev aimed at him and the tall stories Khrushchev told at his expense; he tried to arrange for lunches together; he timed things so they frequently went home from work and receptions in the same car. Khrushchev and Malenkov even moved next to each other on Ostozhenka Street and broke open a gate in the fence between their adjoining houses.

When the rules of the game that he initiated required it, or when he was in particular need of Malenkov's support for one of his schemes, Khrushchev graciously accepted the other's attentions. But the moment the need was past, he made it unequivocally clear that ultimately everything depended on him, and he devised a new ploy for reducing Malenkov's standing. Thus, at a CC plenum on March 14, 1953, Malenkov, at Khrushchev's initiative, was removed from his post of CC secretary. Soon afterward, Khrushchev asked the Presidium to consider doing away with the tradition that had existed since Lenin's time of having the chairman of the Council of Ministers (formerly the Council of People's Commissars), rather than the CC general secretary, chair all Presidium (Politburo) meetings.

Khrushchev behaved irritably at this session. His right nostril twitched. The corner of his mouth pulled toward his ear. His face looked like an angry bulldog's. "Why should Malenkov be chairman of the Presidium? Why must we submit to Malenkov? We have collective leadership. We should have a division of functions. I have my responsibilities; Georgii has his. Well, let him take care of them." Without further discussion or objection, Khrushchev and the principal members of the Presidium settled the question to his satisfaction.

Soon after, Khrushchev called on the obliging Malenkov to propose at a CC plenum that he, Nikita Khrushchev, be elected first secretary of the Central Committee. Thus, by one adroit move after another, Khrushchev succeeded in nullifying the agreement reached over Stalin's coffin to guard against excessive power slipping into the hands of any single CC secretary and to abolish the post of general (first) secretary. In short order, Khrushchev demanded that Malenkov be dismissed from the post of chairman of the Council of Ministers. This was done.[10] But for the time being, Malenkov was no impediment. By virtue of his moral and ethical makeup and his lack of willpower, Malenkov could not and did not want to hold out against Khrushchev.

However different in erudition, political and economic experience, and moral character, Molotov, Voroshilov, Mikoian, Kaganovich, Bulganin, Malenkov, Pervukhin, and other leaders were all representatives of the old school. They were all dedicated body and soul to Marxist-Leninist doctrine; they all placed the party's interests above everything else; they were all sincerely convinced of Stalin's greatness and infallibility; and just as sincerely, they now wanted to revert to collective leadership, "the old way," to meet the party's demands. They believed that all fundamental problems affecting the party and the nation could now be freely discussed and decided within the Presidium, the Council of Ministers, and the CC plenums by majority vote. Not one of them had any ambitions to one-man rule.

But there were two men within the leadership who looked at things far more practically, without a shred of romanticism or sentimentality. They were Nikita Khrushchev and Lavrentii Beria. Both thirsted for power. Both knew that after Stalin's death the machinery of one-man rule was not scrapped and consigned to the annals of history. It was preserved in toto; one only had to master it and start it up again. Like two beasts of prey, they eyed each other, sniffed each other, circled each other, each trying to guess if the other would make the first leap to crush the opponent and sever his jugular with his teeth.

Khrushchev knew full well that of all the top party leaders, Beria was his only serious opponent, the only serious obstacle to his unchecked ambitions. He also knew that he was dangerous. Beria's hands were on the levers that maintained the security of the Kremlin and the government, that provided for all means of official and other communication, and that controlled the special troops of the MVD[11] and border guards. The smallest miscalculation on Khrushchev's part could cost him his head. This was the reason he built an intimate relationship with Beria when he decided, on his own and in strict secrecy, to destroy him. Suddenly, before everyone's eyes, the two became inseparable companions.

Beria gloried in his new position. His power seemed limitless. He could do whatever he wished. Everything was within his grasp. For all practical purposes, there was no one who was superior to him, no real control over what he did.

Stalin was gone. How wonderful! Now he could live—really live— without fear of anyone. He had to know everything that was going on. Everything about everybody. Their most carefully guarded dirty little secrets. He had everyone by the throat. Stalin would have to be exposed, debunked, his memory obliterated. Let everyone know that Beria is no tyrant. He's a democrat. He'd have to write some memorandums right away, proposals for decrees in support of peace, legality, democracy, the sovereign rights of the national republics. And a general amnesty. He'd have to construct a townhouse in Moscow and a luxurious villa on the Black Sea as an ostentatious present for each member of the Presidium. Let everyone know what sort of man Beria is!

His frenetic activity began as soon as the sarcophagus with Stalin's mummified remains was placed in the mausoleum in Red Square. He emphatically let it be known that his views would have to be reckoned with in the sphere of foreign policy. This came as a surprise inasmuch as he had never been much interested in that field before.

To start at the beginning, shortly after Stalin's death a certain Western statesman made a speech that dealt with a whole number of fundamental issues on the international agenda. As minister of foreign affairs, Molotov drafted a reply in the form of a wide-ranging newspaper article. The draft had all the thoroughness typical of Molotov's style: it singled out key issues and put the emphasis where it belonged. I did what I could to help with the article. After that, the text was typeset at *Pravda* and sent to members of the Presidium for discussion. I attended that meeting of the Presidium. Malenkov was chairman. Molotov's article was roundly approved without any special comment. Two or three minor editorial corrections were suggested—that was all. The question seemed settled. But suddenly Beria asked for the floor. "I have some amendments to make."

Beria began to read from a typewritten text—an entirely new article that did not use a single paragraph or a single phrase from Molotov's draft. In his strong Georgian accent, he read page after page, with hardly any expression. The Presidium members exchanged glances of mounting embarrassment and confusion: What should they do? Molotov sat motionless, with an impenetrable look on his face; three of his fingers kept pressing rhythmically on the baize table as though he were crushing a soft piece of bread. Only in Khrushchev's small crafty eyes did I see derisive gloating. From under his eyebrows his gaze shifted from one listener to another, as though to say, "Take it from me, tomorrow it'll be like that on all other questions." I suspect that this marked the moment when Khrushchev began to approach certain members of the Presidium with a scheme for destroying Beria.

Beria's article was written in a racy agitprop style that was replete with clichés. It must have been the work of some half-educated products of some party school, some provincial newspapermen who were close to Beria. Finally he was done. "There," he said, "are my amendments to Comrade Molotov's article." He looked around the table with his dull-gray eyes behind his thick pince-nez. A nervous tic played on his face. Now and then he bent his head back and stared at someone from under his glasses.

Everyone knew that these were not meant as amendments; they constituted a counterstatement. Everyone was silent. The silence went on for a long time. Finally Malenkov, as chairman, said, "Well, all right, let us approve Comrade Molotov's article with Lavrentii's amendments."

There were no objections. Not a muscle moved on Molotov's face.

In June, I had another opportunity to observe Beria as the new international expert. The Presidium was reviewing our relationship with the German Democratic Republic. While his face twitched convulsively and his arms gesticulated wildly, Beria spoke of the new government that was being formed there in the most scathing terms. He berated it in every way. I could not stand this any longer and spoke up from my place at the end of the table: "We must remember that the future of the new Germany is socialism."

Lurching forward as though he had been hit with a whip, Beria shouted, "What socialism? What socialism? We must put an end to this irresponsible twaddle about socialism in Germany!" He spoke with such a scornful mien, with such distaste, as though the very word "socialism" and the journalists who used it were insufferable. I think that was my first and only dialogue with the dreaded minister of state security.

Shortly afterward Beria submitted to the Presidium a "manifesto on the nationalities question." This was an artfully composed document with a good share of demagoguery. In it, Beria addressed party and public leaders and the intelligentsia of the Soviet republics. It was painfully transparent that this "manifesto" was not intended in any way to promote any valid political goals, such as correcting what was wrong and distorted in the relationship between Moscow and the republics in the sphere of socialist construction, or fortifying and expanding further the sovereignty of allied and autonomous republics and the bonds of friendship among the different nationalities. No. Beria was angling for support among the people of the national republics and within their leading strata. "Know that I, Beria, stand for the full and complete sovereignty of all national and autonomous republics. I am for having their leadership composed solely of people of their own nationality. I am for granting every republic the exclusive supremacy of its own language."

Everything in Beria's manifesto was calculated to sow divisions among the various nationalities rather than promote closer relations, to spawn bourgeois nationalism instead of bolstering and furthering an internationalist ethos. Beria's aim was to exploit precisely these antidemocratic, nationalist sentiments to his own advantage.

Yet he knew that first and foremost what was expected of him was some word on the rule of law. The endless arrests and purges completely exhausted the party, the military, the intelligentsia, and the country as a whole. When will it end? When will we see the return of revolutionary legality? When will we be able to breathe freely without constant fear for ourselves and our families? Beria, the man who for years on end was one of those mainly responsible for the reign of arbitrary will and lawlessness in the country, decided to don the mantle of a champion of legality, individual freedom, and democracy. Let every one know that Beria stands resolutely against illegal arrests and cruel, punitive policies and is a supporter of replacing widespread arrests with a program of educational rehabilitation. Thus he will dissociate himself with one stroke from the crimes of the past and will rise before the people as their deliverer from lawlessness and the guardian of socialist law and order.

These ends could be served initially by an amnesty.

On March 27, 1953, the Presidium of the Supreme Soviet issued a decree, "On Amnesty" that Beria had drawn up. Never before had the Soviet judiciary enacted such a broad amnesty. All criminals sentenced to five years or less, all persons sentenced for financial and economic crimes and almost all military offenses, and all male prisoners above the age of fifty-five and female prisoners above the age of fifty were freed from detention, and any other forms of punishment were annulled. All persons sentenced to more than five years had their terms cut in half. All investigations and judicial cases in the above categories that had not yet been subject to court proceedings were closed. In effect, the only people still left in confinement were the relatively few sentenced for particularly serious counterrevolutionary crimes, large-scale embezzlement of socialist property, assault, robbery, and premeditated murder. The remaining masses of criminals were freed, their convictions removed, and their voting rights restored.

The initial public reaction to the amnesty was positive. But soon enough the wave of human beings released from prison began to inundate cities, workers' villages, kolkhozes and sovkhozes, resorts, train stations, and piers. Among the newcomers were habitual thieves, malicious hooligans, hoodlums who were repeat offenders, criminals, men sentenced for rape and grievous bodily injury, swindlers, embezzlers, bribe takers, and other felons. The number of murders, wholesale burglaries, robberies, and violent disturbances soared. Many localities were literally terrorized. People were afraid to go to the movies or the theater. With the coming of night, shutters were secured with heavy bolts, and residents waited anxiously and fearfully for dawn. The turbid torrents of criminality reached as far as Sverdlovsk, Tbilisi, Baku, Kiev, and Leningrad. Finally they broke into Moscow.

Alarm over the situation kept growing, along with sinister rumors that Beria had freed this underworld force with a special purpose—to form a criminal guard for the furtherance of his aims. But at this point something happened that drew a sigh of relief from the entire intelligentsia and the people as a whole.

On April 3, 1953, the editors of the principal Moscow newspapers, I among them, were summoned to a meeting of the party Central Committee. There we were told that a thorough review conducted under the supervision of the Ministry of Internal Affairs had established the spuriousness of all the charges in the so-called Doctors' Plot. This finding pertained, among others, to one of the principal accusers in the case, the Kremlin Hospital doctor Lidiia Timoshuk. It was she who had denounced the illustrious physicians, alleging that they made knowingly false diagnoses in caring for hospitalized party and government leaders and that they prescribed deliberately wrong treatment to bring about the deaths of party and government leaders. "For assistance rendered to the government in the exposure of the doctors-murderers," Lidiia Timoshuk had been awarded the Order of Lenin on January 21, 1953. Now it was announced that Lidiia Timoshuk was a secret agent of the security services and that she had written her denunciations in accordance with the MGB's instructions. These denunciations formed the basis of the charges.

On April 4 the press carried an announcement by the Ministry of Internal Affairs that stated that the investigation into the Doctors' Plot was canceled, inasmuch as the case was based on false testimony, and that everyone implicated in the case was rehabilitated. There is not enough room here to describe the torments that these outstanding Soviet doctors endured, most of whom were in their seventies during their months of detention. The award to the perjurer Timoshuk was withdrawn.

The public greeted the collapse of the Doctors' Plot as the end, or at least the beginning of the end, of that flagrant lawlessness and arbitrary rule that it had lived under for so many decades. Lavrentii Beria, who had been the main producer of these scenarios, with their "conspiracies," "attempts," and "espionage," was now on stage as the guardian of legality, law, and order. To enhance his image he even sequestered some of his cronies in solitary confinement in Lefortovo.

There was a good chance that Beria's new standing would be irreversibly consolidated. That was why Khrushchev decided to act without delay. Procrastination could prove fatal. However, any attempt to get rid of Beria required painstaking preparation and great caution. Beria was in control of security for the entire Kremlin and of all the security agents who were assigned to guard the individual members of the top leadership. He was in command of the border troops, the MGB divisions, and the police. He was in charge of the entire governmental communications network and knew how to use it for his own purposes. (Beria's eventual arrest led to the discovery of a huge number of tape recordings of Politburo members' telephone conversations.) All talk of plans and actions had to take the most conspiratorial forms—taking a stroll in a garden, whispering during the showing of a movie, and so on. Beria had his spies and microphones everywhere.

The most complex and delicate problems were how to get the members of the Presidium to agree to Beria's removal and how to obtain their active participation in the operation. Should Khrushchev confide in all the members or only some? If only some, then whom? Who should be first? Second? What should the order be? Who should be entrusted with the technical side of the operation, and how? All the parts of the conspiracy had to work flawlessly and with machinelike precision. Any snag could be catastrophic. To preserve his power Beria would stop at nothing.

On a later occasion, while reminiscing about the past I asked Khrushchev whether party leaders had been unanimous about the need to remove Beria. Did their plan work smoothly?

"Well," he replied, "what can I tell you? . . . Viacheslav [Molotov] grasped my meaning at once and made it clear where he stood. When I hinted to him, You see how Beria is behaving? Shouldn't we remove him from his present post before the situation gets dangerous? Molotov's look showed me that he understood. He asked only one question: What, just remove him? After a question like that, everything was clear, and we talked candidly.

"Bulganin did not have to be persuaded. He could see how things were.

"The most difficult question seemed at first to be about Malenkov. Everyone knew of his close friendship with Beria. They always came in together, sat together at all presidiums, and left together. You'd think they were joined at the hip. How to approach him? You know, we could ruin everything and place a noose around our own necks.

"But I could that see Egor [Malenkov] wasn't happy. After all, he knew as well as the rest of us that Beria was in a hurry to take Stalin's place and that he could do whatever he wanted with any of us. After those very first Presidium meetings it was clear where he was heading.

"Malenkov was in a tight spot. As chairman of the Presidium meetings, he tried to smooth things over, but he couldn't swing it. You remember how it was. Whatever the meeting, whoever had anything to propose, Beria would come up with a counterproposal. To speak up against him, who the hell knew what that could lead to.

"Finally, I noticed that Egor himself began to feel me out. Once or twice he said to me, cautiously, that Lavrentii was 'causing difficulties.' I gradually realized that Egor had had it, and I took the risk of having a talk with him. Well, I must say, he was like a rock throughout the operation."

"So," I asked, "you acted unanimously?"

With a characteristic snort, puffing his lips out, he answered, "Anastas [Mikoian] was vague, as always. It was hard to make him out. He agreed that Beria's behavior was inappropriate, but at the same time he said, 'After all, he's still all there.'"[12]

I could not tell from this conversation with Khrushchev whether Mikoian had been at least partially aware of the plans. It could be that after feeling him out and being uncertain of his attitude, Khrushchev never brought him into the conspiracy, and that Mikoian learned of the specific agreement in regard to Beria only at the meeting that sealed Beria's fate—all the while repeating the objection, "After all, he's still all there." (It is interesting to note that eleven years later, the operation to oust Khrushchev had to be concealed from Mikoian. At the Presidium meeting where Khrushchev's dismissal was approved, he again repeated, "After all, he's still all there.")

Everyone privy to the plot realized that Beria could not be removed in a democratic fashion—his henchmen could bring the entire state security mechanism, so perfectly maintained all these years, to bear against any party or government leader they chose. Beria could be removed from his posts only by subjecting him and his MGB confederates to sudden arrest and incarceration under guard and by having him remain in strictest solitary confinement while the subsequent bureaucratic and judicial proceedings went ahead.

It could be said that this was undemocratic and unconstitutional. After all, the man in question was the country's first deputy prime minister, a marshal, a member of the CC Presidium, and so forth. Yes, it really was undemocratic and unconstitutional. But by that time, the situation that Stalin's will had created over many years along with the logic of events had reached the point where the party and the state had lost control of the state security agencies. Moreover, these agencies had achieved a position over and above the party and the state; these bosses recognized the orders and authority of only one man—Stalin. In his final years, Stalin himself gazed with fear at what he had spawned, and began to put distance between himself and Beria. His was the dilemma of the wizard who brings evil demons to life and has no incantations to keep them under control.

Who, then, could be entrusted with such a complex and conspiratorial operation against Beria? Under the prevailing conditions in the country, there was only one real force that could bring it off—the army, its top echelon. From among the officers, the plotters selected a group of the most trustworthy people, who could be counted on not to lose their nerve. The group included Marshal Georgii Zhukov; Marshal Mitrofan Nedelin, chief of the Soviet army artillery; Marshal Kirill Moskalenko, commander of the Moscow military district; General Pavel Batitskii, soon to be appointed commander of the antiaircraft defenses of the Moscow district garrison; and several others. Their assignment was to arrest Beria on a certain day at a certain place and keep him securely isolated for the duration of the investigation and judicial review.

Those were the last, solstice days of June. Moscow sweltered in the heat. Like chickens on a torrid day, people went about with their mouths open, gulping greedily for air. Even the nights brought no relief.

Preparations for the mission were in their last stage. The objective was to overcome and remove not only Beria but also his closest aides, who could affect the progress and outcome of the operation. On the eve of the day set for action, there was a meeting of the CC Presidium. Scheduled for the following day was a meeting of the Presidium of the Council of Ministers, which numbered among its members the chairman and his first deputies—that is, the CC Presidium members Beria, Molotov, Bulganin, and Kaganovich. On many occasions and in colorful terms, Khrushchev described for us what happened next.

"After the meeting we went home to our dachas in the same car—Beria, Malenkov, and I. On the way we were kidding around and telling jokes. I wanted our looks and behavior to show that everything was completely normal. All the same I was gnawed by doubts. Had the son of a bitch sniffed out something about our plans? If so, we were done for. He'd head us off and wring our necks like chickens. In those last few days I outdid myself paying homage to him, falling all over myself groveling before him. That evening all this lovey-dovey kept going. Apparently he didn't suspect a thing.

"We dropped Egor off first. I decided to take Beria to his front door so that I could be sure he was home and would stay there till morning, the next morning. I gave him the works. Getting out of the car we strolled about for a long time. I complimented him shamelessly—how he managed to raise such large and valid questions after Stalin's death. . . .

"'Wait, Nikita,' he replied, obviously flattered, 'this is only the beginning. We'll decide on everything. Who can stand in our way now? As for us, our lifestyle is going to change. So will the way we work. I've already explained my proposal to you. You're still wavering, seeing problems where there aren't any. What if I tell my construction people to build a townhouse for every member of the Presidium—one in Moscow or the outskirts, whatever you say, the other in the Caucasus or on the Black Sea. You want one in the Crimea? You want one in Pitsunda?[13] Wherever you like. Townhouses like that will make your mouth water.' Here Beria smacked his lips with relish. 'Give every Presidium member a townhouse as a government gift, as his own property. Let him live there. Let his children live there. Let his grandchildren live there. What, haven't we earned the privilege of bestowing such trifles?"

"You're right, you're right, Lavrentii," I responded. "We must give this more thought. It's a good idea. Let's talk about it one of these days."

"'Well,' he said, 'good night, my friend. Let's get a little sleep. Busy day tomorrow. We'll hold our meeting. Then let's have lunch. . . .'

"I gave him a long and warm handshake. All the time I was thinking, 'All right, you bastard, I'm shaking your hand for the last time. . . . Tomorrow, just in case, I will have a gun in my pocket. Who the hell knows what may happen.'"

But everything went well and according to plan. The Presidium met in the Kremlin at the appointed hour. The agenda was announced beforehand. Malenkov was chairman. As Khrushchev related, "Egor was paler than usual, with brown bags under his eyes. He must have had a bad night. But he exuded confidence and calm." The moment the door closed behind the last member to enter, a group of marshals, all armed, positioned themselves in the next room, ready to carry out their assignment.

Malenkov spoke. "Before getting down to the agenda, we have a proposal to discuss the issue of Comrade Beria."

Beria winced as though from a slap on the cheek. "What issue? What issue? What are you babbling about?"

The carefully prepared sequence took its course. Lavrentii Beria was told bluntly and angrily everything that needed to be told: first and foremost, that he was trying to make himself dictator, that he placed the state security services over and above the party and the government, and that he hatched and implemented his own plans.

At first Beria was stunned. His face twitching convulsively, he gaped with the eyes of a cold fish at one Presidium member after another: What was this? Some intrigue against him? A plot? All he had to do was say the word, and any one of them would be crushed like an ant. He looked frantically about him, as though searching for some secret button that could be pressed, or some ordinary telephone that he could use to bark a brief order for his whole monstrous exterminating machine to go into action. He knew every secret of that machine.

But with every passing moment he sensed, not with his mind but with his chilled innards, that this was no misunderstanding, no inquiry. It was something terrifying and inevitable. When he was told that he was under arrest and would be tried in court, a greenish brown hue spread from his chin to his temples and forehead.

The armed marshals entered the hall. They escorted him to a waiting car. It had been agreed beforehand that he would not be placed in the inner prison at Lubianka or in solitary confinement at Lefortovo. That would invite fatal twists. It was decided to detain him in a special prison of the Moscow military district under military guard. There this state criminal was guarded day and night by a special detail of selected officers under the supervision of Marshal Batitskii. The same day, Beria's closest aides at the Ministry of Internal Affairs were arrested and detained.

That evening I was, as always, in my office at *Pravda,* putting out the next day's issue. There was a ring on the special Kremlin phone. The caller was Panteleimon Ponomarenko, then a candidate member of the CC Presidium.

"Comrade Shepilov? We're all at the Bolshoi Theater. We'd like to know . . . you don't happen to have an article by Beria in tomorrow's paper?"

"No, we haven't received any article by him."

"There isn't any reference to Beria in any connection, even just his name?"

"I don't think so," I replied, "but I'll check through the paper."

"Yes, please do, so that his name doesn't figure in any way in tomorrow's issue."

"Very well."

"Well, as for the rest, until tomorrow."

Although I knew nothing of what was going on, this one call was enough to make me realize that Beria had been toppled.

On July 2, a Central Committee plenum convened in Sverdlov Hall in the Kremlin. Malenkov delivered a report on the Beria case. The plenum lasted six days; spirits ran high.

I rejoiced and was deeply proud of my party, the CC, and its leadership. What a monster the party had laid low! How bravely and shrewdly it had averted the danger of a new Cavaignac![14] Of course, I mused, it was profoundly regretful that such a degenerate had clambered up to the post of Minister of Internal Affairs and the rank of marshal. But apparently those were the ruthless laws of class struggle. Didn't Evno Azef, the leader of the military organization of the Socialist Revolutionaries, become an agent provocateur?[15] Didn't the equally despicable provocateur Malinovskii succeed in becoming leader of the Bolshevik faction in the Duma?[16] We are building socialism, said Lenin, knee-deep in the mire of old society.

After Beria's arrest, we all went about on clouds of happiness. Now there would be an end to all this arbitrariness, all these unwarranted arrests. An end to the sinister activities of the special conferences. An end to the innumerable concentration camps. The marvelous rising structure of socialist society would be swept clean of all the abomination dumped there by the odious turncoats Ezhov, Abakumov, and Beria. We would restore and secure Leninist standards of conduct for the party and nation.

Immediately after Beria and his accomplices were arrested, the CC secretary Nikolai Shatalin was assigned to the Ministry of Internal Affairs with instructions to place everything instantly under his control, to prevent any possible surprises on the part of entrenched Beria adherents, and to begin the process of transforming the ministry into an institution that conformed to the demands of loyalty to the Leninist party and to the authentic moral standards of a socialist country.

Shatalin had been a longtime colleague of Malenkov on the CC staff. For many years he specialized in personnel questions. Right after Stalin's death, at the March CC plenum, he was transferred from the CC, where he was a candidate member, to the CC Secretariat. Now, while hard at work, he was tapped to help out in the state security establishment.

Malenkov's report and the speeches of CC members at the plenum contained many lurid facts attesting to Beria's vileness and criminal activities. It goes without saying that Beria never dreamed that anyone would ever gain access to his secret personal safes in the Kremlin, at Lubianka, and at home. Not for a minute did he ever part with the keys to his safes. Now these safes were forced open. Here lay the fruits of his surveillance of Presidium members, the fruits of the taps on their telephones. Here were the preliminary plans for future denunciations and criminal cases against any targeted party or government leader. Here were extensive lists of names, addresses, and telephone numbers of girls and women who attracted the lascivious glances of this morally depraved executioner. Here were lace handkerchiefs, silk stockings, and trinkets to pay off the partners in the pleasures of this Eros in ministerial guise.

Beria, how generous he was! True, he often ordered his minions to deliver this or that actress, some female secretary or schoolgirl, to his townhouse or one of his secret apartments. This was frequently done. True, on leaving the Kremlin after a day's work, he would often tell his bodyguards to seize and drag into his car a young female pedestrian whose legs attracted his attention. This, too, was done with technical proficiency. But what favors he showered on his conquests! What lavishness! Rare wines and delicacies at the bedside! Embroidered scarves and expensive stockings! And a guaranteed abortion or disposal of the newborn at a state nursery if their carnal delights had an undesirable sequel.

The speakers at the CC plenum advocated a radical change in the utterly intolerable situation that was created over many years, where the state security agencies eluded the collective control of the party and placed themselves above the party and the state. The plenum unanimously found Beria guilty of criminal antiparty and antistate activities that were aimed at undermining the Soviet state, as well as treacherous attempts to place the Ministry of Internal Affairs over and above the government and the party. The plenum voted to expel Beria from the CC and the Communist Party of the Soviet Union as an enemy of the Soviet people.

At the same time, the Presidium of the USSR Supreme Soviet decreed that Beria be dismissed as deputy chairman of the Council of Ministers and as minister of internal affairs and that his case be forwarded to the USSR Supreme Court for review. Sergei Kruglov filled the post of minister of internal affairs.

The July plenum of the Central Committee charged all party organizations to assume unremitting and systematic control over all MVD activities in Moscow and the provinces. The plenum acknowledged the need to brace the agencies of the MVD with party workers and make significant improvements in party and political education among security personnel. We left the plenum happy and elated.

As Khrushchev later related, "One day we got to talking in Beria's presence about the security and authority of our leaders. Beria said, 'If someone dared touch me, there would be an immediate uprising among the troops. The entire people would rise up.'" But Beria was locked up in a vault of the Moscow military district, guarded by soldiers. There was no uprising, and the people rejoiced that the predator had been driven into a cage.

In the initial stage of his detention, Beria was in a state of shock. What was this, a nightmare? Was he imprisoned? Wasn't he the omnipotent Beria? Wasn't it true that only yesterday a single word from him was enough to shatter anyone's life, to lock a person away in solitary confinement or a concentration camp forever, even send him to the execution block? Was he alone behind the thick prison walls?

They had taken away the laces to his shoes, his belt, his suspenders, even his pince-nez (a precaution, apparently, against the possible use of glass lenses for self-inflicted harm). They subjected him to the most humiliating forms of search and inspection, including his dental crowns and anus. In his spluttering indignation, he forgot that thus far they had applied to him only an infinitesimal part of the practices and regulations inscribed in that manual on torture which he had helped write and which had been tested on the flesh, bones, and minds of hundreds of thousands of prisoners.

A seething fury and thirst for action replaced his shock. Like a tiger that found itself locked in a cage, he would jump up from his iron bedstead and race around the cell. "If only I could get to Kobulov, Goglidze,[17] or any of my people at Lubianka, they would tear this vault to pieces." But he knew full well that neither Kobulov nor Goglidze nor any of his loyal henchmen were at Lubianka. They, too, were probably in high-security cells somewhere. He felt that all his blood, the blood of his distant Mingrelian ancestors, was boiling in his veins and scalding his cheeks, his ears, and his heart. He was ready to howl with rage and frustration like a wild animal.

Why did he let them twist him around their little finger? Of all people, that uneducated oaf Nikita Khrushchev! This was his doing. How he posed as my friend! How he shook my hand! Kept declaring his love. . . . And I . . . sensed during those last few days that something was wrong. At times I'd catch the vicious looks he'd surreptitiously throw my way, and then the moment our eyes met a broad smile would spread over his face. How could I have failed to ask myself why he began to seek me out and escort me home? I thought he was trying to ingratiate himself with me out of fear. Ah, now I can see what this kulak is capable of! What if I opened Malenkov's eyes? Because Nikita will soon destroy him as well! Is that where my salvation lies?

Beria conjured up all his creativity to send a secret note to Malenkov.

The note began, "Georgii, do not trust Nikita." But Malenkov quickly read out the note at the CC Presidium.

Beria exerted himself to the limit. But it was all in vain. The trial revealed the terrifying and grave crimes that Beria and his cohorts committed—abuse of power, venal action, and the satrap's total moral decay.

In the face of incontestable facts and irrefutable evidence, Beria, who only yesterday was an angrily erupting volcano, gradually acquiesced. He realized with increasing clarity that there was no salvation for him. It was the end. There would be no miracle. The sense of hopelessness was unbearable. It burned his breast like a red-hot shaft. To dull this pain, he recalled erotic memories from his past.

Here is one about an actress. Beria's bodyguards lay in wait for her at the stage door. Ordered her into their car. Brought her to Beria's townhouse. Made her go through certain procedures in the bathroom. Then, an invitation to the table. Intimacy in an alcove. A sportswoman, movie star, salesgirl, typist, singer, doctor, ballerina, another movie star, stenographer, schoolgirl—the names on an intimate record of depravity that was secreted in one of his office safes came to almost three hundred. Like some medieval miser rummaging through his treasures with a palsied hand, Beria ransacked his memory for the most voluptuous scenes and lustfully reviewed them in his mind. The word "schoolgirl" triggered an episode from the previous year.

With their ever-present discharge of pus, Beria's muddy-gray eyes came to rest on a teenage girl who was walking in the street. She was brought to his lair. The rape led to pregnancy. The girl's mother soon found out about everything. Ignoring the grave danger that loomed over her, she managed to snare the all-powerful dignitary and tearfully begged him to save her daughter. Now something unheard of happened. Hitherto, Beria had never hesitated to make short work of any of his victims who dared divulge the "state secret" of their ordeal or tried to find protection. But now things took a different turn. In a dacha village for MGB personnel on the Vladimirskii Highway, there suddenly appeared a new dacha with a three-meter-high fence. No one, not even the MGB employees who lived in the village, had any idea who took up residence there or what went on behind the fence. They noticed that every day a closed automobile, apparently with food supplies, went through the dacha's impenetrable gate. Any members of the MGB families who came close to this mysterious dacha while picking mushrooms were warned severely by the guards at the gate that it was "forbidden to walk here."

Only on one occasion did a female cook in the mysterious dacha whisper to a woman on the adjoining plot that behind the tall fence resided a "girl with an infant child" and the girl's mother. Now and then, very rarely, someone who "must be a very high official" came for a visit.

What had transpired in the black heart of this phenomenal lecher? A stirring of pity for a teenager ruined for life? Pride that he, Beria, with his history of loathsome diseases, could still father a child? It would be hard to say. All that is known is that on the second day after Beria's arrest, someone rang the bell at the gate of the mysterious dacha and announced loudly through the small window that those within should no longer expect the car with food supplies.

But this was one recollection Beria brushed off. It did nothing to relieve his tormenting sense of doom. He desperately clawed out of the depths of his memory the most erotic images he could find. He tried to revel in all their details in order to arouse his flesh and forget himself if only for a moment. At those moments, the senior army officers on round-the-clock guard duty saw through the peephole how Beria, covered with a rough army blanket, writhed in the ecstasy of masturbation.

On December 23, 1953, a special judicial commission of the USSR Supreme Court that was chaired by Marshal Ivan Konev found Beria guilty of state crimes. The same sentence was handed down to Beria's accomplices: former Minister of State Security of the USSR Vsevolod Merkulov; the former head of an MVD directorate and later the minister of internal affairs of the Georgian Soviet Socialist Republic, Vladimir Dekanozov; the former deputy minister of internal affairs of the USSR, Bogdan Kobulov; the former head of another MVD directorate, S. A. Golidze; the former minister of internal affairs of the Ukrainian Soviet Socialist Republic, Pavel Meshik; and the former head of an MVD investigative bureau for especially important cases, L. E. Vladimirskii. All were sentenced to death and had their property, awards, and military titles confiscated. The sentences were carried out the same day.

After that, work began on eradicating the Beria phenomenon root and branch. Severe punishment was meted out against the former minister of state security of the Georgian SSR, Rukhadze, and his confederates and against the former minister of state security of the Azerbaijani SSR and,

later, first secretary of the Central Committee of the Azerbaijani Communist Party, Bagirov. In December 1953, indictments for grave state crimes
were brought in open court in Leningrad against the former minister of
state security, Viktor Abakumov; the former director of an MGB investigative bureau for particularly serious cases, A. G. Leonov; the former deputy
directors of the same bureau, V. I. Komarov and M. T. Likhachev; and the
former MGB employees I. A. Chernov and Ia. M. Broverman. By decision of the Military Collegium of the USSR Supreme Court, Abakumov,
Leonov, Komarov, and Likhachev were shot. Chernov and Broverman were
sentenced to lengthy terms in labor camps.

The same year, 1953, put an end to extrajudicial bodies like the MVD
special conference, which handed down sentences without judicial review
in violation of revolutionary legality. It sent hundreds of thousands of innocent people to their deaths. The sentencing of Beria and his accomplices
thus laid the foundation for doing away with all forms of arbitrary rule
and restoring socialist legality. That was why Beria's exposure was greeted
with heartfelt joy by everyone—by party and government leaders, the party
membership, the entire intelligentsia, and the whole nation.

Khrushchev shared this general elation, of course. At that time and
in later years, he spoke frequently, at length, and everywhere about Beria's exposure—at meetings of the Presidium and the CC Secretariat, at
CC plenums, at general conferences, at meetings in the Kremlin, and
at innumerable diplomatic receptions. At these receptions, flushed with
ample quantities of alcohol and in the presence of the wives of high officials, diplomats, foreign correspondents, and waiters, he recounted and
smacked his lips over the details of Beria's reign. At first everyone, or at
least many, ascribed this to his "earthiness," his "spontaneity." "After all,
he wasn't raised in a boarding school for daughters of the nobility." "He
never studied diplomacy." "He's a worker. So he's had a few. He was candid
about everything. What's wrong with that?" Of course, after the severity
of Stalin's time, when it was necessary to weigh every action, gesture, and
word at official and unofficial affairs, all this came across as novel. What
it produced was a spate of detailed and colorful dispatches that foreign
diplomats and correspondents sent home: "How everything is changing
in the Moscow Kremlin!"

In all his vivid accounts, Khrushchev did not fail to emphasize his
own special role in Beria's exposure and, on occasion, to stick a few pins

in "certain of Beria's pals." In addition to being happy about the way things turned out, Khrushchev was overjoyed by the outcome of the operation's "business side." With Beria's execution, Khrushchev's path was cleared of the only rival, who, like him, was struggling to assume dictatorial powers. True, in the official ranking of top leaders, Khrushchev had yet to take first place. But things were definitely moving in that direction with lightning speed.

At a joint meeting of the CC plenum, the Council of Ministers, and the Presidium of the USSR Supreme Soviet the day after Stalin's death, Khrushchev was given fifth place within the top leadership, behind Malenkov, Beria, Molotov, and Voroshilov. Now, in July 1953, he appeared in all forms of print to be in third place, after Malenkov and Molotov. But as the saying goes, the first step is the hardest.

Beria and Khrushchev had the same goal—to ascend to the top of the power pyramid. But they went at it along different paths and with different methods. Beria tried to do this by utilizing the all-powerful state security agencies, which were under his sole control. To attain his ends in this manner was realistic. But it had one crucial weakness. In Lenin's day, the Cheka under Dzerzhinskii, and later Menzhinskii,[18] won the respect and affection of the whole country with its heroic, noble, and glorious actions. But then the security agencies entered a new phase. The monstrous lawlessness of 1937–38 and succeeding years and the crimes openly committed by Ezhov, Abakumov, and Beria enveloped the MGB in an atmosphere of fear and universal alienation. A regime built on such a rickety foundation could not count on stability, to say nothing of legitimacy in the eyes of the people.

Khrushchev, possessed as he was by oversized ambition, sought to reach the pinnacle of power by mastering the party organization, through which he thought he could bring everyone and everything under his control. As I described earlier, in line with his plan he demanded that Malenkov, already demoted as CC secretary, be replaced as chairman at meetings of the CC Presidium. Henceforth, Khrushchev chaired both the Presidium and the Secretariat. After that, Khrushchev demanded the restoration of the defunct post of general (first) secretary, which he assumed at the September 1953 CC plenum.[19]

Now all the most important affairs of the party and the country—promotions, appointments, dismissals, and personnel changes that affected all party, governmental, military, cultural, and other leaders—were concentrated in his hands. This enabled him to carry out a large-scale reshuffling of officeholders. He did not base his transfers and promotions on a person's loyalty to the party and the people, education, ability, professionalism, honesty, conscientiousness, or any other worthy political, civic or moral qualities. No. His main criterion for appointing people to the highest positions was the extent to which he could rely on them as his own men.

As a result of this approach, many party and government posts began to be filled by a flock of ignoramuses of questionable professional achievements and moral fiber, persons who were said to have access to and devotion for Khrushchev. To do this, Khrushchev placed the greatest importance on two sectors of the state system—the army and the security services.

Only a few months after Beria's fall—that is, after the first of the year (1954)—Khrushchev, in line with his criteria, succeeded in having Ivan Serov appointed chairman of the Committee on State Security (KGB). He was an utterly amoral and ignorant figure, directly and personally involved in many of the security agencies' past crimes. But he had worked alongside Khrushchev in Ukraine in 1939–41 as people's commissar of internal affairs of the Ukrainian SSR. Serov had remained close to Khrushchev in later years and was ready with a serf's zealousness to carry out any of his lawless instructions and personal whims.

As for the army, the most able marshals and top-notch generals with the most brilliant wartime records and the greatest hold on the people's affection were gradually removed from their posts and turned into figurehead generals. Khrushchev replaced them with commanders in his own image. To entrench his position even further, Khrushchev soon made himself chairman of the Supreme Military Council and commander-in-chief of the Armed Forces of the Soviet Union.

Now, with Beria gone and his reorganization complete, Khrushchev had his hands on the principal levers of party and state control. He could now begin to implement the "reform" plans he regarded as necessary and expedient.

CHAPTER THIRTEEN

Khrushchev at the Helm

FUTURE HISTORIANS WILL EXERT CONSIDERABLE effort to answer many difficult questions and explain many social paradoxes. How did Khrushchev take the helm of state? How should his reforms be assessed? What was his positive contribution to state and society? Did he make a positive contribution? Why, for an entire decade, was Khrushchev able to initiate ridiculous and fanciful projects that were costly to the country without any opposition? How did the Soviet state and society manage to withstand the trampling of economic laws?

One answer that requires a complete break with the doctrines of Marxism and historical materialism would go as follows. Over the thirty years of Stalin's uninterrupted command of the ship of state, no new national figure emerged who was qualified to lead the country in its steady progress toward socialism. As a result, Khrushchev got it into his head to become the newly proclaimed dictator. By removing Beria and other rivals from his way, he achieved his goal. Exercising his one-man rule, Khrushchev launched a "reform program" that had extremely grave consequences for many sectors of the economy, government, and society. This made his fall inevitable.

Real life was not so simple and straightforward. The country's political development after Stalin's death presented a contradictory picture of zigzags; there were great successes and major failures. The new, the progressive, and the hopeful were born in travail. The old and the obsolete fought in retreat and, while decomposing, often poisoned what was new. Nikita Khrushchev cannot be portrayed as a villain of the kind that strode across our provincial stages in the old days. To fully grasp the course and essence of the events of the Khrushchev decade, it is necessary to make allowance for the pressures and counterpressures of the following contingencies, forces, factors, and traditions.

By 1953, when Khrushchev stepped into the main political arena, the Soviet Union had become a mighty industrial and agricultural power. The country's remarkable development provided incontrovertible proof of the superiority of socialism over capitalism. By 1953 the national income of the USSR was 1,367 percent higher than in 1913, compared with a growth rate of 295 percent in the United States, 171 percent in Great Britain, and 145 percent in France. Soviet industrial production was expanding at phenomenal speed. Over the eleven prewar years of 1930 to 1940 and the eleven postwar years of 1947 to 1957—that is, during the twenty-two years when the Soviet Union was at peace before Khrushchev's reforms broke up the entire managerial system—the annual growth in Soviet industrial production averaged 16.2 percent, compared to 2.9 percent in the United States, 3.3 percent in Great Britain, and 2.6 percent in France.

In an unprecedentedly short span, the USSR moved from fifth place in the world as an industrial power in 1913, to second place, and from fourth place in Europe to first place. The advantages of the Soviet system provided a scientific basis for the communist party's confidence, which we all shared, that the country would resolve its basic economic problems and take first place as a world economic power.

The conglomeration of backward, scattered, and individual private farms had been replaced by an extraordinary system of mechanized agriculture, the world's largest—4,857 sovkhozes, 9,000 tractor stations, and 93,300 kolkhozes. Gross agricultural output soared. Village life underwent fundamental changes, becoming more comfortable and civilized. The party led the nation through a radical cultural revolution. All of the country's nationalities and ethnic groups increasingly shared in the growing richness of intellectual life.

Of course, industry and especially agriculture still faced many unresolved problems. Insufficient use was made of powerful stimuli to increase productivity—for example, the provision of economic incentives to every enterprise and worker. Likewise, inadequate use was made of tools for augmenting the growth of public wealth, such as cost accounting, profitability, price controls, and profits in accordance with the law of labor value. Because of that, the USSR lagged badly behind the most developed capitalist countries in productivity, supplies of consumer goods, and the quality of many products. Despite these deficiencies, however, a mighty countrywide socialist economy based on public ownership of the means of production was built in three decades. Unlike capitalism, with its unpredictable nature, the Soviet economy was governed by the laws of planned proportional development and expanded socialist production and growth.

The tampering with economic laws that went on under Khrushchev can—and did—do great damage to the country's economy, but it could not change the nature of socialist production. At the risk of additional losses and setbacks, objective laws must sooner or later make headway, breaking through and overcoming subjective deviations to restore balance.

From an objective standpoint, it can be said—as I said earlier—that Stalin did everything he could to topple the pillars of Leninism, paralyze the party as a vital association of like-minded revolutionaries, and leave to it the sole function of meekly carrying out the great leader's plans and glorifying his infallibility and genius. But the roots of the Bolshevik party had sunk too deeply in the people's consciousness, and its great Leninist traditions were too strong, to permit Stalin to complete his destructive work. The Soviet people's magnificent victory in the Second World War, the incredibly rapid recovery of the national economy from its wartime devastation, and the country's triumphant progress on the road of socialist construction greatly enhanced the party's stature. The party's authority among the people, within the international communist movement, and throughout the world reached its zenith in the postwar period. This put certain limits on Khrushchev's sweeping condemnation of all that preceded him, and placed certain demands on his "reforms." To gain public acceptance, they had to bear fruit at least as well as Stalin's programs. "You're dissatisfied, you're angry, you denounce the past, you trample Stalin in the mud; all right then, show us what you can do." It had to be shown not in words but in practice. The promissory notes eventually had to be honored.

How did Khrushchev's reform campaign begin?

For a considerable period Khrushchev, as I said, did not meddle in questions of foreign policy or express any opinion on the subject. He deferred to Molotov's absolute authority in this field and even seemed respectfully awed before the complexity of international problems. I remember that in one of my conversations with him during that time, he said, "I'm amazed at Viacheslav. What a head he must have for it! Got to keep the whole world in his head. It's good that we have him taking care of things. He's dependable. He isn't going to slip up. He's cautious. You can't go off half-cocked in that business. Yes, Viacheslav . . . what a brain."

In fact, for quite a while Khrushchev did not try to change anything that Stalin had arranged in sectors of the economy, government, and party other than agriculture. Everything done under Stalin he regarded as right and proper, wise and necessary. At any rate, at the time we did not hear him say anything critical about Stalin, his policies, or his actions. On the contrary, he constantly dwelt on Stalin's greatness, wisdom, and the "orderliness" of his rule. When someone eager to curry favor with the new pretender to the throne flattered him, contrasting his "kindheartedness" with Stalin's "cruelty," Khrushchev exclaimed with characteristic flamboyance, "Come on! Stalin—Khrushchev? Why, Khrushchev isn't worth Stalin's shit!" He apparently became so enamored with this imagery and self-deprecation that he repeated the phrase not only in private conversations but at various official meetings.

Prior to the Twentieth Party Congress, Khrushchev was generally reticent when it came to criticizing the past and its leaders. He was consolidating his position and wanted to be liked by all. He was friendly toward the entire top leadership at meetings of the Presidium and the CC Secretariat and did not countenance any abrasive comments or personal attacks. He granted his colleagues broad initiative and authority in their own fields. "I leave it to you. Decide for yourselves. You know more about this than I do. It's not up to me to instruct you." The tone and style of his work impressed everyone. After all, the way things were under Stalin was still fresh in their memory. Everyone in the Kremlin circle who was close to Stalin had lived in an atmosphere of tension, anxiety, and bone-chilling fear. With Stalin's sarcophagus installed in the mausoleum, everyone sighed in relief. Then came Beria's arrest. Everyone said, "How relaxed things have become. . . . How wonderful." Khrushchev missed no chance to emphasize this. Beria's arrest and his role in it were a constant part of his monologues.

To parade his forthrightness, accessibility, and collectivism, Khrushchev had lunch daily with any members and candidate members of the CC Presidium who cared to join him in one of the private halls of the Kremlin. Gradually these lunches became occasions for discussion of various topics, and almost all the top leaders were present. After every meeting and reception, Khrushchev gave a ride in his car to several people going his way.

As I mentioned earlier, right after Stalin's death Khrushchev moved into a townhouse next to Malenkov's near Metrostroevskii Street (Ostozhenka), and they put a gate in the brick wall separating the two residences to make it easier for them to see each other. Before long, Khrushchev decided that his pairing with Malenkov excluded others and was an inappropriate form of collectivism. He ordered a townhouse built for each member of the Presidium, just as Beria had proposed doing in his day. Soon enough the picturesque and popular Lenin (Vorob'ev) Hills were bedecked by a row of luxurious townhouses. Their interiors were done in marble and expensive wood, and they were isolated from the outside world by tall, massive walls, evidently of yellow limestone. The entrance to each house was barred by a heavy steel gate with a small entrance. The garden and gazebo of the Khrushchev residence on the very brow of the Lenin Hills offered a breathtaking view of Moscow spread out below.

All this took place at a time when the housing shortage in Moscow was particularly severe. One of the eccentricities of Stalin's headlong industrialization plans was his patent disregard for housing construction, even though no industrialization program can be sustained at a steady and rapid pace without an adequate expansion of housing. Millions of Muscovites lived cheek by jowl in overcrowded communal apartments, old wooden houses without hot water and indoor toilets, and even barracks and cellars.

Under the circumstances, the older Politburo members, Molotov, Voroshilov, and Kaganovich, long domiciled in the Kremlin, shrank from these novelties and were not keen to move to Lenin Hills in full sight of everyone. But the code of "collectivism" militated against singling oneself out, and soon this glittering array of townhouses was home to the Politburo in toto. A sumptuous athletic center with a swimming pool and other facilities was erected nearby. Here the new householders could pamper themselves with all the bodily comforts of the Roman emperors. Aware of Lenin's Spartan way of life from verbal accounts, writings, and film records, people promptly dubbed this new community "At Lenin's Behest" and *khrushchoby*.[1]

In the period immediately after Stalin's death, Khrushchev, as I said, deferred piously to Stalin's views on everything. On everything that is, except agriculture. In this field Khrushchev counted himself an unsurpassed expert and authority and thought Stalin an ignoramus. When the discussion turned to agriculture, he sighed and tapped first his forehead and then the wooden table with a crooked finger, as though to say that Stalin did not know anything on the subject. After that, he spouted a cascade of proposals about what should be done to assure the lightning-quick development of agriculture.

Agriculture was where he started his reforms. One day, I think it was in July 1953, he summoned me and said we would now lay the groundwork for a CC plenum on agricultural issues. He gave me a general picture of conditions in the villages and his thoughts on how to cure the difficulties and hardships of agricultural production. It would be good, he added, if I would head a group of economists and CC staffers in preparing a resolution that reflected his report to the plenum.

After graduating from Moscow University and putting in several years of practical work, I took a three-year course at the Agrarian Institute of Red Professors. Before and after the war, I published many works on socialist agriculture. On a number of occasions, the Moscow Party Committee and the Central Committee enlisted me to help prepare various papers on agriculture and the economy in general. So Khrushchev's assignment did not seem unusual. Our group was given an office once occupied by the CC secretary Andrei Andreev,[2] where we got down to work.

I believe our group came up with a major and scrupulously scientific study. The draft resolution we produced offered a comprehensive Marxist analysis of socialist agriculture—its advantages and achievements as well as its difficulties and problems. We did our best to sum up the prospects for continued development, focusing on the following requirements: the full mechanization and electrification of agriculture; the use and problems of chemical fertilizer; the general scientific application of agricultural technology and animal husbandry; an expanded grain harvest, which was the basis for all other forms of agricultural production; the central importance of crop growth in farming and more intensive cattle raising; economic incentives for sovkhozes, tractor stations, kolkhozes, and individual agricultural workers; and improvements in managerial and productivity techniques.

Besides our group, there was another group at work on Khrushchev's report to the CC plenum. Because his reports and major speeches came so close together, the work of preparing them acquired a set method and sequence. Under Stalin, every proposal contained in his addresses had the force of a directive. Implementation and reshuffling of personnel followed the speeches. The consequences were often very serious. So a brief digression on how things were done in Khrushchev's time would not be amiss.

His speeches fell into three basic categories. The first kind was impromptu. Khrushchev loved to speak and seized on every occasion to do so. Toward the end of his political career, his passion for speechifying became a pathological verbosity. He not only loved to speak, he knew how to do so. His impromptu speeches were pithy, colorful, and original. He usually made use of many vivid examples, comparisons, sayings, and proverbs. Very often they took the form of vulgarities: "We'll show them what for," "We eat our soup with our spoons and not our shoes," "He crushes flies with his nostrils," and others of that nature. Sometimes when annoyed, he relied on plain obscenities. But his lively, colorful, and pungent language appealed to his mass audience, at least to start with; a more critical reaction came later. Had Khrushchev received a real education, had he acquired a modicum of culture and at least an elementary knowledge of Marxism, he would have been a superb orator. But his mind, when it came to theory, science, and literature, was a tabula rasa. Even in the field of agriculture, in which he was said to be an expert, he hardly read a single book. His knowledge, according to his Philistine outlook, came from "experience."

He saw something on a visit to a sovkhoz or kolkhoz. (He made frequent visits to sovkhozes, kolkhozes, and new construction sites, as he was fond of travel.) He liked what he saw. Immediately, without looking into it or referring to existing studies on the subject, he publicly exhorted everyone and everybody to emulate what he had seen. It later turned out that what he had seen was an agricultural technique that was useful in subtropical areas but absolutely inapplicable in the country's central and northern zones. The same was true of his talks with people. He met and talked with many agronomists, field technicians, and scientists. If he liked a person and found his ideas attractive, he instantly praised him to high heaven and promoted him. With Khrushchev's impulsiveness and incurable bent for improvisation, this reliance on "experience" sometimes had tragic results.

After an impromptu speech, the text went to his assistants Grigorii Shuiskii, Vladimir Lebedev, and Andrei Shevchenko,[3] who called in newspaper hands like Pavel Satiukov and Leonid Il'ichev to subject the text to corrective surgery. Distinctly unacceptable parts were cut out or softened, essential new material was grafted on, and citations from the Marxist classics were inserted in appropriate and inappropriate contexts. The entire speech was cleaned up, smoothed out, and powdered. Since these wordsmiths were mediocre party-school products, Khrushchev's colorful language suffered. It lost its picturesque quality to conform to bureaucratic jargon and newspaper prose.

Now Khrushchev's speech was deemed ready for publication. The next day, over five or six pages, *Pravda* and other newspapers served up the new stew, still hot from the stove.

The second kind of Khrushchev speech was on issues in which his complete ignorance was so obvious that the whole thing had to be written for him. During his initial years in power, such issues included international economics and policies, the world communist movement, literature, art, and ideology. In later years, he laid claim to the irrefutability of his views on all these questions. But thus far the preparation of this second kind of speech was entrusted to the same group of Khrushchev aides, who, depending on the subject, enlisted the help of international experts, writers, and art scholars.

Sometimes Khrushchev was able to master the final product, sometimes not. Putting on his eyeglasses, stammering, and stumbling over difficult words, unfamiliar terms, and names, Khrushchev painfully picked his way through someone else's text as though it were a barbed-wire barricade. At such times, Khrushchev reminded one of a hobbled racehorse led onto a racetrack, or a clever dog forced into a muzzle. He agonized, became irritated, and got nervous. The audience grew bored. Finally, unable to contain himself and dying to speak unfettered by the prepared text, he said, "Well now, let me digress a bit from the text," and began to speak extemporaneously.

If the speech was on foreign affairs, officials responsible for the conduct of Soviet foreign policy squirmed in tense anticipation. What thunderbolt was coming next? What damage would it cause? But the audience sat up. Then the picturesque harangue came. How the French and Belgian factory owners had exploited him in his childhood in the Donbass and how later we "gave it to them." How the American imperialists who sent the U-2 spy plane over Soviet territory now had "their mugs in shit." How "Enzenhower" should be the director of a kindergarten rather than president of the United States. And more of the same.

Having gotten this out of his system, he would suddenly stop short and exclaim, "Well, I've strayed somewhat from the text. I see all the foreign correspondents are hurrying out the door. They're running off to send their telegrams. Khrushchev said this, Khrushchev said that. My advice to you: Less yelping, gentlemen. We've seized God himself by the beard. We'll know how to deal with you. . . . Now, to get back to the text." Sometimes these spontaneous improvisations recurred several times during a speech and exceeded the prepared text in length.

After such a performance, his own contribution was discarded or included in abbreviated or edited form, and the text was published in the press. Oftentimes the impromptu part was clearly unsuitable, but the foreign diplomats and correspondents had already transmitted it to their home offices. Soviet newspapers then came out with a different version from the one that appeared in newspapers abroad; the consequences were predictable and sometimes so serious that they had to be patched up.

The third kind of Khrushchev speech involved particularly important issues on which he considered himself fully competent and in whose timely preparation he felt he should take personal part. Chief among these were reports at CC plenums and party meetings. Here, too, a select group wrote the drafts, although the group was larger in number and of a higher quality. Khrushchev shared his thoughts with the authors. As I have noted, he was semiliterate and did not know how to write. But he gradually developed into a lively speaker. So he made his input by dictating to a stenographer. Often he called the stenographer back while the report was still being prepared to add other thoughts that had occurred to him; he insisted that the new passages be worked into the speech.

That's how it went. Khrushchev had a constant flow of brilliant thoughts. He dictated them almost daily, and they were all included in a

text that swelled in size. That is why Khrushchev's reports were so uni-
formly flabby: they contained everything that came into his mind in the
course of their preparation. That is also why they were so inordinately
long—five, six, eight, even ten newspaper pages in length. At conferences,
plenums, and congresses they took seven, ten, even twelve hours to read.
This gave rise to the famous and popular joke:

QUESTION ON ARMENIAN RADIO: Can an elephant be wrapped in
    a newspaper?
ANSWER: Yes, if the newspaper contains one of Khrushchev's speeches.

It was partially in this fashion that Khrushchev's above-mentioned
report at the September 1953 CC plenum was prepared. It took almost a
whole day to read. The text took up five and a half pages of *Pravda*. The
plenum's resolution took up four. The draft that the group of scholars
prepared remained virtually unused. The resolution amounted to a slightly
condensed version of Khrushchev's speech.

The speech included everything he saw in the countryside, everything
he knew about agriculture, and everything his assistants and statisticians
told him. Despite that, it did not present a fundamental analysis of the
real state of our agriculture nor define the basic issues that had to be resolved to ensure further development. Issues large and small were thrown
together helter-skelter. Some really major questions were not mentioned
at all; for others, the emphasis was put in the wrong place.

It is common knowledge that Soviet agriculture is based primarily
on grain, the foundation for the development of all its other branches.
During the postwar period, shortfalls in grain harvests were particularly
marked, which held back development in all other agricultural sectors.
Malenkov's statement in his summary report at the Nineteenth Party
Congress—that "the grain problem, once regarded as the most drastic and
serious problem we face, has been successfully, decisively, and irreversibly resolved"—was palpably erroneous. Experience and statistics did not
support this conclusion. It was clear that the key to a general expansion
of agriculture lay in a significant increase in grain production and in the
elimination of factors that held it back. Without that, it would be impossible to move ahead faster in the raising of cattle, technology, and the yield
of potatoes and vegetables.

Yet none of this figured in any way in Khrushchev's report at the

September 1953 CC plenum. True, he let fall this sentence: "In overcoming the lag in the raising of cattle and the production of potatoes and vegetables, we must achieve faster growth in the production of grain." But that was a passing interjection. There was no general discussion of the need to increase grain production as the most critical problem lying ahead. On the contrary, the grain situation was presented in rosy colors. "In the field of grain production we have been more successful than in certain other agricultural sectors. Not only have we in a relatively short period of time restored grain production that was damaged by the war to previous levels, but we have increased it. Fields sown with valuable commodities like wheat are growing at a rapid rate." Khrushchev also provided a general assessment of Soviet agriculture. "By and large, we are meeting the country's essential demands for grain, in the sense that our country is assured of adequate supplies, the government has additional stocks, and a specific amount of grain goes for export."

In other words, Khrushchev's report on the state of grain production did not depart from Malenkov's report at the Nineteenth Party Congress. He gave an optimistic picture of a balance between supply and demand in grain several months after Stalin's death; this did not prevent him from repeatedly charging at a later time that "Stalin ruined the villages," that "under Stalin the country was out of grain," that "we were dying of hunger but selling grain abroad," and so on. Khrushchev's report listed all the major and minor problems affecting agriculture, except for the basic and principal problem of grain. In the many party gatherings, conferences, assemblies, and newspaper articles devoted to the proceedings of the plenum, much was said about cattle raising, potatoes, vegetables, grains, and tractor stations—the whole gamut of issues. But the chief and decisive problem of grain was left aside.

Several months later this omission hit Khrushchev himself. The campaign for the implementation of the plenum's decisions was still in its initial stages, and neither in Moscow nor in the provinces had there been enough time to work out measures for putting them into effect; nonetheless, another—special—CC plenum was called in February 1954. Khrushchev delivered a report that took eight hours to read and filled five newspaper pages. This report was titled "On the Further Expansion of Grain Production in the Country and the Development of Virgin and Fallow Land." Now everything was concentrated on the problem of increasing the volume of grain production. The principal means that he put forward as the panacea for agricultural problems was the development of virgin and fallow land. Thus the epic of wilderness reclamation was launched.

The next few years were replete with innumerable CC plenums and Kremlin conferences of rank-and-file and advanced agricultural workers, tractor-station operators, and sovkhoz members. There were conferences by agricultural sectors, regions, and republics, and there were party gatherings. At each meeting, Khrushchev spoke for hours on end. One directive followed another. One remedial measure replaced another, even though the first had not had sufficient time to be fully tested.

Thus, at the CC plenum of September 1953, Khrushchev focused on the country's traditional agricultural regions and set the goal of expanding production through labor-intensive methods—enlarging the productivity of agriculture and the raising of cattle. The need, as he put it, was to "increase the yield in grain, cotton, vegetables, meat, milk, fruit, and so on, for every hectare of land, every hectare of harvest." Yet a few months passed, and unexpectedly the plan for more intensive agriculture was, in effect, dropped for unknown reasons. The old, highly productive regions like Ukraine, the northern Caucasus, the central black-earth belt, the Volga region, and Siberia suddenly became the stepchildren of Soviet agriculture. The virgin lands—there lay the answer! Plowing virgin and long-fallow lands in Kazakhstan, Siberia, the Urals, and other uncultivated regions—there was the solution to all the problems that prevented an agricultural abundance throughout the land!

Did the proposal to claim virgin and long-fallow land for agricultural production make sense? Yes, it did. But it required a thorough assessment of the soils and climates of the regions in question, the long-term average yields in each region or in similar conditions elsewhere, and the available and projected transport facilities. It was necessary to determine what types of crop rotation were right for each region and to make reliable estimates of the economic gain—costs versus revenues—that could be expected in each case. On this basis, one could have reached a conclusion about whether the project was cost effective and, if so, in what regions, on what scale, in what time period, and with the use of what equipment and scientific methods.

But that did not happen. Khrushchev's traits and qualities were such that his approach to the problem was later justly characterized as subjective and arbitrary. He went to Kazakhstan. There he gained firsthand impressions. These gave him an idea. His hyperactive nature demanded its immediate realization. He gave a pungent account of his trip and his impressions that went like this: "You know, I was in Kazakhstan. You drive through the grassy steppe—it's like an ocean! What soil! You come to a ravine, and look—you can see the whole cross-section. A layer of fertile soil two or three *arshiny*[4] deep. Soil like this is lying unused. It's a crime. We have billions of rubles lying here under our feet. Why, Kazakhstan alone could flood not just the whole country in grain but all of Europe as well!"

In February 1954 endless relays of trains, trucks, planes, and other forms of transport began moving their loads of tractors, trailers, and workers to the unpopulated Kazakh steppes to plow up the virgin lands. The valiant and self-sacrificing Soviet people, especially its heroic youth, were ready for anything. There was no shelter, so they lived in tents. There was no regular supply of food and water, so they stoically endured that as well. "The party calls, and it is essential for the nation, so we must overcome all difficulties!"

And overcome they did. One can argue about this monumental campaign to develop the virgin lands. One can hold different opinions about its economic effectiveness on a national scale. One can, and should, criticize Khrushchev's high-handed approach to the enterprise. But it would distort history to deny that the party and government organizations involved in agriculture worked with superhuman will, that hundreds of thousands of citizens voluntarily resettled in unpopulated regions under severe conditions, and that they did everything that was humanly possible and even impossible to claim the desert. The major failings of this gigantic campaign came not from its participants, not from any lack of a sense of duty on their part, but as a result of the strategic concept of the entire endeavor and the means employed to implement it.

In response to Khrushchev's efforts, the words "virgin lands" acquired a sacramental quality. The virgin lands would resolve everything. The virgin lands would yield grain. The virgin lands would produce an abundance of agricultural products. Everything for the virgin lands! The scores of speeches that Khrushchev delivered during this period made it seem as though our old and well-established agricultural regions had disappeared from the map. It was as though mankind were without thousands of years of experience at tilling the soil, and we were the pioneers, starting the history of agriculture from scratch.

A stream of tractors, trailers, trucks, gasoline, seed, and funding flowed toward the virgin lands. For years, the traditional agricultural regions were shunted aside, their supplies of equipment, money, and other requirements reduced to a bare minimum. This happened despite the fact that the older regions—Ukraine, the Kuban, the northern Caucasus, western Siberia, the Urals, the Central Asian republics, and many other parts of the country—were the principal suppliers of agricultural products and commodities. They had the potential for an enormous increase in agricultural output. These regions had enormous advantages: fertile soil, a favorable climate, able workers, an adequate labor force, good communications, well-tested methods of crop rotation and farming in general, and a wealth of experience in large-scale socialist agriculture. Twenty-five years had passed since the great transformation of the village. A new and unprecedented socialist system of sovkhozes, tractor stations, and kolkhozes had taken root and developed. The agricultural economy had quickly recovered from the destruction of the war and moved steadfastly forward. Among the most important decisions and major projects that the party and its Central Committee had approved was the adoption of an integrated and continuing program of developing large-scale socialist agriculture. The program's principal features were as follows: the comprehensive mechanization and electrification of agriculture, with emphasis on large increases in the manufacture of tractors and other equipment and the construction of hydroelectric and thermoelectric stations; the irrigation of wide areas through the use of cheap energy that was generated by a chain of hydroelectric stations along the principal waterways and by the construction of canals and other irrigation systems; the creation of large-scale protective forest belts and other measures to prevent drought; the wholesale conversion of agriculture to scientific methods of modern agronomy and animal husbandry; and the general use of crop rotation, selective breeding, seed growing, segregation of livestock by breeds, and other techniques.

The central purpose of this multifaceted program—its philosophy, as it were—could be summed up with one phrase: the intensification of agriculture. The idea was to go not for an enlargement of arable land but for a steady increase in the yield of existing farms and the productivity of existing animal husbandry, thereby laying the basis for the progressive expansion of the country's supplies of food and raw materials. Shortly before his death, Stalin declared at a meeting of the Politburo, "This is the last time I sign an annual plan for enlarging the area of cultivated land. We must go the way of intensification of agriculture. From smaller acreages we must get bigger yields." Indeed, the agricultural history of the entire world teaches us that intensification is the only right way.

But Khrushchev turned these party decisions and projects on their head. He ridiculed all existing intensification plans: "The Turkmen canal . . . Protective forest belts from sea to sea . . . Crop rotation . . . You have to be—" Making his habitual allusion to Stalin, he tapped his finger on his forehead and then on the wooden table. "How many years have we been dillydallying, like a cat waiting for the gruel to cool, with all these crop rotations? Where has it gotten us?"

The priority shown toward the cultivation of virgin lands marked a turn toward extensive rather than intensive agricultural development, toward the unrestrained expansion of cultivated soil. The whole point was to claim virgin land. This approach lasted the length of the "great decade." The area of virgin and long-fallow land plowed up in the country's arid regions, principally in Kazakhstan, was nearly forty million hectares. In Kazakhstan, the amount of cultivated land increased sixfold from 1913. The technology employed was fairly simple. In the spring, an army with tractors descended on the boundless expanse of virgin and long-fallow land, tilled the soil, planted the seeds, and left. In the fall, columns of combines gathered the harvest. For years on end, the virgin lands had no repair centers, no mechanized threshing facilities, no drying facilities, no warehouses or protective coverings for grain, and no roads. The losses in equipment and crops were colossal.

The switch to extensive tillage restrained the development of agriculture and its technology for a whole epoch. Khrushchev discredited and discarded the concepts of agronomy and crop rotation. Year after year, rye was planted in rye fields, wheat in wheat fields. Any attempt at diversification was abandoned. The use of fertilizer, irrigation, and the rotation of sown lands was never considered. Toadies out to curry favor with Khrushchev plied him with "expert data" that indicated that it was perfectly all right to sow the same strain of seeds time after time in the same soil. Khrushchev brandished this "data" at every conference. But alas, crops do not conform to speeches, even those uttered by the first secretary of the Central Committee.

Despite the tremendous waste incurred, the virgin-land program did produce some harvests in its initial years. The yield was small, but the soil did put forth crops. It was a case of skimming off the topsoil. But then, as any half-competent agronomist might have foreseen, the inevitable came to pass. Neglecting crop rotation and disregarding the elementary rules of agronomy, the practice of sowing the same strain of seeds in the same ground led to the increasingly rapid disintegration of the soil. Millions of hectares of what had once been virgin land began to erode with alarming speed. Black storms sucked up and blew away the soil's richest layers. Enormous stretches of grain fields turned into oceans of weeds. The unwanted stepchildren, the old fertile grain-producing regions, also began to perform unevenly in yield and volume. The supply of grain in the country deteriorated. But the worse it got, the shriller were the pronouncements and promises that Khrushchev made from the highest pulpits: "We'll show the Americans what for! With our agriculture we'll lay them flat on their backs!" Compelled to "show them what for," he devised one miraculous panacea after another.

One day he criticized the rotation system that Academician Vasilii Vil'iams[5] created—letting fields go temporarily to grass—and ended its use everywhere. Instead, he ordered a further expansion, beyond all reasonable limits, of areas sown with grain. He declared wheat his favorite of all grains. Khrushchev waxed rhapsodic on the delectability of pies and buns made from wheat flour. Describing the society of the future, he said, "What is communism? Communism is pancakes with melted butter and sour cream." After the wheat episode, he declared that corn was the monarch of the fields, and corn it was for long thereafter. Khrushchev glorified it not only as all-purpose fodder but as an edible crop. At numerous conferences, he zestfully described the tasty dishes that could be made with corn.

The damage done to the national economy by Khrushchev's fixation on corn is by now common knowledge. He heard somewhere that in the United States corn accounted for a large percentage of grain production. He did not sort out where, how, and why Americans grew corn, yet he seized on corn as the panacea for all of the country's agricultural woes. In hundreds of speeches he demanded that corn be planted everywhere—

from Transcaucasia to Iakutiia and Primor'e.[6] Anyone who disagreed or had doubts was dismissed from office; agricultural authorities who objected were pilloried. Among the common folk, Khrushchev earned the nickname of Kukuruznik. His *kukuruza* [corn] caper turned out to be one of the primary causes of the disorganization and decline of all of Soviet agriculture.

Khrushchev also heard somewhere the well-known fact that sheep in central Russia were prone to hoof fungus. In 1954 a series of agricultural conferences and party gatherings that were national, regional, and republic in scope were held in the Kremlin. Khrushchev unfailingly spoke at each one. We sat and listened as he exclaimed with characteristic passion and dogmatism, punctuating his speech with gestures, "Now they're raising sheep in central Russia. What idiot dreamed that up? Doesn't everyone know that sheep there suffer from hoof fungus? We must clear the region of sheep." At the February 1954 CC plenum, he tore into our animal husbandry workers for raising sheep outside the black-earth belt. "In the non-black-earth regions the number of sheep has increased by 55 percent, in spite of the fact that many of these regions are unsuitable for highly productive sheep breeding."

During Stalin's thirty-year reign, supervisors at all levels became accustomed to accepting the leader's every word as law. His instructions had to be put in effect unconditionally. As the Kremlin sessions gave way to conferences and party gatherings at republic, territorial, oblast, and regional levels, Khrushchev's pronouncements on sheep breeding were passed down from above, becoming more inflexible ("for the sake of clarity") the lower down they went. When they reached the village, kolkhoz, and sovkhoz levels, the sheep hoof infection began to seem more threatening than leprosy, and sheep breeding in Russia began to look almost like a crime.

Khrushchev, of course, was blissfully unaware that coarse-wool sheep had been raised mostly in the central, northwestern, northeastern, and northern parts of Russia from time immemorial. For centuries on end, sheep breeding had produced wool for coarse cloth, felt boots, and boot liners. It provided sheepskin for half-length and full-length overcoats. It shod and dressed the peasantry, the urban working class, and the military. In the nineteenth century, the Romanov species of sheep, the best kind in the world for making overcoats, was bred in the former Iaroslavl' province. But Khrushchev's directive was issued from the highest tribune, and in the central and northern regions of Russia sheep were mercilessly slaughtered.

It took a long time for Khrushchev to admit that he had been "misled about sheep." Such an admission was extremely rare for him. Ignorance usually goes with inflated conceit, which makes an honest admission of one's mistakes extremely difficult. By the time he said that "they misled me about sheep," the number of coarse-wool sheep, including the Romanov breed, had dropped sharply.

Next he discovered the miraculous qualities of peas, and everyone began to grow quantities of them. After the pea craze, he declared that the principal and decisive requirement for improving the entire agricultural system was, first, fertilization and, later, irrigation; and in irrigated fields, the ideal crop was rice. Khrushchev extolled the virtues not of pies, buns, and pancakes made of flour but of the incomparable Uzbek pilaf.

The thousands of persons who constituted the agricultural workforce could not keep up with the new ideas, projects, and prescriptions that swirled in Khrushchev's head and that showered down on them in a cascade of instructions. The state of affairs in the agricultural sector grew steadily more muddled. The government had to dip into its grain reserves. But even that proved insufficient, and it became necessary to import large amounts of grain and flour.

It was part of Khrushchev's style to make startlingly quick promises and set astonishing time limits on the sole basis of his intuition. After making mincemeat of the Stalinist agricultural system at the September 1953 CC plenum, he set this goal before the country: "To raise production levels sharply in all agricultural sectors over a period of two to three years and to provide the population with an enhanced assurance of the availability of food products." Going even further, he set the goal of achieving within the shortest possible time a degree of abundance truly possible only in a fully communist society. "We must set for ourselves," he said, "the goal of attaining a level of nutrition fully adequate on a scientific basis for the complete and harmonious development of a healthy person. . . . We will attain this level of consumption very soon—for some products in two or three years."

But the country saw not two or three but ten years go by; by 1963 the tragic consequences of Khrushchev's idiotic improvisations and economic recklessness in the villages were fully felt. The yield per hectare in grains fell from the 1940 level of 860 kilograms to 830 kilograms and kept tumbling almost to the prerevolutionary level of 820 kilograms. The 1963 grain harvest proved to be the smallest in all the years of the "great decade." Khrushchev was livid. He stopped sallying forth into the virgin lands and carrying on about their miraculous properties. He blamed everything either on Stalin, on the Ministry of Agriculture, on the private holdings of kolkhozniki, where cows and pigs were allegedly gobbling up the grain, or on wrongheaded agricultural methods. He again offered scheme after scheme for achieving "a communist abundance of products." But his credibility among the people quickly eroded. The huge army of party, local-government, and agricultural workers, worn out by the endless reorganizations, despaired about the state of Soviet agriculture.

The government's plentiful grain reserves, which had survived four years of devastating war, were exhausted. The Soviet Union ceased to be an exporter of grains and became an importer. Each year, tons of gold bullion were taken out of reserves that had been built up over decades and thrown on the world markets to pay for large-scale imports of grain from Canada, Australia, and the United States and flour from West Germany. Grain was bought on credit from Romania. On November 27, 1967, the *New York Times* reported that during the Khrushchev era the USSR annually sold between 200 million and 500 million dollars of gold. The country faced the threat of famine. From Transcarpathia[7] to Primor'e, enormous lines formed outside bread stores during the night. Millions of villagers trekked to the cities in search of bread. In many cities and regions, the bread stores adopted a secret rationing system by favoring customers who lived nearby, drawing up special lists of customers, and issuing ration cards.

At a later time a railroad engineer from the Perm district, speaking of Khrushchev, told me: "This 'we'll show them' fellow, he hung bags on the necks of the whole country."

"What bags?"

"Well, you're off to work, to your locomotive, and your wife hangs a bag around your neck. Everybody was sewing those bags that you use for feeding horses. Some out of burlap, some out of oilcloth. You're back from a trip, and you go at once to the food queue. Stand there for twelve hours. Then your wife takes your place. Your turn comes, and they pour some flour made of corn and bran into your bag, or some millet, and maybe a piece of bread, not enough to stave off hunger. And the bread . . . like some kind of putty, the crust just peels off. That's how we lived in those days, with those bags. That's what he reduced the whole country to."

A locomotive stoker from Krivoi Rog,[8] a female teacher from Chuvashiia,[9] an engineer from Briansk,[10] and many others told me similar things. Churchill, I believe, is credited with a well-known quip about Khrushchev: "It takes a lot of talent to leave Russia without grain." This turned out to be one of the principal reasons, if not the main one, for Khrushchev's fall. The political and agricultural issue was posed in the starkest terms: it was either the immediate dismissal of Khrushchev and all his virgin-land, corn, and pea improvisations and the return to scientific methods of agriculture, or an inevitable, national economic catastrophe. The food supply for 200 million persons determined the country's political and economic atmosphere.

I do not intend to provide an analysis of the country's economic situation during those years, nor do I have the resources to do so. I deal only with the situation insofar as it characterizes Khrushchev's style, method, and approach to problems and as it tells us what the khrushchevshchina was and what its social consequences were. This analysis, of course, is essential. The khrushchevshchina was responsible for enormous production delays that cost billions of rubles. It complicated and slowed the entire development of the country. Yet it did not paralyze the people's vital energies, nor undermine the invincible might of the socialist system. Overcoming all objective and subjective difficulties, the nation continued to build, create, and increase its sophistication. The land of the Soviets moved confidently forward.

A few years later, in 1957, I bluntly criticized Khrushchev. In response, he turned loose many of his henchmen to slander and defame me. The most unimaginable inventions and malicious lies were concocted. One example was a speech that the former USSR minister of sovkhozes and subsequently the RSFSR deputy minister of agriculture, Tikhon Iurkin, gave at the December 1958 CC plenum. He eloquently recounted how he and other CC members were present at several sessions of the CC Presidium that were devoted to the virgin and long-fallow land program. "We saw how desperately Nikita Sergeevich was fighting," here he named some names, "who were waging a furious struggle against the party's policy on the cultivation of virgin and long-fallow land, threatening that it would reduce the yield of grain per hectare, which would result in stagnating grain production, and that government expenditures on the virgin lands would far exceed the returns." (See the minutes of the December 1958 CC plenum, pages 408–9.)

He named me among those who were "waging a furious struggle" against the program. This was plainly false. Iurkin knew he was lying. Neither in 1954 nor later did I speak in opposition to Khrushchev's virgin land and kukuruza projects. As an economist and agronomist, it was impossible not to see their grave flaws. But like my generation of communists, I had been raised in the spirit of utter loyalty to the party and the strictest discipline; to express doubts about the party's directives would have been sacrilege. Furthermore, as executive editor of *Pravda*, my job was to provide detailed and accurate coverage and explanations of all of the party's decisions regarding agriculture, including its decisions about the virgin lands. Today, when the passage of time has made everything crystal clear, it would perhaps be flattering to appear in the guise that Iurkin created for me. But as the saying goes, "Plato is dear to me, but the truth is dearer."[11] As a CC member and executive editor of *Pravda*, I attended all the CC plenums and was often present at meetings of the CC Presidium, but I was never aware of any "desperate" or "furious" struggle that anyone waged against tilling virgin and long-fallow land.

We were still in the honeymoon that followed Stalin's death. Everyone did his best to maintain the fullest unity within the leadership, no matter what: do not contradict one another unless absolutely necessary, and yield to one another wherever and whenever possible. Molotov was the only one who expressed any criticism of Khrushchev's virgin-land program. He did not reject the possibility of cultivating some of the virgin lands, but was against doing so widely and recklessly. He did not vote against the resolutions that were submitted at meetings of the Presidium and the CC plenums, but he made specific comments about them and warned against switching from an intensive to an extensive system of agriculture. Even though his practical comments and proposals were couched in the most politically acceptable language, they were rejected.

An event occurred at the September 1953 session of the CC plenum that had a fateful effect on developments within the party and country. Shortly after Stalin's death, as I mentioned earlier, Khrushchev demanded that the post of first secretary of the Central Committee be revived and that he be elected to it. At the September 1953 session, Malenkov spoke in favor of the proposal, and the plenum approved it by unanimous vote. From that moment, we witnessed the rapid and increasingly conspicuous process of privileging the first secretary among the other Presidium members and expanding his role and status. Traditions built up over decades encouraged this trend.

Stalin wielded absolute power. His agreement with or approval of any question settled it once and for all. If someone were lucky enough to be in his presence and hear him express an opinion about something, or make some brief comment, opinion, remark, or even a reply at a meeting or assembly, his words acquired the force of immutable law. Depending on the implication of the opinion, remark, or comment, decisions immediately followed within the Central Committee and the government, and some people were promoted, and some perished.

Lenin saw limitless personal power as the greatest danger to the party and the revolution. As we know, he warned in his last political testament against the boundless power that was concentrated in Stalin's hands as general secretary and proposed that he be replaced.[12] Yet in Lenin's day and for several years after his death, Stalin's power still had its limits; it was constrained by the fact that the party, the soviets, the government, the Politburo, the Orgburo, the Secretariat, and the trade unions were healthy, vital organisms of their own. Stalin's word and opinion became law only by the political exclusion, and later the physical extermination, of anyone who criticized him or seemed likely to do so.

As a result, the role of the general secretary, the post that Stalin held for most of his years in power, assumed gigantic proportions. The sensible division of functions between the CC and the government that had prevailed under Lenin was erased. Even minimally substantive political, international, economic, and cultural questions had to be considered by the CC before any decision could be made by the government. The CC decision depended wholly on the views and orders of the general secretary. The government, in most cases, was left with the sole function of processing the CC's decisions.

This type of relationship between the party and the government, and later between the party and the country's economic institutions and trade unions, began to spread throughout the system, down to the party's regional committees and regional executive committees. On that level too, the opinion and command of the first secretary decided everything. This led not only to an enormous expansion of the bureaucracy and the unnecessary duplication of functions but to the atrophy of governmental, economic, trade union, and other components of the Soviet system.

After Stalin's death, there was never any critical review of the relationship that existed between party and governmental bodies or of the role and place of the general secretary in the country's leadership structure. Having been elected first secretary, Khrushchev simply stepped into Stalin's well-worn shoes and plodded ahead. But there was more to it than that. Stalin realized shortly before his death, either by instinct or by intellect, all the flaws and dangers that were inherent in the system of one-man rule. Perhaps the realization came to him because there was no one in his inner circle whom he saw as a worthy heir. When he was in the company of a few of the inner circle, he sometimes said, "When I die, what are you going to do without me? You'll be done for!" Perhaps it was in the hope of averting such a catastrophe that he agonized during his final years about a new form of collective leadership. I have mentioned his speech at the Nineteenth Party Congress, his swan song, where he called on the world's communists to be standard-bearers and champions of democracy. Immediately after the congress, Stalin proposed the creation of several top-level collective bodies that would provide party leadership in the most important areas of governmental and party responsibility: a standing commission on international affairs that Malenkov would head, a standing commission on military affairs that Bulganin would head, a standing commission on ideological questions, which Stalin would entrust to me, and so on.

Khrushchev did not pursue that idea. He took the well-trodden road that Stalin himself had charted so determinedly over the previous thirty years— the road to one-man rule. In no time at all, all business of any importance had to be cleared with Khrushchev before being submitted to any party or government department. The stock formula of bygone days was revived, but with a different name: "Reported to Nikita Sergeevich," "Agreed on with Nikita Sergeevich," "Nikita Sergeevich approves." That was enough to issue a decree, allocate funds, or appoint someone to a high post.

But the change in name was of enormous significance. Stalin was a thoroughly proficient Marxist. He had gone through the lengthy school of hard knocks and revolutionary struggle. He had vast experience in party and governmental affairs. He was wise and patient in resolving problems. A rash or precipitate decision on his part was almost unheard of. Khrushchev was an utter ignoramus. He was very impulsive. When he became first secretary, he jealously guarded his authority. He regarded any decision reached without his knowledge as sidestepping the party and came down on the culprits with all his ire. He considered a person who disagreed with him on anything, or who made any critical remark, as a person who disagreed with the party and the party's general policy; he promptly charged the offenders with "deviationism." Everything had to be "approved by Nikita Sergeevich."

But no one can know everything. Besides, Khrushchev was barely literate and did not like to study problems in detail. He always had to say something, instruct someone, speechify, dash off somewhere, and clink glasses at formal dinners. When someone sought his counsel or laid some issue before him, he made spontaneous, contradictory, unwarranted, and at times preposterous decisions that he reached by instinct and whim. Yet these decisions became law. Aware of this, all sorts of operators and intriguers, including people in high places, tried to "get Nikita Sergeevich's approval," preferably "at the right moment," when he was "in a good mood," or, even better, when he was "in high spirits." It hardly needs to be said that the party and the country paid dearly—with billions of rubles—for this capriciousness; sometimes his whims changed the course of people's lives. There was no appeal against these decisions: the first secretary's word was law.

In his initial phase as first secretary, Khrushchev tried to be considerate, to get along with the other Presidium members, and to maintain a comradely spirit and the outward forms of collectivism. But looking around him, he gradually came to the conclusion that it was not in his interests to break with the thirty-year tradition of the general secretary's style of leadership. The more he revealed his ignorance, the more he insisted that everyone recognize his absolute monopoly as the representative and incarnation of the party and therefore the state. It was unlikely that Khrushchev knew anything about Louis XIV, but the maxim attributed to the French monarch would be fully applicable in slightly amended form to the upstart leader: *"Le Parti—c'est moi."*

At first subtly, cautiously, and cunningly, and then headlong, Khrushchev moved toward one-man rule. He did not miss a single chance to promote himself. One of the events that contributed to his glory was the celebration of his sixtieth birthday.

It was a clear April day. There was a ring on the special Kremlin phone in my *Pravda* office.

"Comrade Shepilov? This is Malenkov. Could you come over for a few minutes right away?"

I told him I'd be leaving immediately.

Leninskii Prospekt. Gorky Street. Bright sun. Housepainters and janitors washing and painting the residential buildings and store fronts for the coming of May. On the street corners, flower girls with garlands of mimosa, bouquets of snowdrops, and bunches of violets from the Crimea. After Stalin's death, the Kremlin was opened to the public; by the Historical Museum, tour guides called loudly to pedestrians to join them for sightseeing within the Kremlin walls. The Spasskii Gate. There were no longer stringent security regulations that governed entry into the Kremlin. The driver of my heavy ZIS[13] limousine slowed down, and two Chekists gave us a casual salute, allowing us to keep going. Ivanov Square. Inside the building, an elevator took me to the third floor.

Malenkov had only recently completed the renovation of Stalin's quarters for his own use. Everything had a grandiose and solemn look. There was an odor of fresh varnish. Malenkov himself looked tired and worried. There were dark rings under his eyes. He was dressed, as in earlier days, in dark gray trousers and a high-collar "Stalinka" tunic of the same color. (At official diplomatic receptions, however, he had begun to wear a black suit and a shirt with a necktie; he joked that the tie choked him, and tugged at the knot from time to time.)

He greeted me with a kind of fluster and exaggerated attentiveness. His manner of speaking and stance betrayed a certain embarrassment. At that time, I had no idea that Khrushchev had already begun undermining the new premier's political base. Malenkov, however, was apparently conscious of Khrushchev's mole-like activity.

He said, "Here's why I asked you, Comrade Shepilov, to come over. April 16 is Nikita Sergeevich's sixtieth birthday. He's trying very hard. He's doing good work. We discussed this among ourselves and decided to award him the title of Hero of Socialist Labor. I was asked to talk to you so that you would present this properly, the way it should be done, in your newspaper. Of course, you understand."

He kept repeating, incoherently and somewhat sheepishly, that "Nikita Sergeevich is doing good work" and that "the award must be presented in the newspaper in the proper way." I was left with the impression that he spoke so insistently and lengthily so that people would hear that he had praised Nikita Sergeevich for his good work and had gone out of his way to make sure that the newspapers gave this historical event a fitting display.

I said, "Georgii Maksimilianovich! Isn't there a firmly established tradition regarding awards to members of the Politburo? Usually a two-column portrait on the first page, under it the greetings of the CC and the Council of Ministers, and under that the decree on the award, title of hero, or a medal. Shouldn't we abide by tradition in this case, too?"

"Yes, yes, of course," he replied, "but do this well, with style. We want to commemorate Nikita Sergeevich's birthday as befits the occasion."

The next day *Pravda* published the material on Khrushchev's birthday in the time-honored way, and the other papers followed suit. However, some issues of *Pravda* carried greetings to Khrushchev from communist parties abroad. At a session of the Supreme Soviet that was then in session, Khrushchev, unlike any of the other members of the CC Presidium except Voroshilov, who was chairman of the Soviet parliament, was elected to the Supreme Soviet Presidium.

Because Khrushchev had been publicly critical of the big show made on Stalin's seventieth birthday, there was no official celebration in his honor. Unofficially, however, things were done on a sumptuous scale. At a formal dinner that the party and government elite attended, all toasts to Khrushchev as a "faithful student of Lenin and brother-in-arms of the great Stalin" were couched in superlatives. Khrushchev took in all this flattery with obvious pleasure and tried to win everyone over with the most extravagant promises. Once again, for the umpteenth time, he spoke vividly about how he had "bamboozled" Beria and "hung him up by his throat on a hook," and how free life would be now, and what good fortune lay ahead for everyone.

Encountering me several days later, he asked, "Were you at my birthday party?"

"No," I replied, "I wasn't."

"Why not?"

"I wasn't invited."

"Well, I guess my fellows flubbed it."

After becoming first secretary of the Central Committee, Khrushchev enacted a wide-ranging and methodical reshuffling of officeholders throughout the country—from CC secretaries and government ministers to secretaries of oblast and city committees and chairmen of executive committees and economic departments. He said quite explicitly that he had to remove "Malenkov's men" and put in "my own people."

The new appointees were a mixed bag. By his choice or whim, utter mediocrities who appeared by chance were named to the most responsible posts. At times, matters took the most astonishing turns. But after Khrushchev consolidated his position, he was able to do astonishing things without opposition. He took frequent advantage of that to feed his own ego.

Among the hundreds of examples of his absurdities, one concerns Iosif Kuz'min. An apprentice carpenter and metal worker in his youth, Kuz'min graduated from the Military Electro-Technical Academy, and worked at the Prozhektor Factory and later in the party's Control Commission. Then he was put to work for the USSR Council of Ministers on agricultural matters and the government's procurement of farm products (!) and, subsequently, for the party CC on machine-tooling issues (!). Kuz'min was an extremely ambitious type who was unburdened by any lofty moral or ethical principles. When Khrushchev launched his gigantic sovkhoz operation, Kuz'min exclaimed, "Right you are, Nikita Sergeevich," "That's great, Nikita Sergeevich," "Everyone admires your ideas, Nikita Sergeevich, and is waiting for the quickest possible reorganization of the sovkhozes." That made Kuz'min's fortune. At one of the Presidium meetings, Khrushchev suddenly proposed appointing Kuz'min as nothing less than chairman of the USSR State Planning Commission (Gosplan).

As a CC secretary and candidate member of the Presidium, I took the floor.

"From the time Gosplan was organized three decades ago, it has been headed," I said, "by outstanding leaders of the communist party, educated Marxists and economists like Gleb Maksimilianovich Krzhizhanovskii, Valerian Vladimirovich Kuibyshev, Valerii Ivanovich Mezhlauk, and Nikolai Alekseevich Voznesenskii. Now we are asked to appoint Kuz'min. But he is a complete ignoramus in economic theory. How could someone totally unacquainted with political economy supervise the computation of the national economic and budgetary figures, take measures to prevent poor investments, and direct the drafting of the general plan? He doesn't have the slightest concept of what that is all about.

"Our state system," I continued, "has survived quite a few storms. There have been all kinds of reorganizations, including some rather hasty ones. But luckily for us, Gosplan, the brain center of the country's economy, has remained unchanged. This has saved us from many woes. To appoint Kuz'min to Gosplan would doom our national economic planning."

Khrushchev was furious. At the next CC plenum in July, he sputtered about how "Shepilov with his professorial arrogance lit into our wonderful worker Comrade Kuz'min." Kuz'min was appointed chairman of Gosplan. He became a highly important figure in the country's government. But it did not take long for everyone to see the obvious: the emperor had no clothes. Khrushchev simmered down. At one of the Presidium meetings, he announced, "Not only do I not trust Kuz'min with Gosplan and the national economy, I wouldn't trust him in my kitchen."

Kuz'min was quietly shipped off elsewhere.

With his straightforward and practical outlook, Khrushchev had no illusions about the mechanics of directing the party and government. Of course, he constantly spoke about "the decisive role of the masses" and claimed that "we are just the servants of His Majesty, the people," that "the party decides everything," that "we are all state employees and accountable to the party membership," that "we have collective leadership—everything is decided according to the views of the collective, the majority," and so on.

That's what he said. But what he did was exactly the opposite. In reshuffling personnel, he was least interested in encouraging initiative and action among party members and organizations, the soviets, trade unions, and the Komsomol. He often said with cynical candor, "What have the people got to do with it? Whom are we going to ask? They'll do whatever we say." What concerned him most was that party and government institutions wielding direct and real power were staffed with his own loyalists. I noted that after Stalin's death and Beria's execution the man who led the state security agencies was Khrushchev's devoted satrap Ivan Serov. That determined the reshufflings and appointments that were made throughout the KGB. Khrushchev could be sure that no danger faced him from that quarter and that his bodyguards would not suddenly become his jailers. He was always acutely concerned about the choice of top military commanders. So far, it suited him to have Nikolai Bulganin lead the Defense Ministry, a man he called his "friend," "close friend," and so on, in all his speeches. But that was not enough. What followed made it obvious that the way he treated many marshals and generals was based solely on his determination to guard against any unexpected moves by the armed forces.

Khrushchev knew that the high command of the Soviet army took a scornful view of his laughable attempts to portray himself as a great military leader. On a variety of pretexts, he gradually forced the most famous commanders of the Second World War into retirement or made them into "decorative generals"—Marshals Georgii Zhukov, Ivan Konev, Konstantin Rokossovskii, Aleksandr Vasilevskii, Kirill Meretskov, and Nikolai Voronov and Generals Andrei Khrulev, Aleksandr Gorbatov, Markian Popov, and many others. These outstanding and gifted commanders were replaced by mediocrities who were promoted to the rank of marshal and were ready to swear fealty to Khrushchev.

It was precisely for this reason that General Kirill Moskalenko was promoted to marshal and made commanding officer of the Moscow Military District and General Filipp Golikov received a marshal's baton after Stalin's death. Khrushchev knew that when Golikov was head of the Soviet army's Main Directorate for Military Personnel, he was guilty of vilifying and condemning to death many servicemen, and that he had been directly involved in the sinister Leningrad affair. But Khrushchev's magnanimous grant of amnesty to Golikov for his offenses against the Soviet people and to Serov for his crimes in the state security system turned both men into his grateful and dependable supporters.

Golikov, therefore, was not only promoted to marshal but was named head of the Soviet army and navy's Main Political Directorate. However, awareness of his crimes against the military and party personnel in Leningrad gradually spread through the armed forces, the Leningrad party membership, and the entire Soviet intelligentsia. Afraid that he would be brought to trial, Golikov feigned mental illness, and the scandal ended with his removal from his new post. But he kept his marshal's star, and on major workers' holidays he can still be seen standing elegantly on the mausoleum dais or addressing young people as a hero of the Second World War.

The state security agencies, the armed forces, and the Ministry of Internal Affairs became Khrushchev's most important power bases and were where he wanted his most trusted men so that he could supervise them personally and directly. But the immense changes he made in the leadership affected all ministries, ideological centers, republics, territories, and oblasts.

Well-educated, high-minded, experienced, and honest people were often replaced by less qualified, less strong, less cultured, morally and politically questionable types. To questions like "What's going on? Why was Minister X replaced by Y? Why did this important post go to such an unsuitable person as Z?" the answers were "Y worked with Nikita Sergeevich in Ukraine. . . . Z is acquainted with Nikita Sergeevich because of their work together in the Moscow Party Committee." Khrushchev proved a master at exploiting the established system of selecting and appointing people to office, and he perfected it to suit his own purposes. A few years after his election as CC first secretary, the centers of the party leadership and government control in Moscow and the provinces had more than their quota of Khrushchev's men.

It would be wrong to see this all in a negative light. Many of the new appointees, whether young or old, were good, honest men of common sense who did a creditable job. But the most important sectors were seeded mainly with the kind of uncultured, ignorant, and arrogant individuals who came to be known among the people as *khrushchevtsy*. The nation and the people became more and more civilized. But the intellectual, professional, and moral level of the country's officialdom deteriorated, for officials were selected on account of their likeness to Khrushchev and appointed on the basis of his tastes and whims.

The heart of the matter, however, lay not in the selection of this or that individual. A selection process based not on ability and moral qualities but on the principles of "personal acquaintance" and "one of ours" is ruinous for the party and the state. An official named to a post because he is "one of ours" will continue in the same pattern and select "his own." This practice then spreads vertically and horizontally. As a result, every high official will be surrounded by a coterie of "his own men"—"*Riazanskie*" or "*Tambovskie*,"[14] "Ukrainians," persons from the People's Commissariat of Heavy Industry, or whatever—they were chosen because where they came from or where they had previously had work experience was the same as that of the official in charge. Often they were labeled even more precisely: "Ezhov's man," "Malenkov's man," "Khrushchev's man," etc.

A situation like this inevitably breeds a system of mutual protection circles, mutual back-scratching, and mutual sycophancy. No criticism from below can breach the line of defense formed around the top official by "his people." As a result, the man in charge and his performance on the job are beyond any criticism or control.

At the end of the 1920s and beginning of the 1930s, word spread among party activists that the CC Politburo had passed a secret decree forbidding any criticism of the Politburo, its individual members, or the Central Committee as a whole. Stalin allegedly justified the decree on the grounds that in a period of intensifying class and intraparty struggle, the authority of the state's highest bodies had to be absolute. I have not verified this information and do not know whether there really was such a decree that applied to all party organizations, publications, and individual communists. But it is common knowledge that soon after Lenin's death just such a ban became the rule and acquired the force of law. This rule covered the behavior of people at all levels of leadership.

The official motto was "Criticism without fear or favor." Over the years, the party's charter consecrated the right of every member "at party meetings, conferences, congresses, and committee plenums to criticize any communist regardless of his rank." Suppression of criticism was made a serious offense that was punishable by disciplinary action and even expulsion from the party. After Lenin's death, however, the reality was that no party congress, no communist group, and no publication risked criticizing any document or part thereof that was issued by the Politburo or the CC Secretariat, and thus did not hold any Politburo member to account. That could be done only at Stalin's initiative, with his approval, or on his direct orders.

Gradually this ban on criticism worked its way down to the people's commissars and secretaries of party CCs at the republic, territory, and oblast levels. Even with irrefutable proof, no one could criticize any official with impunity if it were known that the person had "support within the CC." Millions of people, for instance, were aware that the actions of Ezhov and his henchmen were leading to the methodical destruction of persons who were the flower of the nation. But to say that aloud would have been suicide. Ezhov continued with his diabolical, clandestine operations until, at Stalin's behest, the guillotine fell on his own neck.

Familiar with all the gears, cogs, and levers of the mechanism that governed criticism within the party, Khrushchev used them constantly to consolidate his personal power. He did not shrink from any falsehood. He was utterly intolerant of any remark directed toward himself or his protégés; the critic was immediately fired from his job, sent off to some post in the provinces or abroad, or made into a pensioner. Putting the man in prison was not an option for Khrushchev. In criticizing Stalin, he had donned the mantle of guardian of legality and could not very well expose his true colors.

Khrushchev promoted new men—the Adzhubeis,[15] Il'ichevs, Satiukovs, and Ponomarevs—who gave him unquestioning support when he undertook his most fanciful reforms. In their words, the tragic years of Khrushchev's one-man rule became the "great decade." They heaped frenzied calumny on anyone who dared raise a voice against Khrushchev's follies. When it became clear that his days were numbered, they naturally abandoned him and excoriated him more vociferously than anyone.

Khrushchev regarded Ukraine as the most important source of personnel for work at the union and republic levels. This view was understandable; Ukraine, after all, had more than forty million inhabitants, a powerful and first-rate industry, a well-developed agricultural system, and a plentiful supply of administrators, technicians, artists, agronomists, teachers, and doctors. Since my student days I had been a frequent visitor to Ukraine. As part of the 4th Guards Army during the war years, I took part in the offensive that crossed practically the whole of Ukraine—from Belgorod to Akhtyrka, Kotel'va, Poltava, Kremenchug, Korsun'-Shevchenkovskii, Uman', Rybintsa, and Kishinev. Enchantingly beautiful are the lands of Ukraine, its boundless fields, its blue rivers, its flowering gardens. Incalculable are the riches there that were created by the hands of man. More melodious than a many-stringed lyre are its language, the lilt of its spoken speech (especially that of Poltava), and its silvery songs. But what impressed me most about Ukraine were its people, a handsome breed, large-hearted, many-talented, and of surpassing goodwill.

In the years since the revolution, the republic's material and intellectual resources and riches had increased greatly, and its corps of workers, who belonged to many nationalities, was seasoned by experience. So it would be natural for Ukraine to contribute generously in manpower to other republics, territories, and oblasts in the Soviet Union. Khrushchev strongly encouraged this. He had spent most of his working life in Ukraine and naturally wanted to see it grow and prosper.

However, his good work in this regard was to a great extent motivated by personal considerations. After being transferred from Ukraine to Moscow, he was vain enough to want the Ukrainian people to regard him as their generous "chief" and "patron." It was this desire that lay behind his many efforts to curry favor with Ukrainian party and government officials, even if the efforts frequently violated the Soviet Constitution. Subsequent events showed how deluded Khrushchev was in thinking that his image in Ukraine was that of a beloved father. Toward the end of the "great decade," the dislike and contempt he created for himself throughout the country was perhaps more pronounced in Ukraine and among Ukrainian government officials than in any other republic or section of the intelligentsia.

One of the ways in which he tried to win over Ukraine was his decision on the Crimea. Planning was under way for ceremonies marking the three-hundredth anniversary of Ukraine's reunification with Russia.[16] This historic date naturally deserved to be marked as a major holiday for the peoples of the Soviet Union, an embodiment of the nationalities doctrine that Lenin articulated. The anniversary sessions of the Supreme Soviets in the Ukrainian Soviet Socialist Republic and in the Russian Soviet Federated Socialist Republic were held in a festive atmosphere. The Ukrainian republic and the city of Kiev were awarded the Order of Lenin. At the Bolshoi Theater in Moscow, Kiev's Shevchenko Theater troupe put on its best operas and ballets. At the Kiev railroad station in Moscow, a cornerstone was laid for a monument commemorating the reunification of the two countries. Gigantic parades and mass meetings took place in Moscow and Kiev.

In short, everything possible was done for the noble cause of strengthening the bonds of friendship between the two largest republics and among all the peoples of the Soviet land. But Khrushchev wanted to present a personal gift on a golden platter so that everyone in Ukraine would know of his generosity and his constant concern for Ukraine's welfare.

A conference on agriculture, one of the many held at that time, was in session in the Great Kremlin Palace and was attended by all the members of the CC Presidium and Secretariat. During breaks, the participants retired to two adjoining rooms for breakfast, lunch, dinner. It was customary during these breaks to discuss and decide on urgent international and domestic issues. One day I was invited to participate.

As one pressing question followed another, Khrushchev suddenly made an unexpected proposal: to have the RSFSR hand over the Crimea to the Ukrainian republic on the occasion of the three-hundredth anniversary of their reunification.

"Russia is far from the Crimea," he said. "Ukraine is closer. It will be easier to take various economic measures. I have already talked to some people about it. The Ukrainians, of course, would give their eyeteeth to have it; they'll be in seventh heaven if we give them the Crimea. With the RSFSR, too, I think we can reach agreement. Only it would have to be done properly: The Supreme Soviets of both republics would have to petition the Supreme Soviet of the union to authorize the transfer. Voroshilov will have to get all this through the Presidium of the USSR Supreme Soviet in the proper way. I take it there are no objections?"

Khrushchev's proposal, of course, was senseless and a gross violation of historical tradition and the Leninist nationalities policy for the party and the state. For many centuries, the Crimea was a battleground in the struggle of the Russian people against the Tatar-Turkish yoke, which had made the Crimea a major international slave market. Ivan the Terrible's campaigns in the Crimea of 1556–59, the battles for Perekop[17] that Russian forces waged under Prince Golitsyn,[18] Peter the Great's campaigns in 1695–96 that gave Russia access to the Azov and Black Seas, the Russo-Turkish War of 1768–74, which put an end to Turkish rule in the Crimea—all these are memorable chapters in the history of the Russian state and the Russian military. It was in the liberation wars in the Crimea that Aleksandr Suvorov, Mikhail Kutuzov, and Fedor Ushakov[19] won their places in history.

In 1918 the Crimea—first the Republic of Tauride,[20] then the Autonomous Republic of Crimea,[21] and later the Crimean oblast[22]—became part of the RSFSR. Over the succeeding years, the region was firmly integrated with the RSFSR on planning, financial, cultural and other levels. But the principal and decisive factor was the region's ethnic composition. Under a socialist system, given the solid bonds of friendship among the different peoples of the Soviet Union, territorial disputes are easily resolved and do not provoke social conflict. The territorial division of the Central Asian republics was conducted in an amicable spirit: Kazakhstan handed over part of its territory to Uzbekistan in a friendly fashion, and other examples abound. But in deciding on any such measure, the party and the government always took into account all the factors involved in order not to infringe on the rights of any nation or any national or ethnic group, particularly if small in size. Under the statutes of the Soviet constitution, even regions with a small but ethnically homogeneous population enjoy, as we know, the status of autonomous national regions. In all cases, the underlying motive was to strengthen the ties of friendship and fraternal cooperation among the different nationalities within the framework of a multinational socialist state.

At the time that Khrushchev proposed handing the Crimea over to Ukraine, the population of the Crimean oblast was 1.2 million people. Of the total, 71.4 percent were Russian and 22.2 percent Ukrainian; other nationalities accounted for 6.4 percent. Yet when Khrushchev said, "I take it there are no objections?" Bulganin, Mikoian, Aleksei Kirichenko,[23] Kaganovich, and others responded with exclamations of "You're right! . . . Approve it! . . . Hand it over!" Only Molotov, standing in the doorway waiting for a telephone call, remarked, addressing no one in particular, "This proposal, of course, is all wrong. But apparently we'll have to approve it."

Thus was born the decree of February 19, 1954, that transferred the Crimean oblast from Russia to Ukraine. The hollowness of the reasons that the decree gave—a shared economy, contiguous territory, economic and cultural ties—was apparent to everyone. All the same, the decree passed. Throughout the Crimea all signs were changed from Russian to Ukrainian, radio broadcasts and newspapers switched to Ukrainian, and so on.

I have dwelt on this comparatively minor political event because it is quite telling. The point is not that Russia was dealt an injury. It is difficult to injure a republic of almost 120 million persons, especially if it was a dominant nation in the past. As always, the Crimea remains the country's Arcadia, its resort area, its granary and flower garden; it is the jewel of all the peoples of the Soviet Union. The point is that this was one of the first examples of Khrushchev's highly personal and arbitrary approach to resolving political questions.

Khrushchev wanted to hand Ukraine an anniversary present and thus polish what he fancied was his already glorious image in that land. What he did was a patent and gross violation of the nationalities policy of the party and the state. Of course, Molotov was not alone with his remark that a fundamental error was being committed and that the action was inadvisable—others, including Russian, Ukrainian, Belorussian, Georgian, and other communists realized the same. However, was it worth having an argument in the Presidium about this—in the honeymoon period after Stalin's death—when everyone agreed to preserve "unity" and not make things more difficult for the leadership? Was it worth it?

For Khrushchev, this episode and several others like it served as trial runs. His crafty, puffy eyes peered into the faces of those around him. Would his bid go over with the Presidium? Yes, it would. Similar gambits did, too. With each success Khrushchev's self-confidence grew, his voice hardened, and his tone became increasingly peremptory. From the reluctance of the others in the leadership to quarrel at the expense of a united front, he drew his own conclusions and took the necessary measures to turn it to his advantage. He deployed his people everywhere and drew the levers of power ever closer; he was helped by the fact that the well-oiled machinery that Stalin had devised to assure his one-man rule was still running perfectly.

The top ranks of party and government workers, the bulk of the intelligentsia, and the people as a whole shared a fervent longing for an end to the old, undemocratic methods of leadership, a return in actual practice to Leninist principles in party, governmental, and public affairs, and an espousal of authentic collectivism. Khrushchev was perhaps more voluble than anyone in support of this. But he used talk of all this as a distraction and profited from the sluggishness and passivity of the others in the leadership. He made increasing use of the old, hardened power mechanism, pulling one lever after another. When people close to the top looked past pressures of daily life long enough to realize that it was time to wake up and take immediate countermeasures, it was too late. The old command system was operating at full throttle, and the man at the controls, Nikita Khrushchev, had a satisfied smirk on his face.

The festivities marking the three-hundredth anniversary of the reunification of Ukraine and Russia culminated in a military parade and mass meeting on Red Square, and a glittering reception that evening in the Great Kremlin Palace. Members of the party CC and the governments of the USSR and the RSFSR, delegates from Ukraine and all the other Soviet republics, distinguished figures in industry and agriculture, representatives of the Soviet army and the scientific and cultural establishment, and members of the diplomatic corps mingled in the magnificent setting of Saint George's Hall.

Khrushchev played the role of host to the full. Proposing toast after toast, downing shot glass after shot glass, he radiated pleasure. The more he drank the more uncontrollable, as always, was his urge to speechify. After the official toasts, the unofficial ones came. In the presence of all the guests, their wives, members of the diplomatic corps, and waiters, he launched once again into a detailed and self-congratulatory account of Beria's arrest and trial. He painted a colorful picture of how quickly we would resolve all our problems, how we would enjoy the fruit of abundance, and how we would progress from what he called "sitsializm" to "communizm."[24]

In the middle of one of Khrushchev's speeches, Molotov walked in. He had just flown back from a foreign ministers' conference in Geneva, and, like Chatskii in Griboedov's *Woe from Wit*, "stepped from shipboard into a ball."[25] Khrushchev broke off, came up to Molotov, gave him a bear hug and several kisses, and raised a toast: "We live and work together in our own country. As you can see, we're doing all right. But poor Viacheslav Mikhailovich has got to deal constantly with the imperialists." He went on at length about Molotov's virtues and his hard lot in life.

It would be difficult to guess what emotions came over Molotov at that moment. His face remained expressionless, his manner reserved. He merely made a slight gesture toward the guests, placed his glass on the table without bringing it to his lips, and moved off to one side.

Just five months earlier we had met in this same hall in equal numbers to greet the New Year. By tradition, the New Year's Eve toast was made by the chairman of the Presidium of the USSR Supreme Soviet, Voroshilov; and the master of ceremonies was the chairman of the USSR Council of Ministers, Malenkov. Then it was Malenkov who greeted the guests, welcomed the members of the diplomatic corps, and made the toasts. Five months had gone by, and Malenkov, Khrushchev, and all the others in the top leadership officially held the same posts they had occupied at that New Year's Eve party, but now even those who were not privy to the "secrets of the Kremlin" could see how the balance of power had changed.

Off to one side, almost alone, Malenkov stood shifting his weight from foot to foot. His deputies, members of the Presidium, and secretaries of the Central Committee gazed at the assemblage in ways that bespoke a wide range of views and attitudes, all marking them as second- or third-level figures. The entire hall was dominated by the voice, gestures, and smiles that were unctuous from the greasy sauces of the man now bearing the title of first secretary. A growing circle of his favorites already addressed him obligingly by the disgusting and sinister appellation that had migrated from the Stalin era, *khoziain*—chief.[26]

CHAPTER FOURTEEN

With Khrushchev in China

THE PREPARATIONS ARE COMPLETED. The itinerary is set. The relevant literature and the latest reports from China have been read. The necessary notes have been made. A diplomatic passport is in my pocket. A ceremonial safe-conduct pass for China is attached. The following statement from TASS appears in the press:

"On September 28, 1954, on the occasion of the fifth anniversary of the founding of the People's Republic of China, a USSR governmental delegation left for Beijing. The delegation includes the first secretary of the CC of the CPSU and a member of the Presidium of the USSR Supreme Soviet, N. S. Khrushchev (delegation head); the first deputy chairman of the USSR Council of Ministers, N. A. Bulganin; the deputy chairman of the USSR Council of Ministers, A. I. Mikoian; the chairman of the Council of Trade Unions, N. M. Shvernik; the USSR minister of culture, G. F. Aleksandrov; the executive editor of *Pravda,* D. T. Shepilov; the secretary of the Moscow Party Committee, E. A. Furtseva; the Uzbek SSR minister of industry and construction materials, Ia. S. Nasriddinova; the USSR ambassador to the People's Republic of China, Pavel Iudin (located in Beijing); and the director of the department of the CC of the CPSU, V. P. Stepanov."

The scheduled time of departure is 3:40 A.M.

Now we are at the central airport. At that time, our crack airplane was the IL-14. We board two of these planes and our journey begins. A flock of special aircraft with a retinue of generals, colonels, navigators, security guards, chefs, and waiters accompanies us on our flight. The airport is ablaze with lights. Final instructions.

Khrushchev is in a good humor. He makes puns, pokes fun as usual at Mikoian, and tells Shvernik to "be ready to dine on snakes." He is obviously pleased with himself. This is his first mission abroad, and he is aglow with the importance of the visit, with his role in it, and with anticipation of the pleasures ahead. Under Stalin, everyone was always on his best behavior and aware of being watched. No one, with the exception of Molotov, who was the minister of foreign affairs, ever traveled abroad. No exceptions. Now Khrushchev decides himself when and where to go, with whom and for how long, at the head of a delegation or alone. He revels in his newfound freedom and power.

Farewell to the escorts. Takeoff. Below us, nighttime Moscow sparkles like a giant necklace on black velvet that is laced with strings of diamonds in squares, loops, and intricate designs. A sharp turn, and we are pointing east. Ahead of us is a journey of 6,200 kilometers: Moscow—Kazan—Sverdlovsk—Kurgan—Omsk—Novosibirsk—Irkutsk—Ulaanbaatar—Beijing. Our ladies, regaled with joking accounts about the hazards of flight, are nervous about the turbulence over the Gobi Desert.

I am feverish with excitement. China is the world's most populous country and one of the principal cradles of civilization, if not the main one. A country of limitless material and intellectual riches. What does it look like? What are its people like? I long for insights into the main currents of Chinese life.

Under the plane's wings, endless piles of clouds look like fantastic giant snowmen. Over Sverdlovsk, we have a view of the city's new airport. Our strong steel bird lurches intermittently in air pockets.

We approach the Siberian capital. A phrase that I recently encountered in Alphonse Daudet's *The Nabob* pecks away at my mind: "Under a pallid, smoky sky webbed by a thin rain, the real world lay as though veiled."[1] How descriptive of Siberia's skies!

At 1:20 P.M. we land in Novosibirsk. Greetings, land of Siberia!

Twenty years previously, during the time of great revolutionary change in our villages, I worked here, in the Chulymskii district, as head of a political department. We decide on a short break, take a two-hour nap, then take off into the Stygian darkness, setting our course for Irkutsk.

Below us is the timeless taiga. Pine trees, cedars, and larches are already sprinkled with snow. We land in a drizzle. It's cold. The hospitable Irkutsk leadership puts up a spacious tent at the airport and invites us in to warm up. Pots of steaming soup made of salmon trout from the Lena River and *omul* and grayling from Lake Baikal give off a heavenly aroma.

Fortified by the hot soup, Khrushchev promptly got on his high horse and began questioning our hosts about their progress with corn. The locals, of course, assured him that corn does wonderfully in eastern Siberia. In some of the model farms, they told him, corn grows to a height of 2.5 meters—they showed him a dried corn stalk that is conveniently hidden behind pots of fish soup—and in others it yields 1,500 centners of cob silage.

Luxuriating in the rich and fragrant fish soup, Khrushchev told the Irkutsk leaders to make sure that every kolkhoz plants no less than ninety hectares of corn the next spring. His listeners assured him that his orders would be carried out. Neither Khrushchev, nor local agriculturalists, nor the Irkutsk officials could have explained, however, why the exact number was ninety hectares.

We put the wet snow and drizzle of Irkutsk behind us. Only the last leg of the flight is left—Irkutsk to Beijing. Over Kiakhta we cross the Soviet-Mongolian border. The initial plan was for a layover in the capital of the People's Republic of Mongolia, but this was later dropped. Beyond Ulaanbaatar we sailed into an airy ocean, an expanse of cloudless blue. A bright sun. We entered the air space of the People's Republic of China. Soon everything was transformed. Under the plane's wings, there was a whimsical mosaic of fields—silver, emerald, yellow, and crimson. There were rice fields saturated with water, tracts of early grain shoots, and fields of cereal ready to be reaped. What a riot of colors! What thrifty use of the soil!

Approaching Beijing we dove into a bank of clouds. The plane's windows streamed with heavy rain. In Moscow it was only 11 A.M.; here it was dusk. Visibility was zero. We descended steeply for landing. It felt as though we were burrowing through wet, black cotton wool. Nonetheless, we made a regulation safe three-point landing.

Our Soviet delegation received a formal welcome at the airport. Among those greeting us were the Central Committee secretary and chairman of the All-China Congress of People's Representatives, Liu Shaoqi; the CC secretary and premier of the Council of State, Zhou Enlai; the CC secretary and deputy premier of the Council of State, Chen Yun; the Politburo member Lin Bozhu; the Politburo member and deputy chairman of the Council of State Peng Dehuai; the deputy premiers Deng Zhihui, Ho Long, Chen Yi, Ulanhu, Li Fujing, and Li Xiannian; the director of the Secretariat of the People's Republic of China, Xi Zhongxun; the deputy chairman of the Standing Committee of the All-China Congress of Representatives of the Nationalities, Guo Moruo; the widow of Sun Yat-sen,[2] Song Qingling; the Dalai Lama and the Panchen Lama;[3] the chairman of the Supreme Court, Dong Biwu; the chief prosecutor, Zhang Dingcheng; the Politburo member, secretary of the Beijing Party Committee, and mayor of Beijing, Peng Zhen; and others.

Subsequently, after the outbreak of the Cultural Revolution,[4] most of the above-mentioned persons were declared to be "contemptible revisionists" and "black dogs." Young demonstrators held aloft placards demanding that the people "smash their doglike heads." But at that time they were Mao Zedong's closest brothers-in-arms.

Khrushchev made a speech at the airport, congratulating China on the adoption of its new constitution and on "electing the great son and leader of the Chinese people, Comrade Mao Zedong, as chairman of the PRC."

We are domiciled in small European-style houses. Everything is very plain, comfortable, and impeccably clean. The soft colors of the household utensils and shaggy Chinese towels are pleasant to the eye. Our rooms have apparently been sprayed with some wonderful essence of aromatic grasses. The next morning we go on a tour of Beijing.

Everything is large in China: its territory of 10 million square kilometers, its population of 600 million, its mountain ranges—the Himalayas, the Tian Shan,[5] the Kunlun,[6] the mountains of Sichuan province. The Yangtze and Yellow Rivers are among the six longest in the world. The Great Wall stretches for 5,000 kilometers. There are many arterial roads, including some extremely ancient ones, like the 6,000-kilometer dirt road from Beijing to Kashgar.[7] There is the 1,782-kilometer Grand Canal, constructed as early as the seventh century, which connects Beijing to Hangzhou.[8] Equally large are the revolutionary changes brought about by the new China in the political, economic, social, and cultural spheres after the overthrow of the Guomindang[9] regime.

Even though we are busy with negotiations, meetings, visits to factories and editorial offices, work on official documents, and other things, I tried to make use of every free minute to take in the sights of this great and ancient country. Beijing is more than three thousand years old. It was founded in 1121 BCE by the heirs of Huang Di.[10] Through the centuries this "Northern Capital" was shaken by many storms and bloody conflicts. It survived the invasions of the nomadic Khitans and the Jurchen tribes of Tungus origin.[11] It was conquered by the Mongols. The grandson of Genghis Khan, Kublai Khan, leveled the ancient city of Beijing and erected a new "Great Capital," Dadu, on its site.[12] Later the Manchu capture of Beijing put an end to the Ming dynasty, which had seen the evolution of the Inner (Imperial) City and the Outer City. The Inner City was surrounded by a mighty wall more than twelve meters in height.

The Qing (Manchu) dynasty lasted almost three hundred years. Within the Imperial City, the Forbidden City was erected and surrounded by a red brick wall; it contained the emperor's palace. The massive walls with their battlements and embrasures defended the rulers from foreign invasions and frequent domestic uprisings.

The Inner City, combining the Imperial and Forbidden Cities, is a masterpiece of architecture and art: royal chambers, pavilions, temples, monasteries, and monuments. Our Chinese friends, acting as tour guides, tell us that Beijing contains no fewer than nine hundred palace halls, pagodas, temples, monasteries, museums, monuments, pagan temples, and altars erected during the Ming (1368–1644) and Qing (1644–1912) dynasties.

Here we are in the Imperial Palace grounds: a countless series of opulent halls that stand apart or are connected by spacious courtyards, stone stairways, and walkways, with an expanse of gardens and parks drowning in greenery and freshened by the coolness of numerous lakes and canals. Each hall is distinctive in form. Carved columns, molded arches, sparkling rooftops of porcelain and gilded tile, walls and ceilings decorated with enamel and paint, precious china—everything is of stunning craftsmanship and artistry. What skill countless generations of enslaved craftsmen must have had to create such inimitable treasures!

Each hall has its own name, often philosophical in nature: the Pavilion of Supreme Harmony, where important state ceremonies were held; the Hall of Meditation; the Hall of Contemplation; the Hall of Spiritual Calm; and so on. Here is the spot where the Asian rulers contemplated and indulged their pleasures; one word from a despot like Kublai Khan was enough to wipe a whole city off the face of the earth and cause thousands of men to lose their heads.

There is more. The Moon Gate that leads to the Forbidden City. The Wall of the Nine Dragons in Beihai Park. The Summer Palace of the Empress Dowager Cixi,[13] set off by a lake with islands of graceful lotus and bevies of swans. The White Dagoba Temple. The Western and Eastern Approaches of Eternal Peace that lead to the tombs of the Chinese emperors.

The southern side of the Forbidden City is dominated by the historic Gate of Heavenly Peace—Tiananmen. It overlooks a huge square of the same name; one of our Chinese friends told us that it is five or six times the size of our own Red Square. In the Outer City, we come upon the bewitching beauty of the Temple of Heaven, built in 1420. Here the emperors, regarded as the Sons of Heaven, gave heaven an account of their activities during the previous year and offered sacrifices so that a wrathful heaven would not punish the country with crop failures and other ills. For centuries on end, the luxurious and sumptuous Imperial City was wrapped in stillness and grandeur. The Chinese emperor was an absolute autocrat. Not only the Forbidden City but the entire Inner City of 111 square kilometers was his personal property. In his magnanimity, he could bestow whole palaces and entire city sections to his favorite dignitaries and to generals who were renowned in battle. But along with their entire households, they could be banished from the Inner City at a moment's notice if the emperor withdrew his favor. As for the common people, they were not allowed to live in the Inner City, and even the palace servants and temple attendants had to leave the imperial sanctum for the night, on pain of severe punishment. Today the Inner City contains the headquarters and residential areas of the people's government. At all the former imperial pavilions and places of recreation, we saw workers, craftsmen, students, members of the National Liberation Army, sailors, peasants, and others who gaze at the palace relics, relax, or stroll about.

The parts of the city where the working people live, especially the Outer City, attested to the old China's painful legacy in housing. Here we saw narrow streets without modern conveniences and dilapidated wooden and mud dwellings that are walled off from the street. Many have no windows, or only narrow, barred apertures of oil paper instead of glass.

The living quarters are often connected both to a workshop, where the craftsman and his family turn out their wares, and to a small store, tiny food stand, or plain stall, where they have them on sale. All aspects of production and trade spill out, as it were, into the street, while the family's private life goes on in the back, in small yards bounded by several small houses. Many Beijing streets are crammed with workshops, stores, and small shops. These are grouped by types. Here we have shoemakers and ivory craftsmen, there potters; farther on there are tailors; still farther there are tinsmiths, jewelers, dish painters, silk embroiders, and toymakers—in other words, masters of all kinds of handicrafts. Side by side with these tiny workshops or intermingled among them: a profusion of stores, shops, stalls, eateries, and portable kitchens.

Especially colorful is the covered market on Beijing's main street, Wangfujing. The stalls of petty tradesmen are most numerous. But there are many large state-owned stores and "mixed" stores, which are funded jointly by state and private capital. Items for purchase are in good supply, of fine quality, and of considerable variety. There are plenty of customers as well, both Chinese and Europeans. The Chinese leadership's current policy in regard to trade and industry is one of peaceful transition from capitalism to socialism.

Beijing bustles with activity. There are all kinds of transportation—a few new cars, vintage streetcars, aged buses, bicycles, horse- and mule-drawn carts, rickshaws, pedicabs, haulers of heavy loads, even curly-haired camels. Strolling barbers, moveable repair stalls of all kinds, vendors offering produce, fruit, candy, soft drinks, and toys, shoemakers with their toolkits, medicine hawkers, magicians, and shamans enliven the streets.

The rickshaws and pedicabs are particularly plentiful; they seem to overflow the streets, squares, markets, and sidewalks. Many of the drivers look gaunt and exhausted, with deathly pale faces. They wait long and patiently for fares. When I referred to them in my talk with Zhou Enlai, he said, "This is one of the legacies of the past. Of course, millions of rickshaws don't make our streets pretty. But we're in no hurry to get rid of them. We need them. For the time being, this antiquated form of conveyance makes it possible for many people to get around and to get on with their lives. With the development of large-scale industry and construction, rickshaws will gradually disappear as a form of transport.

Our socialist industry will absorb the rickshaw drivers and turn them into modern workers."

During our stay in China, we could sense the first great advances wrought by the people's government and the first results of the socialist transformation of the economy—changes that were visible in Beijing. All major industrial and commercial enterprises owned by bureaucratic capital[14] had been nationalized. Millions of artisans were enlisted in co-operatives. Enterprises destroyed by war were reestablished and put to work. Old factories were renovated and new ones built. We felt proud hearing our Chinese friends speak of the Soviet Union's major role in the reconstruction work: more than two hundred first-class metallurgical, machine-tooling, automobile, and other plants had been built with the technical and financial assistance of the USSR. And this assistance was still growing.

Beijing is experiencing a construction boom—of housing, modern schools, hospitals, educational institutions, theaters, hotels, vacation centers, and movie theaters. Its workforce, most of it illiterate, is beginning to acquire an education and modernize. Of course, the city is terribly congested, and a huge number of the houses, streets, and whole neighborhoods are without modern conveniences. But in response to their government's call, the people of Beijing and cities and villages throughout the country are taking heroic measures to make things right.

There is a campaign under way everywhere against the "four evils"—flies, mosquitoes, and mice, which carry disease, and sparrows, which ravage rice and other grains. It is done in typically Chinese fashion: all people, children and adults, take part. A team of kids, having met its daily quota of flies or unfortunate sparrows, presents their remains to the team leader in the evening.

The Chinese people's astonishing discipline, and their full compliance with their government's instructions and orders, has worked miracles. We see many examples of this, both large and small, during our tour. For instance, the exploited people of China starved, lived in abysmally unsanitary conditions, and were prey to ill health and disease for centuries. In line with its basic program for improving the people's welfare, the government has been promoting physical fitness. As something recommended by the government, it has become holy writ and something that has to be carried out to the letter. We saw workers at industrial plants, schoolchildren in front of their village schools, and fishermen on the Pearl River take a break at the appointed hour for a prescribed set of physical exercises.

The inborn discipline of the Chinese, their astonishing industriousness, patience, and complete trust and faith in the government and the communist party, topped by the universal conviction that tomorrow will bring China a life of material plenty and intellectual benefits, has reached a critical mass of enormous dynamism. I had one thought: China is a country of boundless economic potential. It is first or one of the first in the world in resources of coal, tin, iron, manganese ore, bauxite, wolfram, magnesium, and copper. It has gold and other precious metals waiting to be mined. Its manpower is incalculable. Despite this, the annual national income of the old China was negligible—twenty dollars per capita. Now, within a relatively short period, the Chinese will eat their fill and, with our help, will base their economy on the most modern industrial technology; they will begin, in Lenin's words, to "civilize themselves." Then an immense force for progress that the world has never seen will burst forth and carry the commonwealth of socialist countries forward in seven-mile strides.

Alas, the country's development has turned out to be much more complex, difficult, and unpredictable.

A reception and the start of negotiations between the Soviet delegation and the Chinese, who were led by the chairman of the People's Republic of China, Mao Zedong, was set for 3:00 P.M. on September 30 at the Imperial Palace. I was elated: now I would meet the man whose name and exploits were legend. A peasant, soldier, and adherent of Marxism-Leninism and revolution since his youth, Mao Zedong rose to be one of the founders of the Chinese Communist Party and later became the universally recognized leader of the party and the great Chinese people. In the 1920s, he led a series of peasant movements, strikes, and uprisings. Together with Zhu De,[15] he organized the first insurgent units and detachments of the Chinese Peasant-Worker Red Army in the interior of the country. These became the rallying points of the revolution and the bases for a new people's government.

Within the global liberation movement, Mao Zedong won a place for himself as a major Marxist theoretician. In his philosophical works, *On Practice* and *On Contradiction,* he set forth the general problems of Marxist-Leninist dialectics in light of the experience of the great Chinese

Revolution. In treatises like *Problems of Strategy in China's Revolutionary War,* "On Tactics against Japanese Imperialism," "The Identity of Interests between the Soviet Union and All Mankind," *On New Democracy,* and "On the People's Democratic Dictatorship" he described the fundamental problems of revolution and the establishment of a new people's democracy in China.

In 1951 the *Works of Mao Zedong* began to be published in Moscow. Partly in preparation for this trip to China, I gave his books a close reading.

Forty years have gone by since the young Mao joined a revolutionary unit as a common soldier in the city of Changsha.[16] The Chinese Revolution went through stormy periods. The Chinese people made untold sacrifices before the altar of victory. On October 1, 1949, speaking in Tiananmen Square, Mao Zedong proclaimed the establishment of the People's Republic of China. At the first session of the People's Political Consultative Council of China, he was elected head of government. This man who has gone so far, who now stands at the head of the world's largest country, what does he look like? What are his thoughts? How does he see the future?

It is precisely 3:00 P.M. We are gathered in the reception hall. A small number of cameramen and news photographers are busy taking the usual pictures. We are ushered into the conference room and greeted by a densely packed group of the country's leaders.

At its center, and probably a step ahead of the others, stands Mao Zedong. He is tall, taller than any of his comrades, and wears a gray tunic and wide trousers, the type of dress we call *Stalinki.* That was what Stalin used to wear; Malenkov, Kaganovich, and many oblast committee secretaries and other party officials copied him. Some of the other Chinese leaders who join in welcoming us are also dressed in Stalinki. Mao's shoes are of the ordinary black, laced, square-toed kind. One by one, we step up to him, shake his hand, and do the same with the others.

Mao holds himself very erect. A large, clear, unlined face. A big sloping forehead. Straight black hair combed back. A large mole on his chin. He looks very young. His whole image is one of strength, calm, intellect, and nobility; there is not a hint of affectation or fussiness.

With a slight gesture, Mao graciously invites us to the big rectangular conference table. The Chinese leaders sit on his left and right. We take our places farther down; Khrushchev is closest to Mao. The Chinese delegation includes Zhu De, Liu Shaoqi, Zhou Enlai, Chen Yun, Dong Biwu, Lin Bozhu, Peng Dehuai, Peng Zhen, Deng Xiaoping, Deng Zhihui, and Li Fujing. It was in precisely that order that their names were uttered and listed in those days; it was in precisely that order that they sat around Mao.

A decade later, with the outbreak of the Cultural Revolution, Mao's inner circle underwent a radical shake-up. At this early time, however, the Chinese leadership constituted a single collective that was closely knit around their acknowledged and revered leader, Mao Zedong. Of course, even in those days some evidence seeped out of China of competition between Liu Shaoqi and Zhou Enlai. But all the indications were that the issue was not a fundamental disagreement, but the efforts of both men to gain Mao's favor; Mao, aware of the competition, kept both under control and maintained the necessary equilibrium.

In any case, on our first acquaintance with the leadership of the Chinese Communist Party and government, we did not want to focus on any possible division or friction within its ranks. We preferred to view everything through rose-colored glasses. This was facilitated by those positive aspects of the leaders' conduct and actions that veiled everything negative. The two most appealing features that we saw were simplicity and modesty.

The hall in which we met was simple and modest. A large table. Chairs with wicker arms. On the walls, portraits of Marx, Engels, Lenin, and Stalin. That was all. No displays of luxury or pomp, even though we were in the former Imperial Palace. The dress of all the Chinese leaders was simple and modest. Their manners and speech were simple and modest. We soon learned how exacting the Chinese were in evaluating their successes, even though without a doubt the victory of the Chinese Revolution was the greatest blow to world imperialism since the October Revolution. We soon learned how simple, strict, and modest were the Chinese leaders' style of work and daily life. Their pay, living quarters, and family wealth differed little from those of the average Chinese intellectual or qualified worker. That spoke greatly in their favor. In those days, the nominal—never mind the real—pay of our own top leaders was no less than eight or ten times the pay of a highly qualified worker or intellectual. Luxurious apartments, suburban and seaside town houses, and access to free products and cultural services of every kind put the top

Soviet leadership in a very privileged position. Leninist standards and strictness toward oneself in these matters had long been discarded. The applicable principles that Lenin laid down in *State and Revolution*[17] had been consigned to oblivion.

What we saw in China in that regard greatly appealed to me. I wanted to interpret it as evidence of the leaders' closeness to the people and their complete renunciation of everything mercenary and selfish for the sake of altruistic service to the country. Subsequent events showed that in this, too, we viewed things in an idealistic light.

When everyone sat at the table, Khrushchev, on behalf of the Soviet leadership, conveyed his greetings to Mao and the other Chinese leaders. Mao thanked him laconically. Khrushchev asked after his health. Mao answered, "Not bad." A discussion of three hours and twenty minutes follows.

In truth, the speaking was done almost exclusively by Khrushchev and Mao. The others on both sides paid close attention. More precisely, the discussion consisted 90 percent of Khrushchev's unrestrained harangues and 10 percent of Mao's terse replies. Unfortunately, my notes on this and subsequent meetings and conversations with Mao are also very brief, and I cannot claim strict accuracy for my recollections.

The translator for our side was the director of the Far Eastern Division of the Soviet Foreign Ministry, later the ambassador to Japan and the Soviet representative at the United Nations, Nikolai Fedorenko. He told us that Mao always speaks tersely, precisely, graphically, and often in a dialectic and artistic style that is very refined, much like his mellifluous verse. To translate him, Fedorenko said, is a real challenge. Actually, the Chinese told us that Fedorenko has a superb mastery of the Chinese language and literature and interprets Mao impeccably.

After the exchange of greetings, Khrushchev said, "We are delighted and proud of your great successes."

Mao replied, "Successes, thanks to your selfless help."

Khrushchev launched into a verbose explanation that selflessness is not at issue, since strengthening China strengthens our own country. Turning to Mao, he said, "You are overly modest."

"Is it being overly modest," Mao countered, "to acknowledge reality, the true nature of things? No one can deny the enormous importance of your assistance. From the old China we inherited three elements of Chinese culture. All the rest has been done with your help."

He defined those three elements as follows:

"Peking duck." Fedorenko explains to us that Mao uses the term symbolically; it stands for food and the necessities of life in general.

"Mahjong." A game of chance employing ivory tiles that, Fedorenko explains, is a symbol of free time and recreation.

"Tibetan folk medicine." A symbol of people's health and well-being.

Mikoian objects. "From what we read in the *Great Soviet Encyclopedia*, China's great culture cannot be reduced to these three elements. By the way, we have published the entry on China in the encyclopedia as a separate book."

Mao laughs. "Then you'll have to make corrections in the encyclopedia. But joking aside, thus far we have been able to achieve a thing or two with your help. Just recently in this same hall, we received a delegation of British Laborites that Atlee[18] headed." He speaks tersely and pointedly about what the Laborites have grasped about the Chinese Revolution and what they have yet to understand.

Interrupting, Khrushchev described our reception for the Laborites in Moscow. Then he speaks diffusely about Yugoslavia and Tito.

Mao sat still, smoking cigarette after cigarette. He gazed ahead with a stately calm; his smooth, handsome face gives no hint about what he thinks of Khrushchev's rambling narratives. His comrades, too, were motionless; respectful attention was written on their faces. For all of Mao's majestic simplicity, it was clear that in the presence of their leader and teacher, any personal initiative on their part, in word or deed, was regarded as inappropriate.

"Our greatest victory," Khrushchev went on, "was the unmasking of Beria." He recited again the details of the Beria affair from start to finish. He recounted the many crimes that Beria and his MGB minions perpetrated. He provided vivid descriptions of Beria's sordid and lascivious revelries. Smugly, he laid out how he had managed, step by step, to "bamboozle" Beria and arrest and execute him.

Khrushchev spoke with gusto; he got up from his chair and gesticulated. He salted his speech with facetious and vulgarly humorous remarks. It was as if a pig had dropped into the middle of this dignified hall and had its belly slit open, its stench filling the room.

The Chinese maintained complete composure. Mao's face retained its sovereign calm. Only at one point in the story did he turn his head slightly toward his interpreter to ask if he had understood something correctly, thereby inspiring Khrushchev to pour on more color. When Khrushchev's seemingly endless disquisition was over, Mao said, "We, too, had our Beria. It was Gao Gang."[19]

We knew Gao Gang as one of the oldest members of the Chinese Communist Party, one of the organizers of the partisan units in their struggle against the Guomindang clique. In later years, he took part in the liberation of Manchuria, headed the People's Government of the Northeastern Administrative Region, and was a member of the CC Politburo of the Communist Party of China and deputy chairman of the Central People's Government of China. Subsequently, after our breach with China, our propagandists asserted at meetings that Gao Gang had been a loyal friend of the Soviet Union and was destroyed by Mao Zedong for that very reason. Evidently, only the future will reveal where the truth lies.

After Khrushchev's torrent of words came to an end, there was a moment's silence. Then Mao, remaining as motionless as a statue, said something like this:

"We will return to many questions at our subsequent meetings. Now I request that you go out and see the country. The first fruits of our work are more visible in the provinces. Look at everything critically. That should be easier for you, as you observe from the outside. To see into the innermost core of things and discover their dialectical links and governing laws, one must look at them from a distance, in a detached spirit, forgetting about particulars.

"Generally speaking, those who are called upon to lead social movements should step aside from practical work from time to time to get a better theoretical grasp of what is going on and plumb its guiding principles. This is a prerequisite for proper planning for the future. I myself have been wondering whether I shouldn't distance myself somewhat from practical activity in order to think thoroughly about what is taking place. Without that, orderly progress is impossible. As for practical work, let them do it." With a movement of his head and arm, he pointed first at Liu Shaoqi and then at Zhou Enlai.

Five years later, Mao Zedong laid down the mantle of chairman of the People's Republic of China. The new head of government was Liu Shaoqi. A few more years passed, and a slew of puzzling, contradictory, and absolutely fantastic rumors began to filter out of China and spread around the world. Mao ceased making public appearances. Mao stopped publishing his writings. Mao was never or almost never seen. What did it all mean? What happened to Mao? What was going on in China?

According to one version, Mao temporarily abdicated from active leadership and sequestered himself somewhere in Hangzhou[20] to devote himself to philosophy. Another version was that he had suffered a massive stroke and was paralyzed, but that this was carefully kept secret and everything was still done in his name. A third version claimed that he had died but that his colleagues, in fear of internal strife and to preserve the unity of the nation and the party that he had embodied, found a double for Mao; this man appeared infrequently on rostrums and at meetings but remained silent.

Rumors aside, it was true that during that period Mao temporarily put aside all practical affairs and almost never appeared in public. It was during this time that a struggle between two fundamental factions in the ranks of the Chinese Communist Party and the government came to a head. Certain forces in the government bureaucracy and the army that were led by Zhou Enlai and the prominent military leader Lin Biao opposed forces within the party organization that were led by Liu Shaoqi. At that point, Mao stepped out of the mysterious twilight onto center stage. News flashed around the world that he had swum across the mighty Yangtze and was at the peak of his physical and mental powers.

Commenting on this announcement, a Sinologist who had lived for many years in Beijing said to me:

"I wouldn't be surprised if this were a subtle political move, Chinese style. In recent years Mao's policies have suffered one reverse after another. The theory and practice of the 'Great Leap Forward'[21] in industry has collapsed. The premature commune movement in the villages proved impractical. The policy of fanning international tensions and triggering the 'world revolution' in country after country has left China completely isolated. All this gave rise to covert opposition to Mao's leadership.

"Mao decided to let all the opposition groups rise to the surface and reveal themselves in full. To bring this about, he feigned illness, retired from active leadership, and concentrated on the course of events. When all the opposition forces were out in the open, he stepped out of oblivion, and launched the so-called Cultural Revolution."

As the revolution spread, I often thought back to my trip to China and my impressions there, and ruefully asked myself, "How could those subtle, sensible, wise, and seemingly infallible Chinese leaders fall prey to such fanatical cruelty?" Each time I answered with another question: How could Stalin and his companions, well-educated Marxists who went through tsarist prisons, exiles, and hard labor, descend to the crimes of 1937 and subsequent years? Evidently, the truth is that when collective leadership and reasoning are suppressed, and the sense of accountability to the people and society is snuffed out, all democratic forms of leadership within the party and the government become illusory, and absolute power inevitably falls into the hands of one man. History has provided clear lessons about what that leads to.

But these thoughts troubled my mind only later. At the time of our visit to China and our initiation into its way of life, we were filled with admiration for the Marxist erudition and wisdom of the Chinese leadership and the discipline and innate, extraordinary politeness of the Chinese people. Yes, we said to ourselves, a country like this, with party leaders like these, is destined for greatness in the nearest future.

At 7:00 P.M. we attended a solemn meeting in the Great Hall of Humanity and Benevolence to mark the fifth anniversary of the founding of the People's Republic of China. Chinese leaders and heads of delegations from socialist countries occupied a stage that was draped in blue and emblazoned with the emblem of the PRC and the dates 1949–54. I looked at the stage and around the hall, and my heart filled with happiness. How many faithful friends there were of the new China! How mighty a coalition of socialist countries around the globe there was! From now on, this coalition will grow, soar, and determine the destinies of mankind.

Zhou Enlai stepped up on the dais. He spoke tersely, wisely, and precisely, yet in his laconic words one heard the music of creation.

The wounds inflicted by war, he said, have rapidly healed. We have started our five-year plan. Before us lies a great task—to transform China into a socialist state that is free of poverty and the exploitation of one man by another. This task we shall carry out.

He spoke of problems and difficulties. "We must be modest, attentive, and conscientious. Our enemies are braggadocio and conceit." He expressed gratitude to the Soviet Union for its generous and selfless assistance. He called for the study of Marxism-Leninism and the progressive experience of the Soviet Union and other fraternal countries. He then outlined a comprehensive program of struggle for peace.

"It is our firm belief that countries with different social systems can coexist peacefully and that all international disputes can be resolved by peaceful negotiations. . . . We want to live in peace with all the countries of the world. We, of course, also want to live in peace with the United States."

At that time, Soviet and Chinese communists, like communists in other countries, spoke the same language. Yet only a few years later, Chinese leaders denounced the possibility of the peaceful coexistence of countries with different systems as revisionism and a grave apostasy from revolutionary Marxism-Leninism.

The next speaker was Khrushchev. His speech was four times as long as Zhou's. Reading from a text prepared for him, Khrushchev spoke at length about old colonial Asia, the way the Chinese Revolution was made, the tasks facing the Chinese communists in the industrialization of the country and the socialist transformation of the villages, the thousands of years of Chinese culture, the new Chinese constitution, and Chiang Kai-shek.[22] He repeatedly sang the praises of Mao Zedong and quoted Stalin.

This was his first speech abroad. Everything that his aides and consultants wrote for him was elementary and common knowledge, but for him, of course, it was terra incognita. That was why he always demanded that the writers of his speeches deal with everything comprehensively, "from the very beginning"—or, as the quip went among our journalists, "from the Ice Age to the sunburst of the Stalinist constitution." With the text in hand, he gloried in his eloquence, even though he frequently stumbled over long words, Chinese names, and geographic designations. From time to time he departed from the text and started to improvise, throwing in little jokes, facetious digressions, and the most unexpected comments and proposals.

For Khrushchev, the speech in Beijing marked the beginning of a ceaseless flow of speeches in country after country; they were verbose, often boastful, peppered with threats to "crush the hydra of world imperialism," or, by contrast, overly friendly, like his bid to President Eisenhower, "Let's dump all our differences. Gather up your grandchildren and come relax with us. You can count on a real Russian welcome."

In his dealings with political figures in socialist countries in speeches and conversations, Khrushchev gradually adopted an exhortatory, didactic, and peremptory tone that at times could be rude and offensive. This was one of the main causes of the rift in the foundations of the commonwealth of socialist nations. True, during our visit to China, his garrulousness was made more acceptable by the prevailing political climate. The Chinese were in the "meetings phase" of their revolution, as we had once been in ours. Huge rallies and conferences were frequent; speeches, including long ones, were the rule. Aware of this, the Chinese often went to conferences and even the theater with food wrapped in a piece of cloth so they could eat during the program. Consequently, they reacted stoically to Khrushchev's unending speeches, especially since everything that was Soviet and that hailed from Moscow was received with the greatest enthusiasm, gratitude, and affection by all strata of Chinese society.

The gala evening concluded with a display of China's marvelous theatrical art, which is based on traditional forms of Chinese stagecraft that go back thousands of years—to the seventh century BCE, according to written records. Besides the traditional spectacles, we were shown something new: plays in which scenes, songs, and themes of a revolutionary nature were intermingled with traditional forms of Chinese opera that told of peasant uprisings against foreign aggressors. Modern Chinese drama and opera combine declamation, dance, song, acrobatics, pantomime, and sleight of hand to the accompaniment of musical instruments, both stringed and percussion. Stage sets and acting conform closely to theatrical convention, like the disclosure of the characters' civic and moral qualities through the color of their dress and makeup: red for courage, white for villainy and treachery, and so on.

My attempt to share my impressions of the modern Chinese theater and describe some of its aspects will necessarily be skimpy. The very concept of "modern Chinese art" is an abstraction. Over the course of many eras, different schools of song and dance, acrobatics, and farce developed in different cities and provinces of the enormous country. Certain features of one school blended with those of another, giving rise to new movements and styles. For instance, the *Yiyang* theatrical school, which originated and flourished under the Ming dynasty (fourteenth to seventeenth centuries), was characterized by outdoor performances, employed large numbers of actors, dealt with action based on democratic themes, and featured free improvisation and mass scenes depicting war against invaders and popular uprisings. The plays lasted several days and weaved in solo and choral singing, group dances, acrobatics, swordsmanship, and battle scenes.

Quite the opposite was the *Kunqu* school, which was the theater of the aristocracy. Noted for its polished acting and accomplished music that professionals composed, it served as one of the sources for the development of *Jingju,* the Beijing theater of the seventeenth to the nineteenth centuries, which combined the skilled acting and vocal virtuosity of the Kunqu school with the popular tunefulness, colorfulness, and military vigor of the Yiyang tradition.

In the *Zaju* school of the thirteenth and fourteenth centuries, women's roles were performed by men. The Zaju theater produced a brilliant array of female impersonators. As it happened, we were introduced in Beijing to the acting of a world-famous star of that constellation, Mei Lanfang. We also saw colorful and entertaining numbers that were staged by troupes representing ethnic minorities—the Uygurs, the Dais, and others.[23]

On October 1, a military parade and a mass workers' rally took place in Tiananmen Square. A bright sun in a cloudless sky bathed everything in gold. The emblem of the republic and a portrait of Mao Zedong looked proudly down on the proceedings. The troops stood in formation. As at Red Square, the reviewing stand accommodated members of the Central Committee and deputies, delegates from fraternal socialist countries, and prominent public figures.

The celebration was formally opened by Beijing Mayor Peng Zhen, who later was one of the first to be declared a member of a "black band of revisionists." Defense Minister Peng Dehuai read the order of the day, which—as in Stalin's time—concluded with ritual acclamations: "Long live the great leader of the Chinese people, Chairman Mao Zedong!"

Our Soviet group, as well as foreign delegates like Bolesław Bierut of Poland, Kim Il Sung of Korea, and Gheorghe Apostol of Romania, are in the main reviewing stand with Mao and his comrades. Before us, formations representing military schools and academies march by, followed by columns of rifle divisions, naval and cavalry units, and mechanized detachments. Parachutists. Artillery. Antiaircraft batteries. Tanks. The people lining the square give their beloved army a rousing ovation.

The military parade demonstrates that the People's Republic of China has the main elements of a modern army. True, some experts on the subject tell us that the Chinese army is still hampered by certain guerrilla and petit bourgeois concepts. There are no military titles or differentiating insignia. There is no military pay; the serviceman is paid in kind depending on the size of his extended family. Below the rank of battalion commander, he is not allowed to marry. For a commander, orders and decisions are monitored by the party cell in his unit. I said to myself, however, that these are infantile disorders of leftism.[24] They, too, will pass.

Squadrons of bombers and jet fighters roared overhead. Admiring them, I reflected that the Chinese will not have to go through the agonizing phases of industrialization. We will continue to give them high-quality machine tools and entire assembly lines, build them the most modern plants, furnish them with the latest technology, and train their engineers and technicians in our schools. The same for their army. They will not have to design their own weapons, one after another. That would require many five-year plans. We are giving them jet planes, rocket artillery, the most sophisticated tanks, antiaircraft systems, and warships. This help will steadily augment the economic and military strength of both China and the Soviet Union.

How great were the exploits on the socialist road of construction of the Chinese people and of this great man with the big forehead standing several steps away from me! The alliance of two titans like the USSR and China alters the destinies of mankind.

I will never forget the five hundred thousand people who were at the spectacle in the gigantic Tiananmen Square. At the outset of our stay in Beijing, our impression was that the Chinese—men and women, adults and children—were all dressed in the same blue cotton suits, trousers, and jackets. Now Beijing donned its holiday attire.

Here are columns of workers who march by with painted billboards, mock-ups of machinery, and models of factory products. Peasants in festive dress go by with placards that depict the earth's bounty. A sea of flowers ripples over a column of schoolchildren. The various formations representing the different peoples of China are set apart from each other by the style and color of their dress and finery. Then comes a sizeable detachment of lamas in purple robes that are reminiscent of ancient Roman togas, although with their bare arms and shaved heads they are more like the priests of ancient Egypt in Verdi's *Aïda*.

The popular procession lasts a long time. Our picture is taken with Mao right on the dais. Mao is greatly revered by the people. On reaching the main reviewing stand, each column stops momentarily. Hopping gently, arms aloft, the marchers hail their leader with fervent cries and wait for his acknowledgment. Mao slowly raises his right arm shoulder high. Not a muscle moves on his face, sculptured like that of a thinker or military leader. A burst of enthusiasm, and the column moves on. Over the seemingly endless river of humanity float portraits of Marx, Engels, Lenin, Stalin, Sun Yat-sen, Mao Zedong, and other Chinese leaders. Clusters of balloons and flocks of multicolored doves rise to the sky.

But now the square came alive with all the colors of the rainbow. Hundreds of young girls and boys who are clad in silk stood before us in groups. Gracefully and rhythmically they performed a dance symbolizing the gathering of tea leaves. They did other dances employing long silk ribbons and fans. After them came a company of young athletes, who show off their skill at exercises with hoops and pole vaulting.

All this made for a colorful carnival. No wonder Khrushchev kidded Elena Furtseva, the secretary of the Moscow Party Committee, when we were alone at lunch: "So, Elena Aleksandrovna, why don't you learn from the Chinese how to stage a parade? Everything is so formal and stiff with us. Here you have songs, dances, athletic performances." A month later, at our own October festival, a lot of what we saw at the Chinese mass demonstration was copied in Red Square.

In the evening, the square before the Gate of Heavenly Peace teemed with strolling crowds. Once again we joined the Chinese leaders on the government dais, chatting and sipping endless cups of Chinese tea. It was as if all four million inhabitants of Beijing poured into the square. Searchlights, crossing and parting from each other, pierce the sky. Bursts of fireworks shower down in millions of multicolored diamonds. I walked down into the swelling tides of merriment. Dancing. Singing. Magicians. Acrobatics. Stilt walking. Games. Theatrical numbers. Tightrope walking. Everywhere there are mobile food stalls and pushcarts, vendors with soft drinks, sweets, and fruit. Though packed with crowds, the square is orderly; there are no disturbances and hardly any sign of police.

Returning to the dais, I shared my quick impressions with Mao Zedong, Zhou Enlai, and the other Chinese leaders. Mao said, "Of course, we do have some police. But there isn't much need for them. People are relaxing. They're happy. There's no cause for disturbances, so there aren't any. People see to it themselves that public order is maintained. The morality of the masses is the strongest foundation for law and order."

This casual exchange gave rise to repeated discussions within our group. The subject was courtesy. If one may talk of national characteristics and features, our observations and conversations in China left us with the impression that courtesy is a trait inherent in the people of this country. The striking discipline and orderliness that we saw during the popular festivities in Tiananmen Square is one example. Here are a few others:

Two small neighboring houses. Two families. They have been here for a long time. Their grandfathers and great-grandfathers lived here. They all know one another. Over the years, they grew accustomed to each other. They are poor, neither aristocrats nor intelligentsia, poorly dressed and often hungry. Nonetheless, on meeting each other every morning, they bow ceremoniously and greet with the most exalted sentiments. That is the custom, in both city and village.

To all Chinese—not just the intellectuals—any impoliteness or rudeness in word or deed, to say nothing of offense, is immoral. Clearly, Confucianism, which is based on principles like humaneness (*ren*), love and respect for the elders of your family and society, proper conduct among people, and so on, played a key role in conditioning of the national psyche in this way. Genuine nobility stems from the observance of ren, whether you are an aristocrat or a commoner. In any event, China has always been known as a country where order rules, traditions are honored, and old age and authority are respected. For centuries past, the Chinese have been known as the politest and best-behaved people on earth.

I could well understand the predicament in which the executive editor of the newspaper *People's Daily*, Deng To, found himself when he spent time in Moscow as *Pravda*'s guest. He questioned me in detail about how *Pravda* began the practice of criticism and self-criticism in 1917, what form it took in 1918, and how it gradually evolved up to the 1950s. Apparently, Deng To had been instructed by the Chinese Communist Party CC to introduce criticism and self-criticism into the pages of his newspaper. Yet to criticize was to allow oneself to say something negative, unseemly, and accusatory about someone—someone who might not even be an enemy. By Chinese moral standards, this was a strange and psychologically difficult thing to do, especially for an intellectual, poet, and aesthete like Deng To. But Deng To wanted to learn from our experience.

I was able to tell him with a clear conscience how things had been under Lenin: how Lenin himself sometimes exposed and routed the enemies of socialism, yet how he brought tact and care for the rules of debate—the

•

assumption of the full equality of persons with different viewpoints, the right to disagree with Lenin, the right to make views public, and so on— into polemics with persons in his own party and class.

Of course, I could not tell Deng To that after Lenin's death these standards were gradually eliminated. The only kind of criticism Stalin understood was destructive. His arsenal of critical epithets featured invectives like "enemy of the people," "saboteur," "wrecker," and "social fascist." Criticism for Stalin meant his own absolute and unquestioned right to attack and condemn anyone he wanted. Any attempt to defend oneself or state a case was stigmatized as an "enemy sortie" and was punishable by death.

I don't know how far Deng To went in making *People's Daily* more critical, but when the Cultural Revolution broke out a few years later, he was declared to be one of Mao's enemies and a member of the "black band of revisionists," and he perished. According to one version, he committed suicide. According to another, Mao's supporters killed him.

During our stay in China, we felt the characteristic politeness of the country from all sides. Our ambassador, Iudin, liked to talk about the subject.

"Now you, Dmitrii Trofimovich, are the executive editor of *Pravda*. I, too, used to edit newspapers, journals, and books. So we both know how editors operate. How do we usually treat authors? We get a manuscript of an article or story. We read it. Not so hot. We reject it. Sometimes we write and tell the author that it won't be published. More often, we don't tell him anything and let him figure out for himself after much agonizing that his piece was inadequate.

"In China it's done differently. The editors get an article. They read it. It's inadequate. So they write something like this to the author.

"'Our worthy, illustrious brother! We have read your article. We are stunned and blinded by the power radiated by its ideas. We would deem it a great honor to publish your article in our journal, but we are convinced that if we did so, no Chinese would want to read anyone else's work in the future. In view of that, and not wishing to deny readers the possibility of acquainting themselves with other Chinese literary works, we humbly request that you agree not to have your article published in our journal.'"

Ten or twelve years later, our papers began to publish information of the following nature:

"The eminent Chinese woman writer Ding Ling,[25] who in the past suffered under the terror of the Guomindang regime, has fallen under suspicion of being insufficiently devoted to the ideas of Mao Zedong and of adopting a bourgeois outlook. She has been sent to the interior of China for reeducation through labor. There she washes floors, does laundry in communes and barracks, and undergoes constant indignities."

"In Beijing, near the railroad station, a band of Red Guards grabbed an old woman and hung on her neck a placard reading 'Foreign-educated.' (She graduated from a university in Germany.) They then stood her against a tree under a portrait of Mao Zedong and lashed her with their belts until she was bloody."

"'Everything that does not reflect Mao Zedong's ideas must be destroyed.' With that war cry, the Red Guards are rampaging in the interior, wrecking party committees, and beating party workers. They pulled down a monument to Pushkin in Shanghai.[26] Under the banner of struggle against the bourgeoisie and foreigners, they force women to cut off their braids and passersby to discard shoes made in Hong Kong."

Reading this, I wondered what had happened to the traditional and extraordinary politeness of the Chinese. How could the Chinese soil nurture evildoing like that of the Red Guards and the *zao fan*?[27] What upheaval had taken place in the minds of young people and a good portion of others? Why? I answered one question with another: What happened to a good portion of the great German nation, which gave us Marx, Engels, Goethe, Schiller, Beethoven? After all, Hitler, Goering, Goebbels, and Himmler[28] were not the only ones responsible for the monstrous crimes of fascism. Millions of Germans took part in building the death camps and gas ovens, running factories for making products from human skin and hair, and turning large, densely populated regions of the Soviet Union into "desert zones."

What could have corrupted the minds of millions of people to such a degree? Apparently, the most potent poison was the ideology of bourgeois nationalism. "*Deutschland über alles.*"[29] The Germans are a chosen people. Germany is destined by God and history to have dominion over the world. This heady brew of great-power nationalism gave rise to the Nazis, the SS men, the operators of gas chambers, the levelers of villages, and other vandals.

The doctrine of great-khan chauvinism is strongly embedded in today's China. China is allegedly the oldest, the greatest, the mightiest, and, yes, the most cultured country in the world. To the nation's youth falls the great historic mission of transforming not only China but the whole world on the basis of Mao Zedong's ideas. The Western era is ending. The great Chinese era has begun.

My journalistic duties consumed the next two days in Beijing. The *Pravda* bureau was located in the Big Sweet Water Well Alley. A dilapidated wooden house. Oil-paper windows. Everything was quite shabby. The two *Pravda* correspondents, Mikhail Domogatskikh and Viacheslav Ovchinnikov, told me that after the trip to Moscow of the executive editor of *People's Daily,* their working conditions improved somewhat. *People's Daily* helps them with trips around the country and access to information for their dispatches to Moscow. Nonetheless, it is still hard for them to do their job. The weight of the past is still present.

For instance, each trip to the interior requires the permission of the police. The permit specifies where the correspondent may go and for what purpose, how long the trip may last, and whom he may interview. For some reason, the permit is stamped "Emigrant." But since his trip to Moscow, Deng To has also supplied our correspondents with personal letters of recommendation, so they are met everywhere with open arms.

The Chinese authorities, I am told, keep close track of everything about China that appears in our central and provincial presses. They literally count the number of lines devoted to China in our articles and news dispatches, and then they publish exactly the same amount of material on the Soviet Union. They are extremely sensitive to any inaccuracy on our part and to anything that is critical or has to do with the darker side of life in the new China. I try to convince the *Pravda* correspondents—and myself—that none of these annoyances have any fundamental significance, that the Chinese have a keen sense of national pride and are loath to have their poverty exposed, and that all this fussiness will gradually disappear.

At the editorial offices of the *People's Daily,* we received a warm welcome and had a frank and friendly conversation about questions of mutual concern. I was surprised by the poor quality and obsoleteness of their printing equipment and offered to help obtain Soviet technical assistance to modernize the pressroom of the central paper of the CC and the Chinese Communist Party.

On October 2, an exhibition of the economic and cultural achieve-ments of the Soviet Union opened in Beijing. That evening Zhou Enlai was host at a reception for foreign delegates to the anniversary celebra-tions. The exhibition was held in an open space outside one of Beijing's sixteen ancient gates. Its centerpiece is a white marble palace erected by Soviet architects. The building has a splendid entrance, imposing halls that are finished in rare marble and wood, and a sky-blue dome with a golden spire. Snow-white stairs lead to the mezzanine. The interior is decorated with colorful panels, art objects, sculpture, and painting. Every-thing is flooded with light, sunshine, and joie de vivre.

More than ten thousand items demonstrate the Soviet Union's indus-trial might, the improvement in the living standards of its citizens, and the rapid development of cultural life in the sixteen Soviet republics.[30] Our visitors include all the Chinese leaders except Mao Zedong, plus prominent public figures like Song Qingling, the widow of Sun Yat-sen and the head of the Society for Chinese-Soviet Friendship; Guo Moruo, the president of the Academy of Sciences; and many others. The exhibition made a strong impression on our guests and was the object of extraordi-nary interest among the population; the people of Beijing requested more than a million passes before the day of its opening.

Later on, Mao Zedong himself visited the exhibition in the company of his closest comrades and gave the display a lengthy and careful inspec-tion. Before leaving, the Chinese leaders signed the visitors' book, lauded the Soviet Union's monumental progress in all branches of socialist con-struction, and added: "The brilliant successes scored in the economic and cultural development of the USSR arouse the unparalleled enthusiasm of the Chinese people in their construction of socialism and serve as superb models for their education. The Soviet government and people are of enormous, comprehensive, and constant help in our own construction. . . . On behalf of the entire Chinese people we express our gratitude for this fraternal friendship. (Signed) Mao Zedong, Zhou Enlai, Zhu De, Chen Yun, Lin Bozhu, Dong Biwu, Peng Dehuai, Peng Zhen, Deng Xiaoping. October 25, 1954."

Around that time, I made the acquaintance of the Dalai Lama and his deputy on secular affairs, so to speak, the Panchen Lama. I don't re-member what I read about Lamaism as a child, but my impression was something like this:

Far away there is a mysterious country called Tibet. It is filled with monasteries. In its capital, Lhasa, there is a magnificent marble palace on top of a high mountain. In the palace lives an all-powerful creature who rules over all the monasteries and the people of the land. This creature is gray, shaggy, and cruel, with ferocious slanted eyes. With one word from him, the head of an offending Tibetan drops off his shoulders. This mysterious and frightening creature is the Dalai Lama. For some reason, the very words "Dalai Lama" had a sinister ring to my childish mind.

Standing before me now in the flesh was the head of Tibet's secular and religious life, the head of the Lamaist church, the fourteenth Dalai Lama, Tenzin Gyatso, and his right-hand man, the Panchen Lama. What did I know? The Dalai Lama turned out to be a slim youth of average height, with thick, neatly cut black hair, clear pale skin, and dark, almond-shaped, glistening eyes. He was dressed in a long tunic of gold brocade lined in red silk. His face was fixed in a shy smile, as though having left the seclusion of his heavenly palace for the world's hurly-burly, he did not know what to do, where to go, or what to say and asked everyone to pardon him for it.

Tenzin Gyatso was chosen to be the next Dalai Lama in 1940, when he was five years old.[31] I was told about the many dramatic episodes that took place during the selection of the Dalai Lamas over the six hundred years of Lamaist history. After all, according to the Lamaist school of Buddhism, the Dalai Lama is not only the country's civil and religious leader but the living embodiment of the deity, one of the reincarnations of Buddha on this earth. Lamaism absorbed many of the fundamental canons and dogmas of Buddhist theology and differs from Indian Buddhism only in several specific ceremonies and rituals. As with Indian Buddhism, it indoctrinates the worker with a slavish submission to his fate.

But the institution of Lamaism is something special. The lama helps the faithful achieve the state of nirvana, which is the whole object of existence. In Buddhist families, most boys are placed in monasteries, where they are schooled in the rudiments of monasticism; they return to the world adherents of Buddhism; in every Mongolian and Tibetan family one of them enters the Lamaist order. Over time, this order gradually split into numerous cliques. Lamas became a privileged stratum of society that the economic and religious power of the monasteries supported. Their authority knew no bounds. Nonetheless, their fraternity was riven by ferocious strife among different Lamaist clans that represented the competing interests of various monasteries, especially the most influential ones—Drepung, Sera, and Ganden. This struggle became particularly bitter and sometimes bloody during the period that was set aside for the selection of the next Dalai Lama, especially because for many years the selection was tied with the conflicting national interests of great powers like Britain, China, and Russia.

According to traditions and rituals built up over many centuries, the heir to the throne is chosen from among boys born in the twelve months following the death of the previous Dalai Lama. The search for the heir is conducted by influential lamas on the basis of oracles, signs, and a special drawing of lots. This triggers fierce struggles among the different factions and the imperial powers that back them. Over centuries of Lamaist rule, there were cases when the new Dalai Lama was deemed persona non grata for one or more factions. If the objectors won out, the boy was killed, and the title went to a boy from another family more acceptable to the victors, who then acquired full power as collective regents to the throne.

But the fourteenth Dalai Lama could not be eliminated. When the revolution triumphed in China, he was fourteen years old. Two years later he was elected a deputy to the People's Political Consultative Council and thereby acquired immunity. Now, at the Soviet exhibition in Beijing, he stood gazing eagerly at the displays from a distant and unknown world of socialism. We posed together in the doors of the building for a picture to keep as a memento.

I remember a small but amusing incident. We walked into the section dealing with Soviet food production, where Mikoian, as the former head of this branch of industry, began telling us about the growth of food products. Then he took a bottle of champagne off the shelf and offered it to the Dalai Lama. I saw confusion spread over the face of my new acquaintance: What should he do? As a deity who is only temporarily on earth in human form, would it be unseemly for him to accept champagne?

"Take it, take it," Mikoian urged. "It's wonderful champagne. Try it. As good as the French."

The Dalai Lama stretched out both hands and shakily grasped the bottle. At first he pressed it to his chest. Looking around anxiously, he apparently decided that it was wrong for a god to hug a bottle of intoxicating nectar to his breast. So he lowered his arms, and the bottle began to bounce against his legs. I offered to relieve him of his burden and have it delivered later to his residence. The Dalai Lama entrusted the unfortunate bottle to me with a grateful look, and I handed it to one of our bodyguards with the necessary instructions.

The next day, our entire delegation was invited to a banquet hosted by Mao Zedong. The formal part of the evening was followed by a performance of the USSR Folk Dance Ensemble, directed by Igor Moiseev. I always regarded this company as one of our greatest choreographic treasures. It has toured dozens of countries and captivated millions with its artistry. Before the performance began, we told Mao and his comrades something about the dance company, since this was its first appearance in China. Mao then asked me to "take the Dalai Lama under your wing and familiarize him with your art." That was how the Dalai Lama and I found ourselves sitting together in front of the stage.

As always, the Moiseev troupe was brilliant, performing Russian and other Soviet folk dances. The colorful costumes, the youthful esprit, and the amazing skill of the dancers left my celestial neighbor in ecstasy. He bounced up and down in his chair and gave little moans of delight; his cheeks were flushed, and his lips parted with pleasure over his sparkling teeth. While observing him I reflected, "Poor little god! In his confinement in Lhasa, he almost certainly never attained a state of nirvana and bliss comparable to what he is experiencing now, watching the dancing enchantment of Moiseev's young girls."

The company then performed two Chinese numbers, the "Ribbon Dance" and a pantomime. Both were met with an ovation.

After the performance, however, Bulganin and Khrushchev told me that they thought the Chinese audience gave a lukewarm reception to the Russian dances. In selecting his repertory, Moiseev in their opinion, did not allow for the traits and tastes of the Chinese national character: the dances performed by Chinese women are flowing, graceful, restrained, and the Chinese are not used to the "wildness and stomping of our ballerinas." I replied that we presented Russian national dances at their best. But I passed on their comment to Igor Moiseev, who was upset to hear it. Later on, he told me that he took all these factors into consideration when preparing the program and that the company met with enormous success everywhere it went in its tour of China.

We did more than show off our own artistic productions; above all, we sought to gain a better appreciation, in the limited time available, of Chinese art. As I mentioned previously, we were fortunate enough to see several Chinese operas with the famous Mei Lanfang in the lead. Although already past sixty, Mei Lanfang performs the roles of a young beauty, a female warrior, and a naughty servant girl with exquisite delicacy, gracefulness, and femininity. The expressiveness and range of intonations in his voice, the perfection of his singing, and the elegance of his dancing created an image of irresistible power.

On October 5, the Chinese government held a reception in honor of the Soviet experts working in China. Premier Zhou Enlai expressed gratitude in the warmest terms to the large and growing army of Soviet specialists who gave their selfless assistance to the Chinese people in its economic and cultural development. The next day the Soviet delegation began its tour of the country.

CHAPTER FIFTEEN

To South China and Back

WE LEFT BEIJING BY CAR and headed for Tianjin, the port on the Hai River near where it empties into the Yellow Sea. The two cities were just then being linked by a 120-kilometer highway, but since only one side of the road had so far been asphalted, we drove through dust and mud, sharing the thoroughfare with a collection of cars, trucks, bicycles, heavy-laden camels, and carts drawn by horses, donkeys, and mules.

The Beijing plain is a mosaic of fields, orchards, gardens, groves, and reservoirs, with a scattering of poplars, acacias, lime trees, maples, oaks, and, here and there, on the former estates of temples and monasteries, cedars and cypresses. The streams, lakes, and artificial ponds are studded with villages that sometimes comprise only a few houses, clusters of dwellings that belong to artisans and craftsmen, and towns. The villages are poor in appearance, with houses of baked mud or a combination of mud and wood; only rarely is there a tiled roof. Rising next to these miserable dwellings are the imposing and often luxurious estates of landowners, stately temples and monasteries, and rural mansions.

The great Beijing plain is primarily a region of intensive agriculture. Wherever one looks, there are fields of rice, wheat, soybeans, corn, sorghum, oats, barley, and cotton. Because the country's population is six hundred million and its arable land is limited, every square meter of soil must be used for growing foodstuffs. There are no uncultivated spots. We saw some of the tiniest plots of land imaginable, literally a meter long; all were cultivated and tended with the greatest care. Hilltops, hillsides, and knolls—all are under cultivation.

To obtain crops from land like this requires a great deal of hard labor: clearing the hills of stones; terracing the hillsides; contriving primitive methods of drawing water from nearby ponds with buckets and troughs; dividing the water among the different plots; fertilizing the land with buckets of manure sedulously collected even from roads that cattle traverse; and constantly tending every sprout by hand. Yet all this is done, since every handful of seeds is necessary to sustain life. And seeds are by no means the only things necessary. The Chinese have a saying: "We eat everything that grows, walks, swims, crawls, or flies."

Perhaps more than any other country in the world, China makes you feel that nothing is more precious than land, the giver of life. With superhuman effort, every bit of land has been reclaimed from wild rivers, swamps, bogs, ravines, mountainsides, and deserts. Until quite recently, the tools used were mainly the antique hoe and wooden plow. Today they have been replaced by the iron plow and, in state farms and leading co-operatives, by horse-drawn plows and more advanced equipment like combines. But in the villages the main propellant forces remain the mule, cow, and horse—and, in Guangdong province, the water buffalo.

Most of the work is still done by hand: collecting dung and other fertilizer; spreading the fertilizer on the earth; planting every budding sprout of rice individually in a flooded paddy; and watering areas that lack irrigation. Most of the harvesting of rice, tea, peanuts, sugar cane, jute, ramie, tobacco, and bananas is done by hand as well. In China, consequently, every liter of tea and sack of rice represents a far greater investment of human labor than in countries where agriculture has been mechanized. The mechanization of agriculture in China will release gigantic amounts of manpower, which can be put to use extracting the boundless riches secreted in the Chinese soil. Another great resource for the coming industrialization of China is the large class of artisans and craftsmen that are spread from village to village and survive by making various articles by hand.

A constant sight in the Chinese countryside is the family burial mound. For centuries past, the Chinese have buried their dead in their own land, the poor peasants on their farmsteads or on a patch of field, and rich city people in family burial grounds in the city outskirts. Communal cemeteries are rare. That is why the fields around the cities are dotted with small, well-tended, fenced-in burial mounds and gravestones, which grow in number from generation to generation.

Gazing at this meticulously parceled system of agriculture, at this land sown with gravesites, I thought how difficult it would be for our Chinese friends when the time came to industrialize their agriculture and open up their fields to powerful tractors, efficient seeding machines, and modern combines. Where will that kind of technology find room to expand? Yet the question will have to be answered quite soon. In fact, the question has already been posed by the victorious popular revolution, which must transform the production and lives of hundreds of millions of Chinese peasants.

China's rural inhabitants compose 86 percent of the population; by far, most are peasants. The story of the Chinese peasantry is one of centuries of backbreaking toil, mass famines, and high mortality rates caused by natural disasters, malnourishment, and disease. In Guomindang China, three-quarters of all cultivated land belonged to landlords and kulaks. Among those working the land, 70 percent were farmhands and poor peasants, and 20 percent were middle peasants. The overwhelming majority of landless peasants and peasants owning only tiny plots of land were forced to rent land from landlords and rich neighbors at usurious rates. Their farming implements—the hoe and the plow—and their irrigation systems had been in use since the days of slave labor. The searing droughts, disastrous floods, and outbreaks of mass famine brought death to millions and, in some years, tens of millions of peasants.

Apparently, in the face of these facts, Mao Zedong decided to revise the fundamentals of the Marxist-Leninist theory of socialist revolution. The cornerstone of this theory is the doctrine of the dictatorship of the proletariat and the preconditions for the victory of the socialist revolution and the construction of a socialist society. Of all the classes of bourgeois society, only the working class is consistently and unswervingly revolutionary in nature. It is free of the fetters of private property. The peasantry, for its part, is the natural and steadfast ally of the working class, under whose leadership it can make a successful revolution.

Mao Zedong rejected these fundamentals of Marxism-Leninism. He outlined partially and in popular form his new premises in a well-known interview with the French writer André Malraux, who became minister of culture under President Charles de Gaulle in 1959. This interview took place in Beijing on July 3, 1965. In the course of the conversation, Mao spoke more or less as follows:

"Stalin did not understand anything about the peasantry. It is quite possible for peasants to seize power."

When Malraux asked when he came to this conclusion, Mao replied, "I did not come to this conclusion. It was always there."

Mao went on to explain why he had always regarded the Chinese peasantry as more revolutionary in spirit than the working class:

"I once survived a long famine in Changsha. . . . Within a three-kilometer radius of my village, every tree had been stripped of its bark to a height of four meters; the starving population ate the bark. People who were forced to eat tree bark were better fighters for us than the taxi drivers and coolies of Shanghai.

"It is ridiculous to compare your kulaks with the poor in undeveloped countries. There is no such thing as abstract Marxism. There is concrete Marxism, which is applicable in China to concrete reality—to trees that stand like naked people because people stripped off their bark and ate it."

By the time of our visit to China, the agrarian reform movement had essentially run its course. These reforms dismantled the feudal and semi-feudal forms of land ownership and transferred the land to the peasantry. Land, cattle, and farming equipment owned by landlords, temples, monasteries, and other organizations, were taken from exploiters and divided among farm laborers, small tenants, landless peasants, and those with tiny parcels of land. In the interests of rapid agricultural development, rich peasants—kulaks—were allowed to keep their land if members of their own families or hired hands helped till it. Private ownership of land was retained. The right to rent, buy, and sell land and various semifeudal forms of rent were tolerated.

As I was told in one province after another, the agrarian reeducation program was enacted with the active participation of the peasant masses and served as a form of revolutionary schooling. This is how the reform was accomplished:

A group of party and agricultural specialists arrived in a village. Together with all the villagers, they made a careful inventory of all the land, farm equipment, and other property that belonged to the local landlord.

They then looked into the background, activities, and conduct of the land-lord and his family, taking written and oral testimony from the villagers and conducting interrogations. All too often, the picture that emerged was one of unbridled tyranny. One landlord raped a peasant's daughter, another made loans at usurious rates, a third beat a peasant so severely that he left him crippled, and so on. Each accusation was carefully in-vestigated, and the landlord was allowed to speak for himself at a com-munal peasant meeting. Sometimes these outpourings of criticism and self-criticism lasted for days and weeks, as they provided a cathartic means for reeducation and schooling in popular self-government.

If it were proven that the landlord was a criminal, the peasants them-selves decided his fate—exile from the village, death, or some other form of punishment. If there was no proof of any crime, and if the landlord and his family were willing to take on agricultural work themselves, they were apportioned land and farming equipment on roughly the same scale as the peasantry.

As a result of this agrarian reform, some three hundred million farm laborers, small tenant farmers, landless peasants, and those with tiny plots of land received enough land and equipment for viable agricultural production. The working peasant received credits, grain, and other forms of assistance from the state. State farms and cooperatives were set up in the villages. Although a secure livelihood remained a distant goal, the peasants' lot began to improve, and mass famine and death from starva-tion became increasingly rare.

"We no longer eat bark," said Mao, "but we have only one bowl of rice a day."

We stopped at a village as the autumn harvest was under way. The peasants here were relatively well fed. But not all of them could count on being well fed throughout the year. Many of the villagers were worried about making it to spring. As their saying goes, "Yellow and green do not go together"—the supply of grain may not last until the vegetables ripen.

Nonetheless, the agrarian revolution laid the basis for a continual in-crease in agricultural production and an end to the poverty and misery that had been the peasants' lot for centuries. Mao's subsequent proclamation of the "three red banners"[1] and his decision to create artificially unviable communes in the villages threw everything into a shambles and caused China's agriculture to suffer a major setback.

I gaze at the small and smaller plots of arable land and vegetable gardens that are cultivated meticulously and lovingly by hand. I gaze at the humble dwellings, which lack not only electricity but kerosene lamps and which at sundown sink into a darkness that is relieved only intermittently by the glow of family hearths, as though they are all part of a nationwide village of six hundred million souls. I gaze at these Chinese toilers' faces, so windblown, so sunbaked, and now so dear to me, at these chapped, shapely, wonder-working hands. I look at the peasants' faded, patched blue-cotton clothes.

I look, and in my mind I see the boundless grain fields of the Volga region with their columns of first-class tractors and combines. I see the villages of Krasnodar,[2] each one home to thirty thousand or fifty thousand people, each with comfortable urban-style apartments that are filled with radios and television sets. I see the villages of Central Asia lit by millions of electric bulbs. I see Palaces of Culture, schools, hospitals, and the homes of Uzbek and Tajik peasants in the Fergana Valley. I see, somewhere around Poltava,[3] the marvelous holiday garb, little morocco leather boots, and necklaces of girls with multicolored ribbons in their hair.

Remembering this, I think: We still have so many unresolved problems in our villages—backwardness, a lack of amenities, and outright poverty. Nonetheless, how boldly and far we have come in providing the peasant with working and living conditions that are worthy of a citizen of a socialist society! In this respect, the Chinese are still only at the beginning of the road. No matter! China is endowed with a limitless supply of material resources and manpower. The Chinese are imbued with phenomenal discipline. Under proper party leadership, the Chinese peasantry can cover the distance from feudal backwardness to socialist civilization in an unprecedentedly short period of time, however great the difficulties along the way.

But now the rural landscape is behind us. We are in Tianjin. This is the third-largest city in China, after Shanghai and Beijing, with a population of 2.7 million, including 570,000 industrial workers. The city was growing even in the thirteenth century. A hundred years ago, it was occupied by British and French troops and fell prey to imperialist exploitation. It was a major center of textile and food production, woodworking, and other industries; it was a major railway hub and port on the Grand Canal. Yet all its key economic positions were under the control of British,

French, Japanese, Russian, and Belgian concessions. The popular revolution that put an end to all forms of imperialist domination was followed by the construction and renovation of the city's metallurgical, machine-tooling, papermaking, chemical, and other industries.

The secretary of the city party committee had been a student in Moscow at the Communist University of the Toilers of the East, where he attended lectures given by Stalin. Now, together with the deputy mayor and the head of the city labor-union committee, he takes us on a tour of Tianjin. This is a fully modern city of the European type. Multistoried buildings and splendid town houses that once belonged to the sharks of financial capital. Comfortable hotels. Large stores. Today all this is the property of the people. The former British club is now a workers' club. One of the city's finest buildings is now the Palace of Culture. Here is the State Bank, there the campuses of Beiyang and Nankai Universities. Theaters. Music conservatories.

We are shown around a large textile plant that employs seven thousand workers. Once the property of Japanese capital, it is now a nationalized Chinese enterprise. Well-lighted factory shops; clean, polished floors. Female workers in neat factory uniforms. Modern automated machinery. Framed in red cotton, an honor roll of socialist competitors, with portraits of outstanding workers.

We chat with workers, engineers, and management about production goals, working conditions, and wage levels. As always, Khrushchev bustles about, asking questions, trying to show off his technological expertise, and offering instructions on what should and should not be done. His Chinese hosts smilingly nod their heads in unison, agreeing with everything he says. Studying these rhythmically nodding faces that are wreathed in goodwill, their rows of white and yellow teeth evident in fixed smiles, I cannot help but think: They put their whole trust in us. They are so well disciplined that they are in full agreement with what Khrushchev has said to them; they will be in agreement with whatever he and other Soviet people tell them now and in the future.

At lunch in the Palace of Culture, many ardent, heartfelt, and sincere toasts are raised. Everything is suffused with unshakable faith in the undying nature of the Soviet-Chinese friendship.

We return to Beijing after sundown. The villages on either side of us plunge into impenetrable darkness. At midnight, we board a special express train for Shanghai. A perfectly comfortable compartment: two convertible beds, a writing desk, a revolving chair, a large mirror, a sink, and a revolving fan. We are attended by a charming and courteous young woman named Wang. She tells us she has completed eight grades of school and is preparing to continue her education.

The next morning we find ourselves in east China. The density of the 147 million people who live in this coastal area is striking. It is raining, but literally every square meter of the great Chinese plain is alive with intense labor. Peasants in straw covers—men, women, adolescents, and children—and many without protection from the rain are astir in the fields. Here the work of sowing, cultivating, and sowing again goes on year round—rice, *chumiza*,[4] sorghum, peanuts, carrots, lotus, wheat, corn, and potatoes. The lovingly tended earth yields two or three harvests a year.

The Huang He—the Yellow River—comes into view; it is China's second longest, stretching over 3,600 kilometers.[5] Rich in silt from the loess through which it flows, it is as yellow as our Amu Dar'ia.[6] It is a capricious river that every so often changes course. It is a life-giving river, providing millions with their sustenance, but also an unruly river that brings monumental disaster and destroys the work of millions when it overflows its banks and breaches its dikes and dams.

Approaching Nanjing, our train is ferried across the Yangtze River, China's longest (5,200 kilometers)[7] and one of the longest in the world. Here we are in the country's southern capital with a population of one million. As an ancient Asian city, Nanjing in many ways reminds one of Beijing. But here there is more greenery, and the majestic Yangtze gives the city a special charm. The picturesque suburbs bear a certain resemblance to those of our Black Sea garden spots, Sochi and Sukhumi—emerald bamboo groves, giant cedars and plane trees, and a thick carpet of subtropical plants.

The city is a beehive of activity. People are dressed mostly in traditional blue cotton, but many are in wide-brimmed straw hats and straw skirts and coats. The rickshaw pullers are everywhere—in front of stores, at intersections, in the alleyways—waiting patiently for fares.

A handsome road bordered with laurel, bamboo, plane trees, and roses takes us to Purple Mountain, the site of the mausoleum of the illustrious son of the Chinese people, the ardent champion of Soviet-Chinese friendship, Sun Yat-sen. A wide granite staircase with four hundred steps ascends to the mountaintop, where the mausoleum of white marble and granite is capped with blue tiles. A tombstone and a statue of Sun Yat-sen mark the patriot's final resting place. The Soviet delegation placed a wreath on the grave. At the Temple of Azure Clouds,[8] we saw the silver coffin of Sun Yat-sen that the Soviet government sent to China in the past.

A clear morning. The rain has stopped. The air is fragrant with decaying grasses and pine. From the top of the mountain we can see the whole of Nanjing and the sprawling estuary of the mightiest of all Chinese rivers, the Yangtze. Nanjing is a major river port that is capable of berthing large seagoing vessels. Leaving the mausoleum, we visit a mass grave of Chinese revolutionaries. During the years of the Chiang Kai-shek dictatorship, some hundred thousand communists and other revolutionaries were executed here, around Yuhua Tai. We place a wreath before a monument to their memory. Great were the sacrifices that the victory of the Chinese people's revolution exacted!

On the way back to Nanjing, we stop at the tombs of ancient Chinese emperors and marvel at the gigantic statues of fantastic creatures—winged lions and chimera, "guardians of the graves" that were erected in the fifth and sixth centuries. Preserved here since the Ming dynasty are gigantic statues of warriors, government figures, and animals—an incomparable museum of ancient Chinese sculpture.

We continue on our way south, accompanied by the mayor of Shanghai and a group of party workers from that city. During lunch in the dining car, Khrushchev, with true Russian hospitality, plies them with dishes and asks about various aspects of Chinese life, but does most of the talking himself, dispensing advice and instructions on various subjects, mainly agriculture.

The valley of the Yangtze River. A great blue river,[9] the third-longest in the world, equaling the Amazon in length. It finds its source somewhere above the clouds in the icy heights of the Tibetan mountains and rushes down toward the sea. Its basin is home to more than two hundred million people, more than the entire population of the United States; its population density per square kilometer is fifty times the American average.

We are in Shanghai. The streets throb with life, cars glide by, and according to some mysterious rules of its own, my memory evokes a song that I used to sing as a boy a half-century ago.

Peking, Nanking, and Canton[10]
Sat down in a phaeton
And rode off to Shanghai
To buy some Chinese tea.

I am in Ashkhabad, it is evening, and the city, wilting in the scorching heat of the desert, begins to stir. From outside the gates of our yard comes the sound of a rattle. We boys, barefoot, in torn shorts, our skin scratched and chocolate brown, run toward the sound, and come upon a Chinese man and woman attired in their eternal blue-cotton cloth. In her right hand the woman holds a rattle, and from her left dangles a wealth of multicolored fans, paper lanterns, Chinese dolls, and various toys. With a mixture of curiosity and fear, we gaze at her tiny bound feet, which look as though they were fettered in wooden boots. She moves with difficulty; any minute she may fall.

Spreading a thin straw mat on the sun-cracked earth, the man puts down a bundle and lays out a variety of fabrics that are wrapped carefully in canvas—velvet, silk, tussah. Our childish imaginations are fired by their richness and bright colors. "Tussah, tussah, good tussah, buy my tussah!" the man exclaims in a reedy voice, revealing his big yellow teeth. The woman redoubles her rattling to attract customers.

Gradually, people in our building are drawn to the scene. A handsome father with curly hair and dirty, muscular hands, which are never scrubbed entirely clean of the thick oily grime of metal and petroleum, stops by. A mother puts down her great tub of laundry and stands there, staring with pity at the Chinese woman; she goes home and returns with a big bunch of dark violet grapes. The woman accepts the gift with a prolonged, rhythmic, doll-like bobbing of her head.

From his remote, clay-brick cottage, the athletic Nikolai, a hunter and snake catcher, appears on the scene. The large brood of the shopkeeper Arzumanian arrives in a swarm. The commotion lures the tax official Semenkin, a grim character with a mustache yellow from tobacco that makes us tremble, out of his enchanting apartment. The largest part of the audience, of course, comprises us barebellied brats with freckles and shaven heads or matted hair.

The Chinese man pats his merchandise, clicking his tongue and repeating his sales pitch. I am sorry to say that I don't remember anyone in our building buying even an archine of velvet or silk, or a paper toy. Losing hope of selling anything, the man smiles and exclaims: "Tricks! Tricks! Tricks!"

Moving aside several bolts of material, he places two porcelain cups upside down on the straw mat. Digging under his clothes for an ivory chopstick and a small ball, he proceeds with his magic, which always leaves us entranced. The ball mysteriously disappears from under one cup and reappears under the other. Then it disappears altogether and to general cries of amazement reappears in my redhead friend Iurka's ear.

Relishing his success, the man digs under his clothes a second time and brings out a small basket, apparently made from a hollowed-out pumpkin that is covered in bast. Its top is removed, and out of the basket a snake rises. A real live snake. The man takes the snake by the gills in two fingers and inserts its head in his nose. Everyone cries out in fear and astonishment. The snake flicks its tail a few times and emerges partially from the man's mouth. Holding out his soiled hat, the man, with the snake still in his nose and mouth, makes a round of the spectators. Oohing and aahing, the grown-ups place an assortment of coins in the hat. The women bring the vendors and magicians some food. The Chinese couple disappear. For days afterward, we boys argue about what we have seen, and try with saucers and string rather than snakes to reproduce the man's magic.

A dark velvet night has spread over the earth. To cool off, we six brothers often sleep next to our father on the adobe-brick roof. In the spring, grass and even poppies sprout in the cracks. The stars shed their mysterious glow. From the Officers' Club comes the sound of the melancholy waltz "In the Hills of Manchuria." I keep thinking of the Chinese magician. In my mind, I see a collection of curious creatures prancing and hopping around him, vanishing and reappearing in swirls of smoke. The creatures are named Peking, Nanking, and Canton. They drag me somewhere—to the blue mountain, an abyss, or Shanghai for some tea. The phaeton is occupied by the Chinese woman with the rattle, with a snake writhing from each ear. When I clamber into the phaeton, she kicks me in the stomach with a wooden boot, and both snakes stretch their heads toward me. I scream in terror.

My father is peacefully asleep next to me. Silence, broken only by the chirring of cicadas. I press myself against my father's back. Where is

Manchuria? Canton is probably a gentle furry creature. There are lots of lanterns in Manchuria, and ivory chopsticks for magic tricks.

Who could imagine that this barefoot, chocolate-brown youngster with a shaven head, broken nails, and skin scratched from climbing trees would, a half-century later, find himself in the country he had dreamed of in childhood? Who could imagine that I would visit those mysterious, fearsome, and fabulously beautiful cities that we mentioned in our naive and silly song, "Peking, Nanking, and Canton"? And I didn't just visit them. Who could imagine that I would be welcomed there with open arms as a Russian, a Soviet, an emissary of the great socialist union?

We are given rooms in a comfortable hotel, the Shanghai, and taken on a round of visits, receptions, interviews; we sightsee around the city and the port area and take tours of industrial and other enterprises—everything that accrues to a friendly diplomatic mission. At the first opportunity, all of us, including Khrushchev, take the elevator to the rooftop of our seventeen-story hotel. What a magnificent and unforgettable view!

Shanghai, ancient Shanghai, was founded in the third century BCE and has become a gigantic industrial center with a population of six million. The city sits alongside the Huangpu River, a tributary of the Yangtze; its waterfront, Sun Yat-sen Boulevard, and its main street, Nanjing Road, are lined by tall, well-designed buildings: banks, skyscrapers, luxurious homes, restaurants, and movie houses. The crimson city lights play over an assortment of parks and gardens.

To the east and north lie the city's industrial centers, Chapei and Yangzipu, with more than thirteen thousand industrial enterprises; to the south are the shopping districts. Along with Suzhou Creek, which empties into its waters, the Huangpu River teems with ships, barges, and junks. The mighty waterway fades in the purple distance to the west, where thirty to thirty-five kilometers away it flows into the Yangtze.

At one time, Shanghai was situated on the East China Sea and served as a maritime gateway to China. Then the coastal waters were silted up by the Yangtze, and the river delta changed location. Shanghai was left some distance away from the sea but remained the most important Asian port on the Pacific littoral, as the Huangpu remained deep enough to accommodate the largest oceangoing vessels.

We tour Shanghai's various sectors and see the lasting impact of the colonial era on the country's biggest city. More than a century ago, Shanghai was lost to Chinese rule. The country's principal port was declared an open city. Before long, control of customs in Shanghai fell into the hands of the British, French, and American consulates, and the city was carved up into foreign settlements under their own independent governments. These settlements spread over thousands of hectares, swallowing up whole areas of industrial and commercial activity and enjoying extraterritorial rights on Chinese soil. In the English settlement, we were shown a sign preserved from those days: "No Chinese Allowed."

The formerly foreign sectors of the city are filled with luxurious homes, high-rises, spacious stores, cafés, clubs, swimming pools, massage parlors, and dens of vice, designed to cater to any taste and whim, that are no longer in use. We also took in another Shanghai, which in the intervening five years had not yet cast off the legacy of the wretched colonial past, a Shanghai of gloomy alleyways; paltry hovels made of mud, plywood, and tin; and squalid shops and eateries. No wonder the world's worst slums are called "shanghais."

The unfortunates inhabiting these warrens—children and adults— knew nothing of clean air, greenery, or potable water. Millions were born here in abysmal poverty, suffered throughout life from innumerable diseases, and went to their graves, generation after generation, without ever experiencing any of the pleasures of life. These were the haunts of opium dens, whose principal suppliers were the British, and of bands of women who had lost all hope of finding work and were forced into prostitution. Entrenched here were the gambling dens of criminal gangs, who terrorized the defenseless population.

The city party committee gave a formal dinner in our honor. Among those present were the city's officialdom and some members of the elite intelligentsia. Khrushchev ate and drank a lot and, as usual, joked about Mikoian. At every opportunity, he informed his listeners that as a child, he herded cattle, and when older, worked as a miner.

This dinner introduced me to the riches and delicacies of Chinese cuisine. In Beijing we had our own residence and kitchen. Everything was prepared by our own chefs from products flown in from Moscow. Khrushchev was a formidable gourmand on a "Rassian" scale.[11]

Everyone knows how sparing and frugal Lenin and his family were in matters of food. His apartment in the Kremlin reflects this side of his life. Lenin's friends and colleagues relate that even after the New Economic

Policy (NEP)[12] put an end to hunger in the country, lunch for Lenin and his family normally consisted of soup and a light entrée, and supper, of a sandwich and tea with jam. His guests, both Soviet and foreign, had to content themselves with this meager fare. The same austerity and moderation were true of Lenin's closest comrades.

At Stalin's "nearby dacha," the formal dinners that were frequently given for foreign communist leaders, industrial designers, diplomats, military officers, writers, and others were more generous than that. But on the whole, the servings were modest and plain. There was no profusion of dishes. There were no servants: everyone helped himself from a sideboard.

For Khrushchev, food was an extremely important part of life. With his ascension to power, a large army of special servitors was mobilized to satisfy his appetite not only at his Moscow home and dacha but wherever he happened to be. Khrushchev loved rich and fatty food—borscht with chunks of boiled meat, lard, pork dishes of one kind or another, pancakes with sour cream, Ukrainian cheese and cherry dumplings (also with butter and sour cream), meat dumplings, and all kinds of rich and spicy appetizers. He preferred large portions that were accompanied by quantities of vodka and cognac. His food followed him everywhere. Wherever he was—the Kremlin, a CC plenum, a Politburo meeting, a Supreme Court session, the reviewing stand at the Lenin mausoleum, a stadium at Luzhniki, or the Bolshoi Theater—whatever he was doing, he and his retinue could count on a generous hot meal and a wide selection of drinks.

In Beijing, the Khrushchev cult of gastronomy remained in force. One of the little houses in our compound was made into a dining room. Here we gathered at mealtimes to partake of Moscow's choicest delicacies. The minister of state security, Ivan Serov, was put in charge of the culinary arrangements. (He was assigned the same duties during Khrushchev's subsequent travels and at various receptions in Moscow.) Khrushchev was very fussy about food and often bawled out, "Serov! Why is the soup cold?" "Ivan Aleksandrovich! Have you decided to feed us unsalted cutlets?" "Serov! Where's the *vobla?*"[13] Serov, usually seated at the far end of the table, would jump up from his chair, and hurry into the kitchen to get things fixed.

Seeing these scenes and hearing his yelping, I couldn't help but think: What a humiliating, serflike role for this man who is a member of the

CC, the minister of state security, and an army general! Would Feliks Dzerzhinskii have permitted anything like this kind of behavior? Even comparing Dzerzhinskii and Serov insults the memory of that noble knight of the revolution.

On our forays out of Beijing, we ate Chinese food. Helping himself abundantly to all the dishes, Khrushchev lectured us: "Enough, enough with the boiled dumplings and borsht. We must get used to the national cuisine. Let Nikolai Mikhailovich [Shvernik] try some fried snake, and Iadgar [Nasriddinova] some stewed dog." As I had been on a strict diet for stomach ulcers for years, these meals were a real problem for me, since the wide variety of Chinese cuisine includes spicy and rich dishes and many flavorful herbs.

Actually, some of our diplomats who spent years in France, Switzerland, and the United States, and, as the saying goes, had been around, assured me that Chinese cuisine is the most diversified, the tastiest, and the most refined in the world. They admitted that it does surprise you at first with its unusual character, but soon enough you learn to appreciate its incomparable delights. I never presumed to doubt the judgment of these gourmands and comported myself impeccably at these Chinese dinners, as it behooves a guest. The same old-timers told me that at the Chinese emperors' banquets, different dishes were counted in the hundreds. I don't know how many dishes were served at our formal dinner in Shanghai, but I do remember some of them.

For appetizers, we had different kinds of sea slugs, morsels made from vegetables and fish, and, among the more exotic specialties, "thousand-year-old eggs," which were specially preserved in the ground until they began to look like black marble, as well as pickled baby loofah, snails with cauliflower, sea lotus roots, and pigeon eggs in seaweed. My favorite soup was swallows' nest. Our swallows build their nests out of mud; in China they do it out of tiny fish. Prepared and cooked from a special recipe, soup made from these nests is tasty and fragrant. There were also soups made from dried bamboo, sea lilies, and shark fins. The main course brought an endless variety of dishes: shrimp in bamboo puree, octopus coated with rice husks and served with cuttlefish sauce; fried shrimp in swallows' nests; stewed python in a special sauce; shark stomach with sea slugs; "the battle of the tiger and the dragon," which is a dish made of cat and snake meat; and much else. The alcoholic beverages included a kind of vodka that was marinated with seven different kinds of snake. Our Chinese friends assured us that these specially selected snakes heighten the tonic quality of the liquor and, like ginseng, strengthen the body.

Like all our meetings with our Chinese hosts, the dinner proceeded in such an unconstrained, cordial, and friendly atmosphere that we did not feel ourselves to be foreigners. Having seen something of Shanghai's industrial complex, we were more convinced than ever that the People's Republic of China was well on the way to socialist industrialization. The city's foreign industrial enterprises had been nationalized, although a few of them, like those belonging to the British, were left to their owners in order to "retain economic ties" with the countries in question. In addition to expanding traditional forms of light industry, like cotton and silk manufacturing, the new government began laying the foundations for and developing modern heavy industry—machine tooling, chemical, electrical, shipbuilding, construction, and so on.

We were fascinated by what we heard about the Chinese experience in the "peaceful transformation of capitalist to socialist industry." Enterprises owned by loyal bourgeoisie were developing along state capitalist lines. An example was the case of one major Shanghai capitalist, Rong Yiren, the owner of several textile plants, mills, and other factories. After the revolutionary victory, Rong's enterprises were made part of the state sector, but he was left in charge of many managerial, organizational, and manufacturing functions. The government remained in overall control. In compensation for his property and in payment for his work, Rong was allotted almost a quarter of the profits. He was also elected a deputy to the National People's Congress, where he often spoke critically of those entrepreneurs who violated the principles of state capitalism, and exhorted all and sundry to follow his example of loyal collaboration with the people's government.

Of course, even our cursory inspection of China's industry revealed enormous difficulties and unresolved problems. The industrial development of China was still in its early stages. Only now, with extensive help from the USSR, were the foundations laid for many modern forms of production. There was a need for a whole corps of trained workers and engineers. For example, of Shanghai's 1.5 million workers, only 200,000 were employed in heavy industry; the remainder, in effect, were craftsmen and artisans engaged in small-scale manufacturing. Added to that were more than 200,000 unemployed persons.

Still, these difficulties could be overcome. The first five-year plan for China's economic development—1953–57—pointed in the right direction by creating an industrial base and expanding heavy industry, transport, light industry, agriculture, and trade. The Soviet Union was committed to providing economic and technical assistance and to training the scientific and technical personnel required for putting this help to use. Ahead lay a clearly defined and scientifically proven road for transforming China into a mighty socialist industrial and agricultural power. For a number of years afterward, China advanced steadily on this, the only right road.

Subsequent developments like Mao Zedong's invention of the "Great Leap Forward" and the "people's communes," violations of Marxist principle that workers and collectives benefit from the results of their work, and the frenzied outrages that were sanctioned throughout the country under the banner of the Cultural Revolution, threw everything into confusion. China's economy was shaken to its foundations and hurled into the past.

A memorable part of our visit was a boat trip along Shanghai's waterways. Shanghai is an Asian Venice, encompassing the mighty Huangpu River, Suzhou Creek, and dozens of small streams, creeks, and canals. This watery kingdom teems with life. As a port, Shanghai handles about half of China's foreign trade. Gigantic seagoing vessels glide constantly and majestically along the Huangpu. The wharves with their warehouses and cranes stretch for more than twenty kilometers. The port of Shanghai can accommodate and process more than 150 vessels simultaneously.

But most of the boats in these waters are junks. I think it was Zhou Enlai who told us that up to twenty million people live in junks and sampans in China. They are born on their junks, live on their junks, feed themselves from the marine life and grasses of the rivers, and die on their junks. How many people live on junks in Shanghai? No one, of course, has made an exact count. But the mayor told us that when revolutionary forces came to power in Shanghai, the city's water-borne population numbered no less than one hundred thousand.

How disparately the junks served the needs of families and the country! Some are huge, others tiny. Some have engines, others sails or sculls. There are cargo ships and passenger boats, houseboats and fishing boats. They are seagoing and river-bound. Some have awnings; others do not. Some attempt to be elegant floating pleasure houses and brothels; others are dilapidated, with gaping holes in their sides and other signs of extreme poverty. Some are designed to transport valuable goods; others carry manure. Some have a deep draft; others are flat-bottomed. Until recently, these junks were home to the poorest of the poor—rickshaw pullers, longshoremen, common laborers, criminals, and prostitutes. Today, the people's government is gradually leading this humiliated and destitute part of the population to a new life.

Night fell. We are cruising up the Huangpu in a motorboat. The water reflected a million multicolored lights. Moonlight played over the skyscrapers on the waterfront. The river smelled of slime and fish. The bustle of the great metropolis was winding down. Mikoian, Shvernik, Furtseva, the *Pravda* correspondent Domogatskikh, and I decided to wander about the city for the next few hours.

The windows of the larger stores are grated. There are no lights within. But the main streets are well lighted. There is a profusion of illuminated billboards. From the nightclubs and restaurants comes the sound of voices and jazz. Some fruit stores are still open. Street vendors proffer candy, fruit, bottled water, and meat patties. The rickshaw pullers call out for fares. The city hums.

We went into a restaurant. All the tables were taken. From the way they were dressed, the customers seemed to be well off—entrepreneurs, perhaps, or the intelligentsia. There were many Europeans. Mikoian fell into conversation with a European couple, who were here on business from the Netherlands. Many people recognized Mikoian and greeted him warmly.

Now we are on the central waterfront. Here we see luxurious homes, skyscrapers, and banks, once the property of British, Japanese, American, and Chinese capitalists. Among the latter, there is a stellar place that was home to the family of Chiang Kai-shek, one of the four wealthiest families in China—the same Chiang Kai-shek who is now under American protection in Taiwan. Here it's like being on Broadway in New York. A sea of lights. A marble embankment. Decorative shrubbery. Young people, festive and beaming, are dancing on the waterfront to the sound of a harmonica. We were given a warm reception on the dance floor. To the vast delight of the young, Furtseva and Shvernik joined the Chinese in a dance.

Violating protocol, no doubt, we ventured into the British consular compound. It was practically empty, with only one diplomat left. The building had a lovely garden. Either by chance or as a lesson for future generations, the garden was protected by barbed wire. The barricades and the signs "No Chinese Allowed" were graphic reminders of the position once occupied by the Chinese in their own country.

Mikoian, Domogatskikh, and I proceeded to one of the workers' districts. It is midnight, yet here, at a narrow, crooked crossroads, the night shift is busily at work. A group of stevedores sets off on some job. The ubiquitous rickshaw pullers hawk their services. Here and there, portable kitchens operate under the open sky. Something is boiling and frying in those pots and pans. The street peddlers have laid out their stocks of bananas, persimmons, and dried fruit. A vendor plaintively offers his bottles of colored and sweetened soda water. A toothless old man with two baskets of grapes on a pole across his back hawks their contents—a big bunch for three thousand yuan. There is a pleasant aroma of fried meat, smoke, and some kind of fragrant grass.

Mikoian and I sit down at a table next to a group of men. With amazing dexterity they are putting away some kind of noodle soup with their chopsticks. We are served something resembling our *pel'meni*,[14] and cups of rose-colored water.

With Domogatskikh interpreting, we engaged the group in conversation. One of the men is a spinner, the second a glassblower, a third a coolie. They responded to our questions with outward goodwill and pleasure. The word "Russian" has a magical effect. In their every word and action we felt the sincere desire of all classes of Chinese people to please us in some way.

Leaving the industrial bustle of Shanghai behind us, we arrived at one of China's most beautiful spots, Hangzhou, at dawn on October 9. No wonder the Chinese say, "In heaven there is paradise, and on earth there is Hangzhou." This is the principal city of Zhejiang province, which has a population of twenty million. Founded in the fifth century, Hangzhou was the capital of the Southern Song dynasty in the twelfth and thirteenth centuries. From the earliest times it was renowned for its beautiful silks, velvets, fans, and bamboo products. More recently, it was a favorite vacation resort for the foreigners and the Chinese elite. Today, as is only natural, it is a center for sanatoria and vacation homes for urban and rural workers, for Hangzhou is truly paradise on earth.

The city embraces West Lake, a large lake of crystalline purity that picturesquely sits beneath Precious Stone Mountain. Everything is green—palms, banana trees, bamboo groves, weeping willows, chestnut trees, beeches, lacquer trees, perennial oaks, and fruit orchards. Today, going over the many photographs bestowed on me by our hospitable Hangzhou hosts, I think back to the incomparable sights of that magic kingdom. Here is the botanical garden with its luxuriant subtropical plants. There, nestled among cypresses, marigolds, and walnut trees, is a memorial gate. Somewhere else, the causeway that the poet Su Dongpo constructed. Yellow Dragon Cave. Baochu Pagoda. Nine-Lion Rock. A quiet lagoon overgrown with lotus. Brocaded Belt Bridge.[15] The fretted and multistoried Six Harmonies Pagoda. Mount Hua, somehow reminiscent of our twin-peaked Mount Elbrus.[16] Jade Spring with its fantastic large black and yellow fish who are unruffled by our boisterous gestures and exclamations. What blessed silence! The pleasant scent of oak wafts on a gentle breeze.

I strike up a conversation with a group of vacationers from various provinces: a jovial young man who is a rolling-mill operator from the Anshan[17] metallurgical complex; a young woman from a tobacco factory; and an elderly codger with large yellow teeth who is a longtime weaver. "Today," he tells me, "my salary is up 20 percent since liberation. Moreover, taxes have been drastically reduced, and prices have been stabilized. In effect, I make much more than before."

We are at the grave of the eminent eleventh-century military leader Yue Fei,[18] who fought bravely for his homeland against the nomadic invaders from the north but was betrayed and killed by a palace clique. Standing at the approach to the gate to his monument are two cast-iron statues of the traitor and his wife, the couple most responsible for his death. The Chinese revere the memory of the glorious warrior, and hundreds visit his grave every day. But before paying homage to the hero's memory, every Chinese visitor spits on these statues and pelts them with stones and all kinds of filth, so that day after day, year after year these memorials to dishonor stand besmirched.

In later years, I often recalled the statues of these villains and the ritual that sprang up among the people. Prior to Khrushchev's fall, his name became hateful among all strata of the population, people of all ages and walks of life. Old and young referred to him solely as Nikitka, Khrushch,

Kukuruznik, and Grishka Rasputin. I let my imagination wander: If Khrushchev had walked the streets without bodyguards after his ouster, perhaps the people's wrath would have overflowed, and every passerby would have spit in the face of yesterday's lord and master. In all likelihood, however, these were not the factors that prompted Khrushchev's successors to supply this eminent pensioner with an impressive security guard.

It would be wrong to leave China without taking in a Buddhist temple or monastery. Although Khrushchev and Mikoian excused themselves, we took the opportunity to visit the ancient Lingyin Si, the Temple of the Soul's Retreat—which was home to forty monks, the Sixth Contemplation and Jade Spring Monasteries, and some temples.

Buddhism began to develop in China in the first century;[19] in the fourth to seventh centuries, having amassed great wealth in land and other resources for temples and monasteries, the Buddhist religion became a great force. Granted, in later centuries Buddhism began to lose ground to Confucianism, the dominant official religion, but even as late as the twentieth century, it continued to play an influential role in the country's economic and political life. The arrangements and rituals at the monasteries and the Hall of Five Hundred Buddhas,[20] which we also visited, were living examples of how, on one hand, religion attunes itself to the hopes and longings of those who "labor and are heavy-laden" and, on the other hand, how the parasitical classes have been able to manipulate religion to keep the exploited and defenseless in subjugation.

Hundreds of millions of destitute persons have been living and dying in India, China, Burma, Mongolia, Japan, and countries of Southeast Asia on a bare subsistence level. They are destroyed by backbreaking labor. They starve. They are mowed down by epidemics. They lack proper shelter. They are helpless in the face of their children's illnesses. When will there be an end to their suffering? What can be done?

In all its forms, Buddhism answers: Yes, you are suffering. Yes, you are destitute. Suffering is the essence of life. But there are Buddhas [arhats] who have freed themselves from suffering. Gautama Buddha left his palace and wealth while still a young man and experienced all the sufferings of the common man. He was a preacher, an elephant driver, a slave, and even an untouchable. In subsequent reincarnations he was a frog, a turtle, and a jackal. He experienced everything. Soon, prior to finally entering nirvana, he will return to earth to redeem all those who suffer.

He will not be the only one to return. With him he will bring thousands of deities and subdeities, the bodhisattvas, who will help all the needy and burdened to enter nirvana, the state of ultimate bliss.

Approaching the monasteries and temples we saw hundreds of statues of various Buddhas with different faces and in different poses. But all the Buddhas in this group are benevolent deities. Their faces are white, their cheeks plump and rosy, and their lips full and crimson. They have the kindest smiles and capacious, hanging stomachs—evidence of constant and tasty nourishment. Their entire appearance seems to say, you are a pariah, a slave, an unfortunate. But if you submit, if you don't oppose evil with violence, if you cease to resist and rebel, you can attain bliss. The deities and bodhisattvas will help you do so.

The local temple contrived many ways for the believers to make their offerings to the Buddhas, cajoling them into volunteering mercifully and generously on their behalf. We saw these offerings and the smoking incense sticks and heard about the extortions to which the faithful were subjected in exchange for "healings," "exorcism of evil spirits," "cures for infertility," "prolongation of life," "cures for snakebites," and "rainmaking."

But the greatest desire of all is for the coming of the messiah, the advent of Gautama Buddha, who will bring solace to the destitute and establish paradise and eternal bliss in heaven and earth. The Buddhist church keeps the faithful in this state of expectation. In the hall with the famous statue of the sleeping Buddha, we even see a pair of slippers: when the Buddha awakes he can put them on and begin to exist.

But not all the gods are kind. In these same monasteries we see hundreds of statues of the most ferocious creatures, with faces distorted in anger, bared fangs, protruding eyes, and twisted bestial arms. In line with the church's social teaching, these gods threaten people with the tortures of the damned and with terrible punishments for breaking the rules of nonresistance to evil, failing to make offerings to the monasteries and temples, and other transgressions. Moreover, the maledictions and tortures that are the wages of disobedience fall not only on present transgressors but on future generations as well. They will remain in force for thousands of years.

In the monasteries and temples we saw many tour groups of young people. With a meticulousness that is truly Chinese, they listened to everything that they were told about religion, asked questions, and wrote everything down.

In a village near Hangzhou, we visited the former estate of a landlord and prominent merchant. All the rooms are tastefully and luxuriously furnished. The houses are connected by magnificent yards, a garden, and a park. A string of lakes and ponds winds around the estate like a blue necklace. The landlord had twelve wives and was a despot to the peasants. During the people's revolution, he was killed in a peasant uprising. Today this is a vacation center. The management treated us to soup made from freshly caught fish, and fried fish in a sweet sauce.

We return by car to Hangzhou. Fields. Gardens. Once again we were impressed by the care shown toward every foot of arable earth. We pass a nursery devoted to dragon cypresses and palms. Marvelous subtropical vegetation, a little like in our Crimea but more profuse and varied, perhaps because the air is softer and more humid. All this makes me all the more impatient to see the southernmost, tropical city of Guangzhou (Canton), which is China's southern gate and which from ancient times provided the country with trade routes to India, Indonesia, and Indochina. A city with a two-thousand-year history. The city where the activities of the great revolutionary democrat Sun Yat-sen reached their maturation. The city that was the center of many workers' and soldiers' uprisings, and wars against imperialist domination.

Our IL-14 makes a smooth landing at the Guangzhou airport. The whole sky is burnished with blinding sunlight. The air is warmed to thirty-five-degrees centigrade and carries the tropical breath of the East China Sea. Guangzhou residents have never seen snow. The mean temperature in January is fourteen to sixteen degrees centigrade.

Spread out along the Pearl River, the city has a population of more than a million, and it has its own special characteristics, resembling neither Beijing nor Shanghai. The river is yellowish white. The new city has straight, broad avenues and many modern European buildings, whose ground floors have arcades that shield pedestrians from the blazing sun. It is the site of a university that Sun Yat-sen founded thirty years previously, as well as other institutions of higher education, large stores, theaters, lyceums, schools, spacious children's playgrounds, and day-care centers. The old city, with its narrow twisting streets, low houses, primitive workshops, and paltry stores, bears the imprint of "age-old slumbering Asia."

We are on the banks of the Pearl River. In both directions, the waterway is filled with great "floating villages"—tens of thousands of junks and sampans moored next to one another. Our Guangzhou hosts tell us that under the Guomindang regime, the river was home to some 200,000 of the poorest of the poor. Because of the unsanitary conditions in which they lived, they were decimated by serious epidemics, including cholera, the plague, and smallpox. The people's government is taking steps to eliminate these floating villages, but some 50,000 to 60,000 people still live on the water.

We carefully studied the structure of the junk. Every junk and sampan is a home; its rooms are screened off from each other with canopies and planked wooden roofs. Some of the junks are clean and attractively decorated; others are revolting cesspits. On all sides there is the bustle of cooking, laundering, and fussing about with children. We chat with the people on one of the sampans: a hauler of cargo, an ivory carver, a rickshaw puller, and a common laborer. The young women playfully propose a boat ride. Unemployment and need are still rife, and prostitution has not yet been eliminated. The river is full of movement. Large, medium, and small sampans and junks glide silently by. Many of them have sails of different shapes and colors; many of the sails are patched rags. Other craft rely on muscle power; standing in the bow, the oarsman plies his crisscrossed oars smoothly and rhythmically, propelling and steering the boat.

We wander about the streets. There are crowds of people in the stores, small shops, eateries, and minuscule workshops. The stores, shops, and street stalls are crowded with all kinds of goods. There are a few manufactured goods and handicrafts from the old days. There is a row of craftsmen engaged in carving ivory. I approach the owner of one of the workshops.

He is the only worker, the seller of his own wares. He is also the head of a large family. He is a barefoot man of less than average height, in torn and patched clothes. He is all skin and bones, his face sunburned and wrinkled. He has lively, intelligent eyes and the kindest, nicest smile. His entire workshop is the size of a writing desk. A tiny workbench. A hand drill and some small ancient knives and awls. That's all. With these tools he is carving an ivory tower of such intricate work, such artistry, that it could easily be displayed in a museum. I express to him my admiration. In response, the magician's eyes and his work-worn face light up with such happiness that he seems ready to give me in gratitude everything that his skilled hands have created.

I find the same in the neighboring stalls of craftsmen who work with bamboo and silk (they make fans, trunks bound in buffalo hide, boxes, woven baskets, and hats), tinsmiths, furniture makers, toy makers, lacquerers, lace makers, porcelain dealers. I think that if these people with their simple wants, industriousness, and discipline were endowed with the prowess of modern technology, China could flood the world with all kinds of high-quality products. In addition to the Chinese, there are all the others—Russians, Indians, Africans, Americans, French, Italians. How abundant and beautiful life will be when we put an end to the disgrace of private capitalism throughout the world!

Today a typhoon is whipping up the seas. These storms often do great damage, leveling entire settlements in Hainan and other offshore islands and uprooting great tracts of orchards. So far the typhoon is distant, and this anthill of a city goes on with its business.

Physically, the people in Guangzhou look more like the Malays, Indochinese, and Indonesians. Their clothes also set them apart from persons in central and northern China. In Guangzhou and Guangdong province generally, one hardly ever sees people dressed in blue cotton cloth. Most people in Guangzhou wear black. The women comb back their shiny black hair. Many women go to work with infants fastened to their backs by a piece of cloth. The children patiently endure their unenviable lot— having to stare constantly at their mothers' backs. People in Guangzhou wear wide-brimmed straw hats, often adorned with Chinese characters. I bought such a hat. To this day it often reminds me of the distant and marvelous banks of the Pearl River.

The heat becomes stifling. But the city's pulse remains strong. The streets are alive with different kinds of automobiles, rickshaws, bicycles, and carts drawn by donkeys and water buffaloes. Lines of barefoot Guangzhou residents file by with baskets of bananas, grapes, pineapples, peaches, oranges, lemons, and lychees, which are something new to us, fruits with a mixed scent of apricot, pineapple, and tea roses. Everywhere one goes there are stalls, carts, small shops, and movable kitchens with all kinds of edibles and vegetables.

The waterfront is sheer pandemonium—the whooping of stevedores, the honking of automobiles, the clanging of streetcars, and the shrill sound of the electric bells used for directing traffic. What unusual colors, sounds, and scents! In contrast to Beijing and Shanghai, in Guangzhou there are hardly any Europeans, so we attract a lot of attention, particularly from young boys, who excitedly follow us in packs.

When we were leaving Beijing, one of the Chinese leaders told me, "When you are in Guangzhou, be sure to visit the Guangzhou market-place. It's been around for many centuries and has much of interest."

Here we are in the marketplace. Truly an unforgettable sight. Long lines of stalls with foodstuffs—vegetables, fruit, meat, fish. There are some shops with skinned carcasses. They look like mutton. Only their long tails reveal their identity: dogs. The tails are deliberately retained as proof that these are really dogs, for dog meat is more expensive than mutton or beef. Turtles, cats, and some unfamiliar creatures that look like lizards but are covered with reddish fur are on sale in neighboring stalls. All this finds its way onto the dinner table.

When we left for our tour of the country, Mao Zedong concluded his recommendations with a note of caution: "When you are in the south, you will be served snakes. Don't be afraid. Of course, that's true not only of the south. But in the south, it's only natural. If people in Guangzhou did not eat snakes, the snakes would eat Guangzhou."

We are in the snake stalls. The snakes in wire cages are of different sizes and colors. A massive python lies stone still. In other cages, snakes of various kinds have rolled themselves into balls. A customer approaches with a basket made from a hollow pumpkin. The owner lifts the selected snake by the gills with a pronged stick and drops it into the basket. I ask if the snakes are poisonous. The Chinese reply, "Poisonous. We don't eat the nonpoisonous kind. They're inedible."

We saw much of interest in an outlying state farm that grew bananas, pineapples, and rubber. The villages in Guangdong province have a special look to them. The reddish earth here is rich and fertile. The sunshine and moisture make it possible to raise three harvests of different grains annu-ally, and five to seven harvests of vegetables. The principal produce and main source of nourishment is rice. But many other crops are cultivated: tobacco, pineapple, peanuts, jute.

By the time of our arrival, the land reform program in Guangdong had been completed. Land belonging to the big landlords and the top civil and military bureaucracy had been given to the peasants, who banded together in cooperatives. The best of the landlords' holdings were made into state farms.

As everywhere in China, villages in Guangdong are densely populated. One peasant hut adjoins another; their blank walls face the narrow lanes. The yards of these houses are microscopic in size: every arable meter of land goes to cultivation. The interiors are incredibly congested. Wood pillars support a rectangular door frame. Walls are stone, adobe-brick, or clay-brick, depending on the region of the province. Slanting roofs are made of straw or reed in most areas, but in some places they are tile. The hearth provides fire for cooking and warmth for the wide bunks, which are also warmed through a flue. The bunks serve both for eating—low, heated tables are placed on their surface—and for sleeping. In the southern regions, small heaters are often placed outside the door.

Dusk. We are in a pleasant suburb, on the banks of one of the tributaries of the Pearl River. At one time this was the home of prominent industrialists and plantation owners. Sumptuous residences. Marvelous gardens. Tropical plants. In the yard of the house where I stay, there is a yard with a big cage where a family of monkeys turn somersaults and make faces at us. There is the screeching of parrots painted in the brightest hues I have ever seen.

These houses are now the homes of the general staff of the Chinese army. Exactly thirty years ago, Sun Yat-sen and the Chinese Communist Party founded the Huangpu Military Academy outside Guangzhou. The officers who were trained in this academy played a large role in the formation of the Chinese revolutionary army and the war of liberation that the army and the communist party waged in subsequent decades.

On the other side of the Pearl River, there is a row of houses standing on stilts. This river does not create unexpected and destructive floods the way the Yangtze does, but the incoming tide can raise the water level up to two meters. Quite a few houses have had to adapt to this daily rhythm.

That evening there was a formal dinner attended by party and government leaders of Guangzhou and Guangdong province and top military representatives. At last, Mikoian, Shvernik, Aleksandrov, and I braved the national dish, soup made from five snakes, that was recommended to us earlier. To me it tasted like good chicken bouillon. Khrushchev later ribbed us endlessly about our reptilian communion.

During dinner I had an interesting conversation with two party leaders, one from Guangzhou, the other from Beijing. Oddly enough, they couldn't understand each other, so different were their Chinese dialects. But it turned out that both had once studied in Moscow, at the Communist University of the Toilers of the East, and were thus able to communicate in Russian. That drew us together as a threesome.

The dinner passed in a lively and lighthearted atmosphere of mutual trust and sincerest friendship. There were toasts to Mao and Voroshilov, to the Soviet and Chinese armies, to the need for vigilance—we were next door to Hong Kong, after all, one of the largest British naval bases in Asia, a hotbed of provocations against the People's Republic of China—and to everything good. I looked around the table and glowed with happiness. Here we are, Russians, an Armenian, a Belorussian, an Uzbek woman, and Chinese, sitting at a table as likeminded communists and friends. As friends, we are prepared to share everything we have. We discuss matters of mutual importance. We all have high hopes for the future of socialist China. This feeling is indestructible. It will last forever.

Soon it will be India's turn and then Indonesia's turn to rouse themselves. Surely something will be coming from the French working class, with its glorious revolutionary traditions. And Italy? And seething Africa? Today one may say not only from the perspective of history but on the basis of events presently unfolding that the worldwide victory of socialism is inevitable.

Who would have thought that fourteen or fifteen years would go by and the Soviet army in all its might would descend on socialist Czechoslovakia one night and occupy all its cities and regions, and that Czechoslovakian party leaders, including first secretary Alexander Dubček, would be hauled off to Moscow in handcuffs? Who would have thought that somewhere on the unknown and uninhabited Damanskii Island, Soviet and Chinese troops, on orders from their governments, would shoot at each other with automatic rifles, machine guns, and cannons, and that those who distinguished themselves in this fratricide would be decorated with heroes' stars? One could not have imagined such an absurdity even in a feverish delirium.

Night, a violet tropical night. Mikoian, Shvernik, and I decided to go for a walk along the river before bedtime. The river, the gardens, and the groves are flooded with bright, mysterious moonlight. The air is filled with the scent of unfamiliar flowers and plants. The riverbanks shimmer like strands of pearls with the lights of village huts. Like huge, fantastic creatures, dimly lighted sampans creep along the river. No longer can we say, "The bells of age-old slumbering Asia have fallen silent." Asia is moving at full speed toward the radiant future, and no force on earth can stop it.

Awaiting me in my house was a bed draped with mosquito netting wide enough for six and windows that were covered with netting instead of glass. All the same, I was devoured by mosquitoes all night long, for I forgot to tuck in the netting around the bed. The house creaked under the force of the typhoon, now somewhere close.

In the morning, we bid a fond farewell to the Guangzhou leaders, both civil and military, and took off for Hankou and Beijing. During the flight, we saw what rivers could be like in China. The powerful yellow waters of the Yangtze seemed to have flooded the countryside from horizon to horizon. Here and there we saw sandy hillocks and sandbanks, rows of trees, and rooftops rising above the waters. The raging river leveled structures along its path and created foaming whirlpools that swallowed up rafts, small boats with torn sails, uprooted huts, and assorted debris. The dams and dikes swarmed with people, armies of laborers trying to restrict the extent of the flood.

From what we saw, the triumph of the people's revolution placed the ongoing battle with nature on a new foundation. During the previous decades, disorganized and ill-equipped gangs of peasants supervised the work. Millions perished in this uneven war. Now we visited a dam-construction site on the Yangtze River that employed what seemed to be millions of people. We weren't wrong.

The provincial leaders of Hebei province and later our friends in Beijing told us that the valleys of the unruly rivers were being lined by towering dikes hundreds of kilometers long. There were projects for creating reservoirs, strengthening old dikes, building new ones, deepening the riverbeds, reconstructing old canals, building others, and so forth. During our stopover in Hankou,[21] we talked to supervisors and ordinary workers who were engaged in this work, and once again we were deeply impressed by the fantastic scope of their planning, flawless discipline, and the totally unquestioning and respectful attitude of the common people toward the instructions and appeals of the government.

During our few hours in Hankou, the Yangtze flood turned into a national disaster. We were told that the flooded area this year covers 160 million square *mu*[22] and that the number of flood victims was close to 50 million. How much property, cattle, and crops were destroyed can only be imagined. A tidal wave of human suffering!

The government appealed to the people of the stricken provinces to join in the battle against the flood. The plan was to build dikes 1.5 to 2 meters high and dozens of kilometers long and high auxiliary dikes hundreds of kilometers long. Responding to the government's call, the Chinese picked up their mattocks, placed their bamboo poles with baskets hanging from each end across their backs, took bundles of provisions, and went forth to the construction sites. The result was an army of many millions of laborers in the river valleys. The cooperatives, state farms, and local authorities helped with teams of horses and cows. Machinery was still scarce.

It was necessary to see for oneself the full extent of the discipline and enthusiasm the volunteers brought to their task. Since Mao called on them and the government issued its instruction, the work was sacred. It had to be done well and on time. Filling two baskets with earth and hanging them on the pole across his back, the team worker jogs up the dike, empties his load on its crest, and hurries back for more. Thousands, tens of thousands, and millions of people throw themselves into this work with antlike industriousness. Before our eyes, men equipped with the most primitive tools erected great ramparts against future flooding.

A deep bow to you, you humble and patient Chinese laborer!

CHAPTER SIXTEEN

Mao and the Atomic Bomb

WE RETURNED TO BEIJING elated and exhilarated by what we had seen. The friendship between the Soviet and Chinese people was a living reality that would endure for ages. It had already penetrated the fabric of both societies. To understand how important this was for the USSR—and for China—it is necessary to recall that at the beginning of the 1950s, the United States was pursuing a foreign policy of "brinkmanship," maneuvering on the brink of war. The author of this policy was Secretary of State John Foster Dulles, with whom I had occasion to cross swords in later years. Dulles was one of the most militant apostles of aggressive American imperialism; the United States in those years flirted with outright military conflict.

One example was the disgraceful and dangerous operation that American intelligence organized a little more than a year before our China visit, the Berlin affair of June 17, 1953.[1] The purpose of the operation was to have authorities in West Berlin foment mass disorder in the capital and other regions of the German Democratic Republic (GDR) and thereby demonstrate popular discontent with the people's democratic government. The operation was facilitated by the fact that there was essentially no tangible border between the two Germanys at that time, and access to the new Germany from the Federal Republic of Germany (FRG) was relatively easy.

The Berlin provocation was organized carefully and well in advance. To help with the preparations, the Federal Ministry of All-German Affairs established a special center in West Berlin, camouflaged under the name Research Council on German Reunification. All the vultures of the land—former owners of businesses, banks, and industrial enterprises that had been expropriated and placed at the service of the people in the new Germany—flocked to this new council. In addition, American intelligence in West Berlin set up a so-called operational headquarters, which financed the training of mercenary thugs, provocateurs, and saboteurs, including recruits from the fascist League of German Youth.[2]

On June 17, on orders that emanated from the American sector of West Berlin, bands of rowdies poured into the streets and squares of the capital of the GDR, vandalizing and setting fire to state stores and enterprises and attacking government employees. Throughout the day, American trucks conveyed all kinds of fascist scum to the capital from the American sector. American officers barged into East Berlin in their jeeps to direct openly this orgy of sabotage and mayhem.

The provocation was an ignominious failure. But it served as a clear reminder that peaceful coexistence between countries with different social systems did not obviate the need to consolidate the socialist camp and all the forces of peace and democracy; on the contrary, the provocation highlighted its importance.

Returning to Beijing, we resumed talks with the Chinese on various questions about our mutual relations and international issues. Up to a certain point, these negotiations proceeded without difficulty and with unanimous agreement on all points. This was not fortuitous—the Soviet party and government were determined to do away with every trace and vestige of the formerly unequal relationship between the two countries. They sought to reach identical positions with the Chinese on all international issues affecting the interests of China and the USSR. They were fully ready to assist China in its economic development and to enter into the closest economic, technological, and cultural cooperation.

On this score, Khrushchev was resolute. Both before leaving for China and while in Beijing, he often said, "We'll treat the Chinese like brothers. We'll share our last crust of bread with them if we have to. First off, we must rid our relationship of everything that demeans the Chinese. Who came up with this idea for joint companies in China? You know,

Stalin even asked the Chinese to grant concessions to the Soviet Union for growing pineapples. Mao Zedong himself told me about it. He said, 'I told Comrade Stalin, why bother with concessions? If you need fresh or canned pineapples, let us know. We'll grow as many pineapples as you need, and deliver them to the Soviet Union ready to eat.'"

Khrushchev continued, "Did you ever hear anything so dumb?" Then he tapped his forehead with a crooked forefinger. "To hell with all that. Everything Chinese goes back to the Chinese."

Of course, Khrushchev was not alone in these views. Without exception, all the party and government leaders were for close fraternal cooperation with China and for generous help to the Chinese in all spheres of political, economic, and cultural development. So were the Soviet people. This outlook determined the entire course of Soviet-Chinese negotiations and led without any friction to the signing of a whole series of important Soviet-Chinese agreements and a final communiqué.

As that final document made clear, the talks revealed that the two governments were in complete accord on all international issues that were on the table. The two sides agreed to consult with each other on a continuing basis and to coordinate their actions on all questions that affected the mutual interests of the USSR and the PRC. Both parties to the accord condemned the United States for its de facto occupation of Taiwan and support of the Chiang Kai-shek clique.[3] Both sides called for the reunification of Korea and for a special conference to resolve this question.

The two governments also took a common stand in their declaration on relations with Japan. They expressed their opposition to the Treaty of San Francisco that the United States forced on Japan and that left Japan a semi-occupied country.[4] Both sides supported the normalization of relations with Japan and the development of trade and cultural ties with the Japanese people.

To put an end to all special Soviet privileges in China and restore full Chinese sovereignty over all Chinese territory, the Soviet delegation agreed to withdraw all Soviet troops from the joint naval base in Port Arthur by May 1955 and to turn over all military facilities there to China free of charge.[5] In the same spirit, the Soviet delegation offered to transfer to China by January 1955 the Soviet share of investments in the Soviet-Chinese joint companies that were established on an equal basis in 1950 and 1951. This agreement applied to the Association for the Extraction of

Nonferrous and Rare Metals in Xinjiang province, the Association for the Extraction and Refining of Oil in Xinjiang province, the Association for Construction and Renovation of Ships in Dalian,[6] and the Association for the Establishment and Operation of Civil Aviation. All of these companies would now be fully owned by the PRC.

As part of its technical assistance, the Soviet Union agreed to supply China with all necessary technical data and information free of charge, send its specialists for consultation, and so forth. A new loan agreement was also concluded. In addition to the 300-million-dollar loan in 1954, the Soviet Union extended long-term credits to China in the amount of 520 million dollars. The Soviet Union also decided to provide the PRC with assistance in the construction of an additional fifteen industrial enterprises and augment the value of equipment going to 141 enterprises to more than 400 million rubles. (A subsequent agreement in 1956 provided for Soviet assistance in the construction and reconstruction of another 56 enterprises.)

Apart from this enormous financial and technical assistance program, we reached agreement on the joint construction of a railroad line from Lanzhou to Ürümqi and Alma-Ata[7] and on the introduction of direct communication links between China and the USSR. The Soviet government was committed to providing China with all possible assistance in this project. A tripartite agreement was also concluded with China and the Mongolian People's Republic to build a railroad from Xining[8] to Ulaanbaatar and connect it to the railroad that runs from Ulaanbaatar to Soviet territory, thus linking the three countries by a direct line.

At the Second All-Union Conference of the Society of Soviet-Chinese Friendship in 1969, I heard an interesting report by a representative of the committee on foreign economic relations, who summed up the implementation of these and earlier agreements. From 1950 to 1959, more than 400 Chinese industrial enterprises were constructed, renovated, or rebuilt with Soviet help. Among these enterprises were forty-four electrical power stations and twelve integrated metallurgical plants with an annual production capacity of 30 million tons of metal. Over a fifteen-year period, the USSR delivered more than 2 billion rubles of industrial equipment to China, more than 24,000 technical data kits, and more than 4,000 patents, including patents for the most technologically advanced automated assembly lines, rolled-metal mills, machinery, instruments, and technological processes. According to one informed estimate, buying all this documentation on the world market would have cost China more than 4 billion rubles. The Chinese had to reimburse us only for the costs of copying the documents and sending them.

In personnel terms, some 8,000 Soviet experts and more than 2,000 instructors and academics were assigned to construction projects and educational centers in China to train Chinese specialists and pass on their own experience; more than 11,000 Chinese students and 8,000 Chinese workers and technicians underwent training in the Soviet Union in all areas of the economy. Again, according to an informed estimate, Soviet aid personnel provided China with training worth 500 million dollars but were paid only 50 million dollars for their work. The extensive exploration for natural resources and the discovery of new mineral riches were two of their contributions. This is an interesting fact: at the time of China's biggest economic boom, a large proportion of China's industrial products was manufactured with Soviet equipment.

As a result of this economic cooperation, the socialist industrialization of China was placed on a firm footing and promised great benefits to both sides. Then Mao Zedong proclaimed his famous Great Leap Forward, and China's economy went into a tailspin. During our stay in China, however, we all had the highest hopes for the country's vigorous economic growth and were confident that China would now make rapid strides along the socialist road in accordance with objective laws.

Driven by his exalted desire to demonstrate again and again our readiness to do everything in our ability to help China, Khrushchev contrived one surprise after another. Near the end of our stay in Beijing, he offered to give the equipment and technology for creating a 20,000-hectare state farm for grain production. We rallied behind the idea. Moscow gave its approval. The Soviet delegation sent Mao a letter asking him to accept this gift, which included 100 tractors, 100 grain combines, 54 trucks, 9 light trucks, 128 tractor-driven plows, plus seeding machines, assembly lines, electric power stations, radio stations, and more. Mao responded with a warm letter of thanks. More followed. The Soviet delegation gave the Chinese all the machine-tool sets—83 varieties—and all the agricultural machinery that were on display at our exhibition in Beijing. Mao responded with another letter of thanks.

Khrushchev's largess did not end there. Before leaving Moscow for

China, he had ordered the administration of the party CC to assemble from state collections, art studios, and commercial sources an assortment of gifts that could be sent to Beijing with the Soviet delegation. We were invited to view these gifts in the conference hall of the CC Orgburo. The collection included television and radio sets, paintings, miniature painted lacquer boxes from the famous town of Palekh, rifles, clocks, silver tableware trimmed with gold and enamel, jewelry, crystal, porcelain, chess sets made from amber and mother-of-pearl, and much else. All this was delivered to Beijing, and Khrushchev, like Grandfather Frost, dazzled everyone with his generosity.

I sometimes thought that we put our Chinese friends in a difficult position. The Chinese are a sensitive people with a highly developed sense of dignity and national pride. During and after our visit, it became clear that they did not want to be lavished with gifts and favors, either official or personal. For every display of benevolence on our part they sought to answer in kind, which was not always easy.

The mission to China, Khrushchev's first foreign trip as head of a government delegation, set the tone and style for future trips and became food for gossip at home and abroad. This developed in two ways.

First, each of his trips became ever more pompous. His retinue of followers grew larger and larger, with relatives, correspondents, cameramen, and servants of all kinds. He became more and more zealous in bidding for maximum publicity in the press, for news photographs, newsreels, television reports, and flattering biographies. Toward the end of his years in power, some of his trips abroad coincided, as a sort of salute, with the launching of space satellites. All these arrangements created a vast circle of careerists and toadies like Il'ichev, Satiukov, Adzhubei, and Sofronov.[9] The paeans and tributes were so intoxicating that they pushed him to wild and reckless acts.

Second, with his inordinate vanity, Khrushchev became more lavish and extravagant with each trip. China, of course, was a fraternal people's democracy, and each act of goodwill toward it was in our own interests and for the benefit of the whole community of socialist countries. During our stay in China, every move that concerned gifts to the Chinese and the substance of our mutual agreements was cleared in advance with Moscow. But now there were an increasing number of trips to the capitalist countries of Europe, Asia, Africa, and America, and the presents strewn along the way were no longer watches and boxes from Palekh but automobiles, airplanes, fully equipped hospitals, institutes, hotels, stadiums, and hundred-million-dollar loans that were clearly not meant to be repaid. The role of magnanimous benefactor was played not only by the Soviet leader but also by his wife, who kindly began to dispense souvenirs that ranged from expensive automobiles to the rarest treasures of the Kremlin Armory.[10] All constitutional restraints were shoved aside. On his own, Khrushchev showered foreign leaders with presents, everything from luxurious private planes to titles like Hero of the Soviet Union. But all this was later. During our visit to China everything proceeded in a sensible, constitutionally irreproachable, and businesslike manner.

The final receptions were under way. Our ambassador, Pavel Iudin, gave one of them. Led by Mao Zedong, all the Chinese leaders were present. Overcome by the moment, Khrushchev made a passionate speech and proposed emotional toasts; Zhou Enlai gave thoughtful, subtle, and correct replies. Mao, as always, remained glacially impassive.

Everything seemed to be going brilliantly. We were happy knowing that we had accomplished our mission, and were sure that we had taken another giant step toward the establishment of a lasting brotherhood between our two great countries. The outlook for the future could not have been clearer: the worldwide victory of socialism was assured.

Perhaps at that very moment, however, the mysterious historical forces that underlie events were already fashioning a Pandora's box, from which the snakes of misfortune would later emerge to poison relations between the two governments, and dangerously threaten mankind with more bloody internecine wars.

What happened? Officially, nothing. Yet something important occurred.

Apart from the official negotiations, an informal meeting took place at that time between Khrushchev and Mao Zedong. I was not present. Khrushchev gave us only a brief account. But Iudin, who was there, later gave me a detailed account of this crucial encounter.

Mao Zedong made two requests of the Soviet government and Nikita Khrushchev: first, that we give China the secret of the atomic bomb and help the PRC set up the production of atomic weapons; second, that we build China a submarine fleet that was capable of protecting the interests of the PRC from American imperialism.

Khrushchev rejected both requests.

In regard to the atomic bomb, Khrushchev argued that if we were to give the bomb to China, the Americans would give their bomb to West Germany. Mao replied that the relationship between the world's two camps suffered from an imbalance on this score. In the West, the United States was not the only country that possessed the atomic bomb; Britain did as well, and France was either developing it or had already done so. Moreover, everyone knew that all the components of the atomic bomb were ready in secret laboratories in West Germany and Japan, both of which had highly advanced industrial systems. In the socialist camp, the Soviet Union was the only country with the atomic bomb. Khrushchev joked, "But isn't it enough that we have the atomic bomb? We will protect you as well. If anything happens, we will strike a blow on your behalf." In regard to the submarine fleet, Khrushchev was not entirely clear in his response. First he lectured ("You have other things right now to take care of"). Then he tried to make a joke of it. Then he argued that "we have a powerful submarine fleet in these waters. Why do you need one too?" Then he suddenly asked, "Maybe we ought to have a joint submarine fleet?"

"Why joint?" Mao objected. "This is all very vague and indefinite. We are asking you to build us an adequate submarine fleet. We will pay you in full. In case there is a crisis in the Pacific, we agree to put our fleet under your command—please, take over, coordinate our actions with your own fleet's."

One way or another, Mao Zedong's requests were rejected. The point, however, was not that they were rejected but how they were rejected.

Khrushchev was a man of ungovernable passions. In handling governmental and diplomatic issues, he often displayed the customs and manners of a crude Russian merchant. When he took a liking to some foreign leader, he wanted to win him over somehow and thus prove to his colleagues and everyone else that "Khrushchev gets what he wants" and that "Khrushchev can do anything"; Khrushchev's generosity at those moments knew no bounds. He plied his partner with attention and presents. He courted him publicly with hugs and kisses. He was able to declare impulsively that if some governmental treaty or action was unacceptable to his partner, it would be revoked or altered. In his enthusiasm, he sought to prove to us that some American or French official was actually a "good fellow" and a "wonderful guy," that "Stalin had ruined everything" in the business at hand, and that now, as we would see, Khrushchev would make it right. But if the object of his campaign proved immune to his seductions and showed his claws, Khrushchev immediately bristled, and the "good fellow" and "wonderful guy" quickly became a "tough nut" and "diehard imperialist."

Something similar transpired with Mao Zedong. Knowing what China was like, Khrushchev was ready to do everything possible to rid Soviet-Chinese relations of all negative accretions; in this respect, he did a great deal that was right and proper. But Mao Zedong, as the leader of the ruling party of a great nation, was concerned with his own plans and problems; he posed questions that stemmed from his need to implement his plans and resolve his problems.

Khrushchev might have discussed Mao's questions, considered his plans, and presented his own views about the serious difficulties that stood in the way of their realization. In view of the cardinal nature of Mao's requests, he could have done so judiciously, unhurriedly, tactfully, and evidentially in order to avert any suspicions within the Chinese leadership about our undying sincerity and fraternal goodwill. But as always, Khrushchev was impulsive and unrestrained. He lavished his gifts, bear hugs, and bounty, doing everything that, in his opinion, strengthened Chinese-Soviet ties. When Mao Zedong put forward proposals, however, which from the Chinese point of view were also designed to benefit Soviet-Chinese relations and the entire socialist community, but which struck Khrushchev as dubious, Khrushchev immediately bristled, turned didactic, got hot under the collar, and began lecturing Mao. This was the reaction of that old "Rassian," the arrogant merchant out on a binge in a restaurant. In a drunken state, he generously offers to treat everyone, throws down wads of rubles, and tries to kiss everyone, but then—"I do as I please!"—smears his companions' faces with mustard and smashes the restaurant's mirrors.

The Chinese, as I said, are a people with a highly developed sense of national pride and dignity. They had just won a great decades-long revolution and war of national liberation and were not going to play the poor relation to a wealthy benefactor. The only relationship they would have accepted was one between equals. They demanded complete trust and respect for themselves.

Mao evidently sensed an element of distrust and disparagement toward himself and China in the tone of Khrushchev's replies. Subsequent events showed that his suspicions were well founded. What the Chinese discerned as the seeds of condescension in those days of October 1954 later sprouted into Khrushchev's arrogance and rudeness and yielded the most poisonous fruit.

Nikita Khrushchev was developing a taste for power. His improvisations in political and economic affairs were sometimes absurd. His juicy pronouncements assumed the status of Marxist verities. He granted interviews to foreign correspondents. Leaders of various foreign communist parties visited him for talks. "Why not? Am I any worse than anyone else? We're no fools either. Anyhow, you can do anything you put your mind to." Khrushchev's rapid evolution from the self-flagellation that was typical of a *muzhik*[11] ("Khrushchev isn't worth Stalin's shit") to tsarist pretentiousness took place before our eyes. He criticized the Romanian leader Gheorghe Gheorghiu-Dej. He scolded the Albanian leaders Enver Hoxha and Mehmet Shehu. He adopted a didactic tone toward the highly intelligent and educated Palmiro Togliatti. But most of all, he began in time to irritate Mao Zedong.

Over the years, Mao amassed the experience and reputation of an outstanding leader and military commander. He enjoyed unquestioning authority in a country of 600 million people. He was the author of many works that were published in Moscow and elsewhere. He wrote poetry. And now Khrushchev, in a muted tone at first, and only within his inner circle, but progressively more loudly and openly, began to widen and intensify his criticism of Mao Zedong; he even abused the Chinese leader and grossly insulted the Chinese people before audiences of thousands. Suffice it to recall his famous remark that was heard around the world: "They don't have pants to put on, yet they go around shouting their heads off about communism!"

In 1959, Khrushchev made a long-awaited visit to the United States. He had made many unceremonious attempts to visit the United States, remarking frequently at press conferences, "I would, of course, be glad to visit America, but I haven't been invited." Then he was invited, and he returned from the United States in triumph. Khrushchev "settled everything with America." "I said to Eisenhower, 'Let's throw all our differences to the devil. Let's turn a new page.'" I have no doubt that Khrushchev sincerely thought that before his time, our diplomats had grappled many long years with America and negotiated with difficulties and disagreements; but he made one trip to America and "settled everything." Now Khrushchev had Eisenhower in his pocket.

It was in this mood that Khrushchev went to China for the tenth anniversary of the establishment of the PRC after returning from the United States. It was only natural that his triumphal tone and enthusiasm about his American visit met with an icy response from Mao Zedong and his colleagues. Khrushchev was infuriated and lost control of himself; he blasted and lectured the Chinese on various issues of domestic and foreign policy.

Restrained, polite, but decisive in their replies, the Chinese gave the blustering attack a firm rebuff. Khrushchev was offended, "slammed the door," and left China before the anniversary ceremonies. In time his annoyance deepened. After all, at home, where he was called an "outstanding Marxist-Leninist," the panegyrics to his name came thick and fast. Even the venerable philosopher Mark Mitin[12] was working on a book in which he claimed that "Khrushchev is the Lenin of today." Yet the Chinese, supposedly without pants to their name, were presumptuous enough to contradict him.

Khrushchev's irritation had tangible repercussions for Soviet advisers and experts in China.

With extensive and comprehensive help from the Soviet Union, the People's Republic of China was laying the foundations of socialist industry and democratic government and promoting a (lowercase) cultural revolution.[13] Thousands of Soviet workers, technicians, engineers, scientists, instructors, and other experts worked at construction sites, enterprises, laboratories, and research institutes to pass on their experience to their Chinese brothers. Then the Chinese party approached the Soviet party CC with a routine business question about payment for the Soviet experts. The question called for a response, either positive, negative, or with some suggestion about what should be done. But Khrushchev, already upset, was incensed by the fact that the question had even been asked. "We're doing everything for them, and now they ask about some kind of payment!"

Khrushchev ordered the immediate recall of all experts and advisers from China.[14] The CC Presidium endorsed this. All work came to an immediate end, and all Soviet personnel left China. No amount of reasoning or persuasion from the Chinese had any effect. The consequence for many construction projects, enterprises, and construction agencies was total paralysis. The damage to the Chinese economy was enormous. Khrushchev's rage became known first to the Chinese leadership and then to the entire party membership in China. It was one of the subjective reasons for the fateful future conflict between the two countries.

It would be wrong, of course, to suggest that this was the basic cause of the Sino-Soviet split. There were deeper, objective reasons as well. But Khrushchev's intemperance was undoubtedly one of the subjective factors in the development of the conflict; it poisoned the entire atmosphere. Of all the ills that Khrushchev visited on the country during the "great decade" of his rule, the breach with China was perhaps the worst.

But all this was in the future. Having been pampered by the Chinese and having left generous agreements and gifts behind us, we prepared to go home. On October 13 the Soviet delegation left Beijing; all the Chinese leaders except Mao Zedong—Liu Shaoqi, Zhou Enlai, the Dalai Lama, and the others—saw us off at the airport. Khrushchev made a farewell address. Our party went separate ways at the airport. Shvernik, Furtseva, Aleksandrov, and I returned to Moscow. Khrushchev, Bulganin, and Mikoian set off on further travel. They visited the naval base at Port Arthur and the cities of Dalian, Anshan, Shenyang, Changchun, and Harbin.[15] They then stopped in all the major cities of the Soviet Far East, Siberia, and the Urals, and did not return to Moscow until more than a month after their initial departure. Khrushchev was an avid traveler and paid no heed to diplomatic protocol. Arriving in a foreign country, he crisscrossed its territory like a tourist for a fortnight or more, sometimes prompting ironic comments from newspaper correspondents that "the Soviet premier apparently has plenty of free time."

I left China with the warmest feelings for the world's most populous country. As the plane ascended, the capital's labyrinthine streets, the quaint mosaic of the fields, and the sinuous line of the Great Wall passed by under its wings. Good-bye, wondrous land. Good-bye, warmhearted Chinese people. I will return. I will certainly return. And I will see a fully industrialized China, glowing with health and happiness.

Onward, China, and fair be the wind in your sails!

Epilogue

THE ANTIPARTY GROUP THAT NEVER WAS

The following is the transcript of an oral interview with Dmitrii Shepilov that took place in July or August of 1991 at the Arkhangel'skii Sanatorium outside Moscow. It was intended for publication in *Pravda*. However, on the very eve of the publication date, Shepilov, then eighty-six, tried to revise a few phrases but could not make up his mind about the exact wording. The interview remained unpublished.

The interviewer is Shepilov's grandson. Shepilov's responses have been abridged to avoid repetition and edited for style, grammar, and clarity. Ellipses indicate incomplete thoughts rather than elided material.

DMITRII KOSYREV: I've read your published writings of the past few months, and I've read your memoirs, and there isn't a word in them about the most interesting part for the contemporary reader: the June 1957 plenum that cut short your political career. Let's take a look at this. Was there an antiparty group[1] or not? How did it all come about?

DMITRII SHEPILOV: Here's a story. A few months before the plenum, I was at the Kremlin. I was walking in a corridor, and I saw a door open and someone come out of Mikoian's office. Through the door I heard someone speaking agitatedly on the telephone. I went in and sat down. Mikoian continued talking: "You're right, Nikolai, this is intolerable; we can't let this go on." Then he put down the phone and said, "I was talking to Bulganin. You know, Dmitrii Trofimovich, the situation has become untenable. We want to teach Khrushchev a lesson. We can't go on this way. He rejects everything and doesn't take anyone into account; all these are his projects . . . we'll ruin everything. We must have a serious talk about it." I kept silent, not agreeing or disagreeing, because I'd come on a different matter altogether and merely happened to overhear what was going on.

I remember a similar episode. This was during the period when Khrushchev no longer visited me, when we no longer took walks together. I left the house and was walking near our dacha. Suddenly a car stopped and Voroshilov stepped out. "Dmitrii Trofimovich, I'm off to Sergeï's wedding. Sergeï's getting married—Khrushchev's son. Aren't you coming?"

"No," I said, "I wasn't invited."

"Dmitrii Trofimovich, we must do something. You know, it's intolerable: he insults everyone; he humiliates everyone; he stops at nothing."

I said, "Kliment Efremovich, why are you telling me this? You're a longstanding, senior member of the party. You're a member of the Politburo. Why are you telling this to me?"

"But you're our chief ideologue."

"Bah, what kind of chief ideologue am I? Our chief ideologue is Khrushchev. Jesus also has a better claim to this role. As for me, I'm just carrying on with my work, as I'm supposed to. There's no point in telling me this. Ask me my opinion, and I will tell you." I didn't tell him what my opinion was.

KOSYREV: You're describing what was, so to speak, in the air in those days. But today the events of 1957 are presented as a well-organized conspiracy of old men who wanted to see a complete return to Stalinism.

SHEPILOV: Not at all. That's absolutely wrong. There was a rumor quite a while later that Bulganin was the leader of the antiparty group. Other names were also mentioned. I hadn't heard anything about any antiparty group. Everyone simply started saying that we couldn't go on this way and that everything was falling apart. There came a time when something had to be done. The country, the party, trade, the economy—everything was breaking down, everything was going to the dogs. Khrushchev quarreled with everyone, with China as well. . . . There were rumors that at some meeting of the Council of Ministers (Khrushchev himself told me this), Bulganin, the chairman said, "Comrades, we can't go on this way. We're heading for disaster. We've got to get together and discuss it."

But this I heard quite a bit later. I think there was some kind of meeting where they were ready to do something; I don't know who initiated it. But I don't think there was any antiparty group. What is being written today about Mikhail Gorbachev—the way he's criticized, the various remarks and comments that are made about him, the opposition to what he's doing—all this is much more substantial.

As for a return to Stalinism . . . Well, let's not forget the Twentieth Party Congress.

KOSYREV: There are rumors that you were the author of both of Khrushchev's speeches at the congress—both the public speech and the secret one.

SHEPILOV: This was the situation. While we were preparing documents for the Twentieth Congress, I called on Khrushchev and said, "Well, Nikita Sergeevich, what's going on? We're sitting here writing documents." He said, "You know, they gave me this speech to read. Ponomarev and others had a hand in it . . . and I don't like it."

Oh, yes, there was something else. A bit earlier I was ill. That's right. Bleeding ulcers. I was in the Kremlin Hospital. But with the congress coming, I asked them to speed up my treatment, and they prescribed fasting for twelve days. Bakulev[2] and other luminaries took part in the consultation. I fasted for eight days, until the blood tests showed I couldn't go on with that. But the bleeding stopped and I went home. Then I called on Khrushchev, and he told me all this.

I responded, "I can help you, Nikita Sergeevich, if you like. I can at least write the foreign-policy section."

I brought in a few people, Leont'ev among them, and we sat

down and drafted those sections of his speech that dealt with our areas of competence—foreign policy and a few others. That's how he operated. When he got the text, he went over it, and since he didn't know how to write, he dictated. Do you remember how he said at conferences and congresses, "Well, let me depart from the text for a minute," and then digressed? This time, too, he didn't pencil in his corrections but called in a stenographer, dictated whole sections, and then stuffed them back in. Still, by and large, the speech included what we wrote. So it's true that I had a direct and important role in the preparations for the Twentieth Congress. After that, this is what happened.

He delivered the summary report, as he insisted it was his right to do. By then he was running the show. I, too, made my report. During the discussion after his speech, I was sitting next to a column. He came up behind me. "Dmitrii Trofimovich, let's step out for a minute." We went out to the lobby where people could get a bite to eat, and he said, "You see, I did my best to negotiate with these Bourbons"[3]—I knew to whom he was referring—"and speak critically about Stalin at the congress. But they—never! Well . . . the thing is, I want to speak about these issues."

I must say that during the period after Stalin, he and I began to speak frankly to each other about everything during our walks. He told me things that only he knew. That Voznesenskii wrote a letter to Stalin: "You know I'm not guilty of anything, so why am I in prison?" Stalin told Khrushchev, Bulganin, and Malenkov to visit Voznesenskii and talk to him. But apparently he said it in such a tone that . . . Besides, everyone knew that Voznesenskii's fate was sealed after he came out with that book. . . . Khrushchev was very antagonistic toward Voznesenskii because Stalin had thought highly of him, and Voznesenskii could be harsh even toward Molotov. Well, they went to his cell.

"So," I said to Khrushchev, "people think that either Malenkov or Kaganovich—"

Khrushchev said, "That's wrong. When we entered his cell, he jumped up from his chair. 'Comrades, thank you, thank you for coming—at last!' Bulganin approached him: 'We're no comrades of yours!' He hit him so hard on the ear that he fell to the floor."

Those were the kinds of things, terrible things, Khrushchev told me. Bulganin turned out to be such a mediocrity, such a . . . As for Khrushchev and me, in those days our relationship was such that he told me about all these confidential matters. By then we spoke freely; he knew my sentiments.

What was Stalinism? Of course, in those days we didn't know one-tenth of what we learned later; we didn't know that the trouble was not with Kamenev, Zinoviev, and Bukharin but with the fact that so many people were exterminated.

Khrushchev said to me: "You'll help?"

I said, "Yes, I'll help."

You see, when I backed him, I served as a counterweight to his entire past, to the fact that he had always been the first to give his enthusiastic support to whatever Stalin said.

He said, "All right, let's go." We left the congress. I think the minutes would show that we were absent that day and the next. I stayed in my office and he stayed in his; you know, he didn't give me any instructions. He said, "After all, we talked it over. You know everything. Help me do whatever has to be done."

I decided to raise two questions: on foreign policy, where Stalin had erred; and on the issue of the military, since I had spent all of the war at the front. I thought about the price we paid for victory, the twenty million dead. Remember, Stalin first put the casualties at seven million. . . . I dealt mainly with these issues. I personally handed Khrushchev sections that I wrote about that. I'm certain they could be found either in Khrushchev's files, the archives of the Twentieth Congress, or Grigorii Shuiskii's possession in the general affairs section of the Central Committee.

Recently, when I was invited for tea at the Institute of Marx, Engels, and Lenin,[4] they said to me, "Dmitrii Trofimovich, there are rumors that you wrote the secret speech."

I replied, "That's absolutely wrong. I'm neither the author nor the coauthor. This was done at Khrushchev's initiative."

Barsukov[5] said, "All right, was the draft ultimately prepared by Pospelov?"

"I don't know who prepared it."

When Khrushchev began to read the speech, I caught only bits and pieces of what I had written. Some phrases, subsections . . . You could spot them stylistically. . . . I don't know to this day who put it all together. But I doubt that it was Pospelov, because you couldn't find a more zealous Stalinist consumed with such boorish inner rage. Stalin was his icon.[6]

In short, I did what any political staffer would have done: I helped with some of the sections. But it was balderdash when they accused me later of opposing the decisions of the Twentieth Congress. I helped prepare both the public report and the secret one.

About foreign policy? At that time, Khrushchev continued to take me everywhere with him. I was included in the party-government delegation that accompanied him to Yugoslavia and in the whole difficult business of restoring relations with them.[7] This was a good cause, because as Stalin used to say, "All I have to do is move my little finger—and poof!—Yugoslavia." But Khrushchev wanted to make peace.

A delegation was selected. I was included. Khrushchev negotiated with Tito and said the right things. My meetings were all with Kardelj, because Kardelj was regarded as the ideologue, the leader of Eurocommunism.[8] I prepared carefully for these negotiations. I have a whole volume of excerpts, speeches. Tito said to me, "You and Kardelj sort out these questions; meanwhile, we'll deal with other matters."

Tito adamantly demanded a relationship of complete equality and noninterference by the CPSU in the internal affairs of Yugoslavia, and for an end to Stalinism, where everything was prescribed and ordered from Moscow. Tito would not agree to anything else. When his one-on-one talks with Tito began, Khrushchev said to me, "He simply will not accept our guidance, our leading role in the communist world." I said, "Nikita Sergeevich, we don't have to lay claim to leadership in the communist world. We came here to make peace. We don't need to insist on leadership."

So Kardelj and I wrote the declaration, which I recall to this day, on the normalization of relations. Then Khrushchev invited Tito to come to Moscow. A few days before he arrived[9]—my relationship with Khrushchev was then still good—Khrushchev said to me, "Tito is coming. What are we going to do? You know, Molotov worked with Stalin, who said all he had to do was move his little finger and there'd be no Yugoslavia. Molotov supported this. He followed this policy, and all his people helped him. Now Tito is coming, and Molotov is still minister of foreign affairs. We've got to do something. We've got to make some changes. I propose that we relieve Molotov of his duties and appoint Shepilov."

That's how my appointment came about.

Yet Khrushchev's relationship with Tito was the same as his relationship with Mao Zedong. It was the same pattern. At first, reconciliation and a step forward; then—Tito is an opportunist, a reformist, and so on.

But to return to what you said about the antiparty group and the revival of Stalinism. Today you can see the true picture. But after the plenum, things began to accumulate. Khrushchev, of course, knew that I had nothing whatsoever to do with 1937, nor with any of the arrests. That was my main political asset. That was why his formula was the "antiparty group of Molotov, etc., and joining them was Shepilov."

Khrushchev understood that by leaving me in place . . . He said to me, "You dealt me the cruelest blow of all. Because Molotov, Klim [Voroshilov], and the others clung to their posts. They all followed Stalin from start to finish. But you! We were promoting you." So he thought up this formula, figuring that "joining" would be understood as "unprincipled." All the Satiukovs, Il'ichevs, and Fedoseevs came up with the idea that Shepilov counted the votes and decided to join the majority.

KOSYREV: How did it finally end?

SHEPILOV: Someone phoned me and said there'd be a meeting that day at four o'clock. Right. They called a meeting of the Presidium.

KOSYREV: So both the meeting and its subject were a complete surprise to you?

SHEPILOV: The subject? Well, you see, the issue had come to a head long before this: We had to get together to discuss the Khrushchev situation. I don't know who set the time and place. When I got there everyone was in place except Zhukov. Zhukov and I always sat next to each other. Remember, we were very close. . . . He was very much against Khrushchev. When *Ogonek* dug up pictures of Khrushchev standing alongside Zhukov, it was just propaganda. In those days, Khrushchev disparaged the army, saying things like "If a major became a swineherd, he'd be of far more use. Why have we increased the army's ranks?" Zhukov was indignant, saying that Khrushchev didn't understand anything.

After a few minutes, Zhukov arrived. The meeting took place in the hall where Lenin's chair was still in place. Khrushchev took his seat. Zhukov sat nearby. Everyone was in his place.

Khrushchev began, "I propose—"

Malenkov interrupted. "Just a minute, Nikita Sergeevich. Comrades, I propose that before we begin with these issues, we discuss Comrade Khrushchev's violations of the principle of collective leadership. We simply cannot go on like this. In view of this, I suggest that it would be inappropriate for Khrushchev to chair this meeting, nor should I act as chairman in his place."

Khrushchev got up and said, "As you wish, as you wish!" He knew, of course, about everything. Serov kept him informed.

Malenkov said, "I propose that Bulganin chair the meeting."

Bulganin moved over to the chairman's place. "Comrades, what is there to say? You know all the facts. It's intolerable. We're heading for disaster. Everything is being decided by one man. We've returned to the past."

People began to speak, one after the other. My speech was extremely blunt. I began like this:

"The Soviet people and party paid with rivers of blood for the cult of personality. Now some time has elapsed, and we are again face to face with another cult in the making. Khrushchev has stepped into Stalin's bast shoes and is plodding along, breaking them in." I continued, "He is the authority on all questions. He reports at plenums and other meetings on all issues—industry, agriculture, foreign policy, and ideology. He decides everything. And he does so ignorantly and wrongly, to boot."

At this point, Khrushchev retorted: "How many years did you spend studying?"

I replied, "I cost the people a lot of money. I finished ten years

of primary and secondary schooling, four years at a university and at
the Agricultural Institute of Red Professors." I said that I was in full
agreement with the party's policies, that I had no reservations on
that score. But I said there had been a number of actions that I'd
spoken to Nikita Sergeevich about. I tried to persuade him. But
nothing came of it. Nothing was acceptable to him. Things were
going from bad to worse. I reviewed one issue after another. As in
my outburst before Stalin about genetics, I spoke in an emotional
crescendo.

I and others broached another subject at that plenum. Serov
played a major role in this affair. He was a despicable, odious type,
formerly one of Beria's deputies. Yet he became head of the KGB.
He was Khrushchev's favorite. He wallowed in the vilest actions.
When Bulganin spoke at that plenum, he said, "One night when I
wasn't home, they went through everything in my house. One night
was enough for him to wire the whole place." Voices responded,
"They bugged my phone, too!" "And mine!" I spoke about the same
thing.

Some time earlier, Furtseva dropped by to see me. "What's going
on? Everything is falling apart. Everything is being wrecked. Can't
we . . . ?" Whenever she came over—I was on the alert myself—she
whispered, "Let's walk around. They're listening in. Cover the phone
with something."

On the eve of the plenum, two days before it opened, Furtseva
came in, white as a sheet and upset. Apparently it had begun, and
Khrushchev was being kept informed of everything. She says to me,
"I've come to warn you that if you discuss this question anywhere, or
reveal what we talked about, we will grind you into gulag dust. I am
secretary of the Moscow Party Committee. The committee does what
I say. We'll grind you down." I say to her, "Comrade Furtseva, what
are you talking about? It's you who came to see me and complain
about the situation." "I never came to see you," she said.

"So," I said in my speech, "there we were: two CC secretaries.
Neither of us was ever in any opposition faction. Neither of us was
ever involved in any kind of provocation. Yet now we couldn't talk to
each other!"

Furtseva wailed, "This is a provocation!"

I continued, "That's the kind of collective party leadership we've come to."

Note that no one who took part in the discussion, not even those who were named members of the antiparty group, absolutely no one, proposed taking any kind of punitive measures against Khrushchev. Everyone said that the situation was intolerable, that we must relieve Khrushchev of the duties of first secretary, appoint him minister of agriculture, but keep him in the Presidium. Then it turned out that all night long Serov and his boys . . . While we were in session and everyone was saying that we must call a plenum for Monday—this was Thursday or Friday—to oust Khrushchev, Serov's men were rounding up people for the next plenum and scaring them with threats of imminent arrests and repressions. As Molotov and Stalin's other accomplices knew, there was a precedent for such threats.

Here's another important point. Zhukov was sitting next to me when the discussion got heated. He, too, spoke critically. Zhukov prodded me with his elbow and showed me a note on a piece of paper. No one knows about this, of course. He destroyed the note later, but it read, word for word: "Nikolai Aleksandrovich"—that is, Bulganin—"I propose that we bring the discussion to an end. Issue a stern reprimand to Khrushchev for violating the principle of collective leadership, and leave everything as is for the time being, and look again at the situation later."

KOSYREV: Why is that important?

SHEPILOV: Because later people said that Zhukov had saved Khrushchev's hide and that he was for Khrushchev. But it wasn't that way at all.

A few days later, when the whole affair was over and I was no longer in the CC, I ran into Zhukov. I said to him, "Georgii Aleksandrovich, you'll be next."[10] Mikoian told me later that Bulganin had once been, and would always be, an accountant: he showed Zhukov's note to Khrushchev, so it was clear to Khrushchev where Zhukov stood.

What is important is that the whole affair was really poorly planned. That is unpardonable if you want to seriously undertake something. No one asked who would take Khrushchev's place. No one said anything about that. Later there were rumors that they'd presumed they would appoint Molotov. Maybe they talked about that somewhere, but there was no proposal. Apparently, everything was so disorganized that the question never came up. That's simply . . . You know, the whole thing was like an explosion. Was there an antiparty group? I cannot say for sure that there was not. I just don't know. But Khrushchev knew—no one could be that unaware—he knew about my relationship with Molotov and the others and about my role in the preparations for the Twentieth Congress, including his speech.

KOSYREV: In speaking up against Khrushchev, did you realize that his ouster could mean a return to Stalinism?

SHEPILOV: Never. I never gave any thought to it. That is unpardonable. I deserve a lashing for it. I never asked myself: Whom will we get instead of Nikita? It was either naïveté on my part or plain stupidity to raise the question, to go into all the gross violations of the principle of collective leadership, all the nonsensical schemes that were leading us to disaster, but not to ask myself who would be there to take Nikita's place. But I heard from several people—maybe they even discussed it among themselves, since Bulganin had surrounded himself with a kind of Council of Ministers—that we no longer needed a general secretary. Maybe Molotov would have been the leader, but I never heard that. But I never could have believed that Molotov would be placed in charge: at one time he had been in danger of execution himself, and his wife was in prison in chains. Yet he called me and said, "Stop attacking Stalin."

As to whether there'd be a return to Stalinism, here Khrushchev did his best thing. And he'd only begun doing it: there were rehabilitations; cases were reopened; people began to come back from the camps and, still alive, tell everything. In short, by then no one was afraid of a return to the past.

But after the plenum there was a revival of repressions. At some point, it became clear that there was no difference between what Stalin did and . . . True, Stalin had people killed, shot, and tortured, whereas Khrushchev only had them fired or slandered. One example was how he dealt with Baibakov. He publicly berated him in the Hall of Columns—"He's a full-blown Shepilovite"—and sent him off to the Council of People's Economy.[11]

KOSYREV: But why did Khrushchev come down harder on you than the others who spoke up within the Politburo and at the plenum?

SHEPILOV: Molotov, Kaganovich, and Voroshilov were, after all, old hands. They worked for a long time under Stalin and were set in their ironclad bureaucratic ways. I was an innocent. I had returned from the front. I was used to making my own decisions. And on two or three occasions, my emotions got the best of me. The others were used to weighing everything, evaluating everything. And psychologically . . . I thought to myself: Here's another Grishka Rasputin. That kept gnawing at me: a Soviet Grishka Rasputin had appeared! That's the reason why Khrushchev said to me: "You dealt me the cruelest blow of all." He added, "Molotov, Voroshilov, and the others—I kept them in check and criticized them—but you I pushed forward. We promoted you. If you came out against me more strongly than anyone, it must have been on principle." I replied, "It was certainly not on lack of principle."

Of course, all these people . . . What astonished me more than anything was that they remained the same Stalinists they had always been. I've mentioned this before, but I'll go into it in more detail. I was both executive editor of *Pravda* and a CC secretary. The telephone rang. It was Molotov. This was after the Twentieth Congress. He said, "Stop attacking Stalin!" I replied, "I'm not attacking Stalin, but implementing the decisions of the Twentieth Congress." Molotov's wife had spent time in prison—in chains, according to rumor. Stalin said that he trembled before American imperialism. He hung by a thread. He could have been disposed of. Yet he remained the same as he had always been.

I got it in the neck sixteen or eighteen times. Let's count them up. I lost the title of candidate member of the Politburo. I was expelled from the CC. I was dismissed from work. I was transferred to Kyrgyzstan. Then, when I was already at work in Kyrgyzstan, where the people treated me marvelously, Khrushchev gave an order. Razzakov,[12] the first secretary, got up at a party meeting and said, "I was in Moscow, and Moscow reprimanded us: The Kyrgyz party organization is currying favor with Shepilov"—imagine, the entire party of a whole republic! "We're forgetting that Shepilov is in Kyrgyzstan as a political exile."

KOSYREV: What was your position there?

SHEPILOV: Director of the Institute of Economics of the Academy of Sciences. At that time, I was still a party member. I was a professor. I was a general. Khrushchev, however, still kept an eye on me and committed acts of petty vengeance. There was a congress of republic leaders. All directors, including me, were invited. Then a CC instructor arrived from Moscow, summoned me, and said, "I'm sorry. There's been a mistake. It was by accident, purely technical. We did not intend to invite you to the congress." They took away my invitation.

After my operation, they let me stay in Moscow. I worked in the archival section of the Council of Ministers. I tried not to do anything that would make me stand out from the others. I came to work on time. I worked hard. I prepared sixty-eight volumes for publication while I was there. They all passed across my desk: a biography of Lenin, the history of the USSR, the history of the Great Patriotic War, and so on, all during the twenty-two years I spent in the archival section. None of the volumes have my name on them. They are all collections of documents.

For five years after the 1957 plenum, my work was irreproachable. I was a foreign-policy observer at conferences. Then at the Twenty-second Party Congress, seeing that nothing was working out, that things weren't going right, Khrushchev hauled out the antiparty-group business again. Il'ichev called the secretary of the party organization at the archive, Abramov. "You've got a party meeting today? Expel Shepilov from the party." Abramov said, "Why? We don't have anything against Dmitrii Trofimovich. Besides, he's sick in the hospital." "Carry out the CC's orders." They didn't even let me know there'd be a party meeting. I found out that evening. One of the female members dropped by and said, "They've just expelled you from the party."[13]

A short while later, Il'ichev called Skriabin, the academic secretary of the USSR Academy of Sciences, and Nesmeianov, the president of the Academy.[14] "You have a general meeting today? Strip Shepilov of the title of corresponding member." Nesmeianov told me this. Again I wasn't informed.

In both circumstances, consistently with the way things were done then, everything was decided unanimously. Later on, two presidents of the academy—Nesmeianov and Aleksandrov[15]—did what they could to rectify matters.

I know that on the eve of his final visit to Pitsunda, Khrushchev presided at a meeting of the Presidium, not realizing that this would be his last visit and that he was providing a final tally of his work. "In regard to agriculture, things aren't settled yet. But there aren't any arrests. The antiparty group has been smashed—not because they were against me but in retribution for 1937, for the arrests. Of course, we shouldn't have lumped Shepilov in with this affair." Iakov Malik,[16] the CC's general deputy administrator, who was at the meeting, told me this. "Shepilov had no part in the arrests. That's why I want to call him in, hear him out, and appoint him rector of the Academy of Social Sciences."

So you see that he cooled down and realized that if I helped draft the decisions of the Twentieth Congress, then . . . Anyhow, I was expelled from the party on February 21, 1962, and was reinstated by the Control Committee of the party CC on February 18, 1976. On March 22, 1991, I was reinstated in the academy. Even after Khrushchev was gone, Il'ichev was still around.

SELECT BIOGRAPHIES

ABAKUMOV, VIKTOR (1908–54). Abakumov was a longtime official in the Ministry of State Security (the secret police) and its institutional predecessors. He was arrested in 1951 for organizing a Zionist conspiracy. After Stalin's death, he was executed as an accomplice of Lavrentii Beria.

ADZHUBEI, ALEKSEI (1924–93). During the late 1950s and early 1960s, Adzhubei was chief editor of *Komsomol'skaia pravda* and *Izvestiia* and a member of the Central Committee. He was married to Khrushchev's daughter. After Khrushchev's dismissal in 1964, Adzhubei was removed from power.

ALEKSANDROV, GEORGII (1908–61). Aleksandrov, a philosopher, was chief of Agitprop through much of the 1940s. Stalin criticized his book *History of Western European Philosophy* in 1947. From 1947 to 1954, Aleksandrov was director of the Institute of Philosophy. After Stalin's death, Aleksandrov briefly served as minister of culture but was weakened by a sex scandal and the political misfortunes of Georgii Malenkov.

ANDRIANOV, VASILII (1902–78). In 1949, after the purge of the Leningrad party organization following the Leningrad affair (see Voznesenskii entry), Andrianov was chief of the party committee for the Leningrad oblast. After Stalin's death, Andrianov was demoted to USSR deputy minister of state control.

BERIA, LAVRENTII (1899–1953). From 1938 to 1948 and again in the spring of 1953, Beria was the minister of internal affairs (chief of the secret police). From 1946 to 1953, he was also a member of the Central Committee Politburo/ Presidium. After Stalin's death, Beria was executed.

BUKHARIN, NIKOLAI (1888–1938). Bukharin, an old Bolshevik, was the leader of the right opposition during the late 1920s, which argued against ending NEP and collectivizing agriculture. After the defeat of the right opposition in 1929, Bukharin was removed from the Politburo. He was executed in 1938.

BULGANIN, NIKOLAI (1895–1975). Bulganin, initially a Khrushchev loyalist, was minister of defense from 1953 to 1955 and chairman of the Council of Ministers from 1955 to 1958. Implicated in the antiparty group in 1957, Bulganin was removed from power the following year.

DZERZHINSKII, FELIKS (1877–1926). Dzerzhinskii, an old Bolshevik, was the first chief of the Cheka, the secret police.

EZHOV, NIKOLAI (1895–1940). From 1936 to 1938, the period of the Great Purges, Ezhov was people's commissar of internal affairs (chief of the secret police). In 1937–38, he was also a candidate member of the Politburo. Ezhov was executed in 1940.

FEDOSEEV, PETR (1908–90). A specialist in philosophy, Fedoseev worked as a Central Committee staffer from 1941 to 1955, allying himself with Georgii Aleksandrov. Fedoseev later became the director of the Institute of Philosophy (1955–62) and vice president of the Academy of Sciences (1962–67, 1971–88).

FURTSEVA, EKATERINA (1910–74). In 1957, Furtseva became a full member of the Presidium, the first Soviet woman to serve in the party's supreme body. In 1961 she was demoted to USSR minister of culture, allegedly for saying unflattering things about Khrushchev on a bugged telephone.

IAGODA, GENRIKH (1891–1938). From 1934 to 1936, Iagoda was people's commissar of internal affairs (chief of the secret police). In 1938, he was tried alongside Bukharin and others on a host of fantastic charges and executed.

IL'ICHEV, LEONID (1906–90). Il'ichev served as chief editor of *Izvestiia* from 1944 to 1948 and later became a staffer at the Central Committee and the Ministry of Foreign Affairs. From 1958 to 1965, Il'ichev was chief of Agitprop. After Khrushchev's ouster, he became deputy minister of foreign affairs, a post he held until 1989.

IUDIN, PAVEL (1899–1968). A graduate of the Institute of Red Professors, Iudin was director of the Institute of Philosophy from 1938 to 1944. After the war, he served in a variety of editorial positions and became a member of the Central-Committee (1952–61) and, briefly, a candidate member of its Presidium (1952–53). From 1953 to 1959, Iudin was Soviet ambassador to China.

KAGANOVICH, LAZAR (1893–1991). An old Bolshevik, Kaganovich became a member of the Central Committee in 1924 and the Politburo in 1930. During the 1930s and 1940s, he served in a variety of party posts, including as secretary of the Moscow Party Committee (1930–35) and of the Ukrainian Communist Party (1947). A central figure in the antiparty group, Kaganovich was removed from power in 1957.

KALININ, MIKHAIL (1875–1946). A member of the party since 1898, Kalinin became a member of the Central Committee in 1919 and the Politburo in 1926, posts he held until his death. From 1919 to 1946, Kalinin was chairman of the Central Executive Committee (which was, after 1938, the Presidium of the Supreme Soviet), a purely ornamental position often referred to as the Soviet presidency.

KAMENEV, LEV (1883–1936). An old Bolshevik, Kamenev was a key figure in the party's United Opposition against Stalin in 1926–27. He was executed in 1936 after a show trial.

KHRUSHCHEV, NIKITA (1894–1971). During the 1930s, Khrushchev worked his way up the party hierarchy, eventually becoming secretary of the Moscow Party Committee (1935) and the Ukrainian Communist Party (1938). In 1939, Khrushchev became a member of the Politburo. After Stalin's death, Khrushchev emerged as the preeminent Soviet leader, occupying Stalin's former position as first secretary (general secretary) of the party from 1953 to 1964, as well as the chairmanship of the Council of Ministers from 1958 to 1964. The Central Committee removed Khrushchev from power in 1964.

KOSYGIN, ALEKSEI (1904–80). During the postwar years, Kosygin served as minister of finance (1948) and minister of light industry (1948–53). He was also a candidate member of the Presidium in 1946 and 1952–53 and a full member from 1948 to 1952. After Stalin's death, Kosygin was excluded from the Presidium entirely. His political fortunes improved in 1959, when he became chairman of Gosplan, and in 1960, when he again became a full member of the Presidium. After Khrushchev's ouster in 1964, Kosygin became chairman of the Council of Ministers, the preeminent position in the Soviet government.

KOZLOV, FROL (1908–65). After the purge of the Leningrad party organization (see Voznesenskii entry), Kozlov served as secretary of the party committee for the city of Leningrad (1950–52) and the party committee for Leningrad oblast (1953–57). A Khrushchev loyalist, Kozlov became a member of the Central Committee Presidium after the unsuccessful antiparty group coup in 1957. After Khrushchev's dismissal, Kozlov was removed from power.

KRUZHKOV, VLADIMIR (1905–91). A philosopher by training, Kruzhkov served as director of the Institute of Marx, Engels, and Lenin from 1944 to 1949 and was a member of the Academy of Sciences (1953). From 1949 to 1955, Kruzhkov was on the staff of the Central Committee, where he became an important figure in ideological and cultural affairs. He was demoted in 1955 to a position at the Urals State University, allegedly for his ties to Georgii Aleksandrov, then embroiled in a sex scandal.

KRZHIZHANOVSKII, GLEB (1872–1959). An old Bolshevik, Krzhizhanovskii served in a variety of positions in the Soviet government in the 1920s, eventually becoming vice president of the Academy of Sciences (1929–39).

KUIBYSHEV, VALERIAN (1888–1935). An old Bolshevik, Kuibyshev became a member of the Central Committee in 1922 and the Politburo in 1927. From 1930 to 1934, Kuibyshev ran Gosplan. At the time of his death in 1935, he was chairman of the USSR Commission on State Control and deputy chairman of the USSR Council of People's Commissars.

LENIN, VLADIMIR (1870–1924). Lenin was the central figure in the development of the Russian Marxist movement and the founding of the Soviet Union. First arrested in 1895, Lenin spent more than two decades in internal and external exile. He returned to Russia in the spring of 1917, where he oversaw the Bolshevik seizure of power in October. After this date, Lenin was chairman of the Council of People's Commissars.

LEONT'EV, LEV (1901–74). Leont'ev, an economist, became a corresponding member of the Academy of Sciences in 1939. He helped draft the textbook on political economy that Stalin edited after the war.

LITVINOV, MAKSIM (1876–1951). A longtime Soviet diplomat, Litvinov served as Soviet ambassador to Britain (1918), Estonia (1920), the League of Nations (1934–38), and the United States (1941–43). From 1930 to 1939, Litvinov was the people's commissar of foreign affairs.

LUNACHARSKII, ANATOLII (1875–1933). An old Bolshevik and briefly a Menshevik, Lunacharskii served until 1929 as the first commissar of enlightenment.

LYSENKO, TROFIM (1898–1976). A biologist by training, a member of the Academy of Sciences (1939), president of the prestigious Lenin Academy of Agricultural Sciences (1938–56, 1961–62), and a three-time Stalin Prize winner, Lysenko argued for the inheritability of acquired traits. Though contradicting the findings of modern genetics, Lysenko's views in the field of agronomy enjoyed the support of Stalin and Khrushchev.

MALENKOV, GEORGII (1901–88). Upon Stalin's death, Malenkov became chairman of the Council of Ministers, a position he held until 1955. He was also a member of the Politburo/Presidium from 1946 to 1957. A central figure in the antiparty group, Malenkov was removed from power in 1957.

MAO ZEDONG (1893–1976). Mao was the leader of the Chinese Communist Party from 1943 until his death, and the leading political figure in the People's Republic of China.

MIKOIAN, ANASTAS (1895–1978). Mikoian was an old Bolshevik who distinguished himself in the Caucasus in the early years of Soviet power. He became a full member of the Politburo/Presidium in 1935, a position he held for more than three decades.

MOLOTOV, VIACHESLAV (1890–1986). An old Bolshevik, Molotov came to prominence in the 1920s as an ally of Joseph Stalin. He was a member of the Politburo/Presidium from 1927 to 1957 and the minister of foreign affairs from 1939 to 1949. During the final years of Stalin's life, Molotov fell out of favor. Nonetheless, he was one of the key figures in the collective leadership in 1953. Molotov was removed from power after the antiparty group coup in 1957.

NESMEIANOV, ALEKSANDR (1899–1980). Nesmeianov, an organic chemist, was rector of Moscow State University from 1948 to 1951 and president of the Academy of Sciences from 1951 to 1961.

ORDZHONIKIDZE, GRIGORII (Sergo; 1886–1937). An old Bolshevik, Ordzhonikidze came to prominence in the Caucasus during the first years of Soviet power. Ordzhonikidze became a Politburo member in 1930 and led the Supreme Economic Council from 1930 to its demise two years later. After this date, Ordzhonikidze became minister of heavy industry. He committed suicide in 1937, allegedly to protest mass repression.

OSTROVITIANOV, KONSTANTIN (1892–1969). Ostrovitianov, an economist, served as vice president of the Academy of Sciences from 1953 to 1962. In the early 1950s, he helped draft the political economy textbook that Stalin edited.

PERVUKHIN, MIKHAIL (1904–78). One of the young cadres that Stalin promoted to supreme power at the Nineteenth Party Congress, Pervukhin was a member of the Presidium from 1952 to 1957. He was also a deputy chairman of the Council of Ministers from 1940 to 1944 and 1950 to 1957. Implicated in the antiparty group, Pervukhin was demoted in 1957.

PONOMAREV, BORIS (1905–95). Ponomarev, a historian by training, was deputy director of the Institute of Marx, Engels, and Lenin from 1943 to 1944 and a longtime staff member in the Central Committee and a number of other institutions. He became a member of the Central Committee in 1956, where he oversaw relations with foreign communist parties. In 1972 he became a candidate member of the Politburo.

POSKREBYSHEV, ALEKSANDR (1891–1965). Poskrebyshev, a Central Committee staff member in the 1920s and early 1930s, served as Stalin's secretary from 1931 to 1952.

POSPELOV, PETR (1898–1979). Pospelov was a member of the Central Committee from 1939 to 1971 and chief editor of *Pravda* from 1940 to 1949. Pospelov helped draft Khrushchev's secret speech at the Twentieth Party Congress.

SABUROV, MAKSIM (1900–1977). Like Pervukhin, Saburov was one of the young cadres that Stalin promoted to the Presidium at the Nineteenth Party Congress. After Stalin's death, Saburov lost his Presidium post but was appointed chairman of Gosplan (1953–55) and deputy chairman of the USSR Council of Ministers (1953–55). Implicated in the antiparty group, Saburov was demoted in 1957.

SATIUKOV, PAVEL (1911–76). Satiukov was chief editor of the newspaper *Culture and Life* from 1949 to 1956 and *Pravda* from 1956 to 1964. From 1962 to 1965 he was head of the Union of Journalists.

SEMASHKO, NIKOLAI (1874–1949). An old Bolshevik, Semashko was appointed people's commissar of health in 1918, a position he held for more than two decades.

SEROV, IVAN (1905–90). A longtime official in the secret police, Serov served as head of the KGB from 1954 to 1958.

SHVERNIK, NIKOLAI (1888–1970). After Kalinin's death in 1946, Shvernik became chairman of the Presidium of the Supreme Soviet. He was also a member of the Central Committee Presidium from 1952 to 1953 and 1957 to 1966. Shvernik played a central role in the rehabilitation of people repressed under Stalin. As a Khrushchev loyalist, he was removed from power in 1966.

STALIN, JOSEPH (1879–1953). Stalin was the preeminent figure in Soviet politics after Lenin's death in 1924. From 1922 until his own death, he occupied the post of general secretary of the party. From 1941 he was also chairman of the Council of Ministers.

SUN YAT-SEN (1866–1925). Sun was a Chinese nationalist and revolutionary who played a central role in the destruction of the Qing dynasty and the creation of the Chinese Republic. In 1912, Sun became the first president of China.

SUSLOV, MIKHAIL (1902–82). Suslov, a member of the Central Committee Presidium/Politburo from 1952 to 1953 and 1955 to 1982, was the party's chief ideologue during the 1960s and 1970s. He was also editor of *Pravda* from 1949 to 1950.

TROTSKY, LEON (1879–1940). A Menshevik before 1917, Trotsky was, in 1923–24, the central figure in the Bolshevik party's left opposition, which sought to stem the tide of bureaucratization and centralization within the party, and, in 1926–27, the central figure in the United Opposition, which opposed Stalin. Trotsky was forced to leave the Soviet Union in 1929. In 1940, on Stalin's orders, he was murdered in Mexico.

VOROSHILOV, KLIMENT (1881–1969). A hero of the Civil War, Voroshilov became a close ally of Joseph Stalin in the 1920s. Voroshilov was a member of the Politburo from 1926 to 1960, people's commissar of defense from 1934 to 1940, and chairman of the Presidium of the Supreme Soviet from 1953 to 1960.

VOZNESENSKII, NIKOLAI (1903–50). An economist by training, Voznesenskii led Gosplan from 1938 to 1941 and 1942 to 1949. In 1947 he became a member of the Central Committee Presidium. Two years later, he fell victim to the Leningrad affair, with its trumped-up charges that a group of present and former Leningrad party and state officials had conspired to remove Leningrad from the Soviet Union. Voznesenskii was executed in 1950.

VYSHINSKII, ANDREI (1883–1954). From 1935 to 1939, Vyshinskii was the Soviet Union's chief prosecutor and the architect of the show trials of the former oppositionists. From 1949 to 1953, Vyshinskii served as minister of foreign affairs.

ZHDANOV, ANDREI (1896–1948). Zhdanov, a Politburo member since 1939, was the party's chief ideologue in the postwar years. He orchestrated the intellectual and cultural crackdown—the so-called *zhdanovshchina*—that began in 1946. Zhdanov died of natural causes in 1948.

ZHDANOV, IURII (b. 1919). The son of Andrei Zhdanov, Iurii Zhdanov was head of the Central Committee's Science Department from 1947 to 1950. He was briefly married to Stalin's daughter. In April 1948 he publicly criticized Lysenko at a meeting of party propagandists, an episode that Shepilov details.

ZHOU ENLAI (1898–1976). An important figure in the Chinese Communist Party, Zhou served as head of the Chinese government from 1949 until his death. Widely perceived as a moderate, Zhou was a target of the Gang of Four, the political leaders blamed for many of the excesses of the Cultural Revolution.

ZHUKOV, GEORGII (1896–1974). A marshal in the Second World War, Zhukov returned to the Soviet Union a widely popular hero. After Stalin's death, Zhukov became minister of defense (1955) and a member of the Presidium

(1957). Khrushchev removed Zhukov from power in October 1957, allegedly for trying to organize a military coup.

ZINOVIEV, GRIGORII (1883–1936). An old Bolshevik, Zinoviev was a central figure in the party's United Opposition against Stalin in 1926. He was arrested in 1935 for complicity in the murder of Sergei Kirov, secretary of the Leningrad Party Committee, and executed after a show trial in 1936.

NOTES

INTRODUCTION: THE RISE AND FALL OF DMITRII SHEPILOV

1. This was the phrasing in the Central Committee's decree on the June Plenum and the subsequent letter to party members describing the antiparty group. See A. N. Iakovlev, ed., *Molotov, Malenkov, Kaganovich. 1957. Stenogramma iiun'skogo plenuma TsK KPSS i drugie dokumenty* (Moscow, 1998), 566, 578. The phrasing was also the subject of many popular jokes: Shepilov supposedly had the longest name in the Soviet Union.

2. "Sem'ia Shepilovykh (Po pis'mam Iuriia Trofimovicha i Aleksandra Trofimovicha, brat'ev Shepilova, v otvet na ego pros'bu ostavit' vospominaniia ob istorii ikh sem'i)," in *I primknuvshii k nim Shepilov: Pravda o cheloveke, uchenom, voine, politike*, ed. Tamara Tolchanova and Mikhail Lozhnikov (Moscow, 1998), 35–38.

3. Yuri Slezkine, "Lives as Tales," in *In the Shadow of Revolution: Life Stories of Russian Women from 1917 to the Second World War*, ed. Sheila Fitzpatrick and Yuri Slezkine (Ithaca, N.Y., 2000), 22–23.

4. On the events surrounding Iurii Zhdanov's speech, see Ethan Pollock, *Stalin and the Soviet Science Wars* (Princeton, N.J., 2006), 41–71; Nikolai Krementsov, *Stalinist Science* (Princeton, N.J., 1997), 161–69; and Valery N. Soyfer, *Lysenko and the Tragedy of Soviet Science* (New Brunswick, N.J., 1994), 170–82. Iurii Zhdanov does not corroborate Shepilov's claim to have spoken in defense of genetics. See Iurii Zhdanov, "Vo mgle protivorechii," *Voprosy filosofii* 7 (1993): 86–87.

5. On the political economy textbook, see Pollock, *Stalin and the Soviet Science Wars*, 168–211; Pollock, "Conversations with Stalin on Questions of Political Economy," Cold War International History Project, Working Paper no. 33 (Washington, D.C., 2001), 5–13.

6. Yoram Gorlizki and Oleg Khlevniuk, *Cold Peace: Stalin and the Soviet Ruling Circle* (Oxford, 2004), 75–76.

7. William Taubman, *Khrushchev: The Man and His Era* (New York, 2003), 313.

8. Dmitrii Kosyrev, "On mog by vozglavit' stranu," in *I primknuvshii k nim Shepilov*, ed. Tolchanova and Lozhnikov, 32.

9. Mohamed Heikal, *The Sphinx and the Commissar: The Rise and Fall of Soviet Influence in the Middle East* (New York, 1978), 92, quoted in Taubman, *Khrushchev*, 313.

10. Iakovlev, *Molotov, Malenkov, and Kaganovich*, 143. On Kaganovich's banishment to the southern Urals, see "'Tovarishch Kaganovich pretenduet na osoboe k sebe otnoshenie.' Ural'skaia ssylka opal'nogo soratnika I. V. Stalina. 1957–1958 gg.," *Istoricheskii arkhiv* 4 (August 2005): 2–26.

11. Dmitrii Kosyrev, "Emotsial'nyi portret epokhi," introduction to Dmitrii Shepilov, *Neprimknuvshii* (Moscow, 2001), 11–12.

12. Dmitrii Kosyrev, unpublished essay. (This is a revised version of the essay cited in the previous note.)

13. David Nordlander, "Khrushchev's Image in Light of Glasnost and Perestroika," *Russian Review* 52, no. 2 (April 1993): 248–64.

14. Igal Halfin, "From Darkness to Light: Student Communist Autobiography during NEP," *Jahrbücher für Geschichte Osteuropas* 45 (1997): 210–36; Halfin, *From Darkness to Light: Class, Consciousness, and Salvation in Revolutionary Russia* (Pittsburgh, Pa., 2000).

15. Yoram Gorlizki, "Ordinary Stalinism: The Council of Ministers and the Soviet Neopatrimonial State, 1946–1953," *Journal of Modern History* 74, no. 4 (December 2002): 720–21.

16. "Shepilov's Speech at the Congress of Soviet Composers," *Current Digest of the Soviet Press* 9 (May 8, 1957): 17, quoted in different form in S. Frederick Starr, *Red and Hot: The Fate of Jazz in the Soviet Union* (New York, 1982), 249. On the political significance of Shepilov's speech, see Boris Schwartz, *Music and Musical Life in Soviet Russia, 1917–1970* (New York, 1972), 301–02.

17. Kosyrev, "On mog by vozglavit' stranu," 31.

18. Andrei Voznesenskii, "Bez nego ia by ne pisal Ozy," *Nezavisimaia gazeta*, April 15, 1994, p. 7, quoted in Iurii Aksiutin, "Popular Responses to Khrushchev," in *Nikita Khrushchev*, ed. William Taubman, Sergei Khrushchev, and Abbott Gleason (New Haven, 2000), 199. For similar criticism from one of Khrushchev's rivals, see Felix Chuev, *Molotov Remembers: Inside Kremlin Politics*, ed. Albert Resis (Chicago, 1993), 346–69.

19. On the tendency to create binary correlations between the Stalin and Khrushchev periods, see Stephen F. Cohen, *Rethinking the Soviet Experience: Politics and History since 1917* (New York, 1985), 109, 128–34; Anna Krylova, "The Tenacious Liberal Subject in Soviet Studies," *Kritika* 1, no. 1 (Winter 2000): 131–33; Miriam Dobson, "Contesting the Paradigms of De-Stalinization: Readers' Responses to *One Day in the Life of Ivan Denisovich*," *Slavic Review* 64, no. 3 (Fall 2005): 580–600.

CHAPTER ONE. STALIN IS DEAD

1. Mikhail Suslov (1902–82), editor of *Pravda* (1949–50) and member of the Politburo/Presidium (1952–53, 1955–82). During the 1960s and 1970s, Suslov was the Soviet Union's chief ideologue.

2. Mikhail Kutuzov (1745–1813), field marshal who led Russian soldiers in the Napoleonic Wars in 1805 and 1812–13.

3. A fabricated plot, made public in 1952–53, that a group of mostly Jewish doctors had conspired to murder party leaders through misdiagnoses and wrong treatments.

4. The Stalin Prize was the Soviet Union's most prestigious award for cultural and scientific achievement.

5. Region north of Magadan in the Far East where many prisoners were sent.

6. Charges that surfaced in 1949 that top party leaders, including Nikolai Voznesenskii, had conspired to turn the Leningrad party organization into a base for anti-Soviet activities. Shepilov discusses the Leningrad affair in more detail in Chapter 7.

7. In 1952, Stalin created the bureau of the Central Committee Presidium, the innermost circle of Soviet power, to counteract the enlargement of the Presidium at the Nineteenth Party Congress. See Gorlizki and Khlevniuk, *Cold Peace,* 153.

8. *Kharcho* is a Georgian beef stew; *chakhokhbili* is a Georgian chicken stew.

9. Nikolai Ezhov (1895–1940), member of the Central Committee (1934–38), candidate member of the Politburo (1937–38), and people's commissar for internal affairs (chief of the secret police, 1936–38).

10. Nikolai Bulganin (1895–1975), member of the Politburo/Presidium (1948–58), minister of defense (1953–55), and chairman of the Council of Ministers (1955–58).

11. Lazar Kaganovich (1893–1991), member of the communist party since 1911, chief of the Moscow Party Committee (1930–35), member of the Politburo/Presidium (1930–57), and a central figure in the antiparty group in 1957 (which Shepilov discusses in the Epilogue).

12. Maksim Saburov (1900–1977), member of the Presidium (1952–57). Saburov was implicated in the antiparty group in 1957.

13. Mikhail Pervukhin (1904–78), member of the Presidium (1952–57) and deputy chairman of the Council of Ministers (1950–57). Pervukhin was implicated in the antiparty group in 1957.

14. Nikolai Shvernik (1888–1970), a communist party member since 1905 and a member of the Central Committee Presidium (1952–53, 1957–66). Shvernik played a central role in the rehabilitation of people who were repressed under Stalin. On rehabilitation see Chapter 2, note 3.

15. Ivan the Terrible (1530–84), tsar. The tsar-bell, supposedly the largest in the world, was cast on the site in the 1730s. It cracked before it could be hung.

16. Boris Godunov (1551–1605), regent of Russia (1584–98) and the first tsar from outside the Riurikid dynasty (1598–1605).

17. Aleksandr Suvorov (1729–1800), field marshal who fought in the Russo-Turkish War (1787–92), quelled the Kościuszko Uprising in Poland (1794), and led the campaign in Italy against revolutionary France (1799).

18. Petr Pospelov (1898–1979), member of the Central Committee (1939–71), editor of *Pravda* (1940–49), director of the Institute of Marx, Engels, and Lenin (1949–52), and member of the Presidium (1957–61). Pospelov played a central role in researching Khrushchev's revelations about Stalin's cult of personality at the Twentieth Party Congress.

19. Acronym for the Communist Union of Youth.

20. Period associated with Stalin's Great Purges.

21. Maurice Thorez (1900–1964), leader of the French Communist Party.

22. Olga Berggol'ts (1910–75) was arrested in 1937, at the height of the Great Purges, as an "enemy of the people." She was set free in 1939 and remained in Leningrad during the German and Finnish blockade (September 1941 to January 1944). Of the three million people who resided in prewar Leningrad, almost half perished during the blockade, mostly through starvation and exposure.

23. Lev Leont'ev (1901–74), Soviet economist and corresponding member of the Academy of Sciences.

24. In 1960.

25. In 1770 a Russian fleet under the command of Aleksei Orlov defeated the Ottoman navy at the Bay of Chesme in the Aegean Sea.

26. Konstantin Rokossovskii (1896–1968), a hero of Stalingrad. Rokossovskii was the child of a Russian mother and a Polish father and spent part of his childhood in Warsaw. He was imprisoned in the late 1930s on charges that he was a Polish spy.

27. Acronym for the Communist International, an organization dedicated to advancing the cause of socialism internationally.

28. Saifuddin Kitchlew (1888–1963), Indian nationalist and opponent of the 1947 partition of India and Pakistan.

29. Khodynka, a field on the outskirts of Moscow, was the site of the coronation of Nicholas II in 1896. Hundreds of people were trampled to death amid rumors that each person who attended would receive a gift from the tsar. In the wake of subsequent catastrophes and the end of the Romanov dynasty in 1917, Khodynka was popularly recast as an omen of future troubles.

CHAPTER TWO. *EZHOVSHCHINA*

1. *Ezhovshchina*, literally the "time of Ezhov," refers to the period of the Great Purges, 1936–38, when Nikolai Ezhov ran the secret police. Shepilov also uses *berievshchina* and *khrushchevshchina* to refer to later periods of senseless brutality associated with Beria and Khrushchev.

2. Shepilov is using an outdated acronym. GPU, the State Political Administration, was the agency that combated counterrevolutionary activity in 1922–23. The secret police went by several different institutional names during the

Soviet period: the Extraordinary Commission (Cheka), the GPU, the United State Political Administration (OGPU), the People's Commissariat of Internal Affairs (NKVD), the People's Commissariat of State Security (NKGB), the Ministry of State Security (MGB), the Ministry of Internal Affairs (MVD), and the Committee for State Security (KGB).

3. Rehabilitation was the process that began after Stalin's death whereby people who had been wrongfully convicted had their names cleared and their party memberships and civil rights restored.

4. Lenin's published writings include correspondence with and directives to Krumin. See his *Collected Works* (Moscow, 1971–76), vol. 42, pp. 356–57; vol. 45, pp. 220–21, 524–25.

5. A "silver pine forest" on the western fringe of Moscow where city residents could swim in the river and enjoy nature.

6. Rudolf Hilferding (1877–1941), German Marxist and politician.

7. A Trotskyite was a follower of Leon Trotsky (1879–1940), Stalin's chief rival during the early and mid 1920s. Trotsky was critical of the lack of intraparty democracy. After the defeat of the "United Opposition" of Trotsky, Lev Kamenev, and Grigorii Zinoviev in 1927, Trotsky was exiled to Central Asia and eventually deported.

8. German workers and soldiers rebelled in 1918 in the final days of the First World War. They demanded the creation of a socialist republic. The disturbances were quelled in 1919.

9. That is, in a working-class district of Saint Petersburg.

10. Simon Petliura (1879–1926), Ukrainian nationalist and, from 1919 to 1920, before Ukraine was incorporated into the Soviet Union, leader of Ukraine.

11. In February 1956.

12. Ivan Babushkin (1873–1906), one of the first social democrats in Russia drawn from the working class and a founding member of the Bolshevik party.

13. Mikhail Kalinin (1875–1946), longtime chairman of the Central Executive Committee and member of the Politburo.

14. The official history of the communist party that was published in 1938 and attributed to Stalin after the war.

15. This is a double pun on the word *ezh* (hedgehog) and the phrase *derzhat' v ezhovykh rukavitsakh* (to rule with a rod of iron).—Tr.

16. In other words, a person who is no longer useful is no longer wanted. This saying, often invoked in Russian, originated in Friedrich Schiller's 1783 play, *Fiesco, or the Conspiracy of Genoa*.

17. Gaius Mucius Scaevola, hero of the early Roman Republic. According to Livy, when the Etruscans besieged Rome around 505 BCE, Caius Mucius tried to murder their leader. After being captured, Caius Mucius dismissed the threat of torture by placing his right hand in a fire, thus earning the nickname "Left Hand" (*scaevola*).

18. Galicia is a region presently in western Ukraine and southern Poland. At the

outset of the First World War, it was part of the Austro-Hungarian Empire. The reference to the First World War is an anachronism, since the conversation took place before the beginning of the Second World War.

19. Anton Denikin (1872–1947), leader of anti-Soviet forces during the Russian Civil War.

20. A nature preserve in the southern Ukrainian steppe.

21. Aleksandr Serebrovskii (1892–1948), Soviet biologist and geneticist who proposed the theory of the divisibility of genes.

22. Mikhail (1891–1957) and Boris (1895–1951) Zavadovskii, Soviet biologists and geneticists.

23. Gregor Mendel (1822–84), an Austrian biologist and a seminal figure in early genetics who was noted for his study of pea plants.

24. Thomas Hunt Morgan (1866–1945), American geneticist and Nobel laureate who was noted for his work on *Drosophilae*.

25. Nikolai Vavilov (1887–1943) and Nikolai Kol'tsov (1872–1940), Soviet biologists and geneticists.

26. Trofim Lysenko (1898–1976), Soviet biologist who argued for the inheritability of acquired characteristics and denied the veracity of modern genetics. After the Second World War, both Stalin and Khrushchev endorsed Lysenko's theories.

27. Popular nickname for the car favored by the NKVD.

28. Cesare Lombroso (1835–1909), Italian criminologist who argued that criminality was an inherited condition and could thus be discerned in a criminal's physical appearance.

29. Acronym for the Extraordinary Commission, the secret police agency that was created in December 1917. The Cheka's first director was Feliks Dzerzhinskii (1877–1926).

30. Followers of Nikolai Bukharin (1888–1938). In the late 1920s, Bukharin was the central figure in the party's right opposition, which argued against ending the New Economic Policy (NEP).

31. Julian the Apostate was the Roman Emperor Flavius Claudius Julianus (331–63), who converted from Christianity to paganism. "You have conquered, Galilean!" were supposedly Julian's last words, a recognition that Christianity would triumph in the Roman Empire despite his apostasy.

32. Even though Bukharin was the central figure in the right opposition in the late 1920s, the book he cowrote with Evgenii Preobrazhenskii in 1920, *The ABCs of Communism*, was indicative of a younger Bukharin who was to the left of the party on important issues.

CHAPTER THREE. MY FIRST MEETINGS WITH KHRUSHCHEV

1. Officially, the Central Committee discussed the Soviet Union's new election law and a handful of agricultural issues at the June 1937 plenum. In reality, the plenum was dedicated to the rising wave of repression and

vast counterrevolutionary plots that implicated even members of the Central Committee.

2. City in eastern Romania.

3. Bogdan Khmel'nitskii (ca. 1595–1657), Ukrainian military hero and political leader who petitioned Tsar Aleksei Mikhailovich to unite Russia and Ukraine.

4. In 1948 the Central Committee's Bureau (*upravlenie*) of Propaganda and Agitation was renamed the Department (*otdel*) of Propaganda and Agitation. Both went by the acronym Agitprop. Shepilov discusses the renaming of Agitprop in Chapter 6.

5. Vatutin died in 1944 as result of injuries sustained in an ambush by Ukrainian nationalists.

6. Shepilov is referring to P. Bogdanov, *Rasskaz o pochetnom shakhtere: N. S. Khrushchev v Donbasse* (Stalino, USSR, 1961).

7. Kulaks were wealthy peasants.

8. A workers' school, commonly rendered with the acronym *rabfak,* catered to workers who lacked a secondary education but wished to pursue a degree at a university or a technical institute.

9. A participant in a labor movement named for Aleksei Stakhanov (1906–77), a coal miner in Ukraine who became a hero for cutting 102 tons of coal in less than six hours in 1935. After Stakhanov's feat, Stakhanovites across the Soviet Union tried to set production records.

10. *Kh* is a single Russian letter.—Tr.

11. Iakov Sverdlov (1885–1919), a communist party member since 1902 and a central figure in the 1917 revolutions.

12. Anatolii Lunacharskii (1875–1933), a communist party member since 1903 and the people's commissar of enlightenment from 1917 to 1929.

13. Georgii Chicherin (1872–1936), people's commissar of foreign affairs (1918–30).

14. Nikolai Semashko (1874–1949), people's commissar of health in the 1920s and 1930s.

15. Maksim Litvinov (1876–1951), a communist party member since 1898 and people's commissar of foreign affairs from 1930 to 1939.

16. Mikhail Frunze (1885–1925), a communist party member since 1903 and a hero of the Russian Civil War.

17. Gleb Krzhizhanovskii (1872–1959), old Bolshevik. After 1917, Krzhizhanovskii served the Soviet state in a variety of different capacities, eventually becoming vice president of the Academy of Sciences.

18. Nadezhda Krupskaia (1869–1939), wife of Lenin. After 1917, Krupskaia became an important figure in Soviet educational circles.

19. Valerian Kuibyshev (1888–1935), a communist party member since 1904, member of the Politburo (1927–35), and chairman of Gosplan (1930–34).

20. Stepan Khalturin (ca. 1856–82), executed for assassinating V. S. Strel'nikov, a prosecutor, in Odessa.

21. Petr Alekseev (1849–91), sentenced to ten years' hard labor in 1877 at the trial of "The Fifty" (the members of the All-Russian Social-Revolutionary Organization).

22. An 1885 strike in the city of Orekhovo-Zuevo, east of Moscow, at a factory owned by Savva Morozov.

23. The newspaper that Lenin founded in Leipzig in 1900.

24. Manolis Glezos (b. 1922), hero of the Greek resistance in the Second World War who was later imprisoned for his socialist beliefs. In 1943 he helped tear the Nazi flag from the Acropolis, the episode that Shepilov may be referring to. In 1963, Glezos won the Lenin Peace Prize.

25. Aleksandr Fadeev (1901–56), Soviet writer, secretary of the Writers' Union, and author of a novel entitled *The Young Guard* (1945).

26. Karl Friedrich Hieronymus, Baron von Münchhausen (1720–97), German nobleman and writer who was famous for his unbelievable tales.

27. In March and April 1912, workers in the Lena goldfields in northeastern Siberia went on strike. More than two hundred were killed by troops who quelled the unrest.

28. Grigorii (Sergo) Ordzhonikidze (1886–1937), a communist party member since 1903, member of the Politburo, and chairman of the Supreme Soviet of the People's Economy (1930–32). Ordzhonikidze committed suicide, allegedly to protest the mounting wave of repression.

29. Fedor (Artem) Sergeev (1883–1921), a communist party member since 1901 and chairman of the Moscow Party Committee (1920–21).

30. Grigorii Petrovskii (1878–1958), a communist party member since 1897 and a longtime figure in the Ukrainian Communist Party.

31. Alexander Kerensky (1881–1970), a prominent figure in the Socialist-Revolutionary (SR) Party, which enjoyed a great deal of support among the peasantry. Kerensky became prime minister of the Provisional Government in July 1917 and went into exile after the victory of the Bolsheviks in October.

CHAPTER FOUR. ZHDANOV SUMMONS ME

1. A euphemistic way of referring to the power struggle among Stalin's potential heirs.

2. Choir that performs folk music.

3. Georgii Plekhanov (1856–1918), Marxist theorist and founder of the social-democratic movement in Russia.

4. Ferdinand Lassalle (1825–64), German socialist, participant in the 1848 revolution, and leader of first German labor party.

5. Karl Kautsky (1854–1938), German Marxist theorist.

6. François Marie Charles Fourier (1772–1837), French utopian socialist.

7. Aleksandr Bogdanov (1873–1928), Soviet philosopher and writer and a central figure in the proletarian culture (Proletkult) movement.

8. Mikhail Pokrovskii (1868–1932), Soviet historian in the 1920s who reinterpreted Russian history through the lens of class struggle. As Soviet culture

became more conventional and Russocentric in the 1930s, Pokrovskii's work fell out of favor.

9. Mikhail Reisner (1868–1928), prominent Soviet legal theorist.

10. The Living Church was a schismatic group within the Russian Orthodox Church that was headed by Aleksandr Vvedenskii and that sought to liberalize church policy on issues like clerical marriage. The Living Church was often supported by the Soviet government, which saw it as a way to weaken the church as a whole.

11. Adherents of *Smena vekh* (Changing Signposts), a journal that was published abroad in the early 1920s by Russian émigrés. *Smenavekhovtsy* advocated reconciliation with the Soviet state, which they saw as strengthening Russia.

12. Region in northeastern Siberia.

13. Participants in a failed revolt against Nicholas I in December 1825. Decembrists hoped for the creation of a constitutional monarchy.

14. Terrorist organization that assassinated Aleksandr II in 1881.

15. Region east of Moscow along the Volga River.

16. Presently Arbat Street.

17. The address of several academic and cultural institutes.

18. On the sex scandal that disgraced Aleksandrov in 1955, see Z. Vodop'ianova, G. Ivanov, and L. Shishkova, eds., "Elochka i drugie liudoedki," *Nastoiashchee* (May 1999): 5–7.

19. Prior to the creation of the Holy Roman Empire, the Karanthanians (the predecessors to the Slovenes) sought union with the Bavarians to protect themselves from nomadic tribes to the east. Contrary to Shepilov's assertion, however, Slovenes are Slavic rather than Germanic.

20. Shepilov is referring to Charlemagne (ca. 742–814), king of the Franks, who united much of western and central Europe in the Holy Roman Empire.

21. Shepilov is referring to *Ostmark,* the modern German rendering of a vernacular term (*Ostarrîchi*) that designated the core territories of present-day Austria. The term originated in a tenth-century conflict between the Duke of Bavaria, Henry the Quarrelsome, and the German king Otto II over control of the Ostmark.

22. In 1278, Rudolph I defeated Ottokar II of Bohemia and thus brought Austria under Hapsburg rule.

23. The Austrian inquisition peaked under Rudolph II (1552–1612).

24. A rural uprising in 1524–25 that was inspired by the Protestant Reformation.

25. Shepilov is likely referring to the Battle of Vienna (1683), when a combined Hapsburg and Polish army defeated the Ottomans on the outskirts of Vienna. The Austro-Turkish War occurred later (1716–18), but there was little activity in the vicinity of Vienna.

CHAPTER FIVE. AGITPROP UNDER ZHDANOV

1. Fyodor Dostoevsky (1821–81), a Russian writer who was arrested as a young man for involvement in the Petrashevskii circle (see note 3) and sentenced to death. His sentence was commuted at the last minute to imprisonment in Siberia (the subject of *Notes from the House of the Dead*). Dostoevsky's later novels, like *Crime and Punishment* and *The Brothers Karamazov*, celebrate Christian virtues like suffering and humility. In *The Possessed*, Dostoevsky criticized the supposed nihilism of the revolutionary movement.

2. Maxim Gorky (1868–1936), writer who left the Soviet Union in the early 1920s over differences with the Bolsheviks. After his return a decade later, Gorky was officially embraced as the central writer of the revolution.

3. Group organized by Mikhail Petrashevskii (1821–66) that discussed literature and philosophy. In 1849 its members were arrested.

4. Aleksandr Kuprin (1870–1938), Russian writer. After 1917, Kuprin emigrated to the West, where he remained until 1937.

5. Gleb Uspenskii (1843–1902), Russian writer noted for his romantic views of the peasantry.

6. Vissarion Belinskii (1811–48), a prominent Russian literary critic.

7. Vano Muradeli (1908–70), Soviet composer. On February 10, 1948, the Central Committee published a decree criticizing Muradeli's opera *Great Friendship* for being formalist and antidemocratic.

8. City on the Sea of Azov in Ukraine.

9. City northwest of Moscow.

10. Presently Nizhnyi Novgorod oblast, east of Moscow.

11. In 1934.

12. In 1939.

13. Agitprop employees.

14. Vladimir Stasov (1824–1906), Russian art and music critic.

15. Aleksandr Serov (1820–71), Russian composer and critic.

16. Shepilov is mistaken about the dates of the zhdanovshchina. Three of the Central Committee decrees that he identifies were issued in 1946. (See the following notes.)

17. On August 14, 1946, the Central Committee criticized *Star* and *Leningrad* for a variety of ideological deficiencies. At a speech in Leningrad soon thereafter, Zhdanov attacked the writers Anna Akhmatova and Mikhail Zoshchenko. Both were expelled from the Writers' Union.

18. On August 26, 1946, the Central Committee criticized theater officials for staging an insufficient number of contemporary Soviet plays.

19. On September 4, 1946, the Central Committee criticized Leonid Lukov's *A Great Life* for incorrectly depicting Soviet life in the Donbass.

20. Shepilov is referring to the period before the adoption of the Popular Front strategy in 1935, when the Comintern rejected cooperation with socialist parties that advocated nonrevolutionary social democracy. Stalin and the Comintern publicly referred to social democrats as "social fascists" and

rightists. This policy emasculated social-democratic parties at the very moment fascism was on the rise.

21. In the late 1940s, Josef Tito, leader of the Yugoslavian Communist Party, rejected the universality of the Soviet experience and its hegemony over the international communist movement and instead pursued the "national road to communism."

22. In the fourteenth century, the Ottoman sultan Murad I compelled Christian youths from the Balkans and elsewhere to serve as Janissaries, elite military servitors who protected the sultan and other high officials. The Turkish government continued to use Janissaries until the nineteenth century.

23. Abram Deborin (1881–1963), Soviet philosopher. In the 1920s, Deborin argued that science had class aspects and that Soviet scientists had to be vigilant for bourgeois propaganda masked as scientific truth. In the early 1930s, Deborin's ideas fell out of favor.

24. Owing to the thirteen-day discrepancy between the Julian calendar in use in 1917 and the Gregorian calendar adopted later, the anniversary of what we now call the October Revolution was celebrated in November.

25. Similarly, in 1936 the Central Committee denounced Dmitrii Shostakovich's opera *Lady Macbeth of the Mtsensk District*, calling it "confusion instead of music."

26. Presently the capital of Uzbekistan. In 1918 it was the capital of the Turkestan Autonomous Soviet Socialist Republic.

27. Presently the capital of Turkmenistan. When Shepilov lived in Ashkhabad, it was in the Turkestan Autonomous Soviet Socialist Republic.

28. Nomadic steppe people who waged war against the early Russian princes.

29. River in Uzbekistan.

30. Iakov Polonskii (1819–98), Russian poet and lyricist.

31. Shostakovich (1906–75), Scriabin (1872–1915), and especially Stravinsky (1882–1971) experimented with atonal, bitonal, and polyphonic composition, which Soviet cultural authorities often labeled as formalist.

32. Elite dacha community outside Moscow.

33. In 1952 the Politburo was designated the Central Committee Presidium. Shepilov uses the terms interchangeably.

34. Novel by Maxim Gorky.

35. Iraklii Toidze (1902–65), Soviet artist and architect who is famous for his wartime poster "Motherland Calls."

36. Anatolii Iar-Kravchenko (1911–83), Soviet artist and recipient of the Stalin Prize.

37. Nikolai Chernyshevskii (1828–89), a Russian socialist, a populist, and the author of the novel *What Is to Be Done?*

38. From December 1944 to December 1949, Popov occupied both positions simultaneously.

39. Aleksandr Matrosov (1924–43), hero of the Second World War.

40. Petr Vershigora (1905–63) and Ivan Pyr'ev (1901–68) were Soviet film

directors. Nakhimovtsy were naval cadets, named for Pavel Nakhimov (1802–55), a hero of the Crimean War.

41. On the so-called KR affair, see Nikolai Krementsov, *The Cure: A Story of Cancer and Politics from the Annals of the Cold War* (Chicago, 2004).

42. Mikhail Romm (1901–71), Grigorii Aleksandrov (1903–83), Fridrikh Ermler, Mikhail Chiaureli (1894–1974), Grigorii Kozintsev (1905–73), Vsevolod Pudovkin (1893–1953), Leonid Lukin (1909–63), Soviet film directors.

43. Vasilii Beliaev (1902–67), Soviet film director.

44. Stalin is referring to the Baku Commune, the pro-Soviet government that ruled Baku, Azerbaijan, for several months in 1918. In July 1918, Armenian nationalists and moderate socialists expelled the Bolsheviks and their allies, the Left SRs (Socialist Revolutionaries), and invited British forces to protect the Baku oil fields from Turkey. British forces later captured and executed the Baku Commissars in Turkestan.

CHAPTER SIX. ZHDANOV'S DEATH

1. According to the previous chapter, this meeting took place in March 1949, the year Lysenko won his third and final Stalin Prize. Yet Shepilov may be mistaken about the date and context of Nesmeianov's objection. Nesmeianov did not become president of the Academy of Sciences until 1951. In 1949 he was rector of Moscow State University. In addition, it would have been highly unusual, and indeed dangerous, to speak against Lysenko in Stalin's presence so soon after Iurii Zhdanov was disciplined for doing something similar.

2. In May 1946.

3. Genrikh Iagoda (1891–1938), people's commissar of internal affairs (chief of the secret police) from 1934 to 1936. Iagoda was executed in 1938.

4. Viktor Abakumov (1908–54), longtime official in the secret police. Abakumov played a key role in the Leningrad affair. He was arrested in 1951 for allegedly organizing a Zionist conspiracy within the Ministry of State Security and was executed in 1954 as an accomplice of Lavrentii Beria.

5. City in southern Russia on the Black Sea.

6. Shepilov is referring to a conference of propagandists who were charged with disseminating the party's position on genetics.

7. The biological tenets of Ivan Michurin (1855–1935). Michurin was noted for his hybridization of plants and his belief that external factors affected genetic structure.

8. Jean-Baptiste Lamarck (1744–1829), French evolutionary theorist who argued that changes in environment produce changes in organisms.

9. The process whereby the flowering or fruiting of plants is hastened by treating seeds before cultivation.

10. Kliment Timiriazev (1843–1920), Russian botanist.

11. Shepilov is likely referring to the first mass communist *subbotnik* (voluntary labor day) in 1919 among the workers of the Moscow-Kazan railroad.

12. Pasha Angelina (1913–59), founder of the Soviet Union's first all-female tractor brigade.

13. Mariia Demchenko, collective farmer who set a record for sugar beet production in 1935.

14. Evdokiia Vinogradova and Mariia Vinogradova (no relation) were textile workers in the city of Ivanovo, northwest of Moscow. In one shift in 1935 they supervised a record number of automatic weaving machines.

15. Follower of August Weismann (1834–1914), a German biologist who argued that multicellular organisms are comprised partly of germ cells, which pass on hereditary information.

16. Grigorii Rasputin (ca. 1870–1916), Russian mystic who had a great deal of influence in the court of Nicholas II. Rasputin was murdered in 1916 by aristocrats close to the royal family who felt that his influence was malevolent.

17. Popular nickname for Stalin.

18. Shepilov errs in the chronology of these events. Iurii Zhdanov's speech occurred on April 10, 1948, and the Politburo meeting that Shepilov attended was on May 28. See Pollock, *Stalin and the Soviet Science Wars*, 51–52; "Posetiteli kremlevskogo kabineta I. V. Stalina: 1947–1949," *Istoricheskii arkhiv* 5–6 (1996): 35; and Krementsov, *Stalinist Science*, 161–66.

19. Hilly region between Moscow and Leningrad.

CHAPTER SEVEN. THE TRAGIC FATE OF NIKOLAI VOZNESENSKII

1. "Quarantine line," an expression that the French prime minister Georges Clemenceau supposedly coined in 1919 in reference to the new states in eastern Europe that served as buffer against Soviet communism.

2. Petr Liashchenko (1876–1955), Soviet economist.

3. Nikolai Nekrasov (1821–77), Russian poet.

4. Diminutive form of Sergei.

5. Ilya Ehrenburg (1891–1967), Soviet writer.

6. Leonid Leonov (1899–1994), Soviet writer.

7. Mikhail Sholokhov (1905–84), Soviet writer and Nobel laureate noted for his depictions of the Don Cossacks.

8. Alonso Cano (1601–67), Spanish painter, architect, and sculptor.

9. Easternmost region of the Soviet Union, across the Bering Strait from Alaska.

10. Kamensk-Ural'skii, a city southeast of Sverdlovsk (Ekaterinburg) in the Urals.

11. Followers of Grigorii Zinoviev (1883–1936). Lev Kamenev, Leon Trotsky, and Zinoviev formed the so-called United Opposition in 1926–27 to protest the lack of intraparty democracy. In 1936, Zinoviev and Kamenev were executed, allegedly for complicity in the 1934 murder of the Leningrad party boss, Sergei Kirov, and for plotting with Trotsky (then in exile) against Stalin's life.

12. Ivan Serov (1905–90), longtime official in the secret police who helped

orchestrate the arrest of Abakumov in 1951. In 1954, Khrushchev appointed Serov head of the KGB.

CHAPTER EIGHT. A HARD ROAD

1. In 1966.
2. In 1928 fifty-three engineers from the town of Shakhty in the Don region were tried on charges of sabotage. The Shakhty affair marked the end of the policy of conciliation with "bourgeois specialists" and the beginning of the Cultural Revolution (1928–31).
3. In 1930 eight economists and planners from Gosplan and the Supreme Council of the People's Economy were tried for conspiring with the French government to attack the Soviet Union.
4. The trial of Grigorii Zinoviev, Lev Kamenev, and fourteen other persons on charges of conspiring with Leon Trotsky, then in exile, to murder top party officials.
5. The trial of Karl Radek, Georgii Piatakov, Grigorii Sokol'nikov, and fourteen others on charges of "wrecking" the economy.
6. The trial of Nikolai Bukharin, Geinrikh Iagoda, Aleksei Rykov, and thirteen others on charges of organizing an underground terrorist network to assassinate political leaders and wreck the economy.
7. Anthony Eden (1897–1977), British foreign secretary (1940–45, 1951–55) and prime minister (1955–57).
8. James F. Byrnes (1879–1972), US secretary of state (1945–47).
9. Léon Blum (1872–1950), French socialist politician, prime minister (1936–37, 1938), and chairman of the French Provisional Government (1946–47).
10. International conference in August 1956 sponsored by the United States, Great Britain, and France that unsuccessfully sought to negotiate a peaceful settlement to the Suez crisis. After the failure of the London conference, Israel, France, and Great Britain seized control of the Suez Canal in October.
11. In 1950 the Soviet Union sponsored the Stockholm Peace Petition to outlaw the use of atomic weapons. Nearly five hundred million people worldwide signed the petition.
12. Shepilov is mistaken here and indicates as much later in the chapter. The first explosion of a Soviet atomic weapon occurred in Kazakhstan in August 1949. The second explosion, presumably what Shepilov is referring to here, occurred in September 1951 and led to the design for the first production bomb.
13. According to the terms of the Yalta Conference in February 1945, the Soviet Union was allowed to reestablish a naval base in Port Arthur, Manchuria. Prior to the Russo-Japanese War of 1904–5, Port Arthur was a Russian possession. The Changchun railroad (or Southern Manchurian railroad) linked Harbin in northern Manchuria with Port Arthur.
14. Supporter of the Paris Commune, the radical government that ruled Paris for two months in 1871.

15. Ferdinand Foch (1851–1929), commander of the Allied armies in World War I. In 1920, Foch assisted Polish armies in their campaign against the Bolsheviks.

16. Charles Tillon (1887–1993), French communist and leader of the resistance against the Nazis.

17. In Central Asia and Siberia.

18. Shepilov is referring to the wedding-cake structure occupied by the Ministry of Foreign Affairs.

19. Lion Feuchtwanger (1884–1958), German-Jewish writer and critic of the Nazis. The translation used here is from Lion Feuchtwanger, *Moscow 1937: My Visit Described for My Friends,* trans. Irene Josephy (New York, 1937), 3–4, 10–11, 13.

20. The sort of pathetic foolishness that the character Manilov embodied in Nikolai Gogol's novel *Dead Souls.*

21. Mingrelia is a region in western Georgia where the Mingrelian language is spoken.

22. Noe Zhordania and Evgenii Gegechkori were Georgian Mensheviks and nationalists who opposed the incorporation of Georgia into the USSR after 1917.

23. The Jewish Anti-Fascist Committee was created in the Soviet Union in 1942 to rally support against the Nazis. Its chairman was Solomon Mikhoels, director of the Moscow State Yiddish Theater, who died under mysterious circumstances in 1948. At the end of Stalin's life, the Jewish Anti-Fascist Committee fell victim to a wave of official anti-Semitism. Many persons associated with the committee were tried on trumped-up charges, convicted, and executed. See Joshua Rubenstein and Vladimir P. Naumov, eds., *Stalin's Secret Pogrom: The Postwar Inquisition of the Jewish Anti-Fascist Committee* (New Haven, 2001).

24. On the northeast side of Moscow.

25. In 1939.

26. The Kirov that Shepilov is referring to is a small city north of Briansk in western Russia, not the large city of the same name in the northeastern quadrant of European Russia.

27. Emilio Segré (1905–89) and Leó Szilárd (1898–1964) were physicists from Italy and Hungary, respectively.

28. Grandfather Frost (Ded moroz), Russian Santa Claus.

29. Ivan Pavlov (1849–1936), Russian physiologist noted for his research on the "conditional reflex" in dogs. Pavlov showed that certain physiological reactions, like salivation, could be taught.

30. Leon (Levoi) Orbeli (1882–1958), Soviet physiologist, director of the Pavlov Institute of Physiology (1936–50), and vice president of the Academy of Sciences (1942–46).

31. Arnol'd Chikobava (1898–1985), Soviet linguist. In the article that Shepilov refers to, Chikobava argued that the theories of Nikolai Marr should not be

equated with Marxist linguistics, and that language does not develop in tandem with modes of production.

32. The "new teaching" that Stalin denounced was Nikolai Marr's (1865–1934) contention that language, like culture, was part of the Marxian super-structure. According to Marr, change in the economic base of a society (for example, from capitalism to socialism) produced change in the structure of language.

33. Emelian Iaroslavskii (1878–1943), longtime communist party official, editor, and historian.

34. See Eugenia Semyonovna Ginzburg, *Journey into the Whirlwind* (New York, 1967), 5–8. Kazan is about seven hundred kilometers east of Moscow.

35. Stepan Bandera (1909–59), Ukrainian nationalist who played a central role in the anti-Soviet Organization of Ukrainian Nationalists despite being in exile.

CHAPTER NINE. A TEXTBOOK ON POLITICAL ECONOMY

1. Claude-Henri de Rouvroy Saint-Simon (1760–1825), early French socialist.

2. On the political economy textbook, see Pollock, *Stalin and the Soviet Science Wars*, 168–211.

3. The crown of Monomakh is a symbol of the Russian autocracy, supposedly brought from Constantinople to Kievan Rus by Grand Prince Vladimir Monomakh (1053–1125).

4. Stalin is referring to "A Contribution to the Critique of Political Economy," which Marx wrote in 1859.

5. Iurii Zhdanov relates a similar story about Shepilov and Stalin. During the Politburo meeting in May 1948 where Shepilov spoke in favor of genetics, he also endorsed the work of Voznesenskii, who had expanded upon "the science of war economics that Stalin founded." When Stalin heard this, he flatly denied that he was the founder of this branch of economics. See Zhdanov, "Vo mgle protivorechii," 86.

6. Kondrat'evites were followers of Nikolai Kondrat'ev (1892–1938), an econo-mist who distinguished himself in the 1920s in the debate on the "scissors crisis" (so called because it referred to the widening gap between the prices of agricultural and manufactured goods). A defender of the New Economic Policy (NEP) compromise with peasants, Kondrat'ev was arrested in 1930 and executed in 1938.

7. Savva Morozov (1861–1905), a wealthy Russian entrepreneur.

8. As Shepilov indicates below, Gorky continued to travel abroad after this date. Gorky permanently left Italy, his home since 1921, for the Soviet Union in 1933, the date typically associated with his return to Russia.

9. Adam Bogdanovich (1862–1940), Belorussian ethnographer and folklorist.

10. Aleksandr Shcherbakov (1901–45), Central Committee staff member (1932–36) and member of the Central Committee (1939–45) and the Politburo (1941–45).

11. Romain Rolland (1866–1944), French writer and socialist.

12. Village northeast of Moscow known for its painted lacquer boxes.

13. Model prison camp that sought to rehabilitate criminals through labor. The Bolshevskii Labor Commune was widely advertised in the 1930s as a progressive attempt to combat criminality and was the subject of the Soviet film *Journey to Life*.

14. Aleksei Speranskii (1887–1961), a prominent Soviet pathologist.

15. Fedor Khitrovskii, Gorky's friend and later the founder of a museum in Gorky's childhood home in Nizhnyi Novgorod.

16. An ethnic group in east-central European Russian whose members speak a Finno-Ugric language.

17. Group of graphic artists who achieved considerable fame in the 1920s and 1930s for their irreverent and satirical illustrations.

18. Formally, the Tatar Autonomous Soviet Socialist Republic, located east of Moscow along the Volga River.

19. City northeast of Moscow.

20. Maxim Gorky was the pen name of Aleksei Maksimovich Peshkov. Thus, his son's patronymic was Alekseevich.

21. Shepilov is mistaken here. Nadezhda Alekseevna Peshkova (née Vvedenskaia) was the wife of Gorky's son, Maksim Alekseevich Peshkov. Family members called her Timosha.

22. Fedor Chaliapin (1873–1938), the most famous Russian opera singer during the early part of the twentieth century.

23. Nikolai Golovanov (1891–1953), Soviet orchestral director and composer.

CHAPTER TEN. UNDER THE SWORD OF DAMOCLES

1. Mikhail Riumin (1913–54), a longtime figure in the secret police who helped to orchestrate the Doctors' Plot. Riumin was executed in 1954 as an accomplice of Beria.

2. Article 58 of the Soviet Criminal Code pertained to counterrevolutionary activity.

3. Mikhail Tukhachevskii (1893–1937), Iona Iakir (1896–1937), and Ieronim Uborevich (1896–1937) were Soviet military leaders who were executed during the Great Purges.

4. Valerii Chkalov (1904–38), Georgii Baidukov (1907–94), and Aleksandr Beliakov (1897–1982) were Soviet aviators who together accomplished a number of record-setting flights in the 1930s, including a nonstop journey from Moscow to Vancouver, Washington, via the North Pole.

5. In 1934, the Politburo created the Special Board of the NKVD to try "socially dangerous" persons. See J. Arch Getty and Oleg V. Naumov, *The Road to Terror: Stalin and the Self-Destruction of the Bolsheviks, 1932–1939* (New Haven, 1999), 122–23.

6. Aleksandr Solzhenitsyn (b. 1918), Soviet writer and dissident. Shepilov is probably referring to Solzhenitsyn's novella *One Day in the Life of Ivan*

Denisovich (1962), which was the first work published in the Soviet Union after Stalin's death to address the issue of camp life. It is not known whether Shepilov had access to Solzhenitsyn's *Gulag Archipelago,* a work that circulated clandestinely, in samizdat.

7. Reactionary, monarchist, and anti-Semitic political movement in late tsarist Russia.

8. Soviet coeducational youth organization.

9. Karaganda oblast is in north-central Kazakhstan. Taishet is roughly six hundred kilometers northwest of Irkutsk, Siberia. Novosibirsk is in south-central Siberia.

CHAPTER ELEVEN. THE NINETEENTH PARTY CONGRESS

1. Aleksandr Notkin (1901–82), Soviet economist. After the discussion of the draft of the political economy textbook in November 1952 (which Shepilov discusses in Chapter 9), Notkin sent a letter to Stalin raising several concerns about Stalin's comments on the draft and points raised during discussion. Stalin defended his comments in the reply that Shepilov references. See I. V. Stalin, *Sochineniia,* vol. 3 (XVI), ed. Robert H. McNeal (Stanford, Calif., 1967), 246–57.

2. On March 20, 1952, L. D. Iaroshenko, an economist, sent a letter to the Central Committee in which he complained that the summary report from the November 1952 discussion did not adequately represent his views. Stalin responded on May 22 that Iaroshenko's position on the role of productive forces and the relations of production in societal development was "un-Marxist." Stalin was more positive in a September 28 reply to the economists Sanina and Venzher about their input, but he still pointed out their "grave theoretical errors" regarding the economic laws of socialism and collective farms. See ibid., 258–304.

3. River in the northern Caucasus Mountains.

4. From *sokol,* or falcon.—Tr.

5. Alexander Herzen (1812–1870), one of the fathers of Russian socialism. In 1835, Herzen was exiled to Viatka, in northeastern European Russia, after the police broke up a reading circle devoted to the writings of the French socialist Henri de Saint-Simon and the German playwright Friedrich Schiller. Herzen left Russia for good in 1847 and later became a prominent critic of the Russian autocracy through his journal *The Bell.*

6. Since Sorrento is a village in southern Italy, Herzen may be referring to the towering Aleppo pines that are common in the region.

7. Timofei Granovskii (1813–55), Russian academic and Westernizer who was an advocate of Hegelian philosophy.

8. Nikolai Ogarev (1813–77), Russian writer and socialist.

9. In the Second World War.

10. Mir Dzhafar Abassovich Bagirov (ca. 1895–1956), secretary of the

Azerbaijani Communist Party (1933–53). Bagirov was arrested in 1954 and
executed in 1956 as an accomplice of Beria.

11. Otto Kuusinen (1881–1964), old Bolshevik, academician (1958), and longtime
figure in the politics of Kareliia, the historically Finnish region north of
Leningrad.

12. Georgii Dimitrov (1882–1949), Bulgarian communist and leader of the
Comintern (1935–43).

13. Thomas More (1478–1535), English humanist scholar. More coined the
word "utopia" and used it for the title of his 1516 book, where he set forth
his vision of the ideal social and political system.

14. Tommaso Campanella (1568–1639), Roman Catholic theologian and philosopher. In *City of the Sun* (1623), Campanella imagines an ideal society without
private property.

15. Shepilov is mistaken here. Party leaders eliminated the office of general
secretary in March 1953 to ensure a collective leadership. Khrushchev occupied a post that was much the same in function, if not name (first secretary),
beginning in September 1953. Shepilov may be referring to the increase in
the number of Central Committee secretaries and the reorganization of the
Secretariat that occurred in October 1952.

16. In 1966, when Leonid Brezhnev led the party.

17. May 9, 1945, the day hostilities with Nazi Germany ended.

18. An endearing diminutive for Bukharin.

19. Stalin's nickname.

20. Indigenous peoples in northeastern Siberia.

21. Leonid Mel'nikov (1906–81), first secretary of the Ukrainian Communist
Party (1949–53). Mel'nikov became a full member of the Presidium.

22. Vasilii Andrianov (1902–78), first secretary of the Leningrad oblast Party
Committee (1949–53). Andrianov became a full member of the Presidium.

23. Averkii Aristov (1903–73), first secretary of the Cheliabinsk oblast Party
Committee (1950–52). Aristov became a full member of the Presidium.

24. Nikolai Mikhailov (1906–82), first secretary of the Komsomol (1938–52).
Mikhailov became a full member of the Presidium.

25. Nikolai Ignatov (1901–66), first secretary of the Krasnoiarsk regional
Party Committee (1949–52). Ignatov became a candidate member of the
Presidium.

26. Ivan Kabanov (1898–1972), first deputy chairman (1951–52) and chairman
(1952–53) of the State Committee for Material-Technical Supply. Kabanov
became a candidate member of the Presidium.

27. Aleksandr Puzanov (b. 1906), first secretary of the Kuibyshev oblast and city
Party Committees (1946–52) and chairman of the Russian Soviet Federated
Socialist Republic (RSFSR) Council of Ministers (1952). Puzanov became a
candidate member of the Presidium.

28. "Joint" was likely an allusion to the American Jewish Joint Distribution

Committee, a charitable organization that was active in the Soviet Union in the 1920s and 1930s.

29. Nikolai Fedorenko (b. 1912), Soviet diplomat, philologist, and translator.

30. Dmitrii Chesnokov (1910–73), longtime party official and expert on ideological issues.

31. Aleksei Rumiantsev (1905–93), Soviet political economist. Rumiantsev later became editor of *Pravda*.

CHAPTER TWELVE. IN MORTAL COMBAT

1. Historical veracity was a special point of contention in the late 1940s, when Andrei Zhdanov attacked Vano Muradeli's opera for being (among other things) antihistorical.

2. Shepilov is referring to the Austrian State Treaty signed by the United States, France, Great Britain, and the Soviet Union in 1955. It restored full sovereignty to Austria and ended the Allied occupation.

3. On June 19, 1953.

4. In 1947.

5. In 1948.

6. In 1965.

7. Gamal Abdel Nasser (1918–70) created the Free Officers Movement after the 1948 Arab-Israeli War. The movement sought to destroy the monarchy and modernize Egypt. Muhammad Naguib (1901–84) was a central figure in the Free Officers Movement and the first president of the Egyptian Republic (June 1953–November 1954).

8. David Zaslavskii (1880–1965), Soviet journalist and old Bolshevik.

9. Mikita instead of Nikita has a disparaging sound in Russian.—Tr.

10. In February 1955.

11. After Stalin's death, Beria consolidated the Ministry of State Security (MGB) into the Ministry of Internal Affairs (MVD). Shepilov discusses this in Chapter 1.

12. Mikoian is tacitly juxtaposing Beria's mental state with Stalin's.

13. Georgian resort town on the Black Sea.

14. Jean Baptiste Cavaignac (1762–1829), French politician who called for wide-scale repression to destroy the opponents of the French Revolution.

15. Evno Azef (1869–1918), member of the SR party who worked as a double agent for the Okhrana, the tsarist secret police.

16. Roman Malinovskii (1877–1918), Bolshevik who was elected a deputy to the Fourth Duma in 1912. After his arrest in 1910, Malinovskii became a double agent for the police. Malinovskii was executed by the Soviet government in 1918.

17. Bogdan Kobulov (1904–53) and Sergei Goglidze (1901–53), longtime officials in the secret police who were executed as accomplices of Beria.

18. Viacheslav Menzhinskii (1874–1934). After the death of Dzerzhinskii in

1926, Menzhinskii became head of the United State Political Administration (OGPU).

19. Shepilov is ambiguous here about the proper nomenclature for the chief figure in the party. The post of general secretary was abolished 1953 and restored at the Twenty-third Party Congress in 1966. Thus, Khrushchev became first secretary at the September 1953 CC plenum.

CHAPTER THIRTEEN. KHRUSHCHEV AT THE HELM

1. Shepilov's use of the neologism *khrushchoby*, a play on the word *trushchoby* (slums), to describe the ornate villas in Lenin Hills is unusual. In popular parlance, the word was used to describe the monotonous, shoddy, and increasingly ubiquitous five-storied buildings that were built from prefabricated concrete panels in cities across the Soviet Union in the 1950s and 1960s. Shepilov may have intended for *khrushchoby* to be understood in an ironic way when used in reference to the party leaders' villas. If so, it would be an implicit juxtaposition of the perquisites that the elite enjoyed with the reality of daily life for the vast majority of Soviet citizens. It may also be the case that Shepilov was simply unaware of the popular connotations of *khrushchoby* at the time of writing.

2. Andrei Andreev (1895–1971), old Bolshevik and member of the Politburo (1932–52).

3. Along with Oleg Troianovskii, Shuiskii, Lebedev, and Shevchenko were Khrushchev's closest assistants. Shuiskii specialized in general party affairs, Lebedev in ideology and culture, and Shevchenko in agriculture. See Taubman, *Khrushchev*, 366.

4. One arshin is approximately seventy-one centimeters, or twenty-eight inches.

5. Vasilii Vil'iams (1863–1939), Russian soil scientist.

6. Regions in eastern Siberia.

7. Region in western Ukraine, west of the Carpathian Mountains.

8. City in central Ukraine.

9. Region east of Moscow along the Volga River.

10. City southwest of Moscow.

11. Saying attributed to Aristotle (384–22 BCE), a student of Plato.

12. Lenin wrote the document that became known as his testament at the end of 1922 and the beginning of 1923, a year before his death. Lenin was especially critical of Stalin, whom he deemed "too rude" to be general secretary, and recommended that the Politburo remove him from this post.

13. Acronym for the Stalin Factory.

14. People from Riazan and Tambov, cities southeast of Moscow.

15. Aleksei Adzhubei (1924–93), a prominent Soviet journalist and an editor of *Izvestiia* who was married to Khrushchev's daughter.

16. After the Treaty of Pereiaslavl' in 1654, left-bank (eastern) Ukraine was incorporated into Russia. Before the insurrection that Bogdan Khmel'nitskii

led against Jews and Poles in 1648–54, this land was part of the Polish-Lithuanian Commonwealth.

17. Perekop is the name of the isthmus that connects the Crimea to Ukraine.

18. Vasilii Golitsyn (ca. 1643–1714), Russian political figure, diplomat, and military commander who led attacks against the Crimean Khanate in 1687–89.

19. Fedor Ushakov (1745–1814), Russian naval commander who distinguished himself in the Russo-Turkish War of 1768–74.

20. Tauride (Tavrida) is an ancient name for Crimea that originated with the Tavry, a people who likely descended from the Cimmerians and who lived in the vicinity of the Greek colony of Khersones, established in the fifth century BCE. The Republic of Tauride was a pro-Soviet government that was created in March 1918.

21. In October 1921.

22. In June 1945.

23. Aleksei Kirichenko (1908–75), member of the Central Committee (1952–61) and the Politburo (1955–60).

24. Shepilov is mocking Khrushchev's accent.

25. Aleksandr Griboedov (1795–1829), Russian writer and diplomat. In *Woe from Wit,* he satirizes the Russian aristocracy.

26. Stalin was also referred to as *vozhd'*, typically translated as "boss."

CHAPTER FOURTEEN. WITH KHRUSHCHEV IN CHINA

1. Alphonse Daudet (1840–97), French novelist.

2. Sun Yat-sen (1866–1925), Chinese revolutionary who helped topple the Qing dynasty. Despite being one of the founders of the Chinese Nationalist Party (Guomindang, or Kuomintang), Sun was highly regarded by communists as the father of modern China.

3. At the time of Shepilov's visit, the Panchen Lama was Choekyi Gyaltse (1938–89). After the Dalai Lama, the Panchen Lama is the highest ranking figure in Tibetan Buddhism.

4. In 1966, Mao called on Red Guard detachments to seize power from party officials to weed out his opponents. Millions of people were imprisoned or perished in the ensuing chaos. Although Mao halted the Cultural Revolution in 1969, the political infighting in the upper ranks of the party that it masked lasted until 1976, when Mao died and the "Gang of Four" was arrested.

5. Mountain range in Central Asia that straddles the borders of China, Kazakhstan, and Kyrgyzstan.

6. Mountain range in western China and Tibet that defines the southern edge of the Taklamakan and Gobi Deserts.

7. City in the Xinjiang Uygur region of western China.

8. City in east-central China, southwest of Shanghai.

9. Chinese Nationalist Party that Sun Yat-sen helped found in the early years of the twentieth century to press for the abolition of the Qing dynasty. After

the victory of the communists in 1949, leaders of the Guomindang (Kuomintang) fled to Taiwan.

10. The Yellow Emperor who ruled in the third millennium BCE and who, according to myth, is the ancestor of all Han Chinese.

11. The Tungus ethnic group originated in eastern Siberia and northern Mongolia. The Khitans, an offshoot, eventually moved south into Manchuria, and the Jurchens, another offshoot, into Manchuria and northern Korea.

12. Genghis Khan (1162–1227), founder of the Mongolian Empire, which at its peak stretched from eastern China to Persia and the Russian principalities in Europe. Kublai Khan (1215–94) defeated the Han Chinese Song dynasty in 1279 and located his capital in what is now Beijing.

13. Empress Dowager Cixi (1835–1908), de facto ruler of China during the late nineteenth and early twentieth centuries.

14. Enterprises that were owned or controlled by Guomindang officials or people who supported the Guomindang regime.

15. Zhu De (1886–1976), communist military leader and politician who helped devise the guerrilla strategies that defeated the Guomindang.

16. City in south-central China.

17. Book that Lenin wrote while hiding in Finland during the summer of 1917; in it he described the future socialist state.

18. Clement Atlee (1883–1967), British prime minister (1945–51) and leader of the Labor Party (1935–55).

19. Gao Gang (1905–54), communist politician who committed suicide after being purged from the leadership in 1954. With the help of the military, Gao allegedly tried to position himself as Mao's heir.

20. In eastern China.

21. Campaign in 1958–62 to accelerate industrialization.

22. Chiang Kai-shek (1887–1975), leader of the Guomindang after Sun's death in 1925.

23. The Uygurs are a Turkic ethnic group in northwestern China. The Dais are a Thai ethnic group in southern Yunnan province in southwestern China.

24. A similar "infantile disorder of leftism" existed during the Soviet Civil War. The so-called Military Opposition opposed Trotsky's plans to reinstate corporal punishment and the death penalty, end the election of officers, and use specialists (former tsarist army officers) in the Red Army. In 1920 Lenin wrote a pamphlet entitled *Left-Wing Communism: An Infantile Disorder* denouncing this and other leftist factions within the party.

25. Ding Ling (1904–86), Chinese writer and recipient of the Stalin Prize (1951).

26. Shanghai was home to a sizeable Russian émigré population.

27. A word for rebellion that was frequently used in conjunction with the Cultural Revolution.

28. Hermann Goering (1893–1946), Joseph Goebbels (1897–1945), and Heinrich Himmler (1900–1945) were key figures in the Nazi leadership. Goering was

the founder of the Gestapo; Himmler, the head of the SS, was the chief architect of the Holocaust; and Goebbels was propaganda minister.

29. "Germany above all," the first stanza of the German national anthem that was in use during the Second World War.

30. The Karelo-Finnish Soviet Socialist Republic (SSR) was incorporated into the RSFSR in 1956. After this date, there were fifteen union republics.

31. Shepilov is mistaken here. Tenzin Gyatso (b. 1935) was proclaimed the reincarnation of the thirteenth Dalai Lama two years earlier, when he was three.

CHAPTER FIFTEEN. TO SOUTH CHINA AND BACK

1. The "three red banners": the Great Leap Forward (1958–62), the party line, and the people's communes (local administrative units).

2. City in southern Russia.

3. City in central Ukraine.

4. Russian word derived from the Chinese that refers to a kind of grain.—Tr.

5. The Yellow River is more than 5,400 kilometers in length.

6. River in Central Asia.

7. The Yangtze River is nearly 6,400 kilometers in length.

8. The Temple of Azure Clouds is located on Fragrant Mountain outside Beijing, where Sun was temporarily interred after his death in 1925.

9. Shepilov is presumably being more poetic here than accurate. The Yangtze annually deposits millions of tons of silt in its delta and the East China Sea and is not often described as "blue."

10. Or "Beijing, Nanjing, and Guangzhou," in the standard Pinyin transliteration employed elsewhere in this book.

11. "Rassian" (*raseiskii*) suggests a chauvinistic lack of concern about what others think. Shepilov uses it to ridicule Khrushchev's thoughtlessness toward his Chinese hosts.

12. NEP (1921–28) allowed Soviet peasants to sell grain surpluses at market prices, and thus alleviated the food shortages that were endemic to the Civil War. It was also accompanied by a relatively free market in the retail sector.

13. A dried fish.

14. Meat dumplings.

15. It is unclear what bridge Shepilov has in mind. What he calls *most parchovaia pereviaz'* may be Precious Belt Bridge, first built in 816. The bridge is a tourist attraction in the city of Suzhou, northwest of Hangzhou. Shepilov does not mention visiting Suzhou, but he may have been given a photograph of the bridge.

16. Mount Hua, the site of several Daoist monasteries, is in Shanxi province. Like Mount Elbrus in the northern Caucasus, it has more than one peak. Shepilov does not mention visiting Mount Hua.

17. City northeast of Beijing, in Liaoning province.

18. Yue Fei (1103–42), Southern Song military leader who fought against the northern Jin dynasty. Qin Hui, Yue's corrupt betrayer, believed the war was

too costly and convinced the emperor to recall Yue from the battlefront. Qin's wife argued that the emperor needed no reason to execute Yue, since his power was absolute.

19. Buddhism was introduced in China as early as the second century BCE.

20. What Shepilov calls the Hall of Five Hundred Buddhas is conventionally rendered in English as the Hall of Five Hundred Arhats. An arhat is a Buddhist ascetic who is enlightened.

21. One of the three cities constituting Wuhan, which sits at the intersection of the Yangtze and Han Rivers in Hubei province.

22. A mu is equal to 666.6 square meters, or 0.16 acres. The flooded area is thus equal to 10.6 million hectares (more than 106,000 square kilometers), or 26.4 million acres (more than 41,000 square miles).

CHAPTER SIXTEEN. MAO AND THE ATOMIC BOMB

1. Shepilov is referring to what is conventionally called the Uprising of June 17, 1953. On June 16, several dozen construction workers in East Berlin walked off the job when they learned that their pay would be cut if they did not meet new production quotas. The following day, a crowd estimated to be one hundred thousand strong took to the streets of East Berlin; smaller protests were held in other East German cities. With the help of Soviet tanks, the police quickly restored order, but not before killing more than one hundred protesters.

2. Though not fascist, the League of German Youth (Bund Deutscher Jugend) was a conservative, anticommunist youth organization in West Germany that claimed twenty thousand members in 1952.

3. After communist forces in North Korea invaded the South in 1950, Truman ordered American naval forces to protect Taiwan from a potential invasion from the Chinese mainland.

4. Signed on September 8, 1951, by forty-eight nations, the Treaty of San Francisco formally ended the war between Japan and the Allies (but not the Soviet Union). The treaty also determined reparations and the fate of Japan's imperial possessions.

5. Naval base at the southern end of the Liaodong Peninsula in Manchuria. In 1897, Russia leased the base from China, but Russia lost it to Japan in the Russo-Japanese War seven years later. In the closing days of the Second World War, Soviet troops reoccupied Port Arthur.

6. Also known as Dal'nyi (Russian for "distant"), Dalian is a city near the Port Arthur naval base.

7. Lanzhou is a city in Gansu province in north-central China. Ürümqi is a city in the Xinjiang Uygur region in western China. Alma-Ata (Almaty) was the capital of the Kazakh SSR.

8. City in Qinghai province in western China.

9. Shepilov is apparently referring to Anatolii Sofronov (1911–90), a writer of conservative repute and the editor of the magazine *Ogonek*.

10. Museum in the Kremlin that holds many of the treasures of the Russian autocracy.

11. Male peasant.

12. Mark Mitin (1901–87), philosopher, recipient of the Stalin Prize (1943), and editor of the journal *Philosophical Issues* (1960–67).

13. Shepilov is juxtaposing the Leninist notion of cultural revolution (lowercase), which comprised education and enlightenment, with the Maoist notion (uppercase), which relied on coercion and terror.

14. In 1960.

15. Shenyang, Changchun, and Harbin are cities in Manchuria. Anshan is in Liaoning province, northeast of Beijing.

EPILOGUE: THE ANTIPARTY GROUP THAT NEVER WAS

1. Epithet for Molotov, Malenkov, and Kaganovich, the most prominent participants in the unsuccessful attempt to remove Khrushchev from the post of first secretary in June 1957.

2. Aleksandr Bakulev (1890–1967), a prominent Soviet doctor who was chief of the surgical division at the Kremlin Hospital.

3. The House of Bourbon occupied, at various times, thrones in Spain, France, and a number of smaller principalities in Europe.

4. Chief archival repository for the party. IMEL scholars published works on the history of the party and the international communist movement.

5. N. A. Barsukov, historian who specializes in the Khrushchev period.

6. Contrary to Shepilov's assertion, Pospelov chaired a committee that investigated the extent of illegal repression under Stalin and, with Averkii Aristov, drafted an early version of Khrushchev's speech. It appears that Khrushchev and his aides pieced together the final version from the Pospelov-Aristov and Shepilov drafts and a number of firsthand accounts that they solicited. See Taubman, *Khrushchev,* 280–82.

7. In May 1955.

8. Edvard Kardelj (1910–79), longtime Slovenian communist, ideologue, and member of the Yugoslavian Academy of Sciences. Eurocommunism was the relatively moderate political doctrine that many Western European communist parties espoused in the 1970s and 1980s to broaden their popular appeal and distance themselves from Moscow. Strictly speaking, Eurocommunism did not exist when Khrushchev first visited Yugoslavia in 1955. Tito, however, was determined to maintain autonomy from the Soviet Union.

9. In June 1956.

10. Zhukov was dismissed from power in October 1957, allegedly for planning a military coup against Khrushchev.

11. Nikolai Baibakov (b. 1911), chief of Gosplan (1955–57). Contrary to Shepilov's assertion, Baibakov was demoted in 1957 to first deputy chairman of the RS-FSR Council of Ministers. In 1958 he was again demoted, this time to chief

of the Krasnodar Council of the People's Economy. This may be what Shepilov has in mind.

12. I. R. Razzakov (1910–79), chairman of the Kyrgyz Council of Ministers (1945–50) and chief of the Kyrgyz party (1950–61).

13. Shepilov was officially excluded from the party in March 1962.

14. There are a couple of inconsistencies in Shepilov's account of Khrushchev's vendetta. First, Shepilov was excluded from the Academy of Sciences in 1960, before the Twenty-second Party Congress. Second, the academy's academic secretary at that time was Evgenii Fedorov, not Georgii Skriabin (who held the post from 1966 to 1977).

15. Anatolii Aleksandrov (1903–94), Soviet physicist and president of the Academy of Sciences (1975–86).

16. Iakov Malik (1906–80), longtime Soviet diplomat.

INDEX